Readings in International Business

Richard N. Farmer

Robert W. Stevens

Hans Schöllhammer

Dickenson Publishing Company, Inc.,

Encino, California, and Belmont, California

ISBN 0-8221-0072-X
Library of Congress Catalog Card Number: 75-120005
Printed in the United States of America
10 9 8 7 6 5 4 3 2 1

Contents

Introduction

Suddenly in the 1960s and 1970s, everyone seems to be doing it or at least trying to learn how to do it. International business, previously reserved for clerks in the export department, is where the action is now, not only in over 400 of the 500 largest American firms, but also in banks, foreign companies, thousands of smaller firms, and transportation and insurance companies. General Motors, in appointing a new president, pointedly notes that a large portion of his earlier career was spent abroad in various GM affiliates. Young executives who find themselves assigned abroad these days are being rewarded, not exiled, by their firms. Ambitious executives wonder how to get overseas to work with various branches of their firms, not how to avoid being sent there.

The reason for the growing activity is simple. While the truly *one world* may still be far away, existing political, economic, and social patterns in which all firms must work have proven in this generation to be quite favorable to the development of the multinational firm, whose activities span many national boundaries. Chrysler, the Getty Oil Company, and Caterpillar Tractor used to be purely American creations, but now they are globally involved companies. These developments began in the 1950s and even earlier, but went almost unnoticed by the academics of the business community.

Then suddenly we discovered that we live in a world where firms are no longer only national, except in the legal fiction sense, and everyone wanted to know much more about this new type of firm. International business programs proliferated, international stories acquired more than a quarter of the space in general business magazines, and students, who are always sensitive to new straws in the wind, decided to go into international business. But along with students, businessmen and professors have also been internationalized. While students are looking for courses that will prepare them for what's going on, businessmen are intent on finding new management talent that can cope with all kinds of unfamiliar international problems, and professors are on the lookout for new taxonomies, new systems of thought, new case studies that will bring the subject down to manageable proportions. Let's see how each of these three groups sizes up the field.

Realistic students now study international accounting, finance, and marketing, knowing that before any responsible firm will trust them overseas, they must first prove their business and managerial competence in the home office. These students realize that international business requires the same functional knowledge as business in a purely domestic setting. Marketing is a universal business problem, although its form may be modified in different environments; business always needs

1

men with financial skills, although the nature of financial markets can differ between countries; and production has a logical universality wherever it is practiced, even though local customs and problems can sometimes make a great difference. International business alone can be a rather nebulous field, but when combined with solid functional proficiency it can provide very practical training for one's business future. A man who knows how to carry off a delicate financial operation in France for his multinational company will not lack for opportunities, and a person who can see the subtle differences between marketing channels in Bangkok and Boston can be a valuable asset. The process also can be reversible. A person who has successfully marketed his firm's products in Bangkok may have a cosmopolitan point of view, along with a comparative one, which allows him to see in new perspective the Boston situation and to come up with solutions there which purely local marketers have missed.

For practicing businessmen, international business creates frustrations, strange behavioral problems, cultural conflicts—but it also promises excellent profits. It means long nights spent doing homework—studying environments which used to interest only anthropologists or State Department specialists. It means developing a new way of thinking about firms—how they are organized, what cultural excess baggage they carry, and how they might do their jobs better. It involves the real excitement of breaking new ground, of doing things politicians have long regarded as unfeasible, and economists have regarded as improbable.

Sometimes international business has also meant failure. Many firms have gone abroad with glowing hopes and large profit expectations, only to fall flat. An electronics firm moves into Sicily, then withdraws in a few years, out millions of dollars and surrounded by recriminations from local citizens. What had looked very good quickly turned into a mirage. A major American firm takes over the biggest French computer company, and five years later still cannot make any money, although it is in the fastest growing market in the world. What went wrong? Things which worked very well in the United States somehow don't quite fit the foreign environments, and managers have great difficulty in seeing exactly what they missed. Perhaps the scholars can pinpoint such problems, or younger men, trained differently, can do better than culture-bound older ones.

But international business means success as well, often major success. Many firms make much more money on their foreign operations than on their American ones, and foreign expansion can be extremely valuable to any firm. A few pioneer firms who got into international business early now find that half their sales and more than half the profits come from abroad, and their stockholders are rewarded accordingly. Such activities can even work both ways. A brilliant young Frenchman becomes a key executive for a global group with a large computer manufacturer; a German patent, picked up almost by accident in the routine course of operations, turns out to be the key to a whole new product line in America and elsewhere; or close business contacts developed over the years in England result in major sales in the Middle East, as a new consortium builds a major irrigation and power system.

For professors, international business means exciting new ideas. It means working to develop scholarly articles on new business concepts, both for students and for businessmen who are interested in what is going on here. It means developing new cases covering international situations for firms which a decade ago would not have thought of leaving Ohio, let alone the United States. It means preparing new kinds of courses with international flavors, or introducing international materials into existing ones. It means long discussions with students about how best to prepare themselves for careers which would have seemed very improbable only a few short years ago.

It also means frustration and learning, since no one now over 35 ever studied international business systematically. The field did not exist. There are no yellowing, twenty-year-old lecture notes in international business; all of it seems to have happened in the past few years.

And international business means the interaction of students, professors, and businessmen in efforts to figure out what is really going on. New fields attract restless, probing minds that don't mind borrowing extensively from anyone who seems to have a good idea. A businessman must be willing to go down to the university and talk to a class, or to spend some time with a serious doctoral student who just happens to be working on a problem which has bothered the manager for some time. It means that students can get into the act, as when they work with local firms on export marketing problems—often firms who rarely discussed matters with students before.

Slowly things are being sorted out and slowly firms, students, and scholars are discovering common ground, common problems, and common means of attacking problems that are still quite new to most of them. Such evolution potentially involves a whole new way of thinking about business education.

These readings attempt to capture the interest, excitement, and originality of the new trend in business which is making our existing political world look obsolete. What is new and exciting these days in the global picture is the way businessmen are leapfrogging over national boundaries, making the necessary adjustments to what they find on the other side, and incidentally, showing us what a brave, new world could be like. They are actually doing what many politicians and bureaucrats are too timid even to contemplate, focused as these functionaries are on the cramped, narrow little world of petty national states, static economies, and dreary wars without end or purpose.

For more than a century, businessmen have been regarded as plutocrats, exploiters, and men of narrow vision, whose only interest was to take advantage of other people to achieve their selfish ends. A whole theology (Marxism) was built on this premise. But if that's the way it is, why are so many new but underdeveloped countries today clamoring to get private foreign firms to invest in their economies? Why are the older countries of Europe now hastening to modernize their capitalistic institutions, hoping to realize some of the productivity gains the Americans are reaping? Why are countries all over the world suddenly building schools of business as rapidly as they can, confident that such schools will create the trained managers who will increase their countries' wealth? The Russians, along with everyone else these days, are finding the shortage of skilled managers one of their major bottlenecks.

All the world yearns for more wealth, and those who can provide more are today's managers and businessmen, a despised class in other days but now wooed by a needy world. Because we feel that international business is the most important and most rapidly developing aspect of business today, we have selected these readings to interest and inform students in this area.

What is International Business?

International business can be defined as any business activities that take place across national boundaries. Some of the more important types of international business are:

(1) Export and Import Transactions in Goods. This is the oldest and most common situation, where one country sells its products to another. These transactions in international trade are similar to domestic sales, but the act of crossing a frontier can make a major difference in how the sale is handled. Governments can levy import duties or impose quantitative quotas; frequently payments must involve the changing of one currency for another; and often language and trade customs are quite different.

This is a very old part of business—an early international trade transaction is described in *Genesis*, when Joseph in Egypt sold grain to his brothers from what is now Israel. When you use your Philips razor, buy a Volkswagen, or play baseball with a Haitian-made ball, you are involved in this part of international business.

Lots of Americans are involved in this dimension of international business without even thinking about it or knowing it. The Connecticut assembly line worker may be putting together a jet engine for England; the Indiana farmer could be growing soybeans for Japan; the Peoria engineer might be designing a starting motor to go into a tractor for Pakistan; and so on. Even in a somewhat isolationist state like Indiana, about ten percent of all jobs are created by exports, and another two or three percent are created by imports, as when the friendly Volkswagen dealer hires a new salesman.

(2) Licensing Agreements. Many firms that would never think of going overseas, along with many that do, get into the business of licensing their patents and copyrights to foreign firms. A Japanese company may buy rights to produce a patented process for petrochemical manufacture, or a Brazilian company might wish to use certain copyrights.

This process also works both ways, although the net flow favors American firms. Almost any plate glass window made in the past five years is manufactured under English patents involving a new tin float process, as one example. No country has a monopoly on brains, education, or technical excellence.

(3) *Exports and Imports of Services.* When you finally get to take that long awaited European vacation, you may fly with Lufthansa, Air France, or BOAC. Here, you will be buying services from foreigners. When a Frenchman flies to Baghdad on Pan American, he is reversing this process.

Countries sell insurance, management consulting, transportation, and even money services to each other (through bank and other financial institution loans). These services also are very old—Grecian ships carried Roman cargoes to Tripoli two thousand years ago.

(4) *Turnkey Projects.* American contractors often build a complete power installation, road, or irrigation project for a country or firm. When it is finished, the foreign owner takes the key and begins to operate it.

This is a variant of exporting, but here firms are involved in exporting a complex set of goods and services. The expertise and skills of the contractor are put together to create a viable, operating system.

(5) *Management Contracts.* An American firm may contract with a foreign one to provide management skills for a specific period, often including training of local citizens to take over the system within a stated period of time. TWA has managed foreign airlines in this manner for many years. Here the exported item is a service, and one which Americans have in abundance—good management.

(6) *Production and Distribution in a Foreign Country.* The American firm can build factories and distribution systems in a foreign country. This is the most complex and interesting case, since the company now has to adjust its operations to the foreign environment. Instead of worrying about American workers, it now must worry about foreign ones; instead of living with American laws about marketing practices or labor relations, it must adjust to foreign laws.

(7) *The Evolution of the Multinational Company.* These developments have led to the evolution of the multinational company which may operate in dozens of countries while interchanging men, components, and capital between any or all of them. Until this new enterprise arrived on the scene we had seen companies as country-bound, with ownership and management locked into the United States, Great Britain, Germany, or some other country. But when firms began to jump country boundaries in various ways, particularly including building and operating production and marketing facilities in many countries, we discovered that the firm's home country may not matter so much.

These multinational firms may be the forerunners of important international political developments. Politicians and world statesmen speak wistfully of the far future when nations may cooperate and merge; already *firms* are doing such things in their international operations. If the American or French manager is best, he runs the show, not whoever happens to be born in the right country. If the firm needs to cooperate with many local suppliers to get the job done, it does, whether or not there are the proper political treaties or not. And countries reluctantly come along and agree, since one critical factor in multinational business operations is that every participant gains something as a result of his activities. No one gets it all, but all get something. And even the most avid nationalist is inclined to accept the proposition that something is always better than nothing.

These readings will return often to the concept of the multinational corporation. This new development has bothered, encouraged, and frightened many persons around the world, and has given all of us a glimpse of what true international cooperation may be like.

Multinational firms may be a new concept, but at the micro level they must deal with the usual business studies. Products must be marketed, financial arrangements made, production lines designed, control systems established, and so on. But environmental interlocks are different. A multinational firm with a plant in Europe must do most of its labor recruiting in that area, and personnel practices used in Indiana probably will not do. Educational levels and standards are different in Europe, and one cannot operate as if the environments were the same. To insist that junior managers have M.B.A. degrees will only mean that no men are available, since almost no Europeans obtain this degree. Part of the problem is a lack of graduate business schools. To insist on high school education for assembly line workers would also mean that virtually no one could qualify, since relatively few persons in Europe continue school until age 18.

These points may seem trivial, but in each environment one encounters constraints which force the firm's management to operate in a somewhat different manner than they might at home. Few American multinational firms have failed because they forgot that the voltage in England was 220 instead of 110 and did not redesign their electrical equipment accordingly, but some have gone broke because they forgot that English trade unions are quite dissimilar from those in the United States, and they failed to make necessary labor relations adjustments.

Examination of any type of international business reveals one key respect in which local and international business differ. We all know a considerable amount about our own local environment; we have grown up in it, and there is no real need to explore it in great detail when we consider a local business problem. But as soon as a company crosses a national frontier, its environment shifts, and the firm must be aware of how this different environment affects its operations. All firms are interrelated with their domestic environments, but when a two-country problem is introduced it becomes critical to know how this new environmental dimension may affect the internal activities of the firm.

Chart 1 suggests the relevant taxonomy. Here the key environmental factors for any country are listed first (Part A). The first four categories apply to individual countries and break down the relevant part of the environment into four basic kinds of factors. The next three environmental categories indicate the strictly international environmental problems that firms face as they cross national frontiers. These environmental constraints are in effect imposed on the firm.[1]

---

[1] The environmental-internal firm problems suggested here are covered in detail in Richard N. Farmer and Barry M. Richman, *Comparative Management and Economic Progress* (Homewood, Ill.: Richard D. Irwin, Inc., 1965).

Companies, like other citizens, may make suggestions for change or improvement in any part of the environment, and on occasion their ideas are listened to, but for the most part they must adjust to the environment as they find it.

Chart 1

A: *Environmental Factors Affecting Productive Firms*

C_1: *Educational Factors*
C_2: *Behavioral Factors*
C_3: *Legal-Political Factors*
C_4: *Economic Factors*
I_1: *International Behavioral Factors (e.g., attitudes toward foreigners)*
I_2: *International Legal-Political Factors (special rules affecting only foreigners and foreign goods and capital)*
I_3: *International Economic Factors*

B: *Critical Elements of the Management Process*

B_1: *Planning and Innovation*
B_2: *Control*
B_3: *Organization*
B_4: *Staffing*
B_5: *Direction, Leadership, and Motivation*
B_6: *Marketing (policies pursued)*
B_7: *Production and Procurement*
B_8: *Research and Development*
B_9: *Finance*
B_{10}: *Public and External Relations*

The internal operations of the firm suggested in Part B are the things firms must do internally to obtain maximum profit in their operations (or to achieve any other goals the firm may have in mind). These are the decision nodes for managers, or the critical elements of the management process. As we indicated above, the kinds of decisions made within a firm are quite intimately affected by its environment, and good decisions made in New York may not be applicable to the same kinds of problems in Bangkok. The environment and firm decisions are closely interrelated.

On both the macro and micro levels, we are concerned with the adjustment of managements and firms to their environment. This means that we must know a great deal about the environments in which firms operate, and about managerial and firm functions as well. The international business synthesis is to match up these two systems to the ultimate advantage of the firm.

Chart 1 also provides a definition of international business. If a firm is involved in any international activity, it must do the usual business things, such as market, finance, produce, plan, etc. But all of these managerial and firm functions are environmentally related. One does not plan without considering various laws or economic developments; one does not sell securities without taking into account the rules and regulations of the country in which they will be sold; and so on. If you look at the Critical Elements of the Management Process, you will note that in each case, some consideration must be given to the foreign environment. Volkswagen will not sell one car in the United States unless it observes all American auto safety laws; IBM will not sell or lease a single computer in France without taking careful account of various French laws and customs. As the involvement in a foreign economy becomes greater, as when IBM sets up a plant and marketing system in France, the environmental involvement grows.

The study of international business thus involves two interrelated variables. On the one hand, we are interested in finding out what key environmental differences may exist, so that we can adjust to them; on the other, we are interested in how firms do in fact adjust their internal operations to mesh efficiently with these environmental differences. The first question might be, what is French labor law and how does it differ from the American? The immediate follow-on question is, how does IBM handle its personnel problems in France, given these differences?

This set of readings reflects our interest in the environmental problems which firms must adjust to, as well as the manner in which business problems are solved in international situations. Since one cannot cover everything at once, the plan of the book is to oscillate between the macro and the micro aspects of the matter. Part 1 deals largely with the international environment in which firms must operate. Here the questions of balance of payments, trade policy, and international trade theory and practice are covered. While the basic focus is on the environment, the authors have noted effects of rules, laws, regulations, and theory on the internal problems of firms.

Chart 2 suggests both the interrelationships between the environment and internal firm operations and the plan of this book. By putting the environmental factors across the top of the diagram and the business variables vertically, it is possible to see the various possible environmental-internal firm interlocks which are important. Thus one type of international business material which is studied is marketing (B_6). But marketing has interrelationships with the environment in terms of education, behavioral factors, legal-political problems, economics, and so on (the C_1, C_2, C_3, and C_4 blocks on Chart 2). When one studies a marketing problem in various countries, observing the different environments and the way in which they interact with the firm's marketing problems, he is studying one aspect of international business.

Chart 2 also shows the organization of this book. The numbers in the squares indicate the materials with which these sections of the book generally deal. In every case there are interrelationships between various environmental factors and internal firm problems.

Part 2 swings back to internal firm problems in comparative and multinational management. Basic focus here is on how managers react when operating in different environments. Again the environment is not ignored, but major interest is on how a firm's managers plan strategies to meet the complex needs of a multinational operation.

Part 3 returns to the environment, this time focusing on business problems and opportunities created by formation of regional economic groupings. While the major interest is environmental, again some consideration is given to the problems of firms in adjusting to rapid change in their operating constraints.

Chart 2: Critical Managerial Elements and External Constraints

	Educational C_1	Behavioral C_2	Legal-Political C_3	Economic C_4	International Behavioral I_1	International Legal-Political I_2	International Economic I_3
Planning B_1							
Control B_2							
Organization B_3							
Staffing B_4							
Direction B_5							
Marketing B_6							
Production & Procurement B_7							
Research & Development B_8							
Finance B_9							
Public & External Relations B_{10}							

Parts 4 and 5 continue the macro approach, considering environmental problems created by national planning and economic development. Once again the authors raise critical questions for firm managements to consider as they explore changing constraints on firm operations.

Parts 6 and 7 return to the micro-focus, covering problems of international investment and international management. Once more the environmental-firm interlocks are made by various authors as they relate internal firm problems to different business environments around the world.

In teaching international business, we have found that this system of moving from macro environmental problems back to micro firm problems, always considering the way in which the two dimensions interrelate, is very helpful to students. They first observe an environmental situation, then attempt to apply it to a business problem. Thus in Part 1 it is possible to read the articles, then consider what this has to do with the firm. What might an American auto manufacturer do, for example, if foreign tariff barriers on medium-sized trucks are sharply reduced as a result of Kennedy Round tariff bargaining? The firm's response will be both more prompt and more intelligent if it has been aware in advance that such matters are under consideration. Or, to take another case, after examining the problem of too few foreign top executives in American multinational firms, as Professor Simmonds does in an article in Part 7, how might the Board of Directors of a multinational firm carry out in detail its wish to correct the situation? To handle this question, a student must not only know something about the supply of competent managers in various cultures, but also a good deal about personnel planning and selection in large corporations. Each part is designed to give students some information and analysis to make these environment-firm interlocks on their own. This analysis is the essence of international business.

We have found that rapid development in the field of international business has frequently outdistanced textbooks. Hence a collection of readings of this type is planned to supply a supplementary text for international business students and practitioners. Moreover, many useful readings are found in widely scattered and often hard to find sources. Organizing and integrating readings makes it possible for many more persons to read the best of recent writings in this field.

And finally, several of the readings appear here for the first time. These new readings were initially papers prepared by graduate students for courses in international business at Indiana University. Professor Schöllhammer also has written a new paper on French planning for this volume.

Part One

Balance of Payments and Trade Policy

1

Businessmen, both in the U.S. and in many other countries, are widening their horizons today—looking beyond the small, familiar world of the traditional nation-state and reaching out toward worldwide patterns of production, investment, finance, and marketing. They have learned that all people are consumers, no matter what flag may fly above their heads, and that all can improve their skills to become more efficient as workers and managers. In short, businessmen today are reaching outward, determined to play an international role.

But as business leaders turn outward from the comfortable, familiar environs of home they find themselves confronting a host of new and unfamiliar environmental factors. Perhaps the most conspicuous difference in the business environment abroad is that in most foreign countries people speak a different language. True, the large and prosperous English-speaking world still includes (besides England) Canada, the U.S., and the "down-under" countries of Australia and New Zealand, while today English is the major second language in much of the rest of the world including Scandinavia, the Indian subcontinent, and much of Africa and Latin America.

But a successful businessman should speak the *main* language of the people with whom he is in daily contact, and therefore most people preparing for international business careers acquire fluency in at least one modern language besides their own. In internationally-conscious Europe it is not unusual for people to be fluent in at least four languages—English, French, German, and Dutch or Swedish, for example.

Language differences, important as they are, can be fairly easily overcome by learning a new "foreign" language, but some of the other problems that plague international businessmen often prove harder to learn to live with. In this first section we consider two of these problems that are unique to international business—the international trade and balance of payments policies of governments. The changes that occur from time to time in trade policies, needless to say, introduce a new dimension of uncertainty into international business calculations.

A memorable example of the difference for businessmen that changes in national trade policies can make was provided several years ago by the experience of a number of American oil companies. These companies undertook new and expensive programs of drilling for oil abroad, expecting to export the oil they might find back to the vast and profitable American market. After much crude oil was discovered abroad in this way, however, the U.S. government introduced restrictive quotas on American oil imports, and the international companies were left to sell their oil as best they could in lower priced foreign markets.

Not all changes in international trade policy are unfavorable for business, of course. In 1967 when the Kennedy Round of international trade negotiations was concluded American exporters found that the tariffs on their goods in foreign countries had been reduced by an average of some 30 percent, the reductions to take place step by step over a five-year period.

The second major difference between the environments of domestic and international business that we take up in this section concerns changes in countries' international balances of payments. An international balance of payments is the statistical record of all of the flows of money into and out of a country. The net difference between these flows, that is to say, a net *inflow* or a net *outflow*, determines whether the country's holdings of international monetary reserves have been added to or subtracted from during the period.

Under our existing international institutions, it is the behavior of a country's balance of payments that determines, sooner or later, whether its government can continue to fulfill its pledge to maintain intact the international value of the country's currency. If a national balance of payments turns seriously adverse, eventually the country's government will be required to introduce strong corrective measures to defend the currency. These measures usually include disinflationary policies—higher interest rates and tighter money—intended to cut back the level of total demand. At such times many a private firm has had to stand by and see its profits cut to ribbons because the country where it is marketing happens to have had balance of payments problems which it met by cutting back the level of total economic activity.

In international business, a country's balance of payments plays a key environmental role similar to the one played by the gross national product (GNP) for domestic business. In fact, considering the record of the past 20-odd years, we must conclude that balances of payments have been of even greater environmental importance than GNP's because they are subject to more sudden and unexpected changes and, once they signal a threat to the currency, governments have shown themselves very willing to subordinate the interest of international business to the overriding search for currency stability.

International businessmen must be alert at all times to changes in the business environment that arise in the field of international trade policy and in the balance of payments field because changes in either one can result in a sudden expansion or contraction of their markets. All countries are bent upon pursuing their own national goal systems, which may differ in many ways from the objectives that the multinational firm has in mind. For example, a multinational firm may find itself in a situation in which its home country's balance of payments requires the company to remit its profits back home as promptly as possible, while at the same time the balance of payments of the host country, where the profits have been earned, requires that only token profit remittances be allowed to leave the country. One of the fine arts of international business management is learning to thread one's way through regulatory puzzles of this sort.

Such irrationalities seem to be accepted as integral parts of our politico-legal environment today, but hopefully that environment itself will undergo a process of gradual change. Worldwide problems of our day are posing new opportunities for worldwide cooperation in such fields as satellite communications systems, environmental pollution, the arms race, the coming need to harvest food from the sea, and the long standing need for international monetary reform—to mention only a few. We must hope that in days to come governments will be able to internationalize their approaches to problems such as these, much as businessmen have effectively internationalized their approach to serving world markets. If government attitudes move toward more international cooperation, some day international balances of payments may become as unobtrusive and inoffensive as regional balances of payments are today. But in the meantime, balances of payments are neither unobtrusive nor inoffensive, and it is essential that we take the measure of their influence.

An understanding of balances of payments requires at least a minimal involvement with the figures, and in our first selection the staff of the Federal Reserve Bank of St. Louis explains the significance of the major accounts and describes some of the interrelationships among them. Next, Professor Stevens gives us an over-all view of the behavior of the U.S. balance of payments in the 1960s, drawing on his experience in international business at the time the U.S. government's "voluntary" foreign credit restraint program was introduced to curb the flow of business and banking funds from the U.S. to continental Western Europe. (The program was later converted to a mandatory basis.) After surveying the attitudes of international businessmen toward the government's restrictions, Professor Stevens takes a broad look at the over-all U.S. balance of payments problem and concludes that the American attitude toward it has been one of continuous wishful thinking. In his view the problem will not "go away soon," and its persistence calls for a reappraisal of the entire spectrum of the government's international economic and financial policies. Nothing that has happened since this article was published has altered either its major findings or its main conclusion.

International businessmen have benefited greatly from a number of studies of their environmental problems sponsored by the Committee for Economic Development, a prestigious organization of 200 leading American businessmen and educators. The CED sponsors research dealing with problems of public policy that are of significance for business and then, on the basis of its research studies, promotes public discussion of the policy issues involved. One of the most widely quoted research monographs distributed by the CED's Research and Policy Committee was entitled "The Dollar and the World Monetary System." We have chosen a chapter from this important CED report to provide a brief explanation, in clear and simple language, of the role of the U.S. dollar in the international payments machinery.

The U.S. government's program to cut back the flow of American capital to Europe has had a number of unintended fallout effects, none of them more impressive than the powerful stimulus it gave to the rapid growth of the Euro-dollar markets and Euro-bond markets outside the United States. The widespread international use of dollars in these markets is slowly displacing "the dollar's gold backing"—to use an old-fashioned term—as the real source of its worldwide acceptability and usefulness. We have chosen a description of Euro-dollars written by Oscar L. Altman of the International Monetary Fund to cover the emergence of this fascinating new financial market that has so rapidly become a major source of finance for American firms operating abroad.

The remaining items in this section deal with areas of public policy that are crucial in shaping the environment in which international business decisions of the future will be made. Robert L. Kerstiens describes the origins and subsequent development of the U.S. government's foreign credit restraint program. Every public official who has been connected with this program has told us that it is only temporary, and, as an echoing refrain, many business economists continually press for its elimination. However, as the U.S. balance of payments has deteriorated instead of improving, many observers have concluded that the U.S. government's controls on foreign lending and investing are likely to remain intact. The outlook remains clouded by military developments in Southeast Asia because the balance of payments deterioration was mainly caused by the U.S. government's increased military spending there and by the domestic inflation associated with that military venture. Domestic inflation worsens a country's balance of payments because it sucks in more imports while simultaneously lessening the price competitiveness of exports.

Despite the long string of foreign payments deficits and the decline of American international financial strength that accompanied them, the U.S. government maintained its long-established devotion to liberal international *trade* policies. The government restricted foreign investment but not foreign trade. To tell the story of U.S. international trade policy, we have chosen a round-up article on the most recent international trade negotiations conducted under the auspices of the General Agreement on Tariffs and Trade (GATT), the negotiations that were known as "the Kennedy Round."

Finally, we include two articles by Chris C. McEvoy and David A. Wollin on East-West Trade matters. They consider the barriers imposed by the U.S. government on trade with Communist countries and assess the probable gains and losses involved in changing the rules governing this trade.

The specific effects of these broad environmental influences on particular *companies* will, of course, depend upon their individual circumstances. Broadly we may note, however, that businessmen and governmental people concerned with international business matters, by concentrating on the everyday problems of buying and selling, meeting payrolls, planning new investments, and the countless other tasks that go to make up business life, are working on the problems and opportunities that all people share as consumers and producers. Many international businessmen find great satisfaction in the knowledge that, in the long run, their work may have more beneficial effects than the activities of those who earn their livings by keeping alive ancient quarrels.

How to Interpret the Balance of Payments Accounts

Federal Reserve Bank
of St. Louis

The Balance of Payments Accounts are a double entry record of real and financial transactions between U.S. and foreign residents. Because it is based on double entry bookkeeping principles, the balance of payments always balances in the sense that receipts always equal payments. The double entry nature of the Balance of Payments Accounts is shown on the left-hand side of the accompanying table. This strictly accounting balance must not be confused, however, with a meaningful economic balance, because the economic behavior underlying some of these transactions may not be sustainable. For example, the receipt of $1.2 billion in 1967 from the sale of the U.S. gold stock (IV.3.a) can only continue as long as our gold stock lasts. There are two officially accepted measures of our economic Balance of Payments, the *Liquidity Balance* and the *Official Settlements Balance*, which are shown on the right-hand side of the table.

To understand the bookkeeping aspect, it is convenient to divide the Balance of Payments Accounts into four categories: Goods and Services, Private Capital, Government, and Other. These accounts are, of course, linked to one another; an export could be financed by a private bank loan, by a government grant, or by a private gift.

(I)   *Goods and Services.* Merchandise exports and imports are a measure of physical goods which cross national boundaries. Service exports and imports measure purchases and sales of services by U.S. residents to foreign residents. Sales of military equipment are included in service exports, and U.S. military purchases abroad are included in service imports (I.2.a). Investment income from the large volume of U.S. direct and portfolio investment abroad is the largest surplus item in the service category (I.2.b). Next to military, travel is the largest deficit item in the Goods and Services category (I.2.c).

(II)   *Private Capital.* For long-term capital, this records all changes in U.S. private assets and liabilities to foreigners. Net increases in U.S. assets are measured as payments of dollars abroad, and net increases in U.S. liabilities are measured as receipts of U.S. dollars from abroad. Direct investment (II.1.a) by Americans abroad is much larger than direct investment by foreigners in the United States. However, portfolio investment (II.1.b) is about evenly divided. For short-term capital, payments represent changes in all private U.S. assets,

Reprinted from December 1968 *Review*, Vol. X, No. 12, Federal Reserve Bank of St. Louis by permission.

U.S. Balance of Payments, 1967

(In Billions of Dollars)

Transactions	Balance of Payments Accounts			Balance of Payments Measures			
				Liquidity Balance		Official Settlements Balance	
	Receipts	Payments	Balance	Net Balance	Financing of Net Balance	Net Balance	Financing of Net Balance
I. Goods and Services	45.8	41.0	+4.8	+4.8	—	+4.8	—
1. Merchandise Trade (goods)	30.5	27.0	+3.5	—	—	—	—
2. Services	15.3	14.0	+1.3	—	—	—	—
a. Military	1.2	4.3	-3.1				
b. Investment Income	6.9	2.3	+4.6				
c. Travel	1.7	3.2	-1.5				
d. Other	5.5	4.2	+1.3				
II. Private Capital	2.7	5.5	-2.8	-2.8	—	—	—
1. Long Term	2.3	4.3	-2.0	—	—	-2.8	—
a. Direct Investment	.2	3.0	-2.8			-.3	
b. Portfolio Investment	1.0	1.3	-.3			+.3	+.8
c. Bank and Other Loans (Net)	1.1	.0	+1.1				
2. Short Term	.4	1.2	-.8	—	—	-.8	—
III. Government (non-military)	1.4	5.6	-4.2	-4.2	—	—	—
1. Loans	1.4	3.4	-2.0	—	—	-2.5	+.5
2. Grants and Transfers	—	2.2	-2.2	—	—	-2.2	—

U.S. Balance of Payments, 1967 (continued)

(In Billions of Dollars)

Transactions	Balance of Payments Accounts			Balance of Payments Measures			
				Liquidity Balance		Official Settlements Balance	
	Receipts	Payments	Balance	Net Balance	Financing of Net Balance	Net Balance	Financing of Net Balance
IV. Other							
1. Private Transfers	—	.8	– .8	– .8	—	– .8	—
2. Errors and Omissions	—	.5	– .5	– .5	—	– .5	—
3. Changes in U.S. Reserve Assets	1.2	1.1	+ .1	—	+ .1	—	+ .1
a. Gold (outflow is Receipt)	1.2	—	+1.2	—	—	—	—
b. Convertible Currencies	—	1.0	–1.0	—	—	—	—
c. IMF Gold Tranche Position	—	.1	– .1	—	—	—	—
4. Changes in U.S. Liquid Liabilities	3.7	.2	+3.5	—	+3.5	—	—
a. Foreign Official Holders	2.0	—	+2.0	—	—	—	+2.0
b. Foreign Prvt. Holders	1.7	—	+1.7	—	—	+1.7	—
c. Int'l. Organizations other than IMF	—	.2	– .2	—	—	– .2	—
Total	54.8	54.8	.0	–3.6[a]	+3.6	–3.4[a]	+3.4

[a]Figures do not add because of rounding.

Balance of Payments and Trade Policy

while receipts represent only changes in non-bank short-term liabilities. Changes in U.S. bank short-term liabilities are listed under IV.4 along with short-term liabilities of U.S. official monetary institutions.

(III) *Government.* Gross outflow of loans, grants, and transfers for the government were $5.6 billion, and the net outflow was $4.2 billion in 1967. A large share of government loans and grants is tied to purchases in the United States. To the extent that tied purchases would not have been made without the government loan or grant, this results in an increase in exports of U.S. Goods and Services. Thus, the $4.2 billion deficit somewhat overstates the government's real impact on the over-all Balance of Payments deficit.

(IV) *Other.* Private Transfers represents gifts and similar payments by American residents to foreign residents. Errors and Omissions is the statistical discrepancy between all specifically identifiable receipts and payments. It is believed to be largely unrecorded short-term capital movements. Changes in U.S. reserve assets represent official transactions of the U.S. government with foreign governments and the International Monetary Fund. Changes in U.S. Liquid Liabilities represent increased foreign holdings of liquid dollar liabilities of U.S. private and official monetary institutions (banks, the U.S. Treasury and the Federal Reserve).

Balance of Payments Measures

Two economic measures of the balance of payments are represented in the table. The Net Balance column shows the source and over-all size of the deficit or surplus, while the Financing column shows how the deficit is financed or the surplus disposed.

The major difference between these two measures is the way foreign holdings of U.S. bank and Treasury liabilities are handled. The underlying assumption about economic behavior in *Liquidity Balance* is that all foreign holdings of dollar liabilities which mature in one year or less (Liquid Liabilities) are a real claim on the U.S. gold stock. As such, the Liquidity Balance measures the actual decline in the U.S. gold stock and other reserve assets of the U.S. government and increases in all U.S. liquid liabilities to foreigners.

The underlying economic rationale of the *Official Settlements Balance* is that only foreign official holdings of dollars represent a real claim on the gold stock. Foreign private holders and international organizations have a demand for dollar balances as an international currency in the same way as they may have a demand for any U.S. services. Thus, an increase in foreign private holdings of dollars is treated in a manner similar to that of a capital inflow; i.e., included in the Net Balance column rather than in the Financing column. The Official Settlements Balance measures changes in U.S. reserve assets, and changes in foreign official holdings of dollars both liquid and non-liquid. Thus, long term U.S. bank liabilities of $.8 billion and U.S. Treasury liabilities of $.5 billion purchased by foreign governments are in the Financing column.

Wishful Thinking on the Balance of Payments

Robert W. Stevens

The United States' balance of payments with the rest of the world has been in deficit for some fifteen years—in serious deficit for the past eight years. Reflecting this imbalance, our largest banks and corporations are being asked under President Johnson's program of "voluntary" restraints to set aside temporarily their pursuit of maximum profit in international operations until our over-large payments deficit can be replaced by approximate balance.[1]

Actually, the achievement of a workable balance in our international payments is of vital importance to all businessmen. The breaching of liberal foreign economic policies, which has greatly affected (a) private foreign lending and investing and (b) the procurement policies of our foreign aid and military programs, could spread someday to other areas.

Already a "head tax" on U.S. tourists going abroad has been mentioned. But if the international strength of the dollar should come under serious question, even the government's championing of liberal international trade policies—as at present in the Kennedy Round of the General Agreement on Tariffs and Trade bargaining—could eventually be forced to give way. And, of course, if serious trouble should arise in the international economy, even purely domestic economic activity would not be at all immune.

Temporary Restraints

The compliance of U.S. businessmen with the president's program of voluntary restraints has been broadly satisfactory and has confounded the doubts of some skeptics—particularly abroad—who claimed to believe that compliance would not be forthcoming. However, it must be noted that in their public statements U.S. businessmen have nearly always prefaced their support for the voluntary program by pointing out that it is only a temporary measure. In private conversation businessmen close to the operation of the program are even more definite in stating their belief that the effectiveness of the program depends *altogether* on its being temporary.

Reprinted by permission of *Harvard Business Review*. © 1966 by the President and Fellows of Harvard College; all rights reserved.

[1] The "voluntary" restraints were made mandatory on January 1, 1968 and, at the time of writing, were still in effect.

The argument is that it may not be unreasonable to ask businessmen voluntarily to moderate their pursuit of profit in the interest of an overriding national goal for a short time, but that voluntary compliance with such official requests could not be expected to continue over a long period of time.

Spokesmen for the Administration have frequently repeated their appreciation of the fact that restraints on private foreign loans and investments are certainly not in the long-run interest of our balance of payments because they reduce future U.S. income from abroad and probably also repress exports. These spokesmen have also given repeated assurances that the voluntary program of restraint is only temporary.

In its later, mandatory form the program was also said to be temporary, and it was liberalized slightly by the Nixon administration. With estimates of the direct and indirect costs of the Vietnam war to the balance of payments running at $4–5 billion, however, the U.S. deficits continue large, and at the time of writing few observers expect an early end of controls as long as the U.S. remains bogged down in Southeast Asia.

On reflection it seems obvious that if the voluntary program on restraints is to be removed and if U.S. international economic policies in general are to return to a posture of liberalism, the U.S. balance of payments will have to leave chronic deficits behind and move into a position of sustainable approximate balance.

If we do not achieve such a balance in our international payments, more may turn out to be at stake than one's prognosis for liberal economic policies. In the following pages I propose to analyze what has been happening thus far in the 1960s as the basis for trying to decide how likely we are to achieve this balance—soon. In the first part of the article I will examine critically a number of widely held views about the balance of payments. Then I will analyze the trends which I believe have emerged over the six years 1960–1965. Finally, I will summarize as conclusions some of the changes in U.S. policies which seem to be called for by the state of the balance of payments.

Ever since 1958, when our large foreign payments deficits began, it has been common to assume that they are only temporary. This optimistic attitude toward the balance of payments deficits has been taken by Washington officials and by most U.S. businessmen, but it is in marked contrast to the attitude which most people took toward the opposite condition—the shortage of dollars outside the United States—in the 1940s and 1950s. In those days learned papers were written exploring the hypothesis that the world *might* have to face a "permanent" dollar shortage, and it was at least respectable to conclude—as some did—that the verdict was *yes*. But the large U.S. payments deficits which have characterized the years since 1958 have been regarded as temporary aberrations. Therefore, they have not attracted the attention of economists the way the earlier U.S. surpluses did.

Several reasons may be advanced to explain why it was once thought by some economists that the payments *surpluses* might be built into the very structure of the world economy, whereas today it is thought by most people that the U.S. payments *deficits* will soon go away.

Economic Prowess

One undoubtedly powerful reason is that the great prowess of the large, flexible, and highly productive U.S. *economy* might be expected to be reflected in our net *financial* balance with the rest of the world. In the first postwar decade the vast power of the U.S. economy, as compared with that of other nations, was so obvious as to need no elucidation. There was little inclination to doubt on either economic or financial grounds that it was proper for the United States to assume—as gracefully as possible—the economic, political, and military leadership of the world which circumstances and our remarkably productive economy had thrust upon us.

Among other things, it was taken for granted in those days that (a) our foreign aid should encourage greater self-sufficiency and increased productivity in the recipient countries, (b) we should encourage increased U.S. private investment abroad, (c) the substantial devaluation of the European currencies in 1949 would contribute toward a better payments equilibrium, and (d) the United States could assume without too great a strain the military and financial proprietorship of the North Atlantic Treaty Organization. Even so, there were some economists in those years who thought that the world dollar shortage might persist.

Whatever may have happened to the world dollar shortage, it is a fact of life that economic, political, and military attitudes once well established certainly *do* tend to persist. Today, when our economy still remains unrivaled in the world, if the popular premise that economic strength always confers financial strength were sound, then people might still think it "natural" for the United States to be running an international payments surplus, provided various frictions and temporary obstacles to its achievement could be removed. But the simple argument from basic economic strength is not valid, and there is no natural payments balance. A country's balance of payments at any one time depends on many things—only one of which is the productive power of that country's economy.

"Conventional Wisdom"

The mention of temporary obstacles to payments equilibrium suggests a second powerful reason why our foreign payments deficits are generally thought to be abnormal and ephemeral. The United States is still carrying the economic, political, and military leadership of the world which it first assumed about twenty years ago. We have been reminded by Washington officials almost weekly that these "burdens"—they were once called "opportunities"—are not ephemeral but, instead, will require our serious attention for many years.

However, the message has not really sunk in. Most Americans believe today that the United States is carrying *more* than its share of the economic, political, and military burdens of the Western world, and that somehow the inequity which this implies will soon be remedied. This view was expressed in 1959 by President

Eisenhower when he said that the United States was not willing to play the role of "an Atlas trying to carry the whole world." When the inequity of supplying more than our share of economic and military aid to the rest of the world is remedied, many people think, the drain on our foreign payments will disappear and chronic surpluses—or at least approximate balances—will once again be the normal state of our balance of payments. However, there are four main reasons why there is little to be said in favor of this "conventional wisdom" about the U.S. balance of payments.

(1) *Military Grants.* Our military aid to other countries has no direct effect—and never has had—on our balance of payments, since it consists of goods and services transferred to other countries directly; there is no corresponding financial transaction. In recognition of this fact, the U.S. balance of payments is practically always shown after excluding "Transfers Under Military Grants," as they are called in the official statistics, from our exports.

(2) *Aid-Financed Exports.* Our economic aid to other countries has had little direct effect on our net balance of payments in recent years, since it is mostly now tied to our own exports. This fact is depicted in Table 1, which shows the difference between gross and net foreign aid and their relationships to the balance of payments.

Gross and Net Foreign Economic Aid as It Affects the U.S. Balance of Payments

(In Millions of Dollars)

Year	(1) U.S. Government Nonmilitary Grants and Capital—Gross	(2) Portion Spent on U.S. Goods and Services, etc.	(3) Portion Going to Foreign Countries, etc.	(4) Foreign Loans Repaid to U.S. Government	(5) U.S. Government Nonmilitary Grants and Capital—Net
1960	$3,405	$2,279	$1,126	$ 636	$−490
1961	4,054	2,908	1,146	1,274	+128
1962	4,293	3,249	1,044	1,280	+236
1963	4,551	3,737	814	970	+156
1964	4,263	3,578	685	703	+ 18
1965	4,277	3,569	708	902	+194
Average	4,140	3,220	920	960	+ 40

Note: Column 1 = Column 2 + Column 3; Column 5 = Column 4 − Column 3. In Column 5 net inflows are indicated by plus figures, and net outflows are indicated by minus figures.

Table 1.

Column 1 shows the concept of foreign economic aid which appears as an outflow in the usual presentation of U.S. balance of payments statistics. As Column 2 and Column 3 show, however, more than three-fourths of this foreign aid has not involved any direct dollar outflow from the United States. These nonmilitary loans and grants are, roughly to this extent, used to finance our own exports; and the U.S. favorable trade balance, as usually shown, includes aid-financed exports of goods and services along with strictly commercial exports.

In 1965, for example, direct dollar payments to foreigners associated with $4,277 million of government grants and credits were only $708 million, or 16.5 percent of the gross outflow. As Column 4 shows, in 1965 the U.S. government collected $902 million from foreign debtors. Since most of these debts were incurred under aid programs of earlier years, they may logically be offset against new outflows of aid; when this is done, it will be noted (Column 5) that net economic aid has had practically no effect on the U.S. balance of payments in the 1960s.

(3) *Sharing of Financial Burden.* Many of our friends in the other industrialized countries of the world do not agree with the frequently expressed U.S. view that we are carrying more than our appropriate share of the "burden" of economic aid to the less developed countries.

In his intensive study of international aid shares for the RAND Corporation, John Pincus concluded: "The contention that the U.S. is over-paying (in terms of burden sharing) is not strongly supported"—in part because "the U.S. values about one-third of its food aid at two to three times the world-market price."[2] More broadly, it is well known that France spends a larger fraction of its GNP on foreign economic aid than we do (1.5 percent in 1962 compared with 0.9 percent for the United States, according to the study[3]). Pincus also assembled data to show that the U.S. share of the total economic aid extended by eight member countries of the Development Assistance Committee of the Organization for Economic Co-operation and Development *would* be about 69 percent if it were assessed on an average of U.S.–U.K. progressive income tax rates, compared with actual aid commitments by the United States in 1962 equal to only 65.6 percent of the eight-country total.

(4) *Common Military Burden.* It might be argued that, although U.S. military and economic aid to other countries does not cost our balance of payments anything, *our own* military activity in foreign areas—which *is* very costly to the balance of payments—is really being undertaken by us in what we regard as the common interest of the West. If this is so, the argument might run, our allies abroad will soon pick up their "proper" share of the common military activities as we have expanded ours.

As Table 2 shows, foreign military spending has indeed been costly to the balance of payments. Averaging almost $3 billion a year thus far in the 1960s

---

[2] *Economic Aid and International Cost Sharing*, a RAND Corporation Research Study (Baltimore, Md.: The Johns Hopkins Press, 1965), p. 143.
[3] *Ibid.*, p. 135.

(Column 2), the expenditure is larger than the balance of payments deficit itself (Column 1). While this expenditure has had a tendency to decline under repeated efforts by the Pentagon to economize, it increased again in the third quarter of 1965 under the impact of escalation in Vietnam.

U.S. Foreign Military Expenditures, Military Sales, and Balance of Payments Deficit—Liquidity Basis

(In Millions of Dollars)

Year	(1) Balance of Payments Deficit	(2) Foreign Military Expenditures	(3) Foreign Military Sales	(4) Military Expenditures Less Military Sales
1960	$3,881	$3,069	$335	$2,734
1961	2,370	2,981	402	2,579
1962	2,203	3,083	656	2,427
1963	2,670	2,936	657	2,279
1964	2,798	2,834	744	2,090
1965	1,355	2,881	844	2,037
Average	2,546	2,964	606	2,358

Table 2.

Finding it difficult to curb military spending abroad, several years ago the Pentagon stepped up its foreign sales efforts overseas on behalf of U.S. manufacturers of military equipment and supplies. These efforts have resulted in the establishment of a brisk export trade in arms, which has risen from some $200 million to $300 million a year in the 1950s to shipments valued at $844 million in 1965 (Column 3). However, the "net" cost to the balance of payments of U.S. foreign military operations—that is, military spending less these special sales—remains far above the Pentagon's announced target. In December 1962 Assistant Secretary of Defense Charles J. Hitch told a subcommittee of the Joint Economic Committee that the target was to reduce this net cost to $1 billion by fiscal 1966; in the first three quarters of fiscal 1966, the net cost was running at an annual rate of $2.3 billion.

Most of the arms exports have been sold to our NATO allies, and the NATO area also receives much the largest share of total U.S. military spending abroad (62 percent in 1960–1965). Even after deducting our arms sales to them, the U.S. military deficit with our NATO allies in 1965 was $1,037 million, or slightly more than with all other areas combined.

Since more than half of our balance of payments deficit is with those countries who are also our most powerful allies, the argument might run that our deficit will be reduced when they take over what we regard as a more appropriate share of the common burden. But this line of thought neglects several important facts. For one thing, the United States has been bearing the lion's share of the total financial cost of NATO since its inception in 1949. In the early days of the treaty, efforts to find an acceptable burden-sharing formula collapsed completely, and there is no prospect of their being revived. U.S. military expenditures have long been a higher proportion of our GNP than is the case in any other NATO country and our share of the total NATO military budget is about 73 percent—a higher percentage than would obtain under most burden-sharing formulas cited in John Pincus' study.

In other words, for many years our NATO allies have been quite content to see the United States pay most of the financial costs of the organization, and there is no reason to expect them to change their attitude toward this subject. Moreover, one of our two closest major allies is desperately fighting to avert bankruptcy and has been forced by severe financial stringency to *curtail* its overseas military operations several times in recent years. Our other closest major ally no longer regards U.S. foreign military spending to be in its interest and has undertaken to mount a financial attack on the U.S. dollar.

Europe's Inflation

There is a third reason often advanced for believing that the eight-year run of deficits in the U.S. balance of payments "must be" temporary. This is based on economic analysis rather than on seductive arguments about economic strength necessarily implying financial strength or on naive arguments about financial-burden sharing in NATO. The argument is that our main economic rivals in world trade—the countries of Western Europe—are having more trouble with inflation than we are, and that this will certainly lead to an ever-larger surplus in our commercial relations with them.

This line of reasoning, which was the basis of the quite optimistic conclusions reached by Walter Salant and his associates in their important study for The Brookings Institution several years ago,[4] is quite a respectable one in its more sophisticated forms and has been convincing to many people. A major difficulty is that, as Table 3 reveals, it does not seem to be working.

In the argument as sometimes formulated, the fact is cited that the prices of many commodities have risen more in Western Europe, on the average, than in the United States. However, when this argument is based on *consumer* prices, it overlooks the fact that many items which loom large in consumer budgets—such as rent, utilities, and most other personal services—never get into international trade at all. Thus one cannot draw conclusions about international trade based on the behavior of consumer prices.

While Table 3 shows that consumer prices have in fact risen much more in

---

[4] *The United States Balance of Payments in 1968* (Washington, D.C.: The Brookings Institution, 1963).

Europe than in the United States, it also reveals a very real difficulty: export prices (or average values, actually, for the countries shown have risen less than in the United States, and shares of world trade in manufactures have hardly moved in harmony with the consumer price changes at all. Europe has had more inflation than the United States almost continually during the period of our major payments deficits, but our share of world trade in manufactures—which after all is the acid test—has not grown in relation to Western Europe's. Thus another widely used argument for supposing the U.S. balance of payments deficit is only temporary may also be deficient.

Prices and Shares of World Trade in Manufactures—United States and Major Common Market Member Countries

	1958 = 100				Percent	
	Consumer Prices		Export Prices		Shares of World Trade in Manufactures	
Year	United States	Average of Germany, France, and Italy	United States	Average of Germany, France, and Italy	United States	Total of Germany, France, and Italy
1959	101	102	100	95	21.2%	32.6%
1961	103	108	103	98	20.5	35.4
1963	106	118	102	99	19.7	35.6
1965	109	127	106	102	20.4	35.0

Note: Germany, France, and Italy represent the European surplus countries over this time span; they are weighted equally in the indexes. The export price indexes are adjusted for changes in currency par values.

Table 3.

Even if the argument has validity, the question is: How long must we wait for corrective forces to make themselves effective? And it may someday become: How long can we *afford* to wait?

Before leaving the belief that, given time, Europe's inflation will solve our balance of payments problem, we should note that it may be false because it is internally inconsistent.

As our European friends never tire of pointing out, the United States already has a large merchandise trade *surplus* with Western Europe ($2 billion to $3 billion a year), most of it with the continental countries. (Despite a large trade deficit with us, Western Europe continues to accumulate gold and dollars from us, mainly because of large dollar receipts from U.S. private investment, U.S. military activity, and transfer receipts from other areas.) The argument we are considering supposes that the Europeans would acquiesce to a large increase in that trade surplus—say up to a doubling—while our economy grows more competitive than theirs.

But no one who has discussed this matter with continental Europeans would accept such an argument at all. Europeans have long been more export-conscious—and also more gold-conscious—than Americans, and they would not tolerate a huge increase in their merchandise deficit with us. This is aside from the fact that many in Europe would regard such an increase as a Machiavellian trick to augment the resources which U.S. businessmen could then use to finance ever-larger "take-overs" of European industries.

Concepts of Balance

We may now leave this brief survey of reasons which many give to support their belief that the U.S. foreign payments deficit "must be" temporary. I think it is plain that such reasons are made up largely of fallacious logic and wishful thinking. It follows then that, to the extent U.S. government officials believe the present voluntary restraints program will be temporary because pressures on the over-all balance of payments will ease for any of these reasons, to such an extent they are mistaken. And we have not even taken into consideration the 1966 deterioration in our trade balance or the mounting cost to the balance of payments of U.S. activities in Vietnam.

The possibility remains open, of course, that our balance of payments deficits may prove to be transient and may disappear or turn into surpluses for reasons other than those that have been discussed. Sometimes, as we all know, things seem to turn out right but "for the wrong reasons." Partly to search for new insights into our balance of payments—and to uncover such other reasons if possible—I have rearranged the official Department of Commerce statistics in an unorthodox but, I think, analytically helpful way (see Table 4).

The official figures for fiscal 1965 have been revised and considerably expanded as the department has sought to incorporate a number of recommendations put forward by the President's Review Committee on Balance of Payments (the Bernstein Committee) and by other official study groups.[5] The effect of these changes has been to add greater complexity; the latest tabular presentation for the years 1960–1965, for example, consists of nine tables covering nineteen full pages in the *Survey of Current Business.*[6]

My rearrangement goes in the opposite direction—toward more severe concentration into fewer items. Accordingly, I have condensed the official sixty-item main table into only eighteen items, and I have also arranged the lower half of the

---

[5] The Subcommittee on Economic Statistics of the Congressional Joint Economic Committee, The Executive Committee of the Cabinet Committee on Balance of Payments, and the Technical Committee on Balance of Payments Statistics chaired by the U.S. Bureau of the Budget.

[6] Office of Business Economics, U.S. Department of Commerce (Washington, D.C.: U.S. Government Printing Office, June 1966), pp. 24–42.

U.S. Balance of Payments — 1960–1965

(In billions of dollars)

	1960	1961	1962	1963	1964	1965	Average 1960–1965	1st Quarter 1966a
Current Account, Commercialb								
1. Merchandise Trade	+2.9	+3.2	+2.1	+2.4	+3.9	+2.0	+2.8	+1.5
2. International Travel	-0.8	-0.8	-1.0	-1.2	-1.1	-1.2	-1.0	-1.3
3. Private Investment Income	+2.7	+3.4	+3.8	+3.9	+4.7	+5.1	+3.9	+5.2
4. Other Private Services	–	-0.1	-0.2	-0.2	-0.1	-0.2	-0.1	-0.3
5. Net Balance	+4.8	+5.7	+4.7	+4.9	+7.4	+5.7	+5.6	+5.1
Other "Basic" Transactions								
6. Pensions & Remittances	-0.7	-0.7	-0.8	-0.9	-0.9	-1.0	-0.8	-1.0
7. Military Expenditures Less Sales	-2.7	-2.6	-2.4	-2.2	-2.1	-2.0	-2.3	-2.5
8. All Other U.S. Government	-0.7	-0.2	+0.4	+0.1	+0.1	–	–	+0.3
9. Private Long-Term Capital	-2.2	-2.2	-2.6	-3.3	-4.3	-4.6	-3.2	-2.6
10. Net Balance	-6.3	-5.7	-5.4	-6.4	-7.2	-7.6	-6.4	-6.4
Alternative Concepts of Balance								
11. "Basic" Balance (lines 5+10)	-1.6	+0.1	-0.6	-1.5	+0.3	-1.8	-0.8	-1.3
12. U.S. Private Short-Term Capital	-1.4	-1.5	-0.5	-0.8	-2.1	+0.8	-0.9	-0.1
13. Errors and Omissions	-0.9	-1.0	-1.2	-0.4	-1.0	-0.4	-0.8	-0.9
14. "Liquidity" Balance (lines 11+12+13)	-3.9	-2.3	-2.2	-2.7	-2.8	-1.4	-2.6	-2.3
15. Increase in Liquid Liabilities to Nonofficial Agencies	0.5	1.1	-0.5	0.6	1.3	0.1	0.6	N.A.
16. "Official Settlements" Balance (lines 14+15=17+18)	-3.4	-1.3	-2.7	-2.0	-1.5	-1.3	-2.0	-1.0
Line 16 Financed By:								
17. Decrease in Official Reserves	2.1	0.6	1.5	0.4	0.2	1.2	1.0	N.A.
18. Increase in Liabilities to Foreign Official Agencies	1.3	0.7	1.2	1.7	1.4	0.1	1.0	N.A.

a Seasonally adjusted annual rate.
b Excludes aid-financed exports, military expenditures and sales; private investment income includes applicable fees and royalties.
Note: Minor discrepancies are due to rounding.

Table 4.

condensed table (Table 4) to highlight the three alternative concepts of balance which have been widely discussed in recent years. Unfortunately, the rival claims for the different concepts of balance became most insistent just when the problem of imbalance in the accounts themselves—on any of the definitions—became most awkward. By now much of the clamor has died down, but we are left with three concepts of the variable we are interested in. It will be helpful to look at each of the different concepts of balance.

The "Basic" balance, once favored by the Treasury Department, was used for several years by the Council of Economic Advisors and was also the concept used by Walter Salant and his associates in their study for The Brookings Institution. The "Liquidity" balance corresponds to the concept which the Department of Commerce has been using for several years. The "Official Settlements" balance is the one recommended by the Bernstein Committee.

"Basic" Balance

The U.S. balance of payments as measured by the Basic balance has not been seriously adverse in the 1960s. The average deficit has been a little less than $1 billion a year, a sum which—if it were the whole story—could probably have been handled fairly easily by the existing machinery of international finance. However, the Basic balance is not the whole story. As a comparison between it and either of the other two concepts makes plain, it has usually registered less than half of the total U.S. deficits which must be somehow accommodated. (The average Liquidity balance deficit has been some $2.5 billion a year thus far in the 1960s, and the average deficit on the Official Settlements balance has been about $2 billion a year.)

Actually, the Basic balance is not a very useful tool for measuring short-term or even medium-term changes in the balance of payments. One might say that it is "too basic" to be very helpful on a quarter-to-quarter, or even on a year-to-year, basis. It comes into its own when one is interested in decade-to-decade changes. For example, in the first six years of the 1960s the Basic balance has usually shown a modest deficit; it was also moderately in deficit in the early 1950s, but in the 1930s it ran sizable surpluses.

While useful for long-run general statements of this sort, the Basic balance is essentially a synthetic concept from the viewpoint of operational decision making. The reason is, of course, that it abstracts from the net flows of "U.S. private short-term capital" and from all of the unrecorded transactions grouped under "errors and omissions." These two sizable categories must be included if one's intent is to define a net international balance that requires financing.

"Liquidity" Balance

When U.S. private short-term capital and errors and omissions are added to the Basic balance, the result is the Liquidity balance (Table 4)—which corresponds to *the* balance of payments deficit as the Department of Commerce has defined it for several years.

On the Liquidity basis in the 1930s, there was a massive movement of liquid resources into the United States because large inflows of U.S. private short-term capital and large errors and omissions inflows during those troubled years were added on top of the considerable surplus on Basic transactions. While U.S. private short-term capital has tended to flow out of this country ever since World War II, the tempo in the 1960s increased at a great rate until 1965. Then there was a sharp reversal owing to the introduction of President Johnson's voluntary balance of payments restraints which were coordinated by the Federal Reserve banks. This reversal is probably only temporary because (1) there is a tendency for U.S. private short-term capital outflows to rise along with exports, and (2) some capital-short countries in Europe and Latin America—plus Canada and, especially, Japan—have come to rely on the United States for short-term finance.

Errors and omissions, the flow of funds out of the United States which escapes official detection but which must be financed like any other outflow, have been about equal in magnitude to the recorded outflow of short-term capital—averaging about $800 million a year—thus far in the 1960s. These large financial flows—"between the lines" of the official statistics, as it were—constitute a very troublesome problem from the point of view of attaining a workable international financial equilibrium. The reason is that, while errors and omissions remain undetected by definition, they act in a systematically perverse way to intensify whatever imbalance exists at a given time.

In this respect they correspond somewhat to changes in business inventories in a modern industrial country which often go into a strong accumulation phase when the economy is already struggling with price inflation and overfull employment and which may also go into a strong liquidation phase when the economy becomes threatened with deflation and unemployment. However, the record shows that errors and omissions have behaved even worse than this; an analogy to an unsecured and shifting cargo in the hold of a ship fighting its way through a stormy sea is more apt than the analogy to the behavior of business inventories.

Let us look at the record of errors and omissions. In the 1930s, when the U.S. balance of payments was in uncomfortably large surplus year after year, errors and omissions were adding to the difficulty. The undetected migration of funds to our shores got as high as $400 million a year several times in the 1930s (a whopping sum in those days), and averaged over $1 billion in 1939–1940 as World War II hostilities began to break out.

The flow of undetected funds into and out of the United States has continued to exacerbate whatever existing disequilibria there have been in the postwar period. During the most acute phase of the postwar dollar shortage in 1947–1949, for example, undetected *inflows* of $1 billion a year made the problem more acute. Then, from 1951 to 1959, when most people believed our fundamental problem was still one of a world dollar shortage outside the United States, the flow of unrecorded funds *into* the United States averaged $520 million a year.

When it became apparent that the dollar shortage had passed, errors and omissions went sharply into reverse also and, as Table 4 reveals, these undetected funds have contributed an average of $800 million a year toward intensifying our problems during the years 1960–1965.

It is probably inherent in their nature that unrecorded financial transactions should act in this way to complicate further whatever the problems are at a given time. To an unknown extent, the net total of these flows reflects speculative activity—long-term as well as short-term—and it is in the nature of speculative activity that it has a destabilizing effect on markets. Errors and omissions may be telling us that some people, some place, do not think the dollar's difficulties will be short-lived.

There is a point to be made about the sheer arithmetic of errors and omissions. If—and it is a vitally important "if"—the climate of opinion about the U.S. balance of payments could be changed, a considerable part of the problem might disappear just because people would feel differently about it. Based on the record of the past twenty years, if the $800 million average outflow of 1960–1965 could be exchanged for the $500 million average inflow of 1951–1959, the Liquidity deficit would have been cut by two-thirds.

However, this way of looking at the matter really amounts to putting the cart before the horse; unrecorded transactions tend to be a *result* of whatever the climate of opinion happens to be for other reasons, and we cannot *start* to improve the balance of payments in this way. These transactions tend to come last, not first. But this arithmetic is not wholly useless either. It shows that if the dollar can be seen to be strengthening impressively, the process of improvement itself may become self-reinforcing if and when people become convinced that the international financial position of the dollar is as strong and secure as the U.S. economy itself is known to be.

"Official Settlements" Balance

As for this third balance concept, it mainly measures changes in what might be called the net cash and near-money position of the U.S. economy *vis-à-vis* foreign central banks and governments. The Official Settlements assets involved (line 17 of Table 4) are gold, convertible foreign currencies, and our gold tranche position in the International Monetary Fund; the liabilities involved (line 18) are those of the U.S. government, U.S. banks, and U.S. private residents to foreign official agencies.

The last three lines in Table 4 can be used to illustrate the operation of the gold-exchange standard and to show why nearly all economists dislike it so actively. In a word it places the United States in a position where it must assume the responsibilities of a central bank without having any of the authority which such banks must have. On the one hand, the decrease in official reserves may be taken as roughly equivalent to gold—the hard, clanking money of international finance. (In the past six years, 94 percent of the cumulative net decrease in reserves was accounted for by a decline in the U.S. gold stock.) On the other hand, the increase in liabilities to foreign official agencies approximates the liabilities that the United

States "owes" to central banks, governments, and monetary institutions in the rest of the world.

Most of the liabilities held by official agencies abroad are convertible under U.S. law into gold at the wish of the owners, much as member bank deposits at Federal Reserve banks are convertible into Federal Reserve notes at the wish of the member banks. The vital differences between the two cases are more important than their similarities, however, because *within* the United States the Federal Reserve banks have the authority to control the total amount of money in circulation by regulating the total of their own demand liabilities. Since 1935 they have also had the power to prevent a financial panic through a broadening of their powers to lend to member banks—which they also supervise. It is scarcely necessary to point out that the U.S. government has none of this *authority* over the international economy—only the self-imposed *obligation* to pay gold to foreign official agencies at their request.

The U.S. deficit with the rest of the world on the Official Settlements basis has averaged $2 billion a year over the past six years. The rest of the world has demanded settlement for half of this in the form of gold ("hard money") and has accepted paper claims (U.S. liabilities) for the other half. The cold fact is that, whether we like it or not, gold is one of the two ultimate sanctions (the other is military force) in today's ungoverned world; therefore we must look carefully into the play of forces surrounding our gold transactions with the rest of the world.

The first thing to note is that for many years the United States held more gold than it "needed." In the first decade after World War II, we usually had about $22.5 billion of gold; and in 1949, when the European currencies were devalued, we held about 70 percent of the world's stock of monetary gold. The second thing to note is that we have lost gold every year since 1957, at an average rate of about $1 billion per year. Thus over a twelve-year period our stock of gold has fallen by 48 percent, from $22.9 billion in 1957 to $11.9 billion in 1969. At present it amounts to about 30 percent of the world's official holdings.

If, for the purpose of illustration, we suppose that the U.S. balance of payments deficits are *not* temporary but will continue for the next six years at about the 1960–1965 order of magnitude, and if we also suppose that the rest of the world will continue to accept paper claims on us for half of these deficits, then our gold stock will fall by $6 billion, or by a further 43 percent, in the next six years. In that case it would stand at $7.8 billion in 1971—about one-third of its size in 1957. At such a level, our gold stock would almost certainly be smaller than the 1971 gold stocks of several European countries. In this event they would doubtless be quite unwilling to have us continue trying to play the role of nonofficial world central banker. However, under these circumstances we could probably not be relieved of this task on terms that we would find satisfactory. Gold calls the tune in such matters, and we would be expected to comply with the wishes of those who would have it.

Thus it is at least conceivable that, under more or less normal conditions in the world economy, our gold reserves might decline by two-thirds over a fourteen-year period (1957–1971). Given the gold-exchange standard in its present form, at some point in the course of such a decline confidence in the dollar would probably falter. Experience in Britain—which at times has also had to play the role of semicentral banker to the world—indicates that from time to time in the course of a currency's decline people decide they should get out of that currency into gold or foreign claims. At such times, domestic residents read the same grim financial pages that foreigners do, and respond similarly. All who can seek financial havens abroad, insofar as this is allowed or can be arranged.

This hypothetical six-year prospect for our country is distasteful and calls for a more careful look at the forces which come into play around gold in the contemporary world. Such a look discloses that those who manage our international monetary affairs are fully aware that today—as in the days of the mercantilists—a major objective of policy must be to defend the gold stock, and they have acted accordingly.

Since 1960, under the adroit leadership of men like former Under Secretary of the Treasury Robert Roosa, various special financial devices have been brought forward for the purpose of taking some of the pressure off gold. These devices—or "Special U.S. Government Transactions" as they were formerly called in the Federal Reserve Bulletin—have had a favorable cumulative effect of about $5 billion. Foreign governments have paid us about $2 billion in advance on debts which they owed us; the governments which agreed to buy our arms have made payments to us in advance of delivery totaling about $1.5 billion; and foreign central banks and governments who had idle dollar balances which might have been used to buy gold from us purchased about $1.5 billion of special nonmarketable securities from us instead.

No one associated with introducing these special financial devices has claimed that they help to solve our fundamental balance of payments problem. Instead, they have been put forward—like President Johnson's program of "voluntary" restraints—in order to "buy time" until, in the words of the conventional wisdom, our "temporary" deficits are replaced by surpluses or by a sustainable approximate balance. It should be obvious that these special devices cannot be expected to continue providing relief for very long. Moreover, if—for the purpose of illustration—they should all run out and become unavailable in the future, the potential calls on our gold stock would *increase* by some $0.8 billion per year.

Clearly, it is a matter of grave national importance whether the deficits in our balance of payments are—or are not—temporary. And to that question we now return.

Future Developments

The records show that no one has been very good at balance of payments forecasting, and I do not propose at this point to add another forecast to the collection. On the principle that in some sense the past contains the seeds of the future, I propose simply to look broadly at our record thus far in the 1960s—with the aid of Table 4. No effort has been made to quantify small changes or to forecast values for given years. Instead, the purpose of the exhibit is to focus on a few broad categories which will determine, among them, the order of magnitude of the net balance in the future.

It may be that in a balance of payments, as in aesthetic matters, beauty (or its absence) may sometimes be in the eye of the beholder. Other observers might prepare a slightly different version of Table 5. I do not insist that mine is sacrosanct, much less that the trends shown in it should be extrapolated forward for the next six years. My only claim is that these are the trends which I believe are in Table 4, and that if the next six years are to be very different from the last six years, the burden of proof is on the forecaster to tell us what he thinks the differences will be. In the following brief comments, I will explain how I arrived at some of the figures in Table 5, and also why I believe the U.S. balance of payments deficit will not soon go away.

Major Discernible Trends in U.S. Balance of Payments (Net)—1960—1965

(In billions of dollars per year)

1. Merchandise Trade	$0.0
2. International Travel	−0.1
3. Private Investment Income	+0.5
4. Pensions & Remittances	−0.1
5. U.S. Foreign Military Spending	+0.1
6. Private Long-term Capital	−0.5
7. Basic Balance	−0.1
8. Private Short-term Capital	0.0
9. Errors and Omissions	+0.1
10. Liquidity Balance	0.0
11. Nonofficial Liquid Liabilities	0.0
12. Official Settlements Balance	0.0

NOTE: Figures favorable to net balance are indicated by plus figures; figures unfavorable to net balance are indicated by minus figures.

Table 5.

The U.S. commercial merchandise trade surplus (excluding our aid-financed and military exports) followed a U-shaped curve over the six-year period of 1960–1965, averaging $3 billion the first two and last two years, but only $2.25 billion in 1962–1963. No trend, either upward or downward, is visible over the six years. It might even shrink in the six-year period ahead, as it is doing in 1966, especially if we are to have more cost and price inflation relative to our main rivals that we have had in the past.

On the international travel account, our net deficit with the rest of the world grew slightly from year to year in 1960–1965, at an average rate of about $0.1 billion per year.

Private investment income, defined here to include income flows both into and out of the United States on private foreign investments—both direct and portfolio— is easily the only strongly favorable trend item in our balance of payments. As defined, it brought in an average of almost $0.5 billion more each year during 1960–1965. It should continue to grow encouragingly provided limitations on the flow of new U.S. private capital abroad do not repress it.

The net outflow due to pensions and remittances is subject to a slow secular growth averaging a little less than $0.1 billion per year.

U.S. foreign military spending on a net basis declined at an annual average rate of something over $0.1 billion per year under the combined impact of the Pentagon's efforts to economize on spending and to step up arms sales. Whatever one may say about the future development of other balance of payments items, it is clearly government policy to step up foreign military spending; and it is doubtful that the government can sell enough more arms to keep up, even in the present hectic phase of the arms race in many parts of the world.

To indicate a reversal of the trend in this item is easier than to quantify the reversal. Expenditures are said to be up $0.7 billion in fiscal 1966. For the purposes of looking forward, we may suppose that a probable increase in arms sales can be offset by a probable increase in this figure. If so, military spending on a net basis would go up $0.7 billion, and perhaps level off there.

(The heavy role given in my analysis to the government's military, rather than civilian, activities abroad in contributing to the payments deficit is also pointed up—in a different format—in the so-called "gold budget." In the January 1966 U.S. government budget statement, it was estimated in a presentation of the net foreign currency disbursements of all major government agencies that the Department of Defense would account for $2.4 billion of the $2.9 billion which the government expected to spend abroad in fiscal 1967.[7])

In Table 5 private long-term capital lumps together both the inflows and outflows of direct and portfolio investment capital in order to arrive at a single measure of the effect of all private capital flows between the United States and the rest of the world on our balance of payments. It is interesting to note that the average rate of increase in the outflow of these "geese" offsets 100 percent of the average rate of increase in the inflow of the "golden eggs" of investment income in the first six years of the 1960s.

It is well known that the net outflow of private capital from the United States

---

[7] Budget of the United States, Fiscal Year 1967, Special Analysis "M."

has been on the increase sharply in recent years, and it would certainly have been higher in 1965 and 1966 except for (a) President Johnson's voluntary balance of payments restraint program, and (b) high and rapidly rising interest rates in the United States. A sustainable equilibrium in our balance of payments would imply the elimination of one of these special factors and a considerable easing of the other.

How much capital would flow out then? It must be recalled that the United States is by far the largest generator of savings in the world, as well as having by far the most efficient institutions for mobilizing and channeling savings; also all the rest of the world, including Western Europe, is interested in increasing its supply of capital. Should the increase in the rate of outflow of $0.7 billion per year in 1961–1964, for example, be taken as an index to the probable order of magnitude under conditions of no restraint?

On a conservative assessment $0.7 billion per year might be treated provisionally as an upper limit to the annual rate of increase because it includes, among other things, the period when U.S. business was discovering Europe. On the other hand, the calculated 1960–1965 rate of increase of $0.4 billion per year is too small, since it ends with a year of abnormal restraints. Perhaps $0.5 billion or $0.6 billion per year suggests a reasonable order of magnitude for annual increases in a future without abnormal restraints.

Net Balances

The Basic balance shows no trend in 1960–1965. However, if Table 5 is to be used in thinking about developments in 1966–1971, both the military item and the private long-term capital outflow should be adjusted in a direction unfavorable to the balance of payments. Military spending would increase at once by $0.7 billion or, say, at an average annual rate of $0.1 billion in 1966–1971, while the private capital outflow might increase by $0.5 billion or $0.6 billion per year.

For the Basic balance, which was trendless in 1960–1965, these adjustments would imply an annual worsening of $0.3 billion to $0.4 billion in 1966–1971. However, higher income on a rising outflow of foreign investment could well offset part of this deterioration.

Private short-term capital, when the year of the once-for-all inflow—1965—is excluded, turns out to have a U-shape in the five-year period 1960–1965, if one averages the two pairs of terminal years. On this basis it is judged to be without a trend. There appears to be a favorable trend in errors and omissions, particularly when the first and second three-year periods are compared, of about $0.1 billion per year. Liquid liabilities to nonofficial foreign agencies is another line with a U-shape in 1960–1965, when viewed in terms of two-year periods, and is therefore treated as without a trend.

The sum of these various trends when we get to the Liquidity and Official Settlements balances was a favorable +$0.1 billion per year from 1960 through 1965. But the military and long-term capital adjustments suggested above would convert the +$0.1 billion into, say, –$0.2 billion or –$0.3 billion per year or a bit less if one is thinking ahead to 1966–1971.

In short, there has been practically no trend at all in the U.S. balance of payments deficit over the past six years; and if one allows moderate adjustments for known current developments, a slight tendency toward worsening appears. (This statement, and the conclusions which follow, assume that the U.S. government will be able to continue using some or all of the special financial devices which, in the past six years, have reduced the potential calls on our gold stock by some $0.8 billion per year. In the absence of these special government transactions, the situation would become much more critical much sooner.) This absence of a trend over a six-year period does not mean, of course, that the past will necessarily go on repeating itself in the future. At the same time, however, a cardinal principle of economic forecasting is that we must rely on the past as a principal guide to what the future may be like.

Therefore, barring *unforeseen* changes of a favorable character, we must suppose that the balance of payments in the coming six years will be no more favorable than it has been in the past six. In that case, and given the manner in which the gold-exchange standard operates, the United States would probably become financially nonviable at some point during those years.

Against the background of such a proposition, perhaps the most hopeful thing one can say is that—fortunately—the past *need* not repeat itself in the future.

Conclusion

My survey has uncovered interests at stake in the possible future development of the U.S. balance of payments which transcend the profit-making activities of great banks and international corporations. Above and beyond these interests lies a possible danger to the international financial position of the dollar itself and thereby to world financial stability.

A strong implication of my analysis is that this danger will not be dissipated unless we in the United States can manage to free ourselves from wishful thinking and fallacious arguments so that we can come to grips with important policy choices which will have to be made.

The United States is, as the title of Peter B. Kenen's book reminds us, a "giant among nations"; but we should not forget that giants, like ordinary mortals, must manage their affairs prudently and be able to change with the times.

As long as the world outside the United States believed itself to be chronically short of gold and dollars, the United States could afford to be quite a carefree giant—free, that is, from financial limitations on its behavior. But once the dollar became less scarce in the world, the all-important financial basis for this freedom of action disappeared. In the late 1930s, in the 1940s, and in the early 1950s the United States had its day, financially speaking, on the world stage; but thus far in the 1960s the United States—while still an economic giant—has found its financial freedom to maneuver on the world stage steadily reduced.

As someone once put it, when balance of payments limitations began to restrict our freedom of action, "the Americans had to rejoin the human race." But have we really rejoined the human race in the sense of seriously reexamining the fundamentals of our position in the world? Have we not, instead, temporized in the face of what should have been a spur to new attitudes and new policies? Even at the highest levels of government have we not continued to act as if our balance of payments difficulties "must be" transient—while we go on paying out gold under the grim rules of the gold-exchange standard and resorting to "temporary" palliatives in the form of selective policy de-liberalizations?

Market Forces and Government Policies

At least two quite different kinds of economic forces come into focus in a country's balance of payments: (1) impersonal market forces which eventuate in private exports, imports, foreign investment, and so forth; and (2) the financial implications of certain governmental policies such as loans, grants, and the cost of foreign military activities.

Now it is a commonplace observation that corrective economic adjustments which work through impersonal market forces have become quite slow to make themselves felt in the modern world. This is because of rigidities due to such factors as fixed exchange rates, full employment policies, and imperfect competition. The corollary of this proposition is not so frequently stated, however. It is: because these economic and social rigidities inhibit rapid adjustment through impersonal market forces, those basic governmental policies that have important balance of payments effects must be changed much *more* promptly if foreign payments equilibrium is to be reattained within a reasonable period of time. Today the United States is in balance of payments trouble because neither impersonal market forces nor basic governmental policies have changed in the required direction rapidly enough.

If we remain loyal to our liberal philosophy, we cannot resort to direct controls over the market; and therefore if we wish to speed up our balance of payments adjustment, we must operate mainly through those policies of the government itself which largely affect the balance of payments. As evidence of the fact that we have allowed too many of our foreign policies to become atrophied, let me mention only three important policies which have important implications for the balance of payments and which have remained essentially unchanged since they were first adopted to cope with the problems of President Truman's Administration:

(1) When the U.S.-inspired International Monetary Fund started operations in 1947 with scrupulously limited powers, few people recognized that because these powers were so inadequate, the United States would soon find itself replacing the United Kingdom at the painful center of the gold-exchange standard which had proved itself unworkable in the inter-war years.

Today the United States has allowed its international solvency to become dependent on this discredited monetary "system" which allows foreign governments—including those who wish to force us to change our policies—the option of drawing on our gold stock whenever they wish.

(2) In 1949 the United States hastily, but effectively, took the leadership in establishing NATO to defend Western Europe, which, though a vitally important center of the world power, was temporarily weakened both economically and politically. Battle-ready Russian troups under the command of a paranoid old Bolshevik were in a position to march across undefended plains into the industrial centers of Europe, where large, well-organized Communist parties would have welcomed their arrival as "deliverers."

Today the United States still maintains—and heavily finances—NATO as a kind of military proprietorship in Western Europe, still poised mainly to counteract the 1949 threat. Since 1949, however, Western Europe, Russia, military technology, the prestige of Communism, and the U.S. gold stock have changed out of all recognition.

(3) Also in 1949, when President Truman delivered his inaugural address, he added a fourth point suggesting that the United States should extend limited amounts of technical assistance to the less developed countries of the world—assistance which he thought would be adequate to activate their economies.

Today the U.S. Congress is still agonizing anew each year over economic aid to the less developed countries, which is a tiny and steadily shrinking bit of our economic output. We are still lecturing these countries on their "need" to attract U.S. private investment, although scarcely any of them have at any time been in a position to offer U.S. business the kind of investment climate to which it has responded in, say, Canada or Western Europe. Meanwhile, we blow hot and then cold on supporting their long-term development plans which, according to the World Bank, need about 100 percent more aid than we are now supplying. We also try to forget that today the less developed countries have the controlling votes in the United Nations and that many of them face deepening—and terrifying—economic, social, and political crises in the near future.

Propositions for National Debate

These and other foreign policy issues should be subjected to a broad-gauged and urgent national debate looking toward fundamental changes in our international posture which will recognize the changes that have taken place both in the world as a whole and in our own financial position since the hectic—but invigorating—days of the Truman Administration. Such a debate might start around some of the following propositions:

President Johnson's "voluntary" balance of payments restrictions will not work in the long run. Instead, they will embitter relations between business and government while continuing to repress the growth of foreign investment income, which is the only sector of our balance of payments that is showing a significantly favorable trend. Therefore, a target cutoff date should be set for them forthwith. At the same time, Congress must speed permanent changes in tax legislation to (a) encourage businessmen to increase U.S. exports, and (b) attract more foreign capital to the United States.

The Administration should begin conferring actively with foreign governments about ways to improve the effectiveness of overseas capital markets—in less developed countries as well as in Western Europe. Perhaps the international productivity team approach, which became justly famous in the days of the Truman Administration, could be revived to hasten this essential task. After all, it should not be impossible to convince the Western Europeans that they can obtain the advantages of further industrial rationalization by using their own savings as well as by leaving the field open to U.S. capital. There would be gains on both sides of the Atlantic to the extent that an improved European-wide capital market would in this way inhibit the piling up of gold and dollar reserves in Europe.

Further temporizing with the present form of the gold-exchange standard is not in our national interest—however the continental Western Europeans may feel about it. If the de-monetization of gold proves to be the only available alternative, we should move in this direction before those who hoard gold gain the extra power they need to force us to do their bidding.

Our military operations abroad have turned out to be much more costly to the balance of payments than was ever expected. The United States must work energetically for policies of détente in both the West and the Far East—for financial reasons as well as for long-run political and survival reasons. The policy of "containing" Communism by military means which was initiated during the Truman Administration is in need of fresh debate and reassessment today lest it come to be absentmindedly applied to all of the less developed countries—years after it was formulated to oppose Stalin's 100-odd divisions which threatened Western Europe.

Foreign economic aid has been successfully adapted to constraints set by the balance of payments, and it should be expanded—on a "tied" basis while this is still financially necessary. It may stave off the rise of aggressively hostile regimes in the less developed countries, and it could be the single policy innovation for which we will be longest remembered. It is a technique of peace, and the world needs peace more desperately with each new increase in man's power over nature. Whether or not we get peace is partly a U.S. decision (Henry Adams once said that a passion for peace is the chief trait in the American character).

Although the United States has postponed for too long the foreign policy adjustment it must make to the unwelcome situation in its balance of payments, we still have the opportunity to make those adjustments, for the most part on our own terms. At such a time, it is well to recall that the greatest thing about an opportunity is still the ability to recognize—and seize—it.

The International
Payments System and
the Role of the Dollar

Committee for
Economic Development

The smooth functioning of international payments arrangements requires a maximum degree of cooperation among nations because most countries are striving to achieve simultaneously a number of domestic and international goals that have to be brought into some kind of over-all harmony. Individual nations desire to achieve balance in their international payments with a minimum sacrifice of domestic objectives such as full employment and a steady rate of growth at stable prices. At the same time there is a general desire to have balance in international accounts achieved with a maximum degree of freedom of international trade and payments. Such freedom provides the greatest assurance that the world's productive resources will be allocated most efficiently and will result in the highest output of goods and services.

The Adjustment Process

The composition, quantity, and distribution of reserves (and credit availability) are closely related to the adjustment process through which individual nations bring their international payments into balance. All countries desire sufficient official reserves to make it possible for them to finance deficits that may occur in their international accounts. The reserve cushion allows time for deficit countries to take economic measures, while maintaining their fixed exchange rates, to achieve balance in their international accounts with the minimum sacrifice of domestic goals. Countries whose international accounts are in surplus may accumulate reserves or liquidate debts incurred earlier; if the surplus continues for any length of time they should consider measures to rectify the imbalance in their international accounts by, for example, extending credit to other countries and liberalizing their trade policies.

The Ministers of the "Group of Ten" industrial nations participating with the IMF in the General Arrangements to Borrow[1] have underscored the need for mutual adjustment by both surplus and deficit countries if exchange rates are to be maintained and goods and payments are to continue to move freely across national borders:

Reprinted by permission of the Committee for Economic Development. From *The Dollar and the World Monetary System.*

[1] See footnote 3.

The smooth functioning of the international monetary system depends on the avoidance of major and persistent imbalances and on the effective use of appropriate policies by national governments to correct them when they occur. The process of adjustment and the need for international liquidity are closely interrelated. If there is not enough liquidity, countries may not have time to make adjustments in an orderly fashion, and may be forced into measures that are disruptive both to their domestic economies and to international economic relationships. If, on the other hand, there is too much liquidity, the adjustment mechanism may function too slowly and a delay in taking measures necessary to restore balance will in the end be harmful at home as well as abroad. [2]

Countries with balance-of-payments deficits cannot expect countries with surpluses to finance their deficits by granting them endless credits. Ever increasing credits would contribute to world-wide inflation. Moreover, the longer the unbalancing factors are allowed to continue the more damage may be done to the cost structure of deficit countries and the more painful it will be to eradicate them. It is for this reason that early detection and early correct diagnosis of emerging imbalances are important. A recent report of Working Party III of the Organization for Economic Cooperation and Development (OECD) on *The Balance of Payments Adjustment Process* has urged the institution of an "early warning system" to detect these emerging imbalances.

Deficit countries, however, may face very complex and difficult decisions in adjusting their international accounts without at the same time reducing their own domestic rates of growth and employment to socially and politically unacceptable levels. In some cases selective measures directed at external transactions—such as import surcharges, quotas, or capital controls—have been invoked. Indeed, less developed countries with large deficits in their trade accounts and who desire to maintain fixed exchange rates may regard some direct controls as temporarily necessary to protect their reserves.

Generally, the more advanced countries when in deficit for any length of time should seek the proper mix of fiscal and monetary policies to restrain the total level of internal demand; they should also see that efforts necessary to improve the country's productivity are reinforced by wage-price restraint. It should be recognized as it was at Bretton Woods, that on rare occasions adjustment of exchange rates may be required when a country's balance-of-payments deficit reflects "fundamental disequilibrium." But such exchange rate adjustments would not be regarded as a continuing instrument of adjustment among industrial countries. . . .

Although surplus countries feel less compulsion to redress their payments imbalances, they also have an interest in a stable monetary order. In recent years several European nations with surpluses in their international accounts have reduced the resulting internal inflationary pressures by maintaining high interest

---

[2] Point 5, Joint Statement of the Ministers of the Group of Ten, August 10, 1964.

rates and tight monetary policies without undertaking fiscal restraint. But these policies have encouraged inflows of foreign capital, thus tending to increase the balance-of-payments surpluses of these nations. Given an international system that calls for free money and capital markets, a mix of restrictive fiscal measures combined with relatively easier monetary policies would have made the most effective contribution to a stable international payments system at the same time as it dampened excessive domestic demand. Easier monetary policies, especially lower interest rates, would have discouraged capital inflows and could have encouraged capital outflows. Surplus countries also should consider opening their markets more freely to imports as well as to foreign borrowers. Similarly, they might cut away the restrictions on the use by their citizens of foreign currencies for purposes of trade, travel, and investment. Assumption by the surplus countries of a greater share of the defense and aid burdens of the Free World would be another important step in the same direction.

Institutional Arrangements

In its broadest sense the international monetary system embraces all those individual transactions which are conducted daily among individuals, companies, financial institutions, and governments of different countries. Normally buyers and sellers of foreign currencies in one country settle their transactions in the local currency by operating through the foreign exchange market. Only net purchases or sales therefore require transfer across national boundaries. Most of these transfers are settled in the currencies of the major trading countries whose banking facilities are well established and whose money and capital markets provide the major sources of credit. Thus, it is not surprising that the dollar has become the most important international trading currency.

In another sense, the term "international monetary system" may be defined to include all the institutional arrangements and cooperative undertakings[3] through which the individual nations hold their official reserves and settle balances in accounts among themselves, and abide by certain rules of the road for trade and payments.

These official arrangements reflect the desire of the nations to provide an equitable and efficient method of carrying out international transactions. The International Monetary Fund Agreement, among other things, was designed to promote the free convertibility of national currencies with one another. Most of the major countries and many of the others have committed themselves to maintain the exchange rates of their currencies within one percent either side of the par value

---

[3] Among the institutional arrangements are (1) the Articles of Agreement of the International Monetary Fund; (2) the General Arrangements to Borrow concluded by the IMF with the "Group of Ten" major industrial nations; and (3) the General Agreement on Tariffs and Trade (GATT). Cooperative undertakings include, for example, the regular meetings of certain central bank managers at the Bank of International Settlements, and the currency swap arrangements concluded by central banks or governments.

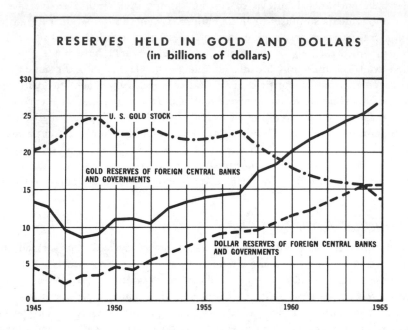

RESERVES HELD IN GOLD AND DOLLARS
(in billions of dollars)

U. S. GOLD STOCK

GOLD RESERVES OF FOREIGN CENTRAL BANKS
AND GOVERNMENTS

DOLLAR RESERVES OF FOREIGN CENTRAL BANKS
AND GOVERNMENTS

Source: Federal Reserve Bulletin.

Figure 1.

declared to the IMF. This rate may be altered only in case of severe imbalance in a country's international accounts. The par value of the United States dollar is $35 per fine troy ounce of gold. The United States is the only country which makes its currency freely convertible into gold at a fixed price whenever requested to do so by foreign monetary authorities, and thus provides an official link between all world currencies and gold.[4]

---

[4] The Federal Reserve Bank of New York stood ready until 1962 as the Fiscal Agent of the United States Treasury to buy gold at $34.9125 and to sell gold at $35.0875 a fine ounce for official monetary purposes. Thus our margin was ¼ of one percent below and above our parity. Since 1962 the Treasury has bought and sold gold at $35.00.

Foreign countries which maintain foreign exchange markets uphold the par value of their own currencies by intervening in the market to buy their own currencies with dollars when their own currencies start falling toward the lower limit of the range. On the other hand, when the exchange rate reaches the upper limit they buy dollars with their own currencies. Thus, if the value of the dollar falls because dollars are in excess supply, then eventually foreign monetary authorities will acquire dollars and may turn them in to the United States Treasury for gold.

Because the dollar is not only the world's leading trading currency but also its prime reserve currency, and used as such by many countries along with gold to settle official debts to other countries, the dollar has become the world's standard of value and the keystone of the world's monetary system. The wide acceptance of our currency reflects the size of our market for goods and services, the size of our capital markets, the high productivity of our economy, the relative stability of the dollar's value, and the dollar's special link to gold. Confidence in the dollar has rested on the nation's fiscal probity, price stability, and liberal traditions.

As stated above, countries today hold their *official* reserves partly in the form of gold and partly in dollars and pounds sterling. They also can count as reserves "Reserve Positions in the International Monetary Fund." This component of reserves is represented by those rights which member countries can exercise "virtually at will" to draw other currencies from the IMF. Additional international liquidity beyond official reserves may be provided through credits obtained on a conditional basis from other nations or the IMF.

Our Deficit and International Reserves

Under current arrangements, additions to the world's official reserves can be made in three ways: *increments* to the world's stock of monetary gold, *additions* to official institutions' holdings of reserve currencies, principally dollars, and increases in drawing rights at the IMF.

Over the past 15 years, reserves of the Free World have increased at an average annual rate of about 2.5 percent. This figure obscures the fact that reserves outside the United States increased at 5.5 percent per year while the United States reserves actually declined. For the period 1958–1965, new monetary gold provided only about 20 percent of the increase in reserves for countries outside the United States. About 73 percent of the increase in reserves outside the United States came from net sales of gold by this country, the increase in United States dollar liabilities to foreign official institutions, and reduction in this country's Reserve Position in the IMF.

The deficits run by the United States and general increases in drawing rights at the IMF have provided the rest of the world with substantial reserves. It might be said that the United States deficits had to be large enough, at least during the fifties, to enable foreign central banks also to build up their own gold reserves, mostly through purchases of United States gold.

World reserves, however, can increase substantially under the present system, without a decision at the international level, only if foreign official institutions are willing to add to their dollar holdings or a large amount of gold is added to official reserves. To the extent that foreigners are unwilling to add to their dollar holdings it becomes impossible for the United States to have a deficit without at least an equivalent loss of reserves. If foreigners choose to convert dollars into gold in an amount exceeding the United States deficit, world reserves would actually decline unless offsetting increases occurred in total official gold holdings or in automatic drawing rights at the IMF.

A critical question, and one to which it would be impossible for the United States alone to give an answer, is how much additional reserves in the form of dollar claims the world's central banks are going to want year by year.

Were the balance-of-payments issues limited to this one question, designing the United States response to its deficit might still be a relatively simple matter. The United States goal would be a deficit exactly equal in size to the world's need for liquid dollar claims. For as long as the deficit did not exceed this amount there would be little danger of an oversupply of dollars leading to purchases of gold by foreigners. However, the United States also performs the role of banker to the world.

During the postwar period the United States has provided the world with reserves by capital outflows and aid which have exceeded the United States current account surplus. Part of these capital outflows have been generated by the process of financial "intermediation" in which the United States, as banker to the world, borrowed short and lent at long and intermediate terms. To the extent that its loans to foreigners were offset by foreigners putting their own money into liquid dollar assets, the United States cannot be accused of over-investing abroad. Assuming there is no crisis of confidence in the dollar, a large proportion of the short-term dollar claims accumulated by foreigners in this process are relatively stable in the sense that they do not necessarily represent a call on United States gold reserves. It should be clear, however, that at times part of these private holdings of liquid dollar assets can and have moved into the hands of foreign central banks and thus have become a claim on United States gold.

The function of the United States as banker is crucial to the health of the international payments mechanism. Financial intermediation performs essentially two functions.

First, it supplies to foreign enterprises long-term loans and investment funds for which they would have to pay more domestically and which they often cannot get in the amount they need at any price. This function performed by American financial institutions facilitates investment and economic growth abroad.

The second function is a necessary counterpart to the first. The United States supplies liquidity to foreign asset holders who put funds in this country at short term because they gain safety, liquidity, and an interest return. Under these conditions foreigners find short-term dollar deposits more attractive than keeping such funds at home. The conditions for these private financial operations are created in large part by the existence of differences in liquidity preferences in one nation's capital and money markets as against another's. Many observers believe that Europeans, for example, have been less willing than Americans to hold their financial assets in long-term, less liquid forms, and to have short-term, rather than long-term liabilities outstanding against them. The resulting trade in financial assets has been an important contributor to growth outside the United States.

How much the banking function contributes to the United States balance-of-payments deficit on a Liquidity basis is difficult to estimate accurately. However, it should be clear that any action we take to limit this banking function will have an adverse effect on investment conditions abroad.

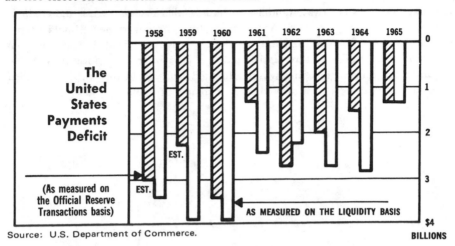

Source: U.S. Department of Commerce.

Figure 2.

Calculating the Deficit

In simplified terms, the international payments of the United States are balanced over a given period (normally a calendar quarter or year) on the *Liquidity basis* when there is no loss of United States reserves (principally gold) and no increase in foreign *official* or *private* short-term claims on the United States. Elimination of the deficit by the Liquidity method of calculation would imply a cessation of growth in deposits and short-term investments in the United States by private foreigners unless our own reserves increased correspondingly.

By the *Official Reserve Transactions* method of calculation the deficit is measured in terms of losses in our reserves plus increases in dollar liabilities to *official* foreign monetary authorities and governments and to international institutions; all voluntary placements of funds in this country by *private* foreigners are treated as capital inflows in the balance of payments, reducing the deficit, not as items financing the deficit as in the Liquidity calculation.

The distinction between *official* and *private* dollar holdings is important. From 1959 through 1965 the growth of world commerce has been accompanied by an average increase of over $700 million a year in short-term dollar holdings of private foreigners. The percentage increase in private foreign holdings of dollars closely paralleled the percentage gain in world trade, suggesting a connection between the desire of private foreigners to hold dollars and the volume of world trade.

We believe that, while increases in liabilities to private foreigners have some importance, the right course now is to aim at eliminating the deficit on the Official

Reserve Transactions basis.[5] If the United States is to continue to play its part in financing growth of world trade, it should not—in the interest of checking gold losses and increases in liabilities to foreign monetary authorities—threaten to eliminate increases in private holdings of liquid dollar assets, of cash and credit to support international business. At the same time the government should keep a watchful eye on trends in the Liquidity deficit. It is recognized that private dollar holdings could represent a potential drain on gold reserves; if foreigners should acquire more dollars than they wished to hold, they could turn them in to their monetary authorities who in turn could cash them in for gold.

---

[5] The charts throughout this statement are consistent with the Official Reserve Transactions basis of calculation.

Euro-Dollars

Oscar L. Altman

It would not be surprising if the Euro-dollar were something of a mystery to those unfamiliar with it. To begin with, it is a comparative newcomer on the international financial scene, dating only from 1958–59. Again, the expression "Euro-dollar market" is rather misleading, since the market is not confined to Europe and does not trade only in dollars. Sterling deposited in Paris is traded in what is called the Euro-dollar market, and residents of the United States borrow Euro-dollars outside the country as well as dollars in it. Small wonder if the Euro-dollar market seems to be a confusing institution, best left to the international bankers who created it and the economists who presumably understand it.

It is, however, also important to people who have no direct connection with it, since all the major institutions which have a part in determining the character of international trade—which facilitate it or hinder it, or which make it more or less flexible or convenient—are important. There is no doubt that the Euro-dollar market, although new and wholly unofficial in character, has become an indispensable part of the international monetary system.

Having grown from virtually nothing to more than $10 billion in net assets in the last eight years, the Euro-dollar market is now one of the world's largest markets for short-term funds—mostly dollars. It is an international market, and it is one of the freest, most competitive, and most flexible capital markets that exists anywhere. Its flexibility is demonstrated by the manner in which, with scarcely a sign of strain, and with little short-term effect upon interest rates, it has handled large in-and-out movements of funds. A notable example is the repatriation of dollars in 1965, which the United States made part of its program of voluntary restraint to deal with its balance of payments deficit. Another example is the large borrowings by Italian commercial banks in 1963–64, amounting to perhaps $750 million, followed in 1965–66 by a reduction of these borrowings and investment of more than $1 billion. The market has survived a number of business failures involving losses of Euro-dollar funds in Germany and the United States that have had considerable publicity; it seems to have tightened its procedures as a result of them.

Reprinted by permission of the publisher from *Finance and Development*, Vol. IV, No. 1 (March 1967).

What Is the Euro-Dollar Market?

The Euro-dollar market is a market, located principally in Europe, for lending and borrowing the world's most important convertible currencies. The currency mainly dealt in is the dollar, but the market also deals in such major European currencies as the pound sterling, the Swiss franc, the deutsche mark, the Netherlands guilder, and the French franc. The professional participants in it are commercial banks, but merchant banks, private banks, and some investment banking firms are included.

Funds flow into the market from forty to fifty countries on all continents; these are owned by official monetary institutions, other government agencies, banks, industrial and commercial enterprises, and private individuals. Funds flow out for investment in a large number of countries, including Japan and the United States. Commercial banks in London, Paris, and other European cities are the principal intermediaries or dealers in the Euro-dollar market, and they "make" the market in the sense that they are willing to accept Euro-dollars in the form of time deposits (since June 1966 a few banks also have been prepared to issue negotiable certificates of deposit) or to make loans or investments in Euro-dollars. It is characteristic of the market that these transactions are made in large amounts, often of $1 million or more, at competitive rates of interest.

The Euro-dollar market attracts funds because it offers higher rates of interest, greater flexibility of maturities, and a wider range of investment qualities than other short-term capital markets; and the market is able to attract borrowers because it lends funds at relatively low rates of interest. It thus renders the financial service of intermediating between owners of funds and would-be borrowers. The market operates with low costs because the banks and other firms that use it are well known, because the transactions are for substantial sums, and because dealings are highly competitive. The low costs are reflected in competitive advantages to both depositors and borrowers.

But this description does not touch upon one aspect of the market that gives it its unique character, namely, that the transactions in each currency take place outside the country where that currency originates. The market for Euro-dollars refers to the market in dollars outside the United States, not to the origin or the character of the dollars being dealt in. The Euro-dollar market in, say, London, thus deals overwhelmingly with titles to dollar deposits, i.e., dollars deposited in banks in the United States. Similarly, the market for Euro-sterling refers to the market for sterling outside the United Kingdom.

The Euro-dollar market (to use this common term to cover all the external markets in all the major convertible currencies) is closely allied to the great network of arbitrage transactions—that is to say, transactions designed to take advantage of differences in exchange rates and interest rates in the different trading centers. Thus, banks may borrow dollars and then lend them; they may borrow deutsche mark, swap them into dollars, and then lend dollars; or they may borrow dollars, swap them into deutsche mark, and then lend deutsche mark. Euro-dollar operations basically deal with the flow of funds from an initial owner to a final borrower, but in the process they affect the level of interest rates in different countries for funds lent for as short a time as one day or for as long as eighteen months. They also influence the exchange rates of the major convertible currencies, and the relationship of the rates being offered for present funds (spot rates) to the rates being offered for the same currency on specified future dates (forward rates). Although Euro-dollar operations *affect* all these other components of the international financial market, they do not *determine* them. All the components of the market are interrelated, and all of them are arbitraged in all directions.

How Are Euro-Dollars Used?

The process of using Euro-dollars and other currencies begins when some bank in the market collects funds in the form of deposits. The bank uses some of these funds in its own operations, and transfers the balance to another bank in the form of a deposit. This process may be repeated two or more times until all the funds are finally used in either of two ways: first, they are lent to a business enterprise other than a bank to finance commercial or industrial transactions; or second, they are used by banks to improve their reserves or liquidity and thus to contribute to their over-all operations.

A large part of the world's international trade is invoiced in, and must be paid for with, dollars and sterling and—to a much smaller extent—in and with the major currencies of continental Western Europe. Therefore, importers have found it useful to borrow Euro-dollars and other currencies when this was cheaper than borrowing their domestic currency—and Euro-dollars have often been notably cheaper than domestic funds. In the same way, exporters have often found it cheaper to finance the period between shipment of their goods, and payment of these goods in dollars or other major currencies, by borrowing dollars rather than their local currency. All in all, a substantial amount of international trade is financed by Euro-dollars.

But while international trade is the usual business of Euro-dollars, not all Euro-dollars are involved in it all the time. Where it is cheaper to borrow Euro-dollars than domestic currency, it is not surprising that some Euro-dollars are borrowed to finance operations or inventories of businesses not directly engaged in international trade, or to carry temporarily parts of new security issues. However, the domestic use of Euro-dollars has not been welcomed by all governments. When a country has domestic interest rates and monetary and credit policies that differ a good deal from the world average, residents can use Euro-dollars to limit their effects or even escape from them. Hence, some governments have, as a matter of general policy, restricted the ability of their corporations to borrow Euro-dollars for domestic purposes while permitting them to borrow Euro-dollars for international purposes. In effect, they have recognized that borrowing Euro-dollars for financing exports, imports, shipping, and the like is a "natural" procedure that strengthens the international trading positions of their corporations, while banning such borrowing would be difficult to enforce, especially where corporations have widespread international activities. Thus, even countries that limit Euro-dollar borrowings (e.g., France and Sweden) may permit a wool or banana importer or a shipping company to borrow Euro-dollars but forbid a department store or hotel chain to do the same thing.

Other countries, however, including Italy, Germany, and the United States, allow (and sometimes encourage) their corporations to borrow Euro-dollars and other foreign currencies. Indeed, a substantial part of all bank loans to Italian corporations is made in foreign currencies, notably dollars and Swiss francs. Corporations in Germany have borrowed large amounts from abroad; and even when such borrowings have been denominated in deutsche mark, the funds for these transactions were probably obtained by borrowing Euro-dollars and then swapping them into domestic currency. In the last two years, U.S. corporations have been strongly encouraged to borrow funds abroad, as part of that country's balance of payments adjustment program.

Who Owns Euro-Dollars?

The "original" owners of the dollars and other currencies initially placed in the market are a widely varied group; they may be individuals, commercial banks, international agencies such as the Bank for International Settlements, or national central banks or monetary authorities; they may or may not be residents of the country where the currency originates.

Until 1965, when the United States first took steps to control the export of capital in order to improve its balance of payments position, a substantial part of the dollars deposited in the Euro-dollar market was owned by U.S. residents. They placed deposits either in Canadian banks (which in turn redeposited part of them with banks in Europe) or in European banks. In response to the current U.S. informal controls on short-term capital movements, most of these Euro-dollar deposits have been repatriated. Moreover, since a large amount of dollars deposited with European branches of U.S. banks is now being put at the disposal of the head offices of these banks in the United States—making these head offices borrowers of Euro-dollars—the United States has become a net debtor to the Euro-dollar market. This situation would, of course, be reversed if money market conditions in the United States became easier and if the balance of payments situation of the United States improved.

Only a small part of the dollar deposits in the Euro-dollar market at the present time is, therefore, owned by residents of the United States. The overwhelming bulk of these deposits represents dollars already owned by foreigners or purchased by them with other currencies. Nonresidents already own large amounts of dollars. At the end of 1965 foreign holdings of dollars totaled $25 billion, of which $14 billion was held by central banks and other governmental agencies outside the United States, $7 billion was held by commercial banks (other than U.S. banks), and $4 billion was held by all other non-U.S. holders.

Central Banks Are Large Owners

In an earlier article, the writer pointed out that, in the summer of 1962, some twenty or twenty-five central banks or monetary authorities had directly or indirectly deposited dollars in the Euro-dollar market. He also pointed out that it was conservative to assume that two-thirds of all the funds in the European markets came from this source. The conclusion that a substantial part of the dollars in the market was owned directly or indirectly by central banks and monetary authorities was considered quite surprising.

At the present time, the number of central banks or monetary authorities that have placed funds in the Euro-dollar market is probably more than twenty-five, but their percentage of total funds has decreased. Yet it is probably fair to say that at least one-third of the Euro-dollar deposits in the eight major European countries at the end of 1965 were owned, directly or indirectly, by monetary or governmental agencies.

The decrease in the proportion of official funds in the Euro-dollar market since 1962 is probably attributable to two factors: foreign official dollar holdings have increased less in this period than foreign nonofficial dollar holdings—by $1 billion compared with $3 billion; and the rate of interest obtainable on funds lent in the United States is now nearly as great as can be earned in the Euro-dollar market.

Other Owners

Commercial banks own a sizable amount of the dollars deposited in the Euro-dollar market. Their funds come from four sources: dollars deposited by their customers; other foreign currencies deposited by their customers and swapped into dollars; domestic currency owned by the bank and swapped into dollars; and dollars borrowed by the bank in the Euro-dollar market and redeposited in other banks at a higher rate of interest or for a more convenient length of time. All these actions reflect the self-interest of the banks and the desire to earn the higher rate of interest available on the Euro-dollar deposits compared with that obtainable on short-term securities in their own countries. The banks may also wish to improve the liquidity of their assets or to obtain a better distribution of the maturities of these assets. The Euro-dollar market provides greater flexibility in these respects than do any short-term money markets except those in the United States and the United Kingdom.

Other business enterprises, particularly those in international trade, may find it profitable to hold excess balances, or even working funds in dollars, partly because dollars can easily be invested and partly because so much of international trade and services is denominated or paid in dollars.

It has sometimes been said that Euro-dollar funds may be borrowed to finance issues of long-term securities in Europe, particularly those denominated in dollars. A more recent and potentially more important development has resulted from these security issues denominated in dollars, particularly the most recent ones by subsidiaries or affiliates of corporations. Many such issues were floated in advance of need, so that the proceeds could be deposited in the Euro-dollar market until they were used to pay for plant and equipment. Thus, through the mechanism of this market, private and institutional holdings of dollars for long-term investment were temporarily converted into additional supplies of short-term dollars for the Euro-dollar market.

The owners of deposits made in sterling are probably broadly similar to those who make them in dollars, though the proportions held by classes of owners are somewhat different. Deposits denominated in currencies other than dollars and sterling probably show a quite different pattern of ownership, since central banks do not hold reserves in these currencies (except for the relatively small amount held in French francs) and therefore cannot deposit them in the Euro-dollar market.

An "Unofficial" Creation

The Euro-dollar market has grown up, and continues to grow, without official favors, subsidies, or tax advantages. The market is so broad, so international, and so competitive that it cannot be controlled or even greatly influenced by any one country. This has important advantages in mobilizing capital, lowering and unifying interest rates, and increasing competition in banking. On the other hand, as we have seen, a number of countries have taken the view that their national economies should be shielded, to a greater or lesser extent, from the operations of the Euro-dollar market. Therefore, individual countries have from time to time increased or decreased the ability of their banks and business enterprises to use the facilities of the market.

Rates of interest charged by banks for loans in Euro-dollars tend to be lower—and sometimes very much lower—than those charged by these same banks for loans made in domestic currencies. Because of the market, large enterprises have access to more banks in more countries. The market has thus intensified banking competition in many countries, and notably those in which competition is restricted by regulation, cartel arrangements, or gentlemen's agreements. This competition has been welcomed in some countries (Italy is one example) because it has tended to lower domestic interest rates, including those charged on loans made in local currency by local banks. In other countries (such as Germany) this competition has been criticized on the grounds that it has fostered unsound banking competition and therefore encouraged the making of riskier loans.

The International Financial System and the Euro-Dollar Market

As well as increasing competition in banking, the Euro-dollar market has had two important effects upon the international financial system.

First, it has strengthened for the time being the position of the dollar, largely because it has made it more profitable to borrow or to hold dollars. As already noted, official and nonofficial holders of dollars have been able to earn higher rates of return in the Euro-dollar market than in the United States; and to the extent that their total holdings are responsive to higher rates of interest they perhaps hold more dollars than they would if there were no Euro-dollar market. And it is obvious that when more dollars are used in international trade and financing, fewer dollars are converted into gold.

Second, the market has facilitated the financing of balance of payments surpluses and deficits. This aspect of the market has not as yet received the attention it deserves. Countries with balance of payments deficits have borrowed funds from the Euro-dollar market to reduce the demands upon their reserves. Thus, when the Bank of Italy in 1963–64 encouraged its commercial banks to borrow in the Euro-dollar market, it shielded Italian reserves from the full effects of a capital outflow and a payment deficit. On the other hand, countries with balance of payments surpluses have been able to minimize the domestic effects of these surpluses (and the growth of official reserves) by encouraging their residents to deposit dollars in the Euro-dollar market directly or through the commercial banking system. This was done in Germany in the early 1960s and in Italy when its balance of payments recovered in 1965–66.

The Euro-dollar market, then, has come to play an important role in providing a mechanism for attracting funds from governments, banks, business enterprises, and individuals, and for lending funds to banks, business enterprises, and individuals, and, directly or indirectly, to governments. In doing so, it has contributed to both private and public international liquidity and it has improved the level and the efficiency of this liquidity.

Is It Here To Stay?

Two related questions are frequently asked about the Euro-dollar market: is it here to stay? and—in particular—can it continue after the United States swings into a balance of payments surplus? The answer to the first question is that the Euro-dollar market has become an integral part of international financial markets, and its functions will have to be performed by itself or by some other market unless the world moves toward financial autarchy.

The answer to the second question is more difficult to state briefly. Because the Euro-dollar market dates from 1958–59, when the United States first developed large balance of payments deficits, it is often assumed that its deficits created the market and that a balance of payments surplus will reduce or even destroy it. But since governments and residents of many countries have found the market valuable and make extensive use of it, the size is not determined by the U.S. position alone. It is also affected by the extent of the balance of payments surpluses of all countries, and by the balance of payments deficits of the major countries with good credit standing that are willing to borrow, or to let their banks borrow.

It seems likely that the operations of the Euro-dollar market would not be significantly curtailed if the United States developed a balance of payments surplus—and, indeed, might even continue to increase.

Advantage & dis.

U.S. Government Restrictions on Foreign Investments

Robert L. Kerstiens

Introduction

For seventeen of the last eighteen years, the United States has had a deficit in its balance of payments. On January 1, 1968, President Johnson in his address to the nation announced, among other measures to help the balance of payments situation, a program of mandatory restraints on business investments abroad. This new program, restricting overseas investments, is the culmination of nearly three years of a program of "voluntary restraint" on this type of investment. In order to reduce the continuing balance of payments deficits, businesses had been asked to voluntarily restrict their direct foreign investments.

The government contended that in the short run, the balance of payments situation would be helped by restraining capital outflows. The business community, in opposition to such restraints, pointed out that, in the long run, the income position of foreign operations would be endangered and that future balance of payments credits in the form of return on overseas investments would be lost. . . . Some overseas investments have been foregone, and some future income returns have been lost; but as of the time of this writing the effect of the voluntary program on future balance of payments credits of income returns has not been substantial. This paper views three main situations:

(1) Arguments for and against the restraint programs, particularly the viewpoint of the business community.

(2) The effects of the voluntary program on the balance of payments and on foreign investments.

(3) The possible effects of the new mandatory program.

The Growth of Direct Foreign Investments and the B/P Problem

The reasons for the great increase in direct foreign investments over the past decade are many and have been well documented elsewhere. Demand, con-

Reprinted by permission of Robert L. Kerstiens.

sumption, and profits in foreign areas, particularly Europe, have been high, and American companies met this growing market by investing in foreign plant facilities rather than by exporting. Also, tariff walls and integrated markets in some instances kept out U.S. exports and necessitated foreign operations if an American company wished to sell to the markets.

A study by the National Industrial Conference Board indicates how production abroad by U.S.-owned subsidiaries has overtaken exports by U.S. firms as the most important means of meeting foreign demand. The value of U.S. direct foreign investments at the end of 1966 was $54.6 billion, with sales of $110 billion, while U.S. exports were about $29.3 billion. Thus production abroad, being four to five times as large as exports, is seen by the NICB as the "primary link between U.S. producers and foreign markets."

Since 1958, the U.S. has had continuing, significant deficits in its B/P accounts with a large part of the debit entries consisting of investment outflows of private capital. However, it is also important that while these capital outflows occurred, substantial returns on overseas investments took place in the form of income remittances, royalties, and fees, and they contributed as credit entries to the B/P accounts. Further, direct investments have some effect on the amount of merchandise exported and imported by U.S. companies. (See Table 1 for these numerical trends.) In every year since 1958, income on investments alone, not counting royalties and fees, was above the direct investment outflows of the same year. Thus it is obvious that restraint programs on capital outflows could help the B/P in a given year; however, the effect of such restraints on future income returns would be detrimental. As will be seen later in this paper, the contribution of direct foreign investment to the B/P is an important factor in determining the usefulness of the restraint programs.

Deficits in the U.S. B/P in the early 1950s were considered necessary by both the U.S. and foreign countries in order to erase the "dollar gap" and the shortage of international liquidity which then existed. But, in 1958, the deficit rose to $3.5 billion and with Europe inflating, pressure was beginning to arise for the U.S. to do something about its continuous deficits. The B/P problem became of immediate concern to the government in late 1961 when European Central Banks were reluctant to accumulate further dollar balances.

In 1962, the method of taxing foreign earnings by American companies was changed in an attempt to bring about faster remittances to aid the B/P. In 1963, to cut down on long-term borrowing in the U.S. by foreigners, the interest equalization tax was proposed and later went into effect retroactively in that year. There was some improvement in the B/P accounts affected in 1963 and 1964, but there was an increase in other private capital outflows offsetting these gains. In November 1964, there occurred a run on sterling and with fears widespread of a devaluation of the reserve currencies, a large, short-term capital outflow from the U.S. took place. The stage was thereby set for new and stricter government measures to rectify the B/P problem.

The Voluntary Investment Restraint Program

In February and March of 1965, the government formulated its voluntary restraint program with the advice and guidance of the business community which was represented by an Advisory Committee of top executives of international businesses. The program was said to be temporary. Also in early 1965, the government initiated a restrictive program on lending abroad by banks and nonbank financial institutions.

Despite the fact that the government in several statements recognized the long-run payoff of direct foreign investment, the Administration decided that current capital outflows could not be afforded at their previously unrestricted levels. Secretary of Commerce, John T. Connor, noted a diminishing returns in restrictions on foreign investments and stated, "The competitive situation of our companies abroad could begin to deteriorate. Beyond that point (unidentified in time), we will have to have a different mix." The voluntary program became effective in April 1965, and was continued until January 1968 in spite of the government's recognition of the deleterious long-run effects on the competitive situation of American companies producing abroad.

The initial program *asked* certain U.S. companies (632 received letters of specifics) to increase by 15 to 20 percent in 1965 over 1964 their already positive contributions to the U.S. B/P. Ways in which companies were asked to assist were as follows:

(1) Avoid or postpone direct foreign investments in *developed* countries in marginal projects and in projects which do not soon result in higher exports and larger investment income. No restraints were called for on investment in *developing* countries.

(2) Restraint financing of overseas investments from funds raised in the U.S. or from foreign earnings that ordinarily would be repatriated.

(3) Arrange to get funds abroad, even if necessary at financing charges higher than in the U.S.

(4) Sell equities in foreign subsidiaries to residents in host countries.

(5) Accelerate repatriation of income earned abroad.

(6) Minimize the outflows of short-term financial funds and arrange for the orderly repatriation of such funds previously invested abroad.

(7) Expand exports to foreign subsidiaries and others.

Thus the basic aim of the voluntary program according to Secretary Connor was "not to restrain expenditures by U.S. companies on plant facilities abroad," but to "minimize the impact of the outflow of funds on the U.S. balance of payments." Capital investment for foreign plant and equipment spending could continue if funds could be raised abroad.

The original goals for B/P improvement were set by the individual companies themselves. Of the companies reporting, the total goal for 1965 was set at a $1.3

billion over-all contribution to the B/P. The program considered that different companies would be in different situations in regard to their past and planned investments and companies were therefore invited to confer with the Commerce Department about their particular situations. The program was somewhat flexible in interpretation.

The program rejected any serious changes in policy such as exchange controls or changes in gold policy. No direct penalties were established for failure to comply. However, the greatest constraint on business was not the program itself but the fear of the lurking alternative of compulsory measures should the voluntary discipline fail to achieve the needed degree of improvement in the external account. And importantly, since the program was emphasized as being only necessary temporarily, companies were given incentive to cooperate.

From its very beginning, the program was frequently being altered, with major revisions occurring before each new year on December 5, 1965, December 14, 1966, and November 16, 1967. With each revision the program was tightened; not because business was not complying with the program but because the B/P still was not being corrected enough. In various reports in *International Commerce* throughout 1965 to 1967, the Commerce Department repeatedly commended the businesses involved for their contributions to the B/P situation; as recently as December of 1967, Secretary of Commerce, Alexander B. Trowbridge, praised the participating firms for their improved showings. So while the government was patting business on the back for a job well done, each revision in the restraint program drove the "knife" of restrictions further into the same back.

The various program revisions tightened the restraint on direct investments in the following ways:

(1) Over-all targets for selected transactions and another special target for direct investment transactions were set *by the Commerce Department*. Direct investments are defined as the net outflow of funds from the U.S. plus the undistributed profits of subsidiaries abroad. The direct investment targets for *each* company in the three major revisions were as follows:

   (a) For the 1965–1966 two-year period, the target was 90 percent of the amount during 1962 to 1964.

   (b) For 1966–1967, the target was 80 percent of the amount during 1962–1964,

   (c) For 1967–1968, the target was 66-2/3 percent of the amount during 1962–1964.

(2) New countries were added to the developed countries list to which investments were restricted (April 1965; December 1965).

(3) More companies were added to the direct reporting list (400 in January 1966).

Despite these increasing limitations on foreign investments, it was repeatedly emphasized that the voluntary program was designed to "moderate, and not to halt, the outflow of U.S. capital, even in the short run." This was the official Administration line, up to the day when the mandatory restraint program was introduced. The voluntary program then, can be seen to have become increasingly tighter in its restrictions on business investments overseas. But as indicated, businesses in the program, for the most part, did comply with the provisions of the program, and the direct investment targets which were set originally by themselves and later by the Commerce Department were achieved.

The B/P and Direct Investments Under the Voluntary Restraint Program

For a number of reasons, including changes in the number of companies and changes in some of the ground rules by the Department of Commerce, results of the voluntary program over the years are not strictly comparable. Over-all improvements in the B/P sought by the Department from the reporting companies were as follows: $1.3 billion in 1965, $3.4 billion in 1966, $2.5 billion in 1967, and $2.6 billion in 1968, and the participating companies did achieve their goals for the first three years. These improvements by all the reporting companies include their contributions by restricting capital outflows for direct investments, by increasing exports, by increasing remittances of earnings, and by returning short-term capital deposits to the U.S. Since all these factors count in the voluntary program as contributing to the B/P, the amounts listed as over-all improvements in the B/P do not indicate that the B/P deficits in those years would have been that much worse without the voluntary program; instead they indicate the efforts of the reporting companies in contributing to the B/P through their overseas transactions. While these efforts on the part of businesses in the voluntary program were significant and influential in lowering the B/P deficits, it will be seen that the total B/P problem was not solved.

Increases in total direct investments abroad did taper off as in each of the three years, 1965, 1966, and 1967. The outflows were about $3.0 to $3.5 billion. (See Table 1.) Each revision in the direct investment outflow in the quarter following revision was at a lower level than in the previous quarter. (See Table 2—arrows indicate revision periods.) The stability in these investments is largely due to the success of the voluntary program's direct investment targets for companies.

While gains to the B/P were made in the capital account as direct investments levelled off, they were lost in other B/P accounts. This is true particularly of military expenditures abroad as the Vietnam War progressed. As Table 2 indicates, in the second quarter of 1965, foreign military expenditures began a steady climb in each quarter which continues up to the date of this writing. Curiously, the second quarter of 1965 is the same period when the program was beginning. Actually, the government in many of its statements has connected the necessity of restraint on direct investments with the Vietnam War, and in many people's minds the two events will end together.

Also, as can be seen in Table 1, the merchandise trade balance fell from $6.7 billion in 1964 to $3.7 billion in 1966. The merchandise balance of $3.5 billion in 1967 indicates that a further decline has been made.

Direct Investments, Related B/P Accounts, and the Liquidity Balance Deficits, 1958–1967

(In billions of dollars)

	1958	1959	1960	1961	1962	1963	1964	1965	1966	1967
Direct Investments	−1.181	−1.372	−1.674	−1.599	−1.654	−1.976	−2.435	−3.418	−3.543	−3.026
Income on Direct Investments	+2.121	+2.228	+2.355	+2.768	+3.044	+3.129	+3.674	+3.963	+4.045	+4.445
Royalties and Fees	+ .246	+ .348	+ .403	+ .463	+ .580	+ .660	+ .756	+ .924	+1.045	+1.126
Merchandise Trade Balance	+3.312	+ .985	+4.757	+5.744	+4.417	+5.079	+6.676	+4.722	+3.658	+3.48
Liquidity Balance Deficit	−3.365	−3.870	−3.901	−2.370	−2.203	−2.671	−2.800	−1.335	−1.357	−3.5

Source: *Survey of Current Business.*

Table 1.

B/P Gains in Direct Investments Lost in Other Accounts

(Millions, seasonally adjusted)

	1964				1965			
	I	II	III	IV	I	II	III	IV
Direct Investments	-451	-548	-664	-772	-1208*	-864	-628	-718*
Foreign Military Expenditures	-744	-732	-694	-691	-671	-716	-754	-785
Merchandise Trade Balance	+1787	+1569	+1640	+1680	+959	+1405	+1255	+1153
Liquidity Balance Deficit	-344	-614	-518	-1334	-818	+199	-457	-259

	1966				1967			
	I	II	III	IV	I	II	III	IV
Direct Investments	-634	-1006	-900	-1003*	-622	-648	-939*	-818
Foreign Military Expenditures	-861	-911	-953	-969	-1045	-1070	-1094	-1110
Merchandise Trade Balance	+1178	+956	+802	+722	+1009	+1154	+1077	+243
Liquidity Balance Deficit	-651	-122	-165	-419	-533	-533	-638	-185

*Indicates times when the voluntary program started and revised.

Source: *Survey of Current Business.*

Table 2.

In regard to the over-all liquidity balance deficits, Table 1 shows that the deficit was approximately halved in 1965 from 1964 as it reached $1.3 billion; in 1966, the deficit continued at a low $1.4 billion. Moreover in 1967, the liquidity balance deficit increased to $3.6 billion, particularly as a result of the fourth quarter's extremely large deficit of $1.8 billion. Even though the voluntary program had already been set to continue into 1968, the fourth-quarter deficit indicated that an even stronger restraint program was necessary.

Other Sources of Funds than Capital Outflows for Overseas Investment

As noted above, increases in direct investment outflows tapered off in 1966 and 1967. Nevertheless, plant and equipment expenditures of U.S. affiliates continued to rise from 1965 to 1967, though it was at a declining rate. (See Table 3.) From 1960 to 1965, capital outflows made up 36 to 46 percent of total plant and equipment expenditures abroad. Table 3 shows that in the years 1966 and 1967 the percentage had declined in both years, reaching as low as 31 percent in the latter year. Assuming that plant and equipment expenditures by overseas affiliates are an indication of the financial needs of the affiliates, the decline in direct investment outflows in 1966–1967 as a percent of total capital needs indicates that other sources of funds were increasingly being utilized.

Direct Investment Outflows as a % of Plant and Equipment Expenditures Abroad, 1960–1967

(In Billions of Dollars)

	1960	1961	1962	1963	1964	1965	1966	1967	1968
Plant and Equipment Expenditures Abroad	3.789	4.122	4.618	5.068	6.199	7.488	8.770	9.9[a]	10.8[a]
Direct Investments Outflows	1.674	1.599	1.654	1.976	2.435	3.418	3.543	3.026	N.A.
Direct Investments Outflows as a % of Plant and Equipment Expenditures Abroad	44%	39%	36%	39%	39%	46%	40%	31%	N.A.

[a] *Survey of Current Business estimates.*
Source: *Survey of Current Business.*

Table 3.

Other sources of funds for foreign affiliates to finance new investment are depreciation reserves, retained earnings of affiliates, and foreign lenders and investors. Retained earnings of affiliates contribute a large portion of new investment funds; these amounts were $1.5 billion in 1965 and $1.7 billion in 1966. The amount of new investments financed by retained earnings is dependent on sales and income and therefore funds from these sources are not necessarily available when needed.

Foreign sources of funds were increasingly being employed as a means of financing foreign investments. Beginning in the middle of 1965, a large increase in the number of bond issues of U.S. corporations and their subsidiaries in the Euro-currency market, and most in Euro-dollars, occurred. The value of the Euro-bond issues was $353 million in 1965, $454 million in 1966, and a lesser rate in the first half of 1967; U.S. corporations and their affiliates made up approximately one-third of the total bond issues during the period.

As a result of the entry of American corporations into this European market, interest rates on Euro-dollars on deposits of an estimated $15 billion and on Euro-bond issues were driven up, especially at the end of 1966. Because interest rates were so high, many American companies sweetened their bond issues by making them convertible into stock. Large internationally known U.S. corporations are usually able to obtain the best terms in the market; however, these rates of interest in 1966 and 1967 were still higher than obtainable in the U.S.

In order to utilize foreign sources of funds, some U.S. corporations set up special financial subsidiaries abroad. These special subsidiaries raised $190 million in 1965 and $600 million in 1966.

Further, subsidiaries increased their loans from foreign banks and other sources as a means of financing investment. Increases in these loans are indicated in the following table (data are in millions of dollars):

1962	1963	1964	1965	1966	1967
114	−36	+74	+178	+474	+513

In summation, it is clear that business had responded to the voluntary program's proposal of employing foreign sources of funds for new overseas investments. Funds were raised by floating bond issues in European markets and by obtaining loans abroad. (Total data to account for how business financed all of its investments in 1966 and 1967 are not yet available.) Over-all, the evidence indicates that the total plant and equipment expenditures during the period of the voluntary program continued to rise, although at declining rates, and with a growing proportion of new investment financed by foreign sources of capital.

The Mandatory Restraint Program

With the fourth quarter 1967 deficit so large, the government came forth with new measures to eliminate the B/P deficits. Among the new measures announced by President Johnson on January 1, 1968 was the mandatory restraint program on business direct foreign investment. It was the first time mandatory peacetime controls were imposed in the history of U.S. capital outflows. The president decreed the mandatory program by executive order under an obscure 1917 Banking Law.

The mandatory program was designed to reduce the deficit in the country's international B/P by $1 billion in 1968 from 1967's figure. Other measures taken to lessen the B/P deficit were: (1) a new program of export promotion by the government; (2) a further tightening of overseas lending by U.S. banks; (3) a proposal to reduce or tax foreign travel by U.S. citizens; (4) a decrease in government expenditures abroad; (5) discussions with foreign nations for elimination of non-tariff barriers; (6) a proposal to increase foreign investment and foreign travel in the U.S.

These latter measures were to reduce the deficit by a total of $2 billion.

The business community is to be further limited by the mandatory program in its freedom to meet its foreign investment opportunities. In the new program, capital outflows for direct investments in 1968 are prohibited except with special government authorization to continental Europe (except Finland and Greece) and to the Republic of South Africa. Further, capital outflows for direct foreign investment are limited to 65 percent of a company's average 1965–1966 investment in other developed nations and in the oil-producing countries, and are limited to 110 percent of a company's average 1965–66 investment in the developing countries.

For a company already operating in Europe, reinvestments annually up to 35 percent of its 1965–1966 investment are allowed.

Also, repatriation of foreign earnings is required according to which of the following two formulas produces a higher figure: (1) the 1964–1966 average percentage of earnings repatriated or; (2) the amount of foreign earnings that exceed a company's direct investment ceiling (in the European case).

No terminal date for the program was established; however, the Commerce Department indicated that it is not anxious to perpetuate controls but that the mandatory program will last at least until the Vietnam War is settled. Criminal penalties and large fines were established for non-compliance.

If plant and equipment expenditures are to be maintained at high levels, the mandatory program will increase the need for American corporations to raise their new investment funds abroad. Already U.S. international businesses are lining up to borrow dollars deposited in Europe. This new demand in the Euro-market has brought out predictions that the rate on long-term Euro-bonds could hit 9 to 10 percent once the new issues being prepared reach the market. Whether supply of funds can be kept high enough to meet this increased demand without these high interest rates or rationing of funds is not certain.

While the new mandatory program will definitely cut back on capital outflows from the U.S. and therefore assist in helping the B/P position in the short run, the longer-run effects could be detrimental to the B/P. If U.S. companies' overseas affiliates are not able, due to limitation of foreign capital markets or due to extremely high interest rates, to get the desired financial resources to expand their operations to meet competitive needs, future profits and B/P credits of income remittances would be lost. Even in the short run, the European recovery now in progress might be adversely affected as high interest rates limit new investment; and this would then have a tendency to cut off some U.S. exports.

Arguments for and against Restraints on Overseas Investment

This section of this paper is largely based on the NICB's study in 1966, *U.S. Production Abroad and the Balance of Payments: A Survey of Corporate Investment Experience.* The NICB's study has attempted to clarify the complicated effects of direct foreign investments on other B/P accounts and has indicated the complex reasons behind foreign investments by American companies. Most of the arguments against restraint programs to be presented here will be taken from this important study.

However, before presenting the arguments it should be pointed out that determining quantitatively the precise effects of the restraint programs is next to impossible. The restraint programs have distorted the free flows of capital, and the ramifications of the restraint program on each particular segment of the B/P will never be ascertainable. Also, changes in the various B/P items are in part due to natural market influences, such as changes in profit levels in overseas operations.

First, arguments in favor of the restraint programs will be presented; arguments against the restraint programs will then follow.

Arguments in favor of restraints on direct foreign investments are as follows:

(1) The restraint programs are justified by the government as *necessary* to assist the correction of the nation's B/P deficits.

(2) Individual B/P accounts can be separated; the restriction of one account, capital outflows, does not affect the others to any great extent.

(3) Only *incremental* earnings would be lost if new direct foreign investments were restricted; the earning position of existing foreign operations would not be jeopardized.

(4) Direct foreign investment and the consequent production and sales of the foreign operation displaces some exports formerly made to the area where investment occurs.

(5) Sales by U.S. affiliates abroad replace exports from U.S. based production to third areas.

(6) When direct investment occurs, U.S. imports increase because the goods that are produced abroad by the new facilities are in many cases sold back to the U.S. The NICB study stated that the disadvantageous B/P effects of foreign investments noted in arguments 4, 5, and 6 were negligible or were related to special market situations.

(7) The restraint programs force the development of European capital markets and take pressure off the U.S. capital markets.

(8) The programs help to educate corporate treasurers in better ways of financing their overseas operations; most firms up to the time of the programs did not consider and did not employ many foreign sources of long-term funds.

(9) The restraint programs, if successful, would lessen U.S. B/P deficits and would decrease the availability of dollars to finance trade; this would make foreigners agreeable to the needed changes in the international monetary system.

Arguments against restraints on direct foreign investments are as follows:

(1) Restraints on foreign investments in present periods have later adverse effects on the B/P in losses of earnings and interest on the foregone investments.

(2) It is not possible to restrict an individual B/P account, such as investment capital outflows, without affecting other B/P accounts, including merchandise and service exports.

(3) Foreign investments boost exports from the parent company and other U.S. companies to the new affiliate or through the affiliate to others.

(4) Incomes, consumption, and production in host countries are raised by direct investments which, in turn, spur more U.S. exports.

(5) Many foreign investments enhance the ability of the U.S. parent company to get needed imports at costs lower than would have to be paid to independent producers of the needed items; this is particularly true in the petroleum and extractive industries.

(6) Continued foreign investments to existing affiliates are necessary to survive competitively. To restrict new investments would be detrimental to the over-all future earning power of the whole company, including the subsidiary.

(7) The use of foreign sources of funds is more costly than U.S. sources, and the company, restricted in getting its capital at home, will either have to forego the investment or accept a smaller profit because of the more costly use of foreign funds.

(8) Bond repayments and interest payments as a direct result of the restraint programs will go to the foreign sources of funds and not to Americans as credits to the B/P.

(9) The reduction in the flow of U.S. capital abroad according to the restraint program is offset by withdrawals and diversions of foreign capital from the U.S. or money that would have gone to the U.S. for investment.

(10) The restraint programs are a reversal of years of government policy of encouraging overseas investments by corporations.

(11) The adoption of capital restrictions by the U.S. could lead other nations to resort to similar restrictions.

(12) The restraints are criticized on the grounds of illegal impositions on the rights of free enterprise.

Effects of the Voluntary Programs

The total effects of the voluntary restraint programs will never clearly be known. As seen, when the restrictions were placed on one account, capital outflows, even a short-run B/P surplus was not possible. The increased military expenditures abroad were not connected with any cutbacks on outflows of capital; but losses in other B/P accounts, such as merchandise trade, could have been due in part to the restraints on capital investments abroad. Because overseas investments in plant and equipment expenditures did continue at a high rate, earnings remittances in the future do not appear to have been affected to any great degree as of yet. However, it is true that some investment has been foregone, particularly by smaller companies which were just beginning or were considering making investments abroad, and some earnings returns have been lost. There will certainly be losses to the B/P accounts in interest payments which will now go to Europeans rather than back to U.S. investors as before the restraint programs. The amount of losses of future income returns and of interest payments to American companies and to the U.S. B/P can only be speculated as no exact quantification is possible. The main point is that continued direct investment abroad does make continued contributions to the B/P in other accounts, and that to the extent that any profitable overseas investment has been foregone, some future returns will have been lost even if they are not measurable.

On the other hand, the fear of losses in business competitiveness in foreign markets due to restricted capital flows appears to be largely unfounded so far. While some smaller businesses may have been forced to forego making investments overseas due to the restraint programs, most established international businesses were able to raise the desired funds abroad for expansion of their plant facilities. Because plant and equipment expenditures continued at higher levels, future earning power of overseas corporations as yet has not been seriously affected. The long-run B/P position of overseas investments return flows has not been seriously affected as yet for the simple reason that capital investment has not yet been restricted to any great degree.

The voluntary program was then successful as far as it went in limiting direct investment outflows, but the B/P position of the country's total payments was not corrected. Some reasons why the voluntary programs were successful in meeting their goals through the cooperation voluntarily of the business community are as follows:

(1) Throughout, the program ostensibly was sanctioned by the business community itself through the Advisory Committee of top international executives.

(2) The programs did not really hurt most companies. Targets on capital outflows for direct investments were not that strict because increases, although more limited with each program revision, were allowed. Also, untapped foreign sources of funds were available to finance desired investments.

(3) Despite the importance of international operations today, the majority of U.S. businesses did not experience the restrictions.

(4) The voluntary program occurred in a period in which profitability on the average of overseas investments was declining.

(5) The programs were emotionally tied to the war in Vietnam which probably most of the business community supported.

(6) Business feared the alternative of direct controls if they did not comply. The premise that governmental public goals of foreign policy are higher than that of economic freedom has long been accepted by the American people and the business community. In World War II, direct controls on industry were imposed and private business had no choice but to comply, to meet the war effort. With the Vietnam War as the accepted policy, the private sector must accordingly pay the price necessary to prevent deterioration in the country's B/P. Had not the Vietnam War occurred, it would probably have been much more difficult for the government to get the cooperation of the business sector.

The Possible Effects of the Mandatory Program

Some of these reasons just noted also explain why the mandatory program was received so calmly by businessmen. Business has assumed that funds will be available abroad and that adjustments to new restraints can be made. U.S. businesses are quite adaptable and ingenious in coming up with new ways to function in meeting their objectives.

As long as most firms are able to finance their new investments at reasonable costs abroad, international businesses will probably continue to acquiesce to, while at the same time seek exemption from, the government's restraint programs. Much depends on how flexible the Department of Commerce is in allowing exemptions.

The mandatory program does have the goal of reducing the B/P by $1 billion, and in this new program, business contributes to meet that goal only by reducing overseas direct investments and by profit remissions. Increasing exports, returning short-term capital deposits, and other measures by business of contributing to the B/P, while still emphasized as being important ways to contribute to the B/P, are not a part of the new mandatory program, as they were in the voluntary program. Also, rather than stabilize or lessen increases of direct investment outflows as under the voluntary program, the new program is more restrictive in that it prohibits capital outflows to certain areas and limits them in other areas. Because the mandatory program is so much more restrictive, it is certain that some profitable overseas investments will be restricted and that some losses in future income returns and B/P credits will be incurred.

The Future of Foreign Investments and Government Restraints

The government has apparently taken the view that future income remittances losses due to its restraint programs are not quantitatively large or that income remittances are not vital to the B/P. Implicit in this viewpoint is that American companies have overcommitted themselves to production abroad. This opposition to expansion of American companies overseas is also expressed by many foreign countries and foreign companies who fear American dominance or American competition.

However, from the viewpoint of American business, it appears that a new structure of business operations is trying to emerge: the multinational business era. Overseas production by U.S. subsidiaries is now four to five times as large as U.S. exports, and the multinational companies involved have a totally different outlook toward foreign investments than does a U.S. governmental official concerned with the B/P.

In the existing B/P system, multinational companies and their global orientations are considered secondary to the needs of the countries involved in maintaining the values of their currencies and providing a balance in exchange flows. As long as national boundaries and separate currencies exist, the multinational companies will have to consider the effect of their operations on the nations involved and on their B/P.

The main key in this conflict of interests is the international monetary system. If the new mandatory program, along with the other new measures, succeeds in substantially reducing the U.S. B/P deficits, then a reconstruction of the monetary system could occur. Multinational businesses would then be in much better positions to conduct their operations without investment restrictions by governments.

But it appears that these more ideal states will not exist anywhere in the near future. The next few years will be difficult ones for the U.S. international businesses as the mandatory program is enforced and as businesses attempt to operate their multinational operations within its restrictions.

Bibliography

"Building a Case for Direct Investment Overseas." *Business Abroad* (November 28, 1966): 9–11.

Christie, Herbert. "Euro-Dollars and the Balance of Payments." *The Banker* (January 1967): 37–43.

Connor, John T. "Goals for '66 Outlined to Aid Payments Balance." *International Commerce* (December 13, 1965): 2–4.

Cutler, Frederick and Lederer Walther. "International Investment of the U.S. in 1966." *Survey of Current Business* (September 1967): 39–48.

"Driving Down the Deficit." *Business Week* (January 6, 1968): 13–15.

Gerrity, John. "The Johnson Administration Sets Out Anew to Pursue Tantalizing Mirage of a Balance of Payments Equilibrium." *The Weekly Bond Buyer for the Capital Investor* (January 8, 1968).

International Commerce. (March 1, 1965): 11–14.

International Commerce. (March 8, 1965): 22.

International Commerce. (March 19, 1965): 19.

International Commerce. (April 19, 1965): 29.

International Commerce. (January 24, 1966): 4.

International Commerce. (May 23, 1966): 20.

International Commerce. (May 30, 1966): 9.

International Commerce. (June 27, 1966): 37.

International Commerce. (December 26, 1966): 24.

International Commerce. (June 12, 1967): 3.

International Commerce. (July 10, 1967): 9–10.

International Commerce. (January 8, 1968): 2–6.

Janssen, Richard F. " 'Sizable' Staff to Enforce Outflow Curbs, Planned as Long as War in Vietnam Lasts." *The Wall Street Journal* (January 15, 1968): 3.

Morgan Guaranty Trust Company. *The Financing of Business with Euro-Dollars.* New York: Morgan Guaranty Trust Company of New York, September, 1967.

"Not Much Pain for Big Business." *Business Week* (January 6, 1968): 16–17.

"Plant and Equipment Expenditures of Foreign Affiliates of U.S. Corporations, 1966–1968." *Survey of Current Business* (October 1967): 16–17.

Polk, Judd, Menster, Irene W., and Veit, Lawrence A. *U.S. Production Abroad and the Balance of Payments: A Survey of Corporate Investment Experience.*

Robock, Stefan H. "Overseas Financing for U.S. International Business." *Journal of Finance* (May 1966): 297–307.

Shirmer, Walter. "An Industrialist's View of Restraints on Industry." *The Balance of Payments Problem: Implications for International Business.* American Management Association, Inc., 1965, 25–28.

United States Council of the International Chamber of Commerce, Inc. *U.S. Direct Investments and the Balance of Payments* (November 1966).

"The U.S. Payments Gap Today." First National City Bank of New York *Monthly Economic Letter* (March 1967): 32–35.

Vicker, Ray. "Dealings in 'Euro-Dollars' Spurt in Wake of U.S. Curbs on Outlays Abroad." *The Wall Street Journal* (January 15, 1968): 1, 17.

"Voluntary Investment Restraint Program Ran 12% Ahead of '66 Pace." *International Commerce* (December 25, 1967): 31.

"Voluntary Restraints Likely to Continue in 1967, Seen as Best Approach in Payments Issue." *International Commerce* (November 21, 1966): 13.

The Kennedy Round and Beyond

Eric Wyndham White

The Kennedy Round of trade negotiations, which have entered their final and decisive phase, mark a climax in the process of international trade cooperation over the last two decades. The restoration of a multilateral trade and payments system stands out as one of the major achievements of postwar international cooperation. The enormous advances in economic activity achieved during that period—and the greater material well-being that this has made possible—have been due to the dynamism and energy which have characterized the process of economic reconstruction within national boundaries. It is, however, significant that this rising tide of prosperity has been accompanied by a constant and spectacular growth of world trade. In this development the international agreements and institutions have provided the essential framework for international cooperation in the field of trade and payments and, among these, the IMF, the GATT—and in the earlier years the OEEC—have played a vital role.

The word "climax" is perhaps misleading insofar as it suggests a summit from which the road forward must necessarily lead downwards. The sense in which I use it here is that of an apotheosis which should cause us to take stock and to prepare the way for perfecting the machinery and methods of cooperation which have proved so fruitful in the past, but which remain increasingly necessary to enable us to consolidate the ground that has been won and to move forward to further advances.

Trade Policies of Regional Blocs

There is every reason to hope that, at the end of the Kennedy Round, a substantial measure of tariff disarmament will have been achieved and that the

From a speech by Eric Wyndham White, published in *World Business* No. 4 (January 1967).

"World Business," a publication of the Chase Manhattan Bank of New York, printed the following excerpts from an address by Mr. Eric Wyndham White when he was Director-General of the General Agreement on Tariffs and Trade (GATT). The address was delivered just before the Kennedy Round of GATT tariff negotiations was concluded on June 30, 1967. It was intended to call attention to some important aspects of international economic relations that would still be in need of improvement. The Kennedy Round negotiations, named after President Kennedy, who had laid the preparations for them, achieved a notable reduction in worldwide tariff barriers.

general level of tariffs will have been so far reduced as to set the stage for a further significant growth in international trade. This would in any event be a step of major importance. Its importance is enhanced, however, by the development of powerful regional trading groups which will shortly achieve their objectives of total elimination of tariffs between the adherent States. I refer in particular, of course, to the EEC and EFTA.

These are such powerful trading groups that unless, parallel with the dismantling of internal tariffs, they proceeded simultaneously with the reduction of external tariffs, there would be a serious risk of substantial distortion of the international trading system. This in itself would be wasteful and would jeopardize the realization of the trade-creating effects which these regional groups undoubtedly have and indeed which, from the point of view of GATT and of international trade, is their major justification.

Further Tariff Reductions

This being said, the question arises whether the Kennedy Round marks the end of the road. In my view, clearly not. In the first place, a successful Kennedy Round will still leave a large number of problems to be resolved, even if only in the limited area of tariffs and other trade barriers and even if one looks at the industrial field alone. Some of these problems are relatively minor; others are far-reaching.

For example, after the Kennedy Round, there will be large numbers of duty rates which will be very low indeed, say 5 percent or less. In modern conditions of industrial production, duty rates of this level often have little or no protective effect and could be described as "nuisance" tariffs. Nuisance they undoubtedly are, since they involve in most countries a series of documentary and other formalities which are more serious than the customs duty itself. These, it seems to me, should be marked out for early elimination.

Secondly, it has become apparent in the course of the Kennedy Round that there are certain sectors of industrial production—characterized by modern equipment, high technology and large-scale production, and by the international character of their operations and markets—where there are evident gains to all in arriving, within a defined period, at free trade. As has been seen in the EEC and EFTA, a "defined period" is extremely important since it provides industry with a clear indication both of the need for adjustment and adaptation to conditions of free trade, and an assurance of a reasonable period in which to make these adjustments.

I therefore see progress in the field of tariff reduction as being best sought through the promotion by the major industrialized countries of a Free Trade Arrangement (FTA) covering (a) the consolidation of all existing duty-free items, (b) the "nuisance" duties I have earlier referred to, (c) certain sectors of industrial activity which are ripe for a move towards free trade, and (d) additional sectors or products on which duties could be eliminated from time to time through negotiation or agreement, or by unilateral action. This would not be an exclusive arrangement since, being negotiated in GATT, the benefits would extend through the most-favored-nation clause to other GATT countries.

Trade in Agricultural Products

Amongst the most complex and urgent questions which confront us is the problem of trade in temperate-zone agricultural products. Largely neglected in the liberalization process, agricultural trade can no longer be left on one side in a forward-looking international trade policy. Here again, international cooperation will have to extend beyond traditional protectionist measures applied at the frontiers. National policies must become the subject of international discussion and negotiation.

Because the aim of national policies in the industrialized countries centers on assuring adequate levels of return to farmers, so as to avoid too sharp a contrast with the growing prosperity of the industrialized population, national and international prices are at the heart of the problem. An alternative has to be found to national policies tending towards self-sufficiency, subsidized exports and the generation of surpluses which have to be marketed by various devices, most of which have, or risk having, a detrimental effect on commercial markets.

Impact on Less Developed Countries

So far, I may be reproached with concerning myself too exclusively with relations between the industrialized countries. These are not, however, as irrelevant to the interests of the rest of the world as is sometimes assumed in polemical discussions. A sustained high level of economic activity in the industrial world is a major prerequisite of rapid growth in the less developed countries.

The greater the resources that are generated in the industrialized countries, the greater will be the amount which they will be able to transfer so as to assist economic development elsewhere. More indirectly, a high level of economic activity is essential to provide a strong demand for the exports of the less developed countries, whether of primary products or the more diversified exports, which find a reasonably receptive market in times of prosperity but are extremely vulnerable in periods of relative decline in the buoyancy of the world economy.

Price-Fixing Arrangements

There nevertheless remains the urgent need to tackle with vigor the pressing problems of the less developed countries, and to pass increasingly from the painful process of diagnosis to that of active remedial treatment. The most urgent problems are those which relate to trade in primary products which, for the time being, constitute the major resource of the less developed countries. Here the central problem is one of the level and stability of prices. As to the level, I remain convinced that this has to be responsive to market forces.

On the demand side, any attempt to fix prices at artificial levels poses a number of problems. The first is feasibility. Unless this trade is to be forced exclusively through governmental channels, it is difficult to see how prices can be dictated by governmental fiat. The second is desirability in the interest of the primary producer. If raw material prices are maintained at artificial levels, a great stimulus will be given to substitution by synthetics and to increased investment in processes aimed at economy in the use of primary raw materials. Those who underestimate this danger might well study post-war developments in the use of raw rubber versus synthetic, and the emergence of manmade fibres as a rival to cotton. Neither case suggests the wisdom of an ill-considered policy of artificial stimulation of the price of the raw material.

On the production side, there are real limitations to the ability of raw material producers—many with an administrative structure which is ill-equipped for even less sophisticated tasks—to control increases of production which are triggered off by a sharp upward movement of prices. The reaction of sugar production to a rise in prices is a mournful precedent of recent date.

Stabilization is another matter. There is everything to be said for a determined effort to bring about a greater stability of prices for the major primary products within a realistic price range; and when this is not possible, for reinforcing the existing arrangements for compensatory financing for primary producers during times of financial stringency arising from periodic declines in the prices of their basic exports.

There remains the problem of the countries who, having had the benefit of sheltered markets in the past, find it impossible to produce remuneratively at world market prices. These countries must be encouraged to shift into more suitable lines of production and, in the meantime, they should be assisted by deficiency payments internationally financed.

Access To Markets in Developed Countries

Every encouragement must also be given to diversification in the primary producing countries. Apart from financial and technical assistance, this implies that the developed countries should be prepared to open their markets to the industrial exports of the less developed countries.

It has been suggested that this policy should be expressed in the form of preferential treatment of these exports. Whilst this idea, conceptually and emotionally, has much appeal it raises a number of very serious complications which it would take a long time to resolve. Above all at a time when the tendency is, in the sectors where the less developed countries are already competitive, for the developed countries to discriminate against the export products of these countries, it may be questioned whether this is—in the immediate future—the most obvious line of attack.

Much can and should be done at once to improve the access of less developed countries to markets of the developed countries. This can be achieved without any of the complications inherent in a preference scheme. The Kennedy Round presents a major opportunity for comprehensive and early action. The extensive reductions of tariffs and trade barriers on products of interest to less developed countries for which the Kennedy Round affords the occasion could be applied immediately, without phasing the reductions over a period of years as is proposed for the concessions as a whole.

Insofar as hesitations in granting concessions of interest to less developed countries arise from the fear that the effective benefits would, in fact, accrue to developed countries, there may be room for negotiation of special arrangements which would obviate this difficulty by limiting the concessions in these cases to products of less developed countries. Finally, although the working hypothesis in the Kennedy Round is a 50 percent across-the-board reduction, this is an auto-limitation for most participants and should not be allowed to rule out deeper cuts for products of special concern to less developed countries.

The negotiations could also be the occasion for sweeping away the remaining discriminatory restrictions on export products of less developed countries. Unhappily, this is an unrealistic target for cotton textiles, where a number of less developed countries are in a position to exploit a competitive advantage—even though probably an ephemeral one. The Long-Term Arrangement on Cotton Textiles, negotiated under the aegis of GATT, is an unhappy recognition of the political problems which force the developed countries to adopt an anomalous and inappropriate attitude towards the less developed countries.

More East-West Trade

Also high on the agenda of international trade problems of the future is trade between the free-enterprise and the socialist economies. So far, this trade has continued to be conducted on a bilateral basis. It has been marginal in volume but is showing an upward trend and clearly has great potential for growth. With this prospect in mind, it is high time to question whether bilateralism is an acceptable, or possible, basis for an expanded trade between the two types of economy. Even in present circumstances, the efficacy of the system may be questioned. It is inclined to compress trade into narrow channels, the free-enterprise economies tending to be limited to furnishing machinery and equipment, and being obliged to accept in return consumer goods which might or might not find a market in normal conditions, or to reserve for the socialist countries a part of their jealously restricted markets for agricultural produce. Hardly a formula for growth.

The Tasks Ahead

If, therefore, we successfully pass the climax of the Kennedy Round there will be no lack of subjects to engage the attention of the international institutions having special responsibilities for international trade. There will be much business—particularly pertaining to agriculture—which will have been hopefully begun in the Kennedy Round, but which will call for follow-up and development.

The Kennedy Round is not only a climax to a period; it is also a doorway to the future, to the translation into practical arrangements of the concept of interdependence, the validity of which grows increasingly apparent in the context of the economic realities which press upon us. Even the greater economic powers can no longer pursue their destinies in disregard of others. Still less can they seek solutions to their economic problems by narrow nationalistic policies. Nor can one escape the impact of the economic difficulties of others. When the bell tolls for one, it tolls for all.

Issues and Prospects of Increased Trade with the Soviet Bloc

Chris C. McEvoy

The history of international law and diplomacy reveals that the business community has had a large hand in civilizing the world. Over two thousand years before Christ, Mesopotamian merchants, experienced in contracts and litigation, organized trading companies to seek business in unknown lands. As the power of trade to improve the lot of mankind became recognized, a body of laws developed to regulate contacts between countries. The "law of nations" evolved slowly, for no country could be forced to abide. The Magna Charta—dating back to the 1200s—contained a section guaranteeing the safety of merchants entering or leaving England. Law is indispensable to trade: differing customs and experiences require the common framework laws provide for mutual trust, cooperation, and agreement. A country that obeys laws only when beneficial to do so violates a cornerstone policy of foreign trade, and the law-abiding nations must retaliate by shunning the betrayer, or dealing at arm's length. This is the position of the free world and the Soviet Union today, and this paper will consider the issues of trading with the Soviets (whether trade *should* be increased) as well as the constraints affecting trade (how much it *could* be increased).

Trade with the Soviet bloc has political, moral, and economic implications. The economic impact is by far the smallest; the difficult questions are political and moral. In terms of total U.S. trade, trade with Russia is negligible; until recently, the high point occurred in 1930 when the Soviets purchased $136 million in goods and sold $21.1 million to the U.S. Some businessmen may wish to forget that business strongly urged recognition of Russia to open untapped markets, and Secretary of State, Cordell Hull agreed, believing trade a way out of the depression. At this time, Russia was the United States' third best customer for automobiles and purchased half of the U.S. locomotive exports. However, trade began to decline after Russia was recognized by President Roosevelt in 1933, and deteriorated when Russia refused to repay $139 million in loans. Lend-lease and other aid during the war amounted to $11.2 billion; in 1945, the Russians refused to join the World Bank and Monetary Fund. In 1947, Russia turned thumbs down on the Marshall Plan. With the Korean War, the United States cut off practically all trade with the Soviet Union. In 1951, the United States asked $800 million to partially settle the Lend-Lease debt. The Soviets offered $300 million which was rejected. Nothing

Reprinted by permission of Chris C. McEvoy.

much happened in the way of trade until 1958 when Premier Khrushchev called for a large expansion in trade. This marked a major turning point in the relations between the United States and Soviet Union so far as trade is concerned.

The Case Against Expanding Trade

Anastas Mikoyan, Soviet Deputy Premier (then), visited the United States in 1959 in search of better relations and more trade. The State Department suggested that if the Russians desired increased trade, they should pay their back bills, allow private firms in the U.S. greater access to producing and consuming units in Russia, respect patent laws, and give up for the moment the idea of long-term credits. The matter of Russia's unpaid obligations to the United States is a major stumbling block. In 1917, after the revolution, the United States loaned $187 million; yet soon afterward, Russia seized $60 million in United States assets. This plus the Lend-Lease debt clearly placed Russia under the Johnson Act—passed in the thirties—which prohibits long-term loans to a country that is in default on its debts to the United States. (Normal commercial credit—as used in the wheat sale—is sanctioned.)

The Russians realize that the unpaid debts are important and have made some attempts to settle. Their recent behavior on the foreign scene is another matter. Russian activity in world markets has been disruptive and has caused strident indignation. Using foreign trade as a cold war weapon, the Russians were by the end of 1960 selling oil at below prevailing prices; in addition, sugar from Cuba was being dumped on the world market as well as chemicals. (By January 1965, Prime Minister Kosygin admitted that fuel has become scarce throughout the Soviet Union; chemicals, of course, are now the subject of a concentrated drive.) Russian behavior has been both predatory and irrational.

Another reason for limiting trade with the Russians is that trade will strengthen their economy. In November 1963, Undersecretary of State, George Ball, asked that credits to the U.S.S.R. be limited to a maximum of five years. To extend credits longer would, according to Ball, aid the Kremlin's policy of subversion and aggression. *Barron's National Business and Financial Weekly* points out:

> From the Soviet Union on down, the Communist bloc boasts a long history of refusing to honor its obligations, a hard-earned record of default which has ruined its credit rating with everyone but Western statesmen. Hence, commerce between East and West today usually adds up to aid, not trade. What is worse, it is tantamount to granting aid and comfort to the enemy.

The extent to which trade "comforts and aids the enemy" is a consideration that is not lightly dismissed. The National Foreign Trade Council has stated that long-term credits to the Soviet Union and the satellite countries represent "unwarranted and unwise foreign aid." The fact that future trade depends on long-term credits make the point crucial. Such credit would permit strengthening of the Soviet empire, and it would be unwise for the United States to subsidize an enemy—one which time and again has demonstrated its animosity and vengeance for freedom.

Russian atrocities are frequently mentioned by those critical of expanding contacts with the Soviet Union. Within the past few years—at a time when a detente was allegedly shaping up—the Russians have arrested a Yale professor and tossed him in jail on the basis of some planted documents; the captain of a wheat-carrying ship was ordered off his bridge at gunpoint in a Russian port; a British businessman who introduced a Soviet official to Western agents was kidnapped and sentenced to eight years for "espionage"; and a great deal of publicity was accorded an incident recently when a German engineer who had detected wire taps used by the Soviets was splashed with mustard gas. What galls critics of the Soviet Union's behavior is that the Russians can get away with behaving in this way and still expect to enjoy the fruits of trade with the free world. The Russians seek the advantages enjoyed by members subscribing to the law of nations while making few of the sacrifices. The root of the problem lies in the Russian government, and there is little chance for significant change. Russian mischief on the world scene is of course well known and well documented. It was to this George Ball alluded when he warned that long-term credits could aid the Kremlin's policy of "aggression and subversion." It is obvious from Mikoyan's visit in 1959 and other visits since that Russia seeks from the West many plants and processes that could easily be converted to war use. Even the strongest proponents in the discussion of trade draw back from agreeing to supply the Russians with war potential. However, it may have already been done. Joseph A. Gwyer, Senior Research Specialist of the Library of Congress, claims that "errors of judgment" by the United States and allies have helped build Russia's war potential.

An argument for increasing trade with the satellites is to weaken their dependence on Moscow. The argument is plausible, but difficult to pin down. In a crisis, which way would the satellite turn? The evidence suggests that the ideological ties are not easily broken, and despite the fact that trade with the West does tend to reduce reliance on Moscow, loyalty prevails within the bloc. Marshal Tito in Yugoslavia has received a great deal of United States aid (and trade) because he had the nerve to stand up to Stalin. Despite massive United States involvement, Tito recently (and apparently willfully) "betrayed" the U.S. by proclaiming the closeness of his views with those of Khrushchev. The American ambassador to Yugoslavia, George Kennan (who is an expert on Soviet affairs), quit his job in disgust. The point is that Tito realized his own tenure is dependent upon maintaining the same conditions and political atmosphere that exist in Russia. Economically, the bloc is still overwhelmingly tied to Russia.

Opponents of increased trade can marshal vociferous support for their cause. Many reasons are more emotional than rational, but since they are widely held they deserve consideration. In the *AFL-CIO News*, union president George Meany's speech on this subject was reproduced: he argued against granting economic concessions to Communist regimes "whose basic aim is the destruction of democracy and the free enterprise system throughout the world." Meany noted that long-term credits were at the base of the campaign to increase trade. Why grant economic concessions without receiving some concessions? Meany received a standing ovation from his audience when he asked, "Why rescue sworn enemies from the snare of their own economic fallacies?"

Labor has been particularly critical of increased contacts with the Soviet Union. In testimony before the Senate Internal Security Subcommittee on March 22, 1963, Joseph P. Drago, president of Local 893 of the International Association of Machinists, told about investigating a sale of machine tools to Russia. Drago was tipped off that some plant machinery was being produced for Russia. The company—Fairchild-Stratos—had done defense work which seemed to heighten the issue. The company refused to cancel the order (for precision gear boxes), pointing out that the equipment was for papermaking and could not be used for anything else. There was union agitation to strike. The International advised Drago to talk with the State Department. At foggy bottom, "behind the grand mahogany desk, and out of the well-padded leather seat came the official 'rationalizations' which we were not looking for. . . ." Drago then went to the Commerce Department with the same result: "We were confronted with the same rationalizations. . . . We were discouraged and dismayed. . . ." The Union made a brief appeal for public criticism and did receive some support. However, the gear boxes were shipped to Russia.

Notably the company's claim that the gear boxes could be used for nothing but papermaking was not at issue. The difference, then, was that the union was against trade in general while the company saw nothing wrong with it. Such opposition to trade regardless of its nature is not rare in this country. *Fortune* notes:

> *A few Congressmen have always been ready to jump in when they suspected that the Administration was turning "soft" on trade with Communism. One of them once remarked that he couldn't understand why Commerce assigned 250 men to the export control operation. If he had his way, there would be only one man in it and he would have only one word in his vocabulary: "No."*

The question of whether trade might benefit the United States more than the recipient is not considered by many people. In Congress . . . is H.R. 4155, "a bill to prohibit trade with Communist nations," being considered by the Committee on Interstate and Foreign Commerce (such bills are introduced every session).

Why the Soviets Must Trade

. . . Nikita Khrushchev was suddenly purged and accused of "harebrained scheming, immature conclusions, and boasting." These charges help to explain the Russian position today. Time and again Khrushchev publicly stated that Russia would surpass the United States in one area or another, and he even gave the date when the event would occur. Khrushchev's boasts began to ring hollow as the sprawling bureaucracy stifled economic life in Russia; yet the boasts opened

Pandora's box by promising the Russian people that they would soon become consumers. To keep these promises—and to accomplish the more immediate task of feeding the people—Russia is compelled to seek outside help.

Evidence exists today to indicate that Russia was and is severely overextended. Good harvests in the mid-fifties, the stunning Sputnik space shot, and the intercontinental ballistic missiles that Khrushchev loved to rattle shoved Soviet prestige to great heights. However, the tremendous economic investment in missiles and space yanked the rug from under the Soviet economy. The light industrial sector was ignored. As a result of putting all of his resources in the military and space basket, Khrushchev's rolling economy began to falter: the industrial growth rate stalled, agriculture plummeted, and the standard of living boasts remained unfilled. These events help explain the cutback in Communist China (which ignited the famous Mao Tse-tung–Khrushchev charges and invectives). Charles J. V. Murphy, writing in *Fortune*, suggests that Khrushchev realized by the spring of 1960 that "the Soviet power base would fail his audacious schemes. It was too small. He had built too soon." It was in 1960 that the decision was made to bluff the world: thus came the Berlin incidents, the Vienna meeting with President Kennedy, and the confrontation over missiles in Cuba. Having misjudged President Kennedy and the American people's determination, Khrushchev then turned to making the best of his tattered economy.

Attention was focused on Soviet farming and consumer goods. To build up these industries, there was only one direction to turn: to the West for trade and credit. As early as 1959 Khrushchev told Americans that he wanted machinery and equipment for making chemicals, petrochemicals, and synthetics. By 1962, the need was even greater.

The Case for Expanding Trade

An obvious reason for expanding trade with the Soviet bloc is that it will be profitable to do so. Businessmen practically by definition seek expanded markets (this activity has brought the prosperity to the free world). Businessmen correctly point out that America's allies sell a great deal to the Russians, so refusing to trade will in no way deprive the Russians of goods. In addition, when a good is sold that is in surplus over here, the benefit is two-fold. Eugene Braderman, director of the government's Bureau of International Commerce, estimates that of the $750 million in goods Russia buys from Western Europe, the U.S. could, with lighter restrictions, walk away with about $250 million (an increase of 1,570 percent over the present $15 million). To keep the figures in perspective, it is noted that $250 million is less than 10 percent of this country's balance of payments deficit. Undeniably, $250 million is preferable to $15 million.

Canada's wheat sales in 1963 whetted American appetites for increased trade. Canada defended the sales on the grounds that trade promotes peace and that if Russia were more dependent on the West, the country would be less of a threat to peace. A similar argument is advanced for trading with the satellite nations. The crumbling of the Soviet monolith is considered good by the free world. The argument is advanced that some of the satellites are apt to be very responsive to trade opportunities with the West. The satellites have resisted directions from COMECON (the Russian payments union that attempted to plan which country should have which industry). This national independence has led some satellites to increase free world contacts. The policy of autarky practiced within the Soviet bloc has been less severe on Russia because of its size. However, many of the satellites have found that for them autarky has required some sacrifices. It is possible that this policy—the cornerstone of Soviet trade policy—could be discarded by some satellites if the lure of trade on more favorable terms were dangled by the West.

The U.S. has traded with the satellites on favorable terms when there has been evidence of independence from Moscow. After Gomulka came to power and made a few independent sounds, President Eisenhower extended most favored nation tariff rates to Polish goods. In addition, he allowed more liberal exports to Poland; Poland is now the United States' biggest trading partner among the Iron Curtain countries. The argument that trading with the satellites has not produced a definitive measure of independence is difficult to refute. Presidents Eisenhower, Kennedy, and Johnson have all had problems with Congressmen who wished to legislate an end to contacts with the bloc nations. It is important that three separate administrations (and two different political parties) have felt these contacts to be in the best interests of the United States. The fact remains that many of the problems now besetting Russia have only recently come to light. It could well be that with these problems—in conjunction with the framework already established for trade—the satellite countries may be encouraged to scuttle such policies as autarky. Progress in this realm can be expected to move at a snail's pace, yet so long as the approach seems reasonable, three presidents have argued that the stakes were too high to ignore.

Proponents of trade note that some of the intransigent Russian attitudes which have discouraged trade are now changing. Patent protection has been one of the thorniest issues. Time and again the Russians have pirated free-world inventions with no royalty payments. Just recently, the Russians have acted to change this. At a meeting in Geneva of the International Union for the Protection of Industrial Property, the Soviet Union announced intentions of ratifying the agreement on patents. The *Economist* notes that Russia's failure to ratify the 82-year-old agreement up to this time has "inhibited patentees in western countries from licensing their processes in the Soviet Union." The Russian need for trade to overcome its shortages may have forced it to behave by Western rules. (However, one interesting school of thought contends that by the time the Russians tore down a machine and made copies it was obsolete.) The *Economist* notes that Russia is research-minded, and ratification of the agreement will allow receipt of royalty payments on Russian inventions. Whether the Russians will respect the agreement is another matter. History is replete with broken promises. Russia's need for western technology is likely to enforce the agreement, however, and with today's communications, breaches would surely be noticed and publicized.

The Soviets further show an eagerness to aid the ideologically despised capitalists. In November 1964, Moscow hosted a meeting of 90 executives from 63 corporations and banks to explore specific problems in trading with the Russians: exporting, importing, licensing, financing, arbitration, dumping, patent protection, and customs procedures.

The possibility that increased trade will "civilize" Russia in dealings with the world is one of the more plausible and appealing arguments. It is possible to use foreign trade as a diplomatic tool, and continuance could be contingent upon good behavior by the Russians. If Russia's plans counted upon certain items from the West, the threat of cancellation might be effective. It was with this idea in mind that in 1961 the possibility of completely halting trade to the Soviet Union was considered by some Congressional committees. According to Philip H. Tersize, acting Assistant Secretary of State for Economic Affairs, the United States might halt all trade with Communist nations if Russia continued threatening vital Western interests. A cessation of trade would injure the Communist nations far more than the United States. However, to use trade as a foreign policy lever, it must exist in enough quantity to make its withdrawal painful. Increasing trade will give the Soviets incentive to get along with the West.

Trading with the enemy is controversial, and talk of liberalization brings out some strong opinions. On the "pro" side, there is a growing number of people in favor of increasing trade. Among businessmen sentiment appears to be strong, according to an opinion survey released by the Senate Foreign Relations Committee: of 125 producers polled, 105 said trade should be increased; only 9 flatly opposed the idea. Sentiment to increase trade is not confined to businessmen. Not long ago, Vice President Hubert Humphrey (then a Senator) asked for a reappraisal of U.S. curbs on trade. Senator Humphrey said, "We refuse to trade in goods that in any way can injure national security." Senator Stuart Symington points out that every other developed country in the free world actively trades behind the Iron Curtain. Symington requested more trade, less aid: "Trade invariably improves understanding." Senator Magnuson in debate has remarked that "trade is usually the forerunner of an increasing ability of people to get along with one another." The Senators asked the Secretaries of Commerce and Treasury whether any free world country other than the United States was not doing all possible to trade behind the Iron Curtain. The answer was no.

Supporters of increased trade can trot out another ally—George Meany—whose name should be familiar because he also appeared in the arguments against trade. To counteract "buy American" furor in 1961, Mr. Meany publicly stated that many Americans and firms were dependent upon overseas trade and thus he did not support "buy American" campaigns. Mr. Meany has every right to point out that he was referring to free-world overseas trade and not trade with Communist nations. However, his point holds for *any* country with whom the United States trades, particularly since two-way trade is necessary with Communist nations. If trade is to exist, the United States must purchase goods from the country involved.

Last, but by no means least, are the opinions of the men occupying the White

House. Presidents Eisenhower, Kennedy, and Johnson all showed an interest in increasing trade with the Soviet bloc countries. Early in the Nixon administration U.S. controls on trade with communist China were relaxed moderately and at the time of writing more relaxations are expected. The opposition to trading with the Communists has been centered in Congress, not at the White House.

Present and Future Opportunities

The United States wheat deal with Russia in 1963 and 1964 broke the ice so far as trade is concerned. The wheat deal was special because it was a one-shot affair; the United States had voluminous surpluses, in no way could wheat be transformed into war material, and (most importantly) the wheat could have been obtained elsewhere. President Kennedy's decision to sell wheat to the Russians was based on these factors, as well as his announced desire (good propaganda material) to help feed hungry people anywhere. Immediately the issue of credit came up, and the Senate rejected government credit assistance to the Russians. Under President Johnson, this position was reversed and the sale consummated. The United States wasn't the only country to make concessions. The Russians, in order to lower the price of the wheat, cut harbor dues for U.S. ships. By March 1964, Russian purchases of American wheat had totaled $134 million, a figure much higher than normal yearly trade with the Soviets. Thereafter, U.S. exports to Russia fell to previous (pre-wheat) levels.

Given sympathetic action by the United States, what is the outlook for increased trade with the Soviet Union? Russia's policy of autarky is a large impediment. The gains and benefits of trade have shown themselves clearly in the free world. The Common Market's growth as a result of removing trade barriers has been astonishing; while the countries of the West have been enjoying the fruits of trade, Russia has kept her block of nations icily aloof. Russia's deep suspicion of outsiders led the country into its autarkic policy; its exports and imports for each country must approximately match. In the multilateral free world, a country only worries about its total trade balance and thus is free to plan its purchases and sales with a greater degree of flexibility. Autarky is vastly inefficient as it forces the Russians to accept goods they do not need or want simply as a balancing proposition. (Russia's dumping of Cuban sugar resulted from accepting far more than the country could possibly use.) Will the Russians abandon autarky? If they expect to stick to their schedules of purchases in the next ten years they will have to. The satellites are even more hampered because of size, and seeing them become more independent economically from Russia would be no great surprise.

Since Russia has few goods the West needs (they have offered iron ore and ant eggs), they will have to rely on gold sales to finance purchases (something the country has always been loath to do). With typical secrecy, the Soviets refuse to discuss materialistic subjects such as gold reserves. However, the *Financial Times* of London early last year "leaked" some statistics:

The Kremlin's gold reserves, excluding liabilities for recent wheat purchases, were estimated at $2.5 billion; special deposits in Switzerland and Lebanon amount to $700 million; COMECON's gold pool (Russia contributed 55 percent) contains $150 million; the satellites have reserves of less than $300 million.

Thus the total gold reserves in the entire Soviet bloc total $5 billion. Recent production of gold in Russia has amounted to $300 million per year. In a three-year plan schedule (1964–1966), production should total $1 billion.

Credit must play a large role in any expansion of trade with the Soviets, yet credit is where the Soviet Union has collected many black marks. Unless the government trading with the Russians guarantees credit extensions, the Russian promise to pay can be placed only at interest rates as high as 9 percent. Finland, Russia's largest "outside" trading partner, held many Russian I.O.U's last year and at one time the amount climbed to $40 million. Austria has also held some large claims; the country was relieved in 1963 when Russian debts were reduced to $7 million from $12.4 million. As with patents, a change in Russian attitudes will have to bear the test of time.

As a means of increasing trade with the Russians, countries of the free world other than the United States have offered long-term credits. This brings up the important question of whether Russia will be able to pay her debts. The Russian planners are known for their sudden, overwhelming and expensive interest in one area at a time. Khrushchev's grand design to improve the chemical industry was predicated on the availability of both technology and credit from the West. There are estimates that by 1970 Russia will be in hock to Western Europe for $3–4 billion! Unlike the United States' payments problems, these claims will not be offset by assets in foreign countries. They will represent cold hard cash owed foreign countries. One wonders whether Russia has demonstrated her good intentions sufficiently enough at this time to warrant such high credit extensions. It is pointed out that owing this much money to Western Europe could allow the Soviets virtually to blackmail Western Europe. To those who say Russia would be foolish to do such a thing, that it would shut off future trade, one has only to consider past Russian behavior that was completely irrational. Too little is known about Russia and the Soviet bloc to predict that this time agreements will be upheld, particularly when those agreements involve such an important chunk of their gold reserves.

As pointed out before, there is still a great deal of edginess in the United States about expanding trade. In 1961 trade increased 80 percent in a certain three-week period. The sharp rise brought raised eyebrows from some Congressmen, and soon after license totals dropped. (This indicates that the licensing function is more closely attuned to home politics than to foreign protection.)

In summary, there are four barriers to increased trade:

(1) Export controls prohibit items Russia wants most (however many of them are available through our allies).

(2) Russian goods have higher tariffs in the U.S. than other goods (Russian vodka—which the Russians recently sought to debase with capitalistic alcohol because they were running short—would meet tariffs 35 percent higher than vodka from France).

(3) Russia needs liberal long-term loans yet under the Johnson Act she doesn't qualify until all old debts are settled (there have been exploratory talks and Russia has offered $400 million to settle the $2.6 billion Lend-Lease loan).

(4) Russia produces little that the U.S. needs or wants.

These points indicate that at the present time the outlook for increased trade with Russia of any great magnitude is out of the question. The future may bring a different picture and it is necessary to look more deeply into the methods of Russian production to ascertain future opportunities.

Opening Russia to trade would be to discover 200 million new customers, one might be tempted to say. In terms of purchasing power, however, Sweden offers a larger market. Russian boasts and predictions of things to come have always been on the fantastically high side, and a consumer market is not anticipated for the near future. It is important to realize that the entire environment is radically different from that in the United States. Russians are paid by the state, and with no profit motive there is little incentive to turn out salable goods. The incentives that exist are based on quantity—a self-defeating concept in an industrial society, and one that prevents Russia from performing up to the standards set in the West. There are other difficulties in dealing with Russia: deliveries from the U.S.S.R. are unreliable; prices are difficult to negotiate with a state monopoly; differences in legal systems make enforcement of terms difficult.

The outlook for the Russian economy is dim, and basically the Communist system is at fault. Professor Evesi Liberman from Kharkov University has been in the limelight recently as the architect of a "Red profit motive" for gauging performance in the Soviet Union. Professor Liberman hotly denies that the theory is anything new, and he claims:

> Denial of profit by socialism and recognition of profit by capitalism has never served as the feature distinguishing socialism from capitalism. The difference is in the way profit is formed, appropriated and used. In the U.S.S.R., profit belongs to society as a whole and is not the sole purpose of production. It is merely the means for raising living standards, for extending and improving production. Under the conditions of a planned economy, profit can and must express actual efficiency of methods of production.

It is obvious that the professor's definition excludes profit as an incentive. Further, when profit is used in conjunction with planned (artificial) prices, it actually measures nothing except the summation of past guesses—guesses which are made by government "experts" who are not paid out of the so-called profits resulting from their work.

The fact that Communism stifles enterprise and growth has become particularly evident in Russia during the past few years. As society in Russia has become more complex, planning has become more unable to keep up. One is convinced of this when viewing the farm situation. Historically, the U.S.S.R. was an exporter of wheat. However, because of managerial ineptitude, old machinery, lack of fertilization, poor irrigation methods, as well as the favorite scapegoat, the weather, production of wheat dropped tremendously (on a bushel-per-acre basis) and the Russians were forced into what must have been humiliating deals with Canada and the United States. Because wheat was in short supply, livestock was slaughtered; this threw the livestock cycle off balance and it was necessary for Russia to import meat. Planning in agriculture is simply unable to keep up with conditions. Russian farmers, in addition, lack the education and initiative of their American counterparts. And, importantly, there are no manufacturers and salesmen in Russia trying to convince the farmer that one product will increase output better than another. A great deal of education is imparted through advertising, a horrendous thought to any practicing Marxist. It is said that Khrushchev came to power as a result of the farm mess; his inability to solve the farm problem was a contributing factor to his ouster.

Recently, Chairman Leonid Brezhnev announced a new farm program:

(1) More rubles will be invested in machinery, fertilizers, buildings, irrigation equipment, and other tools.

(2) "Sharply higher" prices will be paid for grain and livestock (up 50 to 100 percent).

(3) Collective farm grain quotas have been cut from 65.5 million tons (1964) to 55.7 million tons—and the quota will stay at this level through 1970.

(4) Peasants may cultivate private plots, raise livestock, and sell this in the cities.

(5) Consumer goods prices on collective farms will be lowered to the level of city stores.

It is wryly noted that the above program represents "more of the capitalistic carrot than the Communist stick." American farm experts claim "agriculture, much more than other industries, responds to the incentive of capitalism and suffers from the regulation that goes with Communism."

The farm situation suggests that some of the new equipment may come from the West, particularly since the farm-related industry will not be in full swing for some years. The situation in industry is just as bleak as that in farming. In an editorial, *Barron's* examines the Russian chemical plans as outlined by the planners. Russia intends to spend 42 billion rubles ($46 billion at the official rate, less in real terms) in seven years to increase chemical production three-fold—a program that would be difficult for the United States to achieve. It is pointed out that added fertilizer capacity will create scores of interactions and reverberations through the economy; huge new sources of power will be needed. Assistance from the West (up to one-third of the whole project) is an integral part of the plan. If Russia truly expects to buy $2 billion in equipment each year from the West through 1970, much of it will have to be financed on credit. However, $2 billion per year for this period would be a tremendous investment, and even if Moscow offered cash it is doubtful that suppliers could be found. Chemical development is tremendously complicated, with many interactions with other production capabilities (in which the Russians are lacking).

> Complicated chemical processes must flow from a reservoir of broad-gauged scientific achievement; the whole field of petro-chemicals (which is still virtually unknown in the Soviet Union) was pioneered a generation ago by a corporate offshoot of Shell Oil. Chemical development also hinges on other kinds of automation, precision instruments, and rigid quality control—areas where by admission Russia is weak.

Oleg K. Antonov, the designer of the turboprop engine (and a deputy of the Supreme Soviet), writing in Izvestiya in the fall of 1961, complained "the emphasis on quantity rather than quality prevents the State Planning Commission, economic councils and manufacturing establishments from shifting to new and more progressive indices. . ." In another article, Antonov stated that Soviet production tends to be technologically obsolete; inefficiency and waste result since there is no "feedback" in the form of market forces and competition. Where the state has a monopoly, the user has no recourse for defective products.

Malfunctions of Soviet products are widely reported in the press. One Communist journal reported that on April 1, 1962, the country's metal-cutting machine tool inventory was about 2.5 million units. Of this 800,000 were being repaired; 800,000 were in use to machine spare parts, and only the remaining 800,000–900,000 were actually in use in Soviet establishments.

Quality remains a problem because there is no incentive to produce quality merchandise. In Russian plants, the quality inspector is paid less than production workers and is subservient to the plant director. The plant director's salary is in part determined by output, so it is obvious that the inspector is not going to reject very many units. Joseph A. Gwyer of the Library of Congress estimates that "30 percent of all Soviet tractors, up to 60 percent of all automobiles and up to 25 percent of construction machinery is systematically idle because of the substandard quality of parts and assemblies. . . ."

Conclusions

As noted before, the Russians produce little that the Americans need; and because of the constraints of Communism one must conclude there is little hope that output will improve either in quality or desirability. These factors will keep Russia's sales down and will force Russia to curtail imports or dip into gold reserves. However, financing the farm and chemical programs will require vast infusions of outside technology and capital. Clearly, Russia's past policies and practices will have to change.

The issue of expanding trade with Russia thus rests on the question of credit. Should the United States government guarantee long-term loans for Russia? At the present time, this would be illegal under the Johnson Act (but this matter could be simply settled). Those against offering credits point to the past record of financial and moral atrocities; they note that the Russians have not renounced their policy of aggression; they feel that trade will strengthen the country and allow it to pursue its predatory policies with increased vigor.

Those who favor increasing trade with the Russians reply that the Allies have effectively undercut the U.S. position in every possible way. In their thirst for new markets, the Allies have pushed much further than the U.S. wishes in offering sophisticated machines and processes as well as long-term credits. The dike has already beer pierced; the question for the United States is whether it wants to capture some of the Russian market. Where trade needed by the Russians is in surplus in the U.S., trade doubly benefits the United States. Recent Soviet overtures toward becoming a more respectable trading partner—such as the patent agreement—are good omens.

Basically the issue of whether to expand trade with the Soviets can be put into game theory form:

	Increase Trade	Do Not Increase Trade
Russia	+10	+9
United States	+ 3	0

The figures represent measures of "benefit" and are admittedly arbitrary. If trade is increased, Russia benefits by 10 units and the United States by 3 (a reasonable increase would mean little to the total U.S. trade picture). Not increasing trade would hurt the Russians little since they can buy the goods from other countries; thus they still have 9 or 10 units. However, not increasing trade *would* change the position of the U.S. to 0 units. The rational choice on this basis (and game theory is lacking because it ignores other considerations) is to increase trade, particularly up to the point where the Allies can no longer supply what the U.S. will not provide.

Sentiment in the United States is shifting to favor increased trade; the position of the president has already been noted. To study the matter in detail, President Johnson appointed eleven men to a committee which is to look into expanding trade with the Soviet Union and Communist countries in Eastern Europe. J. Irwin Miller, chairman of Cummins Engine Company, is chairman of the committee; other members include Chancellor Herman B. Wells from Indiana University; Nathaniel Goldfinger, AFL-CIO research director; Crawford H. Greenwalt, chairman of duPont; William A. Hewitt, chairman of John Deere and Company; and others. The make-up of this committee is not surprising; trade is not likely to increase in the chemical and farm areas. Johnson has appointed men who have intimate knowledge of these industries.

It is clear that to expect large increases in trade with the Soviet Union would be unreasonable because of many constraints; yet, increasing contacts with Russia will give the West a foot in the door and could be a step in the right direction toward "civilizing" Russian foreign policy. This is the important concern of the United States. Because of its small dollar amount, trade with Russia could be considered much ado about nothing. Clearly, no monumental gain is in store for the U.S. However, the matter of principle is to be considered as the introduction suggests. If Russia is convinced that the wave of the future is cooperation and mutual trust, it *may* become a nation respectful of principles. From this, the world would have much to gain.

United States Legal-Political Barriers to Trade with Czechoslovakia

David A. Wollin

The scent of profit is in the air. Some U.S. businessmen suddenly are realizing the possible potential of the communist market, are suppressing their previously intense anti-communist feelings and are pressing for reduction of legal barriers to trade with the Soviet bloc.

It is the intent of this paper to discuss U.S. legal-political barriers to trade with Czechoslovakia, although explicitly recognizing that other barriers and other Communist nations do exist and do have a relevancy to my discussion. While I had originally hoped to limit the discussion to U.S.-Czech trade, I have found it not possible to ignore the broader topic of U.S.-Soviet bloc trade.

But a descriptive discussion of U.S. legal-political barriers to trade is not complete—one must, in addition, analyze both sides and take a stand on U.S. trade policy. It is the contention of this paper that:

(1) U.S. legal-political barriers have greatly restricted U.S.-Czech, as well as East-West, trade.

(2) The logic for such barriers is no longer valid.

(3) The removal of these barriers and resulting increase in East-West trade would be beneficial to the U.S.

(4) President Johnson in his expected policy statement on East-West trade should recommend removal of these barriers as a path to trade expansion.

Postwar Trade

Czech trade changed significantly, both in commodities and partners, after World War II.[1] Industry in Czechoslovakia was nationalized and, under socialist economic planning, directed toward heavy industry. Exports of machinery, tools and equipment increased rapidly and became the chief Czech exports.

As a member of the Soviet bloc, Czechoslovakia has reorientated trade from West to East. Today her chief bloc trading partners are: (1) U.S.S.R. (50 percent); (2) East Germany; (3) Poland.

Her chief partners outside the bloc are: (1) West Germany; (2) United Kingdom.

Reprinted by permission of David A. Wollin.
[1] "Foreign Trade of Czechoslovakia," *Overseas Business Reports* (March 1964): 8.

It is interesting to note that Czechoslovakia's trade with Germany before the war and East and West Germany after the war has continued at a relatively high level—probably reflecting sociological as well as economic ties between Czechoslovakia and Germany.

Considering the Communist bloc as a whole, the sale of goods by Western nations to Communist nations in 1962 was[2]: (1) West Germany ($750 million); (2) United Kingdom ($393 million); (3) France ($320 million); (4) Italy ($261 million); (5) Japan ($213 million); (6) Finland ($200 million); (7) Canada ($175 million); (8) Sweden ($145 million); (9) Austria ($145 million); (10) Egypt ($135 million); (11) India ($130 million); (12) Australia ($130 million); (13) United States ($125 million) (less than 2 percent of total U.S. trade in 1962).

Present U.S. Policy

According to Dean Rusk, the U.S. policy toward international communism has three objectives[3]:

> *(1) To prevent the Communists from extending their domain and to make it increasingly costly, dangerous, and futile for them to do so.*
>
> *(2) To achieve agreements or understandings which reduce the danger of a devastating war.*
>
> *(3) To encourage evolution within the Communist world toward national independence, peaceful cooperation, and open societies.*

In another statement Mr. Rusk declared[4]:

> *Today we are engaged in a contest with Communist power and ambitions that rage around the globe. . . . Inevitably it involves our trade relations, and for the first time we have faced the need for applying the instruments of economic denial in the absence of a general shooting war. . . . Such policies (trade) cannot be applied in any uniform or simply in terms of either time or geography. . . . Since the Communist nations no longer form a completely monolithic bloc in political terms, it follows that we should not treat them as a monolith in trade terms.*

(The absence of a general U.S. trade policy is demonstrated by the fact that trade with Yugoslavia is subject to less stringent regulation than that applied to Czechoslovakia, while policies toward China amount to total embargo.)

---

[2] "How to Share in East-West Trade," *Newsweek* (September 13, 1963), p. 71.

[3] *Department of State Bulletin* (March 30, 1964): 474–484.

[4] *Department of State Bulletin* (March 16, 1964).

Mr. Rusk adds[5]:

> Our trade policies should be custom tailored to fit the need. . . . We have developed a policy of selective controls in trade with the Soviet bloc:
>
> (1) Deny commodities, weapons, and technology of direct military significance. . . .
>
> (2) We and the NATO allies are also agreed that no free country should become overdependent on the Soviet bloc for critical commodities, such as oil.
>
> (3) The U.S. also prohibits exports. . . of equipment and data embodying certain items of advanced technology that might adversely affect our national security or welfare.
>
> In our trade policies toward the individual countries of Eastern Europe we have sought to encourage tendencies toward greater independence of actions.

Expressing his feeling that trade should be used as a weapon, Mr. Rusk states[6]:

> Trade enables us to exert some influence on the evolution of policy and institutions in this period of accelerating change in Eastern Europe. . . . The use of trade with Communist countries for national purposes is a matter for national decisions. The volunteer efforts of individuals or organizations to impose their private notions on our over-all trade policy can only frustrate the effective use of this essential national instrument.

Apparently contradicting the evidence presented previously under Public Law 480 and the Agricultural act of 1961, he further adds[7]:

> We have never embargoed or opposed the sale of foodstuffs to the Soviet bloc countries.

Summary of U.S. Policy

While the U.S. maintains a different trade policy toward each of the Communist nations, in practice the policy has been mostly uniform for Russia, Eastern Europe, and Czechoslovakia, and has grown mostly out of the "cold war" strategy following World War II. From the preceding chronological discussion it appears that the most restrictive legislation has been the Export Control Act (affecting U.S. exports) and the higher duties for Communist nations (affecting U.S. imports). Many of the

---

[5] Ibid.
[6] Ibid.
[7] Ibid.

other regulations mentioned were reduced to minor importance when the U.S.-Soviet wheat deal set "precedents" by liberally interpreting the Johnson Act, etc.

Sociological Barriers

But U.S. legal-political barriers have not alone been responsible for reducing U.S.-Czech trade. Since the beginning of the "cold war" American people, including American businessmen, have been typically vigorously anti-communist, and thus have felt morally committed not to deal with the Soviet bloc. According to one authority[8]:

> Throughout the U.S. today hundreds of corporations are energetically engaged in programs to "educate" Americans about the nature and threat of Communism. It is hard to fix the cost of the programs... but the total cannot be less than $25 million dollars a year.

It is interesting to note that the $25 million mentioned above amounts to more than the total U.S.-Czech trade in 1963.

Nature of the Communist Trading System

It takes two—the buyer and the seller—to make a trading agreement and similarities or differences in economic, political, or cultural systems of trading partners will determine the ease or difficulties of trade. Aside from the legal-political barriers, there are inherent differences in the economies of Czechoslovakia and the U.S.—and any communist and capitalist nation—which make trade difficult.

Czechoslovakia has a centrally planned economy[9]—control of economic resources and all economic activity is in the hands of the government and is conducted under a system of central economic planning.

Foreign trade is a government monopoly administered by the Ministry of Foreign Trade, whose duties are: (1) to insure that foreign trade is realized in accordance with the economic plan; (2) to conclude commercial treaties and trade agreements and participate in negotiations on payment agreements and tariffs; (3) to issue basic instructions for transport, credit, and trade policies; (4) to cooperate closely with other Ministries who have export requirements and produce goods for export.

---

[8] A. F. Weston, "Anticommunism and the Corporations," *Commentary* (December 1963): 479–487.

[9] "Basic Data on the Economy of Czechoslovakia," *Overseas Business Reports* (December 1962): 27.

The Ministry regulates the demand for imports in accordance with exports, and supervises and requires specific enterprises to respect trade agreement obligations. The Czech government, through the Ministry of Foreign Trade, has established twenty-nine specialized corporations, each of which has the exclusive right to conduct trade in a definite category of goods and services.

In addition, Czechoslovakia and other Communist nations typically conduct trade bilaterally, so as not to complicate central planning, while the U.S. conducts trade multilaterally. Bilateral trading, coupled with a general lack of goods to sell to the U.S., presents difficulties. For the U.S. company to expand exports to Czechoslovakia means either that Czechoslovakia must run a deficit with the U.S. (creating credit and foreign exchange problems) or start trading multilaterally, in hopes of running surpluses with underdeveloped nations to offset deficits with the U.S.

Fallacy of U.S. Policy

It is my opinion that present U.S. restrictions on trade with Czechoslovakia and other Eastern European nations are based on arguments which are economically unsound and militarily dangerous. Presumably we are conducting an economic "offensive" against Czechoslovakia by limiting exports of "strategic" goods to that nation, which she may in turn use to increase her military strength in order to commit Communist aggression. However, the effect of our embargo on exports has been not to deny the Soviet bloc of stategic goods, but merely to make Eastern Europe more dependent on Russia and shift some of Eastern European trade from U.S. to Western European businessmen.

Items denied export, such as beet and cane sugar, are certainly not of strategic significance. The fact is that the nuclear age has arrived and items such as petroleum, which were tremendously important in World War II, are no longer essential to fighting a world war that may last only a few minutes—the 1948 concept of a "strategic good" is no longer valid in 1965. Yet our 1948 concepts resulted in 1948 laws which still restrict 1965 trade.

Therefore, I feel that Congress should reduce legal-political barriers to trade for the reasons specified in the next section.

Benefits of Reducing Barriers

Economic Argument

Hopefully a reduction in U.S. legal-political barriers to trade would result in increased trade. A pessimist might assert that even if legal-political barriers were removed, the other barriers mentioned (differences in trading systems and sociological barriers) would still restrict trade to its present level. However, recent developments do not support the pessimist's viewpoint:

Czechoslovakia and the other Eastern European nations are not only showing signs of becoming more open societies but are also striving to increase trade with the West. After years of emphasizing heavy industry based on imported raw materials to the neglect of agricultural and consumer goods, the Soviet bloc economy went into a serious decline in the early 1960's as demonstrated by the following graph of Czechoslovakia's industrial production:

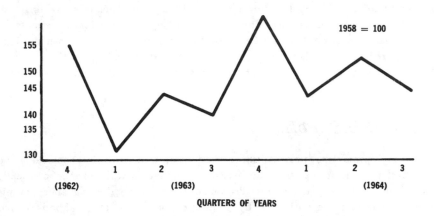

QUARTERS OF YEARS

Because of economic difficulties the bloc has gone through a stage of economic self-examination from 1962 till present as reported by the *Economist Intelligence Unit*[10]:

March 1962. *Because of economic difficulties, prospects of East-West trade continue to be bright. . . . The failure to diversify their engineering industries and to achieve a sufficient degree of cooperation means that Eastern Europe must now import a wider range of capital goods if their economic plans are to be carried out. Since Russia is unable to provide the goods, the industrialized countries of Western Europe are the only alternative sources of supply.*

Sept. 1962. *Countries in Eastern Europe fear that the growth of the Common Market may result in the loss of some of their markets . . . therefore they are attempting to put their own organization (COMECON) on a stronger footing.*

Jan. 1964. *On Jan. 1, 1964, a bank was established by the COMECON countries to facilitate multilateral payments and trade between them.*

---

[10]"Quarterly Economic Review, Eastern Europe, North," *The Economist Intelligence Unit*, March 1962–Feb. 1965.

Sept. 1964. *Poland, Czechoslovakia, and Rumania are fighting for an economic rather than political concept of COMECON.*

Nov. 1964. *In economic and industrial matters there are signs of greater liberalism (in Eastern Europe).*

Feb. 1965. *The COMECON bank appears more successful now and it looks as though it will undertake operations in trade with the West. . . . The planned economies of these countries have reached the point where the adoption of some of the basic principles of a free economy seems to be not only advisable but unavoidable. . . . The countries in this area need more economic freedom to enable them to align their trading relations with the West, to carry out plans for industrial specialization, to find a more profitable basis for intrabloc trade and to create incentives for greater efficiency in industry and agriculture.*

Feb. 1965. *There is a great political controversy raging inside the Czech political party . . . much of the industry is already subject to large-scale economic experiment.*

A recent article in *Newsweek* stated[11]:

(1) *That the Communists want more trade . . . is already painfully clear . . . COMECON has complained that the NATO embargo on strategic trade with the East "puts a brake on the development of our economic links with the capitalist countries."*

(2) *Czechoslovakia and Eastern Europe represent an untapped consumer market to American businessmen. In September of 1964 Skoda, the Czech auto maker, inaugurated a new $220 million plant to produce 100,000 cars annually, 25 percent of which they hope to sell in Western markets. The demand in Czechoslovakia for the 50,000 new Skodas to be sold there was so great that 93,000 Czech car buyers deposited $2770 each in hopes of getting an auto within three years. Presently Czechoslovakia had a total of 200,000 cars for a population of 14 million.[12]*

The American businessman's search for profits is beginning to overshadow his campaign against communism. Ever since the Canadian wheat deal, businessmen talk more and more about the "tremendous potential" of the Communist market.

Apparently the American businessmen want more trade with the Soviet bloc; apparently the Soviet bloc wants more trade with the West; apparently a reduction in U.S. legal-political barriers *would* result in increased East-West trade. But even

---

[11] "East-West, the New Trade Winds," *Newsweek* (Aug. 19, 1963), pp. 38–40.
[12] "Little Red Wagon Heads West," *Business Week* (Sept. 19, 1964), 49–50.

then the question of an imbalance of exports and imports poses a problem. According to many authorities the biggest obstacle to East-West trade is that the Soviet bloc simply does not have enough of the goods we want. While this factor would tend to restrict trade in the short run, evidence supports the long run theory that Czechoslovakia and other Communist nations may be forced to adjust their economies to produce more "exportable" goods.

Assuming that trade *would* in fact increase with a reduction in barriers, would this increase in trade be beneficial? The economist, using free trade theory, would contend that it would. The American businessman, eyeing the 350 million potential customers in Russia and Eastern Europe, would contend that it would. The die-hard anticommunists, using their outdated military arguments, would contend that it wouldn't.

Peace Argument

The time has come not merely to passively "contain" the Communists but to actively pursue a policy of peace. . . . A passive containment policy might not accomplish peace soon enough. Our slowly changing liberalism toward trade with Eastern Europe, beginning with Yugoslavia and Poland, might not accomplish its objectives soon enough.

But how do we actually pursue peace? Certainly an initial and basic step must be an increase in trade relations with Czechoslovakia and the rest of Eastern Europe. This would *not* be a policy of building up the enemy at our expense. This *would* be a policy of establishing business relations in hopes that political and social relations would follow. Trade relations make both sides more dependent on each other, and enlarge points of contact.

In addition, a large increase in East-West trade would disrupt the central economic planning of the Soviet bloc, forcing them to adopt more open economies—if they want to trade. There is also the argument that increased trade with Eastern Europe would reduce their dependence on the Soviet Union, thus splitting up Communist power.

The alliances that have lasted from 1945 until present are slowly breaking up. New friends and new enemies are being made by all nations, and for different reasons than in 1945. The U.S. must not let itself be restricted from changing its relations by a set of economically and politically illogical laws. The U.S. must not sit idly by while Western Europe takes the lead in establishing trade relations with the Soviet bloc. The U.S. must take the lead, because it is economically, politically, and morally our only alternative.

Conclusion

In his State of the Union address, President Johnson declared[13]:

> *In Eastern Europe, restless nations are slowly beginning to assert their identity. Your government, assisted by leaders in labor and business, is exploring ways to increase trade with these countries and the Soviet Union.*

Certainly I hope that the U.S. government does not let events in Vietnam sway its "commitment" to expanding East-West trade.

---

[13] "More Red Trade?" *Newsweek* (May 11, 1964), 71.

Part Two

International and Comparative Management

2

As activities increase, scholars inevitably attempt to explain them with theory. In international management all sorts of processes are developing which, when viewed as isolated individual acts, may make very little sense to the observer. A multinational firm moves all of its financial activities to New York; a manufacturer begins to build tv tuners in Taiwan; another firm fails dismally in its efforts to introduce soups to France. Why do these things happen? Is there any pattern common to all international business which may be used as a tool of analysis here?

In comparing various firms around the world, many differences and similarities are evident. Saudi Arabian firms use American style accounting, while marketing channels in Italy appear quite different from those in England. Here again we try to find the rationale, or underlying pattern.

This section deals with theory and structure in international and comparative management. The writers are trying to isolate the key variables, to determine what is likely to be similar, and why, and what is likely to be different in management in various countries.

Internationally oriented American firms must necessarily deal with both comparative and international management problems. An American manager must often make business decisions about unfamiliar problems in foreign environments, peopled by strangers who may well regard him as an outsider. Thus in the New York office a communication from the Chilean branch asks for permission to settle a labor dispute in a given way. In reading his subordinate's memo, the solution seems peculiar indeed to the American manager, yet perhaps this is the way it should be. How can he know—he may never have been in Chile; yet one major branch of his activities may depend on his getting this and similar decisions right most of the time. How would a manager even begin to sort out endless data to decide what the correct decision should be?

Here we have an example of how comparative management theory might help. In the above case an American manager is operating a branch in a foreign country and culture. Some things are the same, such as manufacturing technology; others may be quite different, such as labor law. If the manager can make relevant environmental-internal firm interlocks with the local environment, he may begin to see solutions to problems which previously were merely masses of confusing data.

In the general introduction to this book of readings, we have already introduced the methodology of comparative management, which is the way internal firm activities interrelate with various environments. The basic approach which most authors are now taking is to figure out which part of the environment most directly and forcefully affects the given internal business or managerial problem, and then relate the decision to this environment.

When first approached, this method seems peculiar to most Americans. We have lived our lives in one environment, and a surprising variety of things which we take completely for granted may not even be present in another culture, or they may be so different that the business decisions made seem totally peculiar. This is particularly true of legal problems, because laws can be so different between nations. Thus one author of this work routinely did things regarding price fixing and service adjustments in trucking which would be felonies in the United States. One such potential felony was giving special prices to major clients. But he was in Saudi Arabia at the time, where such activities were not only legal, but strongly encouraged by the government. An American visitor, familiar with motor trucking regulation in the United States, once sat for two days watching this performance with total amazement. He expected the police to break up the game at any moment.

The point here is that the proper internal business decisions in Arabia were illegal in the United States, and many American firms have similar internal problems. But the way they resolve these problems would seem peculiar to an Arabian also, since the obvious, seemingly correct decisions would not be made. Who was right? Everyone was! The difference in this case was in the environment, not in the abilities or skills of the respective managers.

We have already identified the educational, behavioral, legal-political, and economic blocks of environmental variables which taxonomize the environment for firms. The first article in this section by Farmer and Richman shows how this taxonomy was developed for the first time. As with most academic efforts, the bits and pieces had been around for a long time, and some practical managers already had worked out for themselves a crude similar system to get their multinational affairs managed correctly. What these authors did was to get everything together to see how it all looked in one systematic system, along with suggesting measurement techniques for various countries to focus on what is *really* important for a given problem.

One confusing point is that for country A, some environmental constraints may be critical, while for country B, these are unimportant. Thus for a new African country, the educational constraints, including basic literacy, may be critical, given the poor educational achievements of this population. Whole factories may have to be designed with these constraints always in mind. But the same firm building a new plant in France can ignore most of these, since educational levels in this country virtually guarantee that they will not be critical. But in France the rate in inflation (and economic constraint) may be critical, while in the African country this point can be ignored.

This bothers students and businessmen, since it sometimes appears that managers and scholars are being evasive. If education is important, say so! But comparative management deals with *relative* systems, not absolutes, and one must continuously keep changing his environmental constraint weights, as Farmer and

Richman do, so that the internal firm problems can be seen in their true light. One cannot expect to memorize lists of factors in comparative management and come up with absolute and always true answers. The only correct answer in comparative management is, "It depends . . . "

Comparative management can be a powerful tool for the multinational firm operating in various environments, but it also can be useful in other ways. American firms abroad must deal with local firms as suppliers, potential customers, and competitors. If managers can gain insights into how these local firms operate, and why, it is possible to be more effective in such dealings. To assume that the local water company is just like the one at home, only a bit more quaint, can lead to serious error.

Comparative management also tends to teach tolerance, if for no other reason than that one has to behave properly in any foreign country. One can be violently against public ownership of electric power companies in the United States and give money to politicians who feel the way he does. But if this individual gets to England to start a branch operation, he will be dealing with a publicly owned power company whether he approves or not. As a visitor, he is stuck with local customs. Such experiences can teach all of us a great deal about how the rest of the world works.

Comparative management studies are not yet a decade old, but already the field is exploding, as various scholars and managers add their insights to what already has been suggested. Professor Schöllhammer's article sums up the state of the art after five hectic years of analysis, hypothesis, and conjecture. The field sometimes appears to be riding off in four different directions at once, yet the basic notion of internal-firm—external-environment interlock is a common thread through virtually all writing. Since nothing else is really decided beyond this key point, the reader is invited to join in the debate.

Early explorations in comparative management, including the Farmer-Richman approach, were criticized because managers seemed to be seen as passive agents, responding only to external stimuli like rats in a maze. Given an environment, it would appear that any intelligent manager would always end up in the same place. If this were true, then why not replace the manager with a computer?

But Farmer's article on transportation management in different situations suggests yet another dimension of this field. Here we find many managerial options to get the transportation job done, and regardless of environment several of them might be efficient and useful. Which one should we choose? Here we see another dimension of comparative management—the kinds of managerial strategies which might be adopted, given the environment. The manager does have options, and good managers, while hindered by poor environments, will still do better than poor managers in the same environment. The scissors cut both ways—the environmental blade is one part of the action; the managerial blade is the other. It is impossible to say which one cuts the most.

This section also includes two articles by professional international managers. Mr. Townsend, of the Chrysler Corporation, explains what some dimensions of the multinational management task appear to be from the chief executives' chair. Here, too, the unusual is the ordinary when the firm moves to new environments. Bathing a cornerstone of the new Detroit plant in ram's blood for good fortune would probably result in the responsible executive being certified insane; the same action at the new Turkish plant was a logical and efficient behavioral factor in getting the firm off to a good start.

Mr. Powers of Pfizer suggests how a large American firm goes international and what ramifications such activities have on the entire firm. Firms sometimes begin various international activities as minor, side bet propositions—only later do they come to realize that this step eventually involves the restructuring of the enterprise and the reconstruction of thinking of all top executives. Mr. Powers suggests why this is so.

Travel is said to be broadening, and this is so in comparative and international management. Instead of considering one's petty provincial problems, the whole world becomes your beat. Instead of assuming that anything is always true, one must keep an open mind. And surprisingly, this study turns out to be a two-way street. Instead of carrying your invaluable information to the peasants abroad, it often turns out that they have better solutions to some problems than you have. One gives something—but one also receives. This point comes through again and again in the articles in this section. We may go forth confident that we have all the answers—but we return, thoughtful and enlightened, because we can now compare the way things might be if we weren't trapped so thoroughly in our own environment.

In the end, this may be where one world is located. A major advantage of international business, or any business, is that when deals are made, all parties benefit. No one buys or sells unless it is to his advantage to do so. Perhaps we don't make all the gain, but we always make some. And something is better than nothing. International firms do not have gunboats in the wings, ready to crush those who do not wish to deal; hence they have to learn to cooperate with anyone out there who has something to offer. And when the deal is made, when various parties carry out their part of the bargain, it often turns out that they weren't so bad after all. We can live with those guys—they're tough, but what the hell, we came out all right.

This may turn out to be the most important reason of all for international business and comparative management studies. Chrysler could have refused to spread the ram's blood. This author could have refused to deal with the charming Saudi Arabian with three wives, because in his culture such a man would be immoral. But the ram's blood was spread, and the deal with the polygamist was made—and we are all better off for the experience. In comparing these experiences with political and military adventures the world around, it may become clear that business is far ahead of other groups in building one world. Not the perfect world, but a better one than anyone else has been able to develop. If nothing more comes from the experiment than this, we are well ahead of the game.

A Model for Research in
Comparative Management

Richard N. Farmer
Barry M. Richman

Comparative management deals with problems of management and managerial efficiency in various countries. In exploring management theory to determine what tools and techniques can be utilized in this comparative area, it becomes clear that existing management theory has some serious drawbacks in terms of its orientation and applicability to different types of cultures and economies.

Traditional management theory usually deals with productive enterprises operating in a single environment. Management has been defined in one major work as "the accomplishment of desired objectives by establishing an environment favorable to performance by people operating in organized groups."[1] In this approach, the managerial functions of planning, staffing, direction, organizing, and control within the firm are analyzed. The firm attempts to operate as efficiently as possible in its environment, in the sense of trying to achieve its goals with the minimum use of resources.

Explorations of the management theory jungle[2] reveal that virtually all theories approach the problem of management as an internal problem within a productive enterprise. External factors, if considered at all, are assumed constant in most formulations. Hence, the universalists focus attention on functions and principles of internal management in a given firm in a given environment, seeking to determine how a firm might gain more effective and efficient operations. The various human relations and behavioralist theories of management focus on the persons in a given firm in a stated environment, again trying to determine how the firm might operate better. In a similar manner, the decision theorists, the students of bureaucracy, and social systems theorists, with few exceptions, view the firm as fixed in space and time.

This type of analysis certainly helps an individual firm achieve higher levels of efficiency. No organization is perfect, and close study of its major functions and personnel will usually yield insights into its operations which will increase efficiency. However, this analysis does not attempt to consider the problem of

Reprinted from the *California Management Review*, Vol. VII, No. 2 (Winter 1964). Copyright 1964 by The Regents of the University of California.

[1] Harold Koontz and Cyril O'Donnell, *Principles of Management*, 3rd ed. (New York: McGraw-Hill Book Co., 1964), p. 1.

[2] The various modern management schools are examined in Harold Koontz, ed., *Toward A Unified Theory of Management* (New York: McGraw-Hill Book Co., 1964).

relative efficiencies between firms in different environments. If, for example, an efficient manager of a ball-bearing plant in Pennsylvania were placed in charge of a similar operation in Mexico City, he would initially be less efficient than he was in his American job. The man has not changed, but the environment has. The question of relative managerial efficiency and differences in managerial activity between cultures is the problem to be considered here.

It may also be true that managerial efficiencies may vary between industrial sectors in the same country. Thus railroads may be managed less efficiently than steel companies in a single country. Present management theories can perhaps point to ways of improving efficiency in both sectors, but they fail to explain why the two industries have different levels of efficiency.

Present Theory Inadequate

In effect, most studies of management have taken place within a "black box" labeled *management*, without much concern for the external environment in which the firm may operate. As long as this external environment is about the same for all firms, the approach is valid; however, in cases where the environment differs significantly, present theory is inadequate to explain comparative differentials in efficiency.

Where environments do vary, as is the case between nations, it is necessary to examine the external pressures, or constraints, upon internal management. A manager may perform adequately in his internal direction of his firm, but he is also influenced substantially by external factors in his country which directly react on and influence internal management.

The hypothesis presented here is that in cases where comparative situations are considered, existing management theory in effect assumes the absence of many of the crucial variables. As a result, it is rather inadequate to use as a research tool in the area of comparative management. Our purpose is to develop a new conceptual framework for such studies which hopefully will prove more useful in the analysis of critical comparative management problems.

Efficiency an Objective

General Economic Goals

As a beginning for comparative analysis, it is useful to consider the question of what general economic goals most societies have. Management of productive enterprise does not take place in a vacuum: it may be defined as the co-ordination of human effort and material resources toward the achievement of organizational objectives. The organizational objectives ultimately reflect the desires of people for useful goods and services.

The basic assumption here is that virtually all countries want more goods and services and prefer a higher level of per capita income to less. Or they may prefer the same per capita income they now have, produced with less inputs, in order to enjoy more leisure. In either case, the manager's problem is to become steadily more efficient over time.

Increasing productive efficiency has generally been considered a desirable goal for enterprise managers in most societies. In capitalist countries, improved efficiency means higher profits and greater rewards for firm owners and managers; in Marxist countries, the planners stress firm efficiency so that the country can produce more goods and services with the same inputs. Since a country's total production will be the sum of production of component productive enterprises, the more efficient[3] each firm is, the more efficient the country will be.

National efficiency here can be considered conceptually as an engineering notion, namely:

$$(1) \qquad\qquad\qquad E=Q/I,$$

where E is efficiency, Q is output, and I is input. In economic terms, inputs consist of land, labor, capital, and management. Outputs are useful and desirable goods and services.

Measuring outputs and inputs with the elastic yardstick of money will not indicate real efficiency in any economy. Just as the inputs necessarily must consist of actual labor hours, real capital in the form of machines, plant, and so on, outputs must consist of real goods and services. The physical efficiency of a country will be measured by comparing real inputs and real outputs. Identifying and quantifying inputs and outputs is difficult, since different kinds of things must be added to determine what efficiency is.

However, there is a measure which can be used as a rough guide to managerial effectiveness in a given economy as compared to other economies. Comparisons of gross national product per capita between countries can be used.[4] It would be useful also to include a weighted value of the rate of growth in GNP per year over the past decade in making comparisons, since it is possible that a country will be interested in less income now in order to achieve more later. In part, the portion of GNP invested determines how big it will be in the future, but preparations for the future may not appear in national income accounts. Note, however, that a country could have a high rate of investment and still not get much growth, if the investment were badly directed—which in effect would be saying that management effectiveness is low.

---

[3] The problems of defining enterprise efficiency are great, given the difficulty of measuring variegated inputs and outputs. See Herbert A. Simon, *Administrative Behavior,* 2nd ed. (New York: The Macmillan Co., 1961), pp. 172–197, for a detailed discussion of this crucial point. It is important to point out that the concept of productive efficiency warrants an entire chapter in our book. In this chapter models of both firm and economic system efficiency having universal application will be presented.

[4] For a discussion of the concept of gross national product, see Paul A. Samuelson, *Economics,* 5th ed. (New York: McGraw-Hill Book Co., 1961), pp. 212–237. As with many other aggregate concepts dealt with here, measurement of this item is much more difficult than the basic concept.

Expanded Output

This type of comparison of GNP, growth, and managerial effectiveness begs the question of whether or not a country or culture in fact wants to become more efficient. The implicit value judgment here is that such efficiency gains are desired badly enough so that a culture, given probable trade-offs to get more efficiency, will opt for more efficiency. But if a culture decides not to obtain growth, the entire analysis collapses. In such a case a country could be perfectly managed in the direction of no growth, orienting its energies to other, possibly more esthetic values.

Our argument here is based on evidence from dozens of countries which suggests the contrary.[5] Poorer countries are striving mightily to expand outputs, and development economics, almost unknown twenty years ago, is a thriving branch of general economic analysis. Governments uninterested in development have been overthrown, to be replaced by those who are. International commissions, agencies, and bureaucracies have been organized to deal mainly with rapid economic progress. Wealthy countries worry about their rates of growth, while poorer ones steadily push for improvements in this sector. There are few countries in the world that fail to give at least lip service to the idea of development, and many countries, rich and poor, set national plans of achievement for the next five, seven, or ten years—always with some large per capita income growth indicated. There is overwhelming evidence to indicate that economic efficiency and improvement are desired; this is at least a good working beginning for analysis.[6]

Managerial Functions

The Concept of Managerial Effectiveness

All productive enterprise managers perform the same general managerial functions: planning and decision making, control, organizing, staffing, and direction. This is as true for a large steel company in the United States as it is for a small candy factory in Moscow. The act of managing cannot be performed without engaging in these functions. Hopefully, managers are motivated to perform these functions as efficiently as possible, but as noted above, the measurement of efficiency in a complex economic situation is quite difficult. Thus it is useful to consider the problem as one of determining managerial effectiveness. This may be defined as the degree of efficiency with which managers of productive enterprise

---

[5] The authors have worked, lived, and studied in Canada, the United States, Mexico, the U.S.S.R., Poland, Czechoslovakia, Lebanon, Kuwait, Saudi Arabia, Egypt, and the United Kingdom. Experiences in these and other countries studied have served as a basis for much of the analysis presented.

[6] See Robert L. Heilbroner, *The Great Ascent* (New York: Harper & Row, 1963), pp. 75–88, for a further discussion of this point.

achieve their stated (or given) goals. Subjectively, at least, one can evaluate given enterprises in terms of how well they seem to perform. In the aggregate, for all productive enterprises in the economy, the rough measure of this managerial effectiveness is GNP per capita plus growth in GNP over fairly long periods. A specific act of a manager may not be quantifiable, but results for the whole economic system are.

To get at the question of why management is effective or not, it is useful to consider the relative importance of management in any economic system. Management is the active factor in such a system. A country can have endless resources of all sorts but, unless management is applied to these factors, the production of the system will be close to zero. Moreover, the better the management, the greater output will be. Managerial effectiveness is the critical factor in the economic system.

The basic hypothesis here is that managerial effectiveness determines productive efficiency, or:

$$(2) \qquad\qquad\qquad E=f(X),$$

where E is productive efficiency and X is managerial effectiveness. If managerial effectiveness can be determined, we should be able to say something about the efficiency with which a country converts its inputs into outputs. If efficiency can be measured by a GNP rate-of-growth index, managerial effectiveness should also correlate closely with this index.

External Constraints on Management

In making comparisons of management efficiency between countries with widely different social and cultural environments, difficulties soon arise when traditional types of analysis are applied. We observe two managements in the same sector, and we note that in country A, managers seem far superior to their counterparts in country B. However, we cannot then state categorically that managers in A do their internal managing job better than those in B, since the nature of the external environment facing the two managements may be completely different. A may be a country with ample supplies of highly skilled labor, while B may have serious shortages of this important factor. A may also have a good, low-cost transportation system, while B is faced with transport shortages, high-cost freight movements, and the need to build far larger inventories than in A. A may have an excellent credit system, which allows a competent firm to obtain adequate funds, while B may have no organized capital markets. The result could well be that the presumably inept managers in B are actually doing better than their counterparts in A, given their external constraints.

In such a case it is fruitless to argue that the firm in country B should improve its internal management. This is clearly possible in most cases, but the gains from urging change in external constraints might prove much larger. The point here is that comparisons between internal managements in different cultures may prove useless unless the external environment is also studied carefully.

This external environment may be termed the *macromanagerial structure*. It consists of the crucial external factors which directly influence the activities and effectiveness of firm management.

The nature of the impact of external constraints on internal firm management is shown in Figure 1. The productive enterprise is taking available inputs and creating usable outputs as efficiently as possible. However, the external constraints act on managers to inhibit or aid their effectiveness. These external constraints may generally be grouped into the following sectors: economic, legal-political, socio-logical, and educational. Since managerial effectiveness depends on, or is influenced by, external constraints, we have:

$$(3) \qquad\qquad X = f(C_1, C_2, \ldots C_n),$$

where the C's are the various relevant external constraints.

A second critical point is that many of the external constraints are interrelated. Hence, a culture's view toward managers may well be closely connected with educational achievements, or the efficiency of the commercial banking system may depend at least in part on formulations of business law. The result is an extremely complex set of interrelationships which determine in large part how efficiently a country performs economically.

Ranking Constraints

In an attempt to measure the importance of external constraints on internal managerial effectiveness, the approach here will be to give each major external constraint a numerical value suggesting its relative importance. For any given country, it is then possible to give values to these constraints, relative to other countries. In effect, this will rank various countries in terms of the impact each external constraint has on managerial effectiveness. The scores given will be based on a subjective evaluation of how the constraint affects management—the higher the score, the more assistance the constraint is in making internal management more effective. Hence, if the American central banking system is given a score of 100, the German might have a value of 90, and the Saudi Arabian a value of 10.

Clearly such numerical evaluations are incapable of being refined values of the impact of such constraints. In effect, what is being done is to rank the effectiveness of each constraint between nations. Any observer making the rankings could, with some logic, give somewhat different evaluations of the impact on management of key constraints. The purpose of giving a numerical ranking, however, is to focus on the best available subjective evaluation of a given constraint. Most persons who are familiar with central banking problems would probably rank the three countries above in the same order, although they would give different numerical values to the constraints. But mere ranking fails to indicate that, if a country is really deficient in some respects, it is not just below a second country, but far below it.

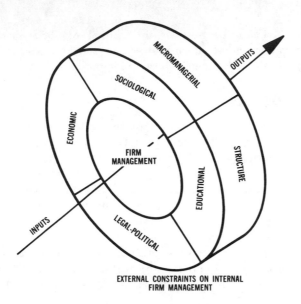

EXTERNAL CONSTRAINTS ON INTERNAL
FIRM MANAGEMENT

Figure 1.

If the constraints are really relevant in determining managerial effectiveness, the scores of the various countries rated would indicate the relative managerial effectiveness in the economy. The score would indicate the relative efficiency of the given economy as well—although this could also be obtained by comparing per capita GNP plus its rate of growth. The evaluation of the external constraints has the additional value, however, of focusing on the reasons *why* a country has poor management. The lower scores on selected constraints point to the corrections needed if improvements in efficiency are to be made. Countries may have similarly low per capita GNP figures for quite different reasons, while, conversely, countries may be relatively wealthy for different reasons. This technique also allows for the evaluation of different economies in terms of specific factors which tend to influence managerial effectiveness. If a given country is strong in central banking and monetary policy, it will prove less important to devote time and skilled manpower to corrections here than in areas where more serious problems exist.

Relative Efficiency

The External Constraints

The list below shows the relevant external constraints affecting managerial effectiveness and their assigned weights. If a given country were perfectly organized from the standpoint of efficient management, it would be rated 500 on the suggested constraint scale. No country could presently receive a perfect score, because no country is perfectly efficient in its management. Note also that as long as there is any technical progress in the natural or social sciences, some improvements in managerial effectiveness over time could be expected. Deterioration could also occur if negative changes occurred in the constraints.

Identifying Constraints

The method of constraint identification was to consider the various pressures in a country which could be seen to have some effect on internal management. There is a danger that this technique will lead to discussions of everything in the world. The variables mentioned are obviously very complex, and detailed study of even a few could take a lifetime. However, if only the portion of the constraint directly influencing management is considered, the task becomes somewhat simpler. Hence, we are not interested in all of law and legal theory but only the portions of law which bear directly on management. Similarly, our concern with education does not include all of pedagogy but only the portion which concerns managerial effectiveness. By focusing our attention in this way, it may be possible to gain some insight into how such constraints actually do affect internal managerial effectiveness.

External Managerial Constraints and Suggested Weights

Educational Characteristics (100)

$C_{1.1}$: *Literacy Level.* The percentage of the total population who can read and write, and the average years of schooling of adults. (50)

$C_{1.2}$: *Higher Education.* The percentage of the total population with post high school education, plus the quality of such education. Numbers and quality of colleges and universities in the country. The types of persons obtaining higher education. (20)

$C_{1.3}$: *Specialized Technical Training.* Types and quality of technical training, including apprenticeship programs, engineering training, technical institutes, company training programs, vocational high school training, and similar. The type, quantity, and quality of persons taking such trainings. (10)

$C_{1.4}$: *Attitude Toward Education.* The general cultural attitude toward extensive education, in terms of its presumed desirability. (10)

$C_{1.5}$: *Educational Match with Requirements.* Whether or not the type of training available in a culture fits the needs of productive enterprise on all levels of skill and achievement. (10)

Sociological Characteristics (100)

$C_{2.1}$: *View of Managers as an Elite Group.* The general social attitude toward managers of all sorts. (10)

$C_{2.2}$: *View of Scientific Method.* The general social attitude toward the use of rational, predictive techniques in solving various types of social, business, technical, and economic problems. (40)

$C_{2.3}$: *View of Wealth.* Whether or not the acquisition of wealth is considered socially desirable. (10)

$C_{2.4}$: *View of Rational Risk Taking.* Whether or not taking of various types of personal, corporate, or national risks is considered acceptable, as well as the general view toward specific types of economic and productive risks. (10)

$C_{2.5}$: *View of Achievement.* The general attitude toward personal achievement in the culture. (20)

$C_{2.6}$: *Class Flexibility.* The possibilities of social class mobility, both upward and downward, in the culture, and the means by which it can be achieved. (10)

Political and Legal Characteristics (100)

$C_{3.1}$: *Relevant Legal Rules of the Game.* Quality, efficiency, and effectiveness of the legal structure in terms of general business law, labor law, tax law, and general law relevant to business. Degree of enforcement, reliability, etc. (30)

$C_{3.2}$: *Defense Policy.* Impact of defense policy on productive enterprise in terms of trading with potential enemies, purchasing policies, strategic industry development, labor competition, and similar factors. (10)

$C_{3.3}$: *Foreign Policy.* Impact of policy on productive enterprise in terms of trading restrictions, quotas, tariffs, customs unions, etc. (20)

$C_{3.4}$: *Political Stability.* Influence on productive enterprises of revolutions, changes in regime, stability or instability over protracted periods, etc. (20)

$C_{3.5}$: *Political Organization.* Type of organization in constitutional terms, degree of centralization or decentralization, pressure groups and their effectiveness, political parties and their philosophies, etc. (10)

$C_{3.6}$: *Flexibility of Law and Legal Changes.* Degrees to which relevant barriers to efficient management can be changed, certainty of legal actions, etc. (10)

Economic Characteristics (200)

$C_{4.1}$: *General Economic Framework.* Including such factors as the over-all economic organization of the society (i.e., Capitalistic, Marxist, mixed), property rights, and similar factors. (50)

$C_{4.2}$: *Central Banking System.* The organization and operations of the central banking system, including the controls over commercial banks, the ability and willingness to control the money supply, the effectiveness of legal policies regarding price stability, commercial bank reserves, discounting, credit controls, and similar factors. (20)

$C_{4.3}$: *Economic Stability.* The vulnerability of the economy to economic fluctuations of depression and boom, price stability, and over-all economic growth stability. (10)

$C_{4.4}$: *Fiscal Policy*. General policies concerning government expenditures, their timing, and their impact; the general level of deficit, surplus, or balance; total share of government expenditures in gross national product. (10)

$C_{4.5}$: *Organization of Capital Markets*. The existence of such markets as stock and bond exchanges, their honesty, effectiveness, and total impact; the size and role of commercial banking, including loan policies and availability of credit to businessmen; the existence of other capital sources, such as savings and loan associations, government-sponsored credit agencies, insurance company loan activities, etc. (20)

$C_{4.6}$: *Factor Endowment*. Relative supply of capital and land (agricultural and raw materials) per capita; skills and ability of the work force. (20)

$C_{4.7}$: *Market Size*. Total effective purchasing power within the country, plus relevant export markets. (20)

$C_{4.8}$: *Social Overhead Capital*. Availability and quality of power supplies, water, communications systems, transportation, public warehousing, physical transfer facilities. (40)

$C_{4.9}$: *Interorganizational Cooperation*. Degree to which various firms, government agencies, unions, and other relevant organizations co-operate with each other to achieve desired mutual goals. (10)

Perfect Score: 500

Effect on Management

Constraint Evaluation

For a given country, the constraints can be evaluated by a person familiar with the general cultural, economic, business, and political environment in the country. Quantification of the external constraints is obviously subjective and difficult, but at least an effective ranking can be accomplished. The kind of evaluation desired is one which tries to weigh the effect of the constraint on internal managerial effectiveness in a country. The lower the assigned score, the greater the impediment to efficient internal management. High scores for given constraints suggest a favorable impact.

This ranking is posed basically only in managerial terms—it is not particularly relevant if a given external constraint aids the development of folk art or literature, for example. While such cultural activities may have a great deal to do with the quality of life in a country, as long as they have nothing directly to do with effective internal management they are irrelevant for our purposes.

The scores achieved by various countries in effect rank the country with other countries of the world. Total scores may be similar, but internal ratings may suggest weaknesses worthy of further study. Hence country A and country B may have identical total scores of 275. However, A rates highly on sociological factors, while B rates highly on economic characteristics. In this case, the strategies to be followed by the countries might be completely different. Both can improve managerial effectiveness, but in different directions. The usefulness of the rating scale is to focus on the kinds of serious problems which require analysis, change, and reform.

The variables noted are constantly changing over time, and it is impossible to pose this type of question in static terms. A country may have a poor but improving legal system, for example. Rapid change may occur when a country makes a major shift in foreign policy. The joining of a customs union such as the Common Market could have this sort of effect—as might the winning or losing of a war.

As a result, it is necessary to consider the external constraints over a fairly long period of time, and to rate trends as well as actualities. A decade should be long enough to consider the major shifts in constraints in this sense. Since change is continuous, rechecks of given countries would become necessary to determine what impact macromanagerial shifts had on managerial effectiveness.

Change in External Factors

The Impact of External Constraints

Examples of how the external constraints affect internal management may serve to illustrate the precise choice of constraints noted in the foregoing list. The basic idea here is that a given firm, with given internal managerial effectiveness, could actually have a gain in efficiency if external constraints shifted favorably. The discussion and examples which follow are intended to be suggestive rather than conclusive, since space does not permit an exhaustive evaluation of every constraint and its implications for managerial effectiveness.

Educational Constraints

The quality and efficiency of any organization depends largely upon the over-all quality of the persons in the organization. Hence the nature and quality of the educational process within a country are critical factors in determining the level of managerial competence. If a manager has to staff only from illiterate, superstition-ridden peasants, he will have a much different organization than the man who has a choice among skilled workers and university graduates. In part, this educational factor consists of formal schooling and scholastic organization, but informal schooling is equally important. The English, with their sparse university population, appear weak in regard to formal education—but also to be considered is the high development of apprentice training available in that country. To produce large numbers of college or technical institute graduates may be worthwhile, but the quality of educational experience, as well as the quantity, is quite relevant.

Basic Literacy

The most important factor of all is basic literacy. Many a genius has been able to educate himself in quite astounding ways, once he was literate—but the competent but illiterate person rarely has a chance to improve himself.

The types of highly educated persons in the culture also affect management. If managers are largely trained as lawyers, their work will likely reflect this education, and the enterprise they run will be quite different from one staffed largely by engineers. If the managers are trained as managers, which outside the United States has been rare, the firm will also be different. And if managerial training is largely informal, consisting of on-the-job training of intelligent, non-college men, results will be still different. In any case, the types of persons available to the firm will in large part determine how well the firm does its job.

The educational complex of a country may also determine technical, as compared to managerial, efficiency. If a country is willing to finance extensive technical education for its citizens, it will benefit accordingly in this complex world. Failure to do so will result in poor performance for many productive enterprises.

Far too many countries have attitudes toward education which result in their educational systems being badly out of step with educational requirements for productive enterprises. Too many lawyers are produced, and far too few engineers and doctors. The familiar result in many countries is to find managers trained as agronomists, engineers serving as accountants, and lawyers working as technicians. The effect on efficiency is clear.

As with the sociological constraints, the problem of evaluating the impact here is difficult. Other things being equal, the firm with the best trained management and work force will be more efficient, and if "best trained" can be evaluated, some insight into the impact of these external constraints on internal management can be achieved.

Attitudinal Values

Sociological Constraints

This set of constraints can also be discussed as a group, although in a detailed analysis the major constraints would be broken down and analyzed independently. It is clear that many of these constraints are extremely complex sets of variables in the environment which tend to affect managerial effectiveness considerably.

The general attitudes toward managers and management will influence the type of management and the leadership effectiveness of managers. Managers may be seen as dynamic, entrepreneurial heroes, capable of performing great feats which enrich the culture and the economy—or they may be seen as cynical exploiters of humanity, concerned only with a narrow view of profits and crass commercial activities. If managers are regarded as heroes, the profession will not lack capable recruits, and managerial competence will tend to improve over time. Educational systems, as well as popular folklore, will reflect this attitude. But if managers are considered only slightly better than mad dogs or vicious exploiters, it is quite probable that the profession will suffer accordingly. So, for that matter, will leadership and productivity.

Closely connected to this point is the way in which alternative elite groups are viewed in the culture. If the traditional elite occupations of the clergy, the central government bureaucracy, the military, and the law are regarded so highly and rewarded so well as to drain off talented young men from management, business organizations will suffer. The impact of such status rankings will not only be reflected in the quality of recruiting of competent young men, but also in the way in which managers see themselves, and in their influence on the society. In some cases, strong admiration for traditional elite groups, plus tight entry controls into these elite professions, may actually help business management, since highly qualified young people may be drawn to management or entrepreneurship as the only high-income occupation open to them in a tightly stratified society. Many European countries have large landed estates once owned by the traditional elite groups, but now serving as country estates for the previously despised managerial elite.

Social attitudes of this sort may also interact with the type of constraints business operations face in other sectors. A country which has small regard for management and business activity is not likely to have a government sympathetic to business problems, and constraints such as tax law, business codes, and similar factors will reflect prevailing attitudes as to the importance of key groups in the society.

Use of Scientific Methods

The general feeling toward scientific methodology will also strongly influence managerial efficiency and behavior. If a country has a strong traditional religious and cultural bias toward non-scientific behavior, it will prove difficult to introduce modern managerial methods, which are based on the same type of predictive, rational view of the world as are the more purely technical devices. A modern manager who operates efficiently spends much of his time trying to predict what might happen and altering his decisions accordingly, much as an engineer or scientist tries to predict behavior in mechanical or scientific phenomena and infers from what will happen how the situation might be altered to advantage. If the culture's view of the world is mystical or fatalistic, such future orientation will prove difficult. Many problems of presently underdeveloped countries stem from this constraint. Being unable to understand scientific methodology, citizens are unable to understand the reasons for the success of the Western economies which have utilized scientific techniques in a wide variety of activities, including management. In a non-scientific culture, managerial and technical recruitment will prove difficult. Even if a few capable men exist, the problem of developing effective work forces will also be hard, since virtually all skilled personnel will require some training in scientific methodology and thinking.

The manner in which society regards wealth also will be relevant in determining the type of management it gets. Wealth can be seen as a passive, asset situation, where money is held mainly by a social class which deserves it for non-productive reasons. Or it may be viewed as a dynamic, income item, growing steadily as the forces generating wealth are steadily improved and expanded. If the prevailing view is the former, management is likely to be held in low esteem. If the rich are highly regarded in the culture, seekers after wealth will not be hard to find, and if management offers a path to riches, the profession will benefit. But if wealth is regarded with suspicion, or if certain kinds of wealth are considered better than others, productive enterprise may suffer. In many cultures, land-created wealth is considered better than industry-created riches, and industrial management suffers.

Rational Risk Taking

The uses of wealth also are relevant. Calvinist-oriented countries typically regard riches as something to be used to create further wealth, while other societies have a much more static notion of the uses of wealth. Conspicuous consumption instead of productive investment can have considerable impact on the manner in which enterprise develops and on the practice of management itself.

The social view toward rational risk taking may also influence the type of management obtained. A society which sees large risks as desirable and acts accordingly will have considerably different managerial attitudes than one where reasonable risks are considered unsound. This attitude, as with others mentioned above, tends to shift over time at varying rates. Often a culture has a sub-group which may directly influence the types of managers and entrepreneurs in the society. The Chinese in Southeast Asia, the Lebanese in Africa, and the Armenians in the Middle East are examples of such sub-groups who seem willing to take bigger business risks than the general population. The impact of such groups on management and entrepreneurship in these areas has been large.

Management will also be influenced by the general social view toward personal achievement. In cultures where personal drive and ambition are regarded as negative values, management will be hampered. If Horatio Alger traditions abound, the reverse will occur. The drive toward achievement may be collective as well. Some countries are known for their almost overwhelming desire to succeed, to achieve *grandeur* in the community of nations. If such achievements require better management of productive enterprises, it will probably be forthcoming.

If the culture deliberately or unconsciously prevents a significant number of citizens from entering the ranks of management, there will be some impact on efficiency. An obvious example is the tendency in most countries to exclude automatically all women from top-level management, thus throwing away half the intellectual potential of the country. Such restrictions as may be connected with race, religion, or social class would also be examples of this type of exclusion. The smaller the pool of acceptable managerial candidates as a percentage of the total population, the less likely it will be that a country will have effective management.

Legal Codes Different

Political and Legal Constraints

The nature of legal constraints on business, such as contract law, patent and anti-trust law, labor legislation, and tax law is relatively clear-cut. Firms operating under Anglo-Saxon legal codes have different rules of the game than firms operating under Napoleonic codes or various forms of religious law. Hence a firm in some Middle Eastern countries must do business under *Shariya* law, which is derived from the Koran. Business cases involving breach of contract and similar matters are evaluated by religious judges, whose major precedent is koranic injunction. Since each case may be decided on its individual merits, precedents seldom are available to indicate what the next decision may be, resulting in considerable uncertainty in business decision making. This legal code also bans interest payments entirely, and the effect of this prohibition on internal business operations can easily be seen.

Defense policy and foreign policy may also have considerable business impact. Americans are familiar with the kinds of differences in organization found in firms dealing mainly with the Defense Department; while one major reason for the remarkable success of West German firms since 1948 is that the very low defense budgets of the Republic have prevented a drain of valuable human and material resources into defense activities. Such foreign policy decisions as trade agreements, tariff rates, and import quotas can literally mean the survival or collapse of many business enterprises. This type of policy also has considerable effect on the price of both inputs and products sold. One major effect of the American fuel import policy, which sharply restricts the flow of low-cost crude oil into the United States, is to raise energy costs for productive firms and lower their efficiencies. No matter how capable a manager may be, he still has higher costs in this sector than many of his foreign colleagues.

Political stability also directly affects firm effectiveness. An enterprise trying to operate in a country which endures frequent revolutions, and which has complete turnabouts in major political policies from time to time, faces completely different uncertainty problems than a country which is politically stable. Where firms can be reasonably confident that present major government policies will endure, their internal effectiveness will be higher.

Countries whose political and legal institutions are straightjacketed by tradition and inertia may have considerable inefficiency caused by their inability to change gracefully over time as economic and managerial requirements change. Firms may find that they are hampered by archaic customs, laws, and traditions, and that they are unable to operate efficiently as a result. All countries are afflicted with this type of problem to some degree, but some systems are much less flexible than others.

Detailed Studies

Economic Constraints

The economic constraints affecting business efficiency have been covered in great detail in studies both by economists interested in determining levels of income in an economy and by development economists.[7] Since management is one key factor of production, the analysis of why it functions as it does, given other external economic conditions, has not been lacking. Hence the economic constraints developed in the foregoing list are taken from various sources in the economic literature, which have noted the significance of these factors in keeping a total economy in the position of having a relatively stable price level, with real income per capita rising as rapidly as possible. In developed countries, the avoidance of recessions and depressions has also been covered exhaustively.

Traditionally, economists have tended to place more weight on the other factors of production than management, assuming managerial effectiveness. Thus in analyses of the American economy, managers of productive enterprises are assumed to behave in a rational manner calculated to improve their profit position and internal efficiency. In the recent tax cut debate, as one example, the assumption was made (correctly) that if $11 billion of additional purchasing power were put into the economy, American businessmen would make the necessary additional sales efforts, invest intelligently in needed capital equipment required for sales expansions, and so on. Precisely how such activities would take place within the firm was not considered in detail by most economists.

The Dependent Variable

Our analysis follows the usual economic analysis in that it is argued that a stable price level, with growing per capita incomes, freedom from recessions, and adequate supplies of capital directed properly to firms needing it are desirable for effective internal firm management. However, here we are proposing that the traditional economic approach be reversed: that is, if the economic constraints are of assistance to business enterprises, the internal efficiency of the firms will be greater, leading in turn to higher levels of per capita income. Management has become the dependent variable around which the economy revolves. There is an interrelationship here between the other factors of production and management which creates an endless interaction between the economic constraints and the efficiency of internal business management.

------

[7] See Ralph K. Davidson, Vernon L. Smith, and J. W. Wiley, *Economics: An Analytic Approach* (Homewood, Ill.: Richard D. Irwin, Inc., 1958), pp. 115–226, for one of many studies of macroeconomics. See Paul Alpert, *Economic Development* (New York: The Macmillan Co., 1963), for one of many examples of modern economic work in the study of income growth.

Examples of how the economic constraints affect internal managerial effectiveness are easy to develop. Consider a situation characterized by extreme price inflation, such as presently is occurring in Brazil. Enterprise planning in this case must necessarily revolve around the prospect of higher prices for both inputs and outputs tomorrow; the firm must steadily try to get out of money (the depreciating asset) and into goods (the appreciating asset). The effect of such external circumstances on the firm will result in management policy which is completely different from efficient management policy in a stable price situation. Such behaviors may both be quite efficient, but they are not the same. An inventory policy considered completely unsound and inefficient in the United States could make quite good sense in Brazil at the moment. Similar impacts could be traced for such external factors as extreme economic boom or deep depression. Firms cannot escape such situations—they must adjust to them, but to argue that these economic factors are unimportant in their effect on internal management would be unsound.

Another example of the effect of economic constraints on managerial effectiveness would be when production is efficient only when the market reaches a given minimum size. Such economies of scale in production influence the organizing, staffing, and planning of a firm operating in an economy where it is unable to achieve minimal efficient size. The firm will be inefficient relative to similar firms operating in countries where such size is easily achievable. Hence a Chilean steel mill may be unable to operate efficiently no matter how good its managers are, while a relatively inept group of American steel mill managers can easily achieve lower costs due to the size of the market.

Analysis of Matrix

A Comparative Management Matrix

It is possible to construct a comparative management matrix using the external constraints developed above. Such a sample evaluation is shown in Table 1. Here the constraints are arranged vertically, with various countries being evaluated listed horizontally. The ratings for each constraint are made for the country, and the totals are added. At this stage, such evaluations are definitely subjective—the purpose here is to demonstrate how a more complete study might be accomplished. However, for our book we intend to use a variety of techniques to assure that our rankings and weights are meaningful. For example, some use will be made of the "Delphi" technique developed at Rand Corporation.[8] In this connection, we plan to get specialists who are expert in a number of countries studied to rank those countries and assign weights to those constraints within their sphere of competence. Through a series of interviews and questionnaires, in addition to our own research,

---

[8] Norman Dalkey and Olaf Helmer, "An Experimental Application of the Delphi Method to the Use of Experts," *Management Science*, IX, No. 3 (April 1963), 458–467.

Suggested Comparative Management Matrix

External Constraints	U.S.A.	U.S.S.R.	U.K.	Mexico	Saudi Arabia
Educational (100)					
$c_{1.1}$	48	45	45	25	6
$c_{1.2}$	15	11	10	5	1
$c_{1.3}$	6	8	9	3	1
$c_{1.4}$	6	9	5	5	5
$c_{1.5}$	8	5	7	5	1
	83	78	76	43	14
Sociological (100)					
$c_{2.1}$	5	8	4	5	6
$c_{2.2}$	35	25	35	25	5
$c_{2.3}$	6	8	5	6	8
$c_{2.4}$	6	3	4	5	5
$c_{2.5}$	12	15	10	10	8
$c_{2.6}$	8	9	5	4	4
	72	68	63	55	36
Political-Legal (100)					
$c_{3.1}$	25	20	28	20	10
$c_{3.2}$	6	3	8	6	5
$c_{3.3}$	10	5	15	12	5
$c_{3.4}$	18	15	20	10	10
$c_{3.5}$	6	5	8	5	4
$c_{3.6}$	6	2	5	5	1
	71	50	84	58	35
Economic (200)					
$c_{4.1}$	30	20	32	28	25
$c_{4.2}$	18	10	19	12	3
$c_{4.3}$	5	6	8	5	5
$c_{4.4}$	5	5	6	5	2
$c_{4.5}$	18	10	19	8	2
$c_{4.6}$	16	12	10	6	6
$c_{4.7}$	19	15	15	8	4
$c_{4.8}$	35	25	30	12	6
$c_{4.9}$	8	4	7	6	6
	154	107	146	90	59
Total (Constraint Index)	380	303	369	246	144
1960 GNP[a]/Capita	$2,300	$760	$990	$280	$110
1951–60 Growth Rate	1.5	4.0	2.0	1.5	2.0
Efficiency Index	405.0	272.6	178.2	37.8	19.8

[a] GNP data derived from United Nations, *Statistical Yearbook, 1961* (New York: United Nations, 1961), pp. 21–38; 486–489. The UN noted that intercountry GNP comparisons should be used with caution because of the statistical discrepancies between countries.

Table 1.

we are confident that meaningful rankings, weights, and values for the countries under analysis will emerge.

Total constraint scores are added for each country and compared to the index of GNP per capita and GNP growth in the past decade. The weight given here is 80 percent for GNP per capita and 10 percent for the growth rate. If the hypothesis that productive efficiency depends on managerial effectiveness is correct, there should be a close correlation between the GNP-growth index and the managerial effectiveness index.

Subjective Ratings

Again it should be noted that the scorings for the various external constraints are completely subjective at this stage. The statistical meaning of the number is nil, although this technique does have the virtue of forcing the investigator to ponder in his own mind the relative significance of various constraints affecting management.[9]

The matrix developed in Table 1 shows that the countries with higher rankings in their managerial effectiveness indices also have higher per capita income, when adjusted for income growth. Note, however, that the United Kingdom actually ranks higher (subjectively) than the United States on political-legal constraints. The relatively less developed countries show weaknesses in all areas, although the degree of weakness differs between them.

Labor Problems

A company doing business in the United Kingdom, as compared to one in the United States, could expect to have considerable staffing difficulties, given the relatively low ranking on educational constraints. Highly skilled manpower for managerial and technical positions is likely to be in short supply. Firms in Saudi Arabia would have serious training problems with labor, given the very low literacy and other educational ratings. They might also be advised to consider their legal position quite carefully, given the low ranking on this constraint.

---

[9] The use of rank order correlation techniques would be more meaningful statistically. See A. C. Rosander, *Elementary Principles of Statistics* (New York: D. Van Nostrand Co., Inc., 1951), pp. 618–629. However, the authors have found the use of numerical evaluations useful as a first approximation, since the analysis to date has been used for subjective evaluation of strong and weak points in a country's external managerial constraints. It is useful to say that the central banking system of the United States is better than that of Saudi Arabia, but it is much more useful to say that the American system is ten times better, even though this latter judgment is quite intuitive and subjective. Where large numbers of countries are ranked, such wide discrepancies probably would not appear, and rank order analysis would be more useful. It should also be noted that the various constraints could conceivably be quantified, although the amount of work involved would be enormous for most constraints.

Those concerned with increasing efficiency in the United States might well ponder the implications of the relatively lower sociological and political-legal rankings, which suggest a mildly antibusiness climate. Russians, on the other hand, would be best advised to consider economic reforms which could improve the effectiveness of productive enterprises. The point here is that the matrix is designed to provide a focus on difficulties which a given country faces. If the rater disagrees with the authors, he is welcome to defend his choice and propose other ratings which could show other difficulties.

Intercorrelation of the various constraints also shows up in the rankings. If a country like Saudi Arabia has a very low literacy rating, it is likely that the country will also rank low on many other ratings, since basic literacy is a necessity for many facets of productive efficiency. It is difficult to imagine a situation where illiteracy would be coupled with a highly skilled labor force.

Hopefully, this type of focus on weaknesses will lead to debate and discussion as to ways and means of correcting deficiencies. If the alleged deficiency is in fact unreal, the problem then becomes one of finding which other factors cause lower per capita GNP figures. Readers are invited to rate countries in which they are interested, to determine if this approach casts any light on managerial problems within the given economy.

Overseas Problems Anticipated

This matrix might also be useful for American firms planning to establish branches overseas. Where weak points emerge in the host country, the firm could anticipate difficulties and plan accordingly. If the educational factors are rated low, the firm can anticipate training and staffing problems of a different type than would be found at home. If the legal structure is poor, careful advance planning with American and local lawyers to avoid difficulties would prove useful, and so on.

A final note is that on Table 1, our efficiency index for the Soviet Union places this country in rank order two, whereas the constraint index places it in rank order three. The reason for this is that the apparent GNP growth rate has been so high in the past decade. Also relevant may be the way in which GNP is measured here—errors in intercountry comparisons can be large. Rather than "adjust" the efficiency index to account for this discrepancy, we have let it stand—to suggest that further work in refinement of the concepts discussed here is very much in order.

Purpose of Analysis

Conclusion

Our purpose in this paper was to consider the kinds of problems which arise when different countries are compared in terms of their relative managerial efficiency. Such discrepancies cannot be explained in terms of existing management theory; thus it is necessary to evaluate the nature of external constraints bearing on management. By examining such constraints, considerable insight is gained into the reasons why various countries have more or less efficient internal management in productive enterprises. This type of analysis has already proved useful to the authors in their examination of various management problems in quite diverse countries, and it is hoped that it will provide some insight into other types of comparative management problems as well.

The Comparative Management Theory Jungle

Hans Schöllhammer

A systematic and comprehensive conceptualization about business management is of relatively recent origin. Scholars reviewing the evolution of management thought[1] generally trace it back to the scientific management movement which gained remarkable momentum with the publication of Frederick W. Taylor's *Principles of Scientific Management* in 1911. From there on the field of business management attracted a great number of eminent thinkers who all contributed in some form to a systematic identification, classification, and interpretation of managerial problems, and thus provided a theoretical underpinning for the management discipline. However, differences in emphasis or neglect of certain crucial aspects led soon to the development of various theoretical orientations, some of which developed as "schools of management," each with its own focus, instrumentarium, and following. Professor Harold Koontz described and analyzed this situation in an admirable article entitled "The Management Theory Jungle."[2] He attempted to bring some order into this "jungle" by grouping the various major contributions to management theory into six schools of thought: the management process school, the empirical school, the human behavior school, the social system school, the decision theory school, and the mathematical school. But whatever the differences in orientation or emphasis of the various management approaches, they have at least one common characteristic: within their frame of reference they perceive the various phenomena under consideration as being universal. For instance, the management process school points out fundamental managerial activities and prescribes general "principles of management" by which managers should let themselves be guided in the efficient discharge of their managerial responsibilities.[3] Similarly, the behavioral school of management emphasizes certain "constants" such as a fundamental incongruency between organizational

---

Reprinted by permission of the *Academy of Management Journal,* Vol. 12, No. 1 (March 1969), pp. 81–97.

[1] See John F. Mee, *Management Thought in a Dynamic Economy* (New York: New York University Press, 1963); John F. Mee, *A History of Twentieth Century Management Thought* (Ann Arbor, Mich.: University Microfilms, Inc., 1963); Claude S. George, *The History of Management Thought* (Englewood Cliffs, N. J.: Prentice Hall, 1968).

[2] Harold Koontz, "The Management Theory Jungle," *Academy of Management Journal,* IV, No. 3 (Dec. 1961), 174–188.

[3] See Harold Koontz and Cyril O'Donnell, *Principles of Management,* 4th ed. (New York: McGraw-Hill, 1968).

and individual goals and prescribes to management a behavior pattern which would minimize the negative consequences of this incongruency.[4]

It can be argued that the explicit or implicit claim to universality of the various management theories has delayed the emergence of a field which is now referred to as international or comparative management. This field is of very recent origin; it emerged as a distinctive entity around 1960 and has since then experienced a very rapid development. The comparative management theory now commands the attention of an increasing number of scholars; many of them are attempting to build a conceptual foundation for this new field by providing a framework for the detection, identification, and evaluation of uniformities and differences of managerial problems in different countries or regions.

In spite of the very recent origin of comparative management as a separate field of research and teaching, there is already a considerable diversity in the theoretical underpinning of this discipline. There is thus a need for shedding some light into what might now be called the comparative management theory jungle. This is the purpose of this article: to review the various orientations of comparative management theory, to point out the strengths and the shortcomings of the different approaches, and to make recommendations for a synthesis.

The Socio-Economic Approach to Comparative Management

This approach starts from the premise that management is the most critical factor for unlocking the forces of economic achievement. For instance, Harbison and Myers see in the manager "the catalytic agent in the process of industrialization; i.e., he acts and reacts with the economic and social environment to bring about economic change."[5] Management thus is considered as a change agent, but nevertheless as an integral part of a particular social and economic system. The emphasis of the socio-economic approach to comparative management is on the interrelationship and mutual influence between a given set of socio-economic conditions and management practices. By investigating in various countries the relative intensity of management utilization as well as the social determinants of managerial activity, the advocates of this particular approach to comparative management attempt to isolate those management-related factors which enhance or inhibit a country's economic status. It is hoped that the results of this kind of an inquiry would allow an explanation and evaluation of the relative level of economic achievement of various countries or societies. In addition, it would provide a basis for the normative prescription of certain managerial behavior patterns if a high degree of industrialization and economic dynamism is to be accomplished.

---

[4] See Chris Argyris, *Integrating the Individual and the Organization* (New York: John Wiley and Sons, 1964).

[5] Frederick Harbison and Charles A. Myers, *Management in the Industrial World* (New York: McGraw-Hill, 1959), p. 17.

The first comprehensive socio-economic approach to comparative management was propagated by Frederick Harbison and Charles A. Myers in their book, *Management in the Industrial World*. The authors' basic assertion is that economic progress and industrialization—"an almost universal goal toward which all nations are marching"—depends on managers, i.e., "human agents who create and control the organization and institutions which modern industrialism requires. They are the ones who build and manage the enterprises which combine natural resource, technology, and human effort for productive purposes."[6] Harbison and Myers then propose to look at management from two points of view: first, an analysis of managerial activities or tasks, and second, an analysis of the managers themselves. With respect to the first perspective Harbison and Myers follow the traditional management literature emphasizing managerial functions such as the undertaking of risk and handling of uncertainty, planning, coordination, administration, supervision, and control. Their proposal for an analysis of the managers themselves has three perspectives: (a) management as an economic resource, (b) management as a system of authority relationships, and (c) management as a class or elite. The first perspective is on the one hand quantitatively oriented by merely recording the relative intensity of management utilization in a given country. On the other hand it is also qualitatively oriented by being concerned with the relationship of management to the productivity of labor and the inherent inefficiencies in organizations caused by dysfunctional managerial behavior such as personal jealousies, rivalries, prejudices, idiosyncracies, nepotism, etc. The second perspective focuses on managerial authority, i.e., the characteristics and peculiarities of the superior-subordinate relationship in a given society. The main questions which Harbison and Myers want to have answered in this context are concerned with how authority is acquired, exercised, and maintained. The third perspective emphasizes a structural analysis in terms of who gets into the management class, by what means, and what is management's relative prestige as well as power in a given society. This model has been used as a guide for describing and analyzing the management situation in a dozen different countries. The results of these studies confirm broadly Harbison and Myers' hypothesis that the relative level of economic activity and achievement is a function of socio-economic conditions which manifest themselves in the relative intensity of management utilization, the peculiarities of acquisition, exercise, and maintenance of managerial authority, and management's relative prestige and power in society.

This kind of socio-economic approach to comparative management has been adopted mainly among scholars theorizing about the conditions for economic development and industrialization, such as Professors David McClelland[7] and

---

[6] *Ibid.*, p. 3.
[7] David C. McClelland, *The Achieving Society* (Princeton, N. J.: D. Van Nostrand Company, 1961).

Everett Hagen.[8] The merit of this approach is that it can rely on a well developed analytical instrumentarium for the examination of those economic conditions and sociological norms which govern or strongly influence managerial behavior patterns. But the results of this approach are frequently ambiguous and do not necessarily lend themselves to the support of predictions or at least normative, prescriptive statements. For instance, the analyses of the management situation in Great Britain, France, and Germany in Harbison and Myers' book reveal substantial differences from a sociological perspective, but from the point of view of an economic preference function no clear conclusion can be drawn as to the impact of the noted differences. Another drawback of the socio-economic approach to comparative management is its macro-orientation, i.e., it does not pay equal attention to individual differences in managerial behavior or interfirm differences in a given society. The strongest criticism is, however, the rather limited focus of this approach: from the broad spectrum of environmental differences it concentrates mainly on those which are of particular interest to sociologists and cultural anthropologists. Particularly this latter shortcoming has led to the second major orientation of comparative management theory for which one might use the term ecological approach.

The Ecological Approach to Comparative Management

The traditional management literature is largely confined to the description, evaluation, and prescription of structural conditions and functional processes from the point of view of an effective utilization of the production factors which the organization employs. It is thus emphasizing the "internal environment" of a firm's operations and takes the external environment largely as given or at least not as being within the realm of business management theory. It seems logical to abandon this position and to focus on the interdependencies and causal relationships between a firm's internal operational conditions and processes and its external environment, i.e., to use an ecological approach.[9] This approach to comparative management attempts to isolate those external environmental variables to which similarities or differences in managerial effectiveness in different countries can be attributed. The business firm is seen as a part of an ecological system in which the external factors have a determining impact on managerial effectiveness which in turn determine firm efficiency and, in the end, aggregate economic efficiency. This emphasis on the interaction between a business organization and its environment makes it necessary to distinguish between various ecological components such as a

---

[8] Everett E. Hagen, *On the Theory of Social Change* (Homewood, Ill.: The Dorsey Press, 1962).

[9] The term ecology was introduced by E. Haeckel in 1867 meaning the influence of environmental conditions on the behavior and development of organisms—see R. C. Stauffer, "Heackel, Darwin and Ecology," *Quarterly Review of Biology*, XXXII (1952), 138–141.

country's sociological, political, and economic characteristics which are conceived as constraints on managerial effectiveness.

The two scholars who first developed and tested the ecological approach to comparative management are Professors Richard Farmer and Barry Richman.[10] Their major hypotheses are that (1) managerial effectiveness is a function of various external environmental constraints, (2) firm efficiency is a function of managerial effectiveness, and (3) aggregate economic efficiency is a function of the efficiency of the individual economic units. With respect to the environmental constraints Farmer and Richman distinguish between four major categories: (a) educational characteristics—referring to the nature and quality of the educational process and society's attitude toward education within a given country; (b) sociological-cultural characteristics—meaning the dominant human attitudes, values, and beliefs and the way these tend to influence economically oriented behavior and work performance; (c) a country's political system, ideology, and specific legal regulations; and (d) a complex set of economic phenomena characterizing a country's level of economic activity, the presence or absence of a supporting infrastructure, etc. Multinational firms are, according to Farmer and Richman, exposed to a fifth environmental constraint category, the "international constraints" which are again subdivided into sociological-cultural, legal-political, and economic factors.

Another major contribution to international and comparative management theory using an ecological approach was made by Professor Roy Blough. As rationale for this approach he declared that "talking with business and government officials in this country and abroad has persuaded me to believe, first that the problems in international business are different from those of domestic business primarily because of the special conditions or environmental factors under which international business operates and second, that some or all of these environmental factors are of substantial concern to those who are interested in the subject of international business, from whatever viewpoint."[11] Blough focuses on three sets of environmental factors and their influence on business decisions: governmental policies, cultural characteristics, and the stage of economic development. Throughout his analysis there is an emphasis on the necessity for a kind of passive, adaptive behavior on the part of the business organization to the dynamically changing environmental conditions.

Whereas Professor Blough considers governmental policies as the major environmental conditioning factor on management activities—giving only scant treatment to the impact of cultural and economic factors—Edward T. Hall, in an

---

[10] Richard N. Farmer and Barry M. Richman, "A Model for Research in Comparative Management," *California Management Review*, II, No. 2 (Winter 1964); *Comparative Management and Economic Progress* (Homewood, Ill.: Richard D. Irwin, 1965); *International Business: An Operational Theory* (Homewood, Ill.: Richard D. Irwin, 1966).

[11] Roy Blough, *International Business: Environment and Adaptation* (New York: McGraw-Hill, 1966), p. V.

admirable study entitled *The Silent Language*,[12] concentrates on cultural and sociological environmental conditions and their impact on international management. Apart from an interesting classification of cross-cultural differences, Hall does not project a comprehensive conceptual model for comparative management studies; but his analysis is nevertheless a good example for the ecological approach to comparative management, i.e., an attempt to isolate major environmental conditions and to examine their relative influence on managerial effectiveness and economic achievement.

A number of empirical studies provide evidence of the conceptual soundness of this approach,[13] but it also has some weaknesses which cannot be overlooked: (1) The emphasis on environmental conditions has the effect that the individual enterprise is regarded as being basically a passive creature of these external "constraints." As a result, there is generally an overemphasis on the necessity for environmental adaptation and not enough attention is paid to the fact that management may choose to act in defiance of certain external conditions. More often than not management uses the business organizations entrusted to them as an instrument for active influence on environmental conditions in order to make them more conducive to efficient business operations. In other words, an ecological approach generally neglects to investigate management's role as a change agent. This does not mean that scholars like Blough, Richman, and Farmer are not aware of the active influence of management on environmental constraints, but they simply tend to discount the potentiality of management's nonconformist role, at least in the short run. (2) Another shortcoming of the ecological approach to comparative management theory, as it has been advocated thus far, is its inability to cope with the fact that practically all environmental conditions are interrelated, yet their impact on business operations is not cumulative and not uniform. Theoretically it is possible—and it makes an orderly, logical impression on the reader—to draw up a list of external environmental factors and separate them into black boxes with labels such as cultural-sociological constraints, etc. However, empirically it is almost impossible to appraise the precise impact of a given constraint category on internal management practices and management effectiveness. As a basis for empirical research, the ecological orientation of comparative management theory is thus operationally defective. It simply allows too much discretion in the evaluation of external environmental phenomena and their influence on management practices.

---

[12] Edward T. Hall, *The Silent Language* (New York: Doubleday, 1959), and "The Silent Language in Overseas Business," *Harvard Business Review* (May–June 1960), pp. 87–96.

[13] See R. F. Gonzales and C. McMillan, Jr., "The Universality of American Management Philosophy," *Academy of Management Journal*, IV, No. 1 (April 1961), 33–41; W. Oberg, "Cross Cultural Perspectives on Management Principles," *Academy of Management Journal*, 1, No. 2 (June 1963), 129–43; E. C. McCann, "An Aspect of Management Philosophy in the United States and Latin America," *Journal of the Academy of Management*, III (June 1964), 149–152.

The Behavioral Approach to
Comparative Management Theory

In the field of business administration and management one finds presently a proliferation of publications which claim adherence to a behavioral approach, and it is thus not surprising that in the comparative management field too a behavioral orientation is being advocated. In general, using a behavioral approach means first the formulation of concepts and explanations about human behavior in dynamic systems of interdependency, and second, the use of scientific methods for the elucidation of information and data analysis pertaining to causal relationships of interpersonal phenomena. Scholars using a behavioral approach to comparative management theory focus on typical behavior patterns of managers in different cultures, their motivation for particular managerial attitudes, and managers' relationships with individuals or groups of individuals with whom they have to interact in the pursuit of organizational objectives.

One behavior-oriented conceptual framework as a basis research in comparative management has been advocated by Anant R. Negandhi and Bernard D. Estafen.[14] Their model consists of three major building blocks: (a) the managerial functions, i.e., planning, organizing, staffing, controlling, and direction and leadership; (b) managerial effectiveness, expressed by such indicators as profitability, change in profits and sales, employee morale, and the public image of the company; (c) management philosophy, which Negandhi and Estafen define "as the expressed and implied attitude or relationships of a firm with some of its external and internal agents such as consumers . . . , company's involvement with the community . . . , company's relationship with local, state and federal governments, company's attitude and relationship with unions and union leaders, company's relationship with employees, company's relationship with suppliers and distributors."[15]

The basic idea expressed in this model is that managerial effectiveness is a function of the managerial practices which, in turn, are a function of management's behavioral characteristics which manifest themselves in management philosophies and policies. This theoretical concept can easily be criticized as being not comprehensive enough, as being arbitrary in the selection of the various factors it includes in the model, and also as being superficial in the sense that the focus is simply on overt managerial behavior as it manifests itself in a few seemingly randomly selected relationships with internal and external action groups. The Negandhi-Estafen model also can be criticized for not expressing any concern about the *causes* of a given behavior. However, in a complex field such as comparative management, the indicated shortcomings of Negandhi-Estafen's behavioral

---

[14] Anant R. Negandhi and Bernard D. Estafen, "A Research Model to Determine the Applicability of American Management Know-How in Differing Cultures and/or Environments," *Academy of Management Journal*, VIII, No. 4 (Dec. 1965), 319–323.

[15] *Ibid.*, p. 323.

approach also give rise to some advantages: (a) the concentration on only a few largely controllable variables facilitates this model's use for empirical investigation,[16] and (b) the concentration on management activities and managerial behavior within individual firms, i.e., on strictly micro-economic aspects in contrast to the other, strongly macro-oriented approaches.

A noteworthy comparative study on managerial behavior, attitudes, and satisfactions has been completed by Professors Mason Haire, Edwin Ghiselli, and Lyman Porter.[17] Their research findings were derived from questionnaire replies by over 3600 managers in 14 countries. The main conclusion of the study is that there is a high degree of similarity in managerial behavior in the various countries, but that there also exist substantial national and cultural differences which account for about 25 percent of the variations in managerial attitudes which the research revealed. This particular study shows very clearly the difficulties associated with large-scale comparative surveys: in order to keep the research cost in bounds the researchers used only questionnaires. Since the questionnaires were—for a vast subject such as managerial behavior—rather short and simplistic, there is a lack of specific information on the motivations for managerial behavior and attitudes in the various countries. In addition, the reliability of a good part of the "factual" answers, for instance about the authority connected with a given managerial position, is open to question.

Another interesting and promising behavioral approach to comparative management is presently being tested under the guidance of Professor Bernard M. Bass who developed a set of ten case exercises on management and organizational psychology.[18] Each of these exercises is centered on a specific managerial problem or behavioral issue such as supervision, organization planning, communication, industrial bargaining, managers' personal life goals, or on the job of a manager as a whole rather than on specific instances. All exercises require either personal or group decisions, and Professor Bass' empirical, cross-cultural research focuses on the decision-making process and the behavioral peculiarities which it reveals. Presently a European as well as a Latin American Research Group on Management sponsor the use of Professor Bass' simulation exercises within the framework of various executive development programs. Trained observers register how executives tackle

---

[16] That this model can lead to meaningful empirical results has been demonstrated by Bernard Estafen in his dissertation, "An Empirical Experiment in Comparative Management—A Study of the Transferability of American Management Policies and Practices into Firms Operating in Chile" (Graduate School of Business Administration, University of California, Los Angeles, 1967).

[17] Mason Haire, Edwin E. Ghiselli, and Lyman W. Porter, *Managerial Thinking: An International Study* (New York: John Wiley and Sons, 1966). See also Haire, Ghiselli, and Porter, "Cultural Patterns in the Role of the Manager," *Industrial Relations*, II (Feb. 1963), 95–117.

[18] Bernard M. Bass, *Program of Exercises for Management and Organizational Psychology* (Pittsburgh, Pa.: Management Development Associates, 1967).

these exercises, what decisions they reach, how they modify their decisions. In this way, an attempt is made to get large-scale, empirically verified, objective and comparable data on managerial behavior in different cultures. This research project should also lead to some specific information about the influence of different behavior patterns on the achievement of business objectives.

Although no empirical results of this research effort have been published yet, this behaviorally-oriented approach as advocated by Professor Bernard Bass and his collaborators is certainly—from a methodological point of view—a very original and promising one. It can be expected that the large-scale observation of how executives of different countries, with different traditions and value systems, tackle and solve universal managerial problems will lead to new, interesting knowledge in the field of comparative management.

Another noteworthy conceptual framework with a behavioral orientation to comparative management is a model proposed by Professor Howard Perlmutter[19] and further developed by Professor Hans Thorelli.[20] Both focus on distinct management philosophies which can be adopted by multinational firms:

Management Philosophy		Dominant Behavioral Characteristic
Ethnocentric	→	regulatory, attitude of superiority
Polycentric	→	permissive
Geocentric	→	cooperative

With respect to a multinational firm an ethnocentric management philosophy signifies that corporate management attempts to implement the same values, policies, sentiments, etc., as adopted by the parent company—regardless of environmental differences. As a result, the various foreign subsidiaries of a firm in which management follows an ethnocentric philosophy have little autonomy; their operations are regulated according to the same guidelines that apply to the parent company. A polycentric management philosophy reflects the corporate executives' awareness of environmental differences and their decision that every foreign operation should be as local in identity as possible. The individual units thus operate in accordance with local norms and environmental conditions. The geocentric management philosophy is truly cosmopolitan in spirit; it leads the company to recognize environmental differences but prescribes an interrelationship with the external conditions on a purely functional basis without any preconceived notion of omniscience at the home office or the foreign subsidiary. The interaction behavior among the various units of such a multinational firm can thus be described as cooperative.

---

[19] Howard V. Perlmutter, "L'enterprise international—Trois conceptions," *Revue Economique et Sociale*, XXIII, No. 2 (May 1965), 151–165.

[20] Hans B. Thorelli, "The Multi-National Corporation as a Change Agent," *The Southern Journal of Business* (July 1966).

Professor Perlmutter and Professor Thorelli proposed this model to find out the causes for the emergence of any one of these three forms of management philosophies and their influence on the managerial effectiveness and organizational efficiency of multinational firms. Both scholars hypothesized that the ethnocentric, as well as polycentric management philosophy, gives rise to numerous conflict situations which will be detrimental to managerial effectiveness, whereas a geocentric philosophy will lead to more desirable results.

The description of the various models advocating an essentially behavioral approach to comparative management shows the breadth and diversity of this particular orientation. Its positive aspect is the direct and explicit focus on managerial behavior and attitudes in different cultural settings. Another advantage is that we have at our disposal a well developed methodology for empirical investigation and a large body of knowledge from the behavioral school of management which gives the behavioral approach to comparative management a head start. However, one must also recognize some dangers: first, a possible overemphasis of socio-psychological relationships, and second, the generation of a large amount of information on uniformities or differences in managerial behavior in various countries may not add up to a consistent, comprehensive body of knowledge of its own called "comparative management."

The Eclectic-Empirical Approach to Comparative Management

Up to date, the largest number of contributions to comparative management can be characterized as eclectic-empirical. They are eclectic in a sense that no attempt is made to develop and test a comprehensive comparative management concept, but rather the authors of these studies adopt a framework which facilitates the practical investigation of certain facets of this broad field. Almost all contributions in this category are based on some form of empirical investigation and describe aspects of managerial attitudes and practices in various countries. Obviously, for a rather new and developing discipline such as comparative management, an eclectic-empirical approach has several merits, the major one being that it leads relatively quickly to a stock of empirically derived knowledge to which many researchers can contribute and from which generalizations can be drawn which in turn provide guidelines for further research.

Although there exist a good many competent contributions which fit into the eclectic-empirical category, only a few should be mentioned as prototypes of this particular approach: a very perceptive study of this sort is Professor David Granick's book *The European Executive*,[21] in which he investigates and analyzes management's role in Great Britain, France, Belgium, and Germany. He pays particular attention to structural characteristics of European industry and its

---

[21] David Granick, *The European Executive* (New York: Doubleday, 1962).

consequences for managerial attitudes, peculiarities of managerial practices, labor relations, etc. By doing so he establishes clearly the remarkable differences in the business patterns among these four countries as well as the managerial differences between Western Europe and the United States. An equally noteworthy study is Professor Granick's comparison of Soviet and American management,[22] a subject to which Professor Barry Richman added an impressive amount of empirical information.[23] A comparative management study with focus on the managerial attitudes toward economic development in the Latin American countries by Albert Lauterbach shows the possibilities and limitations of management as a factor in the economic development process.[24] A somewhat similar study on the managerial situation in African countries by Theodore Geiger and Winifred Armstrong reflects on the various external constraints on the rise of an effective, indigenous managerial elite.[25] Other studies which can be mentioned in this category, dealing only with the managerial situation in one particular country, are by Heinz Hartman, Yusif Sayigh, Cochran and Reina.[26] The importance of these studies is that they are generally in-depth analyses of the management situation in a particular country. The only difficulty is that most of these studies focus on different features, which impairs comparability.

The Roots of the Various Approaches

By outlining and analyzing the four major approaches or orientations to comparative management it becomes evident that there are distinct differences in focus and emphasis among them as well as substantial similarities. It is, however, surprising that there is not a higher degree of commonality among them. In tracing the causes for the differences, it becomes clear that they are partially the same as those to which Professor Harold Koontz attributed the "management theory jungle," namely strictly semantic differences in the definition of comparative management as a body of knowledge, the inability or the unwillingness of scholars to understand each other, and the misunderstandings which are a necessary

---

[22] David Granick, *The Red Executive* (New York: Doubleday, 1960).

[23] Barry M. Richman, *Soviet Management—With Significant American Comparisons* (Englewood Cliffs, N. J.: Prentice Hall, 1965); *Management Development and Education in the Soviet Union* (East Lansing, Mich.: Michigan University, Institute for International Business and Economic Development Studies, 1967).

[24] Albert Lauterbach, *Enterprise in Latin America—Business Attitudes in a Developing Economy* (Ithaca, N.Y.: Cornell University Press, 1966); and "Managerial Attitudes and Economic Development," *Kyklos,* XV, No. 2 (1962), 374–398.

[25] Theodore Geiger and Winifred Armstrong, *The Development of African Private Enterprise* (Washington, D. C.: National Planning Association, 1964).

[26] Heinz Hartman, *Authority and Organization in German Management* (Princeton, N. J.: Princeton University Press, 1959); Yusif Sayigh, *Entrepreneurs of Lebanon* (Cambridge, Mass.: Harvard University Press, 1962); Cochran and Reina, *Entrepreneurship in Argentine Culture* (University of Pennsylvania Press, 1962).

consequence of such a situation.[27] Obviously, semantic difficulties are bound to appear in a field where definitions of certain key terms such as management, management philosophy, authority relationships, and environmental constraints are not universally accepted. More serious than these definitional difficulties is, however, the lack of a clear boundary for what does and what does not belong to the comparative management field; particularly hazy is the delineation toward international business. This kind of "demarcation conflict" is aggravated by the fact that comparative management research is conducted by scholars rooted in a variety of disciplines such as sociology, political science, cultural anthropology, and business administration, each with its own terminology and specific interest.

Apart from these general causes there are additional, more specific reasons for what has been referred to as the comparative management theory jungle: (1) the undue focus on managerial activities and managerial behavior within the boundaries of a national state. Most researchers in comparative management embrace explicitly or implicitly as a first hypothesis the existence of a relative uniformity in the environmental conditions and a high degree of homogeneity in managerial behavior within any given country. That this is not the case in most countries can easily be demonstrated. Consequently, comparative management research which starts from the premise of national homogeneity can easily lead to distorted results, simply because it tends to neglect the frequently considerable interregional differences within a country. (2) The managerial class within any country also shows a great heterogeneity: professional managers, owner-managers, managers of large and small organizations, etc., show great differences in their educational background and do not uniformly embrace traditional norms, nor do they react in a similar fashion to environmental conditions. This diversity lends itself generally to an easy support of all kinds of hypotheses that a researcher may put forward. In short, it is not too difficult to find representative empirical evidence for any type of comparative management approach that has been advocated. For instance, a researcher of French management using a behavioral approach may observe that the large majority of firms are small, family owned, thoroughly organized by noncompetitive agreements. He may see in this situation a reflection of the value system which emphasizes security, protection, stability, insistence on independence, and the maintenance of a family status. He may note that these norms work against a dynamic business climate and against an aggressive market behavior, and he thus finds behavioral causes for managerial inefficiencies. On the other hand, a researcher with an ecological orientation may become quickly aware of the considerable impact of French national economic planning on the decisions of the large enterprises. He may observe the close cooperation between the bureaucrats of the planning authority and the technocrats of the large organizations, and he may find that the largely rational decisions of a relatively few technocrats (who behave

---

[27] Harold Koontz, "The Management Theory Jungle," pp. 182–185.

markedly different from the vast majority of the executives of the many small firms) have a much greater influence on the total level of economic activity than the peculiar attitudes of the mass of small family-firm managers. In this case, both the behavioral and the ecological approach would lead to findings which could not easily be reconciled with each other but would, nevertheless, be supported by representative empirical evidence. In brief, the comparative management theory jungle is, at least in part, a consequence of the heterogeneity of the research object which lends itself to the provision of empirical evidence for various types of conceptual orientations.

The Question of Disentanglement: A Framework for Synthesis

It can be argued that the different orientations in the comparative management field are a sign of a healthy development; different perspectives facilitate a thorough analysis of the relevant phenomena and the attempt to find empirical verification for a variety of approaches adds to the stock of knowledge from which from time to time higher levels of abstraction or a synthesis may be derived. Therefore, the only kind of disentanglement that seems desirable is a successive integration and synthesis of the empirically verified knowledge to which the diversity of approaches has led. In this spirit an attempt is made to propose a comparative management framework which incorporates and synthesizes the various orientations that have been advocated.

It is generally recognized that the logical structure of a theory and of rational inquiry consists of three steps: describing relevant phenomena and providing proper explanations, evaluating the observed phenomena by using certain standardized, objective measures, and formulating generalizations with predictive properties.

I. Comparative Management Elements: The Foci of Description and Explanation	Specific Elements of Investigation
1. Managers as Professionals	a. Number of managers in absolute and relative terms, their age distribution
	b. Analysis of managers' social origin, family background, types of schooling
	c. Analysis of managers by typical patterns of career such as required credentials, typical promotion procedure, personal qualities emphasized, earnings
	d. Managerial mobility (interfirm mobility)
	e. The status of management as a profession
	f. The scope of management, education, and development

2. Managerial Norms and Values

   a. Analysis of managers' personal values in terms of commitment to economic, political, religious, aesthetic, social, ethical norms

   b. Analysis of managers' life goals such as relative importance of prestige, power, security, recognition, independence, self-realization, service, leadership, pleasure

   c. Analysis of business objectives as determined by managers; i.e., relative dominance of such objectives as to make satisfactory profits, to grow, to meet and stay ahead of competitors, to promote good will, to provide service to society, to provide for employee welfare

3. Managerial Actions and Decisions

   a. Analysis of types of functions performed such as planning, organizing, directing, controlling, and the techniques or methods used in the discharge of these functional responsibilities

   b. Analysis of task priorities

   c. Analysis of instrumental activities, e.g., average time spent per day on correspondence, phoning, discussions, writing and reading reports, planning future activities

   d. Analysis of the decision-making process: who gets involved in the major strategic and administrative decisions, how these decisions are reached

4. Managerial Attitudes

   a. Analysis of the relative dominance of certain attitudes, e.g., toward delegation of authority, the use of staff, employment of financial and nonfinancial incentives

   b. Analysis of the predominant patterns of leadership

5. Managerial Conflicts and Conflict Resolution

   a. Analysis of the frequency of interpersonal conflicts in organizations

   b. Analysis of the major sources of conflicts

   c. Means of conflict resolution

6. The Structure of Managerial Relationships Within an Organization

   a. Analysis of the structures of relations of managers with superiors, peers, subordinates

   b. Analysis of the scope and limits of managerial authority, i.e., organizational constraints on the exercise of authority

   c. Analysis of the interplay between individual managers and the organization

7. The Interplay of Management as a System With the External Environment	a. Analysis of the external constraint categories such as geophysical, socio-cultural, legal-political, economic, technological characteristics of the environment
	b. Analysis of the structure of external relationships in particular with consumers, suppliers, competitors, labor unions, governmental authorities
	c. Analysis of the locus and distribution of power in the larger society and its impact on business operations

II. Comparative Management Elements: The Foci of Evaluation

Specific Elements of Investigation

1. The Rationality of Managerial Decisions	Taking into account the boundaries of rationality, the focus of the investigation ought to be:
	a. Analysis of the degree of consistency between stated preference functions (objectives) and related decisions
	b. Analysis of the awareness and application of "sound management practices." The yardstick in this respect has to be the present state of the art, i.e., empirically tested, fundamental management principles which have a clarifying and predictive value in the understanding and improvement of managerial, economically-oriented activity
2. Managerial Effectiveness	Since managerial decisions are subject to the boundaries of rationality, managerial effectiveness can only be determined in relative terms by comparing a firm's performance with that of another firm, the average norms of the industry, and/or the achievements of the entire economic system. For the determination of managerial effectiveness one has to eliminate as far as possible those factors which influence a firm's performance level but which are beyond management's control. Selected quantitative indicators for the determination of the relative degree of managerial effectiveness:
	a. Production criteria usable output per employee, defective output: total output unanticipated equipment breakdown, capacity utilization, inventory: total output goods in process: total output

	b. Marketing criteria rate of growth of sales and market share, Unfilled orders: total output or sales, goods returned: sales sales: inventory, marketing and distribution costs: sales
	c. Financial criteria gross and net profit: net worth return on investment current ratio, debt: equity ratios, cash velocity
	d. Personnel criteria absenteeism rates, personnel turnover rates, accident frequency rates and lost working time
3. Firm Efficiency	Firm efficiency is the relative degree of performance in comparison with another firm, industry norms, and/or the achievements of the entire economic system. Firm efficiency is a function of managerial effectiveness as well as external factors beyond direct managerial control. Major indicators of firm efficiency are:
	a. Organizational productivity (input/output relationships)
	b. Profitability
	c. Any enhancement of a firm's potential for survival and growth
4. Aggregate Economic Efficiency	Aggregate economic efficiency relates to the comparative degree of economic achievement of a country or region. Major indicators for aggregate efficiency are:
	a. Rate of growth of GNP
	b. Per capita income and its rate of growth
	c. Investment efficiency (average rate of growth of real GNP divided by the ratio gross domestic investment to GNP)
	d. Utilization rate of factors of production
	e. Total labor productivity

The model presented thus far indicates the major elements of analysis and evaluation; it is the platform on which a comparative management theory rests. To the extent that this model becomes substantiated with empirically verified information, it becomes possible to draw from it *generalizations with predictive properties*, for example the degree of improvement in managerial effectiveness in response to certain changes in the managerial value structure. However, as far as the predictive properties of empirically derived generalizations are concerned, it has to be borne in mind that they are subject to two major constraints: first, since these generalizations are derived from historical data, new emergent patterns of management behavior or new environmental conditions diminish their predictive value. Second, there is always the possibility of the occurrence of chance events which also can modify the course of development and thus make predictions hazardous. The reason for pointing this out is to indicate that comparative management theory will always be only of a tentative nature, in need of continuous empirical verification and in need of changes as new evidence becomes available. Seen in this light, the proliferation of "the comparative management theory jungle" is a sign of a healthy development of this discipline.

Conclusion

The purpose of this paper was to review, analyze, evaluate, and classify the various conceptual, theoretical frameworks which have been advocated and used in the past decade to advance a theory of comparative management. This was intended as a stock-taking and as a first step toward an integration of the knowledge about comparative management as it evolved in the past few years. This effort resulted in the development of a more comprehensive comparative management model which should aid in a systematic classification of existing empirical findings to which the various comparative management approaches have led thus far. The advantage of this synthesis or unification is that it helps promote the cumulative growth of knowledge and also indicates specific areas where a greater research effort is necessary. The model should also help to minimize the existing biases of the various comparative management orientations, and it should provide a guide for further research.

Management Intensity and Transportation Development

Richard N. Farmer

Transportation development occupies a strategic place in the plans of most of the less developed countries of the world. One sure indication of the underdevelopment is the inadequacy of the transport system. The pattern of transport deficiencies inhibiting development is common in many countries. Industrial and agricultural development is hampered by lack of transport to bring raw materials to likely plant sites; by lack of proper distribution facilities; by inadequate and overloaded ports; and other factors. This problem is recognized in most countries. From one- to two-thirds of most development planning budgets are devoted to transportation facilities,[1] including such capital intensive projects as highway nets, international airports, railroad systems, and ports. The level of planning in transportation development has steadily improved as countries gain increasing insight into their needs.

Missing Ingredient

Development plans typically lay out long run, over-all patterns for future development. Decisions are made as to modes to be utilized, and the details of planning are turned over to engineers for execution. Such decisions often reflect experience in the more developed countries, where all modes of transport have found some use. There appears to be a tendency to see West Germany, England, or the United States as a model of what a newly developing country might be, with their railroads, canals, highways, pipelines, and air systems all engaged in carrying out transportation functions.

The implicit assumption in most plans is that when the new facilities, designed by Western or Soviet engineers, are completed, they will function with the same degree of reliability and economic efficiency as those in the more developed countries. The question of the internal management of the facilities seldom arises.[2]

Reprinted by permission of the publisher from *Academy of Management Journal*, Vol. 8, No. 2 (June 1965), pp. 90–106.

[1] Wilfred Owen, "Transportation and Technology," *American Economic Review*, LII, No. 2 (May 1962), pp. 406–407.

[2] For two of many examples, see H. David Davis (ed.), *The Economic Development of Venezuela* (Baltimore, Md.: The Johns Hopkins Press, 1961), pp. 244–280; H. David Davis (ed.), *The Economic Development of Spain* (Baltimore, Md.: The Johns Hopkins Press, 1963), pp. 169–254.

But visitors to less developed countries are aware that the efficiency of transportation facilities in such areas rarely approaches that in more developed nations. Even within a country such as the United States, the difference in managerial efficiency between different firms tends to be quite noticeable. There is rarely some uniformly high level of managerial efficiency that leads to transportation assets being used at optimum levels. Moreover, it is clear that some types of transportation are harder to manage efficiently than others. If, for example, an airline managed its maintenance as badly as some trucking companies, the air carrier would cease to exist.

It is possible that transportation planners in the newer countries fail to consider the managerial implications of transportation modes. It is easy to conclude that if a given number of trucks yield x ton kilometers, twice as many will yield 2x ton kilometers. What may be overlooked is that more effective management of the existing capital and firms may yield more output at less cost.

The purpose of this paper is to explore some of the advantages which might be achieved through more careful consideration of internal management of transport as well as external planning and control.

Management Intensity

Any country has two major aspects of management to consider in transportation.

The *first* concerns the internal management of transportation firms. Like other companies, transportation firms must be managed properly. Their managements must plan, staff, direct, and control their companies in order to realize corporate goals. It is common to find many transportation firms in any economy, ranging in size from large railroads with tens or hundreds of millions of dollars in capital to one-truck firms with a few thousand dollars invested. Firms may be publicly or privately owned, and railroads, airlines, airports, and ports are often in the public sector. Public ownership, however, does not mean that the firms do not need good internal management. While the objectives and goals of publicly owned firms may differ from private operations, the need to perform necessary business and managerial function is still present.

The *second* concerns the planning of promotional and control activities of the entire system. Governments typically promote transportation in many ways, including direct investment in operating companies, the construction of highways, and building of airports. Governments usually are responsible for the long-run planning aspects of all modes of transportation, which are to be integrated into other development plans.

It is common for governments to control operating transportation firms by means of price, entry, service and safety regulations designed to compel transportation companies to conform to social, economic, and political desiderata.[3] While such restrictions may vary considerably from country to country, virtually all governments maintain some regulatory controls over their transportation companies.

In both of these cases, the managerial and administrative requirements can vary strikingly depending upon the type of companies and system used. The managerial requirements for a large railroad are also large, involving the proper planning and organization of a firm employing thousands of employees, utilizing complex communications systems, and having demanding technical requirements for maintenance and operation of equipment. A complex management hierarchy may evolve to handle properly the difficult problems that will arise in day-to-day operations. On the other hand, a one-truck firm, whose owner is also the driver, has a much simpler managerial task. Many such firms operate all over the world without any of the necessary tools of larger enterprises, such as long-run plans, accounts, demand analyses, or staffing problems. An inland water company, with a towboat and a few barges, would be in an intermediate position in terms of management intensity.

In a similar fashion, the government regulatory and promotional system can vary strikingly in intensity. Some countries have elaborate price-entry—safety-service control systems in trucking which apply to thousands of independent firms. Here the administrators must develop a large, efficient bureaucracy to control properly the complex controls applied to carriers. Literally billions of prices must be checked by competent men to determine their propriety, tens of thousands of trucks physically checked to find safety defects, and service complaints investigated by a competent staff. Proper administration of such controls involves careful and intense administrative organization.[4]

Other countries have minimal controls of this sort. Firms compete without regard for government rules regarding their prices or services. Here the necessary level of governmental administration is minimal, and the requirement for trained staff and competent technicians is small.[5] Both of these systems are feasible, in the sense that they both will permit production of ton and passenger miles, but the level of administrative intensity in the two cases is quite different.

---

[3] A detailed discussion of the evolution and application of government policy in the United States is found in Charles L. Deering and Wilfred Owen, *National Transportation Policy* (Washington, D. C.: The Brookings Institution, 1949).

[4] See Dudley F. Pegrum, *Transportation: Economics and Public Policy* (Homewood, Ill.: Richard D. Irwin, 1963), pp. 251–282; pp. 307–380 for a discussion of the type of detailed controls required in a complex transport situation.

[5] For one example of an uncontrolled environment, see Richard N. Farmer, "Inland Freight Transportation in Eastern Saudi Arabia," *The Journal of Industrial Economics,* X, No. 3 (July 1962), 174–187.

Good management requires investment in much the same manner as physical facilities, although this point is not given nearly as much attention as the problem of capital supply. Managers do not appear fully trained. A complex firm must recruit promising men, spend large sums on their development, and allow them to learn by making expensive mistakes. This process requires both time and money before the firm is managed well enough to operate in a satisfactory manner.

If the various transportation possibilities are considered in terms of managerial difficulty, it can be seen that a large hidden cost is present in every transportation situation. Given a level of managerial competence, railroad transport costs may appear lower than truck—but if railroads require considerably more investment in management than trucking firms, the wrong mode choice could easily be made. Unless some consideration is given to the necessary costs of developing adequate management, all costs are not included in the investment decision.

Scale Economies and Management Intensity

The minimal management requirement for a transport firm in various modes can be determined by considering the smallest economically efficient firm which is feasible, given technical requirements. Most transport plans are concerned with economic efficiency, and the smallest firm desired would be one large enough to yield lowest possible unit costs. This smallest firm in any mode would also be the

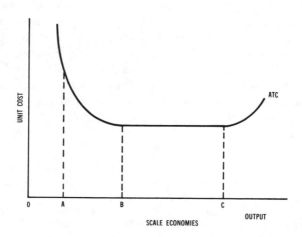

Figure 1.

one which presumably requires the least use of management in that mode. Larger firms might be possible, but they would require more investment in management than the smaller firms. A smaller firm than that which is economically efficient is also possible, but in this case, losses occur because the firm is not big enough.

A number of studies of scale economies in various transport modes have been made which suggest that in most cases, the problem appears as in Figure 1.[6] Very small firms have high unit costs (output OA). At output OB, the firm becomes, in the long run, as efficient as possible, given the technology. Very large firms may be more inefficient, suffering in effect from "gigantomania." The smallest feasible economic firm varies depending on the technology. Thus in motor transport, a one-truck operation appears to be large enough,[7] whereas in air transport, five or more expensive aircraft of the most efficient types are required before the firm becomes optimally efficient.[8] In this latter case, it may be true that a one-aircraft airline requires less management—but this case is economically irrelevant. The proper firm to consider for minimal levels of management is the one large enough to be economic.

The estimated minimal requirements for various types of transport modes are shown in Table 1. It is clear that output is only one variable affecting costs; many other factors including total backhaul possibilities, route intensities and technical design considerations would influence the potential minimum size of any carrier. Hence the figures given in Table 1 should be regarded as estimates rather than precise numbers. But it is clear that firm size can differ widely in transportation, even though the services offered—ton and passenger miles—are the same. It is also true that managerial requirements, in terms of both complexity and cost, of the various minimal firms are also quite different.

---

[6] The problems of scale economies in transport because of its critical importance in policymaking, has been extensively explored in most modes. For motor vehicles, see W. Adams and J. B. Hendy, *Trucking Mergers, Consolidations and Small Business: An Analysis of Interstate Commerce Commission Policy* (Washington, D. C.: U.S. Government Printing Office, 1957); for Rail, John R. Meyer, Merton J. Peck, John Stenason, and Charles Zwick, *The Economics of Competition in the Transportation Industries* (Cambridge: Harvard University Press, 1960), pp. 33–63; for Pipelines, Leslie Coohenbook, Jr., *Crude Oil Pipelines and Competition in the Oil Industry* (Cambridge: Harvard University Press, 1955), pp. 8–32; for Inland water, Meyer, *op. cit.*, pp. 120–126; for Air, Richard E. Caves, *Air Transport and its Regulations* (Cambridge: Harvard University Press, 1962), pp. 55–83; for Ocean Shipping, Walter Oi, "The Optimal Size of Liner Firms," in *The Economic Value of the Merchant Marine* (Evanston, Ill.: Transportation Center, 1961), pp. 278–311.

[7] In unregulated U.S. agricultural trucking, firms average only 1.2 straight trucks and 2.2 tractors per carrier. See Mildred R. DeWolfe, *For Hire Motor Carriers Hauling Exempt Agricultural Commodities: Nature and Extent of Operations*, Marketing Research Report No. 525 (Washington, D. C.: USDA, Marketing Economics Division, ERS) pp. 20–27.

[8] Cave *op. cit.*, p. 59.

Minimum Sized Efficient Transport Firms		
Mode	Output[a]	Net Initial Investment (U.S. Dollars–Millions)
Rail	500.0–1,000.0	$150.00
Motor	0.5–1.5	0.01
Inland Water	1.0–2.0	0.10
Air	100.0–200.0	35.00
Pipeline	10.0–20.0	5.00
Ocean	10.0–20.0	2.00
General Ports	3.0–5.0	25.00
Bulk Ports	5.0–7.0	25.00
Inland Water Ports	0.5–1.0	0.50
International Airports	1.0–2.0	10.00
Local Airports	0.3–1.0	0.50

[a]For carriers, millions of ton miles; for terminals, millions of tons. Passengers and passenger miles are converted to ton miles at the rate of 10 passenger miles equals one ton mile. For source of estimates, see footnote 6.

Table 1.

Evaluation of Management Intensity

The quality and ability of managers required would depend on numerous factors among the transport modes. The more important of these would be as follows:

(1) *Total investment requirements.* The larger the investment, the more complex the managerial problem. Big investments imply large facilities, extended physical plants, the need to operate at relatively high load factors to cover fixed costs, and so on.[9]

(2) *Communications problems.* A one-man trucking firm would have few problems in communicating orders, dealing with customers, keeping track of vital records, or dispatching equipment efficiently. However, a large railroad or pipeline with hundreds of miles of line, thousands of employees, numerous customers and shipments, and difficult problems of control would face a major task of communicating properly with the various persons responsible for effective operations. Workers must be instructed properly; accounting controls must be applied; bills of lading must be routed properly for shipments to be handled correctly; and equipment units must be dispatched safely and quickly. Such communications must be designed to give the relevant managers proper

---

[9] See Frederick Harbison, "Entrepreneurial Organization as a Factor in Economic Development," *Quarterly Journal of Economics,* LXX, No. 3 (Sept. 1956), p. 364, for further perceptive development of this point.

feedback on the nature of problems facing the firm at any moment. This calls for managerial organization of the highest order.

The communications problem is typically intercorrelated with the size of investment, since larger investments typically call for more complex feedback control loops, more extensive documentation of more numerous customer orders, and so on.

(3) Relative technical requirements. The more complex the technology, the greater the need for more effective management to keep the firm in efficient working order. An inland water operator with a simple tugboat and a few barges has a fraction of the managerial problems in this area compared to an airline having very complex jet aircraft and communications systems to operate properly. The level of workers' competence in the airline case must be superior to the water case, resulting in more intensive management staffing. Errors tolerated in the barge situation because the cost is small are not tolerable in the air case. More complex technology typically calls for better management by superior managers—which often is reflected in the managerial pay rates in the various sectors.

(4) Number of workers per firm. A firm employing five men has relatively few staffing or direction problems. One employing 2,000 men operates at a much higher level of complexity. A bureaucracy must be established by management to handle the numerous personnel, payroll, grievance, seniority, and recruitment problems that are certain to arise. Labor bargaining becomes more complex and institutionalized. This problem is interrelated with investment requirements and communications problems as well, since the problems of dealing with large numbers of men often become quite complex in the communications sense.

Labor force quality requirements also tend to rise as the total investment increases.

(5) Maintenance requirements. Maintenance practices tolerable for a trucking line or a small inland water carrier are intolerable for an airline. Safety problems are important here, in the sense that in some technologies, the cost of being unsafe is so high as to preclude such practices. The airline and airport cases are examples of this extreme necessity for safe operating procedures. Yet, typically most complex technologies require similar high levels of maintenance. A pipeline does not present as much a safety as an operating problem—one truck down for maintenance does not close a highway operation, but one leak in a pipeline may cause the entire plant to shut down.

Maintenance management thus has varying degrees of intensity, and management of this function also varies depending on the technology. The cost of this management activity ranges from very little to enormous sums, as in the air case.

(6) General management requirements. In addition to the specific factors noted above, other aspects of management are required in varying intensities. Some

technologies are in a monopoly position (as in the single deepwater port for the country, or the only airport or domestic airline), and hence may require very little marketing effort. Management of the marketing function here requires little more than opening an office to receive customers. Other firms operate in quite competitive environments, as in the case of an international airline competing with airlines of other countries, or a railroad subject to intensive motor truck competition. In these cases, considerable managerial effort must be devoted to marketing. Some firms have very little financial difficulties in arranging for new capital, while others must devote intensive planning efforts to capital outlay proposals. This final factor is a catch-all designed to evaluate subjectively the relative level of managerial difficulty, and hence cost, between various types of transportation firms.

Application of Postulated Scalings

These managerial intensity factors can be evaluated to determine which types of technology are likely to require the most investment in good management. Table 1 attempts to do this by assigning scales of 0 to 10 for each managerial factor mentioned. The more complex and costly the management of each factor, the higher the score.

The evaluations presented are *subjective judgments* based on the author's observations of various U.S. and foreign firms. However, they do tentatively rate managerial requirements of transport firms in various modes. Inland water operations and motor trucking are the least management intensive. This follows from the types of minimally sized efficient firms which can be organized in these industries. Such firms have few employees; they do not need complex, expensive equipment in large quantities; communications difficulties are minimized; and maintenance requirements are relatively small. Railroads and airlines, on the other hand, require large amounts of capital, manpower, maintenance efficiency, and communications organization, and hence are quite difficult to manage properly.

In less developed countries, where managerial talent is always in very short supply, it is common to find the relative efficiencies of the various existing transport modes reflect quite closely this managerial rating scale, with the partial exception of the air sector. The more easily managed modes and terminals seldom present planners with significant problems of expansion or proper services to clients—more commonly, the issue is how to repress this type of competition so that the state railway can survive. Rarely is it necessary for governments to concern themselves about the proper types of truck or inland water terminals, but major ports and airports require constant attention.

The air case is unique in that any firm must be technically efficient to survive. Failure to operate properly means rapid disappearance of aircraft and crews, with the resulting destruction of the firms. However, it is common for national airlines in less developed countries to operate at substantial losses, reflecting in part the less developed level of commercial management, as compared with technical management. Less developed countries, seeing clearly the need for efficiency in this mode, are also more willing to enter technical management contracts with airlines from more developed countries.

Ocean carriers carrying flags of less developed countries are also rare, except when heavy subsidies are paid to cover expenses.[10] This again reflects the relatively complex management required in such cases. Pipelines typically are owned and managed by oil companies in less developed countries, utilizing non-indigenous personnel from more advanced areas.[11]

A further complexity in countries outside the U.S. is that often the firm is publicly owned. These firms do not need less management, but rather more of higher quality. A manager of a private firm can single-mindedly pursue the goal of profit maximization, and his daily activities may reflect the evaluation of each activity on his income statement. A public manager has much more tenuous, and often mutually contradictory goals, and it is much more difficult to integrate routine activities into the vague framework of his instructions. Moreover, a public company often is organized as a government department, rather than an operating enterprise, and employees are more difficult to motivate properly than in the more simple private cases. A publicly owned firm *can* be managed efficiently—but it is quite difficult.[12]

The results of failure to consider managerial intensities in transportation can be seen in almost any country, developed or not. The most vivid illustrations come from the less developed countries. The state owned railway may operate ineptly, often at enormous losses.[13] Ports may handle a fraction of the cargo they might if they were managed effectively. The few ships owned by nationals or the state are typically old, inefficient, and quite marginal in ocean trades. The critical safety functions of airports and airlines are normally done rather well, but other portions of the operation suggest poor management, as the firms lose money, fail to handle their customers properly, and generally show signs of managerial incompetence.

The modes requiring less managerial intensity or skill expand steadily, without serious difficulty. Management of the simpler firms, not needing to pay as much

---

[10] The only large fleets registered in less developed countries are in Liberia (10.6 million gross tons) and Panama (3.8 million gross tons). The large majority of these vessels are owned and operated by foreigners under these flags of convenience. No other less developed countries are in the 15 largest ship-owning countries, whose vessels form 80.5 percent of the total world's fleet. See *A Statistical Analysis of the World's Merchant Fleets* (Washington, D. C.: U.S. Department of Commerce, Maritime Commission, 1962), pp. 137–138.

[11] In the less developed petroleum-producing countries of the Middle East, all major pipelines are owned and operated by foreign concessionary oil companies. See *Middle East Oil Development* (New York: Arabian-American Oil Company, 1956), pp. 17–38.

[12] Some of the more complex issues involved here are discussed in R. Kelf-Cohen, *Nationalization in Britain* (New York: St. Martin's Press, 1959); and V. V. Ramanadham, *Problems of Public Enterprise* (Chicago: Quadrangel Books, 1959).

[13] See J. R. Sites, *Quest for Crisis* (New York: Simmonds-Boardman, 1963), for examples in various countries.

attention to critical maintenance, technical, or personnel problems, prove adept at finding and selling customers. While it may be true that a well run railroad is more efficient than the hordes of motor carrier operators, the usual empirical result is that the motor vehicle operators are more efficient. It is much easier and quicker to develop an efficient small trucking company than a large, complex railroad. If managerial costs are considered, the trucks are often cheaper.

Governmental Administrative Intensity

In addition to considering managerial problems of transport firms, governments must also ponder the role of government as planner, regulator, and welfare creator in the transport field. Historically and traditionally, governments of every description have promoted and regulated transportation to achieve social goals not desired by operating managements.

Government in this case has two basic types of problems. *First*, it must take some role in the planning and construction of routes and terminals for the various modes, including decisions on location of such facilities; and *second*, it may choose to regulate operating companies in order to achieve social goals. The government must typically maintain at least some facilities which are in common use, such as airways and roads.

These activities require organization of government departments to perform the assigned functions. In many cases, the operating management of a state owned facility may be the agency responsible for social goals. It is common to find that the operating managements of airports, railroads, and ports are responsible for planning and maintenance of the terminals and the rights of way they use. This follows from the exclusive use of the facility by the firm, or by companies controlled by the firm (in the case of ports and airports). Roads, airways, and inland waterways are utilized by a variety of firms and persons, including many not in commercial service, and it is usually convenient for a separate government department to handle planning, construction, and maintenance on these routes.

In addition to these technical considerations, many governments also control economic factors in the various modes. The most common economic controls are those over prices, entry of new firms, services offered, and safety. Safety controls are in part technical, although they do have some economic impact on the carrier being controlled.

As with technical controls, it is common to find minimal interference by outside government departments in economic functions of state owned enterprises. The presumed non-profitability goals of such a carrier, plus its assumed social orientation, may lead to the assumption that such controls are unnecessary. Economic controls are applied more to private than to public carriers.

Government implementation of a planning and control system involves considerable administrative cost and, as with internal firm management, this cost will vary sharply depending on the intensity and complexity of the control system being implemented. Price controls may appear proper, but the administrative task of evaluating in detail the billions of transport prices set by carriers may require more high skill administrative and technical talent than most countries have. A safety law governing the operation of motor vehicles may appear to be necessary, but the task of physically examining all of the motor vehicles in the country, to say nothing of enforcing correction of defects found may absorb more mechanics and technicians than are immediately available. The task of organizing a proper police system to enforce entry restrictions in motor carriage can tax any country's organizational and administrative resources. Far too often such laws are passed and remain as dead letters because the necessary manpower and administrative skill do not exist to enforce them.[14] Even in the U.S. such problems present serious difficulties for government officials.[15]

It is quite common for a country to have rather elaborate price-entry-service controls in the motor trucking and other private transport sectors. Countries tend to copy each other, and if England or the U.S. has such controls, other countries follow their example. In some cases, an ex-colonial country will follow the example of the colonial power without much analysis of why such a control system is desirable.

The usual result of such a control system, if effectively employed, is to raise transport prices and restrict transport capacity. One might question whether or not such a system is valid in a country trying to expand real income and outputs. As might be expected, the part of the law which gets the most attention is the portion which restricts competition and keeps prices up.[16] Truck and bus owners are quick to realize the value of a strong political lobby in this situation. Portions of such a system designed to protect the consumers more often than not are ignored and not enforced, given the enormous administrative difficulty of properly operating this type of control system.

Table 2 suggests the level of administrative intensity required in government to plan and control the transport system. In this case, two scores are recorded—the first suggests the investment in good administration necessary to make the system function properly given a reasonably effective price—safety-entry-service control system in the various modes; the second rates the needed administration in a situation where such controls are minimal to public welfare.

In the complete control case, there is roughly an inverse rank order correlation between governmental administrative intensity and firm intensity. The government,

---

[14] For examples see Richard N. Farmer, "Inland Transportation Entry and Rate Controls in the Arab Middle East," *Land Economics,* XXXVI No. 1 (Feb. 1960), 38–40.

[15] See Everett Hutchinson's Testimony in *Decline of Regulated Common Carriage: Hearings before the Surface Transportation Subcommittee of the Committee on Commerce, U.S. Senate, 87 and Congress, 1st Session* (Washington, D. C.: U.S. Government Printing Office, 1962), pp. 250–252.

[16] Richard N. Farmer, "Motor Vehicle Transport Pricing in Lebanon," *The Journal of Industrial Economics,* VII, No. 3, (July 1959), 199–205.

Governmental Administrative Intensity

Mode	RM	RP	P	S	SERVICE	E	MAX AI TOTALS	MIN AI TOTALS
RR[a]		1	8	3	2		14	
		1	1	1				3
MV	5	5	10	8	8	9	45	
	5	5		5				15
IW	5	1	10	8	8	9	41	
	1	1		5				7
AIR[a]	5	3	5	10	5		28	
	5	1		10				16
PL		1	1	1	1	1	5	
		1						1
OCEAN	1		4	4	1	2	12	
	1		1	2	1			4
GP[a]		4	3	2	3		12	
		2	1	1				4
BP		1	1	1	1	1	5	
		1						1
IWP[a]		3	1	1	1	1	7	
		1						1
A-INT[a]		3	3	9	1	1	17	
		2	1	7	1	1	12	
A-L[a]		2	1	7	1	1	12	
		1		4				5

[a]Public Ownership Assumed;
Mode Code: See Table 1;
RM: Route/Terminal Maintenance and Repair;
RP: Route/Terminal Planning and Development;
P: Price Controls on Operating Carriers;
S: Safety Controls;
SERVICE: Service Controls;
E: Firm Entry Controls—Routes, Cargoes, or Equipment Quantity;
AI: Administration Intensity Index.

Table 2.

if it wishes to control the situation completely, must develop an elaborate administration to handle the problem of enforcement for hundreds or thousands of independent entrepreneurs. But if minimal controls are acceptable, the rank order changes significantly.

Tables 3 and 4 show these rank orders. The simplest feasible economic system, in managerial-administrative terms, is a motor vehicle system, with an air system being the most complex.

While the subjective ratings of managerial and administrative intensity may contain significant error, it is not likely that the rankings would change much even after intensive examination. It is possible that some simple international air

Rank Orders of Firm Managerial and Governmental Administrative Intensities in Transport

Mode	Managerial Intensity	Administrative Intensity	
		Maximum	Minimum
RRs	50	14	3
AIR	49	28	16
A-INT	42	17	8
GP	40	12	4
PL	36	5	1
OCEAN	34	12	4
A-L	26	12	5
BP	24	5	1
IWP	16	7	1
MV	8	45	15
IW	6	41	7

Table 3.

Minimum Feasible Managerial-Administrative System Rank Order

Firm		Systems	
IW	13	MV	23
IWP	17	IW	30
MV	23	PL	42
BP	25	RR	53
AC	31	OCEAN	84
OCEAN	38	AIR	115
PL	42		
GP	44		
A-INT	50		
RR	53		
AIR	65		

Table 4.

operation might be designed which would be quite different (and simpler) than the usual pattern, or that a small port in a small country handling significantly less complex general cargo than the average could show simpler results, but the ratings are intended to indicate more lines of analysis than precise evaluations. If a country wants to develop a rail system, it is clear that this will require considerable managerial development as well—the precise amount depending on the size of the system, the way in which it is designed, the type of traffic it handles, the degree of competition it faces, the firm's relationships with its government, and so on. However, regardless of the precise managerial intensity needed, it will be quite high, since railroads of any sort tend to be managerially intensive. Failure to recognize this point can lead to inadequate preparation for management, inefficient operations, and considerable deviation from hoped for performance.

Common Errors in Transportation Planning

Failure to explore the managerial problems inherent in various transportation developments has often led countries to make costly errors. Some of the more common ones are summarized as follows:

(1) It is implicitly assumed that various existing and planned transportation enterprises will be well managed. Capable men will appear to operate the companies effectively. Good management does not just happen—it usually results from good staffing policies and much hard work. Failure to realize that firms can be very badly managed, which results in little or no evaluation of the management problem, leads to costly transportation mistakes.

(2) Varying levels of managerial and administrative intensities are often ignored. The added cost of management in complex systems is not considered, nor is the problem of obtaining enough good managers or bureaucrats to operate the system properly. One of the very real costs for a developing country may not be so much the additional money costs of utilizing better men in transport, but rather the syphoning off in this manner of the quite scarce administrative and executive talent, when it is badly needed elsewhere. If a good man performs well in an unnecessary position, the country is still worse off than it might have been.

(3) As demand for transportation increases, it is assumed that new investment is needed to provide increased capacity. This is clearly true in many cases, such as a situation where new jet aircraft require longer runways, or a region has no modern transport at all. But too often existing facilities are managed so badly that added output might be gained by managerial improvement alone. A port is congested, not because it is inadequate, but because the port director is unable to manage effectively the capacity he already has. A railroad may seem congested, or cars may be in short supply because of poor maintenance, inadequate shunting, or other internal factors. As bottlenecks and congestion occur in growing economies, it is wise to examine closely how existing facilities are managed before making major commitments for new capital equipment, which may also turn out to be quite inefficient because of poor management.

(4) A very common assumption is that the government administrators making structural transportation decisions will be wise, compassionate, and competent. While the majority of government officials may be strongly motivated to perform as best they can, there is no inherent reason why a senior civil servant can somehow make a meaningful decision about a complex engineering report on a new port; decide properly which transport rates should be higher and lower; or compute demand with accuracy far in advance.

Questions of this sort are extremely complex. Few men in the world are capable of being much better than half right most of the time.

(5) It is often assumed, without any evidence whatsoever, that economies of scale exist in all forms of transportation at all times. This belief is not unique to underdeveloped countries. Among others, the British Labor Party and the American Interstate Commerce Commission act as if they also believed it in the case of motor trucking.[17]

The result of this thinking is typically to form motor trucking and buses into very large firms. While some scale economies may be present, there are very real management costs associated with such operations, and again, few countries have enough competent managers to spare for such activities. While *theoretical* scale economies might exist, the one or two truck operators, if they are allowed to compete, typically have much lower *actual* costs—largely because they do not have the intricate management problems of the larger firms.

A further problem is that larger firms in small countries result in monopolies in transport, which also present complex managerial and administrative problems. The major advantage to a country of a competitive system is feedback—if the firm manager is making serious mistakes, his profit and loss calculations will indicate his errors quickly. One does not need cadres of clerks, bookkeepers, and managers to find this out. But a monopoly can go on making mistakes indefinitely—particularly if it also has access to the public purse to cover its losses.

Overlooked here is that the usual measures of scale economies used in economic and business analysis implicitly assume that management will be efficient. If it is not, there is no reason to suppose that the larger firm will be more efficient—and given the naturally more complicated personnel and direction problems inherent in a large firm, it may well have managerial problems that will outweigh any technical gains due to size.

Hypotheses

If the above indication that managerial problems are important is accepted, some implication can be derived for application to the design of transportation systems. An obvious first point is that all transport systems are not equal in terms of managerial costs. It cannot be assumed that any technical system will operate well, unless the country can also insure somehow that the proper types of management of transport firms and administration of the promotional-regulatory framework will be available.

Hypothesis 1. In any developing country, the transport system which is least management intensive will work the best.

"Best" here means closest to optimum economic potential, in terms of both

_____

[17] Pegrum, *op. cit.,* pp. 350–353.

services and cost. From Tables 2 and 3, it can be seen that the simplest system is one utilizing motor trucks and buses and inland water systems. In these cases, there is relatively little investment necessary in management, and firms can be small, local operations run by available entrepreneurs. The very small size of economic trucking and water firms means that in an open entry system, competition will tend to keep prices close to cost, even in small markets.[18] The visibility of equipment and the relative simplicity of firms suggests that in this case entrepreneurs can easily keep up with new developments and innovations, even though the entrepreneurs may possess quite limited education.[19]

It is clear that in some cases cost savings gained from more management intensive technology may be so large as to make it worthwhile. Thus if a country is opening up a large oil field, or developing an iron mining complex that will generate billions of ton miles of traffic per year, pipeline or rail systems may be the only economic modes to use. The problems of obtaining proper management of the transport systems should also be considered as a part of the cost of development.

Hypothesis 2. A simple transport system "spills over" more easily than a complex one, in terms of entrepreneurial and managerial education.

An efficient trucking line can be (and often has been) run by an intelligent illiterate, who is able to learn quite rapidly about the problems of management. The smallest feasible trucking firm is a one-truck, one-employee operation. Managerial problems in this case are relatively simple and easily understood by any perceptive individual. Total firm investment is small, allowing for many persons to enter the business.

In contrast, an airline or railroad is a complex, large organization requiring millions of dollars of capital and thousands of employees. The perceptive citizen who might have been an entrepreneur in trucking can only be a manual laborer in such an organization. Managements are necessarily recruited from the always short supply of highly-trained, well-educated persons available, and only a handful of these ever reach a major decision making position in such a firm. It is common for an enclave consisting of such a large firm to exist for decades in a less developed country without much impact on the local society—just as it is equally common for one truck operator to learn business techniques well enough in trucking to be able to branch out into other business operations.

If the managerial process is so complex that relatively few persons are able to have insights into the problem, the "spill-over" effect on the rest of the economy will be small.

If one of the purposes of development is to develop people as well as economies, such a simple transport system will help significantly in accomplishing this purpose. (The author knows of many entrepreneurs, now successful in the less

---

[18] E. K. Hawkins, *Road Transport in Nigeria* (London: Oxford University Press, 1958), pp. 59–79.

[19] *Ibid.*, pp. 40–50.

developed economies in many other fields, whose major business education started when they bought their first truck.) The high visibility of a motor operation, compared to most other fields, yields big educational dividends—as does the mobility given to the owners. A truck owner sees his country, the way in which it is organized, and new possibilities for expanding his firm in a manner rare in business.

Hypothesis 3. A simple governmental administrative system for transportation is best.

Governments everywhere, including those in the developed economies, are perennially short of high talent administrators. Any government in the modern world has endless critical problems demanding the talents of good men. To waste such scarce talent in trying to regulate a system which might work quite well without regulation seems absurd, yet in many places this occurs.

A major problem here is the history of regulation in the developed countries. It seemed reasonable to control monopolistic railroads before 1920, and many presently developed countries established complex administrative rules to do so. When motor trucks and the other modes developed, it also appeared easier to place them under control, rather than recognize that the competition between many firms might accomplish the regulatory job without controls. The easiest way to control motor trucking flows is to put paved roads in desired locations, not to spend endless man hours trying to force small trucking firms into some predetermined mold. Yet the less developed countries, taking their cues from the more advanced nations, have too often tried to operate their promotional-regulatory government control system in a manner analogous to France, the United Kingdom or the United States. The confusion in transport in these countries suggests that the less developed countries have very little to learn from the advanced countries in this area.

The proper question to ask in considering government promotion and controls in any economy is, "Will this system yield the necessary ton and passenger miles at minimum cost?" If a system having very few control features can accomplish this, it is the system to use—not the one maximizing government employment in the capital.

Hypothesis 4. Where complex transportation facilities presently exist, it is often possible to expand output significantly by improving management of existing firms, rather than making major new investments.

Far too often existing complex transportation firms operate quite inefficiently because management performs badly. Ports operate far below capacity; airlines have load factors well below what might be achieved; railroads find it impossible to raise output with given equipment; and so on. The difficulty here is often managerial ineptness. Instead of purchasing more aircraft at several million dollars apiece, it might be possible to increase utilization rates from, say, two to eight hours per day, thus raising potential output manyfold. But such increases depend on how well the managerial maintenance, scheduling, and other functions are performed. (The author has personally seen outputs of existing equipment in quite underdeveloped areas rise tenfold when proper improvements in management were made.)

Far too often the problem is not in the capital equipment, but in how it is used. Often small investments at the margin result in major gains in equipment productivity. What might be needed is not thousands of new freight cars on a railroad, but a small investment in computational, filing, and allied equipment to better track existing cars and improve their utilization. Or if a fifty-ton crane worth millions of dollars is over-utilized at a part, the required investment may not be another large and expensive crane, but rather a small one to handle little lifts now performed by the larger equipment. Failure to analyze this type of problem properly results in considerable waste and inefficiency in many situations. Before any major commitment is made, it is wise to analyze existing utilization rates and operational systems to determine if internal improvements might not be adequate.

Conclusions

Transportation is unusual in that it offers many feasible technical means of accomplishing the same job. If a country is interested in developing a steel mill, a glass plant, or a soft drink bottling industry, it may be true that no matter how the technical factors are considered, the management intensity of the industry will be relatively constant. One cannot escape the necessity for developing some given minimal intensity of managerial skill and competence.

In transportation, however, it is possible to vary managerial intensitites dramatically, depending on the technology selected. Since it is actually much easier to develop good management in simple situations than in complex ones, it seems reasonable to consider this factor in development planning. If a railroad yields potential ton mile costs of 2.5 cents, but such cost levels are only achievable after ten years of intensive managerial training and development, such managerial factors should be considered in transport planning. The option in such a case might be a trucking system that provides ton miles at 3.5 cents, but where this cost level can be achieved in one year. This latter technique looks more expensive but in the long run it may be much cheaper. When training implications and the avoidance of use of scarce high skill manpower is also considered, the trucking system may be far the cheaper. Though transportation development provided a case in point for this exercise, the management intensity question might well be compared in other settings with possible significant implications.

The Multinational Company: A New Force for World Economic Development

Lynn A. Townsend

I would like to begin by expressing my appreciation to the Society of Automotive Engineers for inviting me to participate in this highly impressive International Automotive Congress and Exposition. It is always a pleasure for any automobile man to meet with your organization, because in a very real sense the automobile industry owes its growth, its world leadership, and its integrity to the great achievements and to the high professional standards of the automotive engineer. I am especially pleased to be asked to meet with you at a time when you are devoting your annual meeting very largely to international considerations.

I am told that the SAE idea is catching on fast in all parts of the world—and I am happy to know that many engineers from other countries are attending this conference and are with us tonight. It is meaningful that John Dyment of Canada is your president—that Mexico is coming on strong and is petitioning for full-fledged membership status in the SAE—and that Japan now has one of the world's most active sister organizations to the SAE, one which actually calls itself a Society of Automotive Engineers in so many words.

Your international meeting comes at a time when the world economy—and the automotive component of that economy—face new problems and new potentials that are far bigger and more complex than those of five years ago, when you held your last international meeting. I would like to express a few thoughts here tonight about this new and changing and highly promising world. I would also like to suggest a few ways in which we in the automobile industry—those who are engineers and those of us who are not—can help to realize the potentials of the new world society that is now beginning to take shape.

Since your last international SAE meeting in 1960, the world has changed in some highly important ways. In 1960, for example, the Soviet Union was still exploiting to the full the propaganda value of its 1957 Sputnik. All over the world, the military and economic offensive directed from the Kremlin looked purposeful and strong. Even though we could see some signs of serious misunderstanding between Russia and China, the combination of the two great Communist powers still looked pretty forbidding.

Today it seems fairly clear that the Communist world is far from unified. It seems clear that the Russian space technology that put the Sputnik in orbit is by no

Reprinted by permission of the Chrysler Corporation.

means as superior to ours as we once thought. And we are seeing unmistakable signs that the Russians are beginning to experiment with some of the features of our capitalist free-market profit system. This is being done, apparently, to put some steam into an economic system that is literally failing to deliver the goods.

Economic Self-Sufficiency

Outside the Communist world some equally important changes have been taking place. Still with us, of course, is the almost universal drive for national economic self-sufficiency and political independence and power. The most recent count showed that there are now 142 sovereign nations on this planet—and this number may have changed since this morning. Of these 142 countries, two-thirds have fewer people than metropolitan New York. And each of them seems to aspire toward having its own army, air force, and nuclear capability—and of course its own automobile industry.

The universal hunger for national sovereignty and self-sufficiency is apparently one of the few constants in our changing world. There is very little likelihood that this nationalistic drive will slow down very much in our lifetimes. People everywhere are proud of their own flag and their own traditions—and very understandably so. They want nothing but the most and the best for their own countries. In my opinion, it is the better part of wisdom to recognize the force of nationalism realistically—and to find ways of adjusting to it and building on it.

In view of the strong and universal trend toward political nationalism in our time, it always comes as something of a surprise to realize that there is an equally strong trend toward regional or continental arrangements which have the tendency to break down artificial economic barriers between nations. The existence of this strong trend toward economic internationalism—providing as it does a counter-vailing force to the continued trend toward political nationalism—may be the most important and most meaningful and in some ways the most hopeful development we are witnessing on the world scene in this second half of the twentieth century.

U.S.-Canadian Trade

The most familiar illustration of the trend toward economic internationalism is, of course, the European Common Market. As we all know, the countries belonging to the Common Market recently took another long step toward the creation of an economic union rivalling that which we enjoy in the United States, when they agreed to establish uniform prices for grain by the middle of 1967. In the years immediately ahead, this agreement will be far from an unmixed blessing for us in the United States. It may present some serious problems for our own farmers and exporters of farm products. However, the agreement does make it possible for our representatives in the present round of trade negotiations to get down to serious bargaining with the Common Market as a whole about trade in farm products. And it also opens the door to concrete negotiations about both farm and industrial products. This could be extremely important for the automobile industry. It gives us some hope for believing in the ultimate creation of a truly international free trade in cars, trucks, components, materials, and services—including engineering services.

This hoped-for development is still a long, long way off. As a matter of fact no one as yet is even talking about it. But here on the North American continent we may be somewhat closer to the creation of a tariff-free common market for automotive products. All of us have known for many years about the economic inefficiency of preserving duplicate facilities in Canada for the production of lines of cars that differ only in the most superficial ways from their U.S. counterparts. And we have recognized that the resulting higher costs have placed a handicap upon Canada's export trade and upon Canada's international balance of payments.

The force of economic logic is beginning to work toward the correction of this situation. Washington and Ottawa are concerned—and we can hope that in the near future arrangements can be made to bring about a more nearly equitable position for Canada in the world market for motor vehicles.

In the years ahead we can expect Canada and the United States to divide the total automotive production of the two countries more nearly in proportion to their population than they do at the present time. Canada's population is now about 10 percent of the population of the United States—but the value of Canada's automotive production is about 5 percent of that in the United States. Through the greater efficiency achieved by specialization and increased volume—and through improved access to the markets of the world—there should be no doubt of Canada's ability over the long run to achieve relative parity with the United States in automobile production.

In this connection, I realize that some businessmen in this country are apprehensive about the breaking down of trade barriers and the creation of more logical combinations of advanced economies. This is understandable. But it is important to remember that this country and its businessmen have never failed to make gains when other countries have become more efficient and more prosperous. Our biggest trading partners are and always have been the countries with the most advanced economies. Every step forward for them is an opportunity for us.

Capitalism vs. Communism

It is important also to remember that with all the progress made in recent years by the economies of the free world and with all the weaknesses demonstrated by the communist economies, the economic system of the free world is still in open and visible competition with that of the communist world. And anything that strengthens the heart of the free world economy in the northern hemisphere, from Japan to Scandinavia—and in the southern hemisphere from Argentina to Australia—will make communism relatively weaker and lessen its appeal.

The struggle between capitalism and communism for the allegiance of men is more visible in some parts of the world than in others. It appears to me, on the basis of my own business experience in various parts of the world, that the country standing right in the middle of this battleground of ideologies is India. Here is the second most populous country in the world. Right across its northern border—hanging there like the sword of Damocles—is the biggest country of all, communist China and its 700 million people. Both countries are fighting a roughly similar struggle against starvation. India's traditions bind it to the West, and so far it has not been an easy victim of communist propaganda. But the Indian economy is only half free. On the one hand it is a planned state-controlled system. On the other it is a private-enterprise, free-market system. Steel, for instance, is in the public sector. Automobiles are in the private sector. The lines are not always sharply drawn.

Much of the Indian economy is aided by Soviet money and technical assistance. Much of it is aided by private and public funds from the United States and the World Bank. No country on earth is a more thoroughly mixed blend of private and state-directed undertakings. This is the true crossroads of East and West. When Kipling said never the twain shall meet, he hadn't seen modern India.

What happens in India is particularly crucial, because it is there that the world's two principal economic systems meet in such direct competition. All of us here tonight know that if we ourselves were Indians, we would be comparing the performance of the free and the controlled systems—inside as well as outside of India. We would pay particular attention to the economic successes or failures of our giant communistic neighbor to the north. And our allegiance would probably go to the system that gave evidence of producing the best results in terms of jobs and food and housing and all the other elements of a rising standard of living.

Private Investment for Growth

The loyalties of hard pressed and hungry populations are pragmatic. I personally am hopeful that we in the West can win and hold the loyalties of people in India and in other countries which, like India, are moving ahead with their economic development. We can get the best results, I think, by doing practical things to help these countries help themselves. This will take the combined efforts of government and private business. Where aid in the form of grants and loans is needed to help the less developed countries build such basic facilities as roads and dams and schools, we should continue to rely on public assistance from the more advanced to the less advanced countries. We can hope other countries will undertake a larger share of the burden now carried by the United States. But by far the greater part of the job of moving the world economy ahead will have to be done through the instrumentality of private business.

The great advantage of private investment is that by combining the technical and managerial skills of the more advanced countries with the human energies and aspirations of the less developed countries it creates an entirely new and mutually profitable and permanent economic way of life. Too often, in past centuries, the more advanced countries considered it to their advantage to keep the less developed countries in their place—playing the role of raw-material suppliers. What we have begun to realize in our time is the enormous gain coming to the developed and to the less developed countries through the mutually beneficial and self-regenerating investment of private capital.

As we all know, in recent years many American companies have been investing heavily in overseas operations. They have done so for many reasons, including the advantages of moving closer to raw materials and to markets for finished products—the need to hurdle the high walls of tariffs and other trade restrictions— and the realization that supporting the economy of a country overseas increases the potential of that country as a market not only for the commodities produced there but also for exports from the United States as well.

We are all aware that this investment has been taking place. But few of us would have reason to know just how big the investment has been. In 1963 U.S. companies invested $4.3 billion outside of this country. This was roughly twice as much as the U.S. government's dollar expenditures outside of this country for economic and foreign aid in the same year.

A study by the Department of Commerce shows that by 1957 U.S. companies had made more than ten thousand investments abroad—and that the total value of these investments at that time came to more than $25 billion. But since 1957 that total has climbed to about $40 billion. This is an increase of about 60 percent in six years.

Put it another way. At the end of 1963, total U.S. private investment outside of this country—by individuals as well as by private business organizations—came to a little over $66 billion. At the end of 1956 the total was $33 billion. This means that in the seven years preceding the end of 1963, private investment by United States citizens outside our own borders grew by as much as it had in all the years previous to 1956.

Effect on Balance of Payments

Now just in case someone is worrying about the effect of all this outflow of investment on our country's international balance of payments, let me give you another fact or two. In the five years, 1959 through 1963, the income returning to this country from all types of U.S. private investments in other countries was 93 percent of the amount invested abroad in those years. And as the world economy grows in strength, the size of this return flow will increase. Moreover, the foreign affiliates of U.S. companies provide an excellent market for the goods we produce in this country. In 1963, those affiliates bought about $5 billion worth of U.S. goods, or nearly a fourth of all our exports.

At Chrysler alone, over the ten years from the beginning of 1954 to the end of 1963, our receipts from exports and earnings on foreign investments exceeded our foreign purchases and investments by more than $1 billion. And there was no single year during this period when our disbursements outside the United States exceeded our receipts.

In other words, private business investments abroad have been a factor of major importance in helping our country to get somewhere near to achieving a balance in our international payments. In this connection, it is important to remember that, owing to the over-all competitive vitality of U.S. business, our country has been enjoying a highly favorable balance of exports over imports. In 1963, for instance, our U.S. merchandise exports exceeded imports by $5 billion. Our over-all international balance of payments problems are caused by other factors.

The economic and financial benefits to our own country of U.S. business investments abroad are very great indeed. But important as these practical benefits are, in the long run it is the contribution of these investments to the cause of peace and international understanding that really stimulates the imagination. Private U.S. corporations with affiliates in many different countries are putting advanced technologies and business practices to work in all parts of the world to raise standards of living and to bring about a more vital interdependence among nations. For want of a better name, these private international business organizations are beginning to be known as multinational corporations. There is nothing new about U.S. companies with widely scattered international operations. But there is something new about the way the greatly increased number of these multinational companies are filling the need of the present world for economic growth and development through the private free-enterprise system.

I would like to say, too, that these multinational corporations are not limited to companies based in the United States. I need only mention the familiar business names Shell and Nestle and Unilever to remind you that the multinational corporation is far from being an American innovation.

The multinational corporation can make available to various countries in various stages of development the financial resources, the engineering knowledge, the management techniques, and the marketing experience they need to move from where they are to something better. The typical multinational company has an extremely wide variety of skills and experience. It provides a reservoir of engineering and management talent which can be tapped to help countries in many parts of the world move toward a realization of their economic possibilities. And being a profit-making organization, in competition with other profit-making organizations, a multinational company has no other choice than to work for maximum efficiency by using the simplest and most economical means to get the desired results. This in itself can be a very major contribution to any developing country.

What all of these facts add up to is the inescapable conclusion that the free world has been laying the foundation for a full utilization of the private competitive business organization as the principal agency of healthy and profitable economic development.

In many different ways the free nations have been working at the bedrock economic and financial problems—trying to create a world climate in which private business can operate effectively. They have been developing new international mechanisms for stabilizing currencies. They have been trying more seriously than ever before to break down tariffs and other barriers to trade between countries.

And they have created international agencies for making funds available to underdeveloped nations to build basic public facilities. The speed with which private investment is growing is the best possible evidence that all that groundwork is now beginning to get results.

We are about to enter the final third of the twentieth century. In my opinion, that period stands an excellent chance of being the most exciting, the most interesting, and the most rewarding periods that the human race has yet experienced. This is not to say we won't continue to have our problems. After all, we have the same old imperfect world, and the same human frailties as ever. We will continue to have our Vietnams and our Congos—on indefinitely into the future. But along with these troubles we will have plenty of constructive activities to keep us encouraged. I am confident we will see deserts begin to blossom with desalinated seawater. We will learn to farm the ocean floor. We will become as familiar with the mountains of the Moon as we now are with the Rockies. And in a thousand other ways we will use science and engineering to build an entirely new and different and better environment for the human race.

Challenge of Change

In the exhilarating period that lies ahead, everyone who is associated with a business organization anywhere in the world is going to have to step lively to keep up with the accelerating pace of change. If this is true for the industrial manager, it is even more true for the engineer. In a very literal sense, the engineer is going to be the architect of a new world. He is going to be privileged to be among the most important makers of history in our time.

From the time of Alexander the Great to the time of Napoleon and right down to our own century, men have tried to force countries into lasting and prosperous federations by military conquest. They failed. I believe we are now entering a period when the slide rule may help the human race to realize the benefits of economic internationalism in a way that could never be accomplished by the sword.

This is the broad picture of the potential that faces all of us as citizens of the world in the years ahead. But for a few minutes let's consider some more immediate possibilities. Let's take a brief look at the automobile business in its international perspective and dimensions and future prospects. Then let's examine a few of the ways in which we as automobile men can help the world measure up to its potential for growth.

World Automotive Growth

Until well after the end of World War II the automobile industry was virtually a monopoly of the United States. As late as 1950, three out of four motor vehicles produced in the entire world were being produced in the United States. But during the past fifteen years the number of cars built in other countries has increased steadily. In 1963, the last year for which world production figures are available, 56 out of every 100 motor vehicles built were built outside of the United States. And while we are talking about the changing shares of world automotive production, it is important to remember that in those same years—between 1950 and 1963—world vehicle production nearly doubled. It increased from 10.6 million to 20.4 million cars, trucks, and buses.

The rapid growth of the world output of motor vehicles in recent years has been due in part to the very substantial investments in other countries by the U.S. automobile industry. At the end of 1963, investments in other countries by U.S. automobile companies totaled approximately $3 billion. And U.S. companies now assemble or manufacture cars and trucks in 98 plants in 37 foreign countries.

Just as impressive as the size of this total investment outside our country is the rate at which it is growing. It is expected that in the two years 1964 and 1965, the amount invested by U.S. automobile companies outside the borders of this country will be increased by well over $1 billion. And this does not include the investments of the many automotive suppliers who have made substantial investments abroad.

What this means is that although less than half the world's motor vehicles are being built in the United States, U.S. automobile companies and their suppliers are participating vigorously in the expanding world market for cars and trucks.

Over and beyond the purely business satisfaction we in this industry can take in the expansion of our overseas operations and in our exports, we can be proud of the contributions we have made to the healthy growth of foreign economies. You and I know, however, that some of the people in some of the countries where we do business have mixed feelings about our presence in their midst. From their point of view, the strength of the multinational American automobile company is something to be welcomed and to be wary of at the same time.

As it moves ahead toward the realization of its great opportunities in the rapidly expanding world market, the U.S. automobile industry may find that its greatest challenge—using the word in its broadest meaning—is political. When it has good relationships with the countries where it does business, a multinational automobile company can thrive at the same time that it helps the host country to prosper. Without those relationships it can find itself thwarted at every turn and operating well below its potential.

Doing Business Internationally

I would like to offer just a few thoughts about some approaches that may be helpful in establishing and preserving good and mutually beneficial relationships between the U.S. automobile industry and the countries where it is doing business.

First—it seems to me to be of the greatest importance for the American automobile company to make every reasonable adjustment to the host countries' programs for attaining their economic aspirations. In other words, we should respect the economic aims of the countries where we do business and work for the fulfillment of those aims.

We at Chrysler have learned there are major advantages in working cooperatively with the people of other countries and adapting our policies and procedures as far as possible to their wishes. We know, for example, that one hundred percent ownership is not necessarily essential to successful operation of a foreign affiliate. We have a number of situations where majority and even minority investments have worked out well for both parties. It was this policy that we followed in making our initial investment in Simca. And we have followed the same policy in, for example, Mexico, Spain, and England. This has worked well for us and—we believe—for the host countries. We think it will continue to work well in the future.

Second—an American automobile company should place as much as possible of the management of a foreign operation in the hands of local people. And when it buys a substantial equity in an existing company, it should disturb existing personnel relationships as little as possible.

More damage can be done to the reputation of an American company in a shorter time by upsetting human relations than by any other means. Some of our personnel practices are being adopted in other parts of the world, but this is a process that cannot be rushed.

It is also important, in this connection, for an American company to observe many local customs that have been hallowed by time. One of our men tells about participating in the laying of the cornerstone of our new plant in Turkey. This ceremony was quite unlike anything you might expect to see here in the Detroit area. But to the people of Turkey it was just as solemn and certainly as meaningful as our own ceremonies are to us. The cornerstone itself was in a pit. Down into the pit went a Moslem priest. With him he took a snow-white ram with gilded horns and hooves. At the right time, and with great skill, he cut the ram's throat in such a way that the cornerstone of our plant was properly sanctified with blood. It was considered a highly successful ceremony because it was performed in the first sunshine seen in weeks—and followed immediately by a good rain which soaked the blood into the earth.

Third—and most important of all—an American automobile company should adapt its operating methods—and especially the technical assistance of its engineers—to the needs of the country where it is doing business.

As I indicated a few minutes ago, it is my belief that the multinational corporation is providing the world with an efficient and rapidly growing private agency for economic development. And it is the engineers employed by these multinational corporations who will carry the responsibility for coming up with the key technical ideas to help the less developed countries move ahead.

To illustrate this general idea with something specific, let me tell you about an interesting experiment in technical cooperation in the manufacture of trucks in Turkey. This experiment, I might add, was conceived and carried out by Chrysler engineering. In that same plant where the cornerstone was sanctified by the blood of a ram, Turkish workers are now fabricating fenders, cabs, and other body components for trucks. They are not using the kinds of dies and presses we use to stamp sheet steel for truck cabs and fenders in this country. They use a simple press-break and shear to cut and form the metal components they need. The tooling cost of this low-volume production process is about one-fifteenth as much as the process used for high-volume production in this country.

The really important thing about this process is that it enables the Turkish people to produce truck components locally. This helps to conserve foreign exchange. It provides training and employment for young men in metal-working skills that can be transferred to other industrial processes. And it gives Turkey a start toward an automobile industry of its own.

It is always a bit difficult for us Americans to recommend technical approaches that are less advanced than those we are familiar with. Engineers especially may find that it goes against the grain to use simple methods when they have been trained in highly advanced techniques. But the greatest service that can be extended to a developing country is to adapt products and processes realistically to the economic stage that country has reached. In countries where labor is plentiful, for example, automation may not be the right first step on the road to progress.

Roads for World Growth

In the last fifteen years we in the automobile industry have learned a great deal about cooperating with other countries to exchange what we know with what they know—to our mutual advantage. This kind of cooperation will keep the world-wide automotive revolution rolling on—to the benefit of people on all five continents. There is still one serious barrier, however, to the continued growth of the automobile industry in many parts of the world. This barrier is the lack of adequate roads and highways for the rapidly increasing number of motor vehicles now being produced.

A few months ago, in Montreal, Wilfred Owen of the Brookings Institution, one of the world's leading authorities on transportation, presented some challenging ideas on the world's need for better roads. I would like to leave one or two of these ideas with you this evening.

In Mr. Owen's opinion, most of the world's resources are lying unused and undiscovered because there is no way to get to them. People in many parts of the world have resigned themselves to poverty—and completely inadequate roads are largely to blame. Hundreds of millions of people still move their goods on the backs of donkeys and camels, and on bullock carts. "They think this is the cheapest way, but actually animal transport costs 40 to 50 cents a ton mile—ten times the cost of mechanical transport." Other people are even worse off than this. They can't even afford animals—and they carry their goods on their own heads.

The imbalance in economic development between nations shows up more clearly, perhaps, in automotive transportation than in any other respect. For example, according to Mr. Owen, North America has only 6 percent of the world's population—but it accounts for 48 percent of its surfaced roads and 55 percent of its trucks and buses. Asia, on the other hand, has 56 percent of the world's people, but only 9 percent of its trucks and buses.

When we worry about all those hundreds of millions of people in other parts of the world who are hungry most of the time, we would do well to remember that one reason for their hunger is that much of the land capable of growing food is out of reach. Moreover, it has been estimated that one-third of all the food that is grown rots in the fields because there is no way to move it to market.

Sad as these facts are, there is some reason to be encouraged. In all parts of the world, nations are laying the groundwork for improved living through improved transportation. In the past fifteen years, for example, the advanced nations have made available $7.5 billion for transportation in the less advanced parts of the world.

It is always encouraging to see the people of underdeveloped countries undertake ambitious programs of self-help. And Mr. Owen tells a story about self-help in roadbuilding that I find very interesting. Let me quote him directly:

> *The most spectacular road-building effort on Earth has stemmed from the Comilla Public Works Program in East Pakistan. This self-help community undertaking has been extended to all of East Pakistan and has resulted in the construction or rehabilitation of 52,000 miles of local roads in two years. This extraordinary accomplishment has been made possible by organizing local farmers and assisting them with tools, engineering advice, and funds from the sale of surplus foods grown 10,000 miles away in the United States.*

Developments like this help all of us here tonight to realize the true meaning of our work. Most of us, perhaps, are automobile men. But in one way or another we are all involved in the task of improving the worldwide system of transportation. Of all the basic work being done in our time to improve the lot of the human race none is more important than this.

It is my belief that you and I—as professionals in the field of transportation—are helping our own country, and in turn the world, to move ahead in the boldest forward thrust of civilization ever seen since the dawn of human history. This is a priceless privilege. Let's dedicate ourselves to making the most of it.

The Multinational Company

John J. Powers, Jr.

Recently, a conservative and distinguished business journal, the *Statist of London*, observed[1]:

> *It takes no great prescience . . . to see that the future lies with a new type of company whose dominant concept will be total internationalism in operations, management, and philosophy.*

In the fifteen-year period from 1950 to 1965, two noteworthy things occurred. Production and sales in the non-communist world outside the United States rose at a significantly greater rate than in the United States. Production of motor vehicles in this period, up 39 percent in the United States, nearly 500 percent abroad. Telephone units up more than 100 percent in the United States, over 200 percent abroad. Petroleum up 74 percent in the United States, 370 percent abroad, and a similarly rapid rate of growth has been achieved also in the office equipment, food, chemical and pharmaceutical industries, to name a few.

During a period of such prosperity abroad, one would expect that exports from the U.S. would have increased substantially and so they did—from about $10 billion in 1950 to about $26 billion in 1965—but something else occurred of even greater significance to America and to the world and this is the second noteworthy event which I would draw to your attention. The book value of U.S. direct investment overseas grew from about $12 billion in 1950 to about $50 billion in 1965 with the result that local production overseas by U.S. based companies rose from about $20 billion in 1950 to about $100 billion in 1965. This is a growth rate of 9.9 percent per year compared with an export growth rate of 5.5 percent. This $100 billion worth of goods produced abroad by American based companies is about four times the amount of U.S. exports and it is clearly increasing all the time. The National Industrial Conference Board calls it "One of the most unusual economic developments following World War II."

What are the reasons for this enormous growth of direct investment and consequent production in overseas markets by American based companies?

Reprinted by permission of Chas. Pfizer & Co., Inc. An address by John J. Powers, Jr., President and Chief Executive Officer, Chas. Pfizer & Co., Inc., before the President's Dinner of the Student Association, Graduate School of Business, Stanford University, April 13, 1967.

[1] *Statist,* February 3, 1967, p. 139.

Primarily, in order to compete effectively in these fast growing markets. To a certain extent government regulations in the host countries may require local production by cutting off or heavily taxing imports of finished goods, or even of some basic materials but, regardless of this, to compete effectively for a good share of any major market requires direct investment in that marketplace in the form of sales offices and warehouses and, at least, packaging and assembly plants, if not basic production units. It is just not possible for a mere exporter to a market to become a major, long-term factor in that market in this second half of the twentieth century. Thus, one who has operated in international markets and made these investment decisions cannot but agree emphatically with the conclusion of the National Industrial Conference Board in a recent study that "... direct investments (abroad) are made in response to the exigencies of the marketplace ... (a company) cannot maintain its market position by merely continuing to send goods from the United States" (pp. 42–43).[2]

It is in its adaptation to these facts of a new worldwide business life that the multinational company is born. But who is this company? Before World War II, there were not very many such companies. Many of those whose names come to mind were foreign owned companies like Unilever, Nestle's, Royal Dutch Shell, I.C.I., Massey Ferguson. Some were American, Standard Oil Co. (N. J.), Singer, Hoover. After World War II, companies of many industries swelled the ranks of those engaged in multinational operations—but most of them were American based, and the rapid rise of this type of activity is sometimes looked on almost as being an American development. To a large extent this is true and I am going to discuss the subject from the point of view of the American based company but, in fact, we are not alone—as indicated by this ringing final paragraph of Mr. H. G. Lazell, Chairman of Beecham Group Limited, in an address about a year and a half ago entitled, "The Role of the International Company."

> I would conclude by submitting to you that we are only at the beginning of a worldwide business revolution, brought about by the international companies; that such companies will inevitably capture a bigger and bigger share of the world trade, and if Britain wants to stay in the International League it must put its international companies on an equal basis with their American competitors.[3]

Of course, it is still true that the *average* American company is primarily oriented to its domestic market. And if there is an international division, it is as likely as not to have junior status in the allocation of managerial and financial

---

[2] A special report from the Conference Board, "U.S. Production Abroad and The Balance of Payments," which is recommended particularly for its analysis of the reasons for American direct investment overseas.

[3] Lazell, H. G., "The Role of the International Company," speech reprinted from *The National Liberal Forum*, November 9, 1965.

resources. In many, perhaps in most, companies there is little incentive to take on the complexities of international business operations. The domestic market seems to offer sufficient opportunity. They react, therefore, somewhat negatively to the proposal to move into distant and unknown places, and to make sizeable expenditures beyond the immediate supervision of U.S. management. It may well be that many companies are right in such an attitude. Their resources are limited and, with adequate potential for growth in the United States and without the depth in management that would permit a breakthrough into international operations, concentration on the domestic market may well be prudent.

For a company, however, which has already realized a good share of its potential in the U.S. marketplace or for a less mature company which discovers an outstanding new product that will attract strong demand everywhere then the case for worldwide marketing seems almost irresistible. To leave competitors to enjoy the growth potentialities abroad would be to concede to them substantial earnings which they can use to compete more effectively everywhere, including the domestic market. And so, for such a company, a beginning is made with exports. But more importantly, the company will inevitably be drawn to make direct investments, first in marketing facilities, sales offices and warehouses and then, as necessary, with plants. And so a company, keyed to expansion under American conditions, will be drawn out of its shell. In a decade or so, a domestically oriented management will find it has a large proportion of its assets deployed around the world—that many of its employees are foreign citizens, that a large amount of its earnings are in foreign currencies, and that it is operating to an important extent outside the jurisdiction of the United States.

In these circumstances, the company finds it has not just grown—it has been transformed. In making direct investments abroad, it has become multinational. In such a situation, though the headquarters of the company is in the United States and though it has the large U.S. market at hand, it must now be managed as a world enterprise. In the long run, the objective must be to make the transition to an organization which treats the world as its market, of which the United States is but one part, and which manages the company's assets and efforts multinationally, in accordance with market opportunities wherever they may be.

As you well know, there is an immense amount of thinking going on now as to the best form of organization for multinational companies. Depending on the nature of the business, there are a number of organizational possibilities, but the discussion of these would require another speech, and another evening. It is, however, worth noting that these organizational changes reflect significant changes in relationships within the enterprise, most broadly the relationship between the parent company and the international division and between the parent and domestic operations. Indeed, it occurs to me that one crucial test of the maturity of a multinational company might be whether the domestic operating organization and the parent company are separate functional entities.

But the change is not only in the organization chart. Again to the degree that the multinational organization is mature, there will be found a change in the attitudes of its people. But, the development of an international viewpoint does not take place rapidly. It must be learned and it must be continuously emphasized. Many people at higher as well as at lower levels must be exposed to new experiences. There must be a continuing supply of men who have participated in both international and domestic operations. And as a continuing part of management development, they must be given the challenge to stretch their minds and from varied experiences to develop a truly worldwide view.

But quite apart from organizational and personnel changes, when a domestically oriented company gradually evolves to the point that it can be described as multinational it must cope with new issues I would like particularly now to direct your attention. Prior to World War II, to all but a very few Americans, international business meant exports imports. The primary problem for the exporter was to find a local distributor. There were tariffs and quotas to be considered; but once these were hurdled the local distributor did the rest. Perhaps he needed financing and a little training, but the investment was minimal. The case now is very different. As I have already pointed out, U.S. multinational companies go abroad to do the job themselves. They put roots down in a country. They add foreign identities to their American identity. They buy land. They hire and train people. They borrow money locally. They negotiate with governments. Their operations stimulate other industries. They bring about developments in housing and education. They may become a part of a national economic development plan or participate in a national program for the expansion of exports or restriction of imports. In other words, multinational companies become committed to their host countries and inevitably play a significant role in their future growth.

It is obvious that a few large investments can have quite revolutionary effects on the developing societies of small countries. Even in developed countries, however, the cumulative impact of U.S. investments can be considerable. They stimulate competition. They change financial institutions and practices. They transform labor-management relations. They alter social habits. They alter power relationships. They break down class barriers. In the United States and abroad, the U.S. company offers opportunities for talented people to get ahead without reference to social background and, thus, adds considerably to social mobility. We are accustomed to this in the U.S. but abroad, where class divisions have been more rigid, the social impact of the multinational company has been more dramatic.

In these circumstances, multinational companies generate tensions. They are agents of change, socially, economically, and culturally. They are pacesetters. They reach across geographic boundaries and overlap political jurisdictions. They do not fit comfortably into concepts developed to explain import and export patterns. They establish new and significant connections between international markets that as yet are hardly recognized in law and diplomacy. Lynn Townsend, now Chairman of the Board of Chrysler Corporation, in a paper on this subject appearing in the October 17, 1966 issue of *NAM Reports* expressed it in these hopeful words:

The existence of this strong trend toward economic inter-nationalism—providing as it does a countervailing force to the continued trend toward political nationalism—may be the most important and most meaningful and in some ways the most hopeful development we are witnessing on the world scene in this second half of the twentieth century.

But the reception in host countries of multinational companies is often mixed. For some reason, they are welcome; and for others, they are resented. They bring employment, but they also bring competition. They import technology and skills, but the foreign connections of these corporations sometimes offend national sensitivities. In some countries, governments have expressed a preference for foreign assistance first in the form of governmental loans, next indirect investments as in securities, and, last on the list, direct investments. The dilemma is evident. All countries want to raise their standards of living but fear some loss of independence if foreign investment is part of the process.

But is this a realistic view? It is true that modernization has a price. But it is not so much the loss of independence as the growth of interdependence. The economic as well as the political history of nations is converging and the multinational company plays an important role in that convergence. I take this as the message of Emile Benoit's interesting article, "Interdependence on a Small Planet," appearing in the Spring 1966 issue of the *Columbia Journal of World Business.* Though countries may be in different stages of development, modern economies show similar characteristics. Computer plants, supermarkets, telephone systems, automobile assembly lines, pharmaceutical production facilities are local expressions of an industrial technology that is not national but supranational. They would quickly become obsolete without the constant feeding with new techniques and new products from abroad, to a large extent brought by the multinational companies.

As I have suggested, multinational companies have not always been welcome by their host countries abroad; and because of national sensitivities, this is not completely surprising. What is surprising is that these enterprises are not infrequently regarded with some hostility by their home governments. It is a curious fact that many men in government and in universities who have done much to build up international institutions in the political and financial fields have, at the same time, failed to see the unique benefits of worldwide industrial enterprises. As Lord Cromer, former Governor of the Bank of England, said so aptly in a recent address in New York, "Although the world has moved forward substantially in international cooperation particularly since the last World War, governmental thinking on international investment has lagged behind that of the business and financial communities."

In the field of international direct investment, practice is clearly ahead of theory and policy and the gap is becoming troublesome. There is a growing number of problem areas requiring that laws and policies affecting world business be reviewed in the light of multinational corporate operations. Multinational companies are urged to become good citizens of the countries in which they operate but it is sometimes difficult for them to satisfy the political and economic demands of conflicting jurisdictions. American based multinational companies owe allegiance to the laws and policies of the United States. It is relevant, however, to raise a question as to how fair it is to the interests of the United States to press jurisdiction over the operations of their subsidiaries abroad. In 1961, for example, there was an effort by the U.S. government, partially successful, to make the foreign earnings of multinational companies subject to U.S. taxes, even when these earnings never leave the host countries. Some foreign commentators have suggested that under the voluntary Balance of Payments program the U.S. government reaches across national boundaries to control local business operations to their detriment. As you know, U.S. laws governing trade with Communist countries, including trade by foreign subsidiaries of U.S. corporations, have been criticized, most noticeably in Canada. And to pose a final difficult issue, to what extent should the U.S. anti-trust laws, confusing as they sometimes can be to us at home, apply to actions of American based companies overseas where such actions fit within the law and the mores of host countries?

But this is not just a matter of U.S. government law and policy. U.S. foreign subsidiaries are often called upon by the governments of host countries to conform to local policies with respect to types of products produced, transfer funds, exports and imports and in other matters which may work against an optimum pattern of global operations.

These issues which I have so briefly sketched involve two broad types of problems. The first is that of conflicting jurisdictions, most clearly posed perhaps with respect to taxes, balance of payments problems, trade restrictions and anti-trust regulations. Such problems have not been too serious as yet, but as the operations of multinational companies grow and become more visible, one need not be a prophet to predict that they will require serious attention. These matters are sensitive. The conflicting claims are difficult to resolve. But their resolution is important to future world development and governments and universities and businessmen should be concentrating their attention upon them now, before they explode in debates heated up by sensitivities always associated with conflicting claims of sovereignty.

The second type of problem involved in these issues is that of conflicting principles of operation of a multinational company, the resolution of which may come close to drawing the line of success or failure for the operation. I refer to the conflict inherent in the concept so often referred to in writings on this subject of maximizing global profits even when this is to the detriment of local profits or other local considerations. *Business Week*, in an article on "Multinational Companies" in its issue of April 20, 1963, was prepared to say, "The goal, in the multinational company, is the greatest good for the whole unit, even if the interests of a single part of the unit must suffer." Others, such as Robock and Simmonds in a fine article in the Winter 1966 issue of Indiana University's *Business Horizons*, at least concede this to be an "extremely troublesome area" involving as it does the transfer of funds, types of production, and employment from one country to another.

There is, however, a most significant point that affects the choice between global and local profits, and as yet, I have seen no one tackle it in this context. In the experience of many of us engaged in international business, a growing global operation must be based on a high degree of decentralization. I hasten to add that I am not trying to settle all aspects of centralization versus decentralization in international operations with that statement. Because I do not yet want to define it myself, I am content for the moment to accept the "deceptively simple maxim: *centralize responsibility for stategic planning and control; decentralize responsibility for 'local' planning and operations*," offered by Clee and diScipio in an article in the *Harvard Business Review* of November-December 1959 entitled "Creating a World Enterprise." But this still means a strong degree of decentralization to the market which could be a region but is more likely a single country unit. And this means a strong delegation of authority and responsibility and, consequently, of the sense of "running a business." It makes possible and should encourage that very critical ingredient, pride in one's work.

How far can headquarters management go then in maximizing global profits at the expense of such a decentralized unit? The first thing to say about it is that there are, of course, great areas of decision where it is unrealistic to opt for the global to the detriment of the local well-being. But there is also a large gray area; and here lies the debate. In this area the local management must realize and appreciate the value of its relationship to the enterprise as a whole. It should be prepared to recognize that there is much merit in the global benefit point of view. But if the essential ingredients of pride and responsibility are to be retained, how far can one go with the global approach? It is this question that dominates my own thinking as I approach the problem of global versus local benefit where I have the freedom to choose between them. (Sometimes law or regulation may decide the issue.) But the question deserves careful study. Perhaps, to some extent, it is a matter of education at all management levels of a multinational company. Perhaps one should reconsider whether the profit and loss statement is in all situations an adequate expression of the success of a local operation. There is some suggestion of this in the *Harvard Business Review* article to which I have just referred when the writers propose that we " . . . must appraise performance against *plan*, not merely against *a single set of arithmetical indicators*." On the other hand, we must also face the fact that we have a world which is steadily shrinking in size as planes and computers compress time and space and make undreamed of things possible. And some argue that this means, as suggested by the previously mentioned article in the *Statist* of February 3, 1967, "the worthwhile plan must be a great deal more than the sum of the ambitions of each local management" to the point that in seeking "profits optimization for the whole group" there must be more not less central control and planning. But, to my mind, the burden of proof should lie on those who would tend to walk back along the path to centralization, for a rather high degree of decentralization has worked spectacularly and the basic reasons for its existence have not been removed by recent developments. I must confess, therefore, that in the end it is difficult to believe that our continued studies of this subject will indicate a return to centralization so much as an optimization of existing areas of central control and planning. Shall we not achieve a *true* maximization of over-all profits of the multinational company by finding the right blend in the resolution of all these conflicts.

It has been said that the function of the entrepreneur is to bring about new and more effective combinations of economic resources. This role involves more than passively reacting to new business conditions. In this era of change the challenge to the multinational company is to act positively to bring about new combinations on a world scale for the better use of economic resources, and to win acceptance and understanding of these innovations both at home and abroad. The *challenge* to government bodies and to you in the universities is to help fashion the proper place for multinational companies in a changing world, so that they may fulfill their potential as engines of world development and betterment.

Unquestionably, we must have the vision to see a completely new world and completely new ways of doing things. The answers do not come easily to the questions I have raised, but there is a great need to grapple with them now, to analyze them in my world and in yours, and by so doing, to establish directions for the tomorrow of the 1970s and 1980s.

Part Three

Regional Economic Groupings

3

The movement toward economic unification and integration, resulting in a variety of international trade agreements, free trade associations, and common markets in different parts of the world, is one of the most significant and far reaching developments of the past fifteen years. Economists have long recognized the beneficial effects of unrestricted international business activities and close international trade and payment relations. However, for centuries the existence of small, separate nations, each jealous of its sovereignty, nationalistic, and devoted to safeguarding domestic business interests against foreign competition, was quite detrimental to close international business interactions.

It was only in the aftermath of World War II that a greater "international mindedness" emerged, which led to the formation of integrated regional blocks within which the economic interchange is relatively unrestricted, whereas the economic barriers toward the rest of the world remain more or less intact. From an economist's point of view this may not seem to be the ideal, but the movement toward regional economic groupings is nevertheless more realistic and easier to implement than *global free trade*, which would result in a worldwide division of labor and thus a complete realization of the principle of comparative advantage.

Particularly the Marshall Plan for European Reconstruction (under which European countries received a total of about thirteen billion dollars in aid from the United States during the decade from 1947–57) provided a major impetus for economic and political cooperation among Western European countries and for closer ties between these countries and the United States. The establishment of a few common, supranational institutions such as the Organization for European Economic Cooperation (OEEC) and the European Payment Union (EPU), formed the basis for further steps toward economic integration among some of the European countries.

In this spirit, for example, the European Coal and Steel Community became operative in August 1952, under a treaty signed by representatives of Belgium, France, Italy, Luxembourg, the Netherlands, and West Germany in April 1951. These countries established an integrated, supranationally administered market for coal and steel devoid of tariffs, quantitative restrictions, or charges with equivalent effect. This genuine integration of a limited but important sector soon led to efforts toward a complete economic integration among these six countries as a first step toward a political unification as well. In a treaty signed in Rome in March 1957 these same countries established the European Economic Community (EEC), also referred to as the European Common Market.

The main stipulations of the Rome treaty, which became effective January 1, 1958, were: (1) The establishment of a customs union. This involved a gradual elimination of all tariffs and other trade barriers among the member countries while establishing at the same rate a uniform tariff schedule and common commercial policies towards third countries. (2) The abolition of all obstacles to the free movement of labor, services, and capital among the member states. (3) The inauguration of a common agricultural policy, a common transport policy, and a coordination of social and fiscal as well as monetary policies. By 1970 practically all of these provisions had been accomplished, frequently ahead of schedule, despite initial skepticism, political disagreements, and several serious crises triggered by such politically oriented issues as the admission of Great Britain into the European Common Market.

Initially Great Britain chose not to join in the integration efforts of the EEC countries whose approach she considered too rigid and too politically oriented. However, she became instrumental to the formation of the European Free Trade Association (EFTA) to which (besides Britain) Austria, Denmark, Norway, Portugal, Sweden, and Switzerland belong. The EFTA was created in 1960 by the so-called Stockholm convention; the member states have merely contracted to remove among themselves all tariffs and other obstacles to trade on industrial goods, but not to set up a common external tariff toward nonmember countries. Compared with the EEC, EFTA's aims are thus much more limited, and therefore the member countries did not find it necessary to establish a supranational structure with political, social, and institutional arrangements. A major unresolved issue is to find some form of economic integration between these two European blocks.

Considering the relatively successful economic integration of the EEC-countries and to a lesser degree that of the EFTA-countries, it is not surprising that their example is followed in other parts of the world. The concept of economic integration has become increasingly attractive to many developing countries which see in these regional groupings an effective and stimulating condition for a more rapid industrialization and accelerated economic development. However, it is frequently overlooked that an effective economic integration effort among various countries requires the existence of certain preconditions. The most important ones are: (1) Not only regional proximity of the member countries but also a well-developed infra-structure, a transportation and communication system among themselves. (2) A reasonably heterogeneous, diversified economic structure within the economic union. An extreme example easily illustrates the importance of this point: if two countries contemplating an economic union should both have coffee as their single trading commodity, then the integration will have practically no effect on their internal trade relations. Particularly some of the economic groupings among developing countries lack a sufficiently stratified economic structure, which reduces the effectiveness of their integration effort. (3) A certain balance in the economic and political strength of all the member countries involved in order to avoid domination or the feeling of inferiority respectively which inevitably would create conflict situations and frictions which again would not be conducive to an integration effort. (4) Economic integration requires an elimination of protective measures among the member countries. This situation may create sudden competitive disadvantages for certain economic sectors in some countries. However, countries can cope better with the negative consequences of the necessary reorientation of economic activities during a period of economic expansion than during a recession. Therefore, the timing of an integration attempt becomes also a very important factor in its success.

Although economic integration is a difficult process, the potential benefits and gains that can be derived from it are quite obvious: Since any form of economic integration results in the reduction and eventually in the elimination of all trade barriers among member countries, there evolves a larger market to which the firms located in this area have unrestricted access. This development allows greater use of external and internal economies, which leads to an improvement in productive efficiency and an intensification of intra-block trade (i.e., the trade creation effect of economic integration). In addition, the formation of economic blocks tends to improve the area's bargaining potential with the rest of the world and stimulates the flow of foreign investments into the area. The potential disadvantages of economic integration stem from the possibility of discrimination against nonmember countries and a restructuring of traditional trade relations, since the liberalization of intra-block trade will inevitably divert a certain amount of trade previously done with nonmember countries to member states (i.e., the trade diversion effect of economic integration). However, it is now recognized that the benefits which can be derived from economic integration generally outweigh by far certain negative effects it may produce.

The readings in this part have been selected to provide a broad perspective of efforts toward economic integration in various parts of the world, to show what problems have to be dealt with, and to indicate how economic integration may affect business activities in general and the multinational firm in particular.

Of any large-scale economic integration efforts the most successful thus far has been the establishment of the European Economic Community (EEC). From this point of view it is worthwhile to review briefly the structural changes in the internal trade relationships of the member countries since the formation of the EEC in 1958 and to point out the most salient issues for future action during the 1970s. The first reading in this part serves this purpose. The statistical tables show the changes that occurred, reflect the relative economic strength of the EEC as compared with other areas of the world, and provide an indication of the gains to which a determined integration effort can lead.

Any economic integration between two or more countries requires some form of supranational organization, i.e., a certain bureaucracy that will work tenaciously toward the integration objectives and that will defend the interests of the community as a whole rather than individual national interests. In the case of the EEC, which encountered numerous political and economic obstacles during its gradual progress toward economic unification, it was the supranational European Commission that provided a good deal of the thrust toward a realization of the provisions in the treaty of Rome. The organizational and institutional requirements of an integration effort cannot be overemphasized; this is the reason for including as the second selection in this part Norman McRae's article, "How the EEC Makes Decisions." This article describes the three major structural building blocks for affecting decisions in the EEC: the European Commission, the Council of Ministers, and the Committee of Permanent Representatives. Of considerable importance and interest are the operating procedures of the supranational European Commission and its interrelationships with the member governments. The article shows succinctly the role which the European Commission plays, and how its role changed as a result of the Community's "crisis" of 1965–66, which was brought about by the French government's refusal to let itself be subjected to majority decisions by the European Commission. An interesting aspect of this article is that it not only describes the institutional set-up for decision making in the EEC, but also the organizational compromises that became necessary during the integration process.

Probably the most controversial (and still unresolved) issue with which the EEC has been faced practically since its beginning is whether Great Britain and other EFTA member countries should be admitted to the EEC and under what conditions. Two of Great Britain's attempts to gain admittance to the European Common Market were rebuffed; but a new effort with the same objective is under way, and this time the chances that Great Britain might become a full member of the EEC are, as the third article in this part points out, much better than the previous times. The article by Philippe Simonnot on "Britain and the EEC" is a balanced analysis of the costs that Britain would incur by becoming a member of the EEC as well as the benefits and advantages it would gain from such an event. The article comes to the conclusion that the substantial costs that Britain would have to absorb by becoming a member of the EEC would be outweighed by a series of economic gains. An expansion of the EEC would thus benefit not only the new members, but the Community as a whole.

The three subsequent readings in this part deal with economic integration endeavors among developing countries. The article by Vincent Cable describes the achievements and the problems of the Central American Common Market (CACM), which includes Costa Rica, El Salvador, Guatemala, Honduras, and Nicaragua. Despite a very successful beginning, the progress toward economic integration among these countries has come almost to a halt, because of both political and economic difficulties. The latter are brought about essentially by an unequal development of the individual member countries; the author therefore suggests the adoption of policies for a balanced growth of the CACM countries supplemented by certain economic and political changes.

The fifth selection in this part deals with the Latin American Free Trade Association (LAFTA), formed in 1960 but which has made very little progress since—at least as compared with the goals that were stipulated at its inception. A major reason for this lack of progress toward economic integration is the heterogeneity in the level of economic activity among the member countries. Attempts are now under way to integrate countries with greater affinity and where the prevailing economic conditions are not too different. The article describes two of these new groupings (the Andean Group and the River Plate Group). Perhaps they can provide a stronger impetus for further economic integration in Latin America.

The last reading in this part reviews and evaluates various economic integration achievements among less developed countries on three continents: Latin America, Africa, and Asia. In asking the question: "LDC Regional Markets—Do They Work?," Ardy Stoutjesdijk comes to an essentially negative answer. He points out that progress toward economic integration among developing countries has been considerably less than anticipated. A major reason for this is an imbalance in the relative economic strength of the member countries and the absence of a supranational institutional framework which could see to it that each member gets its fair share of regionally based activities and thus provide a basis for a balanced development of the member countries.

The European Economic
Community:
Achievements and
Prospects

Richard N. Farmer
Robert W. Stevens
Hans Schöllhammer

The European Economic Community (EEC), consisting of Belgium, France, Germany, Italy, Luxembourg, and the Netherlands, was established by the Treaty of Rome signed March 25, 1957, and became effective January 1, 1958. With this treaty the member countries made a commitment to a mixture of economic, political, and social goals. The main provisions were: (1) to eliminate gradually all tariffs, quotas, and other trade barriers among themselves; (2) to establish, at a similar pace, a uniform common external tariff schedule to apply to imports from the rest of the world; (3) to remove all restrictions on the movement of services, labor, capital, and business enterprises; (4) to establish a common agricultural and transportation policy; (5) to work toward the harmonization of economic and social policies; (6) to assist each other in case of balance of payments difficulties; and (7) to provide for the association of other countries with the Community. All these actions were also envisaged as a step toward a political unification of the member countries.

In spite of numerous crises and controversies which at times overshadowed the integration process, by 1970 the EEC had achieved the first four provisions, it was well advanced on the process toward harmonizing economic and social policies, and it was proceeding with the creation of a monetary union. However, the most important success of the EEC thus far has been the spectacular growth of its internal and external trade.

Internal Trade Expansion

During the first decade of the EEC's existence the trade between the member countries increased from $6.8 billions in 1958 to $28.4 billions in 1968, i.e., a growth of more than 300 percent. Whereas in 1958 the six member countries exchanged 29.9 percent of their total trade with each other, in 1968 it was 45.1 percent. This situation reflects the degree to which the formation of the common market has stimulated the trade among the member countries. The following table shows the magnitude of the integration for the individual countries.

As can be seen, Belgium and Luxembourg have reached the highest degree of integration among EEC countries, depending on the other members for about 65 percent of their exports and 55 percent of their imports.

Intra-EEC Trade in 1968

	In $ Millions		As Percentage of Total Trade of Each Country	
	Imports	Exports	Imports	Exports
Belgium-Luxembourg	4,553	5,249	54.8	64.3
France	6,621	5,460	47.4	43.0
Germany	8,359	9,340	40.7	37.1
Italy	3,709	4,079	36.2	40.1
Netherlands	5,146	4,790	55.4	57.4
Total EEC	26,388	28,918	45.5	44.8

Table 1.

Trade with Third Countries

Since the EEC has to be regarded now as a unified market, it follows that only its trade with third countries (extra-EEC trade) has any significance when it comes to judging its importance in terms of world trade. As the following table shows, the

Shares in World Trade

Imports

	1958		1968	
	$ Millions	Percent	$ Millions	Percent
World[a]	91,600	100	187,200	100
EEC[b]	16,150	17.6	33,550	17.9
EFTA[b]	15,750	17.2	30,400	16.2
U.S.A.	13,200	14.4	33,000	17.6
Japan	3,050	3.3	13,000	6.9

Exports

	1958		1968	
	$ Millions	Percent	$ Millions	Percent
World[a]	86,150	100	167,500	100
EEC[b]	15,900	18.4	35,300	21.1
EFTA[b]	13,300	15.4	24,100	14.4
U.S.A.	17,750	20.6	31,900	19.1
Japan	2,900	3.3	13,000	7.7

[a] World trade excluding intra-EEC and intra-EFTA trade and trade of the Communist countries.
[b] Excluding intra-trade.

Table 2.

EEC's share in world exports amounted in 1968 to over 21 percent, thus exceeding the United States. In the decade from 1958 to 1969 EEC's export to third countries increased by 123 percent and the imports from them by 108 percent. However, in relation to the combined gross national products of the EEC countries, the imports from the third countries declined from 9.7 percent to 9.0 percent.

The increase in EEC's exports to third countries has been largely due to an above-average expansion in the exports of industrial goods, which accounted for about 85 percent of all extra EEC exports.

EEC Exports to Non-EEC Countries by Commodity Category in 1968

Country	Commodity Category						Total
	Food and Raw Materials		Manufactured Goods		Merchandise and Transactions not Classified		
	(a)	(b)	(a)	(b)	(a)	(b)	
Belgium-Luxembourg	13,5	7,9	83,2	8,1	3,3	23,9	100
Germany	5,8	17,9	92,9	48,2	1,3	50,0	100
France	19,9	28,9	79,7	19,2	0,4	7,7	100
Italy	15,7	19,4	83,9	17,1	0,4	6,5	100
Netherlands	36,1	25,9	62,5	7,4	1,4	11,9	100
Total	100		100		100		

a The share of the commodity category in the country's total export to non-EEC countries.

b The share of the particular EEC country in the total EEC-export to nonmember countries of the commodity category concerned.

Table 3.

The above table shows, for example, that about 93 percent of Germany's extra-EEC exports are manufactured goods and only about 6 percent are foods or raw material. As far as the Netherlands is concerned, about 63 percent of its exports are manufactured goods and about 36 percent are agricultural commodities and raw material. The above table also indicates that about 48 percent of all the manufactured goods exported from the EEC area to nonmember countries come from Germany, 19 percent from France, and about 17 percent each from Italy and the Benelux countries.

An increasing share of the EEC countries' export goes to the industrialized countries, whereas the share that goes to the developing countries is steadily declining. The same is true of the imports into the EEC area: a diminishing portion comes from the developing countries, which to a large extent is due to the composition of their exports, i.e., primary products, for which world demand is growing rather slowly. However, the developing countries have increased their share in the EEC's industrial imports from 12.4 percent in 1958 to 15.6 percent in 1968 (amounting to $550 million in 1958 and $2,128 million in 1968).

Geographical Distribution of EEC's Trade

(In Percent)

	Imports		Exports	
	1958	1968	1958	1968
Industrialized Countries	53	56	55	65
Developing Countries	42	37	39	27
Communist Countries	5	7	6	8

Table 4.

A Look Ahead

On the whole, the European Economic Community can look back upon a rather successful progress toward economic unity. As far as the future of this economic block is concerned there are two major issues with which the member countries are now faced: (1) the issue of further integrating their economies, particularly by establishing a monetary union, and (2) the issue of expanding its membership. The latter issue, essentially whether Great Britain and other members of the European Free Trade Association (EFTA) should or could join the EEC and whether some countries of the British Commonwealth should be granted the same preferences the present associated states now enjoy, has stirred many controversies. At present, there is a much more favorable attitude toward an expansion of the Community than in previous years, and positive steps have been taken in this direction. The ramifications, particularly as far as Great Britain is concerned, are discussed in detail in the reading on pp. 201–207.

The other issue, the development toward a further integration among the present EEC members, was given new impetus during a summit conference held at the Hague on December 1 and 2, 1969, when the heads of the governments concerned decided that, the customs union having been achieved, the course should now be set for an economic and monetary union. The first steps toward a realization of this goal have already been undertaken. On October 19, 1970, the Council of Ministers released the text of a plan for the economic and monetary union of the six member countries. The major provisions are:

(1) That the main decisions in economic, fiscal, and monetary matters will be taken at the Community level and that the necessary powers should therefore be transferred from the national governments to the Community, whose decisions will be a reflection of the common interest rather than a summation of national interests.

(2) Since a monetary union implies a full and permanent convertibility of the currencies of the member countries, fluctuations in the exchange rates will be eliminated. This means the plan envisages a permanent fixing of the exchange rates of the currencies involved as a first step toward the adoption of a single currency for the EEC.

(3) As far as the institutional set-up is concerned, two Community bodies will become indispensible: a decision-making body for economic policy matters and a Community system of central banks. These institutions will have the power to make binding decisions within their terms of reference.

(4) The plan also envisages complete economic and monetary unification, to be achieved in stages. The first stage began on January 1, 1970 and will last three years. During this time the member countries will strive for a more effective coordination of short-term economic policies, the adoption of joint medium-term guidelines on budgetary policies, and a further harmonization in the area of taxation. The second stage, to begin in 1974, foresees further adjustments in the coordination of the economic policies and an integration of the various capital markets. The third stage, starting in 1976, would lead to the establishment of a Council of Governors of Central Banks as a step toward the creation of a Community Central Bank with appropriate supranational powers. It would also include the elimination of any fluctuations in the exchange rates of the member countries' currencies as a basis for the introduction of a single EEC currency.

The example of the European Economic Community has shown that economic integration is a slow and difficult process from which, however, substantial economic gains can be derived, both for the member countries themselves and the international community at large.

How the EEC
Makes Decisions

Norman MacRae

The object of this article is to analyse the EEC's present decision-making process, before going on to examine how it might be improved. In the second half of the 1970s, many of Britain's policies are likely to be determined by this mechanism. So we had better start to learn what really goes on in the woodshed. When I had finished staring into it for even a fortnight, I was in some ways quite surprised. There are three main decision-making bodies in Brussels, including an important one which is not really meant to exist. These three bodies are:

(1) The European Commission, the 5,000 European civil servants in the Bâtiment Berlaymont. The first point to make about the commission is that it is the body with the sole real right of initiative within the EEC. The council of ministers meets to discuss proposals put up by the commission, not to initiate policies itself. The second point to make about the commission is that it genuinely wants supranational government for Europe. The council of ministers generally does not.

(2) The Council of Ministers is any council of cabinet ministers from the six countries, called together at Brussels to discuss papers put before it by the commission. The most important councils are usually led by the six's foreign ministers, who meet in Brussels about once a month. At major council meetings, the ministers are surrounded by armies of advisers whispering in their ears; there may be over a hundred people in the room, and the principals are only on a flying visit to Brussels. The council is therefore a very bad decision-making body. It really acts less as a cabinet than as a senate—with the job of saying "yes" or "no" or "try again" to the commission. This has, in practice, thrown a steadily bigger role on what might be called the third real institution of Brussels: the least-publicized cabal.

(3) This third body is the Committee of Permanent Representatives. The six countries naturally each have an embassy or "permanent delegation" to the community in Brussels, and each delegation has grown to a considerable size: usually around twenty-five top class civil servants in each delegation, with representatives of the ministries of finance, agriculture, social affairs, etc.

Reprinted by permission from *The Economist*, London, May 16, 1970, pp. 54–56 (Special Report).

Nominally, these delegations are the "servants, eyes and ears at Brussels of the member governments." In practice, they are much more.

At most times of the year, the committee of permanent representatives meets with officials of the commission on two working days a week in order to discuss matters due to be raised at future meetings of the council of ministers. Where there is unanimous agreement among the permanent representatives or their deputies on points of minor importance, these will be laid before the next council of ministers as so-called "A" points. In practice, this will mean that the point will be accepted by those busy cabinet ministers without further discussion. When matters of greater controversy are in the lists, a sort of war game is declared. We will play a representative one later in this article.

The more one plumbs the workings of the organization at Brussels, the more convinced one becomes that a key advantage for European union is that the mood in this committee of permanent representatives has almost always tended to be more in favor of supranationalism than has the average mood of cabinet ministers and civil servants back home. This fortunate tradition of rather improper bias among men meant to be political eunuchs may owe quite a lot to a historical accident, rather gleefully described by the commission's head of secretariat, Emile Noel, in a recent *Journal of Common Market Studies*. M. Noel explained that the original permanent delegations in Brussels at the dawn of the Treaty of Rome mostly sprang out of

> ... that rather extraordinary "club" which the committee of heads of delegations under the chairmanship of M. Spaak had formed during the negotiations, and which had been both a meeting place of authorised and faithful spokesmen of the six governments and a group of militants (even of "accomplices") dedicated to a vast and noble political undertaking. After March 25, 1957, the "interim committee," on which the same men were practically all to be found, maintained this spirit. Familiarity with this background is necessary for a proper understanding of the Committee of Permanent Representatives.

Still, as jealous governments have had plenty of time to make postings since 1957, this cannot be the sole reason. One has to search for some more convincing explanation of why the tendency in the committee of permanent representatives has never been to report back to the national capitals, "here is the next dodge with which the commission will try to get away"; but has nearly always been to tip the wink to the commission about how much (or how little) supranationalism ministers back home will swallow. Why?

My guess is simply that intelligent men who live permanently in the atmosphere of Brussels—with enthusiasm for unity in the air, and with able and idealistic Eurocrats as their most frequent guests and hosts at dinner parties—tend to get caught in that enthusiasm. The European commission has reason to be happy that they do. It is this, I will argue below, that has helped to keep the powers of initiative in the Berlaymont, even in this period immediately after de Gaulle tried to take them away.

Powers of Commission

The European commission has three different systems for organizing its proposals into action. Starting with the simplest:

(1) The commission has more power than most people in Britain realize to enforce some policies by straight decree. It can issue written orders under about thirty general sub-heads, and these then have the force of law in all member countries. The most important field subject to this draconian procedure relates to the control of monopolies. The commission's very able director-general for competition, a youthful-looking German lawyer called Ernst Albrecht, can issue straight "cease and desist" orders, on the American pattern, against all actions by firms or industries in restraint of competition; and he can then fine any firm that disobeys, subject only to appeal to the European court. In practice, Herr Albrecht discusses matters with national equivalents of the Ministry of Technology before issuing orders, and he is also very willing to discuss matters with the industries and pressure groups concerned. They criticize him as "very academic." This means that Albrecht's anti-restrictive policy is for real. British industry should take note of this.

(2) There are more than another fifty general sub-heads under which the commission can enforce decisions by written order, but has to discuss the matter with some special committee first. Usually, the committee is made up of civil servants from each of the member states (from the Ministry of Agriculture if the issue is particular food prices, from the equivalent of the Board of Trade if it is interpretation of customs duties, etc.). Although the powers of these committees vary, a typical rule is that the European commission can go ahead with its written order unless twelve of the weighted seventeen votes on the committee say it must ask permission from the council of ministers first. This concept of seventeen "weighted votes" appears in many votes in the community; the seventeen is reached because Germany, France and Italy each have four votes, Holland and Belgium each have two, and Luxemburg one.

(3) On more important decisions, however—and particularly decisions that would introduce new policies rather than just administer existing ones—the commission rightly has to get approval from the council of ministers first. At the time of the Treaty of Rome it was envisaged that up to January 1, 1966, decisions should be taken within the council of ministers by general agreement—in other words, by unanimous vote. But after January 1966, the rule was to be that any proposals by the commission could become obligatory on all member countries if they were approved by the council of ministers by weighted majority vote (those seventeen votes again). It was this prospect

which in 1965 so horrified President de Gaulle; and prompted him to bring about the community's "crisis" of 1965–66. Since this has affected the community's decision-making process today, it is important to look briefly at it.

Emperor Attacks Pope

Up to 1965 the commission's manner of operation had been largely determined by the accident of timetables. Discussions at the time of the Treaty of Rome had set January 1st and sometimes July 1st of most years as the dates by which particular features of the treaty's customs union should take effect. As these target dates approached, the commission would tie together a package of proposals, some favoring one country, some another.

For July 1, 1965, the main requirement of the timetable was a regulation for the financing of agriculture: i.e., for the Germans and Belgians to increase their heavy subsidies to France's farms. The president of the European commission at that time, the progressive German lawyer Walter Hallstein, therefore thought this a good opportunity to tie into the package some pieces of supranationalism that France would not like. The bargaining duly dragged on past midnight on June 30th, but everybody thought this was another familiar instance of "stopping the clock." Then, shortly before 2 a.m. on the morning of July 1st, the French abruptly broke off the negotiations; and announced that "solemn obligations had not been fulfilled." To the horror of its partners France withdrew its permanent representative from Brussels to Paris, and started to boycott council meetings and most other committee meetings at Brussels.

President de Gaulle soon made clear what his objective was. From the high pulpit of one of his famous press conferences, he violently attacked the European commission ("this embryonic technocracy, for the most part foreign"), and said that his government could not accept that from 1966 on proposals made by the commission could become binding on France if a majority of the five voted for them. His France would not reopen negotiations in Brussels until "people are ready to have done with the pretensions which ill-founded, Utopian myths raise up."

To this Hitlerian breach of the president's previous pledged word to accept majority voting, the ministers of Europe replied with their usual worried whinny, but some of the people of France responded with a nobler growl. It soon became apparent that the five would seek a compromise with France. They were almost certainly saved from making too abject a one by France's election in late 1965. President de Gaulle was returned, but with a stronger pro-European vote against him than expected.

At two meetings of the six's foreign ministers in Luxemburg in early 1966, the formula for compromise was arranged. All parties signed a communique saying that the five had agreed that "when issues very important to one or more member countries are at stake, the members of the council will try, within a reasonable time, to reach solutions which can be adopted by all the members"; then followed a statement that "the French delegation considers that, when very important interests are at stake, the discussion must be continued until unanimous agreement is reached"; and then an admission in the next paragraph that, "the six delegations note that there is a divergence of views on what should be done in the event of failure to reach complete agreement." This agreement is known in France as the "decalogue." The circumlocution involved surely makes that a slander on Sinai. However, behind the circumlocution, the message was clear. The French had told the others that another crisis might break out if they ever tried to enforce a majority vote against what the French regarded as their vital national interests; and the European commission had been served notice that it had better act much more circumspectly in future.

One of my objects in Brussels was to gauge how decisions really are now taken in the community, after this Luxemburg compromise—or, as I prefer to call it, threat.

A War Game

From the written record, it can be argued that the Luxemburg formula did not alter the process of decision-making at all. Since 1966 some motions have been passed in the council of ministers on a majority vote, sometimes with France in the defeated minority. No protests have come from Paris that France's vital interests have been raped. But this is because, when there are fears that France really would object, a great shuffling of stances takes place further back. Says one disappointed good European at the Berlaymont:

> Under the rule of often-required-unanimity, after the Luxemburg communiqué, everything we propose here has to be decided with an eye on possible liaisons and compromises. Under the rule of majority vote, we could propose from the beginning what we honestly thought was the best solution for the issue itself.

However, the main consequence of this regime of liaisons and compromises seems to me to have been to increase the importance of the committee of permanent representatives, and especially of whoever is temporarily chairman of it.

The chairmanship of the committee of permanent representatives rotates among member countries for periods of six months at a time, in step with the chairmanship of the council of ministers itself. One might expect that this would mean that progress towards any sort of supranationalism would be slow when the French provided the chairmen. But Secretary-General Noel of the European Commission argued with some enthusiasm that "at the community's rate of progress, the six months' period has proved sufficient for getting things done, while too short to allow of abuse"; and also that the chairmanship of the committee of permanent representatives has become a job with a "style":

To define this "style" I would say that the chairman wants his period of office to be marked by some noteworthy community advance and knows that to be active and fruitful it must be imbued with a community spirit. He must therefore—within limits—"keep his distance" from his own country's delegation, which for its part feels that it should be specially conciliatory. Although this balance is perhaps easier to find when a small country is presiding, it has nevertheless been achieved by each chairman in accordance with his own temperament.

It is intriguing to play a "war game," to suggest how some fairly difficult proposal by the commission might nowadays be wriggled through into effect. Say, one with certain supranational overtones, relating to some part of the program for eventual economic and monetary union.

Perhaps the game would begin with a calculated leak from commission officials to the financial attachés on the permanent delegations about what the commission had in mind. When the matter reached the committee of permanent representatives, it would probably be remitted in the first place to the working party of these financial attachés. From this remittance (to men who would already have sounded out their capitals about the commission's likely intention), and after further discussion in the committee of permanent representatives, a fairly lengthy dossier would begin to be compiled. This dossier would show there were (a) some fairly easy points on which agreement between the governments and the commission could be quickly reached; but (b) also political difficulties.

A wise chairman of the committee of permanent representatives will almost certainly operate first by concentrating the discussion on the easy points, in order to get them agreed as quickly as possible. If there is a hold-up on some entirely footling point, then the chairman might conceivably suggest that the committee might proceed to a vote on it; but only on a footling point, one that no country could call an issue of principle. The point about the deterrent threat of a vote is that it helps to concentrate discussion; nobody really wants to be made to look foolish by voting in isolation from all his colleagues on something like the definition of dried peas. The commission has a sad, small file in the Berlaymont of minor proposals that it did not bring through to fruition because "the chairman of the committee of permanent representatives lacked courage to call a vote at the right time." No sensible chairman, however, will call for a vote on the big political issues this first time round. His aim will be that the committee of permanent representatives can report to the council of ministers that (a) the committee is agreed that particular parts of the commission's proposals are to everybody's advantage; but (b) there are also the following major political points which the council of ministers may wish to discuss. . . .

At the first reference to the council of ministers, the ministers will talk about these points in tones of greater or lesser political cussedness or conciliation; and then will almost certainly refer the matter back to the committee of permanent representatives again. Journalists will then stomp out to write stories about how dreadfully atrophied the council of ministers is. Actually, this process of reference to and fro between the committee and the council—perhaps more than once—is an entirely sensible part of the present decision-making process. When the matter returns to the committee of permanent representatives, the delegates there will know for the first time how deeply or shallowly their and their colleagues' ministers (and the civil service advisers back in home capitals) really feel about the issue after having been to Brussels to discuss it. Previously they have merely been able to whisper to colleagues on the committee "the tone of communications from my capital on this has been very stiff"; now they can say "well, you saw how my foreign minister reacted." It is at this second time round that the chairman of the committee of permanent representatives will start suggesting compromises.

Obviously, the commission—which has the sole right to lay proposals before the council of ministers—must be able to reject the chairman's suggestion if it would destroy the purpose of the commission's original policy. But, in practice, the chairman and the commission usually work in cahoots. Although most permanent representatives have their closest contacts with commission officials rather than with the top commissioners themselves, the chairman of the permanent representatives, during his six months' tenure, generally has a long weekly meeting with President Jean Rey of the commission. At these meetings, each side probably leans on the other, and decides what compromises will be acceptable to each. These compromises are then suggested to the council of ministers, and are generally accepted at some time of asking.

My conclusion is that proposals put up by the commission do still get through, but that the crisis of 1965–66 has made everybody more cautious, so that proposals are being trimmed more than before. It would undoubtedly be to the advantage of Europe's efficiency if there were a return to the situation promised before the Gaullist crisis, and if the commission's proposals could be made enforceable by a mere weighted majority vote within the council of ministers.

Perhaps optimistically, I think that there is a prospect that President Pompidou's France may eventually agree to return to this. Inefficiency in the mechanism does not benefit France or anybody else. De Gaulle struck at the principle of majority voting because he had mystic dreams about where he wanted France's foreign and domestic and industrial policy to go. He recognized that a new power was growing at Brussels which in some degree represented the modern forces of technocracy, and that it was liable to clash at some points with his own policies based on the promptings of romanticism. And he certainly was not going to allow a German lawyer called Hallstein to tell the President of France what he could not do in France itself. The battle between Hallstein and de Gaulle was aptly known in Europe as the struggle between the pope and the emperor; the pope at Brussels had great moral force on his side, but very few battalions.

President Pompidou, by contrast, represents the forces of romanticism about as much as does a suet pudding. He is interested in prosaic things, like the technocrats. He may well gradually come to see that the artifical slowing of the process of decision making, which is what the "Luxemburg compromise" amounted to, slows more decision that would be in favor of France than decisions that would militate against it. He may opt for a return to rule by a more efficient technocracy, instead of the present rule by an unnecessarily inhibited one.

Unfortunately, however, I am very doubtful whether a return to prosaic technocracy is going to be enough.

Britain and the EEC: Hesitations on the Threshold[1]

Philippe Simonnot

Britain's businessmen are not fully convinced of the advantages of joining the Common Market. In the first place, they are tired of waiting. Initial enthusiasm has been replaced by a cool appraisal of the advantages and drawbacks of integration, despite the fact that all three political parties back Britain's entry. This is especially true in the city where a common view in banking circles is that "it doesn't matter much one way or the other whether we're in or not. Financial integration has happened already—thanks to the Euro-dollar."

The financial world gives due weight to the government statement that industry's gains will largely be offset by agriculture's losses. This impression was confirmed by a Treasury official close to the Chancellor of the Exchequer: "The advantages and disadvantages are roughly equal, especially if the effect of the progressive lowering of the common external customs tariff is taken into account. British membership in the Common Market is essentially a political issue." He wryly added that "political ministries stress the economic advantages of entering, economic ministries the political advantages."

The Confederation of British Industry quickly sensed the change in public feeling and attempted to rally its pro-Europe members and perhaps change the minds of the others, those whom an official of the National Economic Development Council described as the "peasants of British industry"—the owners of small- and medium-sized firms. These businessmen obviously fear that opened borders and Continental competition will force them to merge or vanish.

By contrast, the enormous and dynamic market offered by the neighboring Common Market tempts the giants of electronics, electrical engineering, chemicals, special steels, man-make fibers, ready-made clothing and distribution. Even so, the temptation is far from irresistible. First of all, these firms are well aware that lowered customs barriers are not synonymous with wide-open markets.

Reprinted by permission from *Le Monde*, Paris (Dec. 31, 1969) and *The Atlantic Community Quarterly*, Vol. 8, No. 1 (Spring 1970), pp. 67–75.

[1] In 1971 Britain is knocking at the door of the European Economic Community for the third time in eight years. Its entry was blocked the first two times by General De Gaulle's France. The prospects of success are greater this time even though public opinion in Britain itself is less solidly in favor of membership than it was before.

The Cost of Membership

Professor Wilfrid Beckerman, head of the Economics Department of University College, London, estimates that it will cost Britain the tidy sum of £1,000 million a year to join the Community. "This figure can be reached in two ways," he said. "The first is by taking the official figures. In 1967, Prime Minister Harold Wilson said the cost of entry would be £500 million. Since then, the pound has been devalued and the Community's surpluses have increased.

"Another way to calculate the cost is by adding up the various elements: £250 million for Britain's contribution to the agricultural financing arrangements; £200 to £250 million for the rise in UK agricultural prices; £100 million for the annual trade deficit with Europe that will occur because our tariffs are higher than those of the Six; another £100 million due to the loss of Commonwealth trade preferences. On top of this we shall lose European Free Trade Association advantages, and the rise in the cost of living, which some estimates put as high as 15 percent, will increase export prices, making us even less competitive on foreign markets."

There is heated debate about such estimates, which contain a degree of guesswork, and the pro-European camp has no difficulty in finding other arguments to put the issue in a less terrifying light. Indeed, Professor Beckerman is even more pessimistic than *The Guardian*, which strongly opposes British entry and has estimated the annual cost at a figure between £400 and £600 million.

The general lack of enthusiasm for integration with the Six might be due to indifference or it may be a question of sour grapes. If a public opinion poll were taken tomorrow, the majority would probably be against entry, as a recent sample survey showed. In the short run, the drawbacks appear to outweigh the advantages. And in the long run? As John Maynard Keynes quipped, in the long run we shall all be dead.

The average Briton is strongly attached to his country's national characteristics. To him, adoption of the metric system is a major token of goodwill to the Continent, at least as meaningful as running a balance of payments surplus for three successive months; and he would be shocked if anybody questioned this. It is true that he is now getting used to the idea that the Commonwealth is practically dead. He realizes that the island of Britain will have to be anchored to the "peninsula" across the Channel. But he is secretly troubled about the future and fears change.

One young businessman said: "We are better off outside the Common Market than in it, for the simple reason that we, like the Americans, can take advantage of the competition among Continental municipalities, who lean over backwards to attract foreign investors."

In view of this, for the export of goods to be more profitable than the export of capital, Britain must not pay too high an entry fee to the Common Market. If, for example, the Community's agricultural policy increased Britain's cost of living and, consequently, wage levels, the large corporations would suffer a corresponding reduction of profits.

The businessman and the man in the street see eye to eye on this issue. The

British consider the Common Market's agricultural policy to be a scandal, or at best a stupid blunder. If there is any one aspect of the Common Market that generates unanimity across the Channel, this is it. Naturally enough, the thought of the Six buried under mountains of surplus butter and drowning in oceans of milk is delightful; but more to the point is the feeling that these difficulties will enable Britain to avoid the imposition of a set of economic rules which run directly counter to economic principles that have been taken for granted since David Ricardo and the abolition of the Corn Laws. Moreover, the British are hoping that the Six will see reason on this during the negotiations.

In a speech before the European Monetary Conference in London last July, Secretary of the Treasury Harold Lever indicated that it would be unrealistic to expect Britain to repay its short-term debts in the near future. He said that the country was suffering the consequences of having acquired capital assets without having made adequate financing arrangements for them. But, Mr. Lever stressed, the assets were there.

Over-all British Debt

Within the over-all British debt the most difficult element to estimate is the volume of short-term indebtedness. Official figures disclose only the "swap" arrangements with the New York Federal Reserve Bank ($2,000 million) and other central banks ($1,500 million), a total of $3,500 million or £1,490 million.

But what is not known is the extent to which the Bank of England has drawn on the credits. Last July *The Times Business News* put the figure at £1,000 million. A certain amount of patriotic feeling among financial journalists concerning sterling should be taken into account however, and it can be assumed that the figure is not an overestimate.

Calculations are further complicated by the fact that the Bank of England also fails to reveal the amount of any repayments it may make. Again, the government has publicly disclosed only a part of the "swap" credits that it has negotiated. Others exist, and they increased the short-term debt to nearly £2,000 million at the end of 1968. This is an open secret, contained in publicly disclosed Treasury figures. During the first eleven months of 1969, however, Britain repaid about £370 million, reducing the short-term debt to a current figure of slightly more than £1,600 million.

The size of the medium- and long-term debt is less difficult to estimate. According to an official statement on November 18, it stood at £3,426 million, which included £1,990 million in debts contracted between 1945 and October 15, 1964, and £1,436 million in subsequent borrowing. Slightly more than half of this debt must be repaid before the end of 1975 and the rest by 2005.

Various statistical checks make it possible to estimate that Britain will have to pay out an average of £400 million a year over the next five years in interest and capital reimbursements. Even official figures put the cost of the medium- and long-term debt at £361 million, comprised of £271 million in capital repayments and £90 million in interest. After 1975 the average annual cost will fall to about £50 million.

It follows that if government achieves its target of the £300 million ʻannual surplus in the balance of payments, Britain will be barely able to meet its long-term debt obligations during the next five years. This year's balance of payments surplus will possibly exceed the target, but it is impossible to forecast the position for the next four years.

Sterling Balances

The sterling balances are sterling reserves held in London by central banks and private persons abroad following debts contracted by the British government during the war. Many central banks, especially those in the sterling area, which mainly comprises Australia, New Zealand, Hong Kong, Malaysia, Kuwait and a number of other oil sheikdoms, have deposited some of their sterling reserves in London under this system.

Until 1968, holders of sterling were tempted to convert their holdings to a stronger currency such as the dollar or the deutsche mark, but the Basel agreement of September 1968 lifted this Damocles sword from the head of Sir Leslie O'Brien, Governor of the Bank of England. This agreement guarantees 90 percent of "official" claims (that is, the sterling holdings of foreign central banks) by pegging them to the dollar, and provides for the dollar convertibility of unguaranteed amounts. Convertibility is secured through a $2,000-million credit from the Bank for International Settlements, which can be drawn on over three years starting in 1968, with repayments to be made between 1974 and 1978.

Some financial experts in the city still believe that in giving up the benefits to be gained from another devaluation in order to keep a part of the sterling balances, and in converting another portion of them from an uncertain short-term liability into a fixed long-term obligation, Britain paid too high a price for the financial security that it sought.

Most observers, however, are convinced that the present recovery is a direct consequence of the Basel agreement. The sterling balances no longer melt away like a snowball in the sun with every report, true or false, of adverse trends. This eliminates one problem for the Bank of England, which has its work cut out in discouraging speculation.

The sterling balances totalled £2,788 million in September 1968, whereas last June they stood at £3,106 million. And although between March and June this year the Bank of England drew on the credit opened by the Bank for International Settlements, this loan has been repaid and the $2,000-million credit remains practically intact.

It should, however, be noted that although the central banks have increased their holdings in sterling balances, those held by the private sector (banks, individuals, etc.) have declined. This is understandable, since they are not covered by the guarantee. But it remains true that, overall, the Basel agreement has worked well, mainly because of the guarantee.

The agreement extends only until the end of 1971, however, and the prospects for further negotiations on the sterling balances is bound to be discussed when Britain and the Six reach the conference table.

Britain's total indebtedness—short-, medium- and long-term debts, plus the sterling balances—is a staggering £8,000 million, whereas Bank of England reserves are scarcely more than £1,000 million. The figures eloquently describe the precariousness of this inverted pyramid.

Even if the sterling balances can be considered to be absolutely frozen, the total debt stands at £5,000 million, of which over £3,000 million is represented by short- and medium-term debts, whose cost far exceeds even the most optimistic estimate of the British balance of payments surplus over the next few years.

Moreover, there should be no illusions about the third-quarter surplus that made headlines in the British press, for figures were based only on the current account and long-term capital movements and did not include short-term capital flow. But in the same quarter the monetary disturbances that followed devaluation of the franc and speculation on the deutsche mark, the Dutch florin, the Belgian franc and the yen led to an outflow of "hot money" totalling £267 million.

As the announced surplus was only £217 million, the Bank of England lost £5 million in reserves and increased its short-term debt by £45 million. In other words, the third-quarter in fact registered a deficit of £50 million and not a surplus of £217 million.

In all fairness it must be added that the stabilization of the international monetary system since October has resulted in the return of an appreciable amount of short-term capital to London.

Compared with the past few years, in which the British debt continued to increase, 1969 has been the year in which Britain, overall, has managed the relative exploit of reducing its short-term obligations by between £300 and £400 million and its medium-term debt by £100 to £150 million.

The Bank of England's prime object has clearly been to free itself from the "gnomes of Zurich" and to lay the ghost of its short-term debt. The fact remains that next year Britain will have to consolidate either its short-term debt, as recommended by Mr. Lever when he was Secretary of the Treasury, or its medium-termed debt, by negotiating an agreement similar to the June 1969 accord with the International Monetary Fund. Without this Britain is unlikely to be able to meet its obligations, totalling £2,000 million, on both fronts. This is another question that is bound to come up in the negotiations on entry into the Common Market.

Technology and Markets

The recently created Ministry of Technology claims that British technology is as advanced as any in the world, including the United States, and that in some fields, including nuclear-produced electricity, it is far ahead.

In itself an indication of how seriously technology is taken in Britain, the ministry covers a wide range of industrial activities. It is clearly too early to appraise the effects of such a high degree of administrative concentration, but there seems to be a certain amount of skepticism among those directly concerned.

It is almost as though the government was unable to resist following, on the administrative level, the trend to concentration in British industry. This trend is reflected in Board of Trade statistics which show a decline of 31 percent, from 1,312 to 908, in the number of companies quoted on British stock exchanges and having net assets exceeding £500,000. The twenty-eight largest companies now account for 50 percent of industry's total net assets. In 1961 they accounted for 39 percent. This trend to concentration has been particularly marked in the food and drink, chemicals, car, textile and clothing, construction materials and electrical industries.

The key economic words in the Britain of today are "concentrations," "merger," "reorganization," etc. And whereas ten years ago Britain was sending experts to Paris to study economic planning, today it is the French who make the pilgrimage to London to examine the famous Industrial Reorganization Corporation.

Mergers in Britain are often carried out through take-over bids and primarily for financial reasons. Industrial output has increased substantially and, as the chart shows, per capita output has increased more rapidly than industrial output from 1967 while employment figures fell.

The biggest increase in output has been registered by the textile industry, followed by the production and distribution of gas, water and electricity. The slowest progress has been made in the car industry, metal working and mines.

Although Britain was the birthplace of the entrepreneur, attention is now focused on American management techniques. This interest is apparent at the Ministry of Technology and the Industrial Reorganization Corp., in the economic press and also in such bodies as the Northern Regional Planning Council. The head of this organization, T. Dan Smith, says he favors American investment in British industry mainly because it brings with it American management techniques.

The problem of economic growth lies in the fact that for a number of years the industrial working population has been static and that, unlike some European countries, Britain cannot draw on labour reserves from agriculture. Thus it will have to rely on increased productivity, to insure that this is not offset by declining employment levels such as have been observed over the past four years.

Economic Advantages

This is an important point in the context of Britain's prospective entry into the Common Market, for if the Six lower their customs barriers to British products there will be less incentive for British firms to set up production facilities across the Channel. Profiting, as in the past, from the Common Market's dynamism, British companies would be able to create new jobs.

On the whole, it seems to be to Britain's advantage to exchange the Commonwealth market for the one offered by the Common Market. In the first place, the traditional British industries are finding it much less easy to sell to the Commonwealth because of tariff barriers and because local industries are becoming increasingly competitive. At the same time, the technologically advanced industries do not, as yet, have a sufficiently extensive Commonwealth market to provide an adequate yield on their enormous capital investments.

Thus, traditional industry is condemned to decline and only the European Six can provide the technologically advanced industries with a profitably expanding market.

The figures speak for themselves. From 1958 to 1968 British exports to the Commonwealth rose by 26 percent, but exports to the Common Market more than doubled and exports to the United States almost tripled.

It thus seems that, despite the reticence, indifference or even hostility of some Britons concerning entry into the Common Market, the move carries with it distinct economic advantages which cannot be ignored and which, taken collectively, probably slightly outweigh the avowed disadvantages.

The short-term effects of membership would almost certainly be unfavorable, but in the long run the outlook is encouraging. The British negotiators are sure to be tough when they encounter representatives of the Six next year, but this will be because they are seeking, as is natural, the best terms possible rather than because, secretly, they want to see the talks fail.

The coming negotiations are likely to mark the end of Britain's long history as a tight little island.

Problems in the Central American Common Market

Vincent Cable

For some years the Central American Common Market (CACM) has been surrounded by a certain euphoria. Rapid growth in regional trade, favorable growth trends in extraregional exports and a relative absence of conflict between members on matters of economic strategy have helped to sustain it. However, two problems in particular have grown in importance and seem seriously likely to jeopardize future progress. (First, all the five countries now face deteriorating payments positions. Second, the fact that this is partly due in certain cases to imbalances in regional trade has brought once again into prominence the issue of 'balanced growth'.) The last attempt to resolve these problems (and particularly the former) was the San José Protocol of June 1968, which imposed a 30-percent surcharge on the common external tariff for non-essential imports and allowed individual countries to impose consumption taxes on a wide range of goods produced within the region: 10 percent on non-essentials and 20 percent on luxuries. The refusal of Costa Rica to ratify this Protocol has created an even more difficult impasse.

Balance of Payments Crisis

The 1960s have generally been a period of economic boom in Central America, with real annual growth rates for 1960–65 varying between 4.0 percent (Costa Rica) and 8.3 percent (Nicaragua) and an over-all annual rate for the region of about 6.3 percent (or about 2.5 percent per head) compared with 4.5 percent for 1950–1955 and 4.4 percent for 1955–60. The increase in growth is explained partly by favorable conditions for the export of primary products and partly by the dynamism of the manufacturing sector, following the liberalization of regional trade.

The deficit on current account in the balance of payments has however increased strikingly, since 1963–64 in particular. In 1967 Honduras, Guatemala and Nicaragua registered record deficits of U.S.$40m., U.S.$80m. and U.S.$50m. (approximate) respectively, while Costa Rica and El Salvador were recovering from record deficits sustained in 1965 and 1966. The cumulative current-account deficit of the region with the outside world now appraoches U.S.$300m., having climbed steadily from a position of near-balance in 1961.

Reprinted by permission of the Bank of London & South America (*Review*, Vol. 3, No. 30, June 1969, pp. 336–346).

This might not have mattered unduly if there had been a favorable trend on capital account. Inflows of private long-term capital and government transfers (aid) have increased steadily and up to 1965 more than outweighed the current-account deficit in all the countries except Costa Rica. However, they have not been adequate and in 1966 (El Salvador) and 1967 (Nicaragua) individual countries had to draw substantially on their reserves. The unfavorable outlook for loans, aid and investment, in view of U.S. restrictions, and the need to service existing debts and investments gives additional cause for concern. Outflows of capital have also represented a problem, explaining the exchange controls instituted in El Salvador in 1961 and Guatemala in 1962.

There are several reasons for the growing trade deficit, which has risen despite an increase in the volume of exports (greater than that in the volume of imports from outside the region for 1960–66), reflecting a rapid expansion in cotton production in Nicaragua and Guatemala, a temporary boom in the banana industry and the expansion of coffee sales overseas. The main factors making for a growth in the deficit are as follows:

(a) The terms of trade for the primary products on which Central America largely depends have deteriorated (though this applies less to bananas than to coffee and cotton), despite a degree of stabilization over the 1964–66 period. Long-term prospects, especially in coffee and cotton, look no better, and there has so far been only slow progress in developing export lines with better prospects, such as fish or meat products.

(b) The low prices are beginning to have an effect on the quantity of some crops produced, while adverse weather has reduced output in others, especially cotton. Also, the International Coffee Organization is making arrangements to reduce the amount of coffee available for export.

(c) Despite a vigorous industrial import-substitution policy, imports from outside Central America have risen from about 18 percent of the total regional GDP in 1961 to 21 percent in 1966. The totals included surprising increases, such as in foodstuffs, of which imports almost doubled over this period. Thus, much of the increase in demand attracted imports from outside the region, though this varied greatly according to the type of product.

(d) The ratio of consumer-goods imports from outside Central America to total consumption fell from 9 percent in 1961 to 6 percent in 1966. Much of this decline was accounted for by regional trade in manufactures, which has served the important function of cushioning the supply of consumer goods at a time of relatively declining import capacity. There are, however, great variations between the countries: Guatemala imports very little in finished consumer goods while for Honduras and Nicaragua the import-consumption ratio is 10 percent and rising, though an increasing share of the imports is being supplied from the CACM. Imports of durable consumer goods are becoming more important, and it is difficult to manufacture these products locally with significant local value added. There have been increased imports of higher-grade textiles and artificial fabrics, replacing locally produced cheap cottons to some extent.

(e) Only very recently has the CACM moved into its "second stage" of local production of the more advanced intermediate products, though by 1964 chemical fertilizers and petroleum fuels had become the most important and fastest-growing products in regional trade. Large-scale production of pulp and paper, and possibly of steel, will begin in the next few years. Meanwhile, imports of these products from outside the region have also continued to rise (from 6 percent to 8 percent of the aggregate GDP in 1961–66) and the further import substitution proceeds the greater is the derived demand for chemical and fuel imports, which is only satisfied locally after a lag—if at all. The manufacturing process itself sets up further import requirements and this may become an additional, rapid and costly addition to the balance of payments, unless full and prompt advantage is taken of the "linkages" that present themselves.

(f) Similar considerations apply to imported capital goods, which constitute 40–50 percent of total fixed investment. For those industries that package, mix or assemble imported ingredients or components, the cost to the balance of payments of the imported components and machinery may be no less than the exchange saved on importing the final product. This problem, especially if the proliferation of assembly plants is not halted, can be expected to intensify as there is nothing remotely like an indigenous machine-tool industry in Central America for standardized machinery, not even on a small scale. Some progress, however, has been made in producing building materials locally; cement has been manufactured in Central America for several years.

(g) The Central American countries have usually suffered an unfavorable balance of payments on invisible account, especially Guatemala and El Salvador, because most shipping charges, insurance and other services are covered outside the region. Tourism has scarcely developed in Central America, and until it does one cannot expect to see this imbalance reversed.

There are thus several factors at work. Some of them, such as the growing demand for fuels and capital goods, and some intermediate goods, are predictable and unavoidable concomitants of industrial growth. Imports of certain consumer goods are avoidable, however, and continued growth of the market, or import controls on luxury items, should eliminate them—though the need for agrarian reform and assistance to the small farmer may be a precondition for eliminating imports of foodstuffs. The problem of increasing exports of primary products is a long-term one of shifting investment into products which enjoy a more elastic demand in the world market, and Central America has so far made little progress in this direction. The same is also true of the development of tourism. Thus, Central America is running into a serious and rigid balance-of-payments problem for which the solution lies mainly in long-term structural changes.

Problems of Unequal Development

For at least two of the five partners the problem is aggravated by the way in which the CACM has affected trade flows within the region: Honduras and even more Nicaragua are running increasing deficits with their partners. If all world trade were freely multilateral, an imbalance with one or another country would not matter in the least as imports would come from the cheapest source, but in a common market, with a generally high external tariff like Central America's, there is a difference in that the deficit countries are buying at higher prices than on the world market ('trade diversion') and when the subsequent payments are settled in convertible currency (as they are) the deficit countries are granting the surplus countries a foreign-exchange subsidy. Also, if the deficit country buys from its partner and this involves giving up a policy of producing for home consumption in the absence of a common market, then additional opportunities for exchange saving (as well as employment generation) may be foregone, though there may be a price saving to offset this. Of course, this is only one side of the picture: the deficit countries also export to the CACM and where their industries depend on that market there is a gain to the national balance of payments while the process also involves the mobilization of unemployed resources at home. In fact, in the absence of the CACM, the country would normally have had to import from somewhere, because its domestic market was inadequate for local production. Thus the Nicaraguan caustic soda plant, for example, is both import-saving and export-creating for Nicaragua, because of the operation of the Common Market. So, even if a country runs a deficit with its partner it may still be sharing positively in the over-all savings of foreign exchange generated by common market industrialization, and there is no strong reason to assume that this is not happening in Central America, though clearly the distribution of gains is far from equal.

No one so far has tried to quantify the benefits and losses to the various participants with anything like the thoroughness that has been shown in East Africa, for example. The following analysis is a very superficial account of the factors which should be taken into account. It presupposes that the union is generally beneficial, and it is a fair starting point to ask what are the net benefits that can be obtained. There is superficial evidence in the high rates of growth of regional trade in manufactured products, but to what extent does this result from the Common Market? Much trade would have taken place in any case, with improving transport links and increasing incomes from the agricultural export sector. An increasing amount of trade is in products with a very low local value added, and produced largely outside Central America. Nevertheless a large amount of the increased trade must have stemmed from the elimination of internal trade barriers and the equalization of the external tariff, and the effect of these on import-substitutive industrialization, though further research is needed to assess its quantitative significance.

Economic theory would lead us to argue by looking at "static" and "dynamic" effects separately. The first is normally concerned in terms of the trade-off of gains from more efficient specialization through trade (as opposed to autarkic production) and the costs of buying from possibly more expensive neighbors (as distinct from the world outside). The situation ruling at the inception of the CACM was suited to trade creation, in the sense that there was existing installed capacity in the traditional industries (textiles, foodstuffs, shoes and clothes) which was inefficiently used in the fragmented market. The CACM brought about greater competition, fuller use of capacity and greater specialization. The cost of living has risen very slowly in Central America and prices of textiles and other traditional goods have fallen or remained constant, as have those of cement and construction materials; all of this indicates that trade has led to a rationalization of industries. The opposite effect, of trade diversion, occurs where a country switches its source of imports to a more expensive common market source, often of poorer quality products, and this is particularly likely in the case of the more advanced industrial products requiring large plants and substantial protection. If one looks at the trade between Honduras and its partners it can be seen that Honduras runs a surplus on foodstuffs which depends very little on the Common Market (with virtually no help from the external tariff) and a substantial deficit in manufactured goods, which include several items at least that are highly protected. (This is also true of Nicaragua.) It would seem that net trade-creation benefits accrue to the more industrialized economies of El Salvador, Guatemala and Costa Rica, whereas Honduras and Nicaragua experience more trade diversion, assuming that the latter countries would otherwise have continued to import their manufactures from overseas instead of producing their own supplies. As Honduras and Nicaragua are now establishing industries like pulp and paper and caustic soda, which need much more protection than simpler manufactures such as footwear or clothes, they will inflict trade diversion on their partners. There is also another factor: trade creation may lead to the elimination of inefficient plants in the high-cost producers; this has affected Nicaragua especially. As the Central American countries, except perhaps Honduras, suffer from severe unemployment, the cost to the individual economies may outweigh the benefits of obtaining a cheaper product, and for this reason the trade creation/diversion concepts are of reduced significance.

The argument for common markets in developing countries and for the continuation of the CACM hangs substantially on the "dynamic" effects. These may be subdivided into *consolidation, expansion, new industry* and *external* effects, with the underlying assumption that common markets help the process of industrialization by import substitution to a level that would not otherwise be possible. The first factor, *consolidation*, relates to the scope for production-line specialization between competing plants mainly in traditional consumer products: this is known to have been important in the Central American textile industry, especially in El Salvador and Guatemala. The second, the *expansion* of existing plant in the same kind of industry, also relates to the scope for economies of scale. The third point refers to the possibility of establishing *new industries* that would not be viable nationally. The limits of the "threshold" capacity for certain investments are difficult to define because techniques and definitions of viability both vary, but attempts have been made by ECLA to identify industries that could be set up: pulp and paper, caustic soda and sulphuric acid, sheet glass, glass bulbs, tires and tubes, fertilizers and an integrated steel mill. A great deal has been done in investment in new industries: tires (Guatemala and Costa Rica), plastics (several), sulphuric acid and superphosphates (El Salvador), wire and cable (El Salvador), caustic soda and insecticides (Nicaragua), and refined oil products (all countries); most of these products, except perhaps refined oil products, depend on the CACM. Fourthly, there are *external* economies in the form of improved skills, improved transport and amenities which have derived from the CACM-based industries in industrial centres such as Guatemala City. Dynamic effects from new industries and external economies have become increasingly important in recent years.

The less-developed members of the CACM have made several complaints about the distribution of these benefits. Firstly, it is argued that new industries have been attracted to the traditional industrial centres because of external economies and other agglomerative features. This means that the traditional industrial areas, which have roads, water supplies, trained labor, and housing for managers, attract investment which itself helps to create more infrastructure and reduce the initial and operating costs for other investors; it is a virtuous circle until congestion begins to reduce the benefits.

With one or two exceptions (a modern textile factory in Honduras and the caustic soda and insecticide complex in Nicaragua) most large new projects appear to have been set up in El Salvador, Guatemala or Costa Rica. Where major projects have been earmarked unofficially for Honduras—the pulp and paper factory for one—it has been very difficult to implement them, presumably because of poor roads, lack of skilled labor and slow project preparation. It can also be said that in some cases smaller plants, which at least from the point of view of size could have been established in Nicaragua or Honduras on their national markets alone, have been set up in El Salvador or Guatemala (the term "shiftability" was applied to such industries in East Africa). The implicit assumption behind Nicaragua's threats to withdraw from the CACM is that several of these "shiftable" industries could be attracted to Nicaragua if it did not have to compete with the external economy attractions of the traditional locations.

Another attempt that has been made to provide a theoretical framework for the arguments about unbalanced growth is that of Dr. Gunnar Myrdal, who has distinguished "spread" and "backwash" effects generated by the rapidly growing regions, which would normally be the most industrially advanced. The spread effect depends on the fact that rapid growth to some extent generates a demand for the products of the poor and lagging regions. The backwash effect occurs when the developing area generates an attraction for capital (and labor if it is in short supply) from the poorer areas. In a case of marked regional disparity the backwash effect could be strong and the spread effect weak. In Central America it is clear that Honduras, which is less developed in terms of GNP per head, level of skills and industrial base, has enjoyed some spread effects in the form of increased agricultural exports to its partners. Nicaragua, which started from a low income level and a weak industrial base, has accelerated very rapidly mainly on the basis of cotton exports outside the region; it now has a higher income per head than El Salvador or Guatemala and can expect to improve its regional trade balance with exports from the large milk-products and caustic soda plants now operating. It seems that there has been a strong if temporary negative spread effect away from Nicaragua, because its primitive peasant agriculture and low level of industrialization have resulted in an overspill of domestic demand to the other common market countries. On the other hand it seems that Nicaragua's rapid growth has not made it more attractive to investors, doubtless partly because of high labor costs.

Backwash effects are probably very small in Central America, because there is little factor mobility. A more important point is that the CACM countries are competing for scarce capital resources, and overseas investment which might under planned development have gone to Honduras or Nicaragua has gone to the other states, because of historical location factors. Guatemala, which has 40 percent of the Central American population and 30 percent of the GDP, and a relatively large capital city, is a natural focus of activity in spite of its political instability. El Salvador has a traditionally dynamic private industrial sector which attracts investment more easily than agriculture, and also abundant cheap labor; too much overseas investment is discouraged and local participation is encouraged. Costa Rica has advantages of superiority in skills and level of industrial achievement and political maturity, but financial mismanagement has offset this to some extent.

As regards the commodity composition of regional trade, Honduras is an importer of finished and semifinished manufactured goods and exports largely agricultural products, though not enough to balance trade; it also exports substantial quantities of timber and some cement and chemical products. Honduras, it would seem, attracts as yet relatively few "dynamic" benefits, though probably the rise in its agricultural exports is by way of a spread effect; unfortunately agricultural exports are growing slowly and divergences are therefore widening.

In Nicaraguan trade with the CACM, there are serious imbalances in all sectors except for vegetable oils and raw materials, which reflect dependence on the cotton crop and its by-products. There will be a large output of chemicals for export from the new caustic soda complex, but at present Nicaragua runs a surplus only on minor manufactured items such as records, plywood and *machetes*. Thus far Nicaragua has gained relatively little from regional trade, and even the spread effect is negative.

The trade between Guatemala and El Salvador is the main element in regional trade, and though El Salvador dominates the chemical and manufactured goods categories, the trade pattern is not seriously unbalanced. It is important to note that whereas El Salvador has not, like Guatemala, run large net trading surpluses with its partners it has, as one of the main exporters of manufactured goods and an importer of food products, enjoyed the lion's share of the "dynamic" benefits. This was also increasingly true of Costa Rica, though it was held back by late entry into the CACM and a peripheral location; its main exports so far are fertilizers and some consumer goods, and it earned a relatively large regional surplus until its regional trade was driven gradually into deficit by uncertainties about its currency.

Policies for Balanced Growth

It cannot be said, however, that the CACM has entirely overlooked the question of "balanced growth," though it has never been clear whether active redistribution to the less-developed members was intended, or merely action to limit widening divergencies—perhaps more the latter. It was accepted in principle in 1958 that a completely free-market choice of investment location would lead to widening inequality, and both the Central American bank (BCIE) and the integration industries agreements were examples of an interventionist approach stopping short of integrated industrial planning.

By the end of 1968, the BCIE had disbursed U.S.$145m. Nicaragua and Honduras have been the two largest recipients, and the Bank's long-term importance perhaps lies in the provision of infrastructure, especially in Honduras. But the importance of the Bank can be exaggerated; most of its funds are provided by international and U.S. organizations, which would in any case have offered aid. Also, it is difficult to identify cases that the Bank actively promoted, or where it made the difference between a project starting or not. It should be stressed also that in Honduras at least the bottleneck is only partially financial; it is also one of skilled manpower.

The Integration Industries Agreement (1958) and the subsequent Special Industries Agreement (1963) giving concessions and what amounted to a monopoly position to important growth industries have had a very marginal effect. Under the first agreement the only industries to be classified have been a plate glass industry for Honduras (not yet established), the caustic soda complex in Nicaragua (heavily criticized because of its cost and its low added value) and the tire and tube factory in Guatemala. The main reasons put forward for this failure are the attitude of the U.S.A. (a principal source of funds) to the creation of multinational monopolies, the administrative complexities of the schemes, rivalry between competing areas and the unwillingness of investors to accept interference with their commercial choice of location. There has however been a recent revival of interest, with six more applications going forward.

The conclusion cannot be escaped that, despite their expressed concern, the five countries have not wholly accepted the principle of limiting, in the interest of greater balance, their freedom of choice in industrial policy. They have competed vigorously for investment by means of generous tax concessions[1] and no sanctions such as comprehensive licensing have been instituted to control location in the

---

[1] Until the entry into force in March 1969 of the Central American Industrial Incentives Agreement and its protocol granting Honduras preferential treatment.

region. As a result, most new industries have been attracted to Guatemala, El Salvador or Costa Rica; the Honduran projects—pulp and paper, plate glass and an integrated iron and steel plant—remain in the discussion stage while plans are being prepared elsewhere for competing installations.[2] Other projects, such as petroleum refining, have been multiplied in all the five countries as a result of over-generous concessions. Honduras is now permitted to offer more favorable concessions but the efficacy of this remains to be seen; if effective, the incentives can only lead to further duplication.

Partly as a result of this vigorously competitive attitude to overseas investment, the five countries are all faced by revenue problems. They are already relatively lightly taxed (8 percent of GNP in Guatemala to 12 percent of GNP in Costa Rica in 1965) and dwindling import duties provide a relatively large proportion of government revenue. Countries like Honduras and Nicaragua, which have substantially changed their source of manufactured imports to CACM partners, feel that not only do they forego the economic benefits of integration but also the financial benefits of self-sufficiency. This is politically touchy but something of a red herring: any policy of import substitution, regional or national, must result in the reduction of tariffs, some of them substantial revenue earners, and though the CACM limits the imposition of other taxes to compensate, there are many alternative approaches, such as raising income tax, which would capture for the governments some of the benefits of rapid industrial growth. In fact generous tax allowances, which have nothing to do with the Common Market *per se*, are one of the main causes of revenue problems and, as a great deal is wasted in the duplication of the projects, the allowances are economically unnecessary. A more rational allocation of industry would help to solve both revenue and balance-of-payments problems.

Economic and Political Solutions

There have been several key issues confronting the Central American countries over the past year. Seen in this light, the San José Protocol does not seem adequate. It might help to solve the relatively minor revenue problem, which could be solved more easily by raising income tax, tightening up on concessions, introducing property taxes, or levying export taxes on surplus commodities. The revenue effect of the San José import-duty surcharge is uncertain and will only be really effective if the effect on the volume of imports is small, which makes little sense from a balance of payments point of view; in increased direct taxation there is no such conflict of interest. The taxes on locally produced goods could help revenue and also reduce the protective effect on the increased import duty; otherwise there would be an additional incentive to produce, very uneconomically, various luxury

---

[2] See *Bank of London & South America Review*, Vol. 3, No. 30, June 1969.

consumer goods: on the other hand they could be used against products from other CACM countries, thus hampering regional trade. The increased duty makes Central America an even more heavily protected area than before, hindering future links with the LAFTA; it may also hinder new investment, and raise the cost of present plants, unless remission for imports necessary for industry is speedily and extensively obtained. Finally, the San José taxes may have inflationary effects if prices are given a permanent upward twist, though presumably it is intended that the measures should have the opposite effect, of reducing real incomes and therefore expenditure. So, as a revenue measure the Protocol is almost certainly tending in the wrong direction—away from direct taxation; the improvement to the over-all balance of payments resulting from reduced expenditure is unpredictable and may be achieved at high cost to the economies.

This does somewhat oversimplify the problems of trying to make a coordinated approach to several problems simultaneously within the CACM, which rules out such devices as devaluation by some of the members or the introduction of severe exchange restrictions: a surcharge on extraregional imports is easily and quickly imposed and does not in itself disturb trade within the community. Nevertheless one must regret the absence of more imaginative revenue measures; of different balance-of-payments protection measures (coordinated money supply and consumer credit restriction was a possibility); and of anything to help solve the growing imbalance problem which has its origin mainly in the unrestricted location of industry, and which can only really be overcome by a reactivation of something like the Integration Industries Agreement, and possibly financial compensation.

Thus also the basic political weakness of the CACM is revealed. It has been based essentially on a tacit alliance between technocrats in the governments and Ecla, on one hand, and the businessmen on the other. Politicians, in power or out, have been happy to be associated with economic progress, but have so far not been called upon to make a deeper political commitment. The present situation calls for politically difficult decisions: a more resilient and more exigent tax structure; land reform to stimulate local agriculture; greater willingness to sacrifice pet industrial projects so as to allow neighbors to catch up; more will to control the location of new foreign-owned plants; a readiness to tackle balance-of-payments problems in a deteriorating world market without attacking CACM partners. If Central America is to proceed successfully, it will need a greater degree of political involvement than has hitherto been demonstrated.

The LAFTA and Subregional Groups

William Beltrán

Since 1963 Latin America's progress toward economic unity has been slow and hesitant. It is now pertinent to evaluate recent achievements in this field, and to make a tentative assessment of the changes in direction and strategy that are taking place.

The LAFTA, which was formed in 1960 and today comprises all the South American republics and Mexico, had as its original aim the setting up of a free trade area through gradual liberalization, by 1973. In 1967, however, at the OAS meeting in Punta del Este, the horizon was enlarged to include the establishment of a common market by 1985, to unite the CACM and the LAFTA. Unfortunately the complexities of this venture have not yet been resolved, with the result that the probability of the Lafta's achieving its objectives by 1973, or of a Common Market being set up by 1985, seems remote.

The obstacles to regional integration are essentially structural in nature and present immediate difficulties, which will become more intractable and offer greater resistance as the scheduled date of 1973 approaches. They are the principal factors behind the delays experienced in liberalizing trade, both in granting new concessions on the "national lists" and in securing agreement on the second 25 percent (by value) of regional trade to be transferred, to the "common list."

Recent Achievements of the LAFTA

The eighth ordinary conference of the LAFTA, held in Montevideo from 21st October to 17th December 1968, produced, however, surprisingly favorable results. In all, 732 concessions were granted, of which 526 referred to new products and 206 to additional tariff cuts for products previously negotiated. In contrast to the large number of concessions granted in 1968, negotiations produced only 451 concessions in 1967, 501 in 1966, and 580 in 1965. As might be expected, the three largest countries in the Association—Argentina, Brazil and Mexico—accounted for more than 70 percent of the concessions granted in 1968. Also, nearly 60 percent of the concessions negotiated in national and special lists at the eighth conference originated in sectorial meetings held during 1968. This is a much higher

---

Reprinted by permission of the Bank of London & South America (*Review*, Vol. 3, No. 31, July 1969, pp. 425–429). Mr. Beltrán is on the staff of the Bank of London & South America.

proportion than the 25 percent negotiated in this way at the seventh conference, which assembled in Montevideo on 23rd October 1967.

The negotiations for the compilation of the common list have proved much less successful. The first quarter of the list, comprising 175 products which together made up just over 25 percent of the total value of trade between member-countries from 1960 to 1962, was finally agreed upon in 1964, after more than six months of negotiations. The second of the triennial rounds has not been completed, with the result that the full program of trade liberalization has little chance of coming into force by 1973.

Change in Direction

The limited scope of the LAFTA, and the nonachievement of its relatively modest objectives, have led to gradually diminishing confidence in its value. The problem is whether a free trade area can provide sufficient safeguards and incentives to enable the "less-developed" republics of Latin America to profit from the increase in intraregional trade, so as to develop their own economic expansion and social welfare; experience so far suggests that it cannot. The structural differences exist not only between member-countries but also within the individual republics. In addition the principle of reciprocity of benefits and the special safeguard clauses for the smaller and less-developed countries have been insufficient to ensure an over-all equitable growth. The "development gap" exists, and to all intents and purposes has become larger in recent years; this state of affairs has given rise to movements towards subregional integration, as embodied in the Andean and River Plate groups. The change in direction can be explained partly by the growth of economic nationalism, and also by dissatisfaction with the LAFTA's progress, coupled with the desire of the less-developed countries to face up to, on equal terms, the three more powerful economies of Argentina, Brazil and Mexico.

The Andean Group

The agreement formally setting up the Andean Group was signed in Bogotá on 26th May 1969, almost two years after the first meeting of the joint committee of representatives of the Andean countries in Viña del Mar in June 1967. Six countries (Bolivia, Chile, Colombia, Ecuador, Peru and Venezuela) are interested in the project, but only the first five signed the agreement.

Venezuela was actively represented in all the negotiations but, because of pressure from its private manufacturing sector, abstained from signing. The main argument offered in favor of abstention was that duty-free imports from the other five countries, with their lower labor costs, would have a detrimental effect on the Venezuelan economy. At first sight the claim seems reasonable: on purely economic grounds it could be argued that, in the short term, Venezuela's new industrial sector would lose more than it would gain from joining the Andean Group. In the long term, however, the advantages of forming part of a common market would outweigh the short-term disadvantages; a certain degree of rationalization will inevitably take place but this must ultimately be for the good of the Group as a whole. Venezuela has decided differently, though there is an 18-month grace period during which it can obtain full founding membership, if a different view comes to prevail.

The total population of the five Andean Group countries is about 53m.; the total area is nearly half that of the U.S.A. and, as an economic unit, the combined market will be larger than in any country in Latin America except Brazil. Annual income per head in the group ranges from U.S.$160 in Bolivia to U.S.$510 in Chile.

Under the terms of the agreement all restrictions on intraregional trade are to be eliminated by the end of 1970. This refers to all products already included or to be included in the "common list" of the Montevideo Treaty, and also commodities not yet produced in the member-countries. This procedure does not apply, however, to products that the contracting parties wish to consider under special industrial development schemes.

The Andean Group will also adopt a common external tariff for its foreign trade by the end of 1980, in two stages. Firstly, before 31st December 1970 the Economic Commission of the Group is expected to approve a draft for a "minimum" common external tariff, whose primary objectives will be to ensure adequate protection for subregional products; to establish progressively a subregional preferential margin; and to facilitate the adoption of the common external tariff and increase productivity within the region. From the end of 1971 the contracting parties will begin negotiations on the draft, so as to bring the minimum common external tariff into force by 31st December 1975. Secondly, a proposal for a complete common external tariff, to be prepared by the Administrative Council of the Group before the end of 1973, will be submitted to the Economic Commission for consideration and approval, and by 31st December 1974 the member-countries will begin to negotiate the common external tariff on an annual, automatic and across-the-board basis to ensure that the scheduled date of 1980 is maintained.

If the Andean Group serves its intended purpose, a large volume of the five countries' imports from the developed countries will be replaced by purchases among the member nations. The loss to the developed countries' trade may be balanced to some extent by the strengthening of the over-all economy of the Andean Group; it is expected that this will produce a demand for capital goods in quantities that the five countries individually would not have required. It is estimated that if the Andean Group can match the rate of growth in intraregional trade recorded by the CACM in its first five years, total intraregional trade will expand from about U.S.$100m. at present to U.S.$500m. by 1975, ten years before the Latin American Common Market conceived by the meeting at Punta del Este is due to come into effect.

The River Plate Group

The drive towards subregional economic integration was also evident when on 23rd April 1969 the Foreign Ministers of Argentina, Bolivia, Brazil, Paraguay and Uruguay signed a treaty in Brasília for the economic integration and joint development of the River Plate Basin, which will become effective after ratification by the five countries concerned.

The treaty has as its primary objective the "geographical integration" of the region on an infrastructure basis; plans for building port installations, improving communications systems and exploiting energy resources are all under consideration. Furthermore, the door remains open for closer economic integration by means of commercial and industrial complementation agreements, which at present seem to be one of the more hopeful signs of economic cooperation in Latin America.[1]

Conclusion

Whether to concentrate on free trade on a regional level, or on subregional economic integration, as preliminaries to setting up a Latin American Common Market, constitutes South America's latest economic dilemma. The Montevideo Treaty has already revealed its inherent weaknesses, whereas subregional integration, apart from that in Central America, is still young. The near future will show whether the affinities of the countries forming the subregional groups are strong enough to provide an adequate framework for greater progress toward full continental integration.

Appendix

Industrial Complementation Agreements

Agreement on data-processing equipment signed by Argentina, Brazil, Chile and Uruguay on 20th July 1962.

Agreement on radio and television valves signed by Argentina, Brazil, Chile, Mexico and Uruguay on 18th February 1964.

---

[1] For a list of the industrial complementation agreements signed to date, see Appendix.

Agreement on domestic electrical equipment signed by Brazil and Uruguay on 2nd June 1966.

Agreement on chemical products signed by Argentina, Brazil, Colombia, Chile, Mexico, Peru, Uruguay and Venezuela on 19th December 1967.

Agreement on petrochemical products signed by Bolivia, Colombia, Chile and Peru on 28th July 1968.

Agreement on household appliances signed by Argentina and Uruguay on 27th August 1968.

LDC Regional Markets:
Do They Work?

During the late 1950s and early 1960s, a large number of developing countries in Asia, Africa and Latin America decided to follow the example of Western European countries which had, within the framework of economic integration schemes, recovered rapidly from the devastating effects of the Second World War. Through integration, it was hoped, higher rates of economic growth would be attainable and rapid industrialization made possible.

The attractiveness of economic cooperation to the governments of developing countries is considerable since most of these countries have small domestic markets by any economic standard. The developing world now totals about one hundred independent, non-communist countries, of which two-thirds have a population of less than ten million and an average population of only three million. More than half have a gross national product of less than one billion dollars and an average gross national product of only $400 million.

Sustained and rapid economic growth on the basis of small domestic markets alone is impossible. In these situations, the opportunity to export is crucial. Traditionally, the less developed countries (LDCs) are exporters of massive quantities of agricultural products and industrial raw materials, but for most of the agricultural commodities export prospects are far from favorable. Exports of manufactures from less developed countries to developed countries are usually small, although a few successful exceptions should be noted (Taiwan, Hong Kong, among others).

On the whole, production of goods in developing countries takes place on too small a scale, as a result of which production costs are relatively high. On top of this, producers in industrialized countries often enjoy substantial protection. It seems natural, therefore, that developing countries should look among themselves for markets, particularly markets for industrial products, which would enable them to pursue their policy of industrialization. Partly as a result of promotional work done by the regional commissions of the United Nations (Economic Commissions for Latin America, for Africa and for Asia and the Far East), economic integration appeared to be an attractive framework for economic cooperation among developing nations. In some cases, as in East Africa and in Central Africa, the

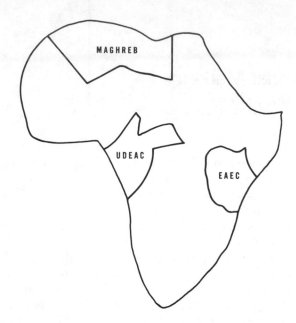

countries could confine themselves to restructuring cooperative schemes inherited from the colonial period, but in most, entirely new schemes had to be set up.

A number of these plans have now been functioning long enough to warrant an assessment of their performance. Have they brought the benefits they were supposed to bring? If they failed to do so, and there appears to be growing disenchantment among both cooperating partners and outsiders who are asked to support them financially and technically, why did they fail? Are the prospects for successful economic integration among developing countries as poor as many observers claim? If so, are alternative forms of economic cooperation more attractive?

The experience of six LDC regional markets may provide some answers to these questions. All other existing integration schemes are excluded because they are of too recent origin or because they exist in name only. The six to be discussed are:

(1) East African Economic Community (EAEC)—Kenya, Uganda and Tanzania;

(2) Central African Customs and Economic Union (UDEAC)—at present Congo (Brazzaville), Gabon, Cameroon and Central African Republic (Chad left the Union in 1968);

(3) Maghreb Common Market (Maghreb)—Algeria, Tunisia, Morocco and Libya;

(4) Central American Common Market (CACM)—Guatemala, Nicaragua, Honduras, El Salvador and Costa Rica;

(5) Latin American Free Trade Area (LAFTA)—all the South American republics plus Mexico;

(6) Regional Cooperation for Development (RCD)—Turkey, Iran and Pakistan.

Regional but Small

Although the six are designated regional markets, some of them are still small economic units. Table 1 gives figures on population and gross domestic product. EAEC, UDEAC and CACM are definitely small markets; only RCD and LAFTA have attained substantial size in economic terms, while the Maghreb occupies an intermediate position. While data relate to a recent year, due to statistical problems they should not be taken to represent more than rough orders of magnitude.

The Economic Size of Six Regional Markets

Grouping	Population (Million)	Gross Domestic Product (Billions of U.S. Dollars)
East African Economic Community	30.0	2.5
Central African Customs and Economic Union	8.5	1.0
Maghreb	33.0	7.5
Central American Common Market	14.0	4.0
Latin American Free Trade Area	220.0	90.0
Regional Cooperation for Development	180.0	27.0

Population data are for the year 1967; GDP relates to 1965/66.

Table 1.

Institutionally, all schemes are very similar. The policy-making authority consists of either the Heads of State or Ministers, with an executive committee preparing most of the recommendations to be approved by the authority. The committee is usually assisted by a varying number of commissions and sub-commissions as well as by a secretary general with a permanent secretariat. In no case, however, have the cooperating countries been prepared to delegate any decision-making power to a supranational authority. This factor and the lack of sufficiently qualified personnel to prepare good regional studies have generally hampered progress toward a regionally integrated economy, particularly in the industrial field. However, most of the integration schemes at present in existence are well structured, at least in principle.

Since the promotion of intraregional trade is one of the major objectives of regional integration schemes, progress on the abolition of restrictions on trade is one of the major indicators of a scheme's success. At the same time, wide divergencies can be noted in the scope of the integration agreements, and complete freedom of intraregional trade is usually seen as a long-term objective only. The current situation can be summarized as follows: in two (RCD and Maghreb), trade liberalization has not yet begun and is being preceded by a number of other measures; in three (LAFTA, CACM and UDEAC), trade liberalization has begun but is not yet completed; and in one case (EAEC), a virtually completed common market, the pressure of circumstances has compelled acceptance of the principle of trade discrimination vis-à-vis partner countries. In order to avoid too great imbalances in intraregional trade and to give some protection within the regional market to the industrially less developed countries of Uganda and Tanzania, the latter two countries can, under certain circumstances, impose so-called transfer taxes on imports from within the regional market. Although such transfer taxes have a temporary character, they obviously conflict with the principle of regional free trade.

Trade liberalization itself does not necessarily lead to actual trade. Not only might trade be physically impossible because transport and communications facilities are lacking, but also countries might have a similar economic structure, producing more or less the same commodities. For this reason, some countries have preferred to build up complementary industrial sectors first—as in RCD—and free trade subsequently.

Another factor which has proved an important obstacle to the growth of intraregional trade is the absence of a monetary agreement among partner countries, which would regulate the currency in which balances arising out of intraregional trade would be settled. A convenient arrangement appears to be one where a clearing mechanism is set up through which balances are paid in convertible currency.

In general, both within and between regions, large variations in trade can be noted. In East Africa, Central Africa and Central America, intraregional trade is undoubtedly important. Within each of these groupings, however, it is clearly more important to some countries than to others. For example, 35 percent of Kenya's trade in recent years was directed at its common market partners, while for Tanzania this proportion reached only 7 percent. Similar variations occur in Central Africa and Central America, although they are less marked. In LAFTA, intraregional trade has constituted a considerable proportion of total external trade in the case of Paraguay and Argentina, but for all other countries it is less than 10 percent. Most of the products traded intraregionally are raw materials and semiprocessed commodities.

Where intraregional trade is important, it is difficult to say whether it is dependent on the integration agreement. In other words, available evidence seems to suggest that much of the trade taking place at present would have taken place anyway, even in the absence of trade liberalization. The fact that manufactures occupy a relatively minor position in total intraregional trade, rarely exceeding 20 percent of the total, seems to point to the conclusion that in terms of industrialization, economic integration has not yet brought many benefits.

Industrialization

Most developing countries have now achieved a modest degree of industrialization. Although generalizations in this respect are dangerous, it can be said that the pattern of industrial growth in most of these countries is often similar. This is obvious. Unless specific resources permit a different pattern, the first industrial ventures will be directed toward the domestic market, and all the countries being poor, the structure of demand will be more or less the same.

A cement factory, a brewery, some light metal working, processing of agricultural products and some textile manufacturing are among the typical components of a young industrial sector. Whenever this general picture emerges, it is clear that regional integration will pose a number of important problems. If all intraregional trade is freed, the various small industries will become competitors, and without corrective measures, the existence of some might be threatened. Obviously, no country will be prepared to let this happen, and all would seek protective measures within the region.

Secondly, the wider market will open up possibilities for new investments in the industrial sector. Without intervention these would be located in the country which is most attractive economically—although culture, politics and climate also play important roles. In most regional markets, this tendency has led to a substantial concentration of industrial and other economic activities within the integrated area, resulting in widely varying rates of growth for the different industrial sectors. Tensions have run high on this issue, and numerous forms of compensation and correction have been introduced. On the whole, however, the impact of corrective measures has been disappointingly small, and the unequal distribution of new industrial activity and growth within an integrated area is without doubt the greatest danger threatening the viability of economic integration schemes.

A third factor of importance relates to the size of the industrial sectors of countries embarking upon a policy of economic integration. If the market is large, as in the case of LAFTA, there is a good chance that one or more countries are industrially more advanced than others in the same region. Following trade liberalization, the industrially backward countries by definition cannot protect new domestic industry from regional imports, which will in most cases harm local industrial development. There seems to be little point for a country in that situation to join an integration program, unless it receives special tariff concessions or unless certain regionally oriented industries are, by mutual agreement, located within its borders. Depending on the degree of advancement of the industrialized partners, such industries might be difficult to identify.

Problems Common to All

Most of these problems have in fact occurred among the six integration programs. In UDEAC the distribution of industries serving the whole of the customs union appears uneven. They can be easily identified because such enterprises are exempt from all import duties and internal indirect taxes and are subject to a unique regional tax. In 1965, thirty firms received such favorable treatment, of which eighteen were located in Congo (Brazzaville), six in the Central African Republic and six in Chad.

In 1968, Chad and the Central African Republic left the customs union, partly

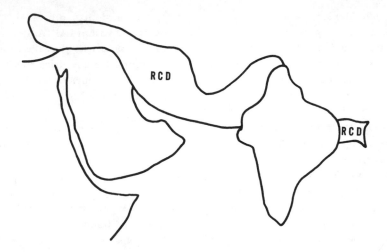

as a result of alleged unfair distribution of costs and benefits within the integration plan. The latter country has now rejoined the customs union. On the whole, there seems no doubt that location in UDEAC of those industries which serve more than one country's market has been the most frequent source of controversy in that region. Congo, Cameroon and Gabon have resisted industrial coordination strongly, preferring fiscal compensation measures, while Chad and the Central African Republic have strongly insisted on some kind of industrial allocation, given their natural disadvantages as inland states.

In East Africa, uneven growth rates of the industrial sector have been repeatedly subjected to corrective measures of all kinds. The East African experience shows clearly how difficult it is to set up an effective compensation plan if some of the preconditions to successful integration are not fulfilled. Corrective measures of a fiscal nature never fully satisfied anybody. A plan whereby various industries were allocated by country failed, partly because Kenya never ratified the agreement, and partly because investors for those industries allocated to Tanzania and Uganda were not forthcoming. At present, a highly complicated internal transfer tax system is in operation, designed to give some protection to Uganda and Tanzania, vis-á-vis Kenya, but it is too early to evaluate its success. In addition, the East African Development Bank is supposed to favor industrial investments in Uganda and Tanzania.

In the Maghreb, no progress whatever has been made in concrete terms with respect to common-market-induced industrial development. The industrial sectors of Algeria, Morocco and Tunisia are to an important extent competitive, and it has proved difficult to devise some system whereby trade is gradually freed, and future industrial growth is of a complementary rather than a competitive nature.

In LAFTA, the different degrees of industrialization among member countries have proved a major handicap to progress in the field of integration. Argentina,

Brazil and Mexico are industrially much more advanced than the other LAFTA members, and it was soon clear that without protection within LAFTA, the smaller countries would not be able to benefit in terms of industrial growth. A special status was accordingly granted to them. Three categories of countries now exist in LAFTA: developed members, less developed members and members with insufficient markets, the latter two groups of countries being entitled to special treatment on the scheduled abolition of tariffs.

So far, these measures have not led to more impressive rates of industrial growth, and the establishment of the Andean Group within LAFTA, comprising Bolivia, Chile, Colombia, Ecuador and Peru, reflects to some extent the dissatisfaction felt by these countries with the present LAFTA scheme.

In Central America, the common market has probably had a positive effect on industrial growth. Several industries have been established which probably would not have been without a guaranty of regional free trade for their products. However, wide divergencies are present here in terms of industrial growth: El Salvador growing fastest (and with initially the largest industrial sector), and Honduras staying hopelessly behind. Special measures have now been taken to aid Honduran industrialization, but they have not yet had the desired effect.

In RCD, an entirely different approach to integration has been chosen, one which has avoided remarkably well most of the problems that more conventional approaches have invariably developed. It was decided that, before any trade could be freed, complementary industrial sectors had to be set up in the three countries and good transport links established. Accordingly, the countries have proceeded to select a large number of industries which would be viable on a regional basis only and determined their location. So far, each country believes that it is getting its fair share of industrial growth. UNCTAD has now completed a study on liberalization and expansion of intraregional trade in RCD. It was discussed during a joint session of the Ministers of Planning and of Commerce in June 1970.

By and large, in all the regions achievements in the field of industrial growth have been smaller than expected and significantly higher regional trade has not been attained. Recent studies in East Africa, for example, show that few industries are dependent on the common market. What seems to have taken place in most integration programs, with the exception of RCD, is that industrial development plans have continued to be based on effective domestic demand for industrial products rather than on regional demand, intraregional trade prospects being treated similarly to extraregional trade prospects. Such cases reflect a lack of confidence on the part of national planners in the continuation of access to the markets of regional partners.

Achievements

Although the record of performance with respect to industrialization, one of the major objectives of economic integration, is not impressive, a number of achievements may be noted in other fields. Some of these relate to the preconditions of effective integration, such as good transport and communications links. Large investments have been made in these fields, and in some cases a common administration has been set up to this end. A common airline, common postal and telecommunications facilities, common customs administration and some form of integrated technical and university education system are often in operation. Where they exist, they have generally been found to be beneficial to partner countries.

However, again due to conflicts with national objectives, some of these common services have been gradually dismantled—particularly in East and Central Africa, where they were initially most important—and replaced by national institutions. In East Africa, for example, the East African Currency Board was replaced by three national Central Banks, and the University of East Africa is gradually being divided into three national universities. In Central Africa, the common postal and telecommunications agency was discontinued, as was the central administration of customs revenue. The University of Brazzaville, initially a regional institution, is gradually becoming a national university. In all other regions, including Central America, common infrastructural projects and the operation of common services began much later and are in the process of being built up.

The question thus arises whether regional integration is, for developing countries, a convenient policy to accelerate economic growth. A major problem in answering this question is the difficulty of ascertaining with any degree of accuracy what would have happened to the economic development of the countries concerned had they not joined an integration plan. Trends in rates of growth of total production and trade are usually too erratic and too dependent on factors having little to do with economic integration itself to serve as a guideline. The identification of all effects related to economic integration is usually impossible due to data limitations. Moreover, some might argue that it is too early to judge.

In some of the smaller developing countries, the possibility of efficient production on the basis of the domestic market alone still exists, or in economic jargon, the import-substitution potential is not yet exhausted. Capital (foreign and domestic), technical skills and managerial ability are much more important constraints on economic growth than is the limited domestic market. As the effect of economic integration on the supply of these factors of production is uncertain, the benefits of the policy of economic integration may be very small. They will arise only when efficient import-substitution is no longer possible.

Although this argument certainly reflects the planning philosophy in many developing countries, there is an important counter-argument. The possibility of efficient import substitution on a regional basis is bound to be larger because the advantages of economies of scale can often be secured through specialization and because industries might be viable on a regional basis but would not be so in separate domestic markets. In the RCD, viability forms the group's basis of existence.

Mechanism Lacking

What seems to be lacking in the other regions is not so much the awareness of these potential benefits, but the lack of a well-designed mechanism which would guarantee that each country gets its fair share of regionally based activities. Ambitious timetables, initially agreed-upon to free intraregional trade, subsequently conflict with national economic planning objectives. The obvious step to take, therefore, seems to be the adoption of a regional investment policy in which the major goal is harmonization of national objectives and regional investment possibilities.

At present, regionally based projects are considered mostly on an individual basis, and this practice must necessarily lead to controversies regarding project location. Rarely is a package of different industries considered so that each partner can have its fair share of regional activity. A regional investment policy would be an effective means to achieve the benefits of regional specialization. To a large extent, it would render unnecessary the complicated compensation agreements which now appear to be required.

The form which such a policy would take varies from case to case. Most countries would be reluctant to delegate supranational powers to a regional planning office, which would have to remain a coordinating agency. It would study industrial and other opportunities on the basis of the regional market and determine the location of projects, keeping in mind the requirements of regional balance. A strict adherence of partner countries to an approved regional investment plan would be required, and cooperation from outside would be highly desirable.

The success of regional investment planning depends very much on the implementation of the plan, and it is likely that a regional investment bank would have to be established to channel investment funds. It is crucial that each country receive what it considers its fair share of new investment, and if private investment does not come forward, the financing may have to come from the regional investment bank. Foreign aid donor countries could play an important role, but foreign private investors should also be encouraged to cooperate. With respect to the latter, it might be necessary for the regional planning agency to have authority to grant industrial licenses, so that foreign private investment will also take place in accordance with the regional investment plan.

Part Four

Economic Planning

4

"National economic planning," a term broadly used to denote various government initiated forms of programming the economic activities of a country in order to achieve specified national objectives by optimal means within a given time period, has become a key term in modern ideological and economic concepts. The first systematic application of economic planning was the Soviet Union's formulation of a Five-Year Plan in 1928. In Communist countries economic planning is necessarily an integral part of the economic-political system; but in free enterprise economies, too, national economic planning has become recognized as an effective tool for influencing and coordinating decisions of individual economic agents and public authorities in order to achieve such national goals as a high rate of growth or balanced regional development more efficiently than through the unplanned interaction of the market forces.

National economic planning can be extended or limited in scope; it can be used for various purposes and by different economic systems. This "flexibility" means that national plans reflect the technical, socio-ideological, legal, and political constraints under which they are prepared and implemented. It is, however, useful to distinguish only three different categories of planning:

(1) *Comprehensive versus Partial Planning.* Comprehensive planning denotes the development of a comprehensive, integrated blueprint which covers all aspects of economic activity, securing a full and balanced use of available resources and coordinating individual business activities. Partial planning, on the other hand, refers to a situation where only the key sectors of the economy or certain aspects of their activities, such as investments, are predetermined; the rest remains unplanned.

(2) *Discretionary versus Formalized Planning.* National planning becomes formalized when it is based on a comprehensive, dynamic model of the economy which allows the calculation of the required size of certain variables (e.g., volume of investments) in order to achieve certain goals (e.g., a specific rate of economic growth). Planning becomes discretionary when key plan variables are uncertain. In this situation, the planners must use their discretion in making direct decisions on planned variables, taking into account stochastic relations. Discretionary planning generally implies a greater margin of error because the plan is largely the result of a collective process of trial and error.

(3) *Imperative versus Indicative Planning.* Imperative planning is the prevalent form in Communist type economies, characterized by the absence of private

enterprises, the disregard of the price mechanism for determining the allocation of resources, and highly centralized decision making. Under these conditions, a national plan, whose objectives are subordinated to political-ideological considerations, embraces practically all economic activities. It is implemented by means of direct orders, and noncompliance evokes sanctions. Indicative planning, on the other hand, presumes the existence of private enterprise and guarantees individual freedom of choice; the market mechanism remains operative. Most important, the plan focuses on the general interest and is approved in a democratic fashion. For the individual decision maker, indicative planning provides a frame of reference containing data about anticipated developments in the economy which allow him to make his own future oriented decisions on a less uncertain basis than would be the case in the absence of a national plan. For the public authorities the indicative plan is a framework for the consistent and coordinated application of economic policy instruments and of certain incentives which are applied in support of the stated plan targets.

Each of the three pairs of plan characteristics must be perceived as the "extremes" on a given scale. Among these extremes, or pure forms, there are many possible combinations and variations. No functioning planning system can be characterized by these extremes alone. It is always somewhere in between, although not in a static but rather in a dynamic sense, since every workable planning system must continuously be adjusted to new requirements and changing conditions.

Most countries in the western world, industrialized or economically under-developed, have adopted some form of national economic planning; countries such as France, the Netherlands, Sweden, India, and Japan have been practicing national planning for about two decades. Even in the United States we can observe a good deal of program planning for specific large scale projects by federal, state, and local governments as well as some form of national economic policy planning. In general, national economic planning in the western world tends to be indicative; with the exception of France and the Netherlands the countries' planning efforts are more discretionary than formalized, and in most countries one can observe a tendency to make the successive plans more comprehensive.

There is no question that the existence of a national plan influences in one way or another every economic unit operating in the area for which the plan has been formulated and implemented. For the individual decision maker a national plan thus becomes at least to some degree an "external constraint" which he ought to take into account in order to make decisions. Consequently, business executives, regardless of their personal disposition toward the idea of national economic planning, should choose to be ignorant of neither the benefits nor the potentially adverse effects of national plans. Particularly for the international firm, a thorough knowledge of the anticipations and stipulations of a national plan can provide a wealth of information to facilitate its environmental adjustment and enable it to minimize potential conflicts with governmental authorities. Especially in countries with sentiments favoring economic nationalism this latter aspect of a national plan's usefulness can be of very critical importance for the efficient functioning of a multinational business concern.

The first selection in this chapter, by Richard H. Kaufman, provides a broad survey of the major issues concerning national economic planning in mixed economies. It shows diagrammatically the essential variables of a national plan and the process of its formulation. The article also reflects on the proper planning objectives and the experiences with planning in European and underdeveloped countries.

The second selection deals specifically with national economic planning as an instrument used to achieve a more rapid economic progress in developing countries. In this respect Albert Waterston's article focuses on the necessary preconditions for successful development planning such as the adoption of realistic plan targets, a sustained governmental commitment to the idea of national planning, and the use of economic incentives rather than direct controls in order to get a commitment to the plan targets by private decision makers. In addition, the article contains recommendations for organizing the planning effort and appropriate forms of foreign technical assistance to improve the planning effectiveness in the developing countries.

The focus of the third selection is on national planning in the industrialized, open economies of Western Europe. Professor Bela Balassa describes and analyzes the planning experience of France, the United Kingdom, and the Netherlands. In this connection he shows the limitations of national planning and reflects on the prospects for the development and execution of supranational economic plans for the European Economic Community.

The final selection concentrates on the interrelationship between national planning and business decision making in France. Professor Schöllhammer's article first provides a characterization of the nature of French-type planning; then it shows the relative impact of the national plans on major business decisions and analyzes the positive as well as negative effects of French planning for the individual firm.

Economic Planning
in Practice

Richard H. Kaufman

Economic planning has been adopted by many countries as a means for improving economic growth. Almost every European nation has had an economic plan, as do most underdeveloped countries. And through the Alliance for Progress, the U.S. encourages the Latin American countries to undertake programs of development planning.

Yet the use and abuse of planning has occasioned widespread controversy wherever it has been practiced. Even many of its original supporters have become concerned with how it has actually turned out. And there is much uncertainty as to why performance has fallen so far below expectations.

What Planning Means

Economic planning is a very difficult term to define since it has been applied in so many different ways. Certainly the type of comprehensive economic planning practiced in the Soviet Union differs sharply from the kinds used in the economies of Western Europe. And the less developed countries have chosen forms of economic planning which lie somewhere in between.

Soviet-type planning is a means for achieving political objectives. The state controls the factors of production. Wages and salaries are politically determined, and state monopolies run such activities as foreign trade. Planning is an integral part of the economic system, with directives issued from the top—from the central planning agency down to each factory.

In free-enterprise economies, on the other hand, planning may serve as a guideline, a general forecast or a budget for government investments that outlines the sectors to be developed if the economy is to achieve a projected growth rate. Private initiative and property are held in high regard, and fulfillment of the plan depends mostly on the economic activity generated by private enterprise. Here planning has a marginal, although not necessarily unimportant, influence on economic life. And the instruments used to influence the economy are generally the same as those of traditional economic policy.

Plans similar in some respects to the Soviet model have been adopted by a

Reprinted by permission of Richard H. Kaufman from *World Business,* No. 1, July 1966 (The Chase Manhattan Bank, N.A.).

number of less developed countries, such as India and Pakistan, with their comprehensive five-year plans and central planning authorities. In other countries, such as in Latin America, planning relates chiefly to public sector projects, such as road and school construction. And although the public sector tends to loom larger here than in the market economies of advanced countries, the private sector still accounts for the bulk of economic activity.

It is difficult to evaluate the contribution of planning to over-all economic development since economic growth is often only one of its objectives, although of course a very important one. The first French plan, at the end of the Second World War, concentrated on the reconstruction of certain basic sectors, such as steel, cement and electricity. One of the main objectives of the Pakistan plans is to reduce income disparities between its East and West provinces.

The current Spanish plan also seeks to reduce regional income differences by establishing seven zones of industrial development. A high priority on accelerating the rates of industrialization is given in the latest Turkish and Greek plans. The current Indian plan seeks to achieve self-sufficiency in food grains. And most of the development plans in the less developed countries have objectives of achieving high levels of employment and reducing income disparities among social groups.

Planning—The European Way

Despite these many goals, some generalizations do appear to be in order as the evidence on the effectiveness of planning in the free world tends to mount. Economic planning appears to have proceeded relatively smoothly in the four developed countries of Western Europe which have practiced it the longest— France, Norway, the Netherlands and Sweden.

Much of the relative success of European plans has been due to favorable economic conditions. As a result of strong economic growth, the early French plans were instrumental in improving the country's infrastructure—highway, power and rail facilities, for example. In Norway and the Netherlands, plan targets were generally exceeded, especially planned investments, growth rates, productivity improvements and foreign trade performance.

The way in which these plans were formulated and implemented was also conducive to their success. France's first plan, the "Monnet Plan" of 1947–1951 which extended to 1953, was based on the realization that the country needed to modernize productive facilities. "Modernisation ou decadence" became the battle-cry. Only when France had developed her administrative and statistical facilities and achieved more planning experience did the Government undertake more comprehensive economic planning.

French planning has been called "indicative planning." Although it embraces the entire economy, there are no direct controls over private firms. Indeed, through a series of consultations, the private sector participates in plan preparations and is also important in its implementation. Businessmen now welcome planning because it gives them a chance to discuss their industries' prospects with their competitors, the Government and labor. As a result, the private sector's wariness of planning has been generally reduced and many businessmen regard the plan as a useful document for guiding their investment decisions. Most importantly, the plan also serves to coordinate public sector investments.

Another feature of the French plan is that the planning authorities present the Government with several alternative growth rates and their implications for the economy. Thus the Parliament can select the alternative which best suits its policy objectives.

Like France, Norway's plans represent the action program of the Government. By contrast, in the Netherlands the plans do not carry official sanction; and in Sweden they are closer to economic forecasts than to programs for action. The Dutch and Swedish plans are drawn up with the help of the private sector, while in Norway there are no such consultations. Indeed, although the Norwegian plans include targets for the entire economy, they are really government programs and are operational only within the public sector. The Dutch plans attempt to foster a climate favorable to investment and higher productivity, and only influence the aggregate levels of demand and output. The Swedish plans have very general objectives and seek to outline economic trends and problems. They have no specific details or prescribed targets.

Britain's six-year National Plan calls for a 25 percent growth in GNP between 1964 and 1970. It represents a projection of the kind of growth the country ought to achieve, based on assumptions about productivity growth and labor force increases. However, Britain's balance-of-payments problem has necessitated defla-tionary measures, which make it highly unlikely that the plan's target can be reached.

Indeed, the European plans have not always proceeded smoothly, as evidenced by France's intermittent struggle with inflation that was won only last year when the planning goals were suspended and orthodox monetary policies were applied. What's more, it may be said that European planning has an inherent inflationary bias. Relatively high growth targets are set to induce investments, the governments borrow freely in order to fulfill the plans, and monetary stability is treated as something that will take care of itself once the plans are fulfilled and productive capacity is expanded.

Also it is evident that economic growth rates of countries which used some sort of economic planning were no higher, and in some cases substantially less, than European countries which did not plan, such as West Germany. But because planning has had limited objectives in Europe, errors or deficiencies have not substantially hindered economic performance.

Japan's planning is similar to that in Europe. The plans are essentially long-term forecasts that serve as guideposts for economic policies. Private sector targets are not goals which must be met, but rather expectations of future conditions. They have proven to be useful to businessmen as guides to their own investment decisions.

Planning in Less Developed Areas

Planning is quite different, however, in the less developed countries of the free world. Many of them have adopted plans which are much more extensive than in the developed countries of Western Europe and Japan, often due to growing population pressures that threaten already low income levels. But their plans have been much less successful in terms of what they hoped to accomplish. In addition, because of the drastic structural changes implied in their plans, errors and deficiencies tend to have serious effects on their economies.

There are many reasons for this unfavorable situation, and they represent the problems inherent in less-developed countries—inadequate administrative and technical skills, over-ambitious demands for development, lack of statistical data, high degree of sensitivity to agricultural changes, and often unstable political conditions. A recent book, *Development Planning* by Albert Waterston, a staff member of the World Bank who has studied economic plans extensively, details many of these general problems.

Political Problems. Changes in government leadership are frequent in less developed countries, and new leaders often do not support previous plans. Also the desire of many political leaders for trappings of modernity has led to the building of steel mills and nuclear reactors which have imposed an undue burden on the economy.

Administrative Problems. Few underdeveloped countries are able to cope with the tremendous administrative difficulties which development planning brings, especially when a basic change in the structure of society is desired. Plans are often too large or complex in relation to a country's ability to implement them. And administrators tend to be more concerned with how quickly they spend money in order to meet plan targets than with how well the money is spent.

Planning preparation and implementation are further hindered by a lack of coordination between planning officials and other government agencies, each jealous of its own functions. And burdensome administrative controls and regulations are frequently used to force private sector activities in directions dictated by the planners.

Economic Problems. Although major planning problems appear to be political and administrative, there are also formidable economic obstacles. Because of the many structural changes desired, plans often call for substantial increases in savings; yet incomes are relatively low. And the need for accelerating investments conflicts with the frequent demands for enlarging social spending and for boosting incomes of poorer regions and groups.

A shortage of well-prepared, productive projects also hinders the fulfillment of planning objectives and often inhibits the effective utilization of foreign assistance. Although agriculture is the key sector in all underdeveloped countries, economic planners either give it low priority or have so far been unable to accelerate its growth. And agricultural deficiencies have wrecked many a plan.

A basic economic problem is that development plans tend to be much too large either in relation to the domestic or foreign resources for financing planned expenditures or to the countries' abilities to absorb the large and rapid changes projected. For example, Morocco's five-year plan aimed at an annual increase in GNP of over 6 percent compared to an average increase of only 1.5 percent in the preceding eight years. The plan was abandoned after two years. Guinea's three-year plan, 1960–63, called for annual increases of 16 percent in GNP, of 70 percent in industrial output and of 60 percent in investments. The goals were not achieved. Indonesia's eight-year plan sought to triple electric power output, quadruple cement production and quintuple oil output. And Bolivia's ten-year plan and Nepal's five-year plan were so overambitious that they were never put into effect.

Planning Problems. Another set of imposing problems affects the ability of the planners to guide their countries' economies. In most underdeveloped countries there is a lack of trained statisticians and technicians, as well as inadequate statistics on which to formulate plans and assess their progress. Therefore, the more advanced forms of economic analysis, such as input-output tables, are of little value. And even where more or less accurate data are available, it is most difficult to make reliable projections because economic and social changes alter the relationships between major variables. For these reasons, the calculations of planners are subject to a considerable degree of error.

Planning in Perspective

The result of all these formidable problems has been to impair the success of economic planning in the underdeveloped countries relative to the mainly indicative plans in Western Europe and Japan. This experience suggests how economic planning might be made more effective.

In particular, many countries need to realize that the comprehensive type of economic plan which encompasses the entire economy may be unmanageable. Often they attempt to make drastic changes in their countries' economic structures before they have obtained adequate supporting information, before institutions are formed to ease their efforts, and before they have gained the necessary experience through the use of partial planning, such as integrated public investment projects. Also they tend to formulate plans without consultation or advice from the private sector, whose support is vital for the fulfillment of the plan. In such circumstances, chances of success are remote.

There is also a tendency for planning agencies to set what they believe should be the country's goals. In doing so they usurp the function of the political leaders and often increase hostility to the plan. The proper function of planners is to indicate alternative courses of action and what these alternatives mean in terms of growth rates, employment levels, investments and other key variables. Then the political leaders may select the course closest to their own policy objectives.

And economic planners tend to forget that the preparation of a plan is the first step in the planning process, not the last one. A plan that is excellent on paper is of little value to a country unless it can be properly implemented. Planners have shied

How Plans are Made in Country X

A Simplified Illustration of a Typical Development Plan

NOTE: The figures below are in billions of dollars and represent the planned results expected in 1970, the last year of country X's five-year plan. Those figures in black indicate the aggregate values which planners would expect as a result of the planning goal of a 7 percent annual growth rate for the economy. The figures in blue represent those same values under a less ambitious objective — a 5½ percent annual growth rate. Percentage figures in parentheses are annual growth rates during the five-year plan period 1965-70.

GOAL No. 1 — Gross domestic product is to grow by 7 percent per year and would total $46.0 billion at the end of the plan.

GOAL No. 2 — Gross domestic product is to grow at a slightly lower rate, 5½ percent per year, and would total $40.2 billion at the end of the plan.

STEP 1
To determine the contribution of individual sectors of the economy to the proposed GDP level. Physical production targets are also set to help achieve stipulated values.

STEP 2
To allocate domestic and foreign resources among alternative uses. The strategy here is to devote as much resources as possible to investment, since this is a key determinant of growth.

STEP 3
To ensure that there is sufficient domestic and foreign finances for the selected investment level.

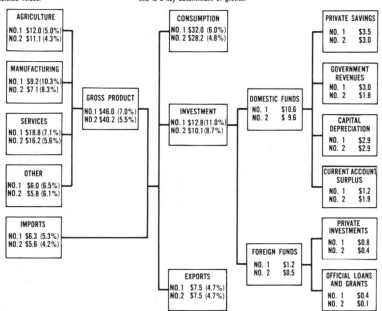

The planners of country X first seek to determine what a growth rate of 7 percent would mean for the economy. They calculate that it would require an average annual growth in the manufacturing sector of 10.3 percent as well as growth rates of 5 percent or more in the other sectors. If such sectoral growth targets exceed levels which can reasonably be expected even with stimulatory government policies, the plan's objectives might have to be lowered.

But even if these targets are physically possible, there may be other problems which could cause a change in plan objectives. In particular, financial resources may not be adequate to cover the planned investment. Country X's plan requires a significant investment expansion to help achieve the 7 percent growth target. This involves domestic savings of $10.6 billion in 1970 and foreign capital of $1.2 billion.

A 5½ percent growth objective would require less domestic and foreign funds, as well as have less of an inflationary impact on the economy. And by needing fewer imports, it would help the balance of payments.

The government authorities who must ultimately decide which plan to adopt are faced with a serious dilemma. Although the second plan may be more realistic and more attainable, incomes will not rise as fast as under plan one. And the pressure of expanding population requires rapid economic growth just to prevent incomes from declining. Also the leaders of country X may feel it is politically unwise to reject a plan which promises, at least on paper, to achieve a higher income growth. Thus, they may accept the first plan and hope that somehow additional finances will be found, and that methods can be devised, to accelerate the growth of the various sectors of the economy.

away from such considerations as something outside their responsibility. As a result, a number of plans have never gotten off the ground and many others were delayed while the authorities considered how to proceed.

Finally, it is important to note that countries can develop without an extensive planning machinery, as witness Japan, Mexico, and Israel.

Planning can indeed stimulate economic development. Its forecasts and indicators can provide businessmen with a rational basis for their investment decisions. And planning objectives are more likely to be realized by giving incentives to private enterprise than by restricting them in favor of government activities. Planning may also serve to co-ordinate public investment projects in order to develop the economy's infrastructure with maximum efficiency.

In these ways, planning can make a constructive contribution to economic growth. But countries which continue to choose comprehensive plans that are beyond their capabilities will continue to suffer serious economic dislocations.

A Hard Look at Development Planning

Albert Waterston

In an attempt to determine where, when, how, and why development planning has been successful, a small group within the World Bank has since 1958 been examining data for countries throughout the world—over 100 countries, developed and less developed, in Africa, Asia, Europe, and the Americas, including socialized as well as mixed-economy countries. Out of this great assemblage of raw material, a comprehensive comparative study was published in December 1965.[1] Those who are interested in development planning are now able to consider not only how it *might* be done but how in fact it *has* been done.

While countries about to start planning their development can learn much from the planning experience of other countries, few make use of this experience: this is the first lesson of the study. The reason, in part, is that the experience of other countries is not known; but mostly, it is because countries will not be guided by the experience of other countries, since they consider their own political, economic, and social conditions to be unique.

Yet the study reveals that most countries not only encounter the same planning problems; they make the same mistakes. They frequently confuse the mere formulation of a plan with planning, fail to take adequate account of what can be done, and hence plan for less than is realistic in some sectors and more than is realistic in others. They have their planners take on extraneous tasks which divert them from planning, set up unsuitable planning machinery, set it up in the wrong places, and so forth.

Plans versus Planning

Planning has undoubtedly promoted development in many countries. But postwar history reveals that there have been many more failures than successes in carrying out development plans. Indeed, among developing nations with some kind of market economy and a sizable private sector, only one or two countries seem to have been consistently successful in carrying out plans.

Except for short periods, most countries have failed to realize even modest

---

Reprinted from *Finance and Development*, pp. 85–91, Vol. III, No. 2 (June 1966). By permission.

[1] Albert Waterston, *Development Planning: Lessons of Experience* (Baltimore, Md.: Johns Hopkins Press, 1965).

income and output targets. What is even more disturbing, the situation seems to be worsening instead of improving. In Asia, where countries' experience with planning has been greater than that in any other region, the rates of growth in the early 1960s fell short not only of targets but even of the growth rates of the 1950s. The situation is not very different in the other continents.

While most countries with development plans have not succeeded in carrying them out, some countries without national development plans or national planning agencies have been developing rapidly. For example, Mexico between 1940 and 1955, when it had no planning agency or plan (and even until now, since in fact it has no plan to which the government adheres), maintained an annual average rate of growth of 5–6 percent. Israel, which had no plan before 1961 and still does not have one which the government follows, has been able to maintain an even higher growth rate. Puerto Rico has become a showcase of development without benefit of a development plan. And among the more developed countries, Germany, without plans, has increased income and output at least as rapidly as France with plans.

It could be contended—and I do contend—that if these countries had had development plans they might have done even better. But the fact is that a country can develop with or without a plan.

A development *plan*, however, is not the same as development *planning*. Planning as a process involves the application of a rational system of choices among feasible courses of investment and other development possibilities based on a consideration of economic and social costs and benefits. These may or may not be put into writing in a "plan." Those who equate a development plan with development planning—and they are many—confuse what should be a product of the planning process with the process itself. A plan can play an important part in the planning process when it makes explicit the basis and rationale for planning policies and measures. But if a plan is prepared before the process has begun in earnest or is unable itself to generate the process, it is likely to have little significance for development.

Importance of the Political Factor

Why are so few development plans carried out? Lack of government support is the prime reason. This lack of support manifests itself in many ways, among them the failure to maintain the discipline implied in plans and the failure to adopt appropriate policies for carrying them out.

Sustained governmental commitment is a *sine qua non* for development; this is cardinal. Pakistan's experience, for example, gives dramatic evidence of the overriding importance of government support. Although the planners of Pakistan's First Five-Year Plan produced a development plan with targets well within the limits set by economic and financial resources, the Plan did not get very far because it did not have help from the government. Given support from a strong and stable leadership, the Second Five-Year Plan overfulfilled its main targets.

Experience in other countries has been similar. In the nineteenth century, Japan, with fewer resources than Burma, China, India, or Indonesia, nevertheless became the most industrialized country in Asia. In large part, this was because of sustained effort supported by a determined government. In the twentieth century, the histories of such diverse countries as the Republic of China, Israel, Mexico, Mainland China, the U.S.S.R., and Yugoslavia give ample evidence of the importance to a country's development of firm and continuing support from a stable government.

Economic Incentives

Until the political leaders of a nation become committed to development, the people themselves are unlikely to show much interest. If a country's leaders make development one of their central concerns, experience shows that the people's interest can be obtained. But except on occasion—for example, during or immediately after a war or other catastrophe or upheaval—interest is not likely to be obtained through appeals to their patriotism, devotion to abstract ideals or altruism, or panegyrics about individual or group accomplishments. Direct government controls over economic activity, or threats of imprisonment or other punishment, are also generally ineffective.

The evidence teaches that the best long-run method of getting people to act in such a way as to achieve plan objectives is to make it profitable for them. Where governments have replaced administrative controls by economic incentives, the result has usually been accelerated economic activity. In Pakistan, for example, government officials as well as outside observers agree that administrative restraints hampered industrial growth during the First Plan period. They also agree in attributing the high rate of industrial progress during the Second Plan period largely to the reduction of government controls over imports and foreign exchange and the introduction of a system of tax incentives and bonuses which encouraged businessmen to expand capacity and output. In Pakistan's agriculture, also, the use of incentive prices played an important part in increasing production.

Since the early 1950s, when Yugoslavia replaced centralized controls based on the Soviet model with decentralized management of the economy, that country has evolved a system of economic incentives based on tax, credit, and price policies by which workers and enterprises are rewarded in accordance with their efficiency. These incentives have done so much to raise production that other Eastern European countries, notably Czechoslovakia, but also Poland and Hungary and even the U.S.S.R., are moving toward the Yugoslav system.

In contrast, many governments in countries with mixed economies rely on direct controls and administrative intervention in the private sector in preference to incentives, and often depress their economies as a result. The problem now is how to get the mixed-economy countries to readopt the system of economic incentives that the socialized countries seem to be taking over from them.

Separation of Plan Formulation from Implementation

Economic development is so difficult that, if political leaders are not very deeply committed to it, the plans which they approve are not carried out because no provision is made for carrying them out. Prime Minister Jawaharlal Nehru of India, who as Chairman of the Indian Planning Commission showed an uncommon grasp of planning problems, once pointedly remarked, "We in the Planning Commission and others concerned have grown more experienced and more expert in planning. But the real question is not planning, but implementing the Plan. . . . I fear we are not quite so expert at implementation as at planning. . . ." This statement is notable not only because it recognizes—correctly I think—that the problems of plan implementation are more difficult than those of plan formulation, but also because it distinguishes—wrongly I believe—"planning" from "implementation."

The word "planning" is often used, as it was by Prime Minister Nehru, to refer to the formulation of plans, but not to their implementation. The conceptual separation of "planning" from "implementation" is more than a question of semantics: it is symbolic of an attitude which is unfortunately prevalent among planners. Experience shows that nothing hampers the success of development plans more than the separation of plan formulation from provision for implementation. Planning cannot leave off where plan formulation ends and action to execute a plan begins. Every target must be accompanied by policies and measures which have been devised specifically to fulfill it; otherwise it becomes only a forecast or projection.

The link between the targets of a plan and the policy and other measures required to attain them is one which many planners and political authorities find difficult to grasp. There is frequently a lack of understanding in developing countries that investment is not enough to ensure growth, that appropriate policy, administrative, and organizational measures are almost always more important for development than is higher investment.

Most plans are prepared in central planning agencies whose officials have little authority over economic policy that is formulated elsewhere. Consequently, one often finds countries where tax, price, monetary, and credit policies impede rather than help to realize plan objectives. For instance, in Pakistan's First Plan, agricultural price policy discouraged farmers from planting crops whose output the Plan sought to increase.

Discounting Overambitious Plan Targets

A planner may not be able to do much about a government's administrative inefficiency and its lack of political commitment or will to develop. But if in preparing his plans he ignores these critical factors, which together constitute the main limitations on the ability of most less developed countries to realize their economic possibilities, he ends up by separating his activities and the plans he formulates from the real world that has its being outside of national planning agencies.

This is precisely what happens in many less developed countries. National development plans are based on a country's economic potentialities or its needs as determined by population growth, and are little related to the country's administrative capacity, or to the government's will, to carry them out. In these countries, plans are not so much blueprints as hortatory instruments. It can hardly be surprising, therefore, that most planning aims are never achieved. Because the aims are related to what is possible or desirable, with little regard to what is likely, they are usually set so unrealistically high that they never have a chance. For instance, in Bolivia's Ten-Year Development Plan for 1962–71, the target of average annual increases of 9.2 percent in gross national product in the first five years may have been economically possible, but it was far beyond the country's administrative and political capacities. The Government wisely abandoned it as overambitious.

If planners are to set realistic targets in their plans, they must somehow find means to *measure* administrative inadequacy and the lack of political will to develop, so that they can "discount" the unduly optimistic targets set when plans are formulated solely on the basis of economic potentiality. This sounds difficult, but it is not impossible. For example, it is possible to quantify the cost of administrative inefficiency, in terms of money and time, on the basis of past discrepancies between original estimates and actual performance in projects and programs. By deflating the estimates by a factor based on past errors, such adjustments can go a long way toward closing the gap between promise and performance.

Similarly, it is possible to quantify a country's political will to develop if planners set up for each major area of policy (e.g., taxation, credit, investment, money, and incomes) feasible alternatives, including the effects of each on development, from which political authorities can make a choice before a plan is drafted. In the process of selecting the alternatives which best suit them, the political authorities will be supplying specific information about the extent to which they are prepared to adopt policies and other measures for furthering development which, collectively, can be said to constitute a veritable measure of their "will to develop."

If the three basic elements that enter into the planning process—economic potential, administrative capacity, and political will to develop—are all taken into account in formulating plans, planning aims are bound to be more in line with a country's real capacity to achieve its economic potentialities.

The Projects Problem

The current artificial separation between the formulation and implementation of plans accounts for the failure of planners, concentrating as they do on aggregative planning, to recognize soon enough that the weakness in most developing countries is not the lack of an elegantly integrated comprehensive plan based on economic potentialities but the lack of well-planned individual projects that can really be carried out. For example, after eighteen months of work on Bolivia's Ten-Year Plan, the planners found themselves in the embarrassing position of conceding that "the principal deficiency that will be noted in the formulation of the present Plan is the small number of specific investment projects . . ."[2] needed to execute it. Similar statements can be found in the plans of many other countries.

Because it usually takes several years to identify and prepare a sufficiently large number of good projects needed to implement a plan, it is too late for planners to become concerned about them after a plan has been prepared or even when it is being formulated. Unless preinvestment and investment studies of projects for implementing a comprehensive plan are sufficiently advanced, it does little good to prepare such a plan. Yet all too often this is exactly what happens. Few projects are carefully worked out before the work of implementing them begins. As a result, many projects and programs are not carried out at reasonable cost and in reasonable periods of time. Attempts to reduce the time spent in preparing projects frequently result in the choice of low-yield projects; substantially increased costs and delayed construction because of technical or other problems that were not foreseen; poor phasing of raw material, transport, staffing, or other requirements; failure to provide adequate financing; shoddy construction; and inability to make full use of completed projects.

Only a few of the less developed countries are fully aware of the need for selecting soundly conceived projects with potentially high yields, defining their scope with clarity, estimating their national currency and foreign exchange requirements with a sufficient degree of accuracy, and laying down realistic schedules for their execution; even fewer have the administrative capacity and the political will to cope with these needs and, especially, to carry out the projects in accordance with carefully developed programs of action.

Changing the Planning Mix

One reasonable conclusion to be drawn from experience is that it may be desirable to reverse the usual proportions of the planning mix. Planners have almost invariably concentrated on aggregative planning rather than on the proper preparation and execution of projects, but experience shows that countries with well-prepared projects coordinated by sound budgetary procedures and controls can dispense with comprehensive plans, at least for a time, and still maintain high rates of growth. It seems clear, therefore, that improvements in project preparation and budgetary controls, where needed, are at least as urgent as the preparation of aggregative plans.

---

[2] Junta Nacional de Planeamiento, *Plan Nacional de Desarrollo Economico y Social, 1962–1971: Resumen* (La Paz, Bolivia, 1961), p. 24 (author's translation).

These findings obviously have an important bearing on the sequence in which planning problems ought to be attacked. If the planning process is to be realistic, planners must not start, as they often do, with a series of theoretical abstractions of planning as it *ought* to be, and they must not try to force these ideas in an inhospitable environment where governments are unstable, not genuinely committed to development, or otherwise unready for aggregative planning. Instead, while not forgetting the long-run objectives that theory demonstrates to be desirable, they must—at least at first—attune their plans to "things as they are."

Improving Planning Organization

Since effective projects should be prepared in the agencies that will actually carry them through, the organization of programing units in these agencies should get much higher priority than it now has in many developing countries, perhaps even higher than central planning agencies. Improved budget offices also may be more important in these countries than improved central planning agencies.

Changing Technical Assistance

The type of technical assistance needed for preparing technically and economically sound projects, and executing and operating them, differs from the type of technical assistance that has been supplied for aggregative or comprehensive planning. Aggregative planning is a business for economists who need only a modest knowledge of agricultural and industrial techniques; but project preparation requires engineers, agronomists, and other technicians, including some who are capable of translating financial costs and benefits into economic costs and benefits.

Because the preparation, execution, and operation of projects involve many people in a government, it is becoming imperative that foreign technical assistance be largely made up of "demonstrators" rather than "doers." Doers can be used for a few special purposes, but only demonstrators working on the job with groups of government employees actually engaged in project preparation and execution can hope to train in a reasonable period the large numbers of workers who must become involved in project preparation, execution, and operation.

What I have written is not an attack on comprehensive planning. Ideally, planning should be undertaken "from the top down" as well as "from the bottom up." But experience reveals that in most countries planners begin with the first and rarely get around to the second. Since planning from the bottom up is essential to development, while planning from the top down is not, it seems sensible for a country to begin with the preparation of sound projects and sector programs and, with these as a foundation, to advance toward comprehensive planning as rapidly as circumstances permit.

Planning in an Open Economy

Bela Balassa

The word "planning" has been used to denote a wide range of activities from the central management of the economy in the Communist countries to government-sponsored forecasts by private groups in Sweden. In a more restricted sense, we speak of planning if the allocation of resources among individual industries is directed—or substantially influenced—by the government whose actions are based on a comprehensive blueprint relating to a period of several years. This definition includes within its scope planning in Soviet-type economies and in several of the developing countries, as well as planning on the industry level in developed market economies.

It is suggested here that planning, as understood in a narrower sense, is inward-looking in character: it can best be applied in countries whose economy is more or less closed to foreign influences and it provides an inducement for reducing reliance on international trade. To begin with, the uncertainty of plans and forecasts increases with the degree of openness of the national economy. While information on interindustry relationships can be utilised to derive a feasible pattern of production associated with a growth target in a closed economy, disappointed expectations in regard to exports and unforeseen changes in imports will give rise to discrepancies between plans and realisation if the foreign trade sector is of importance. Correspondingly, the chances for plan fulfilment can be increased by limiting dependence on international exchange.

In this paper, I will consider the implications of the "openness" of developed market economies for planning on the industry level. In this connection, first I will examine the experience of certain European countries in planning the level of foreign trade, its composition, and the balance of trade. Next, we will examine the limitations of planning in open economies and the implications of Common Market's establishment for French planning. The paper will close with a discussion of the prospects for planning on the EEC level.

European Experiences

A consideration of the plans of various countries suggests a tendency to underestimate the level of foreign trade. While demand for primary products can be

---

Reprinted from *Intereconomics Monthly Review of International Trade and Development*, published by the Hamburg Institute for International Economics, No. 3 (March 1967), pp. 75–80.

estimated as a function of national income or the production of various branches of manufacturing, international exchange in manufactured goods involves intra-industry specialisation, when the uncertainties relating to the latter may, in part, explain the observed underestimation of the level of trade.

The French Third Plan

The French Third Plan can serve as an example; in this case, exports to countries outside the franc area had been estimated at 17.5 billion francs and imports at 16.3 billion francs for the terminal year of the plan 1961, while actual exports were 22.4 billion and imports 20.6 billion. And although one may argue that during the period of execution of the Third Plan the planners faced a special situation by reason of the two devaluations and entry into the Common Market, the volume of trade has again been underestimated in the Fourth Plan: between 1961 and 1964 imports rose by 49.2 percent instead of the projected rate of increase of 16.7 percent, while the relevant figures for exports are 21.5 and 14.8 percent.

At the same time, changes in total exports and imports often cover large interindustry differences. Thus, even if exports and imports are correctly estimated for the economy as a whole, production and investment plans in individual industries will be disappointed if export demand exceeds expectations in some industries while others have to contend with smaller exports or larger imports. Deviations from projected trade values will affect domestic production directly, as well as indirectly, through input-output and multiplier-type relationships. An indication of the direct effect can be provided by comparing actual production and trade figures with the estimates contained in the plan. In the case of the French Third Plan, the deviations went in the same direction in six out of nine manufacturing industries, and in three cases—automobiles, naval construction and aircraft, and construction materials—unplanned changes in the trade balance had a considerable effect on production (Table 1).

Its poor trade performance accounted for the entire shortfall of production in the automobile industry; actual production fell behind the planned figure by 433 million francs, while the discrepancy in the trade balance was 564 million francs. Similar results are indicated for a number of other commodities, too, if the data are appropriately disaggregated. Besides the well-known case of refrigerator imports from Italy, we may mention the experience of the organic chemical industry where the expansion of imports restrained the rise of domestic production. It may be added that the production figures show the influence of domestic and foreign uses and, in cases where the two moved in opposite directions, the data do not reveal the direct impact of trade on production.

A further consideration is that the trade balance in the national plans is generally taken as a target rather than accepting the independent estimates of exports and imports. Thus, the trade balance postulated in the plans provides a constraint for the estimation of trade flows and requires the—often arbitrary—

Differences Between Forecasts and Realisation in
Manufacturing Industries During the Period of the
French Third Plan (1958–61)

(Million francs in 1956 prices)

Manufacturing Industry	Production[a]	Trade Balance[b]
Food Manufacturing	−1336	−297
Construction Materials and Glass	+ 195	+120
Production and Transformation of Metals	−1150	+121
Electrical and Nonelectrical Equipment	+ 738	−199
Automobiles, Motorcycles and Bicycles	− 433	−564
Naval Construction and Aircraft	+ 493	+290
Chemical Products	+1934	+ 54
Textiles, Clothing and Leather	− 998	−196
Wood, Paper and Other Industries	− 45	+435
All Manufacturing	− 602	−236

[a] At production prices.

[b] Excluding customs duties.

Source: J. Benard, C. Roux, and C. Girardeau, "L'exécution du IIIe Plan français: Essai de mesure et d'analyse", *Bulletin du CEPREL,* (July, 1964), 96, 103–4.

Table 1.

modification of the trade projections. Adjustments are usually made in regard to exports so that the global export forecast included in the plan becomes a residual as well as a target. Few efforts have been made, however, to indicate the price changes that would be necessary for reaching this target, and to ensure the consistency of the assumptions underlying the export and import forecasts.

United Kingdom, the Netherlands

In the United Kingdom, note has been taken of the lack of consistency in the assumptions made by the National Economic Development Council in regard to exports and imports, and the projections of the Cambridge Growth Project are also open to criticism. In the latter case, exports are regarded as an exogenous variable and competitive imports become a residual, inasmuch as a balance-of-payments constraint is imposed on the model and complementary imports are estimated as a function of the output of individual sectors.[1] But although the forecast of exports, as well as that of competitive imports, involves implicit assumptions regarding prospective changes in prices, price changes are not explicitly introduced in the model and the consistency of the underlying assumptions is not ensured.

By comparison, in the Netherlands it has been proposed to apply a general

---

[1] Richard Stone, "British Economic Balances in 1970: A Trial Run on Rocket," *Colston Papers* (London, 1964), pp. 75, 77, 82.

equilibrium model that incorporates consistent price assumptions and does not include a balance-of-payments constraint. Instead, equilibrium between potential and actual production is assumed to be ensured by the choice of the appropriate level of autonomous expenditure (government expenditures and residential construction).

The Dutch model represents an advance in the handling of the foreign trade sector and could be further improved upon through appropriate disaggregation. But, for the purposes of projection, the model is as good as its assumptions—in the present case the assumptions relating to the future growth of the world market, the share of the country's exports in this market, the elasticity of substitution between domestic and foreign merchandise, and changes in relative prices in the world economy. The realism of the assumptions means, in the first place, that these are consistent with assumptions made in the plans of other countries. There are indications that this is not the case for industrial countries that are presently engaged in preparing long-term plans. Estimates on the expansion of the world market would agree only by chance, and the tendency to assume unchanged or increasing shares for individual countries results in an "oversubscribing" of future sales. This tendency in turn, finds its origin in the desire of the countries under considerations to improve, or at least to maintain, their balance-of-payments position. We find here the counterpart of the observation according to which by reason of the conservative ways of judging the balance-of-payments position in individual countries, on the world level a substantial deficit is shown. Correspondingly, a summation of planned trade balances would show a substantial surplus that could materialise only if aid to less developed countries was greatly stepped up.

Much has been said about the error-possibilities associated with the estimation of substitution elasticities and it does not need to be repeated here.[2] Uncertainties are even larger in regard to price trends, as indicated by differences in the projection of prices in France and the Netherlands: while the preliminary version of the Fifth Plan calculates with a slight fall in the export prices of manufactured goods in the 1965–70 period, in the Dutch model import prices of manufactures were assumed to rise by 5 percent between 1962 and 1970.

The Limitations of Planning

In the previous section, I have examined various error possibilities associated with the projection of trade in the national plans. These error possibilities augment uncertainty for individual industries and enterprises, while the lack of a common methodology and the tendency to project improvements in the trade balance of developed countries lead to inconsistencies in balance-of-payments forecasts. In turn, the relative importance of these errors for planning and business decision

---

[2] Cf. e.g. G. H. Orcutt, "Measurement of Price Elasticities in International Trade," *Review of Economics and Statistics* (March 1950), 117–32; and A. C. Harberger, "Some Evidence on the International Price Mechanism," *Journal of Political Economy* (December 1957), 506–21.

making will depend on the degree of "openness" of national economies. For individual industries, the openness of the national economy means that projections on future sales involve a considerable degree of error by reason of the uncertainty associated with future trends in production and consumption abroad, of which foreign trade is but a reflection. These errors are magnified in regard to investment decisions that respond to changes in production over time.

At the same time, the opening of national economies makes the activity of individual industries and enterprises more sensitive to changes in international price-relationships. On the one hand, buyers will react to relatively small changes in prices; on the other, foreign competition will restrain price increases, whereas in a closed economy oligopolistic firms could raise prices in the event of a wage inflation.

Given the uncertainty introduced by foreign trade, the planners can hardly guarantee the correctness of projections for individual industries in an open economy, and doubts arise concerning the desirability of government intervention in business decisions since ultimately the profit of the enterprises will be affected. At any rate, while in a closed economy selective measures can be used to validate the forecasts and constrain enterprises to follow the directives of the plan, under OECD and GATT regulations the scope for the application of such instruments is greatly limited. The possibilities for employing measures that discriminate among domestic industries, and between home production and imports, further diminish in the framework of the European Common Market and the European Free Trade Association.

Moreover, with the reduction of trade barriers and the movement towards integration in Western Europe, entrepreneurs increasingly take account of developments elsewhere in making their production and investment decisions. There appears to be a tendency for specialisation in narrower ranges of products and the production process itself is often subdivided between the manufacturers of different countries through the exchange of parts, components, and accessories.

These considerations indicate the limitations of planning in the private industrial sector of open economies. It appears, then, that industrial countries have to make a choice between fully participating in the world trade-network and planning in the private industrial sector. This choice is especially acute for small countries where the cost of protection and the obstacles to planning are the greatest.

It is hardly surprising, therefore, that small countries, such as the Netherlands, Norway, and Sweden, generally refrain from the application of non-neutral measures in regard to manufacturing industries.[3] As Professor Svennilson expressed

---

[3] Cf. C. A. van der Beld and P. de Wolff, "Exercise in Medium Term Macro Forecasting for the Netherlands Economy," paper presented at the Centre International d'ètudes des problémes humaines, in Monaco, in May 1964; P. J. Bjerve, "Government Economic Planning in Norway," Working papers from the Central Bureau of Statistics of Norway, 1963; and Ingvar Svennilson, "Long-term Planning in Sweden," *Skandinavska Bank Quarterly Review,* 3 (1962).

it, "the philosophy of this approach is closely linked to the factor of uncertainty. Roughly 25 percent of Swedish production is exported and imports have a corresponding share in supplying the home market."[4] In Norway, the present situation has come about as a result of a "de-planning" undertaken following the early postwar period when the government had a number of instruments at its disposal for controlling production and investment. Finally, in the Netherlands planning has been confined to short-term policy-making, and long-term models have been used only for purposes of forecasting.

The Experience of France

The experience of France is also of interest. Before the acceptance of obligations in the OEEC and entry into the Common Market, the French applied fiscal and credit measures of a discriminatory character to ensure plan fulfilment and to shelter domestic industry from foreign competition. With the opening of the French economy, however, these instruments have increasingly fallen into disuse. At the same time, industrialists have come to orient their activity in a Common Market framework, and have reasserted their independence from government intervention.[5] To avoid a further erosion of the planners' authority, some commentators have suggested that the methods of French planning be "transplanted" and utilised on the Common Market level.[6]

But are the conditions for planning of the French variety fulfilled in the Common Market? Robert Marjolin, the Vice-President of the European Community in charge of matters of economic policy, has pointed out that "planning, including programme planning, presupposes an economy whose relations with the outside world are limited or can be restricted should the necessity arise."[7] At the same time, the openness of the EEC, measured as the ratio of foreign trade to value added in the production of traded goods, is about 20 percent, comparable to that of the French economy, taken by itself. Moreover, notwithstanding the trade diversion the Common Market's establishment might have entailed, trade with non-member countries as a percentage of value added in the production of traded goods has continued to increase: this ratio was 16.5 percent in 1953, it rose to 19.0 in 1958 and to 19.6 in 1963.

The figures indicate that international trade is of considerably greater importance for the European Common Market, taken as a unit, than for the United

---

[4] *Op. cit.*, p. 77.

[5] See, e.g., the declaration of the Counseil National du patronat français, made public on January 19, 1965.

[6] Cf. e.g., Jean Boissonat, "A la recherche d'une planification européenne," *Economie et Humanisme* (November-December 1961), 66–82; and Jean Bénard "Le Marché commun européen et l'avenir de la planification française," *Revue économique* (September 1964), 756–84.

[7] *Bulletin of the EEC* (July 1962), 12.

States where the ratio of trade to value added in the sectors producing traded goods barely exceeds 10 percent. And while in 1959 the average share of exports in the output of manufacturing industries was 14.1 percent in the EEC, the share of exports is higher in the fastest-growing industries: machinery and transport equipment (21.2 percent) and chemicals (16.7 percent). The share of external trade in manufacturing output may increase further in connection with the observed process of intra-industry specialisation among industrial countries, and these developments would be accentuated if the tariff negotiations undertaken in the framework of the Kennedy Round were successful.

It would appear, then, that the Common Market, too, faces a choice between a liberal trade policy and planning in the private industrial sector. In this connection, a comparison with the situation existing in France before the "opening" of its economy will be of interest. In 1953 the proportion of foreign trade outside the French market area to value added in the production of traded goods was only 10.8 percent in France, i.e., about one-half of the ratio shown for the Common Market in 1963. Moreover, the French used quotas, subsidies, and various other discriminatory measures to shelter domestic industry from foreign competition and to favour one industry over another. Thus, the Government could effectively intervene in the private industrial sector, while the pre-conditions of such an intervention have increasingly disappeared as the French economy has become more open.[8]

Programming in the EEC

Given the higher proportion of foreign trade in national income, the lack of application of quantitative restrictions, and its lower tariff level, a shift towards protectionism would be necessary in the Common Market to provide the same "environment" for planning that existed in France in the mid-fifties. Some observers believe that such a shift is, indeed, in the offing, and interpret the pronouncements made by officials of the Community as indicative of a tendency towards planning on the industry level—and hence towards protectionism. According to D. Swann and D. L. McLachlan, for example, programming in the EEC will develop in the direction of bringing "a direct influence to bear upon the production and investment decisions of the private sector."[9]

In support of this proposition, the authors argue that Marjolin's assurances to the contrary should not be taken at face value since "Marjolin believes in planning, and he is not the only Commissioner to hold such a view."[10] They further maintain

---

[8] For a detailed discussion, see my "Whither French Planning?", *Quarterly Journal of Economics* (November 1965).

[9] D. Swann and D. L. McLachlan, "Programming and Competition in the European Communities," *Economic Journal* (March 1964), 90.

[10] *Op. cit.*, p. 90.

that pronouncements by the EEC Commission and Marjolin on this subject are ambiguous,[11] and conclude that "an even stronger argument for believing that EEC programming will tend in the direction of direct influence on private entrepreneurial decisions . . . is based on the fact that the progressive establishment of the customs union weakens the effectiveness of the national programmes; so much so that those responsible for national programmes regard programming at the EEC level as being indispensable."[12] In the opinion of the present writer, however, Swann and McLachlan's conclusions are based on a misreading of the evidence.

Their first argument is mind-reading, pure and simple, and can be dismissed as such. In turn, references to ambiguity in the pronouncements of EEC officials reflect a lack of understanding of developments in the thinking of the responsible authorities in Brussels. This progress finds expression in the apparent discarding of the term "planning" in favour of "programming" after the first Marjolin speech in Arcachon on May 25, 1962, and in the subsequent interpretation of programming as a growth policy. It is also suggested by a careful reading of published material. Thus, Marjolin does not speak about "the probable and desirable distribution of the increase of GNP" among individual industries as the authors imply[13] but among the large sectors of the economy, such as agriculture, mining, and manufacturing.[14] At the same time, a broad sectoral policy does not necessarily entail direction or intervention in the production and investment decisions of private enterprises; in fact, Marjolin disclaims any intention of "limiting in any way the freedom of the enterprises, who will rest entirely the masters of their production and investment decisions."[15] This theme is further developed in the policy proposals of the Community made public on July 25, 1963. This document expressly excludes interference with decisions made by private enterprises from the scope of programming in the Common Market.[16]

Finally, while pressure is brought on the Commission from some quarters for introducing planning in the private industrial sector on the Common Market level, one should not forget the counter-pressure that comes from countries with a tradition of liberal economic policies, such as Germany and the Netherlands. At the same time, with the lessening of government intervention in the private sector in France, the French patronat, too, has come out for further "de-planning." One may doubt, therefore, that in the absence of a radical change in the present economic situation of the Common Market, the proponents of Community-wide planning in private industry would carry the day.

---

[11] *Op. cit.*, p. 91.

[12] *Op. cit.*, p. 91.

[13] *Op. cit.*, p. 81.

[14] "Rapport général," in La Programmation économique dans les pays de la C.E.E. (Rome, Consiglio Nazionale dell'Economica e del Lavoro, 1962), p. 28; p. 54 in the Italian edition.

[15] *Ibid.*

[16] Communauté éonomique européenne, Commission, Politique économique à moyen terme de la Communauté Brussels, 1963.

The Prospects for Planning

These considerations raise serious doubts concerning the desirability and the feasibility of planning in the private industrial sector of open economies, including the Common Market. In the face of the uncertainty associated with foreign trade and the limitations of instruments available to governments under GATT and OECD regulations, the introduction of planning in this sector would presuppose a shift towards protectionism which would not fail to have adverse consequences for the world economy.

This conclusion does not mean, however, that industrial countries should adopt a negative attitude toward all forms of planning, using the term in a more general sense. One can hardly object to preparing long-term forecasts for the industrial sector in the framework of projections for the national economy, for example, provided that no coercive measures are used to insure the implementation of the forecasts. This is planning's function as "generalised market research," the virtues of which Pierre Masse, the Commissaire général of the French Commissariat général du Plan, has often extolled.

Long-Term Projections

At the same time, long-term projections would provide information on the government's economic policy and its future claims on resources. But, in the opinion of the present writer, the main function of planning should be to provide a framework for coordinated and rational action on the part of the government in regard to activities where the price mechanism does not appropriately evaluate needs and objectives, and appreciable differences between private and social productivity exist. Prices do not serve as a yardstick for choosing among private and public goods, or for determining the composition of public spending. Differences in private and social profitability are also observable in the so-called semi-public sector (agriculture, transportation, and energy), in regard to regional policy, and may pertain to the choice between social and private profitability.

As regards the latter, government intervention can be considered desirable if private decisions do not lead to sufficient investments to reach a growth rate accepted as a target. Such interventions are undertaken in practically all industrial countries, usually on an ad hoc basis, and take the form of tax policy or provisions for accelerated depreciation. Similar considerations apply to basic research that is generally regarded as a par excellence case of differences between social and private profitability.

The determination of the volume and composition of public spending is a further consideration. This involves the evaluation of collective needs and the development of methods that can be utilised for effecting a choice among them. Efforts in this direction have been made, e.g., in France, although it has been noted that the plan succeeded much less in the public sector than in market-oriented activities.[17] Part of the explanation may lie in the fact that while prices provide a yardstick for choice among private goods, no similar mechanism exists in regard to public goods. Little is known about the productivity of public investment in fields such as education, for example, and methods for effecting a rational choice among various forms of public consumption are yet to be developed.

Lack of Coordination

A related problem is the lack of coordination among public agencies and administrative organisations that is observed, to a lesser or greater extent, in all industrial countries. In the absence of appropriate methods for evaluating the needs and demands of the various agencies and organisations, decisions are often influenced to a considerable extent by the relative bargaining power of these organisations. The difficulties of coordination are augmented by the apparent desire for aggrandisement on the part of heads of ministries (France, Japan), autonomous agencies (Belgium), public enterprises (Italy), and conflicts are often observable in the relationships of central and local authorities, too (Norway).

Planning can also have usefulness in the case of agriculture, transportation, and energy that can be regarded as part of the semi-public sector. Governments everywhere intervene, to a lesser or a greater extent, in agriculture but these interventions often respond to demands made by pressure groups rather than reflecting a conscious long-term policy. Yet a rational policy for agriculture can hardly be formulated without considering the future demand for and supply of foodstuffs and agricultural raw materials at home and abroad, trends in productivity, and the need for transferring manpower from agriculture to industry. Similarly, transport and energy policies should be based on an evaluation of future needs as compared to availabilities.

Differences in private and social profitability may further be associated with interregional differences in economic development, and in the postwar period several of the industrial countries have undertaken policies aimed at assisting undeveloped and declining regions. These policies have often lacked coordination, however, and little attention has been paid to their cost in terms of alternatives foregone. Thus, efforts have been made to support the economy of declining regions or to develop regions with poor natural resource endowments, thereby reinforcing the rigidity in the locational structure. With regard to Sweden, it has been suggested, for example, that by reserving government assistance "primarily for localities with high unemployment, or where a relatively small proportion of the population is employed in manufacturing industry, the Committee (in charge of regional problems) has probably selected with a high degree of precision regions

---

[17] Jean Bénard, "Le Marché commun européeen et l'avenir de la planification française," *Revue économique* (September 1964), p. 764.

with especially poor natural facilities, and thus also with limited development potential."[18]

A rational policy would take account of the long-term development potential of the economy, and would aim at facilitating the process of transformation rather than hindering it. This, in turn, would require the evaluation of possible costs and benefits that can hardly take place without establishing a consistent framework for decision making. Regional economic policy in Norway appears to be moving in this direction by favouring larger and stronger units instead of trying to help small, unviable communities as in the past, and by attempting to avoid the possibility that local authorities outbid each other in attracting industries.

It would appear, then, that the recent emphasis on planning on the industry level in developed countries has been largely misplaced. In the face of the uncertainties associated with foreign trade and the limitations of policy investments available to governments under GATT and OECD regulations, government intervention in the private industrial sector has little to commend it. On the other hand, long-term planning has a useful function in the public and semi-public sectors. It would ensure the rationality and consistency of government decisions in the public sector where prices do not provide a yardstick for choosing among alternatives. Further, a conscious long-term policy would appear desirable in the semi-public sector—agriculture, transport, and energy—where ad hoc interventions, taken often in response to special interests, give rise to inefficiencies. This shift in the objectives of long-term planning cannot fail to have a beneficial effect on the economies of developed countries.

---

[18] Assar Lindbeck, "Location Policy," *Skandinavska Ranken Quarterly Review*, 2 (1964), 46.

National Economic Planning and Business Decision Making: The French Experience

Hans Schöllhammer

In spite of the famous statement of the 1930's—"we are all planners now"[1] —national economic planning (broadly meaning a method of organized social action designed to achieve certain specified over-all objectives within a given period) versus individual or corporate freedom of decision making has remained the topic of many lengthy and inconclusive discussions. At the root of the debate is the conflict between the public authorities who are committed to a normative, official plan and the largely uncommitted individual decision makers of the business sector on whose cooperation the implementation of a national economic plan would depend. So far, this interrelationship between macro-economic planning and micro-decision making has been almost exclusively treated in a general, philosophical, and, to a certain extent, political manner.

It is perhaps natural that national planning is looked upon with mistrust in a free market economy. One reason for this is the association of national planning with the political and economic regime of the Soviet Union, which was the first country to develop a comprehensive and systematic five-year plan in 1928. Opponents of national economic planning claim that it is inevitably the first step on a "Road to Serfdom,"[2] because it always involves some form of intervention, manipulation, and coercion,[3] even if the national plans are indicative rather than imperative. This unavoidable by-product of national planning, it is argued, tends to inhibit entrepreneurial initiative as well as organizational flexibility, which leads to a decline in economic productivity and ultimately to dictatorship "because it is the most effective instrument of coercion and, as such, essential if central planning on a large scale is to be possible."[4]

The proponents of national planning generally emphasize the inherent weaknesses of the market mechanism which create the need for the elaboration of an over-all plan to provide the individual decision maker with sufficient information

---

Reprinted by permission from *California Management Review*, Vol. 12, No. 2 (Winter 1969), pp. 74–88.

[1] Evan Frank M. Durbin, "The Importance of Planning" in G. E. C. Catlin, ed., *New Trends in Socialism* (London: Dickson and Thompson, 1935), p. 147.

[2] Friedrich A. von Hayek, *The Road to Serfdom* (Chicago: University of Chicago Press, 1944).

[3] Henry Hazlitt, *Government Planning—Economic Growth* (Zurich: International Freedom Academy, n.d.), pp. 2ff.

[4] von Hayek, *op. cit.*, p. 70.

to relate his decisions to those of the rest of the business community in the pursuit of a common preference function such as a high rate of growth or a high, stable rate of employment. A national plan, it is pointed out, is a kind of large-scale market survey which provides business executives with consistent information about future developments and anticipated governmental actions. It conveys not only what is probable but also what is desirable; it shows what the objectives are and specifies the means by which the public authorities intend to attain them. Consequently, business executives can make strategic decisions under reduced uncertainties, which results in less wastage, a higher economic efficiency, and increased freedom in the form of wider opportunities for growth of the individual firm in an expanding and coordinated economy.

In addition, proponents of planning point to three factors which have operated in recent years to increase the attractiveness of national economic planning:

(1) The growing proportion of expenditures and investments controlled by the government.

(2) An increasing planning consciousness, particularly among the larger business enterprises.

(3) Improved means for collecting and processing large quantities of macro-economic data quickly and efficiently.

This kind of deductive reasoning has not led to any satisfactory solution of the dispute between opponents and proponents of national economic planning mainly because it does not provide any specific, quantitatively oriented answers to some basic questions:

To what extent are strategic and operational decisions of business firms actually affected by the existence of a national economic plan?

How strong is the impact on the affected decision-making areas?

Are there any factors by which the impact of the national plan is conditioned?

What is the relative importance of these factors?

What are the actual advantages and disadvantages of a national plan for the individual firm?

Do the advantages outweigh the disadvantages or vice versa?

Answers to these questions must be found in order to come to a fair judgment about the desirability or nondesirability of national economic planning in a free market economy.

The French economy, basically a market economy, has been subject to planning for more than two decades, and the French system of planning has attracted considerable attention. Among the industrialized nonsocialist countries France has gone furthest in planning its economic affairs. Its system has been in effect for more than twenty years and can be used as a model in attempting to find specific answers to the questions above by investigating the interrelationship between French national planning and the decision making of French business firms. This article presents the pertinent findings of such an investigation, based on in-depth interviews with more than two dozen business executives and on information obtained through questionnaires completed by executives of almost 400 French firms.

The Nature of French Planning

There has been a continuous planning evolution since the First Plan was drawn up in 1947. Methods and techniques have been improved, the emphasis of the plans changed, and their scope extended. The major evolutions have originated from the changing economic conditions to which the general objectives of the successive plans were geared. However, the broad lines of the system and the planning approach have changed little. There is always concern about achieving a maximum rate of growth, balanced regional and sectoral development, and an emphasis on investment activity. In addition, the planners aim to make the plan as comprehensive as possible and, most important of all, the plans have to be compatible with the democratic system and the concept of a free market economy. The methods used for reconciling the requirements of a general economic plan under the constraints of a free market system are described by the authors of the First French Plan as those of a "concerted economy." All those social and economic forces who later put the plan into practice are called upon to help prepare it. It is hoped that the plan, because it forecasts and influences their decisions, brings about enough consistency among individual decision makers and consensus among decentralized objectives to become substantially self-realizing.

Despite their evolutionary nature, French plans have always retained the following characteristics:

(1) The plan is worked out in terms of branches of activity and not of companies or products. It does not dictate a course of action to private enterprise—it is not a control device—it simply states the general objectives fixed for economic and social development and the particular goal for each branch. Within this framework each firm is free to choose its own target. A firm can maintain its position within its branch, can enlarge it, or can diminish it. The firm acts on the basis of better information, but at its own risk. The plan is only an "instrument d'orientation de l'économie" and "should provide the individual investors with an idea about the expected economic development which can be used as basis for appropriate decisions."[5] The public authorities intervene only where there is a danger of imbalance on an economy-wide or sectoral scale.

(2) French planning seeks to draw on the expertise of all major decision-making centers in the nation. In the First Plan, Monnet was already using the expression "concerted economy." He realized that because of the proverbial

---

[5] *Project de Rapport sur les Perspectives de l'Économie Française en 1961* (Paris: Commissariat Général du Plan, 1956), p. 5.

French individualism the plan would only be successful if it were a combined effort in which all French were associated, directly or indirectly. This spirit is reflected in the structural organization for the preparation of the plan, particularly in the "Planning Commissions" which are perhaps the most significant feature of the French planning system. Organized apart from the French Planning Commissariat which is basically the permanent administrative organ of the French planning system, these planning commissions are made up of representatives of the major social categories which have a determining influence on the economic life of the country: executives of private and public business enterprises, representatives of industrial associations, labor unions, and the civil service. The role of the commissions is threefold:

They are a source of information about past activities and future prospects of their sectors, and the data which they supply provide the basis for the final synthesis of a national economic plan.

They indicate measures which the public authorities and private decision makers should follow in order to accomplish the stated sectoral and national targets. They also formulate recommendations which, in their view, are likely to improve the conditions which are necessary for an effective achievement of the plan's objectives.

They review the implementation of the plan, analyze deviations between plan targets and actual accomplishments, and come up with revisions or additional recommendations.

For the Fifth Plan, which covers the period from 1966 through 1970, thirty-one planning commissions with a total membership of over 2,000 persons exist. There are twenty-five vertical commissions which are organized on an industry basis, such as steel, chemicals, mining, energy, and transportation, and deal only with the sector entrusted to them. The six horizontal commissions deal with problems common to the whole economy and are responsible for synthesizing the data supplied by the vertical commissions and for preserving the fundamental equilibria: the production equilibrium, financial equilibrium, manpower equilibrium, and balanced regional development.

Table 1 shows the steady increase in the number of commissions and in the number of people involved in planning. Table 1 indicates that the employers and their associations play a major role in the commissions. The high percentage of civil servants within the planning commissions is explained by the relatively large size of the public sectors and the civil servants' active involvement in the supervision of the plan's implementation. Table 1 also reflects the increasing participation of the labor unions.

(3) As far as the implementation of the national plans is concerned, the French planning authorities have at their disposal a large armory of instruments which can be used to put the plan into action and to enforce compliance with its

Professional Repartition of Total Membership of Planning Commissions

	Business Executives[a]	Professional Organizations[b]	Farmers and Farm Managers	Labor Union Representatives	Civil Servants and "Ex-Officio" Representatives[c]	Other Experts	Total
First Plan (8 Commissions)							
Number of Members	108	59	19	77	118	113	494
Percentage of Total	22	12	4	15	24	23	100
Second Plan (22 Commissions)							
Number of Members	137	5	21	34	184 –126	133	730
Percentage of Total	19	13	3	5	42	18	100
Third Plan (21 Commissions)							
Number of Members	119	140	22	52	201 –188	170	892
Percentage of Total	13	16	2	6	44	19	100
Fourth Plan (26 Commissions)							
Number of Members	211	248	20	114	202 –330	254	1,379
Percentage of Total	15	18	1	8	29	19	100
Fifth Plan (31 Commissions)							
Number of Members	406	430	67	291	457 –145	299	2,095
Percentage of Total	19	21	3	14	29	14	100

a Including nationalized industries.

b Formal groupings based upon industry or occupation, e.g., trade associations and industrial associations.

c Every commission has a certain number of ex-officio members (*membres de droit*) who are civil servants, such as the Director of the Budget, the Director of the Treasury, and the Director of the National Bureau of Statistics.

Table I

prescriptions. Generally, a peculiar mixture of psychological, structural, institutional, legislative, and administrative arrangements make the plan work. The most important are the large public sector which accounts for almost half of the total fixed capital formation, the credit controls, and an array of fiscal incentives for those business endeavors supporting specific plan objectives.

In general, the French approach to implementation of the plan has been characterized as one that uses sticks and carrots, "where there are more carrots than sticks."[6] Indeed, French government authorities have shown great readiness to make use of incentives to stimulate adherence to the plan's provisions. Where the incentives for implementing the plan are insufficient, they are supplemented by authoritarian regulations and direct interventions, such as the necessity for permission to build a plant, governmental approval of prices for certain products, or the stipulation of certain requirements for obtaining credit. However, French governmental officials, as well as planning authorities, regularly emphasize that they do not favor using their power of coercion to implement the plan. For instance, Valery Giscard d'Estaing, while Minister of Finance and Economic Affairs, stated in Parliament that all resources of persuasion should be exhausted before direct governmental interventions and pressures in favor of the realization of the plan are taken. He stated further that "if recourse to public resources should prove necessary in exceptional circumstances, the State would withdraw its participation as soon as the desired ends were reached. . . ."[7]

The Impact of French Planning on Decision Making

Every business enterprise has certain functional decision-making areas to which top management pays relatively more attention than to others. In general these areas are those which are particularly critical for the attainment of the company's objectives. With respect to these areas the management is obliged to anticipate future developments and to plan appropriate actions more carefully than for noncritical areas. Empirical investigations have shown that, apart from purely technological production problems, the most critical issues with which business executives are confronted are generally the firm's investments and related financial commitments, marketing strategy decisions, and research and development activities. Decisions related to these four areas are almost always interrelated, but they are frequently reached independently. An investigation of a representative sample of 371 French business executives' perception of the intensity with which their decisions and/or actions in the four mentioned critical areas are affected by the provisions and projections of the French national plan, led to the results shown in Table 2 and Figure 1.

---

[6] Jacques H. Dreze, "Some Postwar Contributions of French Economists to Theory and Public Policy," *American Economic Review,* LIV:2 (June 1964), 52.

[7] Valery Giscard d'Estaing, "Speech in the National Assembly, May 29, 1962," *French Affairs,* No. 139 (June 1962), 17.

	The Influence of the National Plan is			
	Very Important	Important	Of Little Importance	Of No Importance
On Investment Decisions	31%	33%	15%	21%
On Financial Decisions	26	33	23	18
On Marketing Decisions	15	24	35	26
On R & D Decisions (Allocation of Funds)	11	11	20	58

[a] Percentage of total number of answers provided by 371 French firms.

Table II

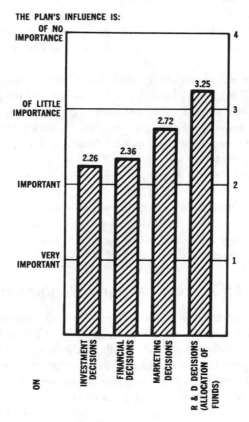

THE PLAN'S INFLUENCE IS:

Figure 1

Table 2 and Figure 1 show very clearly that the French national plans exert their greatest influence on business investment decisions, followed closely by financial decisions. The influence on market strategy decisions is considerably lower, and it is relatively insignificant as far as R&D decisions are concerned, even though thirty-nine firms stated that the national plans exert a very important influence on their R&D decisions.

An examination of those factors which French executives generally take into account when faced with investment decisions revealed four conditions. In order of diminishing returns these are: market expectations; access to the money or capital market; technological developments; fiscal privileges which the French planning authorities offer as incentives for certain decisions that are regarded as supporting the objectives of the national plan. Except for technological developments, the French planning authorities have direct control over these conditions, and it is thus not surprising that in general the French national plan affects business investment decisions rather strongly.

First, the production and investment targets which the plan represents influence market expectations by providing a rather clear picture of what the market will be like. The company can determine its place in the coordinated growth of the economy and move in the direction indicated by the plan. The plan thus creates a climate of confidence that a certain growth target will be attained, which goes a long way toward the actual accomplishment.

The second powerful means is the government's control of the banking apparatus. The banking system is bound to take account of the planned targets and provide financial means, particularly for those operations which conform to the targets. Since the majority of the large enterprises, which mainly determine the level of economic activity, depend on outside finance, it is obvious that the national plan exerts a strong impact on them.

The third reason for the particular influence of the plan on investment and financial decisions can be found in the existing system of incentives which the planning authorities grant to those firms whose activities are in conformity with the objectives of the plan. This leads to the conclusion that the influence of the national plans is largely a function of the means which the planning authorities can bring to bear in implementing the plan.

Conditioning Effect of Company Characteristics

Obviously, French national plans do not affect all business enterprises in the same manner. Which factors other than those directly plan-related condition the impact of the plan on the strategic decisions of the individual firm? An empirical investigation of these factors provided evidence that the personal attitudes of executives (either in favor of or against planning per se) play a rather insignificant role in this regard. Much more important are certain company characteristics, such as: size of the company; ownership situation (whether the company is privately, publicly, or foreign owned); type of business (whether it is in a capital- or labor-intensive industry); marketing orientation (whether the firm supplies the domestic market only or foreign markets as well).

The conditioning effect of these four types of company characteristics can be seen in Table 3 and Figure 2. The influence profile in Figure 2 clearly shows to what extent the differences in intensity with which business executives take account of the plan are caused by the operational characteristics of their enterprise.

The decisions of executives of large organizations are more strongly influenced by the plan than those of executives of small or medium-sized firms. For a majority of the large firms the influence of the plan is important, whereas for the small firms it is of little, if any, importance. Thus, it is a comparatively small but influential group of executives who take the plan seriously and who assure its relative success. Almost all of these executives are intimately familiar with the plan and contribute their expertise to its preparation. The findings of this investigation provide clear support of Andrew Shonfield's assertion "that the activity of planning, as it is

Summary of the Perceived Impact of the French National Plans on French Firms[a]

| | The Plan's Influence is | | | |
	Very Important	Important	Of Little Importance	Of No Importance
Size of Enterprise				
Small	5%	16%	31%	48%
Medium	16	25	32	27
Large	31	31	23	14
Control of Equity				
Private Ownership:				
French Control	22	28	26	24
Foreign Control	14	21	38	27
Public Ownership	51	31	12	4
Type of Business				
Capital-Intensive	24	27	25	24
Labor-Intensive	18	28	31	23
Marketing Orientation				
Exclusively Domestic	26	25	23	26
Mainly Domestic (Limited				
Export Interest)	22	32	25	21
International Orientation	20	21	35	24

[a] Percentage of total number of answers provided by 371 French firms.

Table III

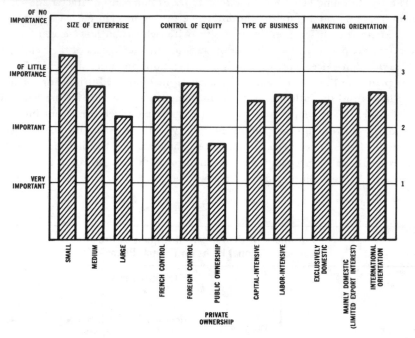

THE PLAN'S INFLUENCE IS:

OF NO IMPORTANCE

OF LITTLE IMPORTANCE

IMPORTANT

VERY IMPORTANT

SIZE OF ENTERPRISE | CONTROL OF EQUITY | TYPE OF BUSINESS | MARKETING ORIENTATION

SMALL | MEDIUM | LARGE | FRENCH CONTROL | FOREIGN CONTROL | PUBLIC OWNERSHIP | CAPITAL-INTENSIVE | LABOR-INTENSIVE | EXCLUSIVELY DOMESTIC | MAINLY DOMESTIC (LIMITED EXPORT INTEREST) | INTERNATIONAL ORIENTATION

PRIVATE OWNERSHIP

Figure 2

practiced in France, has reinforced the systematic influence exerted by large-scale business on economic policy."[8]

Particularly striking is the difference in impact on French-controlled versus foreign-controlled firms. The profile indicates that executives of foreign-controlled firms let their decisions be influenced by the French plan to a substantially lesser degree than the executives of private firms under French control. This fact reflects:

The relatively greater independence of foreign-controlled firms from particular national environmental conditions of which economic planning is just one.

The necessity for multinational firms to make decisions which take account of their particular international constraints and which subordinate, if necessary, nationally oriented considerations to their international aspirations.

The relative newness of a large percentage of foreign-controlled enterprises in France whose management is either against "state planning" as a matter of

---

[8] Andrew Shonfield, *Modern Capitalism* (London: Oxford University Press, 1965), p. 139.

management philosophy or whose management is "neutral" but hasn't yet had time or found it necessary to acquaint itself with French planning.

Even though differences in impact on capital-intensive versus labor-intensive firms are not spectacular, the profile shows that capital-intensive organizations are more strongly influenced than labor-intensive ones. This is mainly due to the preeminent position of investments in capital-intensive firms. Since investment decisions are more strongly influenced by the plan and since investments play a more important role in capital-intensive firms than in labor-intensive organizations, the former must necessarily be more strongly influenced by the national plan, a situation which is borne out by the findings.

Differences in the market orientation are not very significant as determining factors for the degree of influence which the national plan exerts. Firms which supply the domestic market only and those which have only limited export interest show practically no difference at all. However, multinational firms or firms which depend to a large extent on exports show that they take less account of the plan than the domestically oriented firms—obviously because their decisions are influenced by developments abroad.

The very existence of a national economic plan and the way in which it is prepared and implemented create certain conditions. To the extent that these conditions are conducive to a better attainment of the firm's objectives, they have positive effects. Conversely, they have negative effects to the extent that they are detrimental to the attainment of the firm's objectives.

In general, a national economic plan can have positive effects on: the information available to the firm; the firm's level of business activity; the firm's relationships with various social groups; and the impact of competition. Other less direct positive effects can be seen in such areas as economic education and the coordination of government and business decisions and long-range planning.

The Information Effect

Business decision making requires a continuous flow of data, and many authors have emphasized the increasing demand for information in this era of accelerated changes.[9] One advantage of the national economic plan for the individual firm is thus the fact that management is provided with an increasing amount of consistent information. The plan as a source of information has three major properties:

(1) Since the government is committed to implement the plan, it represents a set of authoritative knowledge which can be relied upon to a large extent. This reduces uncertainties and consequently facilitates appropriate decisions in light of the anticipated development.

(2) Using an input-output approach to national planning and taking account of certain balancing conditions such as financial equilibrium and manpower

---

[9] Norbert Wiener, *Cybernetics* (New York: John Wiley, 1948), p. 187.

equilibrium means that the plan is also a set of coherent, logical information which gives the decision makers in the individual economic units reassurance that it is safe to "play the game."

(3) The plan not only provides an extension of the field of cognition of economic interrelationships, but also provides an increase in the length of foresight in time. In particular the long-term projections, such as the twenty-year "plan horizon" of French national plans, indicate trends of developments or processes which are anticipated far in the future and are occurring so slowly that any single decision maker on the firm level could hardly be aware of their existence. Also in this respect the plan for the individual firm has the advantage of reducing uncertainties of future developments and provides a basis for timely adjustments to anticipated changes.

The Dynamism Effect

Built into any form of planning is the drive for achievement. The French national plans are no exception. In fact, they are noted for consistently stating targets which at the outset seem hardly attainable, taking into account such constraints as monetary stability and external equilibrium. But for the individual businessman who is striving to retain the firm's relative competitive position and who is told what the expansion of his sector must be in order to achieve the over-all target growth, this acts as an incentive for expansion and consequently has a dynamic effect on the level of business activity.

However, the stipulation of a high-growth target alone is not sufficient for injecting dynamism into an economy. In addition, it is necessary that the business community be confident that the growth target will actually be achieved. In France, where public authorities control about one-half of the total investment activity and where there exists a large armory of other means to insure the implementation of the plan, there has thus far been little widespread doubt or distrust that the growth target could be attained.

In this connection the plan is a vehicle to make those on whom the level of economic activity largely depends growth-conscious and thus more dynamic. Comparing the presently prevailing business attitudes of executives of large organizations with the somewhat complacent well-documented attitudes of their predecessors in the first half of this century, one cannot fail to notice the change in pace; French businessmen credit the plan with being at least partially responsible for this inspiring dynamism and vigor.

The Harmonization Effect

It can be hypothesized that the French planning system, which calls for representation of the various social groups in the planning commissions, reduces social and industrial conflicts by creating a "social dialogue" which leads to a better understanding of each other's problems. In this way the plan becomes the basis for arbitration between the interests of wage earners and those of employers. This point of view emphasizes the democratic content of French planning procedures and regards the plan as a useful common denominator of policy making among various social groups and classes.

However, the plan or national arbitration force between employers and unionists seems up to now to have been only an ideal and not a reflection of the actual situation. In the words of François Perroux:

> To argue today that the Plan is an organ of social dialogue and collective creativity would be saying far too much. But to assert that it could not become this would be to deprive it of its most powerful source of energy and to refuse it its finest flight.[10]

The Positive Impact on Competition

It has been repeatedly pointed out that the unique feature in the institutional setup of French planning is the planning commission, which includes representatives of the major firms of each individual industry sector; representatives of industrial associations; and civil servants, trade unionists, and other experts. French planners have frequently stressed the advantages of the "dialogue" which this system enables and its coordinating and interpreting effect. For instance, Pierre Massé pointed out that French industry, by avoiding the buildup of excess capacity, has achieved the same production with a lower level of investment than that necessary for the same results in other countries, and consequently, this has resulted in the aggregate in a higher return on investment in France.[11]

The dialogue in the commissions has been interpreted, especially by American commentators, as a euphemism for collusive agreements, an activity which is regarded with suspicion. It has been frequently stated that the commissions' meetings provide an opportunity for restrictive business practices, such as sharing out investment or production quotas, particularly among oligopolistic units. The work of the planning commissions does indeed appear to imply that some agreement is reached between firms on planned investments, production, exports, and other important variables. "Here," David Granick states, "it seems to me we have the essence of French planning. It is the planning of each industry by its own members, acting as a great cartel, with the civil service sitting in on the game and sweetening the pot."[12] S. Wickham, a French economist, phrases it this way:

> If, for instance, iron and steel industrialists meet in a restaurant to discuss production of various types of steel plates with a view to agree on their respective productive capacity, this is cartelization.

---

[10] François Perroux, *The IVth French Plan (1962–1965)* (London: National Institute of Economic and Social Research, 1965), p. 71.

[11] Pierre Massé, "National Planning and Business Enterprise in France," in G. A. Steiner and W. M. Cannon, eds., *Multinational Corporate Planning* (New York: Macmillan Company, 1966), p. 158.

[12] David Granick, *The European Executive* (New York: Doubleday, 1962), p. 154.

> *But, one will say, if they meet exactly for the same purpose in a conference room supplied to them by the government, with a civil servant acting as secretary, then everyone will praise this practice as avoiding duplications in the productive apparatus of the country and promoting full employment of fixed capacity.*[13]

In short, the planning commissions are regarded by some as the most useful part of the French planning machinery and by others as the potentially most dangerous part, because company representatives who work together in a commission may agree to share new markets and consequently may refrain from struggling too hard to alter their share of existing markets, and price competition may become extremely gentlemanly.

Two statements summarize very appropriately the effect of the planning system on interfirm competition. When asked how he feels about the planning procedure which leads to "ententes" and a reduction of competition, Massé replied that ententes between firms are not new and would happen even if there were no plan. However, "if they are going to happen anyhow, it is better that they should happen in the context of economic growth, and within the range of planning authorities."[14]

Granick expresses explicitly what Massé implied with his statement. "A cartel can plan for expansion—indeed this is the most profitable type of programming when conditions are appropriate—and this is what the great combination of French cartels called 'the Plan' has in fact done."[15]

Other Positive Effects

There are other effects which are not widely recognized among the business community because their influence is less direct and because they have only a long-range payoff. The two most important effects of this kind can be termed education and coordination effects.

Officials associated with the Planning Commissariat have pointed out that the national plan itself as well as the procedure for its development serve a useful educational function. The plan is an instrument of economic education for government officials, business executives, and, to a certain extent, labor leaders, opening their eyes to the economic interdependencies in a complex situation.

Ideally, the plan is a coordinated set of anticipated developments related to decisions to attain the envisaged objectives. In recent years the plan has become more and more the framework within which the various decisions as related to governmental economic policy are taken. This coordinating effect of the plan, which refers primarily to governmental economic decisions, has an important

---

[13] S. Wickham, "French Planning: Retrospect and Prospect," *Review of Economics and Statistics*, XXXV:4 (Nov. 1963), 341.

[14] PEP, *Economic Planning in France* (London: Political and Economic Planning, 1969), p. 231.

[15] Granick, *op. cit.*, p. 155.

secondary effect on the business community in the sense that it increases the degree to which business executives can rely on the plan and thus is another factor in reducing uncertainties over future developments.

There can also be negative effects on an individual firm. To the extent that the intentions of individual companies in a certain sector correspond with the development as planned by the planning authorities, there is little occasion for conflict, and the plan will be implemented without resort to "corrective" or coercive means. But, if the plan advocates appreciable changes which individual firms have not anticipated or for which their motivation to comply is low, it creates difficulties for both the planning authorities and the individual firms. In general, the plan can have adverse effects on traditional behavior; investment schedules; the firm's profit-making capacity; the firm's competitive situation domestically as well as internationally; and the firm's or the sector's relative importance in the economy.

Adverse Impact on Traditional Behavior

Economic historians have repeatedly pointed out particular value standards and behavioral characteristics which are typical of the majority of small family-owned French enterprises. The preoccupation of the typical French firm with security and its concern with staying independent of outside influence is in direct conflict with some of the explicit or implicit objectives of the plan, which emphasizes industrial expansion and efficiency in the utilization of resources. For instance, in the directives for a selective lending policy which were issued in 1963 and are still in force, the banks were asked to respect the aims of the plan and to favor certain types of operations, such as regroupings of firms, which would lead to greater concentration and specialization.

Obviously, the plan's emphasis on efficiency, economies of scale, and industrial expansion is in direct conflict with the traditional conservative behavior of a majority of small family-owned firms. Since the governmental authorities provide inducements for compliance with the plan's objectives in the form of access to credit, differential tax rates, or subsidies, the firm that doesn't let itself be "induced" may soon find itself at an impossible competitive disadvantage.

This means that ultimately most French firms are forced either to sacrifice their traditional objectives of security, financial independence, and family control, and adopt the more dynamic objectives which the plan advocates—such as growth and efficiency—or to continue to cling to an outdated but time-honored mode of behavior and be faced with a high probability of losing out competitively.

Adverse Effect on Intrasectoral Competition

The impact of the plan on the competitive situation of an individual firm can be twofold. It can increase as well as reduce interfirm competition, and either situation can have negative consequences for individual firms in the sector.

First, the French plan states the investment and output targets for a sector, and obviously there are instances where most of the firms in the sector try to secure the largest share of the planned expansion for themselves. The attempt to grab the lion's share of the market leads to systematic overinvestment and the buildup of excess capacity. This in turn leads to keen competition among firms, which generally has an adverse impact on the companies' profitability and eventually on some companies' survival particularly if their financial backing is not very stong.

From a macroeconomic point of view such a situation seems quite beneficial since it increases efficiency, reduces excess profits, and guarantees an optimum allocation of scarce resources. But, for the individual firm—or even for a majority of firms in a particular sector—the situation created by the existence of a national plan clearly has serious negative effects on the achievement of the firms' general objectives.

Second, one of the major concerns of the French planning authorities has been and still is that of gaining the cooperation of the various economic and social forces which can make the plan's objectives become reality. In this regard particular attention has been paid to the strategic sectors of the economy (the so-called basic industries) and the large corporations, which can be used for coordinating or coercing the actions of the smaller firms in the same branch. In most cases the representatives of the enterprise sector in the various planning commissions come from large firms.

It is obvious that the planning machinery can also be used for the self-interest of the industry, particularly by the larger firms to enhance their economic and financial power over the smaller firms. The larger firms generally can gain relatively more from the plan than the smaller ones because they can more readily gain special concessions for their cooperation with the plan in the form of differential tax rates or special depreciation allowances, and because they can more easily get access to the sources which provide working capital and long-term capital for development. In this regard, Chamberlain points out that "a kind of 'unholy alliance' may grow up between a government and the major private power centers."[16] This indicates that the plan provides a basis for changing the competitive situation between small and large firms in the sector in favor of the latter. Therefore, from the point of view of many small enterprises, the plan has an adverse impact on their relative competitive positions.

Adverse Impact on Intersectoral Competition

Criticism of the French national plan as "not neutral" has a long tradition and is not surprising in view of the fact that each of the successive plans favored certain sectors or economic activities. For instance, it can be shown that the emphasis of the national plan on the basic industry—the agricultural sector, the export-oriented

---

[16] Neil W. Chamberlain, *Private and Public Planning* (New York: McGraw-Hill Book Company, 1965), pp. 191–192.

industry—has been detrimental to the equal development of other industries and therefore the various "priorities" which successive plans pursued were justly criticized by those who did not belong to the preferred sector. The national plans' intersectoral discrimination effect means disadvantages for individual enterprises in nonpriority sectors as, for instance, when they cannot get the loans they would like to have for expansion. Obviously, preferential treatment of certain sectors over others is a sensible approach to using scarce resources in order to assure the attainment of certain primary targets. From the point of view of the economic system as a whole, there is thus little justification in classifying type of intersectoral discrimination as a negative effect, but it does create disadvantages for firms which are not in a priority sector.

Negative Consequences of Governmental Enforcement of the Plan

It has been pointed out that the planning authorities have direct or indirect control over a large arsenal of means for influencing the activities of the business community in the plan's direction. Among the most powerful means are selective controls over capital issues, over long-term borrowing from credit institutions, over medium-term borrowing from banks, over the selective distribution of bank credit, and over the various forms of tax privileges. The individual firm which must rely on outside finance and whose intended activities are limited by lack of the necessary financial means because of some plan-related considerations, rightly blames "the plan" for having a negative effect on its operations.

Obviously, the financial strings are potentially the most powerful to enforce compliance with the plan, and thus from the point of view of the business community the most negative effects of the plan are related to the financial considerations. However, it cannot be overlooked that other means which are employed to achieve the targets of the plan, to the extent that they are of a restrictive nature, have negative effects also. It can easily be seen how administrative, authoritarian controls, such as price controls, requirements for construction permits, special approval before a net business above a certain size can be established in the Paris area, and required permits to establish refining and distillation plants, are constraints on the free development of business activity and thus exert a negative influence.

Relative Importance of Positive and Negative Effects

French national planning offers a variety of advantages but also has negative effects. The utilization of the positive effects and the realization of the negative effects are largely conditioned by the firm's operational characteristics and the general orientation of the plan. Executives of the multitude of firms show great differences in their responsiveness to and cooperation with the plan. There are those who can afford to ignore it. There are those who cannot afford to ignore it but do so nevertheless and pay a certain price for it, and there are those who are more or less familiar with the plan and cognitive of its favorable and unfavorable implications.

French business executives who claimed to have a high degree of familiarity with the plan and related information were asked to evaluate the various effects of the plan. A total of 158 executives responded to this request; 14 of them were executives of small firms, 19 of medium-sized firms, and 125 of large firms. This somewhat unusual distribution reflects precisely the differences in plan-consciousness among executives of the various categories of firms. A surprising result—at least at first sight—is the fact that the separate tabulation of the evaluation of the various effects of the plan on the three sizes of firms showed practically no differences. This indicates that executives, to the extent that they are familiar with the plan and take account of its provisions, have largely the same perception of the importance of the various effects.

The results of evaluation are summarized in Table 4, Figure 3, and Figure 4, which provide a clear picture of the French executives' appreciation of the positive factors of the national plan and also shows their apprehension with regard to the more disagreeable aspects of planning. It indicates that a large majority of those French executives who stated that they take account of the national plan when reaching strategic decisions perceive that the most noticeable advantage is derived from the fact that the plan supplies them with a large amount of consistent information, at practically no cost, about anticipated developments in the economy as a whole and in the various sectors. It is especially with regard to investment and financial decisions and to a lesser degree with respect to marketing decisions that the information effect of the French plan facilitates appropriate decisions so that they are consistent with the anticipated over-all development.

The magnitude of the information effect of the plan can be questioned, especially in view of the fact that a majority of the executives of small- and medium-sized firms make no use of it at all. However, it must be recognized that effective utilization of the potentially available information requires competent persons who can relate the general information which the plan offers to a firm's specific situation. But in small firms one seldom finds executives who make competent use of the plan, and almost always these firms either do not have the resources for or are prejudiced against qualified staff services that could analyze a complex set of aggregate data in order to extract what might be relevant for the firm. The apparent ignorance of the plan among executives of smaller firms cannot, however, lead to the conclusion that the information effect is negligible, particularly in view of the fact that executives of the large firms attach so much importance to it. Instead, we are led again to the conclusion that the French plan could be better utilized if the channels of communication between planning authorities and smaller firms were improved.

The investigation of the positive effects of French planning has also provided evidence for the French business executives' perception that the plans and the ways they are put into action are conducive to a high level of business activity and

Effects of the National Plan and Their Relative Importance[a]

	Perception of the Effect as			
	Very Important	Important	Of Little Importance	Of No Importance
Positive Effects				
Information Effect	34%	61%	5%	0%
Dynamism Effect	38	35	16	11
Harmonization Effect	0	8	43	49
Effect on Competition	4	14	47	35
Education Effect	0	5	20	75
Coordination Effect	26	47	18	9
Negative Effects				
Discrimination Effect (Intersectoral)	3	10	40	37
Discrimination Effect (Intrasectoral)	11	10	37	42
Financial Means Used to Enforce Compliance as Inhibitors of Company Operations	31	43	20	6
Administrative Means Used to Enforce Compliance With the Plan as Inhibitors of Company Operations	6	21	53	20

a Percentage of total number of answers provided by a representative sample of 158 French business executives.

Table IV

economic dynamism. From this evidence one can conclude that the traditional accusation against economic planning as being detrimental to individual initiative is a fallacy, at least in the context of French-style planning. Influential French executives seem to recognize that the growth orientation of the French plans generally supports the growth objectives of the individual firms. In addition, they seem to realize that the Plan is an important instrument for a coordinated, systematic application of economic policy means, which further enhances its "dynamism effect."

From the point of view of the individual firm, a reduction in intercompany competition is generally considered a desirable state of affairs. It has been argued that the French planning system, which invites competitors to elaborate jointly on their future decisions, is an officially sanctioned mechanism for collusive agreements. A majority of French executives, however, disclaim that French planning has such consequences. For any outsider, particularly someone who

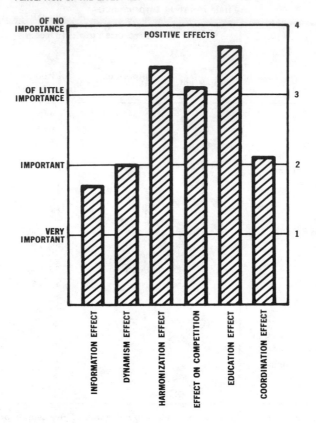

OF NO IMPORTANCE

POSITIVE EFFECTS

OF LITTLE IMPORTANCE

IMPORTANT

VERY IMPORTANT

INFORMATION EFFECT

DYNAMISM EFFECT

HARMONIZATION EFFECT

EFFECT ON COMPETITION

EDUCATION EFFECT

COORDINATION EFFECT

Figure 3

believes in the benefits and efficiency of antitrust regulations as they exist in the United States or Germany, this seems rather unbelievable. But it must be recognized that the majority of French business executives traditionally subscribe to a maxim of "live and let live," and they are thoroughly organized in professional associations. Seen in this light, it seems true that the French planning system itself is of little consequence with respect to interfirm competition, and there is little empirical evidence for claiming that it fosters collusive agreements among competitors.

Still another potentially positive effect of the French planning system has not materialized to the extent that was expected. It was hoped that the French approach to planning would provide a basis for a harmonious resolution of problems between the social classes. However, the empirical evidence so far allows only the conclusion that this expectation remains an ideal. But it should not be

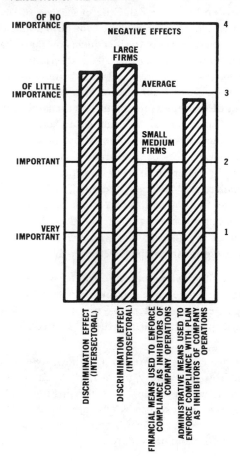

PERCEPTION OF THE EFFECT AS:

OF NO IMPORTANCE

NEGATIVE EFFECTS

LARGE FIRMS

AVERAGE

OF LITTLE IMPORTANCE

SMALL MEDIUM FIRMS

IMPORTANT

VERY IMPORTANT

DISCRIMINATION EFFECT (INTERSECTORAL)

DISCRIMINATION EFFECT (INTROSECTORAL)

FINANCIAL MEANS USED TO ENFORCE COMPLIANCE AS INHIBITORS OF COMPANY OPERATIONS

ADMINISTRATIVE MEANS USED TO ENFORCE COMPLIANCE WITH PLAN AS INHIBITORS OF COMPANY OPERATIONS

Figure 4

overlooked that the plan could indeed be a national arbitration force, and it must necessarily become so if income planning and planning in monetary terms are to have any meaning.

With respect to the potentially negative effects, the investigation led to the conclusion that in general French business executives feel most severely hampered by the planning authorities' control over external financing. The French banks' lending policy, i.e., the extension of loans primarily for activities which are in conformity with the plan, is the single most powerful factor in making a large segment of business executives "plan-conscious."

From the point of view of smaller firms a negative effect of the French plan is its alleged discrimination in favor of large enterprises. Executives of the small- and medium-sized firms on the one hand feel that the Plan fosters intrasectoral discrimination, whereas on the other hand the executives of large firms seem to be quite unaware of this effect. There is evidence for both points of view. However, a careful analysis of the situation leads to the conclusion that what the executives of smaller firms perceive subjectively as the plan's discrimination in favor of large firms is in reality an outgrowth of the small firms' ignorance in plan matters. As a result, the smaller firms do not make use of the various advantages and positive effects which the plans offer in the same manner as the larger firms do.

Alleviation of the intrasectoral discrimination effect of the plan among executives of smaller firms can only be achieved by increasing their cognition of it and by making them aware also of the gradual change in managerial attitudes among executives of the larger firms. The executives of the larger firms have become more aggressive and efficiency-minded, whereas a majority of the executives of small French firms still adhere to a more traditional, complacent, "live and let live" management concept.

From the analysis of the positive and negative effects of French planning on company operations, two general conclusions can be drawn:

(1) To secure the positive effects and advantages of French-style planning generally requires an active endeavor on the part of the firm's management, whereas the negative effects materialize much more "automatically" and can hardly be avoided, particularly if the firm has to rely on external sources of finance.

(2) In total, the positive effects of French planning outweigh the real or imagined negative effects. This is certainly the major reason for the rather favorable attitudes toward French planning and the institutional setup among the majority of those business executives who are cognitive about their country's planning effort. As a result, French executives either laud or ignore but rarely oppose their country's planning system.

This situation does not prevent the executives from voicing strong disapproval of certain plan-related innovations or changes which they feel would create more difficulties and disadvantages than benefits. Numerically, those executives who actively support French planning may be relatively small in comparison with the total number of business executives, but there is no doubt that they represent mainly the large firms, and their attitudes therefore carry considerably more weight than the rather neutral or ignorant attitudes of the others.

The Relevance of the French Experience to the United States

There are some who believe that national planning will never play more than a rudimentary role in our free enterprise system. On the other hand, many people see a growing planning-consciousness in the United States. For instance, in specific large-scale projects by federal, state, and local governments, a good deal of program planning as well as some form of national economic policy planning, more for the purpose of direction than for promotion of development of certain industrial sectors towards explicitly stated national aims, can be observed. Those who believe that a free market system in our age will be successful only if it is supported by substantial elements of long-range forecasting and planning, see a promising development in this increasing planning consciousness at the national level.

In fact, considering the complexity and interdependence of such large-scale programs as the space program, the development of water resources, the construction of the interstate highway system, programs for urban renewal, and the necessary expansion of the ground facilities for air transportation, it becomes obvious that some form of coordinated, long-range national plan is necessary. It seems untenable that the decisions with respect to such far-reaching programs should be made largely in response to external pressures or by sheer drifting. There is ample justification for some form of systematic long-range national planning which would lead to an elaboration of national goal targets, and the means which are necessary to accomplish them within a given time period. Otherwise it will only perpetuate what Secretary of Labor Willard Wirtz has characterized in these terms:

> ... what we are doing really right now is flying the most powerful economic machine in the history of mankind, and I mean to include all of our scientific and technological developments, and we are flying it by luck, by instinct, with almost no instruments at all in the cockpit. ...[17]

The periodic development of long-range national plans could provide a very suitable instrument panel in the cockpit of our economic "flying machine." The question is: Can we learn anything from the French planning experience? Obviously, since any national planning system must be tailored to the specific economic, social, and political conditions of a country, a duplicate of the French system is quite out of the question. However, certain principles which have proven their worth should be considered:

(1) The repeated extension of the so-called plan horizon for the successive French plans has shown the value of systematic long-range projections for a period of up to twenty years. These projections are synchronized with the conceptualization and design of a broad spectrum of choices so that decisions conditioning the future can be made in a coherent manner and do not risk involvement in contradictory situations.

(2) Jean Monnet's idea that a national plan must be derived by a national consensus is certainly a relevant one, although not easy to implement, as the

---

[17] Quoted by Norman V. Peterson in "A National Plan for Century III," *Journal of the American Institute of Planners*, XXXIII:4 (July 1967), 224.

French experience has shown. Nevertheless, a continuous effort has to be made to guarantee that national planning is a collective endeavor, which means that all those who are instrumental in implementation of the plan should also be involved in its preparation. This calls for a particularly active participation by the business community which can provide essential data and information for sectoral projections. A synthesis and harmonization of the various sectoral projections would then lead to a national plan which would become the framework for a coordinated application of our economic policy instruments and would provide a basis for effective corporate planning and decision making. This form of national planning, which results from an extensive and organized exchange of information among all the social forces and decision-making centers in the economy, constitutes neither an intrusion into the freedom of private enterprise nor a reduction of competition between the individual firms; competition will only take place at a more enlightened level.

(3) The French planning system has demonstrated its viability because of its built-in flexibility which has enabled it to respond quickly to new conditions and problems as they arise. Flexibility must certainly be a major characteristic of any national planning system in a free market economy, and it refers particularly to the administrative apparatus, the selection of targets, and the means which have to be applied in order to accomplish the desired goals. One must always keep in mind that there is nothing sacred about national planning; it is only a tool designed to achieve certain specified national objectives in an optimal way. As a tool, national planning can be extended or limited in scope, used for various purposes, and applied under different economic systems.

In addition to these considerations, it is important to recognize—regardless of one's own opinion about the relative merits of national planning—that the methods and procedures which have been developed and tested for national planning purposes can make a significant contribution to increasing the effectiveness of business planning. These methods and procedures can play an important role in devising effective planning systems, particularly for large and conglomerate enterprises. This too is a facet of the interrelationship between national and business planning.

Part Five

Development Questions in International Business

5

The international scene of our time is dominated by the ever-widening gap between the advanced countries and the less developed countries (LDC's). About two-thirds of the world's population lives in LDC's, with only about one-third in the comparatively rich countries of North America, Europe, Australia, and Japan. The usual measure of economic development is GNP/capita, with about $400 or so being a common line of demarcation between "advanced" and "underdeveloped." This is a rough and ready guide, however; the truth is countries can be arrayed in a continuum running from the very rich such as the U.S., Sweden, and Switzerland to the very poor such as some of the newly independent countries of central Africa.

Most of the LDC's are in Africa, Asia, and Latin America, and there are many reasons for their great poverty. Unfavorable climates, lack of natural resources, past eras of exploitation by colonial powers, deeply rooted cultural attitudes that are not congenial to economic activity, inbred behavioral responses that discourage wealth accumulation, and many other factors have been cited to explain why the processes of self-sustaining economic development have simply been frustrated in most parts of the world.

The underdeveloped countries show great variety of political structure. Some are newly independent after long years of colonial servitude, as in Africa; others have been politically independent for over a century, as in Latin America. Some are tiny ministates as in the West Indies; others are huge, thickly populated world powers as China and India. Nearly all have a similar economic structure in that agriculture usually accounts for some two-thirds or more of GNP, while manufacturing industry and those service industries that are characteristic of the advanced economies are severely "underdeveloped." In most of the LDC's the average productivity of labor is very low, investment capital is scarce and often uneconomically employed when judged by the standards of modern industry.

In the view of the traditional economist, the LDC's seem to have plenty of labor, and some have more than enough land, but all appear to be short of capital. Since capital accumulates from year to year out of a people's additions to their savings, and since in the LDC's there is relatively little margin left over after current consumption to be devoted to savings, it is sometimes said the LDC's are poor because they are poor. That is, being poor they have low incomes, which means that saving will necessarily be small, making for a low level of capital formation; and because there is an insufficient growth in the stock of capital, they remain poor.

While this line of reasoning undoubtedly has direct applicability to many LDC's, our matrix goes far beyond it, enabling us to pinpoint many other factors that may be blocks to economic development. By appraising an environment in terms of the four C's, we look at more than just economic factors. We look also at political-legal factors (is the government strong enough to govern and is it staffed by reasonably honest men?) and—perhaps of special importance for the LDC's—we look at educational and behavioral factors (are the workers literate, are there opportunities for training in business and engineering subjects, do people accept work as a dignified way to spend their time, do they have a cause-effect approach to life, etc.).

The constraints in our matrix were selected because they help tie together the micro and macro factors in the environment and because they are directly relevant to the effectiveness of business management.

The international businessman must be interested in the LDC's for many reasons. In the broadest sense he is interested because the hordes of under-nourished, underhoused, short-life-expectancy people in these countries might well be, under other circumstances, his customers. If only the blocks to their economic progress could be removed, they could enjoy greater productivity and greater purchasing power, and they would comprise a gigantic addition to world markets for goods and services. In a narrower sense, he may be interested in the LDC's because some important international businesses have direct interlocks with LDC's. The petroleum industry, for example, often cited as the prototype of international business, depends heavily upon oil supplies in the Middle East, the Caribbean Sea, Africa, and, increasingly, southeast Asia. Other minerals such as tin, copper, iron ore, alumina, and others bring modern businessmen and LDC people together—to say nothing of the growing markets in the LDC's for capital goods of all kinds. Finally, multinational firms are increasingly farming out the manufacture of components to LDC's where low-cost but capable labor is readily available to assemble transistors, build cabinets, etc.

Many LDC's proclaim their devotion to what they call "socialism," as in India, much of Africa, and the Arab world, because many of them have had unfortunate experiences with past colonialism, which they often identify as "capitalism." But these broad label words may mean quite different things in different countries, and western-oriented businessmen have often earned comfortable profits in countries that have opted for various kinds of over-all economic plans. If the expatriate business, perhaps a manufacturing subsidiary of a multinational firm, adapts itself to the goals of the host country, introduces modern concepts of management and skills into the LDC environment, and in other ways makes a contribution to the host country's economic development, it is likely to be welcomed in the private economic sector of most LDC's, even though the host government may be carrying out government-directed planning in closely related economic sectors.

In fact, many LDC's realize that the large professionally managed firms of the economically advanced countries have mastered the art of generating income on a large scale and are beginning to study the operations of these firms to learn the secrets of their success. Thus many international businessmen may find themselves and their operations made the subject of study by LDC planners. Great benefits may flow from the transmission of management and engineering skills from the economically advanced countries to the LDC's in this and other ways. The nitty-gritty of successful economic development requires, at the level of the individual firm, great attention to management details that are readily familiar to most western-oriented businessmen.

Thus, the international businessman in an LDC travels back and forth on a two-way street—learning how to adapt his managerial skills to an environment that may be quite different from the one in which they were developed, and at the same time imparting to others his own attitudes toward work and toward managing business organizations. The exchange can be a beneficial one, and when the conditions are right, it can spark an economic takeoff for the underdeveloped country.

The readings in this section include several gems in the field in international business writing that have successfully stood the test of time. We lead off with Edward T. Hall's classic article on "The Silent Language in Overseas Business." With unforgettable charm Mr. Hall makes us aware that much of our day-to-day communication with other people takes place, not by the use of formal language, but by way of signs and signals that we silently send back and forth to one another, often unconsciously. These methods of communication are culturally acquired, however, and in international life they may sometimes badly misfire. No one who reads Hall's lines on the silent languages of time, of space, of things, and of friendship and agreements is likely to need to be reminded again of their importance.

Another timeless insight into the ways of international business is provided by Ranjit Singh Bhambri's discussion of "Myth and Reality about Private Enterprise in India." He helps us understand why, in the world's largest democracy, "it has become almost—a habit with literate Indians to blame the commercial classes and the financial interests for the country's economic backwardness." In a country which has not attached much value to private enterprise as a way of life, businessmen have been unpopular, it seems, mainly because they have failed to carry out some of the most vital functions that we in the U.S., for example, count upon business to perform. For at least a brief and enlightening moment, West meets East in Mr. Bhambri's perceptive article.

Few selections from the literature of international relations succeed so well in helping us to see ourselves as others see us, as does our third article, "The African Image of Higher Education in America," by Margaret Y. and John P. Henderson. It is disturbing to read how seriously our good intentions may miscarry, especially when they are supplemented by African students' direct experience with American racial prejudice. Some of the students whose experiences are described by the Hendersons may someday be sitting across the negotiating table from American international businessmen.

Government-to-government foreign aid as we have known it for the past 20–30 years is largely an American invention and sooner or later most international businessmen come into contact with some aspect of foreign aid. We are fortunate to have two distinguished practitioners of the art of foreign aid among our contributors. Frank M. Coffin, who has participated in foreign aid activities as a Congressman, an AID mission director, and as U.S. representative in the aid operation of the Organization for Economic Cooperation and Development (OECD), describes succinctly some of the activities that take up an AID mission director's day. In a second article, reprinted from the *New York Times*, former Ambassador to India Chester Bowles describes for us "What Foreign Aid Can and Cannot Do."

Professor John Fayerweather was one of the first research scholars to turn his hand to the problems of international business. We have selected one of his many stimulating articles, "19th Century Ideology and 20th Century Reality." In it he reflects upon the rising tide of nationalism that has engulfed our world and the challenges it poses for multinational companies. Professor Fayerweather cannot claim to "solve" any problems in this uncertain area, but by breaking a problem down into its component parts for separate study, he helps to clarify possible approaches to solutions.

In a final selection, Professor Harry G. Johnson foresees a continually inadequate flow of government-to-government foreign aid in years to come, which he thinks will shift the emphasis in economic development to what can be done by private companies. Professor Johnson surveys some of the new problems likely to arise if the multinational company is to be cast in the role of an agent of economic development.

The Silent Language
in Overseas Business

Edward T. Hall

With few exceptions, Americans are relative newcomers on the international business scene. Today, as in Mark Twain's time, we are all too often "innocents abroad," in an era when naiveté and blundering in foreign business dealings may have serious political repercussions.

When the American executive travels abroad to do business, he is frequently shocked to discover to what extent the many variables for foreign behavior and custom complicate his efforts. Although the American has recognized, certainly, that even the man next door has many minor traits which make him somewhat peculiar, for some reason he has failed to appreciate how different foreign businessmen and their practices will seem to him.

He should understand that the various peoples around the world have worked out and integrated into their subconscious literally thousands of behavior patterns that they take for granted in each other.[1] Then, when the stranger enters, and behaves differently from the local norm, he often quite unintentionally insults, annoys, or amuses the native with whom he is attempting to do business. For example:

> In the United States, a corporation executive knows what is meant when a client lets a month go by before replying to a business proposal. On the other hand, he senses an eagerness to do business if he is immediately ushered into the client's office. In both instances, he is reacting to subtle cues in the timing of interaction, cues which he depends on to chart his course of action.
>
> Abroad, however, all this changes. The American executive learns that the Latin Americans are casual about time and that if he waits an hour in the outer office before seeing the Deputy Minister of Finance, it does not necessarily mean he is not getting anywhere. There people are so important that nobody can bear to tear himself away; because of the resultant interruptions and conversational detours, everybody is constantly getting behind. What the American does not know is the point at which the waiting becomes significant.
>
> In another instance, after traveling 7,000 miles an American walks into the office of a highly recommended Arab businessman on

---

[1] For details, see my book, *The Silent Language* (New York: Doubleday & Company, Inc., 1959).

whom he will have to depend completely. What he sees does not breed confidence. The office is reached by walking through a suspicious-looking coffeehouse in an old, dilapidated building situated in a crowded non-European section of town. The elevator, rising from dark, smelly corridors, is rickety and equally foul. When he gets to the office itself, he is shocked to find it small, crowded, and confused. Papers are stacked all over the desk and table tops—even scattered on the floor in irregular piles.

The Arab merchant he has come to see had met him at the airport the night before and sent his driver to the hotel this morning to pick him up. But now, after the American's rush, the Arab is tied up with something else. Even when they finally start talking business, there are constant interruptions. If the American is at all sensitive to his environment, everything around him signals, "What am I getting into?"

Before leaving home he was told that things would be different, but how different? The hotel is modern enough. The shops in the new part of town have many more American and European trade goods than he had anticipated. His first impression was that doing business in the Middle East would not present any new problems. Now he is beginning to have doubts. One minute everything looks familiar and he is on firm ground; the next, familiar landmarks are gone. His greatest problem is that so much assails his senses all at once that he does not know where to start looking for something that will tell him where he stands. He needs a frame of reference—a way of sorting out what is significant and relevant.

That is why it is so important for American businessmen to have a real understanding of the various social, cultural, and economic differences they will face when they attempt to do business in foreign countries. To help give some frame of reference, this article will map out a few areas of human activity that have largely been unstudied.

The topics I will discuss are certainly not presented as the last word on the subject, but they have proved to be highly reliable points at which to begin to gain an understanding of foreign cultures. While additional research will undoubtedly turn up other items just as relevant, at present I think the businessman can do well to begin by appreciating cultural differences in matters concerning the language of time, of space, of material possessions, of friendship patterns, and of agreements.

Language of Time

Everywhere in the world people use time to communicate with each other. There are different languages of time just as there are different spoken languages. The unspoken languages are informal; yet the rules governing their interpretation are surprisingly *ironbound*.

In the United States, a delay in answering a communication can result from a large volume of business causing the request to be postponed until the backlog is cleared away, from poor organization, or possibly from technical complexity requiring deep analysis. But if the person awaiting the answer or decision rules out these reasons, then the delay means to him that the matter has low priority on the part of the other person—lack of interest. On the other hand, a similar delay in a foreign country may mean something altogether different. Thus:

> In Ethiopia, the time required for a decision is directly proportional to its importance. This is so much the case that low-level bureaucrats there have a way of trying to elevate the prestige of their work by taking a long time to make up their minds. (Americans in that part of the world are innocently prone to downgrade their work in the local people's eyes by trying to speed things up.)
>
> In the Arab East, time does not generally include schedules as Americans know and use them. The time required to get something accomplished depends on the relationship. More important people get fast service from less important people, and conversely. Close relatives take absolute priority; nonrelatives are kept waiting.

In the United States, giving a person a deadline is a way of indicating the degree of urgency or relative importance of the work. But in the Middle East, the American runs into a cultural trap the minute he opens his mouth. "Mr. Aziz will have to make up his mind in a hurry because my board meets next week and I have to have an answer by then," is taken as indicating the American is overly demanding and is exerting undue pressure. "I am going to Damascus tomorrow morning and will have to have my car tonight," is a sure way to get the mechanic to stop work, because to give another person a deadline in this part of the world is to be rude, pushy, and demanding.

An Arab's evasiveness as to when something is going to happen does not mean he does not want to do business; it only means he is avoiding unpleasantness and is side-stepping possible commitments which he takes more seriously than we do. For example:

> The Arabs themselves at times find it impossible to communicate even to each other that some processes cannot be hurried, and are controlled by built-in schedules. This is obvious enough to the Westerner but not to the Arab. A highly placed public official in Baghdad precipitated a bitter family dispute because his nephew, a biochemist, could not speed up the complete analysis of the uncle's blood. He accused the nephew of putting other less important people before him and of not caring. Nothing could sway the uncle, who could not grasp the fact that there is such a thing as an inherent schedule.

With us the more important an event is, the further ahead we schedule it, which is why we find it insulting to be asked to a party at the last minute. In planning future events with Arabs, it pays to hold the lead time to a week or less because other factors may intervene or take precedence.

Again, time spent waiting in an American's outer office is a sure indicator of what one person thinks of another or how important he feels the other's business to be. This is so much the case that most Americans cannot help getting angry after waiting thirty minutes; one may even feel such a delay is an insult; and will walk out. In Latin America, on the other hand, one learns that it does not mean anything to wait in the outer office. An American businessman with years of experience in Mexico once told me. "You know, I have spent two hours cooling my heels in an executive's outer office. It took me a long time to learn to keep my blood pressure down. Even now, I find it hard to convince myself they are still interested when they keep me waiting."

The Japanese handle time in ways which are almost inexplicable to the Western European and particularly the American. A delay of years with them does not mean that they have lost interest. It only means that they are building up to something. They have learned that Americans are vulnerable to long waits. One of them expressed it, "You Americans have one terrible weakness. If we make you wait long enough, you will agree to anything."

Indians of South Asia have an elastic view of time as compared to our own. Delays do not, therefore, have the same meaning to them. Nor does indefiniteness in pinpointing appointments mean that they are evasive. Two Americans meeting will say, "We should get together sometime," thereby setting a low priority on the meeting. The Indian who says, "Come over and see me, see me anytime," means just that.

Americans make a place at the table which may or may not mean a place made in the heart. But when the Indian makes a place in his time, it is yours to fill in every sense of the word if you realize that by so doing you have crossed a boundary and are now friends with him. The point of all this is that time communicates just as surely as do words and that the vocabulary of time is different around the world. The principle to be remembered is that time has different meanings in each country.

Language of Space

Like time, the language of space is different wherever one goes. The American businessman, familiar with the pattern of American corporate life, has no difficulty in appraising the relative importance of someone else, simply by noting the size of his office in relation to other offices around him:

> Our pattern calls for the president or the chairman of the board to have the biggest office. The executive vice president will have the next largest, and so on down the line until you end up in the "bull pen." More important offices are usually located at the corners of buildings and on the upper floors. Executive suites will be on the top floor. The relative rank of vice presidents will be reflected in where they are placed along "Executive Row."
>
> The French, on the other hand, are much more likely to lay out

space as a network of connecting points of influence, activity, or interest. The French supervisor will ordinarily be found in the middle of his subordinates where he can control them.

Americans who are crowded will often feel that their status in the organization is suffering. As one would expect in the Arab world, the location of an office and its size constitute a poor index of the importance of the man who occupies it. What we experience as crowded, the Arab will often regard as spacious. The same is true in Spanish cultures. A Latin American official illustrated the Spanish view of this point while showing me around a plant. Opening the door to an 18-by-20-foot office in which seventeen clerks and their desks were placed, he said, "See, we have nice spacious offices. Lots of space for everyone."

The American will look at a Japanese room and remark how bare it is. Similarly, the Japanese look at our rooms and comment, "How bare!" Furniture in the American home tends to be placed along the walls (around the edge). Japanese have their charcoal pit where the family gathers in the *middle* of the room. The top floor of Japanese department stores is not reserved for the chief executive—it is the bargain roof!

In the Middle East and Latin America, the businessman is likely to feel left out in time and overcrowded in space. People get too close to him, lay their hands on him, and generally crowd his physical being. In Scandinavia and Germany, he feels more at home, but at the same time the people are a little cold and distant. It is space itself that conveys this feeling.

In the United States, because of our tendency to zone activities, nearness carries rights of familiarity so that the neighbor can borrow material possessions and invade time. This is not true in England. Propinquity entitles you to nothing. American Air Force personnel stationed there complain because they have to make an appointment for their children to play with the neighbor's child next door.

Conversation distance between two people is learned early in life by copying elders. Its controlling patterns operate almost totally unconsciously. In the United States, in contrast to many foreign countries, men avoid excessive touching. Regular business is conducted at distances such as 5 feet to 8 feet; highly personal business, 18 inches to 3 feet—not 2 to 3 inches.

In the United States, it is perfectly possible for an experienced executive to schedule the steps of negotiation in time and space so that most people feel comfortable about what is happening. Business transactions progress in stages from across the desk to beside the desk, to the coffee table, then on to the conference table, the luncheon table, or the golf course, or even into the home—all according to a complex set of hidden rules which we obey instinctively.

Even in the United States, however, an executive may slip when he moves into new and unfamiliar realms, when dealing with a new group, doing business with a new company, or moving to a new place in the industrial hierarchy. In a new country the danger is magnified. For example, in India it is considered improper to discuss business in the home on social occasions. One never invites a business acquaintance to the home for the purpose of furthering business aims. That would be a violation of sacred hospitality rules.

Language of Things

Americans are often contrasted with the rest of the world in terms of material possessions. We are accused of being materialistic, gadget-crazy. And, as a matter of fact, we have developed material things for some very interesting reasons. Lacking a fixed class system and having an extremely mobile population, Americans have become highly sensitive to how others make use of material possessions. We use everything from clothes to houses as a highly evolved and complex means of ascertaining each other's status. Ours is a rapidly shifting system in which both styles and people move up or down. For example:

> The Cadillac ad men feel that not only is it natural but quite insightful of them to show a picture of a Cadillac and a well-turned out gentleman in his early fifties opening the door. The caption underneath reads, "You already know a great deal about this man."
> Following this same pattern, the head of a big union spends an excess of $100,000 furnishing his office so that the president of United States Steel cannot look down on him. Good materials, large space, and the proper surroundings signify that the people who occupy the premises are solid citizens, that they are dependable and successful.

The French, the English, and the Germans have entirely different ways of using their material possessions. What stands for the height of dependability and respectability with the English would be old-fashioned and backward to us. The Japanese take pride in often inexpensive but tasteful arrangements that are used to produce the proper emotional setting.

Middle East businessmen look for something else—family, connections, friendship. They do not use the furnishings of their office as part of their status system; nor do they expect to impress a client by these means or to fool a banker into lending more money than he should. They like good things, too, but feel that they, as persons, should be known and not judged solely by what the public sees.

One of the most common criticisms of American relations abroad, both commercial and governmental, is that we usually think in terms of material things. "Money talks," says the American, who goes on talking the language of money abroad, in the belief that money talks the *same* language all over the world. A common practice in the United States is to try to buy loyalty with high salaries. In foreign countries, this maneuver almost never works, for money and material possessions stand for something different there than they do in America.

Language of Friendship

The American finds his friends next door and among those with whom he works. It has been noted that we take people up quickly and drop them just as quickly. Occasionally a friendship formed during schooldays will persist, but this is rare. For us there are few well-defined rules governing the obligations of friendship. It is difficult to say at which point our friendship gives way to business opportunism or pressure from above. In this we differ from many other people in the world. As a general rule in foreign countries friendships are not formed as quickly as in the United States but go much deeper, last longer, and involve real obligations. For example:

> It is important to stress that in the Middle East and Latin America your "friends" will not let you down. The fact that they personally are feeling the pinch is never an excuse for failing their friends. They are supposed to look out for your interests.

Friends and family around the world represent a sort of social insurance that would be difficult to find in the United States. We do not use our friends to help us out in disaster as much as we do as a means of getting ahead—or, at least, of getting the job done. The United States systems work by means of a series of closely tabulated favors and obligations carefully doled out where they will do the most good. And the least that we expect in exchange for a favor is gratitude.

The opposite is the case in India, where the friend's role is to "sense" a person's need and do something about it. The idea of reciprocity as we know it is unheard of. An American in India will have difficulty if he attempts to follow American friendship patterns. He gains nothing by extending himself in behalf of others, least of all gratitude, because the Indian assumes that what he does for others he does for the good of his own psyche. He will find it impossible to make friends quickly and is unlikely to allow sufficient time for friendships to ripen. He will also note that as he gets to know people better, they may become more critical of him, a fact that he finds hard to take. What he does not know is that one sign of friendship in India is speaking one's mind.

Language of Agreements

While it is important for American businessmen abroad to understand the symbolic meanings of friendship rules, time, space, and material possessions, it is just as important for executives to know the rules for negotiating agreements in various countries. Even if they cannot be expected to know the details of each nation's commercial legal practices, just the awareness of and the expectation of the existence of differences will eliminate much complication.

Actually, no society can exist on a high commercial level without a highly developed working base on which agreements can rest. This base may be one or a combination of three types:

Rules that are spelled out technically as law or regulation.

Moral practices mutually agreed on and taught to the young as a set of principles.

Informal customs to which everyone conforms without being able to state the exact rules.

Some societies favor one, some another. Ours, particularly in the business world, lays heavy emphasis on the first variety. Few Americans will conduct any business nowadays without some written agreement or contract.

Varying from culture to culture will be the circumstances under which such rules apply. Americans consider that negotiations have more or less ceased when the contract is signed. With the Greeks, on the other hand, the contract is seen as a sort of way station on the route to negotiation that will cease only when the work is completed. The contract is nothing more than a charter for serious negotiations. In the Arab world, once a man's word is given in a particular kind of way, it is just as binding, if not more so, than most of our written contracts. The written contract, therefore, violates the Moslem's sensitivities and reflects on his honor. Unfortunately, the situation is now so hopelessly confused that neither system can be counted on to prevail consistently.

Informal patterns and unstated agreements often lead to untold difficulty in the cross-cultural situation. Take the case of the before-and-after patterns where there is a wide discrepancy between the American's expectations and those of the Arab:

> In the United States, when you engage a specialist such as a lawyer or a doctor, require any standard service, or even take a taxi, you make several assumptions: (a) the charge will be fair; (b) it will be in proportion to the services rendered; and (c) it will bear a close relationship to the "going rate."
>
> You wait until after the services are performed before asking what the tab will be. If the charge is too high in the light of the above assumptions, you feel you have been cheated. You can complain or say nothing, pay up, and take your business elsewhere the next time.
>
> As one would expect in the Middle East, basic differences emerge which lead to difficulty if not understood. For instance, when taking a cab in Beirut it is well to know the going rate as a point around which to bargain and for settling the charge, which must be fixed before engaging the cab.
>
> If you have not fixed the rate in advance, there is a complete change and an entirely different set of rules will apply. According to these rules, the going rate plays no part whatsoever. The whole relationship is altered. The sky is the limit, and the customer has no kick coming. I have seen taxi drivers shouting at the top of their lungs, waving their arms, following a redfaced American with his head pulled down between his shoulders, demanding for a two-pound ride ten Lebanese pounds which the American eventually had to pay.

It is difficult for the American to accommodate his frame of reference to the fact that what constitutes one thing to him, namely, a taxi ride, is to the Arab two very different operations involving two different sets of relationships and two sets of rules. The crucial factor is whether the bargaining is done at the beginning or the end of the ride! As a matter of fact, you cannot bargain at the end. What the driver asks for he is entitled to!

One of the greatest difficulties Americans have abroad stems from the fact that we often think we have a commitment when we do not. The second complication on this same topic is the other side of the coin, i.e., when others think we have agreed to things that we have not. Our own failure to recognize binding obligations, plus our custom of setting organizational goals ahead of everything else, has put us in hot water far too often.

People sometimes do not keep agreements with us because we do not keep agreements with them. As a general rule, the American treats the agreements as something he may eventually have to break. Here are two examples:

> Once while I was visiting an American post in Latin America, the Ambassador sent the Spanish version of a trade treaty down to his language officer with instructions to write in some "weasel words." To his dismay, he was told, "There are no weasel words in Spanish."
>
> A personnel officer of a large corporation in Iran made an agreement with local employees that American employees would not receive preferential treatment. When the first American employee arrived, it was learned quickly that in the United States he had been covered by a variety of health plans that were not available to Iranians. And this led to immediate protests from the Iranians which were never satisfied. The personnel officer never really grasped the fact that he had violated an ironbound contract.

Certainly, this is the most important generalization to be drawn by American businessmen from this discussion of agreements: there are many times when we are vulnerable *even when judged by our own standards*. Many instances of actual sharp practices by American companies are well known abroad and are giving American business a bad name. The cure for such questionable behavior is simple. The companies concerned usually have it within their power to discharge offenders and to foster within their organization an atmosphere in which only honesty and fairness can thrive.

But the cure for ignorance of the social and legal rules which underlie business agreements is not so easy. This is because:

> The subject is complex.
> Little research has been conducted to determine the culturally different concepts of what is an agreement.
> The people of each country think that their own code is the only one, and that everything else is dishonest.
> Each code is different from our own; and the farther away one is traveling from Western Europe, the greater the difference is.

But the little that has already been learned about this subject indicates that as a problem it is not insoluble and will yield to research. Since it is probably one of the more relevant and immediately applicable areas of interest to modern business, it would certainly be advisable for companies with large foreign operations to sponsor some serious research in this vital field.

A Case in Point

Thus far, I have been concerned with developing the five check points around which a real understanding of foreign cultures can begin. But the problems that arise from a faulty understanding of the silent language of foreign custom are human problems and perhaps can best be dramatized by an actual case.

A Latin American republic had decided to modernize one of its communication networks to the tune of several million dollars. Because of its reputation for quality and price, the inside track was quickly taken by American company "Y."

The company, having been sounded out informally, considered the size of the order and decided to bypass its regular Latin American representative and send instead its sales manager. The following describes what took place.

The sales manager arrived and checked in at the leading hotel. He immediately had some difficulty pinning down just who it was he had to see about his business. After several days without results, he called at the American Embassy where he found that the commercial attache listened to his story. Realizing that the sales manager had already made a number of mistakes, but figuring that the Latins were used to American blundering, the attaché reasoned that all was not lost. He informed the sales manager that the Minister of Communications was the key man and that whoever got the nod from him would get the contract. He also briefed the sales manager on methods of conducting business in Latin America and offered some pointers about dealing with the minister.

The attaché's advice ran somewhat as follows:

(1) You don't do business here the way you do in the States; it is necessary to spend much more time. You have to get to know your man and vice versa.

(2) You must meet with him *several times* before you talk business. I will tell you at what point you can bring up the subject. Take your cues from me. (Our American sales manager at this point made a few observations to himself about "cookie pusher" and wondered how many payrolls had been met by the commercial attaché.)

(3) Take that price list and put it in your pocket. Don't get it out until I tell you to. Down here price is only one of the many things taken into account before closing a deal. In the United States, your past experience will prompt you to act according to a certain set of principles, but many of these principles will *not* work here. Every time you feel the urge to act or to say something, look at me. Suppress the urge and take your cues from me. This is very important.

(4) Down here people like to do business with men who *are* somebody. In order to be somebody, it is well to have written a book, to have lectured at a university, or to have developed your intellect in some way. The man you are going to see is a poet. He has published several volumes of poetry. Like many Latin Americans, he prizes poetry highly. You will find that he will spend a good deal of business time quoting his poetry to you, and he will take great pleasure in this.

(5) You will also note that the people here are very proud of their past and of their Spanish blood, but they are also exceedingly proud of their liberation from Spain and their independence. The fact that they are a democracy, that they are free, and also that they are no longer a colony is very, very important to them. They are warm and friendly and enthusiastic if they like you. If they don't, they are cold and withdrawn.

(6) And another thing, time down here means something different. It works in a different way. You know how it is back in the States when a certain type blurts out whatever is on his mind without waiting to see if the situation is right. He is considered an impatient bore and somewhat egocentric. Well, down here, you have to wait much, much longer, and I really mean *much, much* longer, before you can begin to talk about the reason for your visit.

(7) There is another point I want to caution you about. At home, the man who sells takes the initiative. Here, *they* tell you when they are ready to do business. But, most of all, don't discuss price until you are asked and don't rush things.

The Pitch

The next day the commercial attaché introduced the sales manager to the Minister of Communications. First, there was a long wait in the outer office while people kept coming in and out. The sales manager looked at his watch, fidgeted, and finally asked whether the minister was really expecting him. The reply he received was scarcely reassuring, "Oh yes, he is expecting you but several things have come up that require his attention. Besides, one gets used to waiting down here." The sales manager irritably replied, "But doesn't he know I flew all the way down here from the United States to see him, and I have spent over a week already of my valuable time trying to find him?" "Yes, I know," was the answer, "but things just move much more slowly here."

At the end of about thirty minutes, the minister emerged from the office, greeted the commercial attaché with a *doble abrazo*, throwing his arms around him and patting him on the back as though they were long-lost brothers. Now, turning and smiling, the minister extended his hand to the sales manager, who, by this time, was feeling rather miffed because he had been kept in the outer office so long.

After what seemed to be an all too short chat, the minister rose, suggesting a well-known cafe where they might meet for dinner the next evening. The sales manager expected, of course, that, considering the nature of their business and the size of the order, he might be taken to the minister's home, not realizing that the Latin home is reserved for family and very close friends.

Until now, nothing at all had been said about the reason for the sales manager's visit, a fact which bothered him somewhat. The whole setup seemed wrong; neither did he like the idea of wasting another day in town. He told the home office before he left that he would be gone for a week or ten days at the most, and made a mental note that he would clean this order up in three days and enjoy a few days in

Acapulco or Mexico City. Now the week had already gone and he would be lucky if he made it home in ten days.

Voicing his misgivings to the commercial attaché, he wanted to know if the minister really meant business, and, if he did, why could they not get together and talk about it? The commercial attaché by now was beginning to show the strain of constantly having to reassure the sales manager. Nevertheless, he tired again:

> *What you don't realize is that part of the time we were waiting, the minister was rearranging a very tight schedule so that he could spend tomorrow night with you. You see, down here they don't delegate responsibility the way we do in the States. They exercise much tighter control than we do. As a consequence, this man spends up to 15 hours a day at his desk. It may not look like it to you, but I assure you he really means business. He wants to give your company the order; if you play your cards right, you will get it.*

The next evening provided more of the same. Much conversation about food and music, about many people the sales manager had never heard of. They went to a night club, where the sales manager brightened up and began to think that perhaps he and the minister might have something in common after all. It bothered him, however, that the principal reason for his visit was not even alluded to tangentially. But every time he started to talk about electronics, the commercial attaché would nudge him and proceed to change the subject.

The next meeting was for morning coffee at a cafe. By now the sales manager was having difficulty hiding his impatience. To make matters worse, the minister had a mannerism which he did not like. When they talked, he was likely to put his hand on him; he would take hold of his arm and get so close that he almost "spat" in his face. As a consequence, the sales manager was kept busy trying to dodge and back up.

Following coffee, there was a walk in a nearby park. The minister expounded on the shrubs, the birds, and the beauties of nature, and at one spot he stopped to point at a statue and said: "There is a statue of the world's greatest hero, the liberator of mankind!" At this point, the worst happened, for the sales manager asked who the statue was of and, being given the name of a famous Latin American patriot, said, "I never heard of him," and walked on.

The Failure

It is quite clear from this that the sales manager did not get the order, which went to a Swedish concern. The American, moreover, was never able to see the minister again. Why did the minister feel the way he did? His reasoning went somewhat as follows:

> *I like the American's equipment and it makes sense to deal with North Americans who are near us and whose price is right. But I*

could never be friends with this man. He is not my kind of human being and we have nothing in common. He is not simpatico. If I can't be friends and he is not simpatico, I can't depend on him to treat me right. I tried everything, every conceivable situation, and only once did we seem to understand each other. If we could be friends, he would feel obligated to me and this obligation would give me some control. Without control, how do I know he will deliver what he says he will at the price he quotes?

Of course, what the minister did not know was that the price was quite firm, and that quality control was a matter of company policy. He did not realize that the sales manager was a member of an organization, and that the man is always subordinate to the organization in the United States. Next year maybe the sales manager would not even be representing the company, but would be replaced. Further, if he wanted someone to depend on, his best bet would be to hire a good American lawyer to represent him and write a binding contract.

In this instance, both sides suffered. The American felt he was being slighted and put off, and did not see how there could possibly be any connection between poetry and doing business or why it should all take so long. He interpreted the delay as a form of polite brush-off. Even if things had gone differently and there had been a contract, it is doubtful that the minister would have trusted the contract as much as he would a man whom he considered his friend. Throughout Latin America, the law is made livable and contracts workable by having friends and relatives operating from the inside. Lacking a friend, someone who would look out for his interests, the minister did not want to take a chance. He stated this simply and directly.

Conclusion

The case just described has of necessity been oversimplified. The danger is that the reader will say, "Oh, I see. All you really have to do is be friends." At which point the expert will step in and reply:

> *Yes, of course, but what you don't realize is that in Latin America being a friend involves much more than it does in the United States and is an entirely different proposition. A friendship implies obligations. You go about it differently. It involves much more than being nice, visiting, playing golf. You would not want to enter into friendship lightly.*

The point is simply this. It takes years and years to develop a sound foundation for doing business in a given country. Much that is done seems silly or strange to the home office. Indeed, the most common error made by home offices, once they have found representatives who can get results, is failure to take their advice and allow sufficient time for representatives to develop the proper contacts.

The second most common error, if that is what it can be called, is ignorance of the secret and hidden language of foreign cultures. In this article I have tried to show how five key topics—time, space, material possessions, friendship patterns, and business agreements—offer a starting point from which companies can begin to acquire the understanding necessary to do business in foreign countries.

Our present knowledge is meager, and much more research is needed before the businessman of the future can go abroad fully equipped for his work. Not only will he need to be well versed in the economics, law, and politics of the area, but he will have to understand, if not speak, the silent languages of other cultures.

Myth and Reality about Private Enterprise in India

Ranjit Singh Bhambri

Widespread criticism and suspicion of the activities of businessmen have been a striking feature of public debate on economic and social affairs in India since 1947. It has almost been a matter of habit with literate Indians to blame the commercial classes and the financial interests for the country's economic backwardness. In spite of the generous contribution of businessmen to the Congress Party funds, and the close association of Mahatma Gandhi with many prominent industrialists, the business community found itself under thick clouds of public hostility after independence.

Relations between commercial and industrial organizations and the government deteriorated gradually after the Congress Party assumed power. The speeches of some members of the government and the Congress Party often contained sweeping criticism of various activities of the business community. When he addressed the Federation of Indian Chambers of Commerce and Industry in 1949, Mr. Nehru argued that Indian capitalists and industrialists gave the impression of frailty and feebleness. They were "not big enough to face the problems of the day," he suggested. He warned them, too, that "if your demands come in the way of the good of the masses, your demands will be completely ignored."[1] His statement expressed clearly the popular assumption that Indian businessmen are interested only in making large profits for themselves, with complete disregard of the public interest.

The death of Sardar Patel in 1950 removed the most powerful defender of the businessmen's point of view in Mr. Nehru's government. State participation in direct industrial production has been increasing in the last few years. The government has started new industries under its control. Certain sectors of the economy have, for strategic as well as ideological reasons, been reserved for public enterprise. Moreover, the government has increased its control over the day-to-day activities of private firms.

In December 1954 the Lok Sabha (the lower house of the Indian Parliament) passed a resolution which accepted the "Socialist pattern of society as the objective

---

Reprinted from *World Politics*, Vol. XII. No. 2 (January 1960) by permission of the publisher.

[1] Jawaharlal Nehru, *Independence and After: A Collection of the More Important Speeches, from September 1946 to May 1949* (Delhi: Publications Division, Ministry of Information & Broadcasting, Govt. of India, 1949), p. 189.

of social and economic policy." The Congress Party passed a similar resolution at its annual conference held at Avadi in January 1955, and declared itself in favor of the establishment of a socialist pattern of society in India.

Much space has been given to discussion of the exact meaning of the phrase "socialist pattern of society" and the implications of recent government legislation for the future of private enterprise in India. That the Congress Party does not propose to nationalize all means of production is obvious. This was made clear by Maulana Azad (the late Minister of Education, Natural Resources, and Scientific Research) when he introduced the above-mentioned resolution at the Avadi session of the Congress Party. He said: "I would like to draw your attention, especially at this time, to the deliberate use of the phrase socialist pattern of society. This is most important because we want to have a socialist pattern and not socialism."[2] The authors of the second five-year plan put the matter more precisely: "The accent of the socialist pattern is on the attainment of positive goals; the raising of living standards, the enlargement of opportunities for all, the promotion of enterprise among the disadvantaged classes and the creation of a sense of partnership among all sections of the community. These positive goals provide the criteria for basic decisions."[3] Moreover, the government's agricultural policy suggests that the distinction drawn between "socialism" and "socialist pattern of society" is important. It is well known that the Congress Party is committed to the principle of the abolition of the Zamindari system and the distribution of land among the peasants. It is therefore self-evident that as long as India remains a country of thousands of villages, as long as the majority of her people derive their livelihood from the land, private enterprise will remain the predominant form of production in the economy.

But the proper role of private enterprise in the fields of industry, large-scale distribution, finance, and foreign trade has been a subject of keen controversy in the last ten years. The activities of the government in these sections of the economy have taken various forms. Numerous state-owned plants have come into existence. These plants are owned either by government departments (e.g., Chittaranjan Locomotive Factory and the Integrated Coach Factory at Perambur) or by public corporations specially created to run them (e.g., Hindustan Aircraft Ltd., Sindri Fertilizers and Chemicals Ltd.). In some cases the government has entered into partnership with certain foreign or Indian firms (e.g., Hindustan Machine Tools Ltd., Hindustan Shipyard Ltd.). The state has acquired controlling shares in some firms. Air transport, the Imperial Bank of India (now called the State Bank of India), and the insurance companies have been nationalized in recent years.

These state activities have increased the importance of public enterprise in the

---

[2] *The Statesman* (New Delhi, January 20, 1955).

[3] Planning Commission, Government of India, *Second Five Year Plan* (New Delhi, 1956), p. 24.

Indian economy. It has been estimated that in 1950–1951 the book value of capital assets in the public sector of organized industry was Rs. 440 million, in contrast to a book value of "productive" assets of Rs. 11.1 billion in privately owned factory establishments—a ratio of 1:25. As a result of increased investment on government account, by 1960–1961 two-thirds of the total capital invested in organized manufacturing will be privately owned and one-third government-owned.[4]

These steps have been taken with the intention of accelerating the pace of industrialization, which has been the overriding national objective since 1947. It is widely assumed that private enterprise is too weak to accomplish this heroic task. Until 1956 at least, it was common practice to warn private enterprise that in order to survive it must make the greatest efforts to increase output, particularly the output of industrial products. In their published statements, businessmen of course accepted the prime national objective. But they argued that the policy of nationalism created an atmosphere inimical to expansion. Furthermore, excessive regulation of industry, in their view, could not encourage the private initiative and enterprise on which the success of the ambitious plans for the industrialization of the country depended.

In India this particular debate is not just another ideological discussion of the relative desirability of private enterprise and state activity in the field of production. The tone of this debate and the nature of the arguments used by both sides are determined by the economic environment and aspirations of the Indian people. It is abundantly clear that the place of private enterprise in Indian industry, and the concrete meaning of a "mixed economy," will depend upon the opinion of the public, particularly the educated elite, during the next few years. We must therefore ask ourselves why and how the public came to acquire a negative and hostile attitude toward private enterprise. If this attitude springs from deep-rooted cultural factors and ideological reasons, the private businessman may be allowed to continue only for a short period until the government finds it convenient to take over the industries in the private sector. But if this attitude is based on the past economic performance of Indian businessmen, changes in their performance will surely determine future policy. In the latter case, the present economic policy of the government, owing to its effect on the performance of private enterprise, will become the most important factor in the determination of public attitudes and hence of future economic policy toward private enterprise.

The vast majority of men have always viewed with a mixture of admiration, envy, and suspicion the activities of those who accumulate large fortunes and create industrial empires. The businessman in fact has never been a popular figure. "Dislike of him," writes Professor T. S. Ashton, "runs a continuous thread, through nineteenth century literature, showing up most strongly in the writings of Ruskin and his followers, but visible also in those of novelists and essayists, who much

---

[4] George Rosen, *Industrial Change in India* (Glencoe, Ill.: Free Press, 1958), pp. 13–14.

preferred the ways of gypsies and tramps to his."[5] Even in the United States of America, big business is very often suspect in the eyes of the public merely because of its size. Exploitation by the large corporations and financial interests was a familiar complaint of United States farmers until very recently. Likewise, there is a widespread feeling among the Indian peasants that landlords, traders, and moneylenders are largely responsible for their poverty. Yet the Indian peasant believes, no less strongly than the American farmer, that the right to own private property is an inalienable human right.

Western writers on India have often tried to explain the popular dislike and suspicion of business success, and the slower rate of growth of Indian industry, in terms of the supposedly antibusiness leanings of Hindu religious and social thought.[6] This is a pathetically weak explanation. It is based on a rather superficial acceptance of the opinions which are expressed publicly. In any society there is inevitably a gap between what is said and what is practiced. But his gap tends to be unusually wide in India, where paying lip service to certain principles which are in practice disregarded is only too common. For example, in their public speeches, spokesmen of the Congress Party almost habitually declare their faith in Gandhian principles, yet the economic policy of the party is based on principles which are in the exact contrary of Gandhi's economic philosophy. Social life in India is in many ways a vast ritual. Without a careful analysis of the beliefs of the people, it is quite easy to reach misleading conclusions on this question. Religious principles, however important, do not explain the hostility of the public to Indian businessmen.

It is important to realize that specific criticism of businessmen and their practices is voiced mainly by the educated classes. The habit of criticizing the Indian businessmen has come to be regarded as an occupational disease of the elite. It is this section of the population which is responsible for the formulation of public opinion and for government policy. To explain that policy we must inquire why this section of the population came to adopt an attitude of hostility toward business. Their views cannot, of course, be explained in terms of their adherence to Hindu religion and thought, which do not place a high value on the accumulation of riches. By and large, educated Indians dislike most of the economic manifestations of "Hindu culture." They admire Western societies for their higher standards of

---

[5] Professor Ashton goes on: "They (the businessmen) were variously portrayed as ostentatiously rich or poor-spirited and mean; in either case they were far too much pre-occupied with money. . . . It was an obvious duty to expose (them), and so, a generation or more ago, journalists and others, especially in the United States but also here (i.e., England), took with enthusiasm to what came to be known as muckraking. It was an easy way to public esteem and literary fame." *Business History*, 1, No. 1 (December 1958): 1.

[6] E.g., Helen B. Lamb, "The Indian Business Communities and the Evolution of an Industrialist Class," *Pacific Affairs*, XXVIII, No. 2 (June 1955): 101-16.

living and they admire the Soviet Union even more for having achieved a remarkable rate of economic growth in the last few decades. It is thus absurd to suggest that the Indian intellectual does not consider the pursuit of wealth a respectable activity because it is against "authentic" Indian values.

Educated Indians are not hostile to business, not even big business. They have been hostile to Indian business—quite a different thing. For over a generation they have regarded rapid industrialization of the country as the only way of eliminating poverty and modernizing the country. Indian businessmen, in their opinion, have failed to achieve a satisfactory rate of industrial growth. An outside observer may consider the achievement of Indian industry before 1947 quite impressive, while the condition of agriculture would seem appalling to him. The educated Indian will not deny this. He may take pride in pointing out that even before the Second World War India was regarded as the tenth most important country in the world, and was the second largest in Asia (next to Japan) in terms of total industrial output. He may even concede that this achievement, in the face of opposition from a hostile government, deserves a word of praise.

But all these qualifications do not upset his main argument, that Indian industrial output per capita still remains one of the lowest in the world, and that it could have expanded more quickly. Even the backwardness of agriculture is due, in part, to the very slow pace of industrialization. In the first half of the twentieth century, industries in every other developed country were creating more and more jobs and taking people off the land. But in India very few jobs were created in industry or other nonagricultural occupations in this period. By 1947 manufacturing industries employed barely 2.4 million workers.

The number of Indian businessmen who invest their capital in industry still remains deplorably low. Most of them have accumulated fortunes in money-lending, trade, and speculation. This excessive devotion to trade and speculation has produced the common belief that Indian businessmen are only interested in "unproductive" enterprises.

Lack of vigor, of initiative, and of willingness to take risks have come to be regarded as the distinguishing feature of most Indian businessmen, who have concentrated on activities yielding quick and large profits, and have been traditionally shy of investing in industries which bear fruit over a long period and are most beneficial to provide all the help and encouragement in setting up an industry. The feeling has arisen that the government should assume many of the business risks while private enterprise earned all the profits. Yet any interference by the government in the activities of the firms has provoked the charge that attempts to regulate industry will discourage enterprise and initiative.

Furthermore, various writers have argued that, until recently, most Indian businessmen have shown very little sense of social responsibility, either toward their employees or toward consumers. Their taste for conspicuous consumption is well known. They have seldom contributed to the promotion of education or welfare.

The standard of business honesty among them is reputed to be very low.[7] It would be difficult to find many businessmen in India who believe that the purpose of economic activity is to meet the needs of society most efficiently. Accumulation of personal fortunes, according to their view, is the main aim of business.

This picture of the average Indian businessman—interested in trading, speculation, and quick profits, lacking other initiative and enterprise, shirking the risks of investments which pay in the long run, displaying little concern for the welfare of his employees and almost no sense of social responsibility—is, though exaggerated in some ways, substantially correct. But neither Western nor Indian writers on this subject have recognized that these drawbacks are not peculiar to Indian businessmen. In all underdeveloped countries, businessmen are guilty of all or most of the shortcomings that have been attributed to the Indian businessman. In Latin American countries today, businessmen display a marked lack of classic capitalist vigor and enterprise; they have a strong taste for speculation, and their capacity for conspicuous consumption is perhaps second to none. In eighteenth-century France or England the standards of business honesty were not very high, and in Russia, in the nineteenth century, these standards were, according to Professor Alexander Gerschenkron, "disastrously low."[8] In England an almost complete lack of a sense of social responsibility toward employees was a notable aspect of the businessman's psychology in the early days of the industrial revolution. Recent research into the economic history of most industrialized countries, and factual material relating to poor countries which has been accumulated in large quantities, strongly suggest that some of the defects of the Indian business community should be ascribed less to the peculiarities of Indian culture, as many Western writers have done, than to the underdeveloped state of the economy.

Educated Indians, on the other hand, seem to forget that a lack of social responsibility, enterprise, and initiative has been perhaps the outstanding feature of all aspects of social life in India in the last few decades. As individual members of an amorphous society, businessmen have not been guilty of anything with which the majority of Indians could not be charged. Of course, businessmen have in the past shown a strong dislike of risky enterprises. But the educated classes are the worst offenders here. The tendency of literate Indians to go in for safe government jobs requiring hardly any initiative and almost no risk is too well known to need any elaboration. The universities have tended to produce a type of mind which is

---

[7] I have talked with hundreds of small traders and shopkeepers (in North India) who seriously argue that honesty and success in business do not normally go together. Many of them strongly believe that rich businessmen owe their wealth either to good fortune or to greater dishonesty. Even some sophisticated Indians have suggested that wealth cannot be accumulated by honest means. For an interesting example, see the anecdote from *All India Congress Committee Economic Review* (April 1, 1956), quoted in Charles Andrews Myers, *Labor Problems in the Industrialization of India* (Cambridge, Mass.: Harvard University Press, 1958).

[8] In Bert F. Hoselitz (ed.), *The Progress of Underdeveloped Areas,* (Chicago: University of Chicago Press, 1952), p. 18.

happy and satisfied only in familiar grooves, and they have only just begun to analyze seriously the social and economic problems facing the country.

Moreover, it is not generally realized that private initiative is not in itself a sufficient remedy for the economic ills of underdeveloped countries. In emphasizing these factors, the critics of private enterprise are unconsciously subscribing to the oversimplified laissez-faire theory that, once the immense potential of free, pioneering, individual initiative is released, economic growth will automatically be assured. Before 1947 conditions in India were unfavorable to the rapid expansion of industrial enterprises. There were, of course, very sound economic and political reasons for the inability of individual businessmen to undertake larger risks. Market opportunities in India were rather limited until recently, except for a few industrial products; and the resources of most businessmen were not large enough to provide the basic overhead facilities necessary for balanced growth. Except during the brief period of the Second World War, the British Raj did not see the need for rapid industrialization of the country. Hence the government was neither ready nor willing to provide the thrust for an effective industrial revolution. It is not entirely the fault of businessmen that they did not show any willingness to undertake greater risks in so hostile an economic environment.

Both the economic climate and the performance of private enterprise have changed appreciably in the last few years. During the Second World War, the British government encouraged the production of industrial goods in India to facilitate its war effort. Moreover, a shortage of imported products increased consumer demand for the products of Indian industries. But industrial production did not increase much during this period. The index of industrial production rose only from 100 in 1937 to 120.0 in 1945. What increase occurred was mainly due to the fuller utilization of existing industrial capacity. Further expansion in capacity was not possible in this period because new machinery, usually imported from industrial countries, was largely available. The index of production fell back to 109 in 1946 and to 102.4 in 1947. The political and economic situation after 1947 was very uncertain. Most industries were working well below their full capacity. It is generally argued that, as a result of the uncertainty, industrial production did not show any marked upward trend till 1953.

During this period relations between the government and private enterprise were deteriorating gradually. In 1952 Mr. Sarkar, a past president of the Indian Chambers of Commerce and Industry, wrote that "businessmen are now under suspicion everywhere. We are fast losing goodwill."[9] Various commentators suggested that the behavior of industrial production in this period provided a convincing proof that Indian businessmen were completely lacking in initiative and could not be effective agents in the industrialization of the country. Mr. Asoka

---

[9] N. R. Sarkar, "My Days in the Federation," *Silver Jubilee Souvenir* (Calcutta: Federation of Indian Chambers of Commerce and Industry, 1953), p. 197.

Mehta, the Socialist leader, popularized the phrase, "Indian capital has gone on strike." Businessmen, on the other hand, played up the issue of nationalization. The government was blamed for creating uncertainty about the future of private enterprise. It was seriously argued that no increases in production could take place in this uncertain economic environment.

The volume of industrial output increased after 1953. According to the revised index, industrial production increased from 100 in 1951 to 105.6 in 1953—a gain of only 5.6 points. But in 1954 the index jumped to 112.9 and in 1955 to 122.1. For the first four months of 1958 the index of industrial production stood at 141.2. These figures show that in 1953 private firms started to increase production at an impressive rate. The performance of private enterprise has been very satisfactory in the first three years of the second five-year plan. Most industries in the private sector passed their targets. The total investment allocated to the private sector over the entire plan period was in fact carried out in the first eighteen months. The sharp increase in the volume of capital goods imported on private account in 1956 and 1957 was perhaps the chief cause of the foreign exchange crisis.

Moreover, the number of private registered companies has increased by more than 125 percent since the Second World War. These indices of the growth of private enterprise provide some evidence in favor of the hypothesis suggested above, that the lack of vigor shown by private enterprise may have been due to lack of a favorable climate before 1947.

However, the sources of the strength and weakness of private enterprise in India have not been properly understood either in India or abroad. This lack of understanding is most obvious in the statements of Indian industrialists. The nationalization of the Imperial Bank of India and the insurance companies, and the policy of increasing control over private firms, embodied in the Companies Act of 1955, were extensively criticized by businessmen. This is, of course, a perfectly natural reaction on the part of those who believe in the efficiency and virtue of private enterprise. But the main argument advanced needs careful analysis. Up to the promulgation of the Industrial Policy Resolution of April 1956, prominent businessmen argued in their public speeches that the policy of the government was generating uncertainty, sapping the confidence of private enterprise, and might arrest the growth of production. But the behavior of industrial production in the private sector between 1951 and 1956 shows quite clearly that production was scarcely affected by the climate of uncertainty; instead, it fluctuated in direct relation to the level of public investment. In the years 1951–1953, a period of slack demand and low level of public investment, most industries were working below full capacity. According to the *Monthly Statistics of Selected Industries in India*, in 1952 and 1953 nearly half the industries were working at less than 50 percent of their capacity. A substantial increase in the volume of public investment in 1952 increased monetary demand for consumption goods. Industrial production therefore showed a very impressive recovery after 1953 and private investment also increased. It is clear that the production policy of most firms was not affected by the feeling of acute uncertainty which was a common theme in the speeches of businessmen in the period 1953–1956.

The claims made on behalf of private enterprise have been modified in the last three years. Whereas previously it was argued that the government was destroying the springs of private initiative, the current theme is that private enterprise has done remarkably well *in spite* of the socialist policy of the government. In one of his speeches, Mr. J. R. D. Tata, chairman of Tata Iron and Steel Company, Ltd., declared: "I feel the charge that free enterprise in India has shown no initiative in recent years is particularly hard to take. I for one am in fact surprised at the amount of initiative displayed *considering the discouragement and disincentives to which it has been subjected.*"[10]

The ideas expressed by Mr. Tata are shared by some economists in India and in the United States. For example, Mr. Wilfred Malenbaum, chairman of the India Project of the Center for International Studies at Massachusetts Institute of Technology, wrote recently: ". . . Indian industry in the last few years has demonstrated a vigor and vitality worthy of industry in the most developed lands. This vitality has been clearly manifest in the private sector, *despite* India's commitment to a socialistic pattern of society and a policy of increasing nationalization in its industrial mix."[11] Moreover, it is argued that industrialization will now proceed faster if the state gradually withdraws from the sphere of economic activity and the policy of an almost crippling regulation of industry is reversed. However, a closer investigation of the events of the last five years suggests that these conclusions are unwarranted. Private enterprise has done well *not in spite of, but because of,* the various activities of the government since the inauguration of the first five-year plan. Public investment in power, transport, communications, and various other industries has created considerable purchasing power. It is this purchasing power which makes possible the boom in the comsumer goods industries owned almost entirely by the private sector.

Part of the confusion in this controversy arises from a basic flaw in the accepted theory of investment to which businessmen generally subscribe. It is widely assumed that there is a fixed amount of investible resources available in an economy at any period. This assumption is the basis of the theory that investment undertaken by the state can take place largely at the expense of private investment. Experience, however, suggests that this assumption of a "fixed" amount of investible resources holds good only in a totally planned economy. In a mixed economy, on the other hand, the flow of investible resources can vary within fairly wide limits. The amount of investment that one firm will find profitable to undertake depends upon the planned or expected investments of other units in the economy. Theoretically, it is possible that the state, in order to raise revenue and finance investment, may impose such a high rate of taxation that private enterprise

---

[10] *Economic Weekly* (Bombay, January 1956): 51; italics added.
[11] Foreword to Rosen, *op. cit.*, p. xv; italics added.

becomes both unable and unwilling to undertake any saving and investment. But all the available evidence suggests that so far neither the rate of taxation nor the pattern of government investment has reduced the opportunities for expansion of private enterprise in India. In fact the complementary nature of private and public investment has proved important in at least two basic ways. First, public investment has created the purchasing power without which production of consumer goods remains unprofitable. Second, public investment is slowly creating those overhead facilities, like transport, communications, and power generation, which are necessary to the smooth operation of all industries. In principle there is no reason for investment in overhead services not being undertaken by private firms. But in the case of India, and indeed of all underdeveloped countries, even the most ardent advocates of private enterprise will concede that the provision of these services is beyond the limited resources of private enterprise.

Furthermore, the Indian government has provided various direct stimuli to encourage the expansion of private investment. The taxation policy makes liberal allowances for ordinary and extra depreciation, and enables firms to recover a large part of their investment in new capacity during the early periods of the plant's life. In addition to the depreciation allowance, an investment allowance of 25 percent is given by the taxation authorities and losses may now be carried forward indefinitely. Tax policy touching reserves and dividends affects saving and encourages firms to increase investment. The institutional framework for the provision of industrial finance has been widened. A National Industrial Development Corporation has been set up to encourage the growth of new industries. Special credit facilities are provided for the small- and medium-sized firms which find it difficult to raise capital through the usual channels. Moreover, the machinery of import control has been thoroughly overhauled, and tariff policy is being used as an instrument of industrial development to provide new industries with such protection as is thought to be desirable.

In fact, private enterprise in India has never before received such generous treatment from the state. As a result, it has served the country rather well in the last few years. There is, of course, no doubt that the government has increased its control over the operations of all private firms beyond a certain specified size. Firms have to secure licenses to import goods from abroad. The output prices of certain specified industries, like cement and paper, are directly controlled, and profits are not allowed to rise above a proportion considered "fair" by the administrators. Moreover, the employment policy of the firm is not regarded as an exclusively private problem but is subject to strict government supervision.

The multiplication of controls in recent years has caused serious concern in business circles. The major criticism of this policy is that it leaves little room for personal initiative. While it cannot be denied that recent company legislation has been rather unwise in certain respects, a general increase in the degree of state control of economic activity is inevitable in a planned economy. The requirement of export licenses and permits for expansion becomes a regrettable necessity in an economy which is trying to develop as rapidly as possible with hardly any reserves of foreign exchange. The 1957 exchange crisis, brought about by the excessive enthusiasm of private enterprise, has not led to a smooth rate of economic growth. A certain degree of restraint and co-ordination, implicit in a system of controls, is essential to rapid economic development.

It is necessary to emphasize that the published statements of businessmen and their actual performance tell two quite different stories. The economics system has assimilated the various government measures quite comfortably. The speeches of businessmen should not blind us to the real source of their recently acquired strength. A reference to government-generated uncertainty has become as much a matter of habit with the company chairman as an avowal of faith in the socialist pattern of society with the cabinet minister.[12]

These changes in the performance of private enterprise in Indian industry clearly call for a revision of some popular notions about Indian businessmen, and about the proper role, strength, and limitations of private enterprise in the course of economic development.

The Indian businessman, like businessmen in all free societies, is interested in increasing profits. But the sphere of economic activity in which maximum profits can be realized depends upon the economic environment, which varies from one society to another and changes during the course of economic development. Indian businessmen have habitually devoted most of their energy to trade and speculation because in an underdeveloped country, and especially in the face of competition from more efficient industries in developed lands, industrial investment is unprofitable.

In the last ten years the government of India has managed to create a more favorable economic climate. Individual businessmen, in the pursuit of private profits, are gradually devoting their energies to the building-up of industries. It is entirely misleading to suggest that businessmen have suddenly acquired a new vitality and vigor which they lacked only a few years ago. The more important aspect of recent economic evolution is that increases in effective demand and the umbrella of protection provided by the state have reduced the degree of risk involved in industrial investments. In other words, risks have become more nearly proportionate to the small scale of Indian businesses. Of course, the desire to reap quick profits in trading and speculation is still very much in evidence. Habits acquired over a number of generations do not change in a decade. But the process of transformation has already started and will no doubt gather momentum in the course of the next few years. It is becoming more fashionable to invest in industries. And as the volume of industrial activity increases, the relative

---

[12] Government control of private activity cannot, of course, be increased indefinitely without harmful effects on the volume of production. My point is that, so far, increasing government control and "government-generated uncertainty" have hardly affected the level of productive efficiency. If anything, these measures have helped to improve the performance of the private sector by creating the general feeling that private enterprise is on trial.

importance of trade and speculation will decline. More than that, in an expanding economy these activities acquire a new and useful meaning. They can no longer be described as unproductive.

We shall do well to remember that Indians have not attached much value to private enterprise as a way of life. To them, it is merely an agent of economic growth, a method of achieving a higher standard of living for the masses. On the other hand, strong dislike of private enterprise is very thinly spread among certain sections of the public. The economic policy of the government is based on markedly empirical and pragmatic considerations. The men in office have so far shown themselves quite untinged by any doctrinaire preference for state action for its own sake.[13] The slogan of "a socialistic pattern of society" and the threat of nationalization only remind the businessman that he must fulfill a useful role, use his economic power with consideration, and acquire a new sense of responsibility. Accumulation of private wealth can no longer be the only business of business.

It should be obvious that in the democratic framework of India, the place of private enterprise in industry and the concrete meaning of the term "mixed economy" will depend upon the attitude of the electorate and, above all, of the articulate and restless educated classes. The developments of the last five years, and the relative success of private enterprise, have taken the sting out of public criticism of businessmen. The thesis that educated Indians disliked business success because of some deep-rooted cultural reasons was not, of course, based on a serious analysis of the facts. In fact the level of industrial output has become a very popular topic of discussion and Indians have developed a remarkable taste for the study of statistics.

As private enterprise becomes more successful, and more responsible, it is also becoming more respectable. These factors are bound to have a considerable impact on future economic policy. If India remains a mixed economy, most of the credit for this will no doubt go to Mr. Nehru's government, whose pragmatic policy created an economic climate in which personal initiative and enterprise could harness and create resources, build up productivity, and fulfill the most important social needs.

---

[13] The following quotation from one of Mr. Nehru's speeches (delivered in the Lok Sabha, May 23, 1956) shows that maximum economic growth is the guiding principle of the economic policy of the government. Replying to doctrinaire socialists who urged nationalization of all Indian industries, Mr. Nehru said: "The whole philosophy lying behind this Plan is to take advantage of every possible way of growth, and not, by doing something which fits into some doctrinaire theory, imagine we have grown because we have satisfied some textbook maxim of a hundred years ago." Planning Commission, Government of India, *The New India: Progress Through Democracy* (New York: Macmillan 1958), p. 52.

The African Image of
Higher Education
in America

Margaret Y. and
John P. Henderson

One of the most bewildering and frustrating aspects of an American professor's experience in Africa is the realization and reiteration of the low esteem with which higher education in America is viewed by Africans. While young Africans are quick to grasp at any means of obtaining a university education abroad, those with private backing and those with the highest qualifications tend to seek admission to British and other European institutions. Throughout the echelons of government and education in the former British colonies of West Africa, where American educators are now living and working and whence the United States is drawing increasing numbers of American-supported scholarship students, American education is openly deprecated by Africans and British alike.

This attitude is especially perplexing in the British, because it is so often expressed by individuals whose academic attainments are well below the level and the standard of reputable American schools, and because, in recent years, British education has moved so markedly in the direction that the United States took early in this century. But the dogmatism with which Africans revere British institutions and shrug indifferently at American universities provides a "cultural shock" for which most of us are ill prepared, especially when one's European-trained African colleagues display serious inadequacies of academic background and little current knowledge of research in their fields.

Gradually, as the weeks slip into months and the months into years, the realization dawns that the African image of American education is very different than that of English education. The English experience was conditioned by tradition and by their experience as British subjects, while until very recently the black African was not made welcome at many American universities. While African students obtained academic and professional degrees at Oxford, Cambridge, Edinburgh, Dublin, and London, their countrymen in America studied at Virginia Union, Morehouse, Tuskeegee, Bethune-Cookman, Langston, Atlanta, Howard, and other segregated schools of the American South. On this contrast, and on the insistently superior attitude of the Britisher, whom he has known far longer and more intimately than the American, the African built his image. And now, though hundreds of Africans are studying in more representative American schools and the quality of our best institutions is becoming more widely known and respected, the African, with indi-

---

Reprinted by permission of Margaret Y. and John P. Henderson.

vidual exceptions, still underrates the American degree and the man who holds it, and will most readily accept principles and policies that favor British academic tradition over American innovation in his own educational system.

This depreciatory attitude has serious implications, first because the United States is now wooing large numbers of African students and is not drawing the best-qualified among them; secondly, because American educational philosophy has considerable relevance for developing countries which is not being projected effectively, despite the expenditure of sizeable foreign aid funds in scholarships to African students and in academic advice and assistance within African countries; and thirdly, because this attitude is not limited to the former British colonies of West Africa but is indicative of the reputation of American education abroad.

Since World War II more foreign students and teachers have come to the United States than ever before and the nation has become increasingly involved in international educational endeavors. In 1955 the American Council on Education's Commission on Education and International Affairs was affecting the "international prestige of the United States." Five years later a special publication of the Department of Health, Education and Welfare confirmed that these adverse attitudes indeed existed and had not improved in the course of subsequent experience. Rather, the problems related to the educational image abroad had increased and the greater international involvement of the past decade had tended to reinforce the poor reputation of American education, "particularly in Africa and the near East."

Reporting the findings of a conference on "Foreign Understanding and Interpretation of United States Education," the HEW bulletin provided a fairly detailed analysis of some of the problems involved. The most significant factor which the conference identified was the "double standard," enabling foreign students to obtain American degrees without performing at the scholastic level normally required of American students. Its recommendations, however, were almost entirely limited to improve publicity abroad.

Perhaps the role of the United States Office of Education is properly a public relations or information function, but no amount of public relations can erase the image sustained by a notably inferior product. And the dubious practices within the educational system that produces that product depend, not upon the foreigner's understanding of the American ideal, but upon the American university's understanding of the problems and the practices that are damaging its reputation abroad.

The First Source

The initial problem is, in a sense, a public relations one for it arises, historically, in the differences between the American approach to higher education and the classical academic tradition which has prevailed in Europe. Misunderstanding of those differences has created a false stereotype of higher education in America as amounting to modern, mass mediocrity, with neither tradition nor standards of excellence. Widespread ignorance and misinformation about American education are most prevalent in areas where Western European systems are well entrenched, as in the British system in English-speaking African countries.

There are, of course, some rather basic differences in the British and American concepts of the role of education. We have traditionally differed in our concepts of who should be educated, and for what purpose, and we have differed significantly in the institutional structure of education. While the United States is bound to suffer in any comparison which puts the best British academic institutions against our poorest colleges and universities, a more subtle comparison had influenced the British, the African, and even our own image of the quality of American education. For centuries the British have reserved their academic institutions to a small community of scholars drawn from among the hereditary elite of a much more hierarchical society than our own, while the United States has moved unswervingly in the direction of what is now widely known as "the land-grant philosophy," extending higher education to the sons and daughters of the working man. While the British established a wide range of professional, technical, and vocational institutions, entered at various levels of primary and secondary schooling, we in America absorbed more and more of these specialized functions into the structure of our colleges and universities, in a system which sought both to broaden the base of liberal education and to provide the specialized training required in a rapidly changing society.

Not only has the sheer weight of numbers augured inferior quality in the minds of proponents of the classical academic tradition, but the content of our curricula has appalled the British scholar. For even though we have a different task for our universities than have the British, and other Europeans, we are nonetheless judged by their standards. The result is that American college graduates are compared, across the board, with British scholars, while their true English counterparts, as identified by the economic and social functions of the individual, often are not university graduates at all but hold secondary school degrees and/or specialized certificates of training in vocational and technical fields. An American insurance salesman or accountant is likely to have a broader and more extensive education than the Englishman who performs the same job, and is better rewarded within his economy, but the fact that he shares a university degree with those of more intellectual pursuits tends to deprecate both the degree and the American intellectual in the eyes of the British.

Since World War II persistent pressures upon the educational system have wrought radical changes in England. The number of universities and the size of the student population have increased prodigiously and with this growth, the curricula have changed as well, to serve a broader segment of English society. The trend follows the American pattern and the new universities are referred to, somewhat facetiously, as the red-brick schools, while the term, Oxbridge, is applied to the venerable colleges of Oxford and Cambridge. A popular story current among English scholars goes:

> *When you enter an Oxbridge classroom and say, "Good morning," the students reply, "Good morning, sir," but when you enter a red-brick classroom and say, "Good morning," the students write it down.*

The story reflects both the "snob appeal" of the traditional institutions and the skepticism with which the university community views the new developments. Nevertheless, those responsible for educational policy, who concern themselves with the changing educational needs of the society, are electing a pattern which they know to have been successful in meeting like needs across the Atlantic. Similarly, first-rate British academicians are well aware of the attainments of American scholars and the quality of graduate and undergraduate training in America. But their students are less likely to be, and the general public, even less so, for just as reputation tends to lag accomplishment, general opinion lags professional awareness. In West Africa, the attitudinal lag is necessarily still greater, for educational systems in the former colonies lag the "Mother country" by thirty or forty years, and many of the few who get beyond primary school do so by archaic systems of home study and centrally administered certifying examinations.

Today, however, education is *the* most vital concern of Africans. Although governments may allocate a higher proportion of their resources to other aspects of economic development, individual Africans seek, and value, education above all else. In Nigeria, which encompasses half the population of tropical Africa, the development of rural amenities is a major concern of the village councils, the townships plague the regional governments for the siting of industries in their areas, and the regional governments stress the development of agriculture and expansion of employment in their policies and planning. But the young Nigerian looks to education to place him on the road to success.

In the former British colonies liberal education was, of course, the only means of upward mobility. Where British rule was indirect, hereditary chieftains retained considerable power, prestige, and reward, and access to the ladder was limited. Therefore, in such areas as Northern Nigeria, ruled through the ancient Emirs of the Moslem tribes, education in English encroached little upon the teaching of the Koran in Arabic. But where more democratic processes of indigenous rule existed, as among the Ibos of Eastern Nigeria, the British employed direct rule and the African, by means of education, could gain a place in the lower realms of government and administration. Gradually, in the decades preceding independence, more and more Africans progressed up the educational ladder and made their way into European universities. In the nineteen-twenties they began journeying to America for academic training and when they did so, the differences in the British and American educational systems began to operate in a new way to foster the already prevalent notion that only a second-rate education could be obtained in the United States.

Confirmation of the Stereotype

The earliest African students in America were immediately confronted with the double standard in its most direct form, the segregated college. While the Negro colleges in the United States have filled a great need and have played a part in raising the level of attainment of the American Negro, they have done so under severe handicaps. These institutions have operated with poorly trained faculties and pitifully inadequate facilities, and have drawn their students from among the most ill-prepared in the nation. They have lacked classroom space, library books, laboratory equipment, and most of all, they have lacked contact with the mainstream of academic life in America. They have worked in isolation from the intellectual community, excluded from the academic and professional associations and cut off from the cross-fertilization of ideas generated within the white institutions. That they produce a brand of education inferior to that of the more representative American schools has been inevitable.

The American-educated African leaders who emerged during the struggles for independence attended these segregated colleges. Dr. Nnamdi Azikiwe, President of the Republic of Nigeria, was one of the first and he was followed by many fellow-Ibos. There was greater wealth among the Yorubas of Western Nigeria, which enabled Yoruba students to journey to the more prestigious institutions in England. Also, the Yorubas were more involved with the colonial government, seated at Lagos in the West, so that they received more encouragement and financial assistance from the British.

The "been to's" who returned from England as gentlemen and scholars, studied English literature and British Constitutional Law and tended to be conservative politically because the status quo placed them in a privileged position. But those who journeyed to the less expensive and more accessible schools in America, often financed by the pennies and shillings amassed among the peasants of their home village and the clan organizations of the wage-earners in the towns, had a quite different experience. Far from being ensconced in the gentlemen's digs of King's or Trinity, with stewards to serve them and an ancient tradition of deference to bolster their self-esteem these students lived and studied under the poorest conditions America had to offer the aspiring scholar. Many of them worked at menial jobs, living from hand to mouth while they acquired the coveted degree. Azikiwe who attended Storer College at Harper's Ferry, West Virginia, then Lincoln University, worked his way as a dishwasher and as a small-time boxer.

These students returned to Nigeria with a healthy respect for the American's willingness to work and with a much different set of values than the "been to's." But they soon found that their hard-earned degrees were not valued. They could not obtain employment in the colonial government, their English-trained countrymen looked down upon them, and they were not equipped to prove their merit in the educational field. Representative was one man who returned from a segregated college with a Ph.B. (Bachelor of Philosophy) degree and took a position as English teacher in the sixth form of a secondary school. The students soon protested his inability to guide their studies and he was transferred to a lower form. Later, he was dismissed for incompetence.

Many of these American-educated Africans turned to politics. Cut off from the limited opportunities open to the indigenous population and fired with American ideas of freedom and equality, they stirred the smoldering seeds of nationalism. As Azikiwe rose to prominence he praised American education, encouraged Ibos to seek it, arranging financial assistance for many of them, and enlarged his political prestige and following with American ideological influences. Another Easterner, the now infamous Orizu of Onitsha province, capitalized on his American education and the growing nationalism by developing a racket which enabled him to establish a profitable transport business before he was prosecuted and jailed.

Returning from the United States around 1951, Orizu toured Nigeria lecturing on a greater tomorrow for those who studied in America. He described the British educational system as perpendicular, while the American system was horizontal and more adapted to Nigerian conditions. Orizu collected vast sums from would-be students for which he guaranteed them admission and scholarships in American universities. Some of his victims never left Africa, but some actually went to the States to find that no arrangements had been made for them. Many, even if they lacked the requisite educational background, managed to obtain degrees from segregated colleges, from "degree mills" that fleece unqualified students, and from various night schools and correspondence courses that exist outside the accredited educational structure.

Thus, despite Azikiwe and other prominent African graduates, the reputation of American education was not altogether enhanced by the Africans who studied in America prior to the days of United States interest and aid in Africa. While the favorable publicity of the nationalists attracted some well-qualified African students who were able to gain admission to reputable universities and have achieved distinction, for every one of these there were many others who attended segregated schools or obtained specious degrees from unethical, unaccredited institutions.

The December, 1958, issue of *Nigerian American University News*, published by the United States Information Service, provides a directory of Nigerians who attended American colleges and universities. A total of 171 graduates, dating back to 1928, are listed. Of these, 56 percent attended Negro colleges, 26 percent went to third-rate teachers' colleges and similar institutions, and 18 percent studied at Ivy League schools, Big Ten universities (including Chicago) and large state universities of the Great Plains and Pacific Coast. The list is undoubtedly incomplete and those who obtained various diplomas from unorthodox institutions are, of course, excluded.

During the past decade, African attendance at first-rate universities in the United States has sharply increased, partly because American universities have become more integrated, but also because the universities, the Federal Government, and various foundations have solicited African students and provided financial assistance to them. But the best-qualified English-speaking African students still prefer England. At the University of Nigeria, largest of the new African universities, it is freely assumed that a graduate or staff member who cannot gain admission in England can always go to America for his graduate training. One British lecturer there, when queried about the scholarship qualifications of an assistant lecturer in his department, said he did not think the boy was very promising. But when he learned the young man had applied to the University of California at Berkeley, he said, "Oh, well, he won't have any trouble getting a Ph.D. in the United States."

The University of Nigeria was founded by Azikiwe in 1960. It is located at Nsukka in the Eastern Region and probably has the highest percentage of American-trained academicians to be found in Africa. More than one-quarter of the eighty-five African faculty members, not all of whom are Nigerians, studied at segregated schools in the United States, but twenty-nine obtained advanced degrees at mainstream American universities. Many of them are committed to the American approach, but greater prestige is tacitly accorded to the European degrees of their African colleagues. Not all the European-trained African faculty attended first-rate institutions either, but this in no way alters the status structure, for though American influence is strong at Nsukka, the inferiority of the United States' image persists.

The university was launched with substantial USAID support in the form of academic advisors and administrative personnel and has proclaimed an educational philosophy closely allied with that of the state universities in America. It has instituted four-year degree programs and American systems of coursework and scholastic evaluation, though generally not of curriculum development. There is probably not a student at Nsukka who did not first apply to the University College at Ibadan where, until this year, external degrees for the University of London were awarded in a three-year program with elaborate distinctions as to first-, second-, and third-class honors.

The first graduating class at Nsukka were allowed on the basis of certain prerequisites, to complete their degrees in three years, but few were able to do so with honors. As commencement day, June 1963, approached, the graduating seniors became increasingly worried, tense, and generally belligerent. They had opposed the administration on many minor points of difference between the innovations at Nsukka and "what is done at Ibadan," and now they were about to enter into competition with Ibadan graduates for jobs in the federal ministries, the regional governments, and the expatriate firms who conduct most private enterprise in Nigeria. Many feared their "ordinary" degrees from an untried institution would gain them only the crumbs, and some felt that to graduate without honors was a disgrace they could never live down.

As far as is known at present, Nsukka graduates have not experienced any difficulty in finding employment. It is too soon to judge how well their performance will speak for the American approach at the University of Nigeria, just as it is too soon to judge the quality of higher education that will develop there. The university's problems are legion, not the least of them being skepticism toward American innovations and the conflicting concepts of educational policy among its faculty, which includes more than twenty nationalities with Americans, British, Indians, and Nigerians predominating. However, the first graduating class achieved thirteen of the fifteen highest ratings in the 1963 Western Regional Civil Service examinations and morale has improved accordingly. The university is undertaking teaching and research programs in certain fields, notably agricultural sciences, that are unique in West Africa and may well prove to be its most significant, and most American, achievements in the next decade. In other fields, American leadership has been less outstanding.

"Seconds" for Export

There are currently an estimated 5,000 African students in the United States. Many of those now returning from American universities with advanced degrees are attaining recognition and will project a better image of American education in the future. But unfortunately, the double standard does not end with segregation; our educational export to Africa continues to be inferior to the home product in most cases, partially because misunderstanding is a two-way street. Some of the difficulties, however, stem from misplaced enthusiasm and from the purely procedural problems of administering international educational endeavors.

A major reason for the inferior quality of the scholastic achievements of foreign students in the United States is the reverse discrimination, practiced by individual professors if not by policy, which applies lower standards to foreign students in consideration for handicaps of language, educational background, and sometimes color. This practice, which has constituted a double standard within our best academic institutions, is encouraged and reinforced by misinformation and ignorance among American educators of the very differences from which the undesirable stereotype of American education initially arises. Because American faculties and educational administrators are badly informed about the educational policies and institutions of other countries, the academic credentials of foreign students are often misevaluated. Unqualified foreign students are admitted to both graduate and undergraduate programs and many foreign students, whatever their qualifications, are improperly placed.

The result is that professors find themselves confronting a growing body of foreign students, drawn mainly from underdeveloped areas, who are almost uniformly in serious difficulties. Ill-prepared for the work they have undertaken, they are invariably under strenuous pressure to do well. They must not fail their families at home, and they must not fail to meet the scholastic averages required for financial assistance from the various sources which subsidize their studies. These circumstances exert undue pressure upon the individual professor, who soon learns that the foreign student cannot cope with his subject at the expected level. Often, in order to proceed at all, he must lower his expectations to align them with the student's limitations. Many consider this practice unethical, yet the pressure comes not only from the student, but from the university administration as well, and some professors believe they are doing the student a service.

An economist at a midwestern university once informed one of his colleagues that he had given a "B" to a floundering Korean student. "He didn't really earn it," the professor said, "but he just can't handle the language and I felt sorry for him. It's better for him to go home with a degree, even if he hasn't learned much."

Multiplied many times in a single student's career, incidents like this one produce poorly educated foreign graduates of our academic institutions. The pressures are greatest with graduate students and the malpractices most devastating. No American student could get through a reputable graduate school without earning "A" grades in his field of specialization. But foreign graduate students have been known to obtain degrees with dubious "B" averages in their coursework. Some of the practices related to student research are equally damaging. The research projects undertaken by foreign graduate students all too often deal with problems within their own countries. Knowing little about many of the subjects proposed, sympathetic professors will approve a topic that does not lend itself to systematic study. Statistical data and historical records may be lacking and the American professor's lack of acquaintance with the country in question hinders his ability to guide the student's efforts. The resulting document may not contain a thesis at all, yet because the student has worked hard and it is difficult to evaluate his results, he will get by. In this way the student obtains a doctorate degree without ever learning to perform scholarly research. Neither as an academician, nor in government or industry will he ever be a good advertisement for higher education in America.

These problems are not unique to American universities. Acquaintance with British- and European-trained Africans and Asians makes abundantly clear the fact that other advanced countries are equally guilty of downgrading admissions and degree requirements for students from the underdeveloped areas of the world. However, it is a practice that the United States can ill afford if the existing image is to be overcome, and it is a practice that runs counter to the interests expressed by the expenditure of thousands of American dollars in international educational programs. Yet the double standard seems to apply not only to foreign students but to Americans interested in underdeveloped areas.

An American graduate student at one of our largest universities recently made a flying trip to Tanganyika. After a three-week tour of spots of local interest, he returned home and wrote a thesis which earned a Master's degree in sociology. The thesis, copies of which were later circulated in East Africa, also earned the ridicule of knowledgeable people in the area for its assumptions, its data, and the level of analysis were superficial, inaccurate, and on the whole, naive.

At Accra, in December 1962, flocks of American graduate students attended the Pan Africanists Conference, first of a series planned to bring together scholars of African culture and development. Many were financed by the Ford Foundation and all were filled with fresh-checked enthusiasm. They introduced at the conference all sorts of ill-conceived ideas for research that afforded great amusement to the old Africa hands attending. It was frequently expressed that the

United States was wasting money in supporting such projects since they detract from the body of knowledge rather than contribute to it.

This kind of thing is especially detrimental to the image of American education in that it affirms the already entrenched prejudices, substantiating the assumed mediocrity of American scholarship. Personnel stationed abroad add their share to the process. Americans teaching in the institutions of higher learning in under-developed areas often display inadequate or inappropriate training and experience which would not qualify them for similar positions in good institutions at home. This, of course, is also true of Europeans in underdeveloped areas. Nevertheless, it occurs not only among Americans recruited independently by foreign institutions but among those participating in extensive programs financed by federal or foundation funds and administered through reputable universities.

One of the difficulties here is an all-too-familiar one in academic circles. Because those scholars most engrossed in the subject matter of higher learning are not interested in purely administrative work, academicians have all but abdicated the decision-making role in the administration of our large and complex educational institutions. Faculties are careful to guard certain prerogatives in the determination of educational policy, but one does not find academicians engaged in the management and operational tasks of the university or administering educational projects abroad. It is the faculty who recruit and evaluate new appointees to the academic departments within universities, but the recruitment, interviewing, and placement of academic personnel abroad is usually handled by professional administrators.

Generally these administrators are well-educated people who may hold advanced degrees. However, they are not involved in the primary tasks of a university—the imparting of knowledge to students and the pursuit of knowledge through research. In conducting foreign educational programs they must, inevitably, make decisions that are essentially academic in nature, evaluating needs and selecting personnel in diverse fields with which they are only superficially acquainted. The result is that American educators abroad seldom have been evaluated for the assigned task by their professional peers and are often appointed for the wrong reasons. Thus, despite the high salaries and elaborate perquisites offered as inducements, international projects are not always graced with first-rate academic personnel. Those who are poorly qualified or whose professional abilities are inappropriate to the work at hand fail to gain the respect of foreigners and consequently, both the luxuries they enjoy abroad and the educational system they represent are resented.

The Inescapable Conclusion

As the United States becomes increasingly involved in international education, many of the problems discussed here will resolve themselves to some extent. Ten years ago the opportunities for American scholars to work abroad were far less numerous than now. This being true, fewer academicians concerned themselves with problems that required extensive research in foreign countries. More and more competent specialists are now developing such interests and thus can be attracted to educational posts abroad. Growing knowledge, sophistication, and professional competence will be focused upon international endeavors in the 1960s and the persistent image will fade and flicker with changing shape and intensity.

The crucial element in the contemporary projection of the American educational image is the double standard in all its manifestations. As academicians become more involved in teaching and research abroad and educational administrators gain experience in the conduct of international projects, coordinated effort can improve the techniques of dealing with the problems of evaluation and placement. But the size and complexity of these problems should not be underestimated for they are closely related to the double standard. The question of admissions criteria for foreign students is perhaps the most significant and the most thoroughly knotty single issued involved.

Most foreign students are convinced that American universities have low admissions standards and the weak scholars among them believe that the double standard for performance will enable them to get by. They are not without evidence for this since many foreign students who have been refused elsewhere and could not gain admission to universities in their own countries have been admitted to institutions in the United States. Both our reputation abroad and our standards within the classroom suffer when this happens. Presumably the practice could be eliminated by more rigorous admissions standards, but the solution is less simple than it sounds.

The question of whether admissions standards are or should be lower for foreign students is difficult to answer. Actually, the expectations and demands of foreign applicants usually exceed the recognition their credentials are given. However, if American universities insist rigidly upon their normal admissions criteria they are likely to admit few foreign students and thereby to lose the very essential cross-cultural influences these students provide. Underlying all of the difficulties are the essential uniqueness of the American educational system and the mutual misunderstanding of the ways in which it differs from the patterns followed elsewhere in the world. Few admissions officers and registrars have sufficient knowledge to evaluate foreign applications accurately for a web of similarities and differences in terminology and institutional structure hinders the adjustment of American criteria to fit foreign credentials.

Seldom do foreign applicants have educational experience equivalent to that specified for American students, and comparability of educational background is not easily discerned. For example, few of the students at the University of Nigeria have completed formal secondary-school programs. Many qualify for entrance by means of General Certificate Examinations, for which they studied on their own and by correspondence after completing primary school. Only someone thoroughly familiar with both the American secondary school system and with the level and content of the African certification systems could properly evaluate these students for admission to an American university.

The African Scholarship Program of a number of first-rate institutions in the United States has introduced greater control in the selection process by requiring college board examinations. However, the screening of credentials cannot be completely eliminated. Comparability is most difficult to determine for students from countries where indigenous systems are most developed because of the diffusion of educational institutions and the numerous diplomas, certificates, and degrees which are similar in terminology but entirely different in content from American educational awards. The general confusion sometimes produces farcical results. One African recently obtained a Ph.D. in fine arts after two years' residence at a thoroughly reputable American university. He had previously earned no formal degree at any institution of higher learning, but having acquired his "union card," he is now teaching in a university. Because Africans are less concerned with learning *per se* than with the symbols of learning that lead to economic advancement and social status, incidents like this make American education popular, but it is a popularity coupled with contempt.

Better publicity abroad that seeks to inform foreign peoples of the true nature and attainments of American scholarship may well counteract some of the prejudices born of ignorance. However, no amount of publicity can counteract the attitudes based on experience and direct knowledge of an inferior educational product of the United States. Only better informed university professors, administrators, and admissions personnel can improve the calibre of our educational export. And while the problems of evaluation and placement are complex and have serious repercussions, it is the standard of performance within our universities and colleges and on the job abroad that is crucial. Thus, the onus is upon the university professor himself, who ultimately must be held responsible for the quality of higher education in America.

A Mission Director's Day

What follows is a composite day—a representative rather than an average one—drawn from the experiences of several Mission Directors.

7:30–8:00. During breakfast young student from upcountry drops in, seeking funds for visit to U.S.

8:00–9:00. Gives once-a-week lecture at University School of Business Administration in "Business Finance."

9:00–10:00. At Embassy for Country Team meeting. First problem—What action, if any, to take on left-wing press attack in morning papers that U.S. seeking to overthrow new government. Concludes that attack is reaction to indelicate and misleading article in major U.S. publication.

Second problem—Since new government's policies in formative stage, asks Ambassador if, in next talk with head of government, he would lay groundwork for later talk with Finance Minister on a tax study recommendation which had reached the talking stage with the former administration.

10:00–12:00. In Mission office. Reads morning cables and mail from Washington. Groans as he learns that top prospect for post in education adviser was offered promotion by his university and decided not to leave. Sighs as he reads priority cable asking for complete report for use in Congressional hearing of all work done under an A.I.D. contract for past five years. Notes arrival dates of an inspection team, three senators, newspaper feature writer, and a group of businessmen.

Reads reports from staff, including notes for his call later in day to Minister of Health. Because of disruption in government due to elections, country has not put up its share of funds for anti-malaria work. If money not available by weekend, all spraying stops.

Edits carefully biweekly progress report to Washington. Drafts letter to new Minister of Finance, outlining items to be discussed at hoped for meeting.

Session with Mission's agricultural water resources engineer to discuss draft of report on scheme for irrigating a critical and arid part of the country. Compliments him on thoroughness and imagination. But points out that tone of report, as written, carries implications that U.S. might be preparing to finance the project. Engineer agrees rewriting is needed.

Witness for Aid by Frank Coffin. Copyright © 1964 by Houghton Mifflin Company. Reprinted by permission of the publisher, Houghton Mifflin Company.

12:00–1:00. At Government Building with Minister of Health. Minister not aware anti-malaria work stoppage imminent. Promises to make delinquent payment immediately.

Since this is first discussion with new Minister, discusses current problem posed by government's plan for two new hospitals. Closes by saying a public health nurse in every village will do more for nation's health than five new hospitals. Minister points out political appeal and prestige value of hospitals. Asks if A.I.D. would give budgetary help for at least one hospital. Receives flat no.

1:00–2:30. Lunch at home for vice-president of large U.S. corporation interested in investing in country.

2:30–3:00. On way back to office, calls on secretary of the President's committee for education. Has heard that he and others feared U.S. trying to impose its own pattern on curriculum of new Teachers College. Assures him that our only goal is to see the college develop, adapting the best from the developed world to the special needs of the country.

3:00–6:00. In office. Sees Administrative Officer. Stenographer, recently arrived from U.S., complains of lizards in her room. Wants to go home. Agriculture Division pressing for more space.

Desk work: dictates, signs mail and outgoing cables.

6:00–7:00. Reception at Embassy for members of new government.

7:00–9:00. Attends regular monthly evening meeting of American businessmen sponsored by Embassy.

Businessmen optimistic about further investments.

9:30–10:00. Reads local press. Asks wife how family is doing.

What Foreign Aid Can and Cannot Do

Chester Bowles

Why does the United States, in view of its many domestic burdens, provide loans, grants and technical assistance to promote economic development in Asia, Africa and Latin America? What can the United States reasonably expect in return for such assistance?

If our primary objective is to assure unquestioning support for our foreign policy objectives or servile gratitude toward a beneficient Uncle Sam, we should have abandoned the foreign-aid program long ago. We can no more purchase the loyalty or gratitude of sovereign nations than we can buy the loyalty and gratitude of individuals.

To Help Themselves

What American aid can do and in many parts of the world is doing is to enable those developing nations which are prepared to help themselves build their own solid foundations for independence and national growth. Although we may be angered on occasion by criticism of American policies by the very nations we are striving to help, we should not allow our irritations to obscure this central objective.

In this framework the more relevant questions, it seems to me, are the following: Is the recipient nation using American aid efficiently? Is it making an honest effort to tax its people fairly? To encourage widespread land ownership? To grow more food? To expand its exports? To root out corruption? To reduce its rate of population increase? To stimulate individual initiative?

Such criteria, in my view, are essential to the development of a realistic and mutually advantageous relationship between the aid-giving and the aid-receiving nations.

Against this background let us look at the record of our foreign-aid program in India, the population of which totals more than half of all the non-Communist developing nations combined.

Casual visitors to India are struck with the awesome poverty and squalor. Millions of Indians are still inadequately fed, while millions more cannot read or write. There are large slum areas in most Indian cities. Consequently, it is not surprising that many observers have come to look at this Asian nation as a bottomless pit.

However, on the positive side of the Indian balance sheet are some impressive economic accomplishments which have recently been obscured by the impact of two serious droughts in succession. Since the early 1950's these accomplishments include the following.

Achievement in India

India's steel production has been increased sevenfold.

India's electrical power capacity is now five times what it was in 1953 and it will double again in the next five years.

India's fertilizer industry is now growing steadily.

India's tax system is being revamped to provide greater incentives for foreign investment and for individual initiative.

Malaria has been reduced from 100 million cases annually to less than 50,000 in 1966.

Four times as many youngsters are now going to school.

More than thirty million acres have been added to the fifty million under irrigation in 1953.

This year nearly sixteen million acres of farmland are being planted with new high yielding wheat and rice paddy seeds.

A vigorous nationwide program has been launched in an attempt to reduce India's annual population growth from the present 2.4 percent to 1 percent by 1971.

These basic achievements, made possibly by American and other foreign assistance and by a generally able Indian administration, have created a solid base for further development; indeed, many American and Indian economists are persuaded that with normal rains and continuing foreign aid India may become self-sufficient in food grain by 1972 and able to do without foreign governmental assistance by 1977.

To Prevent Vietnams

Although our minds and our national budgets are primarily focused on Vietnam, it is important that we strengthen our efforts to help prevent new and even more costly Vietnams from developing elsewhere. Well planned and sensitively administered American aid coupled with an effective effort by the recipient nations themselves can help harassed new governments create nations that their own people feel are worth defending.

To assist this evolutionary movement toward political independence and self-sustaining, economic growth is the only valid purpose of American assistance to the developing nations—and it should be reason enough.

19th Century Ideology
and 20th Century Reality

John Fayerweather

One of the more distressing features of our day is the continuing conflict between two of the strongest and potentially most constructive forces in modern society: nationalism and the multinational corporation. From time to time the conflict erupts in spectacular form in expropriations of property—electric utilities in Brazil and Castro's sweeping takeover of U.S investments in Cuba. But more common and actually of greater over-all importance are a multitude of lesser points of conflict—over the share of capital and control a foreign company may hold in a local venture, the degree of regulation foreign governments exercise over foreign operations and many other facets of overseas business.

While each of the points of conflict has some specific logic in itself, underlying them all is the massive sentiment of nationalism limiting the ability of sincere men on both sides to act dispassionately. For example, the question of how much profit a foreign company should be permitted to repatriate is debatable in rational economic terms. On the one hand, there are the rights of the contibutor of capital to a payment for the use of his money. On the other, there are pressing demands in the host country for importation of capital equipment and the materials needed for economic development. But anyone who observes negotiations on this issue it is readily apparent that emotional value judgments are often controlling. The foreign investor is not just receiving "a payment for the use of his money," a cold, economic-legal concept. Rather hc "is draining the host nation of its wealth," a phrase emanating from a politically sensitive mentality attuned to the feelings of the general populace. As often as not, in developing nations with colonial pasts, there are further undertones of "the obligation" of the west to finance development regardless of reward, in order to compensate for excessive profiteering and failure to support development in earlier periods.

Thus, no matter how effectively we may deal with the cold logic of the problems confronting the multinational corporation, we cannot hope for a major breakthrough on many of the critical issues unless the nationalistic component of the conflict is resolved. This is no simple problem, and there is little indication that we are yet even close to solving it. It is the purpose of this article to try to clarify the character of the problem. I propose to look carefully at the nature of both nationalism and the multinational corporation, defining the elements in each which

Reprinted from *Columbia Journal of World Business* (Winter 1966): 77–84 by permission.

are pertinent to the problem and considering the direction in which each might evolve to reach some greater accommodation with the other.

What lies at the heart of the conflict between nationalism and multinational business? To answer that question we had best look at the essential characteristics of each.

Nationalism as we know it is of quite recent origin. While it had assorted early forebears, it was not firmly established until the beginning of the nineteenth century. Prior to that time patriotism, i.e., loyalty to one's country and its monarch, existed. But nationalism goes a good deal beyond patriotism and did not emerge until the majority of the populace achieved a real identification with the state through the middle-class revolutions. A citizen might admire, respect, and love his king and feel emotional ties to his country, but feelings of a quite different order were tapped when the people felt that the nation and its government were truly theirs.

Although nationalism is relatively new, its psychological roots are not. Nationalism is a new manifestation of a fundamental human trait. The key motivation at work is the quest for security, reinforced by other social satisfactions which come from participation in a group. From earliest times these feelings have brought people together into groups with a high degree of internal cohesion and sharp separation from external elements. Social scientists use the term "we-group," which aptly describes the attitudes of the participants. They feel a strong identification with the group, thinking of it and acting in it on a "we" basis and treating those who are not in the group as a distinctly different category: "they," "outsiders," "foreigners." The individual is raised in the traditions, culture, and values of the we-group. He is expected to and generally does willingly accept them and give them strong emotional loyalty and support. Doing so contributes greatly to his own security, for he gains both emotional and physical security from the sense that his group is good and right and strong.

Basis of New Nationalism

For centuries these feelings found their main expression in groups which lived in relatively close physical proximity—the family, the clan, the tribe, the village, and even the city-state. These were units in which the individuals could effectively share in a common life and have a sense of participation in the group. There were larger government units to be sure, but the mass of people were too poorly educated to have much knowledge of or sense of unity with "countrymen" beyond their immediate community, and they had too little participation in the government to feel full indentification with it. But there was nothing in the psychological forces involved which inherently limited we-group attitudes to small units, and two important changes, reinforced by other developments, brought forth the new nationalism: mass education and popular government.

As literacy became more common, facilitated by the printing press, people became better acquainted with the world around them and found in this knowledge an identification with the language, traditions, literature, culture, and often religion of their national group as distinguished from the foreignness of other peoples. Concurrently the rise of the middle class was being fostered by economic growth and by the new social structure associated with the industrial revolution and large-scale manufacturing. The middle class soon developed a strong interest in the functioning of the national government and a capacity to participate in it which superseded that of the feudal-landowning aristocracy.

These limited observations, of course, gloss over a quite long and difficult transition. But in broad outline we can see how and why the we-group psychology was elevated to the national level. From its middle-class base in Europe and North America, nationalism has now spread, in this century of popular government, mass communications and independence movements, to every part of the globe and deep into the ranks of the lower classes, leaving only the more primitive tribal groups outside its influence.

This historical review has two implications for the future. First, since the underlying psychology of nationalism is basic, it will not disappear. Second, changes in the way in which this psychology is manifested may occur. We must look therefore at the developments under way in the world today to see where they may be leading.

Following this train of thought, one's instinct is to look for signs that we are moving toward a yet broader span of we-group structure—the family, the tribe, the city, the nation, now an international cohesion. And, indeed, there are numerous things we can point to which seem to fit the requirements for such a transition. Mass communications media are making people all around the world aware of each other and familiar with their ways of life. There has been a steady growth of what might be called international subcultures. Teenagers, for example, in virtually all countries share tastes in hair styles, music, and the like. To at least a limited degree they show a mutual identification rising above national affiliation. We have similar trends among international businessmen, scientists, chess players, radio hams, and assorted others.

The increasing integration of the world economy is also an encouraging sign. Just as the emergence of nationalism coincided with, and apparently was related to, the economic suitability of the nation-state as the industrial revolution got under way, our modern economy seems to require a cohesion and cooperation among nations. The Internatioanl Monetary Fund (IMF), the General Agreement on Tariffs and Trade (GATT), the European Economic Community (EEC), the Latin American Free Trade Association (LAFTA), and similar mechanisms rising above national sovereignties are critical to world trade and thus to the welfare of people in all nations.

The Threat That Binds

But despite these favorable elements, there are some reasons for doubting that we are on the threshold of a true international we-groupism. First if we look at the past, we find that no we-group has ever existed without a "they." The need for security is generally accepted as a critical motivation in the individual's commitment to the we-group. While a person may need security in relation to the unknown or in isolation, his concern about tangible external threats is strong and its absence removes a significant support of any we-group affiliation. The communist threat has created a degree of cohesion in the free world, but these ties are limited by the affiliation of large portions of the populations of many countries to communism. It is hard therefore to visualize the peoples of the world being drawn together tightly in the absence of a threat from outer space.

Likewise, for all the development of international subcultures, the differences among the nations are still very great and in important respects show little sign of diminishing appreciably. In such vital respects as language, religion and cultural values the Indian, the Japanese, the German and the American are still a very long way apart. One cannot therefore readily conceive of the rise of an international we-groupism strong enough to rival the national variety.

Nationalism is especially strong in the area of business, chiefly because of the heavy influence external business has exerted on the internal social and political affairs of many nations, especially the less-developed ones. This is the dominant theme in Richard Robinson's searching historical analysis of the effect of western investment.[1] Animosity toward foreign investment is therefore part of the nationalistic tradition which binds these peoples together. Thus we start at a tremendous handicap in proposing that multinational business affairs become disassociated from nationalism.

Hope from History

On the other hand, it is hard to ignore the historical affairs of many nations, especially the less-developed countries, where historic patterns tended to synchronize with the basic economic and business system which was desirable for the effective use of the technology of the day. Throughout history, business institutions and political structures have evolved in constructive directions both independently and in their mutual relations. New forms of business units have appeared which were effective in utilizing the technology of the times, and political systems have developed which were appropriate to prevailing economic conditions.

In the Middle Ages, for example, the simple manufacturing technology which for the most part functioned effectively within quite limited geographic areas was satisfactorily utilized by the artisan system. The city, supplemented by the guild, provided adequate social services and control for the artisan economy. As wealth and regional interchange grew, the great trading companies appeared, and at the same time national governments capable of such complementary roles as protection

---

[1] Richard D. Robinson, *International Business Policy* (New York: Holt, Rinehart & Winston, 1964), pp. 1–44.

of shipping emerged. The industrial revolution brought with it the large, publicly owned corporation, with its capacities for bringing together large amounts of capital and operating huge production facilities serving major marketing areas, and the parallel evolution of stronger national governments which built the essential infrastructure and maintained broad controls over business.

If the multinational corporation is in fact beneficial economically, there is a supposition here that government policies and the national sentiments behind them will in some way be adjusted to accommodate it. In speculating about ways in which this might happen another feature of past history is worth observing. Throughout the prenationalistic eras, various forms of internationalism have existed. There have been administrative unifications like the Roman and Ottoman empires in which bureaucracies recruited locally served what were for those times truly international systems, despite the gulf between their masters and the local we-groups to whom they had an initial loyalty. Likewise, in the Renaissance period in Europe the elite, the intelligentsia, were in a sense a distinctive we-group unto themselves, separate from the masses. They spurned localism in favor of a common mission in a unified Catholic society. Can international business and the government officialdom that must work with it around the world achieve such a sense of unity and disassociation from nationalistic patterns? At the moment we can only speculate. But the prospects will certainly be influenced greatly by the extent to which the multinational corporation proves of benefit to the world community.

In examining the benefits conferred by the multinational corporation, we are of course focusing on the social utility of the organization, not on its business efficiency. This distinction is important, for what is profitable for the company, even in a sound long-term view, is not necessarily beneficial to society as a whole. We hope it may be, but we have to prove it.

Is the multinational corporation socially useful, and if so, in what form? Some people have suggested that the hope for the future of international business lies in the creation of a "supranational" corporation chartered by the United Nations, with its headquarters in some center with minimal national character (like Luxembourg), owned by stockholders of a broad range of nationalities and managed as a true world enterprise without partiality to any country. While this is an appealing ideal conceived in conjunction with a transition from nationalism to internationalism, its inadequacy as a means of minimizing the conflict with nationalism is readily apparent. It is effective in removing the impact of the nationalism of the home country of the multinational corporation, but it really does nothing to alter relations with other countries. The supranational corporation is still an outsider, still a "they," whether it be of United States origin or United Nations origin. If and when the peoples of the world start to transfer their we-group emotions to the United Nations in substantial measure, then the device may be really meaningful. But we have seen that this is not a promising outlook, and in its absence I would suggest that the idea has to be viewed with considerable skepticism. Moreover, the change may amount in large part to a fiction, if as seems likely, the capital and management of the corporation still come from a limited number of major industrial countries. Furthermore, for all their negative comments about foreign capital, many nations may have considerably more confidence in the beneficence and responsibility of highly developed business communities than in the qualities of a floating corporation chartered by a very weak government institution and presumably virtually free of over-all government control. This is not to say that the concept may not in fact prove sound, but only to emphasize that at the moment it is unduly favored by the age-old advantages of "the grass in the next pasture."

Can the Ties Be Loosened?

I think therefore that we should more logically look in the other direction; namely, whether to minimize the conflict with nationalism, the multinational corporation could evolve into a system of national units whose external ties are nonexistent. This is a contradiction in terms and is an unlikely, if not definitionally impossible, outcome. External ties are basic to the concept of the multinational corporation. They are the channels along which benefits flow. One can legitimately ask whether these ties can be reduced or severed without at the same time diluting the benefits. Yet since any progress along these lines would cut down on nationalistic antagonisms, it seems worthwhile to consider the extent to which we may move in this direction.

The multinational corporation's external ties may for convenience's sake be subsumed under four main headings, representing the basic flows within a business organization: product, finance, technology and management.

Product Flow. The social utility of the flow of products from one country to another scarcely needs defense. A host of scholars since Adam Smith and Ricardo have so established the concept of comparative advantage that the fact of the flow of goods into a country is thoroughly accepted.

The identification of products with the external multinational corporation by trade names and brands is another matter. In the less-developed countries and to a degree in more advanced industrialized areas like Europe, U.S. companies have found that their brand names are profitable assets because United States industry in general and they in particular have a reputation that attracts consumers. This is seemingly inconsistent with the "anti-they" attitude of nationalism. Suffice it to say that foreign nationals tend to be ambivalent: as practical consumers they want the specific brands, but as nationalists they feel constrained to attack their entry. Polish hams in the U.S. may be a reverse example.

Do multinational brands serve a socially useful purpose? This is a difficult question that cannot be answered clearly. On the surface the value is not apparent. But digging deeper one may suggest that the comsumer acceptance the brands achieve is an important vehicle for market expansion and economic development. We enter here into the question of whether a number of aspects of aggressive commercial marketing make significant contributions to the expansion of a national economy. Theory in this regard is still crude and inconclusive, so all we can do is leave it as an open question.

A final question is whether control of the marketing process must remain in the hands of the home office. It should be noted that the marketing function is one which traditionally has been most readily transferred to independent local businesses. That is, multinational companies both at home and abroad have turned over a large part of their distribution to local wholesalers, import merchants, dealers, and the like. However, we also observe that corporate efficiency motives have led many firms to withhold the marketing of at least the first level of distribution in foreign markets from local firms. Their objectives have been to sell more aggressively, to provide better direction of dealer organizations and other ends which add up to "better" distribution. Thus, in judging whether these penetrations into foreign nations have social value, we are back again to the unanswered question of the contribution of marketing to economic development.

Finance Flow. The imput of capital and the return of earnings are fundamental to private business interest in foreign operations. In Europe and other highly industrialized areas, it is doubtful whether the imported capital is of significant value to the host nation, but in less-developed areas it has an acknowledged beneficial role. Indeed, both the U.S. government and the receiving nations have made major efforts to increase the flow of capital. There is the theoretical possibility that capital needs might be supplied by indirect investment; for example, by purchase of stock of local companies by U.S. investors. The practical prospects in this regard are not good, however, as portfolio investments in the less-developed areas are still living down the adverse experience in the interwar period.

The chief vehicle for inducing a capital inflow but moderating the nationalistic reaction against it is the joint venture—a partnership of foreign and national capital. This may be a partial answer but it appears to dodge the issues, especially when, as most new nations prefer, the foreign company interest is limited to less than 50 percent. First, any arrangement which uses local capital to substitute for part of the investment a foreign company might make reduces the net inflow of needed external capital. Second, in the opinion of the majority of multinational companies a joint venture is managerially less effective than one with single control and may thus weaken the contribution to industrial growth. This is another complex subject which we can only leave as an open question.

It seems reasonable to conclude that the industrialized nations can manage without large capital infusions from abroad. The policies of Japan in the post-war era have followed this general line with success. But in the less-developed countries the social value of inputs of capital tied to managerial control to assure their effective use seems beyond question.

Technology Flow. The flow of research-derived technology for use in products and production processes would seem to provide the strongest basis for the multinational corporation, both in buiness terms and in terms of social value. Certainly it is in the fields where technology counts most that international firms have been strongest—chemicals rather than textiles, office machines rather than bread, etc.

The economic efficiency of doing research in a limited number of centers rather than duplicating it in every country of the world appeals to simple logic. We may have a cross flow of technology between developed areas, as we do between Europe and the United States. But since it seems almost certain that the less-developed nations will lag behind in technology for many years, the technological flow between the developed and developing will be predominantly in one direction.

Can this flow be severed from ownership through licensing agreements? The existence of a vast number of such arrangements is ample proof that it can be done. But we are again confronted with a practical block and a theoretical question. Most large companies would prefer to control the operations rather than turn their technology over to others. They feel that they can do a better job, especially in the developing countries where many of the potential licensees are at a generally lower level of managerial competence than their own organizations. This leads to the same type of question we encountered in the marketing area. If the multinational corporation can do a better job of implementing the technology, is it not the more desirable vehicle for development of the national economy?

Managerial Flow. The substance of this part of the multinational business is hard to describe in concrete terms, especially to the antagonistic nationalist. Yet it has a real meaning. The ability to blend a group of people together into an efficient business organization and to formulate and execute effective policies is recognized as one of the main strengths of the industrialized economies. The application of this competence in foreign countries has given many multinational corporations a basis for superiority well beyond what their products, capital or technology could provide. The social value of inflows of this managerial skill is certainly attested to by the way all countries have sought to draw on the management skill of the more developed. Consider, for example, the multitude of invitations to U.S. management professors and consultants to work in other countries, as well as the activities of the International Executive Service Corps. And while there is the possibility that the inflow might be provided by individual contributions rather than through the organizations of multinational corporations, there are so many proponents in government and academic circles, as well as business, of the thesis that an integrated, going organization is the best transmission device for managerial know-how that one must accept this as a strong presumption.

After we have looked at each of the components of the multinational corporation's activities, there is still something more to be considered in appraising the value of a unified business organization. Just as there is a historical evolution toward large we-groups, there is steady progression toward larger business organizations in which capital, technology and management are integrated with varying degrees of vertical control in the acquisition and distribution of products. We know that this progression has not excluded the existence of smaller enterprises and that a number of enterprises can coexist. It is not impossible therefore to conceive a world in which all corporations would be confined to their own national borders, but would engage in exchanges of products, capital, technology and management skills by arm's length bargaining. But this conception runs counter to the trend of history. It is far easier to accept what we see today as the natural evolution—great corporations efficiently accomplishing these flows through their own integrated operations spreading across national borders.

These views of the component flows and integrated character of the multinational corporation give us a basic perspective on its capacity to accommodate to nationalism. The outlook does not appear highly promising. This is not to say that the corporation cannot act in ways which minimize the effects of nationalism. Much has already been written by this author and others about the practical actions which companies may take to meet nationalistically motivated desires, including the use of local nationals in management, employment of local capital and sympathetic relations with foreign governments.[2] While the details of these actions involve numerous questions, I am here accepting them as obvious and sound basic policies. The present analysis has been pitched to a different level. My concern is that even after we have implemented these basic policies to the point which is typically sound from a business efficiency point of view, we find that the external ties remain so significant that the conflict with nationalism retains a solid core of substance.

Is Conflict Permanent?

My purpose has been to examine the fundamentals of the structure of the multinational corporation to see whether a quite different concept could be conceived which would achieve both business efficiency and social utility. The picture as I have drawn it does not suggest this to be the case. But it should be cautioned that we do not have the type of well-documented, thoroughly analyzed research we need to reach considered conclusions on many aspects of this subject. My primary aim has not been to reach conclusions but to outline the character of the issues and the ways in which we may usefully think about them. As a conclusion it is adequate therefore to observe that there is a very hard core of conflict between nationalism and the character of the multinational corporation and that it is difficult to see how this conflict can be ultimately eliminated.

Where does this leave us? Will the conflict be a permanent one or will a pattern of mutual accommodation evolve? No one really knows. Taking a final look backward, however, we can find encouragement in the way other conflicts within society have found resolution, at least to a fair degree. For example, there is an apparent conflict between the acquisitive, materialistic character of modern industry and the tenets of Christianity. Yet, the two have been effectively married in Western Europe and Anglo-Saxon countries by the Protestant Ethic, which in

---

[2] For example, see my article, "LRP for International Operations," *California Management Review* (Fall 1960): 23–29.

giving religious sanction to hard work encouraged industrial productivity and justified the rewards of industry on this earth. John D. Rockefeller could thus feel no basic conflict in being a good Baptist and making millions of dollars. Likewise, the conflict between job security and the advance toward higher productivity has been always with us, whether in the English Luddites, who smashed textile machinery in the 1810s, or the railroad featherbedding issues of the 1960s. Yet labor has increasingly recognized the social utility and ultimate benefit to itself in more productive industrial methods. In a few notable cases it has even provided leadership in introducing labor-saving devices, e.g., John L. Lewis in the coal industry.

The proposition that the activities of the multinational corporation within various nations have social value has not been proved here, but it does appear to have strong support. If it is valid, then our historical perspective gives encouragement that a resolution of the conflict with nationalism will evolve. Although the change may come through some broad movement from nationalism toward political internationalism, it is more likely to occur through a mutual recognition of self-interest on the part of businessmen and business-oriented government officials around the world, a decline in the nationalistic preoccupation with business affairs, and a reduction of the external ties of the multinational corporation in each nation to the minimum that is clearly socially useful.

The Multinational Corporation as a Development Agent

Harry G. Johnson

During the past twenty years or so the large multinational corporation—and primarily the U.S.-based international company—has emerged as a potent agent of economic transformation and development, not only in the more laggard "developed" countries but also in the developing countries of the world. Both economic theory and economic policy have been slow in recognizing this phenomenon, which has excited a mixed reaction of welcome to the increased efficiency brought about by foreign direct investment in a country and of dislike and fear of what is seen as the growth of foreign economic domination over a country's destiny. Thus far, welcome for solid economic advantages has outweighed xenophobia, in practice if not always in political pronouncements.

In the developing countries, the "crisis of aid" with which the Pearson Commission was concerned has made it necessary to take a strongly positive view of what the multinational corporation can contribute to the promotion of economic development and to look to private foreign investment as an important element in the development process. While the Pearson Report calls for a substantial increase in both the overall total of aid as now conventionally defined and the proportion and total of official aid, contemporary political circumstances make it extremely unlikely that official aid will increase on the scale recommended. It is more likely that official aid will decline even in absolute real terms and that increasing emphasis will be placed on preferential trading arrangements and on increasing private foreign investment. This prospect makes it necessary to consider the scope for and limitations of the promotion of economic development by private foreign investment, and more specifically by direct investment by the multinational corporation.

Heretofore, development promotion has been considered a major responsibilty of government, requiring extensive economic planning and some degree of effective government intervention in and control over the private sector of the economy, including the activities of foreign corporations. The planning approach to economic development, supported by official foreign aid, has not worked noticeably well in the past, as the Pearson Report documents. This is the major reason why the foreign aid required to support the continuation of that approach is unlikely to be forthcoming in the future, and why the emphasis in development policy will probably shift towards increased reliance on private competitive forces.

Such a shift of emphasis will, if it is to work effectively to promote development, require political willingness to accept the fact that the multinational corporation is not like government. The corporation cannot tax the public to obtain resources to be spent on what are considered politically desirable types of development, but instead is motivated by the desire for profits and constrained by the need for profitability. A profit-motivated development process will be different in character from a development process planned by politicians and bureaucrats. In particular, such a development process may conflict sharply with mounting concern about social justice in the distribution of income.

"Social justice" requires the redistribution of income from those who are capable of producing it to those who are not, at its best in the hope that the latter will eventually become capable of rendering an adequate contribution to the productive process. Profit-motivated development, by contrast, entails rewarding those capable of productive contribution to the extent of that contribution as a means of stimulating the development of further productive potential.

In concrete terms, reliance on foreign direct investment to promote development can mean highly uneven development, at least with respect to the direct impact of development. The corporation's concern in establishing branch operations in a particular developing economy is not to promote the development of that economy according to any political conception of what development is, but to make satisfactory profits for its management and shareholders. Its capacity to make profits derives essentially from its possession of productive knowledge, which includes management methods and marketing skills as well as production technology. It has no commercial interest in diffusing its knowledge to potential local competitors, nor has it any interest in investing more than it has to in acquiring knowledge of local conditions and investigating ways of adapting its own productive knowledge to local factor-price ratios and market conditions. Its purpose is not to transform the economy by exploiting its potentialities—especially its human potentialities—for development, but to exploit the existing situation to its own profit by utilization of the knowledge it already possesses, at minimum cost of adaptation and adjustment to itself.

The corporation cannot be expected to invest in the development of new technologies appropriate to the typical developing country situation of scarcity of capital and abundance of unskilled, uneducated, illiterate labor and in the mass training of blue-collar, white-collar and especially executive local personnel. It has at its disposal an effective technology appropriate to the capital and skilled-labor-abundant circumstances of the developed countries as well as access to the capital and skilled-labor markets of the developed countries. Hence it will invest in technological research on the adaptation of its technology and in the development of local labor skills only to the extent that such investment holds forth a clear prospect of profit.

Development Incentives

While the multinational firm has an incentive to invest in the transformation of the local economy only to the extent that such investment promises greater profits, the incentive may nevertheless be sufficient to induce a substantial contribution to development. Two particular incentives are especially important in this connection. First, labor skills imported from the developed countries are extremely expensive in comparison with the cost of training local labor, especially as the cost of training is largely either the labor-time of teachers or the labor-time of students, both of which are infinitely cheaper in poor countries than in rich ones. The foreign company will thus have a large profit incentive to train a local staff rather than import foreign labor.

Second, given the complex input-output relations characteristic of modern industry and the dependence of profitable utilization of the product on the knowledge of the user, the firm may have a substantial incentive to invest in the diffusion of productive knowledge in two directions: to the local suppliers of the inputs needed in its production process and for which it demands quality standards superior to the customary standards of those industries and to local customers who may have to be taught the technology of using the firm's products effectively.

These two incentives can be simply illustrated by reference to two examples related to the improvement of agricultural production: firms interested in the distribution and sale of canned foods have a strong commercial interest in teaching farmers to produce a high-quality standardized product as efficiently as possible, while firms that produce fertilizers, farm machinery and other agricultural inputs have a strong commercial interest in teaching farmers how to use these inputs efficiently to increase their farming profits.

These incentives are important aspects of the potential role of foreign direct investment as an agency for the promotion of economic development. Self-interest and the private profit motive can serve the social interest and may do so more effectively than governmental activities (such as agricultural research stations) that are nominally directed at the social interest but not subjected to the hard test of generating visible profits. Still, the implication is that the main contribution of foreign direct investment to development will be highly specific and uneven in its incidence. In particular, the direct and visible impact is likely to be the training of a relatively small number of local employees for jobs on the factory floor and in the company offices and the creation of a relatively tiny elite of higher income people in a general environment of low income and heavy unemployment. Any more general influence in promoting development will have to stem, on the one hand, from the exemplary value for local enterprises of the existence of efficient, well-managed, science-based subsidiary firms and their production of skilled local workers and executives who can be attracted into local enterprises and, on the other hand, from the ability of the state to use corporate and individual income taxes levied on foreign firms and their employees to finance education and other developmental expenditures.

It is worth noting, in this connection, that the limitations on the potentialities of foreign direct investment as an agent of economic growth derive in part from social considerations that are generally accepted as just by well-intentioned people but in fact serve to inhibit the development process. These are the considerations that sanction both the legitimacy of trade union organization as a means of obtaining "a fair rate for the job" and the desirability of legislation directed at ensuring "fair" wages and working conditions in industry.

Foreign firms are excessively sensitive to local demands for "decent" wages and working conditions and for pay comparable to what similar workers and executives earn in the advanced countries. This sensitivity is reinforced by the fact that skilled and educated people are more mobile internationally than unskilled and uneducated people, as a result of the discrimination in immigration laws in the advanced countries in favor of talented immigrants as against the unskilled run-of-the-mill. But the effect of the social insistence on the payment of "fair" wages is to overprice the labor in question in relation to its social opportunity cost, to inhibit development by taxing it with the obligation to pay unneccessarily high wages and to discourage efforts to develop more unskilled-labor-intensive methods of production.

This is, in fact, a fundamental point about the development process that is too little appreciated. Human societies are essentially conservative. They resist change until it has occurred and then attempt to capture and institutionalize the benefits of change within the traditional framework of social relationships. By so doing, they inhibit change in the name of social responsibility. To the extent it complies with these social processes, the multinational corporation cooperates in the social attempt to prevent economic change and to stop economic growth from taking place.

Conflict

Increasing reliance on the multinational corporation as an agency for promoting economic development is likely to exacerbate problems that have already appeared in the relations between the nation-state as a powerful political entity with a bordered geographical domain and the multinational corporation as a powerful economic entity with an unbordered world market domain. These problems appear in one form or another as a conflict between the sovereignty of the national state and the economic liberty of the large firm, or as a conflict between the claims to sovereignty of different national states, specifically the headquarters nation of the investing corporation and the nation within whose borders the investment occurs.

The former conflict involves a clash between the nation-state's politically derived ideas of what development is and how corporations should behave. The latter conflict involves a clash between the claims of nations to exercise sovereignty both over all activities within their territorial borders, whether of citizens or foreign residents, and over all activities of citizens whether conducted within their borders or not—a clash which focuses on the extraterritorial exercise of national power.

Both conflicts involve the overlapping of domains and the dispute of rival sovereignties inherent in this overlapping. They can be resolved in the long run only by a formal or informal division of powers such as prevails in a federal state. At the present time these conflicts are, and for some time ahead will be, aggravated by two factors.

The first factor is the philosophy of authoritarian nationalism, which has been the unhappy legacy of European political philosophy to the contemporary world, accepted automatically by European thinkers who also regard themselves as socialists and progressives. This political philosophy is aped without second thought by developing-country thinkers who in turn regard themselves as anti-imperialists and radicals. This philosophy generates two blindly emotional attitudes unhelpful to rational understanding—deep suspicion of the profit motive and the market system and unquestioning belief in the superiority of the political over the economic process in the selection of economic decision makers and the formulation of economic decisions. Both attitudes irrationally favor the claims of national sovereignty over the claims of corporate enterprise.

However, the nation-state is territorially limited and the corporation is not. Competition among nation-states for the economic favors of the corporation and the xenophobic character of the nation-state itself will tend to prevent the formation of a conspiracy or cartel of nation-states to exploit the economic potentialities of the multinational corporation in the service of national power. The long-run trend therefore will be toward the dwindling of the power of the nation-state relative to the corporation. To survive as an effective influence, the political process will have to move in the direction of world government. The Pearson Commission's recommendations for changes designed to increase the power of the World Bank are unconsciously aimed in that direction.

The second factor is inherent in the dominance of U.S.-based corporations among the multinational corporations. This dominance has two important inplications. The first is that, rightly or not—and usually wrongly—such corporations will be regarded with suspicion as political agents of the U.S. government rather than as instruments through which shareholders (who may be of all nationalities) are seeking to maximize their profits. The second implication stems from the special nature of the relation—ideologically if not always in practice—between business and government in the United States. The U.S. version of free enterprise (more accurately, the mixed economy)—reinforced by the gigantic size of the U.S. economy—entails a greater independence of business in relation to government, and correspondingly a greater necessity that political control over corporate activity be exercised by law and in the open, rather than covertly by conspiracy and backscratching among specialized members of a recognized and homogeneous political, economic and cultural national elite that is characteristic of most other countries.

Hence, conflicts both between the political interests of the government of a nation and the economic interests of a U.S. corporation investing in it and between the political interests of the U.S. government and the political interests of other national governments in the foreign activities of U.S.-based corporations will be more apparent and provocative of public discussion than is the case for relations between governments and multinational corporations of other nationalities. Relations between other governments and their multinational corporations command less public attention. In the long run, again, the problems of national sovereignty over the multinational corporation and of conflicting national sovereignties with respect to its foreign operations will have to be resolved by some sort of international agreement on a code of company and governmental conduct; but first it will be necessary to reconcile the conflict between U.S. and other views on the proper relation between the corporate enterprise and national government.

Judging by past experience, political criticism of the local activities of a multinational corporation will comprehend every major aspect of its operations and involve, for the most part, naive and economically debatable assumptions about what the corporation should be doing in the national interests of the country. Thus, insistence on the employment of more local workers and executives and on the participation of local shareholders, nominally motivated by opposition to "discrimination," may well create large unearned incomes for a few nationals at the expense of the efficiency of the company's operations and thus at the expense of consumers. Insistence on purchase of a high proportion of inputs into the production process from local sources, designed to diffuse development and encourage industrialization, may similarly burden consumers with excess costs, inhibit the achievement of scale economies by the company and dissipate scarce local entrepreneurial talent in socially unproductive enterprises.

The corporation is more likely than civil servants to have an accurate judgment of the country's comparative advantage. Its preference for imported inputs may reflect that knowledge. It is important to remember that the high productivity of the modern corporation is achieved largely through specialization on its own small part of the production process, made possible by its ability to rely on the quality and reliable flow of inputs purchased from component suppliers. To force the corporation to develop the capacities of local suppliers may put it into a new kind of business for which it is not organizationally or technically equipped.

In similar fashion, criticisms of corporations for failing to export enough, usually attributed to market-allocation agreements in contravention of the national interest, frequently represent failure to recognize the logical implications of insistence on cost-raising import-substitution policies and the maintenance of an overvalued currency.

Finally, criticisms of the corporation for an alleged failure to conduct sufficient research and development locally usually entail both a failure to appreciate the economies of the production of useful new knowledge and a covert attempt to raise the rental value (salaries) of a country's already scarce supply of scientifically competent personnel. In all of these criticisms there is an evident element of confusion in understanding the role and incentives of the corporation—which are to minimize cost by obtaining its human, material and knowledge inputs from the cheapest possible source—and the role and incentives of government—which are to use the monopoly revenue it derives from its control of the tax system and the power it derives from its legal authority to reallocate resources in an economically inefficient fashion to serve politically determined ends and primarily to purchase political support.

Conflicts between governments over the multinational corporation center on the issue of extra-territoriality—specifically, the application of U.S. antitrust and trading-with-the-enemy laws to the trade of foreign subsidiaries of U.S.-based companies with other foreign countries and the application of U.S. balance-of-payments policies to the financial operations of such subsidiaries. In this context it should be noted that U.S. policies are more visible than those of other countries but are not necessarily more reprehensible purely on that account. The fundamental issue is the dual claim of the nation-state to sovereignty over all residents and all citizens. This issue necessarily brings nation-states into conflict with one another and should be seen, not in terms of the traditional categories of "American imperialism," "colonialism" and so forth, but in terms of a more general and fundamental problem of reconciling the traditional and anachronistic concept of the "isolated state" with the economic—and political—facts of a rapidly integrating world economy in which there is increasing mobility of goods, capital, labor (at least educated labor) and knowledge. In the long run, there will have to be one world, politically as well as economically.

Part Six

International Investment

6

Some thoughts about the terminology of international business will serve well to introduce this section dealing with international investment because, in the investment field especially, terminological blocks have sometimes stood in the way of understanding.

Until quite recently, *international trade* has been the term widely used to describe all aspects of *international economic life*. In the economics departments of most universities, courses in international *economics* are still labelled international *trade* and many people, in fact, still use the phrase in this broad, generic sense. But as the readings in this volume make clear, the term *international trade* is far too narrow a one to use in describing all international economic activity. International *business* is a better over-all term, and once we are clear on this important point of terminology we can fit international *trade*, international *investment*, and many other subjects into place as relatively specialized aspects of the general study of international business. In an organization chart, the various branches of international business might relate to one another in the diagram on p. 350.

Terminological problems are important in considering international investment because its rapid growth over the past 20-odd years is making it in some respects a more important aspect of international business and economic life than international trade, particularly for the U.S. For example, Americans' net earnings of investment income from abroad have long since out-distanced our merchandise trade balance as a source of net receipts in the U.S. balance of international payments. By 1969 U.S. net earnings of private investment income from abroad had risen to the impressive sum of $6.3 billion compared to a U.S. merchandise trade surplus of only $0.6 billion.

International investment is customarily divided into two main types, portfolio and direct, as shown in the chart. Portfolio investments are held by their owners for the purpose of collecting the income on them, as the term itself indicates, while direct investments are held for the purpose of exercising managerial control. American foreign investments of both types have risen sharply in recent years but in this section we are concerned only with direct investments—the foreign operations of companies such as IBM, General Motors, and the large international oil companies rather than with, for example, the bonds of Canadian provincial governments held in the portfolios of U.S. banks and insurance companies.

American private direct investment has been one of the fastest growing sectors of the U.S. economy over the past 20 years, growing more than twice as fast as total U.S. output and almost twice as fast as U.S. merchandise exports. The growth

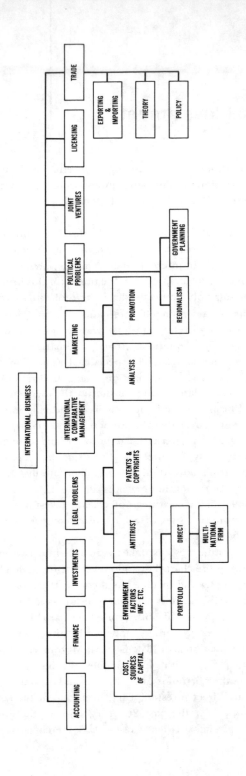

has been so great on a cumulative basis that the value of sales abroad by American-owned firms is now about *five* times as large as the value of U.S. merchandise exports. This means, of course, that for many individual American companies, their foreign *investments* are much more important to them than their foreign *trade*.

Accompanying the rapid growth of private direct investment, we have witnessed the rise of a new form of business organization, the multinational company. This new term is being applied to private business enterprises that have come to regard the world as their appropriate area of operation. They are companies, in short, who are carrying on business right across national boundaries as if the latter did not exist. A multinational company may be incorporated in one country, have production facilities in one or more other countries, raise most of its capital in yet another one, and market its products in still others. American-based oil companies that market in Western Europe and Japan refined products derived from crude oil produced in the Middle East or Venezuela illustrate such multinational companies. Similar examples can be found in other industries—automobiles, computers, farm machinery, and electrical generating equipment, to mention only a few.

Many people whose thought patterns about international business were established through their study of international trade theory find it difficult to reconcile these new multinational companies with the more traditional orientation of international trade theory. David Ricardo stamped economic theory with his own penchant for rigorous, abstract logic in the early nineteenth century, and ever since then international trade theory has sought to explain "why nations trade with one another." However, "nations" do not "trade"—businessmen do—and in recent years businessmen have been increasing their international *investment* and *production* more than their international *trade*. Therefore the old image of countries viewed as colored-in areas on maps, exchanging barter-like a few surplus commodities with other countries is no longer the most realistic model. It relied upon the formal assumption that the factors of production—land, labor and capital—were free to move easily from industry to industry within individual countries, but that *between* countries, they were absolutely immobile. This rigorous, formal model of international trade was never a very accurate reflection of what it was supposed to describe in the nineteenth century, and it has far less correspondence to the world of today.

International investment involves us in the study of the international *mobility* of capital, in defiance of the traditional theoretical postulates. And when we go on to an examination of multinational firms, we find their managements actively deploying not only goods and services and capital funds but also patents, copyrights, technical skills, and—most important—managerial talent itself, virtually anywhere in the world. The traditional formal analyses of international trade have no categories for such activities as these, of course, because they were *excluded by assumption*. The new multinational companies have grown up mainly in the U.S., or perhaps we should say they have grown *out of* the U.S. In part this is because Americans seem to have a comparative advantage in the art of business management, a factor of production, incidentally, that was almost wholly ignored by the classical economists.

Among the readings in this section we have included a few which make their points so clearly and cogently that they have met the test of time. Our first selection, by Professor Behrman, is one of these. He considers the macro-aspect of private foreign direct investment, providing a lucid account of the mainly beneficial effects it is presumed to have on the economies of the home country and the host country, respectively. Experience shows, however, that despite its many supposed advantages, foreign private direct investment has aroused opposition in many host countries because it involves "control by foreigners" who also take funds out of the country in the form of profit remittances. In our second selection, Professor Ray Vernon contests the widely held opinion that foreign private investment still consists of enclaves in the less developed countries that do not benefit the host countries' economies. His evidence indicates that, although this has been true of some private foreign investments in the past, more recently relations between investors and host governments have been changing to the benefit of the host countries.

Next, we look into the internal decision-making processes of multinational companies as Judd Polk reports on a pathbreaking survey of investment decisions that he conducted under the auspices of the National Industrial Conference Board. Polk found that competitive marketing strategies played a larger role, and marginal financial calculations a smaller role on the average, than might have been expected. W. D. Hogue throws further light on the foreign investment decision-making process by noting the different environmental factors that are bound to influence different types of industries. He reminds us that if we are to study decision making we must be clear about who the decision makers are.

The main thrust of American foreign private direct investment in the 1960s was toward the European Common Market, and it occasioned wide-spread and sometimes resentful discussion among Europeans who felt that they were being invaded by American business. In our next selection, Christopher Layton concludes that American investment has had a net favorable impact on the Common Market. In a 1968 best-selling book, the French journalist and political figure Jean Jacques Servan-Schreiber urged Western Europeans to meet *The American Challenge* on its own ground by updating their business and governmental institutions.

The country in which American companies have had by far the largest proportional impact is Canada. American investors have been dominant in a number of Canadian industries for many years but the American presence did not become politically controversial in Canada until about 15 years ago. In 1968 an academic task force headed by Professor Melville H. Watkins issued an analysis of some of the harmonies and tensions that exist between Canadians and the American multi-national firms. As he reports in his selection, Professor Watkins was surprised by the political ripples that his report caused both in Canada and the U.S.

Most observers agree that the less-developed countries could benefit greatly from more foreign private direct investment if terms satisfactory to both the investors and the host governments can be worked out. Now and then, however, misunderstandings and conflicts of interest between the two lead to seemingly intractable impasses. In such extremities, a proposition that might point the way toward a resolution both sides could accept is set forth by Peter P. Gabriel in his article entitled "The Investment in the LDC: Asset with a Fixed Maturity." In a final selection, Professor Emile Benoit reminds us that we all live under conditions of "Interdependence on a Small Plant," and, as Professor Benoit reports, international investment of a modified sort is even beginning to take place between Western capitalist countries and Eastern Communist countries.

Economic Effects of Private Direct Investment

J. N. Behrman

This chapter will analyze the effects of U.S. direct foreign investment on the economies of the host countries and upon the U.S. economy. We are concerned in particular with the effect of these economic impacts upon policy issues relating to the promotion of U.S. direct investment as a means of accelerating economic growth abroad. . . . Although we have drawn many of our examples from the experience of U.S. investment in the industrialized countries of the world, the discussion in this chapter is oriented mainly to determining the potential effects of external direct investment in less-developed countries.

Effects on the Host Country

The discussion of the effects of direct investment on the host country is organized according to the following topics: (1) additions to the real resources of the economy; (2) the impact on output, market structures, and prices; (3) the shifts in resource use and factor rewards; (4) the potential rise in GNP and real income; and (5) changes in international trade and payments.

Additions to Real Resources

The additions to real resources are three: personnel, techniques, and capital.

Personnel. The underprivileged nations are characterized by a lack of adequately trained managerial and technical personnel.[1] Although many are trying to remedy this through educational efforts, there is an immediate need for such individuals. Direct private foreign investment helps to meet this need through either the actual transfer of officials or the training of local personnel by visits of U.S. officials and technicians abroad or by trips of foreign personnel to the parent company.

The value of personnel transfers is not only in the addition to the existing stock of managers and technicians, but in reorienting domestic personnel toward their

---

Reprinted from Mikesell, R. F. (ed.), *U.S. Private and Government Investment Abroad;* Oregon: University of Oregon.

[1] Evidence of the nature and extent of this lack is provided in Harbison and Myers, *Management in the Industrial World* (New York, 1959), chapters on India, Egypt, and Chile. See also John Fayerweather, *The Executive Overseas* (Syracuse, N.Y.: Syracuse University Press, 1959).

roles in enterprise and production. In many countries, individual initiative in striving for increased efficiency or better products is not so widespread and deeply inculcated as in the United States. An important contribution of foreign personnel is to improve the efficiency of local operators as well as to expand the technical or managerial forces.

The manner in which the personnel are transferred has an important effect on the results of the transfer. Thus, if the personnel sent maintain a continuous and direct tie to the parent corporation, they keep up with both the management and production techniques employed by the home plant. Moreover, the parent company should have an interest in seeing that the most effective personnel are sent abroad to train their own successors. At the other extreme, if the personnel are merely hired by the foreign company to help in an individual capacity, the technicians or managers take only existing knowledge with them; and there is no carry-over of continuing technology nor a fund of company experience from which to draw. Between these extremes, the "managing agency" arrangement provides a close identity of the managing firm with the interests of the (independent) recipient company; at the same time it supplies a fund of knowledge and personnel from which the local unit of the agency may draw.[2] Closer to the parent-subsidiary relation is that of minority participation, with the U.S. partner providing temporary management. The long-run benefit of this relationship to the host country consists of training local nationals to take over entrepreneurial and technical functions, thus diversifying employment oppotunities and upgrading the jobs available for local citizens.

Techniques and Research Developments. When a firm transfers personnel or capital abroad, techniques of various sorts are made available for increasing productivity in the foreign country. Foreign firms not only benefit from the knowledge of well established processes and techniques but also from the research continuously carried on by U.S. enterprises. Research is the keystone for growth, providing both the new products and the new techniques which raise industrial productivity. The advantage of a tie with an American company (or any technically advanced company) is that the results of research are obtained without large financial outlays.[3]

---

[2] The relative advantages and disadvantages of these forms are discussed by J. S. Fforde, *An International Trade in Managerial Skills* (Oxford, 1957), *passim.*

[3] See J.H. Dunning, *American Investment in British Manufacturing Industry* (London, 1958), p. 167. Dunning estimates, for example, that of the $1,600 million which American industry spent on private (i.e., nongovernmental) research in 1955, 25 to 30 percent was made directly available to British companies; this $400 to $500 million was more than twice the estimated sum spent by the whole of British industry on private research. As a result of these contributions from parent companies, 25 percent of the 205 associated companies studied by Dunning maintained no separate research and development departments; 56 percent did some applied and development research; and 19 percent did some basic research on their own.

It may be considered a disadvantage not to have research facilities developed in the host country so that it may benefit from the training of research personnel and added employment for technicians. Such an objection is less relevant for the underdeveloped countries. Moreover, in recent years U.S. firms have been establishing research facilities in Britain, Continental Europe, and Japan, where personnel are readily available and ideas are as readily generated as in the United States.[4] Thus, in the longer run, the host country stands to gain from the creation of research units either within existing American subsidiaries or separately for the benefit of the parent corporation and all its subsidiaries.

It is from the *idea* of progress and the techniques of how to obtain it that we obtain the stimulus to economic growth. In some backward areas, the idea of progress is itself unknown; some languages in Africa simply do not have a word for "progress," and some have no word for "work." But once the desire for progress arises, it is readily associated with the demand for new techniques. Where techniques have been stagnant for centuries, the slightest change may make radical improvements in production—such as from the sickle to the scythe. However, for the newly industrializing countries, there is need for techniques somewhat simpler than those used in many areas of the more industrialized countries, e.g., simple water pumps, housing construction methods, simple pictorial teaching devices. Nevertheless, the introduction of these techniques requires men with ideas and the ability to apply their knowledge to specialized problems. Additions to the stock of technical knowledge, therefore, are substantial supports to the economic growth sought in the less-developed countries.[5]

Capital. The addition to the productive capital resources of the recipient country is not measured simply by the outflow of capital from the investing country. Not only are profits reinvested, but there is a substantial mobilization of domestic capital as well. The transfer of personnel and new techniques from the parent firm also enhance the productivity of local capital.

The basic inpact of direct investment is to raise the potential for economic growth through the placing of additional real resources in the command of the host country. The remainder of this section analyzes the results, internally and externally, of the transfer of these resources.

Production, Market Structures, and Prices

One effect of the addition of real resources is to alter types of products made and their costs in various industries. The market structure in the industry affected may also change; and, as a consequence of these changes, prices are likely to alter.

---

[4] *Business Week* (Jan. 3, 1959), reported that European research laboratories were being established because of lower costs and different ideas of technicians there.

[5] Examples of the techniques transferred to Latin America by U.S. companies may be found in Simon Rottenberg's study of "How United States Business Firms Promote Technological Progress" in the National Planning Association's series on *Technical Cooperation in Latin America* (Aug. 1957).

Production. Production will undoubtedly increase with the addition of a new plant or company in an industry of the host country, with the expansion of a line of products in an established company, the addition of totally new products, or through a reduction of costs and a consequent increase in sales of existing items. Different production results occur, however, according to which of these is the stimulus to greater production.

Supposing the transfer of personnel and techniques to be directly cost-reducing, the effect on production depends on the net movement of the cost schedule (i.e., the gross reduction as offset by the cost of acquiring the transferred resources) and the schedule of demand for the product. Given a net reduction in cost, the increased output, however large or small, will raise the satisfaction of consumers by providing additional quantities at lower prices.

The introduction of a new product involves an entirely new set of cost factors and an entirely new demand pattern. Existing demand may be shifted to the new item from substitutes or from other expenditures. Given this shift, it is presumed that welfare is raised over the previous situation, but by how much cannot be determined. If the new production raises real output and disposable income commensurately, a substitution of demand need not take place; the consumer merely has more income and more products to spend it on. However, the introduction of new products provides a "better" product-mix from which the consumer may choose, thus increasing his satisfaction.

Market Structure. The structure of the market in which the products are sold may be altered in the direction of either greater competition or greater concentration. Sellers of close substitutes would, in either event, suffer greater competition.

A move to competition would arise if the resources transferred were placed in an already established industry and were of the cost-reducing type. Such an inflow would "upset the balance" in the industry by providing some plants (new or old) with techniques or assets which the others did not have.[6] The recipient company would obtain more of the business. Notwithstanding the possibility of an expansion of total sales, other firms would suffer a reduction in profit or of relative market share. They may seek ways of meeting the competition, complain about "foreignization," or seek similar resources from abroad themselves.

In his study of U.S.-affiliates in Britain, Dunning measured the competitive impact of the entrance of new companies, or new techniques and assets made available to the Anglo-American firms, on market share, profits, and comparative productivity. He concluded that "the evidence, such as it is, would strongly suggest that the U.S. firms are more efficient than their competitors—and particularly so in the foodstuffs, tools and cutlery, and pharmaceutical industries. In only six cases

---

[6] For example, Dunning reports that, as a result of access by U.S.-affiliated companies to greater research and development expertise, "a British competitor is clearly shown to be at a potential handicap." *Op. cit.,* p. 173.

out of fifty-five were there indications directly contrary to this hypothesis."[7] Dunning also concludes that on the basis of the enhanced competition and the innovating responses of the British companies "the trans-Atlantic associations enjoyed by such firms have brought very considerable advantages in the form of technical and managerial knowledge. As far as can be judged, these benefits show themselves in terms of rising shares of the total market, favorable comparative productivity figures and higher income-asset ratios. We know, too, that such industries are amongst the most dynamic and productive of all within the U.K. economy; that their rate of productivity and capital growth is well above average; that they are amongst the most successful export industries; and that their attention is particularly directed to those variables making for rapid technological progress."[8]

It is because of the greater competitiveness of the U.S.-affiliates that some industrial groups in Japan and Brazil have opposed both the entrance of U.S. companies and affiliation with them; they do not want the competitive situation upset.

The impact on market structure does not stop with the industry primarily concerned. Both suppliers and customers find that their methods of doing business and their competitive performances are altered by the demands and techniques of the American companies. These demands have accelerated the adoption of more modern techniques in materials handling, in processing of supplies and in packaging and shipping goods.[9] An added benefit may be an elimination of high-cost "marginal" producers with consequent benefits to the consumer—so long as a monopoly is not created. However, in many of the less-developed countries, the government is not willing to see these companies fail and efforts are made either to maintain prices (thus increasing the profits of the company assisted from abroad) or to prevent an influx of foreign firms which will upset the market.

---

[7] Dunning found that trends in market share seemed to favor American companies in the chemical and pharmaceutical fields; the British had the advantage in the tools and cutlery, mechanical engineering, and abrasive trades. Of 115 American firms reporting on sales, over half claimed that their share of the market had risen since the war; 25 percent reported a constant share, and 13 percent reported a falling share. This trend was confirmed by a calculation that "the post-war growth of employment in U.S.-financed firms has been four times that of manufacturing in general." Calculations on profits were less conclusive. Comparative income trends showed the rate of profit growth of U.S.-affiliates to be substantially higher than that of U.K. competitors in the fields of beverages and food, scientific instruments, and miscellaneous industrial groups; U.S.-affiliates lost ground relatively in other fields, such as rubber products, chemicals, pharmaceuticals, mechanical engineering, and motor vehicles. Dunning, *op. cit.*, pp. 179–187.

[8] *Ibid.*, p. 194.
[9] *Ibid.*, p. 224.

If the resources transferred were for the introduction of a new product in an established industry, the results might well be a reduction in the sales of close substitutes made by others, leading to a concentration of production in the hands of the recipient company. If the resources are used to introduce an entirely new industrial activity, there is no competition save for the income of the ultimate consumer. The impact on others is not felt directly, and there is less of the "disturbed" response indicated above, despite the fact that some producers will find their costs rising.

Tendencies to monopoly in the market may sometimes be strengthened by the procedure of licensing under patents and trademarks. The recipient company is frequently given an exclusive right to manufacture the new product or employ the new process provided by the U.S. licensor. The monopoly provided is a legal one and is extended for the purpose of encouraging invention and innovation as well as maintaining product quality. Monopolistic tendencies also arise from governmental inducements to the foreign investor which provide either exclusive tax benefits or protection from import competition.

Prices. The effect on prices of a cost-reducing or a product-introducing foreign investment or licensing operation cannot be determined in advance unless something is known of the market structure into which the product enters. The monopoly privilege extended by patent or trademark coverage may permit maintenance or increase of the price as a result of improved quality (or market differentiation). Output may still be expanded with a shift in the demand resulting from changed preferences, induced by advertising and better sales techniques.

There may also be a direct effect on price arising from the type of remittance made for the transferred resources. Different forms of payment for a license, technical aid, or capital may have different effects on pricing. For example, a royalty based on output would tend to be included as a given percentage of costs for all levels of output, and one based on net sales would be deducted from price at various levels (thus affecting marginal revenue). Both of these methods alter the optimum point of production and change the price of the product as compared to a method of payment which did not alter the optimum level. At the other extreme, a return in the form of a share of net profits, as under an equity interest, may not have any effect on optimum output or price.

Though there is little information on the pricing techniques employed by American-affiliated firms, Dunning was able to obtain some information on price reductions resulting from American investments in Britain. One executive of a British firm bought by an American company after World War II reported that "but for the association of an American parent concern and the exchange of technical and marketing expertise, the firm's chief product would, without a doubt, be retailing at a price somewhat around 60 percent higher than the current selling price." However, after a study of prices in Britain over five years in the mid-1950s, Dunning concluded that there was insufficient evidence to show that U.S.-financed companies were either "more price-conscious or more scientific in their price-fixing methods than U.K. competitors."[10]

In sum, it may be stated that the transfer of real resources is likely to cause an increase in production and employment; it tends to cause an improvement in the quality of the commodities produced in the industry and by its suppliers;[11] it is likely to disrupt existing market conditions, but in different ways, depending on the extension of exclusive rights and on the previous market conditions; and it will probably reduce market prices. The distinct benefits to the consumer include the following:

(1) He obtains a better adapted product, and market demands are given closer attention by the U.S. firm.

(2) He obtains better servicing of the product.

(3) He obtains new and different products, which although available as imports, might not be known to him for lack of informative advertising.

(4) He obtains the products at a lower price—as a result of a removal of transport costs which would otherwise raise the price from between 10 to 30 percent, a removal of a tariff duties averaging between 10 and 20 percent, and in some cases a reduction of production costs under those in the United States.[12]

Resource Shifts and Factor Payments

In the less-developed countries, a substantial proportion of the labor supply as well as other productive factors are either unemployed or underemployed. On the other hand, in Western Europe the U.S. investor finds labor and other productive factors more or less fully employed. Resource shifts resulting from foreign investment have different impacts on factor prices and upon domestic industry depending upon these and other structural conditions.

Resource Shifts. As capital and technology move into a given industry in the host country, there is additional demand for labor, materials, and land, as well as

---

[10] Dunning's study showed that "the Ford, Bakelite, Hoover, Hedley, Heinz, Bird's, Blaw-Knox and Evans Chemical companies have been amongst the leaders in their respective industries in the drive to keep prices down and cut profit margins. The Hoover Company, for example, has helped to stabilize the prices of domestic electrical appliances by marketing its own products at a cost between 25–30 percent above the pre-1939 level, whilst in its 1955 annual report, the Heinz Company stated that its average prices between 1947 and 1954 had been raised by 47 percent compared with an average food price increase of 81 percent. Between 1953 and 1954 this same company's prices actually fell, when those of other manufactured foods rose by 2½ percent. Another subsidiary's main product is retailed at 25 percent above pre-war cost compared with an 85 percent increase of that of its main competitors, whilst until recently, the price of razor blades was actually below that charged before the war." *Op. cit.,* p. 188.

[11] See Rottenberg, *op. cit.,* pp. 45–56 and 60–75.

[12] Dunning estimated that "in probably *nine cases out of ten* the British consumer is able to buy his product at a lower price than if it were imported." *Op. cit.,* p. 233.

for domestic capital funds. There is a flow of previously unemployed resources into the enterprise; or, there is a shift from less well-paid endeavors to the new enterprise, with unemployed resources moving into positions which were vacated.

Assuming less than full employment, it is conceivable that there is merely an increased demand for a variety of domestic factors and that the shifts cause no great hardship on any industry.

On the other hand, if there is relatively full employment *or* if the new enterprise adopts cost-reducing methods of production and sells in competition with domestic producers of the same or similar commodities, it is probable that marginal producers in the industry will be forced out of business. This will release resources which can be taken up by the new firm without inflationary pressure.

If the international transfer of resources involves an introduction of a new product, the shift in domestic resources is from other industries or unemployed areas into the new undertaking. Again, it is conceivable that no producer is adversely affected. But, the consequent rise in costs of factors may force some existing enterprises out of business.

It is for these reasons that there have been complaints in some of the developing countries that domestic enterprise and initiative is being swamped by U.S. enterprises. Thus, when a domestic company enters a new field of production and opens the market, a U.S. company may enter with more efficient techniques and thereby lower costs. In bidding for domestic resources and cutting costs (and prices), foreign enterprise may edge the domestic producer out of business and stifle that very (domestic) initiative which foreign private enterprise is supposed to foster.

There is little empirical evidence of the distinct impacts on resources used by U.S.-affiliated companies. Some aggregate information is available for a few areas, however. The expanded demand for raw materials and domestically produced equipment is shown by Philipps' study of U.S.-affiliates in West Germany: the 51 companies responding indicated that they purchased nearly 80 percent (average) of their raw materials and 90 percent of their equipment in Germany. Total purchases of materials and equipment were estimated at $1 billion in 1958—nearly half of the total outlays by U.S.-affiliates in Germany.[13]

The less-developed countries sometimes encourage domestic purchasing by foreign firms through prohibitions on imports, or by requiring that within a given period following the beginning of operations a certain percentage of the value of the output must constitute domestically produced components.[14] Purchases of domestic materials in Latin America by U.S.-affiliated firms during 1955 totalled

---

[13] E.A. Philipps, "American Direct Investments in West Germany Manufacturing Industries, 1945–1959," University of Illinois M.A. Thesis (Jan. 1960), p. 39.

[14] Brazil permitted a number of automobile firms to be established under an agreement that they would produce (or purchase from other domestic suppliers) components equal to a minimum percentage of the total value of the product within a given number of years.

about $1.8 billion. Of this amount, manufacturing enterprises spent nearly $700 million, or 40 percent of the value of their sales; petroleum companies spent over $400 million; and agriculture, mining and smelting, and public utilities another $400 million. These sums constituted sizable additions to demand for domestic resources. However, they were concentrated mostly in Argentina, Brazil, Colombia, Cuba, Mexico, and Venezuela.[15] The 1957 Census of U.S. investments overseas (including Canada) showed purchases of domestic materials and services in the foreign countries of $17 billion, of which $11 billion was by manufacturing companies.

Further evidence is seen in the impact on employment. The 1957 Census showed over three million persons employed abroad (including Canada) by U.S.-affiliates. About one million were employed in Latin America and about 1.1 million in Europe, with an estimated 670,000 employed in Canada. Excluding U.S. personnel, of the total employed by U.S. firms in Latin America, 37,000 were supervisory, professional, or technical personnel in all industrial groups; of this total in Europe, 61,000 were supervisory, professional, or technical personnel; and of the total in Canada, 35,000 were in these categories.[16]

The added demand for resources, resulting in higher factor payments, has not always been welcomed—as in periods of overfull employment in Europe, but it has been eagerly received in most of the less-developed countries.

Factor Payments. The effect of resource shifts is to increase the factor payments when resource supplies in one geographic area or specific category becomes tight. There is likely to be a gradual increase in payments to *all* domestic factors, including capital! Though it is usually argued that the inflow of capital will reduce the return to capital in the recipient country,[17] the fact that foreign investors increase the demand for domestic capital casts doubt on this conclusion. This is more readily seen when a joint venture is involved, but it is also true for those wholly-owned subsidiaries which borrow on the domestic market for short-term and other capital needs. Thus, there is no immediate reduction of returns to capital; rather, there may be an increase. A partial offset to the increased demand for capital arises from the higher volume of savings generated by the new enterprises, and by the higher level of national income.

Wages are also likely to rise in the long run; short-run increases will occur mainly in the industry which is receiving the inflow of foreign resources, as a consequence of bidding away existing labor and skilled foremen. The availability of unemployed labor will tend to keep general wage rates down, however. Also, the

---

[15] Samuel Pizer and Frederick Cutler, *U.S. Investments in the Latin American Economy,* (Washington, D. C.: Dept. of Commerce, 1957), p. 16.

[16] *U.S. Business Investments in Foreign Countries* (Washington, D. C.: U.S. Dept. of Commerce, 1960), p. 122. (Hereafter cited as *Census, 1957.*)

[17] The analysis that leads to the conclusion of diminishing marginal returns to capital in the host country is usually based on static assumptions and does not take into account complementary demands for capital and other factors.

increase in the supply of capital with rising returns will tend to cause a substitution of capital for labor, thus limiting the tendency for wages to rise in the short run. However, in the longer run, as productivity of labor increases in the newly formed industries or in those receiving new technology, wages should rise, supplemented by the general pressure of rising employment. If, in the short run, wages do not rise with productivity, capital formation is faster; the greater use of machinery will raise productivity and wages in the long run. Finally, in many of the less-developed countries, union activities, often with the support of government, assure that wages and fringe benefits are pushed up rapidly even though unemployment remains high.

Empirical evidence indicates that American-affiliated companies (especially new companies that are wholly-owned) tend to pay higher than average wages in foreign countries. The average compensation per employee in Latin America for all American-owned enterprises was about $1,600 in 1955. There were wide variations between industries and countries, however. For example, petroleum companies paid about $4,200 per employee; public utilities about $1,750; mining about $1,500; and manufacturing about $1,350; agriculture was about $900, reflecting part-time employment. Venezuela topped the list with an average of $6,000 per employee, with Chile, Colombia, and Cuba also above the average.[18]

U.S. investment has exerted pressure to raise wages in time of labor shortage, such as existed in Britain after World War II. Dunning's observations of this phenomenon are worth recording:

> Skilled labour of the kind required has been a very scarce commodity since the war, and the tendency for many American subsidiaries to pay well above the current wage rates to attract the necessary numbers has caused certain older-established firms in the surrounding areas to have some misgivings about the desirability of such investment, particularly when comparative wage spirals develop to the detriment of the firms who can least afford to pay. However, this problem is—or should be—essentially short-term in character and can only be attributed in part to the presence of U.S.-financed companies, as the influx of new firms demanding unfamiliar production techniques and types of labour has been a general feature of the post-war development of such areas.[19]

Although some local enterprises may complain of the competition for the limited labor supply, the required adjustments may benefit both workers and consumers. Thus Dunning reports the jute industry which lost labor to new U.S. firms in one area was required to raise its wages and improve working conditions in order to stay in business. This was accomplished through the introduction of new

---

[18] Pizer and Cutler, *op. cit.*, p. 20.

[19] Dunning, *op. cit.*, p. 300. Although wage rates of many U.S.-affiliates are deliberately set higher than competitive rates of U.K. companies, they are still frequently one-third to one-half lower than those paid by the U.S. parents *(ibid.*, pp. 254–255).

machinery and modern managerial methods—to the benefit not only of the workers but also of the consumer.[20]

GNP and Real Income

The increased production arising from the introduction of a new product or the expansion of sales of existing products, and the increase in factor payments, are all reflected in a larger gross national product in the host country. Thus, production outlays and foreign taxes paid by U.S. direct investment enterprises abroad equalled $31 billion in 1957 (excluding imports from the U.S. and depreciation, goods purchased by trading companies and intercorporate sales of petroleum). Of this total, only $1.5 billion was for interest and foreign payments; $4.5 billion was for direct and indirect taxes (60 percent in petroleum), $18 billion for materials and services, and $7 billion for wages (50 percent manufacturing). The increase in wages raises consumer demand, widening the market and providing support for further expansion. The expansion is spread to secondary industries serving the U.S.-affiliates; this expansion brings internal economies. External economies are gained through rising demand for materials and widening of the market.

Internal Economies. The primary internal economy which results from an import of foreign capital and skills by an affiliate is that of a cost reduction, which in turn tends to reduce prices and increase sales. This result, however, requires that a portion of the reduction in costs is passed on to the consumer. A second internal economy arises from the gradual spread of the imported technology throughout the industry affected. Not only are the products examined by competitors, but it is impossible to keep all the new processes secret, though key ones may be kept from competitors for some time. Part of the spread of technology comes through a transfer of personnel within the industry affected. These transfers increase with time; shifts of key personnel transfer managerial and production skills regardless of attempts to withhold them. Part of the spread also comes from transfer of production techniques and management methods to a supplier or customer of the U.S. affiliate.[21]

Still another internal economy resulting from the inflow of new techniques or the use of newly patented inventions under a license arises from the necessity of competing firms to "build around" the patent or special knowledge. There are few patents which cannot be duplicated either through some slight change or through a

---

[20] *Ibid.*, p. 302.

[21] See Dunning, *op. cit.*, Chapter VII; see also Rottenberg, *op. cit.*, Chapter IV. For example, training supplied by *Stanvac* both in its organization and company schools in many operations becomes disseminated throughout the whole economy. See "Stanvac in Indonesia," *United States Business Performance Abroad,* National Planning Association, (June 1957), pp. 70–78; see also other National Planning Association studies in the same series, especially "Casa Grace in Peru," pp. 22–44.

different means of achieving the same end. The necessity to do so in order to stay competitive introduces other elements of cost reduction and leads to a potential expansion of the industry, with consequent additional cost reductions as the scale of operations increases. Alternatively, competitive pressure may be put on companies not affiliated with a foreign partner to acquire a foreign affiliation in order to obtain the advantages of foreign technical knowledge and skills or of additional capital to employ cost-reducing methods of production and marketing.

External Economies. The increased production in a given industry will give rise to a demand for greater supplies of raw materials, improved labor skills, power facilities, better roads and transportation for the materials and finished products. These demands, when met, will bring forth a supply of "economic overhead" facilities which will be useful to a wider range of industries than those receiving the foreign resources. The demand for trained labor by foreign enterprises will, in the long run, improve the supply of such labor for other enterprises by creating a demand for additional training and educational facilities.

In the private sector, the expansion of industry in one area tends to increase activity in others. This is particularly true of the supplying industries.[22] The multiplication of activities in different manufacturing areas is exemplified by the introduction of the automotive industry into Brazil and Argentina. Local assembly soon leads to diversification of manufacturing through production of parts, machine tools, dies, accessories, and complementary items such as industrial engines. Gradually local materials and skilled labor are more extensively employed.

In addition, new merchandising methods such as those introduced in Latin America by Sears, Roebuck and International Harvester will alter demand patterns and cause an expansion of secondary industry providing diverse consumer items.

These contributions should be emphasized in view of the increasing concern in the host countries about the large share of investment directed to extractive industries, especially when the processing of the raw materials takes place in the already industrialized countries. Although there are frequently extensive social-welfare and community-development contributions made by the extractive enterprises, they do not have the same impact on economic growth as does a more diversified industrial activity.

External economies and the advantages they give to diversified and accelerated economic growth have led some countries to stress the use of domestic laborers for more highly skilled and responsible positions. There is an upgrading of workers and managers with the increase in skills and an opportunity for many to be trained in the United States. This upgrading extends to other industries in the country as personnel move to different employments. The improvement in the quality of personnel will have salutary effects on the quality of public administration which in

---

[22] See, e.g., Rottenberg, *op. cit.,* pp. 61–65 and National Planning Association studies on *Sears, Roebuck de Mexico* (1953), pp. 39–45; and on *Creole Petroleum in Venezuela* (1955), pp. 34–36.

turn will be highly beneficial in the development programs of the less-developed countries.

International Trade and Payments

The rise in GNP, shifts in resources, and changing factor payments will affect the long-run composition and direction of international trade and the balance of payments.

Trade. The shift in resource use in the host country from relatively labor-intensive enterprises to those which are more capital-intensive brings a realignment of the comparative advantages in international trade. Resource compositions are made more nearly similar as a result of the inflow of foreign capital, personnel, and technology. The basic differences in factor endowments will stem mainly from differences in raw materials and the training of labor (or the attitude of labor and management toward their jobs). These last differences will in time be removed or modified and the differences in raw material availability will be reduced by world trade in these items. It may be expected that the less-developed economies will gradually be enabled to duplicate the pattern of production in the more industrialized countries.

This result will lead to a reduction of trade in items formerly exchanged between these two groups and an expansion in new lines. This has already been seen in the shift in composition of trade among the industrial countries. The developing economies will begin to process their own raw materials, and they will want to export the semi-finished or finished goods, rather than re-importing them from the industrialized countries. Conversely, apart from the flow of basically indigenous commodities, the trade which occurs will probably be among goods producible in many countries but made competitive because of specialization to gain economies of scale through serving a wider market. Comparative advantage will rest less on specialization by entire industrial groupings and more on specialization in production of separate items within an industrial category which permits cost reduction.[23]

This shift in the basis of trade has two effects on the potential gains from trade. First, it will increase the relative gain from trade in those items not produced in the importing country (e.g., coffee from Brazil for electronic equipment from the United States) compared to the gain from trading similar items (e.g., luxury goods which are readily substitutable at home). The larger proportion of trade in items which are producible in many countries means that the threat of a reduction of trade loses its strategic importance, but it may still involve a sizable loss of the gain from trade.

---

[23] Thus, Britain may have an advantage in new ideas and manufacturing costs while the U.S. companies show an advantage in application of ideas prior to the manufacturing stage and in commercialization and marketing. Since elements of the U.S. advantage can be transferred, manufacturing occurs in Britain. Any loss of this cost advantage will cause a relocation of industrial activity.

Secondly, with the growing similarity in factor endowments, these endowments become less important than demand patterns, techniques, and scale of output in determining comparative advantage. Differences in demand and output volume can be the basis for comparative advantage even with similar factor endowments (especially with varying cost conditions over different levels of output). Reliance on the wider world market and specialization in serving it will, therefore, maintain comparative cost differences, which will make possible a diversified trade provided restrictive commercial practices do not intervene. It cannot be concluded that the gains from trade will be reduced unless it is shown that both the comparative advantages are narrowed and the volume of trade is reduced. Both the volume of and the gains from international trade in the future hinge on whether the new investments and new structure of production lead to efforts at self-sufficiency through similarity of production among countries or to product specialization despite increasingly similar stages of industrialization.

Maximum economic specialization will not occur automatically if predominant reliance is placed on private direct investment. Investment does not necessarily move into those areas which constitute the comparative advantage of the host country. First, the comparison of returns by the investor is between returns in his own country and those in the host country *within* the industry in which he operates. It is seldom questioned whether returns would be greater in another pursuit—though they *are* frequently greater in another industry even within the United States. The entrance of foreign investors into the exploitation of local resources has not been wholly based on a calculation of comparative returns within the host country, but on the desirability of holding or gaining a world market and the "necessity" of developing alternative sources of raw material supply.

Even if the foreign investor sought the enterprise in which the return to capital is largest, it is not necessarily found in the export sector. The export sector is usually made up of commodities relying on intensive use of the more abundant factor of production. Returns to capital in export industries of underdeveloped countries (mostly labor-intensive) are not relatively high compared to returns to capital in other enterprises in the country. Thus, capital inflows could as readily be directed (if along lines of maximum return to capital) into import competing items; or, if into exports, the investor may alter the technical coefficients of production by changing factor supplies and thereby factor payments. The flow of private investment need not, therefore, follow lines of comparative advantage and increased specialization.

Governmental intervention is also likely to reduce specialization. The usual policy is to favor import-competing production and a broadening of the export list. An expansion of import-competing production means the domestic production of items now most efficiently obtained through exporting to pay for goods which are relatively cheaper abroad. The advantages of trade are sacrificed for the advantages of internal and external economies. Whether or not there will be a net gain depends on the specific items produced and the ability of countries to develop export markets for new products, some of which they were only recently importing.

The elimination of trade in certain goods and the rise of trade in new products will undoubtedly alter the direction of trade. Since the less-developed countries are each, in their own way, duplicating production in the already industrialized countries, they will find it difficult to market many of these items to the industrialized countries. They may then turn to regional trade preference associations so as to expand their export markets, at some cost to the exports of the industrialized areas. Regional preference will be added to national protection to cause a decrease in the exports of many commodities from the advanced countries. These barriers to trade will force a redirection of trade of the industrialized countries through both a change in the composition of trade and the partners in trade. However . . . , regional preference arrangements among the less-developed areas may provide the only solution to the problems of rapid industrialization for countries whose traditional primary commodity exports to the rest of the Free World are growing very slowly or stagnating.

It is for the above reasons—pointing to the need for flexibility and a widening of the world market to absorb the required changes—that efforts should be made to keep the markets of the world as open as possible and to prevent a rise in the over-all level of protection. If new items must now be traded and new channels of trade be found, the desired results can be achieved only with a fairly free movement of goods and materials over the world.

Payments. The aggregate payments position of the capital-exporting and capital-importing countries will be altered according to the net change in the exports and imports, as discussed above. Immediately the balance of payments will be affected by imports needed for production by the newly established firms. This is particularly important in the less-developed countries which must import much of their capital goods, but even countries such as Germany require imports for manufacturing production. For example, the fifty-one firms responding to Philipps' inquiry of U.S.-affiliates in Germany indicated that imports of raw materials and equipment accounted for nearly 19 percent of their total purchases in 1958. The drain on foreign exchange from these demands are, of course, offset by direct exports from the same firms and exports facilitated by others through the domestic availability of additional manufactures.[24]

---

[24] Sales of fifty-five U.S.-affiliates in West Germany in 1958 went 30 percent into exports (over half to Europe). Generalizing this percentage to all 132 U.S.-affiliates in Germany would mean some $650 million earned by them from exports each year—or 7 percent of total German exports in 1958. The net contribution to Germany's foreign exchange earnings from the operation of U.S.-affiliates was estimated at $343 million (dollar equivalent), or about 20 percent of West Germany's total balance of trade (exports less imports) in 1958. However, most of this was with Europe, since imports by U.S.-affiliates from the United States were greater than sales by them to the United States. Because of the kinds of products manufactured, Philipps considered that U.S. investment in Germany has not been directly import-substituting but has expanded the domestic sector, releasing German capital to move into the export sector to pay for rising imports. Philipps, *op. cit.*, pp. 38–40. Philipps cautions the reader on the roughness of these calculations; they represent merely general orders of magnitude.

Dunning estimated in his study that U.S.-affiliates in Britain had saved the British consumer about 100 million pounds in 1954 which would otherwise have had to be spent for dollar imports if the same goods had been consumed.[25] The imported cost of the same goods would have been 600 to 650 million pounds, or four times the 1954 imports of manufacturers from the United States, or, 15 percent of the total import bill of the United Kingdom for that year. Most of the investment in the United Kingdom since the war has been in import-substituting items; thus, the Fawley Refinery presumably cut the import bill of the United Kingdom by $300 million during the period 1952 to 1955, and local manufacture of carbon black saved more than $10 million per year.

Since not all of the imports substituted would in fact have been purchased and some of the output of U.S.-affiliates would have been met through British companies, the reduction of the drain on foreign exchange was probably less than the amounts indicated above. On the other hand, U.S.-affiliates in Britain have exported substantial amounts of goods, mainly to countries other than the United States. In 1954 exports of U.S.-affiliates equalled 275 million pounds, or 12 percent of total U.K. manufacturing exports,[26] turning most of these items from net imports (prior to World War II) into net exports in the mid-1950s. It may also be noted that U.S.-affiliates exported more than the average for their particular industry in two out of three cases. These exports arose out of a replacement by U.S.-affiliates of exports lost by the parent company as a consequence of the discrimination against dollar goods and out of the worldwide marketing connections of the parent company. In addition, exports are expanding because of the worldwide demand for the types of goods produced by U.S. firms generated by industrialization in the less-developed areas.

The growth of the international corporation is also a factor in expanding exports; through it, there is a sort of product specialization, with one plant or branch producing all of the company output of a given type and exporting throughout the world, even into the United States. This specialization is buttressed by the existence of lower production costs in many subsidiaries, which leads to turning over world export markets by the U.S. parent company to the foreign subsidiary. Thus, there is market-sharing in operations which does not require, and is not controlled through, agreements but which follows lines of the most efficient production and marketing. U.K.-subsidiaries of U.S. companies generally export to the Commonwealth with the U.S. parent company supplying the Western Hemisphere market; however, the majority of the U.S.-affiliates abroad also sell some items to dollar markets. During 1950–56, when total British dollar sales rose by 65 percent, dollar sales of U.S.-affiliates doubled.

---

[25] Dunning estimated that the £500 million of goods and services sold by U.S.-affiliates required £25 to £30 million of dollar imports; whereas if the same goods had been produced in the United States and transport and duties paid, they would have cost the British consumer £600 to £650 million—a net sterling saving of £100 to £150 million and a dollar saving of around 600 million. (*Op cit.*, p. 291.)

[26] *Op. cit.*, p. 293.

The exports of the United Kingdom have expanded through sales not only by the U.S.-affiliates but also by suppliers of these subsidiaries. Some of these British companies have been asked to supply the U.S. parent with similar products or to supply other foreign affiliates of the U.S. parent. In addition, the attention which British firms paid to the export market has been sharpened by the existence of U.S. subsidiaries driving for export sales.

In sum, exports by U.S. affiliates have made a significant contribution to the British balance of payments and have been the channel for the import of financial capital as well. A similar development has occurred in Germany and other Continental countries.

It may be expected, as is occurring in Mexico for some items, that U.S. manufacturing affiliates will add to the exports of less-developed countries, but such an expansion may be long coming in countries such as Brazil, where production for the local market is the main incentive. Of course, the difference in incentives (between domestic and export markets) would be reduced by easier access to world markets and by the creation of common markets or free trade areas among the less-developed countries.

There is an offsetting outward flow of funds as a result of the capital inflow. A direct charge on foreign exchange earnings arises through the payments for personnel, licenses, and earnings on invested capital. In most countries, there is a fairly close scrutiny of the "burden" of such payments, and contracts for import of U.S. capital and technology will not be approved for dollar payment if the government considers the burden too great. . . . In some instances, however, the gain from exports of the newly introduced product more than offsets the drain from payments to the U.S. investor; for example, earnings from exports of transistors and transistor radios by Japan equalled payments to the United States for *all* technical assistance (licenses) during 1958.[27]

---

[27] The relevant data for Latin America are as follows: U.S. companies exported some $2.1 billion worth during 1955, of which over half was to the United States; these exports were 30 percent of total Latin American exports and more than one-third of all exports to the United States. Over half of the dollar exports generated by U.S.-affiliates (either in sales to the United States or to other countries for dollars), which amounted to nearly $2 billion, came from petroleum. To this addition to exchange earnings of Latin America must be added some $150 million of net capital inflows by the U.S. companies, for a total of nearly $2.3 billion. Offsetting this inflow are imports of about $700 million for materials, components and equipment, some $560 million of which was from the United States. Imports of capital equipment by U.S.-affiliates amounted to $141 million (half for petroleum development), an amount equal to 17 percent of all capital goods imports by Latin American in 1955. Another outflow of exchange was through remittances of income and fees, amounting to $680 million, two-thirds of which was in branch profits of petroleum companies. In sum, earnings of $2.3 billion were offset by expenditures and remittances of $1.4 billion, leaving a net addition to Latin America's exchange earnings of $900 million in 1955. To this must be added an undetermined portion of the $2.8 billion of local sales which substituted for imports. (See Pizer and Cutler, *op. cit.*)

In addition to these direct payments, pressure on the exchanges may arise from a high or rising propensity to import as real and money incomes increase. In many of the less-developed countries there is a fairly high marginal propensity to import (a relatively elastic income demand for imports) so that rising incomes increase imports considerably. The same increase in incomes also tends to withdraw potential exports from the world market.

These trends may be contained by direct and indirect controls, and they may be fully offset through the growth of export capacity and by import substitution. One cannot say what the net effect of foreign investments in manufacturing on external payments will be either for the capital exporting or for the capital importing countries.[28] Nor is it possible to predict the over-all effects on world trade and the gains from trade. The effects on trade and payments will depend upon the pattern of investment and upon national and regional commercial policies. We may emphasize again that liberal commercial policies of the nations concerned are essential to the realization of the benefits from the flow of direct private investment.

Impacts on the U.S. Economy

An analysis of the effects of direct investment outflow on the U.S. economy is perhaps more complex and less amenable to empirical investigation than a consideration of the effects of foreign investment on a capital importing country. The discussion in this section is limited to: (1) the direct costs of and returns from sending personnel, capital, and technology abroad; (2) the effects on factor payments in the United States; (3) changes in the pattern and volume of international trade; (4) effects on the balance of payments; and (5) the broader policy implications of these impacts. The approach in this section is largely empirical and deals mainly with the impacts on specific sectors of the economy. . . .

Direct Costs and Returns

The direct costs of foreign private investment in subsidiaries or in licenses can be measured according to the value of the real resources transferred. They include personnel, home office time, research and development, and capital; these should be more than matched by the discounted value of the direct returns for the endeavor, to be profitable to the U.S. investor.

---

[28] Transactions of U.S. direct investment enterprises abroad with the United States in 1957 added about $1 billion in foreign exchange to host countries' resources. Of this, a net of nearly $800 million accrued to Canada, and nearly $1 billion to Latin America, while Europe and other areas paid a net of nearly $800 million to the United States. (See *Census, 1957,* Table 57). However, it must not be assumed that the net funds accruing to foreign countries are without further effects on their balance of payments. Latin America, especially, does not add the dollars to exchange reserves but employs them for imports of capital goods for economic growth.

The costs of personnel sent overseas are frequently borne by the recipient in that both transportation and salary are paid by the receiving company. But there are also some direct costs in the loss of experienced personnel, both managerial and technical, by the parent company. A cost may also be incurred by reason of the necessity of "keeping open" at home a position of equal rank and responsibility for the official who has gone abroad. Given these unmeasurable costs of sending personnel, it is difficult to determine the benefits over the burdens for transfer of managers, and also, to a lesser extent, of technicians. The shorter the stay abroad, the more readily calculable the costs but the less readily calculable the returns.

Many parent companies allocate a portion of head office time and expenses to the subsidiaries abroad. This is done because of the amount of executive time required to handle relationships with the subsidiary. But the allocation is somewhat arbitrary unless detailed time checks are kept. In view of the opportunity for certain officials to take "all-expense" trips abroad each year, however, it is unlikely that there will be a demand for a close accounting of returns and costs in this area!

The allocation of research and development expenses to foreign operations is equally difficult—in concept and in practice. The familiar problem of joint-costs arises vis-à-vis each development forthcoming as well as the division between foreign and domestic uses of research costs "fixed" in accord with the domestic operations of the company. Any allocation of such costs would appear highly arbitrary.

The cost of capital transferred can be more closely determined through comparison with *expected* returns from use of a similar amount in other pursuits. Again, precise calculations are impossible and expectations may be greatly disappointed or fulfilled many times over. . . . However, it is difficult to generalize regarding over-all profitability of foreign investment because of wide differences between industries and from country to country. If we exclude petroleum, differences in earnings at home and abroad do not appear to be substantial. Over the period 1950–1958, it appears that average earnings were slightly higher for U.S.-affiliates in Europe than average earnings in the United States; thus, average earnings ratios over the period show the United Kingdom at 17.2 percent, Belgium at 13.5 percent, Germany 11.9 percent, Italy 10.7 percent, Netherlands 10.3 percent, and France 10.1 percent.[29] Higher profit margins abroad mean that a smaller volume of business will often add more to total profits than the larger domestic sales.[30]

---

[29] Various articles by Samuel Pizer and Frederick Cutler in the *Survey of Current Business* (Jan. 1954, Aug. 1956, Aug. 1957, Sept. 1958, Aug. 1959). See also Chapter III of this volume. Of 56 U.S. companies in Germany responding to the survey by Philipps, 16 reported earnings less than those of the parent company in the United States (mostly in machinery and automobiles and petroleum) and 25 reported earnings either slightly higher (14) or much higher (11) than in the United States, 12 reported them about the same, and 3 had operations too new to permit an evaluation.

[30] Companies with both large and small operations abroad have reported them as contributing a share to profits greater than their proportionate sales volume. One company official was reported as stating that his West European subsidiary was "as least twice as profitable as our domestic business." (*Business Week,* Jan. 3, 1959).

Earnings ratios in Canada and Latin America have been consistently lower than average U.S. ratios, since 1955. The Department of Commerce asserts that: "In general, there is much less difference between domestic manufacturing returns, as a whole, and returns on direct foreign investments in manufacturing, than there is between the various categories of manufacturing (chemicals, machinery, etc.) within the United States."[31] This attests to the view that investment abroad is as much induced by an expanding market for a given product line (industry output) as by *differentially* high earnings.

If there is in fact a differentially high rate of return on foreign investments by U.S. companies in Europe, it is probably attributable to two elements of the postwar picture. First, U.S. operations have had to give up some of their export markets and the subsidiaries abroad have been able to take over established nondollar markets without the heavy initial expenditures for developing the market. This is evidenced by the export activity of some British affiliates of U.S. companies.[32] Second, manufacturing costs are lower in many foreign countries, while the commodities sold in third markets are frequently sold at U.S. prices.[33]

Calculation of returns is made difficult by the fact that not all returns are monetary. . . . Many U.S. investors expect some return in the form of reverse flow of technical knowledge and patent rights. More significantly, however, for some companies the returns take the form of lower prices for imports or of favorable prices for exports in transactions with overseas affiliates. In sum, a determination of direct costs is, as yet, not possible with the accounting techniques employed, and some returns are not calculable. Therefore, precise comparisons of costs with returns to determine profitability is literally impossible. Though we may leave the decisions as to whether to take the risks attendant upon a miscalculation of costs and returns to the individual corporations, it does not necessarily follow that their determinations will redound to the benefit and advantage of the U.S. economy— even if they make correct decisions from the viewpoint of maximizing private profits. Under some circumstances, foreign investments may reduce the national gains from trade, or the social gains from investment at home may be larger than those from investing abroad.[34]

Factor Payments

Although there are sizable transfers of resources overseas, only the use of personnel and capital are lost to the U.S. economy. These "losses" have a

---

[31] *Census, 1957,* p. 51.

[32] Dunning reports that several U.S. companies depend on their U.K. subsidiaries to supply most of their overseas markets, making the United Kingdom one of the largest suppliers in the world of American-designed products. (*Op. cit.,* p. 311.)

[33] Dunning asserts that "the *marginal* cost of producing for export is less in this country [United Kingdom] than the *marginal* cost of expanding production in the U.S." (*Ibid.,* pp. 311–312.)

[34] For a discussion of national gains from foreign investment, see Chapter XVIII of this volume.

significant impact on factor payments. And even the shifts of technology (which involve no "loss" of know-how to the U.S. economy) have an indirect repercussion on factor payments in the United States.

Since there is a reduction in the supply of personnel and a widening of the market for managerial and technical talents, the reward to this factor in the United States should rise relative to other returns. The same result should occur for capital, even if the returns abroad are not greater than at home. The diminished domestic supply and enlarged demand, as the world market is served, should raise the marginal returns in the United States and thus increase the relative share of capital.

If management and capital are to receive higher *relative* shares, labor must accept a smaller *proportion* of the total product. Currently in the United States there is a growing appreciation of the effects of private foreign investment on wages *and* on the movement of capital overseas. Commenting on the effects of rising wages on the international balance of payments, Professor P. T. Ellsworth has written that:

> There is the additional danger that American firms, in an effort to hold their markets abroad in the face of high and rising wages at home, will export their capital and their techniques and combine them with cheaper and more docile foreign labor. (Such a migration of American industry, especially toward the European Common Market, has in fact been going on at an accelerating rate in recent years. In part, of course, its aim is to surmount the tariff of the Common Market.) From this lower-cost foreign base, these firms can then export in competition with their parent American organizations in third markets and even into the American market. (This trend, too, is already making itself felt.)
>
> Should such competition from foreign domiciled American firms become serious, the logical result would be strong and probably successful pressure for protection, from both labor and management. The general public, in its role as consumer, would then be completely helpless; inflationary forces would be compounded; and the national interest in expanding world trade would be sabotaged. Such an outcome would be intolerable.[35]

There is little doubt that, in terms of its *relative* share, labor is not benefited from the expansion of direct foreign investment by American business in competitive enterprises abroad. However, labor should not be concerned simply with its *relative* share, but rather with its *absolute* rewards. With the decline in import prices and the improved efficiency of production which will be required to adjust to changes in world trade, laboring groups could benefit in terms of *real* income, provided there is a net gain in the real national product from the direct foreign investment. This net gain will arise partly from an expansion (or maintenance) of the volume of exports and from income receipts from abroad.

---

[35] "From Dollar Shortage to Dollar Glut," *Michigan Business Review* (Mar. 1960), p. 14.

Pattern of Trade

There are four major characteristics of U.S. foreign trade which are being affected by the growing volume of direct foreign investment: aggregate volume, volume compared to domestic production and to production abroad by U.S. associates, composition of trade, and geographic direction of trade.

The volume of U.S. exports is directly or indirectly increased by the capital expenditures of U.S. enterprises operating abroad. A portion of the expenditures may be for capital equipment supplied by a U.S. firm which serves as domestic supplier of similar equipment. Even if the bulk of the expenditures financed by the U.S. capital outflow are made for local labor, materials, and equipment, the added purchasing power will lead to larger U.S. exports. Indeed, if the U.S. capital outflow is to provide additional real resources abroad, other than adding to reserves, the capital must be transferred through an export surplus. On the other hand, the transfer of earnings on the invested capital and payments for services or licenses reduces the host country's capacity to import. Although the periods of capital outflow and remittance are different for particular investments, the continuous process of foreign investment and remittance sets up opposing forces on the U.S. balance of trade. Recently, remittances of earnings from direct investment and fees under licenses have been well above the level of the outflow of U.S. private direct investment each year. For the postwar period as a whole, receipts have exceeded direct investment capital outflow by a substantial margin. . . .

Although the process of continual foreign investment tends to expand trade somewhat, this may be offset by an increase in the production of commodities abroad which are competitive to U.S. exports. Total production by U.S. associates abroad has been estimated by the Department of Commerce at $32 billion in 1957 or about twice the volume of U.S. exports. A continuation of the trend of foreign production is likely to reduce still further the *relative* importance of U.S. exports.[36] U.S. foreign trade has not increased at the same rate as gross national product over the past several years, and with the large amount of U.S. foreign investment going into manufacturing and the creation of regional economic associations abroad, this trend will probably continue. Although the absolute level of U.S. exports will increase, the rise will be gradual and not so fast as production of goods abroad by U.S. associates or as GNP within the United States. Foreign trade is, therefore, likely to become *relatively* less important—without diminishing the critical role of some foreign sources of raw materials supply or foreign markets for U.S. exports of a wide range of both agricultural and industrial products.

---

[36] A McGraw-Hill estimate forecasts sales from overseas operations of U.S. companies at $60 billion in 1968 compared to exports from the U.S. of $25 billion; the same figures for 1958 were $30 and $17 billion and for 1949 were $12 and $12 billion (*Business Week*, Jan. 3, 1959). Assuming a 4 percent increase in GNP exports would have barely kept pace while overseas sales would have risen over 7 percent per year.

In addition, the composition of trade is likely to change. U.S. trade with highly industrialized countries will be dominated more and more by new products and by specialized high-technology items. Exports of consumer goods are decreasing relative to capital goods items to the less-developed countries. The more industrially advanced of the newly developing nations are beginning to produce their own capital goods and durable consumer goods items. As economies diversify and produce domestic substitutes for a wide range of imports, the nature of import demand will change. There will be an increased demand for industrial specialties while exports of standardized commodities will tend to fall. This shift in composition to higher value items will offset some of the other forces tending to decrease the value of trade.[37] Commercial exchanges between nations will take on more and more the character of trade in new ideas, i.e., new processes, special skills, and techniques. Once a foreign market for a new product is established, production will move to the foreign market by means of the transfer of patents, skills, and highly specialized equipment.

Considerable specialization among nations will no doubt remain in raw materials. Shifts in domestic production toward industrial items in the newly developing countries may mean a movement in the terms of trade in favor of agricultural commodities. It may be wise for the United States, which has a comparative advantage in production of foodstuffs and cotton, to give increasing attention to exports of agricultural items. However, national foreign trade policies for agriculture are everywhere more protectionist than for other items. Again, the commercial policies adopted are most important in permitting the shifts which are likely to be required by nations involved in direct investment.

Balance of Payments Effects

A complete analysis of the impact of direct foreign investment on the U.S. balance of payments involves a consideration of not only the relationship between capital outflow and the remittance of earnings, but also the effects on imports and exports, including the terms of trade. Insofar as the direct balance of payments effects are concerned, direct foreign investment appears to have made a substantial contribution to the U.S. balance of payments position. Throughout the postwar period, from 1946 through 1960, U.S. balance of payments receipts from direct investments abroad totalled $23.9 billion (including reinvested branch profits), while total direct capital outflow was $14.3 billion, leaving a net gain of $9.6 billion. Moreover, receipts from direct foreign investments has exceeded direct capital outflow in every year but three between 1919 and 1960; direct capital

---

[37] For example, International Harvester has found that sales by subsidiaries abroad replaced its former exports, but that total export sales have dropped only slightly because of a shift to more complex and expensive items not made by the subsidiaries (see *Business Week,* Jan. 3, 1959).

outflow was slightly higher than income in 1928, 1929, and 1931. The reason for this record is that a substantial proportion of earnings on foreign investment are reinvested abroad, sometimes over 50 percent, and U.S. foreign investments generally have been profitable. Moreover, the book value of direct private investments has grown from $3.9 billion in 1919 to well over $30 billion in 1960.

This does not mean that if during any particular year the government had halted new direct capital outflow, our net balance of payments position might not have been improved *for that particular year.* However, direct investment must be regarded as a continuous process, and any attempt to shut off the flow of direct investment capital abroad is very likely to redound on earnings within a few years so that, say, over a ten-year period there would be a net loss of foreign exchange from the restrictive action. This is because firms operating abroad are continually finding opportunities for profitable investment in one affiliate while perhaps reducing their commitments in others. Restrictive actions in the form of capital controls would reduce this flexibility and hence reduce the opportunities of profitable foreign investment.

When it comes to assessing the indirect impact of direct private investment on the U.S. balance of payments, we run into factors which are difficult, if not impossible, to quantify. As we have seen, direct investment tends to increase the market for certain exports. At the same time U.S. firms operating abroad produce commodities which compete with U.S. exports or are shipped to the United States in competition with domestic production. On the other hand, direct investment in raw materials, of which the United States is in short supply and must import from abroad, tends to improve our terms of trade and, hence, our trade balance. It cannot be said, however, that direct investments abroad in industries which compete with U.S. exports are necessarily harmful to our balance of payments position, because in the absence of U.S. direct investment in these industries, local or other foreign firms may undertake the investment. For example, if a U.S. firm builds a plant in Brazil which might otherwise have been built by a German firm, the U.S. balance of payments may be better off, both because the U.S. firm is more likely to use U.S. equipment, materials, and services, and because of the contribution of the direct investment to U.S. foreign exchange earnings. This may be true even though in either case the direct investment involves a loss of direct U.S. exports of the product. It should also be said that U.S. direct investments abroad frequently provide a market for commodities and services of complementary industries which may be supplied from the United States. Investment in sales and distribution operations and in plants which assemble U.S.-produced components often result in an expansion of the market for U.S. exports. In a growing number of industries, in fact, it is impossible for a country to maintain and expand its markets abroad without investment in distribution facilities, warehouses, maintenance, packaging, or assembly. If some components can be produced more cheaply abroad, it may be necessary, in order to compete with foreign products, to produce those components as a means of maintaining the market for the bulk of the commodities that may be produced in the U.S. plant. Hence, there is a very close relationship between direct investment and exports, and in many fields the choice between taking orders for shipments abroad and going abroad to participate in some part of the production process is simply not open.

Policy Implications

Assuming no substantial increase in restrictions on foreign investment by capital importing countries, either in Western Europe, Canada, or in the major industrial countries of Latin America, it seems likely that direct investment activity will continue to rise, both in terms of the value of foreign investment and in the number of foreign affiliates. The movement of capital, enterprise, and techniques will not only change the pattern of world trade, but will probably grow at a faster rate than U.S. exports. (Undoubtedly, the increased trade among regional trading associations, such as the European Common Market and the Latin American Free Trade Area, will be at the considerable expense of imports from outside the regional groupings.) The United States can do little to stop this development. Even if it should decide to restrict the transfer of direct capital abroad, it would not help its own position because firms from other countries would take the place of U.S. enterprise. The shift in the pattern and character of trade from standardized industrial commodities to high technology and new commodities, and the tendency for movements of capital, enterprise, and technology to substitute for trade in commodities, requires that we maintain as a nation a high degree of flexibility of our industry in order to adjust promptly and efficiently to these dynamic movements. This flexibility must permeate all sectors of the domestic economy—both export and import competing industries—and involves a greater willingness of our producers to make such investments and affiliations abroad as are necessary to maintain or expand their markets. Given these conditions, it does not appear that a case can be made either for subsidizing U.S. investment within Europe or for restricting it. Government assistance which provides better information on market conditions and investment opportunities abroad for U.S. firms would appear to be highly desirable.

There remains the question of whether any efforts should be directed toward *encouraging* the outflow of direct investment as a means of promoting growth in less advanced economies. . . .

Foreign-Owned Enterprise
in the Developing
Countries

Raymond Vernon

Nearly two decades ago Hans W. Singer published a well-known paper elaborating the proposition that foreign investments in the export industries of the less-developed countries were of little or no benefit to those countries.[1] This was not the first time that such a view had been advanced. But prior to the 1940s the proposition had rarely been taken very seriously in the conventional economic circles of the West. The cases of North America and Australia, which had depended so heavily in their early stages on export-oriented foreign investment, seemed a sufficient refutation of the generalization.[2] Singer's article, reasonable in tone, apolitical in content, had the effect of fortifying the concerns which already were being expressed by economists in many countries. North America and Australia, according to the new view, were special cases. These areas had been open spaces, unencumbered by traditional social and economic structures, and to them came literate, well-trained, well-capitalized immigrants. Capital shipped from abroad could be productively coupled with the manpower that went along. Innovation and adaptation could be anticipated in the ordinary course. In sharp contrast, export-oriented investment in the less-developed part of the world of the mid-twentieth century was managed by remote foreign interests in an unchanged setting of economic stagnation; such industry could realistically be thought of as nothing more than an enclave of the rich importing countries, rather than as part of the exporting nations.

Reprinted from *Public Policy* (Vol. 15, 1966), Harvard University Press by permission.

[1] Singer, "The Distribution of Gains between Investing and Borrowing Countries," *American Economic Review*, Vol. II, No. 2 (May 1950). See also J. H. Boeke, *Economics and Economic Policy of Dual Societies* (New York: Institute of Pacific Relations, 1963), a classic study of the subject.

[2] The economic literature of foreign investment in the nineteenth century, with special emphasis on British investment, is skillfully and succinctly summarized in Ragnar Nurkse. "International Investment To-day in the Light of Nineteenth-Century Experience," *Economic Journal*, Vol. LXIV (December 1954). The United States role as a capital exporter in the nineteenth and early twentieth century is summarized in Cleona Lewis, *America's Stake in International Investments* (Washington: Brookings Institution, 1938). A summary of European direct investment, with special emphasis on the role of the Dutch in the East Indies, appears in *Report on Management of Direct Investments in Less-Developed Countries* (Leiden: H. E. Stenfert Kroese, 1957). Other general sources especially relevant to this article include D. M. Phelps, *Migration of Industry to Latin America* (New York: McGraw-Hill, 1936); Michael Kidron, *Foreign Investments in India* (London: Oxford University Press, 1965).

The thesis in the Singer article, so clearly and persuasively stated, was re-echoed in many places following its publication. Its impact could be seen in the publications of the United Nations and in many academic journals. Hardly had the revised generalizations been made, however, when indications began to appear that the role of foreign investors in the less-developed countries, whatever it may once havy been, was changing. Foreign investors in less-developed areas, it appeared, were being pushed by events into still another stage, yet to be fully defined. The process of updating the picture of the foreign investor's role has now been going on for some time.[3]

First of all, it is beginning to be clear that enclave economies have sometimes set in motion a series of political and economic forces that operated in the end to break open the enclave. Second, there is evidence to suggest that the less-developed countries by a process of threat and bargaining are rapidly learning how to improve their relative position vis-à-vis the foreign investor. Finally, there are indications that both the identity and the objectives of the foreign investors in the less-developed countries are changing in ways which are reducing the conflict and increasing the reciprocity of their interests with the less-developed countries.

These are rather formidable propositions. As a preliminary to exploring them, it may help to review a little more fully just what concerns policymakers and economists regarding foreign investment in the less-developed countries.

The Debate over Foreign Investment

Any debate on the role of foreign private investment is ordinarily an emotion-charged affair, laced with historical sensitivities and ideological overtones. The concerns of the less-developed countries are expressed not only in economic terms but also in political ones.[4] Their worries relate not only to the behavior of the investors themselves but also to the behavior of the governments behind the investors. Nevertheless, the economic issues need to be well understood.

It does not require many words to describe the classical economic case *for* foreign investment in the less-developed areas. The transfer of foreign capital to a less-developed economy, according to conventional theory, represents a response to the fact that the marginal productivity of capital in the less-developed economy is

---

[3] As an example of the complexities being introduced in the analysis, see a very thoughtful piece by Chandler Morse, "Potentials and Hazards of Direct International Investment in Raw Materials," in Marion Clawson (ed.), *Natural Resources and International Development* (Baltimore: Johns Hopkins, 1964). In quite another vein, see Dudley Seers, *The Mechanism of an Open Petroleum Economy* Paper No. 47 (New Haven: Yale University Economic Growth Center, 1964).

[4] A superb survey of the literature on the subject of foreign investment as it relates to Latin America appears in Marvin D. Bernstein (ed.), *Foreign Investment in Latin America* (New York: Knopf, 1966), pp. 283–305. See also Raymond Vernon (ed.), *How Latin America Views the U.S. Investor* (New York: Praeger, 1966).

higher than it would be at home. The money transfer sets in train a transfer of real foreign resources. In economies in which saving rates are low and import propensities are high, the transfer process is completed in a comparatively short time. In addition to the goods and services that are the counterpart of the capital flow, a certain amount of technology, managerial skill, or training facilities may accompany the capital. Since the foreign investor usually must receive his return out of the output that his investment generates, his activities cannot fail to contribute to the growth and well-being of the less-developed country.

The objections entered against these simple propositions fall under a few major headings.[5] One of these is the view that a large part of the foreign claims that arise from foreign investment are generated without any net transfer of real resources into the economy. In 1964, for example, the equity interest of United States private foreign direct investors in their subsidiaries, affiliates, and branches in Latin America, Asia, and Africa increased by $3.3 billion; yet the added funds coming from the United States amounted to only $565 million, the rest of the increase coming out of the net income and depreciation reserves of the subsidiary firms and from non-United States capital sources.[6] Thus, the argument goes, less-developed economies contributed to the growth of foreign claims largely out of local savings and local resources.

Even if the foreign investor *does* bring his capital from abroad, however, there is a fear that his contribution may be offset by the abortion of other investments in the country. The foreigner's project may, for instance, discourage the expansion plans of domestic entrepreneurs, leading them either to spend their savings on consumption goods or to export their capital abroad. The foreign-owned enterprise may attract the best brains and skills from the trained indigenous work force, thus diverting existing entrepreneurial and managerial talent away from local enterprise. Moreover, the elite indigenous cadre that has been drawn to the foreign enterprise may be denied the opportunity for further learning on the job, since the topmost jobs in the foreign firm are reserved for expatriates. The result is that the resources seemingly provided by the foreign-owned enterprise are offset by a loss of resources in the rest of the economy.

Despite these demurrers and others, the critics of foreign investment generally agree that foreign investors may at times be providing something of value to the less-developed countries. When this is the case, however, foreigners are said

---

[5] What follows is a synthesis of economic arguments derived from many sources. It omits some arguments relating to foreign investment and places others in a context slightly different from the original formulations. Some arguments appear in the sources quoted in the various footnotes of this article. Others are found expressly or by implication in the writings of Prebisch, Singer, Myrdal, Bhagwati, and others.

[6] U.S. Department of Commerce, *Survey of Current Business* (November 1965), p. 15, Table 1. Unfortunately, "non-United States capital sources" are not broken down in the data to distinguish capital originating in the advanced countries from that generated in the less-developed countries. My guess is that such capital is largely raised in the host countries.

generally to be getting more for their contribution than it is worth. There may be real doubt if the flow of resulting economic benefits to the host country exceeds the flow of resulting costs.

On casual first analysis, this would seem to be a very difficult position to sustain.[7] After all, economic benefits can be stated in terms of returns to the various factors of production: to land, labor, and capital. And these returns, in the aggregate, cannot be greater than the net value added by the enterprise in its operations in the country. Foreign capital, therefore, cannot get more in payment than a share of what it has been instrumental in producing; the rest goes to land, labor, and government, which presumably are mainly local factors.

This kind of analysis, however, is usually rejected by the less-developed countries. The return to foreign capital, they say, is a monopolist's return, reflecting the scarcity of the product in the less-developed country. On the other hand, the return to land (as in the case of petroleum or of mining) is usually less than its economic value because the foreign concessionaire is in a position to exercise monopoly coercion. The return to labor, it is contended, is far less than labor's marginal contribution because the pool of unemployed labor in less-developed areas can be thought of as infinitely elastic, thus pressing down the going wage to Malthusian levels. As a result, most of the value added is distributed to the monopoly capitalist; and what he gets may well exceed the economic worth of the output.

When nonreplenishable resources are involved, the indictment takes a slightly different form. The use of a country's nonreplenishable resources, the argument goes, is not necessarily better than having the resources lie idle for a time. The country may be better off postponing the exploitation of the resources until some later date when the exploitation can take place on better terms to the country. The opportunity cost to the host country from a proposed investment, therefore, may exceed its return—especially if the proposed investment is to be made on the terms offered by foreign investors.

Another kind of argument to the same end has to do with the welfare effects of the output of foreign enterprise. Foreign enterprise, the argument goes, tends to produce frivolous items—items whose contribution in welfare terms is low. Nevertheless, the return to the foreigner must be serviced in the end out of the economy's productive capacity. Eventually, therefore, the economy may have to deprive itself of other items which would make a much higher welfare contribution; medicines in the future may be sacrificed for soft drinks now.

Two added grievances are worth elaborating.

One of these stems from the recognition that the currencies of most of the less-developed countries are overvalued. A foreign investor in a less-developed

---

[7] The reasoning that follows is elaborated in many forms by various economists. For a representative exposition, see E. T. Penrose, "Foreign Investment and the Growth of the Firm," *Economic Journal*, LXVI (June 1956), 220–35.

country, with a profit in local currency, accordingly has a claim on more United States dollars than he ought to have. Besides, so the argument runs, the terms of trade by which the less-developed countries exchange their goods with the advanced countries and acquire their foreign exchange are adverse, both in the static and in the dynamic sense. Because of high import restrictions in the advanced countries, the less-developed areas are obliged to accept poor prices for their exports. And the terms of trade grow progressively worse for all the familiar reasons that have been associated with Raul Prebisch and the Economic Commission for Latin America (ECLA).[8] Accordingly, the servicing of foreign claims proves more and more costly in real terms as the years progress.

As this discussion suggests, the contending views in the debate are based on some fairly extensive assumptions of fact. A few of the assumptions can be tested in part by objective data. However, most of them are of the sort that stubbornly resist objective test; the opportunity cost of diverting the best local talent to foreign-owned firms, for instance, cannot easily be measured, nor can the gains in upgrading such talent for future use in the country.

In any case, the less-developed countries' view of foreign direct investment is not the outcome of a systematic totting up of pluses and minuses; it is much more an intuitive leap to a critical conclusion based upon the prevailing interpretation of the history of foreign investment.

Foreign Investment in Raw Materials

The prevailing interpretation of the history of foreign exploitation of raw materials in the less-developed world is that, with a few exceptions, it has been exploitative and degrading for the host country. The historical evidence itself, however, suggests a much more complex set of conclusions.

During much of the nineteenth century, there appears to be a superficial correspondence between the facts of foreign investment and the Marxist theories of the role of colonies in the capitalistic system. The Dutch concentrated their investment largely in the East Indies, the British largely in the British Empire, the United States largely in smaller neighboring countries. Of course, not all investors conformed to the Marxist generalizations. For instance, the British *rentiers* who purchased huge quantities of Latin American securities during the nineteenth century were usually the victims of their own excessive ignorance and enthusiasm, prey to the energetic salesmen of London's investment banking firms.[9] And the European immigrants who ventured into Latin America, backed by capital from home, bore little resemblance to the Marxist caricatures.

---

[8] See Werner Baer, "The Economics of Prebisch and ECLA," *Economic Development and Cultural Change*, Vol. X, No. 2, Pt. 1 (January 1962), 169–82.

[9] J. Fred Rippy, *British Investments in Latin America, 1822–1949* (Minneapolis: University of Minnesota Press, 1959), contains an excellent summary of the era.

Still, despite the notable exceptions, Marxist doctrine may have been more right than wrong in describing the *intent* of foreign investors in raw materials. As far as the entrepreneur was concerned, one hoped to find the raw material and to export it out at lowest possible cost, with minimum exposure to the country whence the raw material was drawn.

Intent is one thing, however, and performance another. Some of the historical evidence suggests that it is difficult to prevent a seeming enclave from having profound repercussions in any society. In some cases, the repercussions may be systematically arrested or contained (witness the cases of the Belgian Congo and the Dutch East Indies prior to independence); in other cases, the consequences may not flow fast enough to match the growing impatience of the political forces in the country. But movement exists; and, when measured in historical perspective, it sometimes seems very rapid indeed.

A classic case of the putative export enclave which proved to have built-in destabilizers is represented by the Peruvian guano era, from 1840 to 1880.[10] Guano was a raw material of great value, isolated on some offshore islands, worked largely by imported Chinese coolie labor, shipped mainly to foreign markets, financed principally by British capital. On the face of it, nothing could be better suited to an insulated enclave operation.

Yet the effects of the guano industry on Peru's mainland economy were pervasive. About half the proceeds went to the Peruvian government. For two or three decades, these proceeds were redistributed among favored Peruvians in the wasteful pattern characteristic of the time; but, thereafter, they served as the seed money for an orgy of railroad building that opened up the Peruvian interior. Some part of the funds generated by the guano industry went to the creation of a local contracting industry and to the creation of a comparatively modern mercantile and banking system. Despite the key importance of foreign labor and foreign capital, the guano trade profoundly affected the structure of the Peruvian economy.

Another case that is commonly represented as the classic foreign enclave economy is the Porfirian era in Mexico from 1876 to 1910.[11] My reading of the growing body of historical evidence covering the period is that foreign investors in raw materials had the quite unintended effect of greatly altering the physical infrastructure and the social structure of the country. The railroads that were built to ship ore out of the country soon drew the bulk of their business from internal

---

[10] The account that follows is based mainly on the work of Jonathan V. Levin, *The Export Economies* (Cambridge: Harvard University Press, 1960).

[11] For many decades after Diaz fell from power, most of the publications describing the period consisted of polemical tracts—brilliant, impassioned, persuasive tracts, in many cases, but not objective works of scholarship. Today, as a result of a decade or more of hard, grubby work by a team of economic historians in Mexico, we have a much fuller and much more complex view of the period than ever before. The results of this work are being published in a series of volumes, under the title *Historia Moderna de Mexico*, by Editorial Hermes in Mexico City.

domestic traffic; the utilities that initially looked to the mines as their major customers soon were producing their power principally for domestic customers. While miners were recruited at cruelly low wages, their employment visibly increased the going wage for labor in hacienda agriculture and even created absolute labor shortages in the areas near the mines; the training of foremen and technicians in the export industries increased the ranks of a competent, frustrated, embittered middle class; the availability of reliable sources of ores and fibers was a spur to a rapidly growing industrial complex based on home markets. These are among the major forces that soon thereafter accounted for Mexico's Revolution.

Still a third major episode reflecting the role of foreign investment in the development process is afforded by the case of Venezuela. Until the late 1950s, that country was typically cited as the case *par excellence* of the pure dual economy, displacing Indonesia as the preferred illustration. Per capita income had been rising rapidly for some time in the country, spurred on by several decades of heavy investment in petroleum and other raw materials. But the popular view of this increase was that it was taking place entirely in the "enclaves"—in the camps of the foreign oil companies and in the headquarters of the bureaucracy in Caracas.

By the late 1950s, observers began to sense that the economic walls surrounding the enclave had broken down. The 1961 census provides some indication of the extent of the process. Table 1 presents a few obvious welfare measures for five states in Venezuela.[12] These states, largely by-passed by the foreign investors, would ordinarily be thought of as the "backwash areas" of the growing Venezuelan economy.[13]

It is difficult to reconstruct precisely the flow of cause and effect which produced the changes shown in Table 1. It is hard to be sure whether the upward movement in the "backwash areas" was achieved principally through the backward integration of the oil camps, through the industrial import-substitution programs of the government, through public investments in infrastructure, or through a combination of such forces. But any authoritative analysis will surely ascribe a significant role to the direct and indirect consequences of the oil operations.

No one in the modern epoch would be inclined to use the Peruvian guano era, the Mexican era of Porfiro Diaz, or even the Venezuelan oil pattern as a model for economic development strategy. On the other hand, it is important to be clear that isolation is not an inevitable feature of an export enclave and may not even be characteristics. Even if the export-oriented foreign investor can find some way of achieving physical isolation, it is doubtful that he can maintain it for very long under modern conditions.

---

[12] The census showed a number of other welfare measures, and all followed the same general trend.

[13] "Backwash" is a concept made popular by Gunnar Myrdal, reflecting the view that some areas are positively injured by growth elsewhere in the less-developed country. See his *Rich Lands and Poor* (New York: Harper, 1957), pp. 27–29.

Selected Welfare Measures in Selected "Backwash" States of Venezuela, 1950 and 1961

		State of Cojedes	State of Lara	State of Sucre	State of Tachira	State of Yaracuy
Percent of population. 7–14 years attending school	1950	42.9	43.4	47.0	49.5	40.8
	1961	65.1	66.0	75.1	68.9	67.3
Percent of population. 10–14 yrs., literate	1950	36.6	38.8	42.5	52.8	37.6
	1961	61.0	66.6	66.4	70.4	64.1
Percent of homes with electricity	1950	18.2	26.0	19.6	36.9	n.a.
	1961	30.8	48.8	36.6	48.4	43.4
Percent of homes with running water	1950	17.4	18.7	16.9	36.2	20.6
	1961	28.4	40.1	24.8	69.1	40.1

Source: *Noveno Censo General de Población*, February 26, 1961 (Caracas, 1965). n.a. = not available.

Table 1.

The history of export-oriented enclaves in independent countries suggests that, whatever the terms of the original arrangements may be, built-in political forces oblige all parties to regard those terms as being constantly subject to renegotiation. The tendency of host governments constantly to try to better their terms with concessionaires had, of course, always been present in some degree. The speed with which this pressure grew and the nature of the demands made by different governments varied enormously from country to country. But the general directions have been clear enough. The history of the petroleum industry serves as a reasonably good illustration of the trend.[14]

In the business of oil concessions, the norms of the early twentieth century were represented chiefly by investments in Mexico and the Ottoman Empire. In those days, prior to World War I, concession contracts were almost exclusively concerned with the size of royalties and other taxes. And these cannot have exceeded 10 percent of the companies' net profits at that time, if they were that high.

From 1910 to 1938, the oil companies were subjected to continuous pressure by host governments, especially by Mexico. As a result, the division of profits shifted somewhat in favor of host governments. In 1938, however, the foreign oil producers in Mexico, scandalized by increasing Mexican demands, held out so stubbornly and intransigently against further concessions (wage concessions, in this case) that they were nationalized.

---

[14] For a good general history of the oil concessions, see J. E. Hartshorn, *Politics and World Oil Economies* (New York: Praeger, 1962).

Yet scarcely five years later, the oil companies were settling for terms in Venezuela which seemed much more disadvantageous to them. In 1943, the industry renegotiated its arrangements in Venezuela on a basis that was popularly described as a 50–50 division of profits; that is to say, the monetary value of all the oil companies' local tax commitments plus social expenditures was roughly equal to their after-tax profits.

Once the 50–50 formula had taken hold, it became the floor from which the oil countries negotiated with concessionaires. By 1966, through one amendment and another, the share taken by the oil countries rose to a much higher level. The precise provisions for enlarging the oil countries' share were varied and ingenious, designed in part to obscure the fact that the 50–50 line had been breached. As a result, a 60–40 split or better became the *de facto* rule. And the end of the continuous process of renegotiation and repartition seemed nowhere in view.

While the split of profits was being shifted between the oil companies and the host governments, the patterns of operation of the oil companies were being shifted as well. By 1965, the Iran operating companies (which were being subjected to the strongest pressures) had placed Iranians in 50 percent of their 150 topmost jobs. And more than half the purchases of the companies was being arranged through local Iranian commercial channels.[15]

Nor does petroleum seem to be a special case. The position of the foreign copper companies in Chile, while perhaps a bit in advance of the general situation, points the direction. For a long time before World War II the Chilean government had been pressing the foreign copper companies for better terms. These pressures bore obvious fruit. An ECLA study published in the early 1950s showed that the portion of the export value of the companies' output retained in Chile rose from 12 percent in 1929 to a high of 57 percent in the middle 1940s.[16] After 1950, the pressures continued. Income-tax rates applicable to the foreign companies were pushed upward. By 1965, having gone about as far as it could hope to go in that direction, the executive arm of the Chilean government secured agreement on an equity interest in the operations of one of the major foreign producers and a lesser interest in the other.

The redistribution of equity, in fact, is taking place in many different forms. In Mexico, the government precipitated such a redistribution by granting heavy tax concessions to companies with Mexican majority partners. In Brazil a redistribution

---

[15] Information provided by letter from the office of the operating companies in Iran. For other illustrations of the same pattern, see David H. Finnie, *Desert Enterprise* (Cambridge: Harvard University Press, 1958). See also in the National Planning Association series *Business Performance Abroad*, the following volumes: *Stanvac in Indonesia* (1957) and *The Creole Petroleum Company in Venezuela* (1955); and on raw materials other than oil, *The Firestone Operations in Liberia* (1956), *Casa Grace in Peru* (1954), *The United Fruit Company in Latin America* (1958), and *Agrifor and U.S. Plywood in the Congo* (1965).

[16] ECLA, *Economic Survey of Latin America, 1949* (New York: United Nations, 1951), p. 280.

**Operations of Petroleum and Mining Subsidiaries of
United States Firms in Less-Developed Areas, 1957**

(In Millions of United States Dollars)

	Petroleum[a]	Mining[b]
Total Sales	4758	1079
Local	1504	186
Foreign	3254	893
Local Payments	2741	792
Materials	1002	302
Wages and Salaries	462	185
Income Taxes	728	172
Other Local Payments	609	133
Foreign Payments	1716	200
Goods and Services	570	76
Remitted Profit	1146	124
Depreciation and Depletion	301	87

[a] Covers Latin America and the Middle East only, since operations elsewhere are heavily weighted by refining and distribution activities.
[b] Covers Latin America and Africa only, since operations elsewhere are heavily weighted by smelting and refining activities.
Source: Samuel Pizer and Frederick Cutler, *U.S. Business Investments in Foreign Countries,* Washington, D.C.: Government Printing Office, 1960.

Table 2.

on similar lines by a major foreign iron-ore producer was undertaken without apparent duress. While extrapolation always carries an element of danger, this is a case in which the projection of past trends into the future seems safe enough.

Quantitative summaries of phenomena of this subtle sort always contain elements of distortion. Besides, the best summary figures in this case are already badly dated, reflecting the situation in 1957. Still, the figures shown in Table 2, with one or two caveats, demonstrate that the foreign raw-material operations in the less-developed economies are very far from an isolated enclave operation. By 1957, responding to one pressure or another, the petroleum and mining operations of United States firms in the less-developed world had become well embedded in the local economies.

Foreign Investment in Manufacturing

The history of foreign investment in manufacturing facilities in the less-developed world has taken rather a different course from that in raw materials.

Before World War II, there were occasional cases of foreign private direct investment in manufacturing facilities in the less-developed areas of the world. But most of the cases that come to mind for that period tended to be one of two types:

they were direct offshoots of some raw-material activity (sugar refining in Cuba, metal smelting in Chile); or they were accompanied by the permanent migration of foreign management personnel, so that in a generation or so the firms had become indigenous (breweries and textile mills in Mexico and Brazil).

Nevertheless, even before World War II, nearly fifty large United States companies, including such prominent names as the Ford Motor Company, Otis Elevator, International Harvester, and United Fruit, had established manufacturing facilities in Latin America, varying from assembly and packaging operations to much more significant processing.[17]

In the period after World War II, the forces pushing foreign manufacturing subsidiaries into the less-developed areas grew more obvious and more compelling. For one thing, the absolute size of markets in such areas grew, as incomes and populations increased. Perhaps more important, however, was the policy of heavy import restrictions which was pursued by most less-developed countries, a policy which confronted the producers and exporters of manufactured goods in the advanced countries with the choice of investing in the less-developed areas or losing their markets. At the same time, the policy offered the tantalizing promise (sometimes not realized in practice) of monopoly profits in a protected market. Under the circumstances a number of foreign entrepreneurs chose to invest.[18]

The local policies followed by such companies, of course, were not always to the liking of host governments. The spotty available data indicate that while some of these manufacturing firms invited local partners to share in the equity, others insisted on maintaining 100 percent control.[19] While many firms staffed their key management posts with local personnel, others reserved a few critical positions for expatriates from the home office.[20] While some assiduously sought out, developed, and financed local suppliers of materials and services, others preferred to import as much as they could for as long as they were allowed.

Unlike the foreign producers of raw materials, however, the investors producing for the local market were not free to retreat, physically or spiritually, to the

---

[17] Phelps, *Migration of Industry to Latin America.*

[18] My own crude classification of the United States foreign direct investment in the less-developed countries suggests that of the $16 billion so invested as of 1965, $5 billion was local-market oriented, $7 billion was oriented primarily to export, and the remainder was not easily classified.

[19] Reasonably up-to-date figures on ownership distribution for manufacturing subsidiaries and affiliates controlled by foreigners in less-developed countries are not to be had. There is no doubt, however, that the dominant and the preferred pattern is that of the wholly owned subsidiary. See. W. G. Friedmann and George Kalmanoff, *Joint International Business Ventures* (New York: Columbia University Press, 1961), pp. 13–38; Samuel Pizer and Frederick Cutler, *U.S. Business Investments in Foreign Countries* (Washington, D. C.: Government Printing Office, 1960), pp. 101–2.

[20] John Shearer, *High Level Manpower in Overseas Subsidiaries* (Princeton: Princeton University Department of Economics and Sociology, 1960).

concept of the enclave economy. Whether they realized it or not, they were bound up with the growth of the country. While foreign investors might desire security and stability, they could not encourage stagnation. That critical fact did not eliminate all the possible points of conflict between national interests and foreign business interests, but it did help a little.

Swiftly, the foreign-owned manufacturing companies became linked with the economies of their host countries. A combination of formal and informal pressures and inducements had brought these companies to a state of total involvement in the local economies. The case of the automobile companies in Latin America illustrates just how far the process has gone. By the mid-1960s, foreign producers in Brazil and Argentina, responding to local regulations, were buying or making about 90 percent of their vehicles by weight in the local economy.[21] In Mexico, the proportion was lower—perhaps 60 percent; but this was largely the result of Mexican official insistence that foreign producers should turn out local copies of the "latest" United States automobile.

Once more, we have to turn back to 1957 in order to obtain comprehensive figures reflecting the linkages of foreign-owned manufacturing firms in the less-developed areas. As Table 3 shows, all but an insignificant proportion of sales was for the local market. More than four-fifths of the inputs were locally acquired.

There is no reason to suppose, however, that the foreign investment in manufactures in the less-developed areas will always confine itself to the penetration of local markets. Elsewhere, I have spelled out in some detail both the incipient process and the supporting evidence which seem to suggest that the less-developed countries may once more see a growth in foreign direct investment devoted to export—but this time to the export of industrial goods.[22] Any boiled-down version of the reasoning and evidence is bound to be a trifle unsatisfactory. Briefly, however, the expectation is based upon a number of mildly heretical conclusions about the absolute advantage of the less-developed countries in producing certain kinds of industrial goods.

Picture a highly standardized product in which price competition is keen. The technology of the product is well developed and readily transmittable; it can, in fact, be embodied in plant and machinery, to be put in place by foreign technicians on a turn-key basis. Assume that external economies are unimportant in the operation of the installation and that the product is of sufficiently high value by weight so that shipment costs are not prohibitive. Assume, too, that the

---

[21] However if all the imported elements were accounted for, such as the rubber in the tires and the iron ore in the steel, the domestically generated proportion of final value in each of the three countries would probably be considerably lower.

[22] A detailed version of the argument appears in two papers of mine: "International Trade and International Investment in the Product Cycle," *Quarterly Journal of Economics*, Vol. LXXX (May 1966); and "Prospects and Problems in the Export of Manufactured Products from Less-Developed Countries," Contributed Paper No. 2 (United Nations Conference on Trade and Development, Geneva, Spring 1964).

Operations of Manufacturing Subsidiaries of United States Firms in Less-Developed Areas. 1957

(In millions of United States dollars)

Total Sales	2,788
Local	2,660
Foreign	128
Local Payments	2,323
Materials	1,464
Wages and Salaries	418
Income Taxes	101
Other Local Payments	340
Foreign Payments	403
Goods and Services	328
Remitted Profits	75
Depreciation and Depletion	62

Source: Pizer and Cutler, *U.S. Business Investments in Foreign Countries.*

Table 3.

productivity of labor in the less-developed country is not so low as to dissipate the competitive advantage of a low money wage and that the cost of capital to the enterprise is not so high as to obliterate the remaining advantages.

This list of requirements, as I have observed elsewhere, is formidable, but it is not prohibitive. Now that the less-developed countries are showing signs of turning their emphasis from import-replacement to export-promotion, we may well see a heightened interest in exploiting the export situations that show promise.

Of course, one need not accept foreign-owned plants in order to promote industrial exports. The Japanese based their early export efforts on precisely the sort of product envisaged here: standardized in nature, based on a technology that was readily transmitted, highly price competitive, yet sufficiently valuable by weight to be able to absorb ocean freight costs. But the Japanese successfully resisted foreign ownership of their plants.

Some of the less-developed countries may manage to copy the Japanese pattern, thereby avoiding foreign ownership. But the pattern requires an unusual capacity for the mobilization of domestic savings and for the application of modern technologies. Taiwan and the Philippines come to mind as cases that seem for the present to accept foreign export-oriented investment on these grounds; both countries offer illustrations of the standardized, price-sensitive, high-value industrial product being manufactured by foreign investors for export as well as for domestic use. A few cases of the same sort are to be found here and there in Latin America, though not many. It remains to be seen whether the less-developed countries and the foreign investors will find a common basis for extending the pattern on a larger scale.

Patterns for Projection

Where have we come so far in the argument? Not a great distance, one has to confess. The summary just presented has not measured the benefits of foreign investments, in growth and payment terms, against their costs. It has not pinned down the income-redistribution effects of such investment. It has not settled the question as to whether such investments generate benefits for the nation which escape the static benefit-cost calculation. Yet, on the whole, the historical account does raise doubts about the major formal arguments directed against such investments; and it does so by querying the validity of some of the premises on which such formal arguments are based. Foreign enclaves have great difficulty in maintaining their enclave status. Foreign investors, whatever the original terms of their entry, have proven peculiarly vulnerable to the renegotiation of such terms in favor of the host country. Foreign manufacturers catering to the local market have been obliged to concern themselves about the growth of the country.

It is possible to push the exposition still one small step further. Here and there one finds a number of systematic studies, conducted under reasonably objective auspices, which have tried systematically to assess the costs and benefits of foreign direct investment for the host country. Some of the studies deal with individual projects.[23] Some deal with a total economy, either building up their conclusions impressionistically with bits and scraps of data or resorting to the simplifications of the econometric model to draw their conclusions.[24] Most quantitatively oriented studies of this sort, whatever their technique, conclude that there are large net benefits in foreign direct investment.

Nevertheless, the best of these studies is not a very rigorous test of the hypothesis that foreign direct investment makes a positive (or, for that matter, a negative) contribution to the economic development of the less-developed areas. Nor is this inadequacy a reflection upon the quality of the researchers. It stems rather from the inherent difficulty involved in measuring the medium-term or long-term effects of such investment.

With time, there will be more studies and better ones. I am inclined to suspect, however, that the improvement of our understanding of the consequences of

---

[23] For one of the better analyses of this sort, see H. D. Huggins, *Aluminum in Changing Communities* (London: André Deutsch, 1965) which contains in Chapter 5 a careful analysis of the impact of the foreign-owned aluminum industry on the Jamaican economy. See also Marvin D. Bernstein, *The Mexican Mining Industry, 1890–1950* (New York: State University of New York, 1964).

[24] See, for instance, Chi-ming Hou, *Foreign Investment and Economic Development in China, 1840–1937* (Cambridge: Harvard University Press, 1965).

One of the more difficult studies to classify from this point of view is "Economic Developments in Venezuela in the 1950s." *Economic Bulletin for Latin America*, Vol. V, No. 1 (March 1960), 21 ff. The data in the article seem to indicate that foreign investment had a major beneficial role in the rapid development of the country. But the article understandably tends to stress principally what still remains to be achieved.

foreign direct investment in the less-developed countries is likely to leave most of the basic measurement problems unsolved. And, in any case, whatever the improved understanding may be, it is likely to have scarcely any effect upon the policies of those countries toward such investment.

Right or wrong, the prevailing view of the intellectual and political leaders of most countries in the less-developed world is that foreign private direct investment at best is something to be tolerated temporarily.[25] Right or wrong, my guess is that they will continue to think so; if not for economic reasons, then for political ones. It would be a mistake to underestimate the predominance of the view or the tenacity with which the position is held.[26] And, at least in my judgment, it would be a mistake to assume that the governments of the advanced countries can do much to change this view, assuming they wish to try.

If one is obliged to accept the general view that the less-developed countries are less than joyous over their need for foreign investment, can anything systematic be said regarding the trends and variations in such views and the probability that such views may give rise to hostile action? It would be absurd to expect some formula that could have projected the expropriatory actions of Cuba, Egypt, Indonesia, Ceylon, and Guinea over the past ten or fifteen years. One general proposition worth considering, however, is that nations have their strongest motivation for suppressing their hostility to foreign private direct investment at a time when their domestic alternatives appear fewest and least obvious. As human resources and capital build up within a country, its leaders have more frequent occasion to ask whether foreign entrepreneurs are contributing something indispensable to the country's resources or whether they are simply pre-empting the business opportunities and the productive resources of the less-developed country at the expense of local entrepreneurs. It may be this factor which explains why, in dealing with private foreign direct investors, Mexico is more demanding than Central America, Argentina and Chile more firm than Paraguay and Uruguay, Nigeria more determined than Liberia or Ghana. The proposition also suggests that it may only be a matter of time before some of the more compliant countries begin to assume a more demanding negotiating position.[27]

---

[25] For samples of this sort of opinion, see Claude McMillan, Jr., R. F. Gonzalez, and L. G. Erickson, *International Enterprise in a Developing Economy* (East Lansing: Michigan State University, 1964), especially Chapter 4; John P. Powelson, *Latin America* (New York: McGraw-Hill, 1964), especially Chapter 4; V. L. Urquidi, *The Challenge of Development in Latin America* (New York: Praeger, 1964), Chapters 4, 8.

[26] Of course, the intensity of such views varies from country to country. The Indian position, for instance, is somewhat less clearcut than the typical Latin American view. See Kidron, *Foreign Investments in India*, Chapters 3–4. But the generalizations in the text will probably serve.

[27] There are signs that the demands are already growing, for instance, in Central America. See Miguel Wionczek, "A Latin American View," in Vernon (ed.), *How Latin America Views the U.S. Investor.*

If there is any major factor that may blunt or defer the increase in pressure on foreign direct investors in the less-developed areas, it is the growth of regional trading areas, as epitomized by the Latin American Free Trade Association and the Central American Common Market in particular. The development of the markets has set two forces in train, each pointing in a different direction. Countries with the hope of dominating the market through their exports (notably Mexico in LAFTA) not unnaturally have asked themselves how best to keep effective rivals out of the area; and the most threatening rivals, as Mexicans have seen it, are obviously the affiliates or subsidiaries of foreign-owned companies located in the territory of another LAFTA member. On the other hand, countries which have felt less sure about the ability or willingness of their indigenous firms to take advantage of LAFTA's opportunities have asked themselves how best to improve their chances in the area; and some have thought of foreign-owned facilities as their most effective means of exploiting the new situation.

The struggle between these two viewpoints has yet to come to a head. It is already clear, however, that the positions of the disputants will be greatly conditioned by the principles suggested earlier. The foreign investor will gain his support from those countries which see no clear alternative to supporting him; and he will encounter hostility from the countries that see a domestic alternative. Perhaps this is the one general working rule that can be taken away from a review of this sort. Ideologies aside, the interest groups in any nation, less-developed or otherwise, usually share the view that they have the right to be masters in their own house. It is only when the cost of implementing that view is large, evident, and painful that the view is voluntarily suppressed. The battle may use the semantics of ideology, but the motives it reflects are universal.

The Market Environment
of Investment Decisions

Judd Polk

Irene W. Meister

Lawrence A. Veit

It is a commonplace of economic doctrine that if a factor of production is allowed to move to a use in which its yield will be greater than its present yield, total production is bound to be increased. In keeping with this basic proposition, capital ought to be employed where the rate of return is highest, and the proper direction for the movement of capital is from lower to higher rates of return.

In a free market economy the traditional economic task of the businessman in investment is to deploy the resources at his command in such a way as to maximize their yield. The correct movement for capital is from lower to higher yield; the businessman's motivation for his decision is to facilitate that movement, within the typically narrow limits of choice open to producers already committed to a given range of production and subject to supervening competitive considerations.

In these simplified terms, the penalty for defying or miscalculating the line of activity that would afford a higher yield is relative loss, which in time is translated into some sacrifice in capital growth, if not actual capital erosion.

As a matter of economics this proposition is true insofar as capital, or any resource, is free to move, and is true for international as well as domestic movements. In short, the only reasonable reply to the question "what motivates capital?" is "the rate of profit." The relevant element of philosophy that accompanies this economic principle is that public policy best serves the chosen economic objectives of the country by bolstering the freedom of resources to move to their most productive uses.

A more specialized application of this rationale for the freedom of resource movement has become one familiar line of interpretation of the current balance-of-payments difficulties of the United States. Again simplifying, the argument runs that since higher profit is the reasonable motivation for investment, the rapid and growing movement of U.S. capital abroad reflects the sensitivity of U.S. capital to the higher rates of return available abroad. It should be noted here that up to this point at least, this line of argument seems manifestly supported by facts already noted: direct investment abroad has been impressive in size and in rate of growth throughout the post-World-War-II period. Generally speaking, rates of return on investment abroad appear to have been higher than domestic rates of

Reprinted from *U.S. Production Abroad and the Balance of Payments.* © National Industrial Conference Board.

return, though the differential has been narrowing. The advocates of this argument continue that because investors are motivated by the higher foreign rate of return, *only the differential profits would be sacrificed if new investment were slowed down or terminated.* Since, it is argued, it is the nature of investors to commit funds now for the sake of returns later, the balance of payments of the country would be improved in the short run by postponing investment which could not earn offsetting returns over that short run. This line of analysis would, of course, tend to support a program of governmental *restraints* on private investment abroad. The reasoning relies also on the validity of the inference that additional investment abroad serves only to gain, over time, additional profits, and that only additional profits would be sacrificed if the investment were not made.

The businessmen interviewed in this study reject this inference. Their almost universal reaction is that their investment decisions are made in response to competitive necessities that affect the entire earning position of their operations abroad. To firms with existing operations abroad—and these firms account for well over half of new investment outflow—"new" investment is not readily distinguishable from investment to modernize or to improve facilities, and even in cases where this distinction might be made, the investment is nonetheless made in support of the companies' over-all competitive position. As will be seen, their direct investments are made in response to the exigencies of the marketplace; capital is a necessity for the development and service of their markets. So, while profit is correctly seen as the motivation of investment, few instances were encountered where a company executive felt that further investment could cease or be materially slowed down without prejudice to the entire earning position. It was in connection with this latter point—the effects of investment interruption—that company executives expressed their fear that current policy is based on a misunderstanding of investment operations.

What are the major factors underlying investment decisions, as they emerge from discussion with company executives?

Broadly speaking, the growth of manufacturing investments is directly related to economic development abroad and the collective desire of U.S. business to participate in this promising growth. Such a statement, however, glosses over a great variety of individual decisions involving a host of considerations which fully explain the nature of the investment transactions and their effect on the balance of payments. Furthermore, while the classical economic considerations of the function of costs and profits in utilization of capital play an important role in the decisions, the most prominent recurring theme in this study is the overriding importance given by investors to marketing strategy and competitive position.

Environmental Factors

Virtually all U.S. manufacturing companies start with an initial bias in favor of manufacturing within the United States where conditions are better known and risks are generally smaller than they are abroad. Therefore most decisions to invest abroad are precipitated by factors which are beyond company control but which make it impractical for the company to serve foreign markets only through exports from the United States. Many of these factors are matters of intervening foreign—or U.S.—government policies, while others pertain to foreign economic developments.

The evolution of most companies' international business typically follows this pattern: First the company introduces its products, builds an export market, and develops demand. It is to be expected that as soon as the market becomes well established and sizeable it will be lost to the company as a straight export market because of foreign balance-of-payments problems and/or competitive local production. The alternatives for the company are to "lose" the market to itself by activating production facilities on the spot, or to lose it to others—it cannot maintain its market position by merely continuing to send goods from the United States. In many less-developed countries local manufacturing is initiated by residents or other foreign companies, and U.S.-company exports to a given market are rendered noncompetitive by protective devices. In developed areas, notably in Europe, the emphasis is on local and foreign competitors who, having plants on the spot, are in a position to take advantage of changes in terms of volume and type of products demanded, and can supply customers faster and better than a company that depends on slower and costlier long-distance supply lines. The company thus becomes adjusted to a transition toward manufacturing abroad as a natural process of international operations and one necessary to the maintenance of its position in foreign markets.

The main environmental factors affecting investments observed in this study are described below. No attempt has been made to indicate their relative importance. Some do, as subsequent comments will indicate, loom more importantly than others, but such weighting can be misleading because in a given case any one of these may be critical.

Foreign Government Actions

The many broad policies of governments to encourage domestic production have tended to give preferential status to domestic output as against foreign production, and therefore to foreign investment as against imports. In the case of less-developed countries, the actions taken in pursuing these policies are likely to be particularly directed toward fostering industrial development or conserving (allocating) foreign exchange.

The more important forms of government action affecting investment decisions, as recounted in company interviews, can be grouped under seven main headings:

(1) Limitations on Investment. It is common practice in less-developed countries, especially the smaller ones, to restrict the number of companies that are allowed to set up factories to produce a specific product. The objective is to limit the amount of foreign exchange used for importation of machinery, and to assure that those who do manufacture will have a large enough market to support their plants. The manifest risk of being excluded from a given national market frequently

leads a company to take the initiative in investing sooner than it would have done for strictly commercial or economic reasons. A frequently recited experience is that of having decided too late; once restrictions are in force, a company is likely to be prevented from making an investment needed to maintain its market position—a move that frequently its competitors had been able to make, because they had acted earlier.

A characteristic experience is that of a company that was reluctant to invest in many of the less-developed, riskier countries during the early years after World War II. As a result, local competitors got started in some of these countries and the company was frozen out. Its most serious loss of a market occurred in India, which had been a large export market for the company, but which was lost to a new local firm undertaking the manufacture of a competitive product. Since then the Indian government has refused to permit this U.S. company to set up a competing factory. As a result of this and similar experiences, the company is now taking the initiative in setting up manufacturing in a number of less-developed countries sooner than strictly economic consideration would justify so as to keep ahead of government restrictions. This factor is not as directly significant in more developed countries, although it is found there also, often in subtle forms. For example, local manufacturers or governments find, on observing the successes of U.S. marketing of imports into the country, that local production is feasible, and warranted by previously unrecognized local demand.

(2) Protective Tariffs. Despite the international drive to reduce tariff levels the imposition of duties to protect new local ("infant") industries has been the key factor in many decisions to start U.S. manufacturing operations abroad. Tariff rates were often mentioned as reasons underlying a number of new investments in Europe and in other developed areas.

Company experience has confirmed the importance of choosing between building European factories within the boundaries of the Common Market or in one of the seven countries of the European Free Trade Area. This problem of choice has been frequently solved by building two new manufacturing plants. Other customs unions and trade areas, especially those in Latin America, are beginning to present similar problems of location, but so far they are less evident in company experience; national tariff walls remain more important than regional trade policies.

(3) Import and Exchange Controls. The power to exclude or to limit imports of specific items is one of the common devices used to foster local manufacturing, and such restrictions thus serve as incentives to invest. On the other hand, companies have now had sufficient experience with shortages of needed imported materials attributable to exchange controls, so that the presence of import restrictions frequently not only deters imports but local production as well.

The experience of a U.S. company that has Brazilian operations may serve as an example: In the early 1950s the company found that it had a huge amount of receivables in local currency on hand that had been derived from the importation of U.S. materials by its local plant, and for which the government would not supply foreign exchange. As a result, the parent company took a 50 percent interest in the local plant in which it had previously held only a small equity and with which it had a licensing agreement. It continued to supply raw materials for the plant despite the fact that it was not allowed to convert its local currency revenues into dollars. Subsequently when it appeared that another company was to build a local raw materials plant which the government would protect by cutting off imports of these materials from the United States, the company decided to set up a raw materials factory, again utilizing substantial blocked funds. The cost of local products in this case appeared to be higher than that of imports but, given the foreign exchange situation, the company's only alternative to local manufacture would have been to go out of business in Brazil.

Another pertinent experience is that of a company that had been supplying virtually all of the Mexican market with a certain type of equipment when the Mexican government, under its generally admired program of industrialization, suddenly terminated further importation on the grounds that local requirements could be met out of induced local production. This assumption was at best premature, as indicated in the U.S. company's records of sharply increased sales to Mexican border areas that can only be explained as indirect exports to Mexico. But one of the critical factors in the complicated and still continuing negotiations to establish Mexican production of this type of equipment within the industrial program was the lack of a local supply of metal of adequate quality, and hence the need for assurance of import permits for this type of metal. It must be presumed that this difficulty will in turn lead to the construction of metal works capable of producing the required raw materials.

Among financial restrictions, the ones most often cited by companies as a cause of concern are those limiting the remittance of profits and, to a lesser extent, transfers of capital to the United States. Of similar importance are regulations affecting royalties and management fees, which are sometimes hard to distinguish from profit remittance, both in company thinking and in foreign-exchange-control practices. . . . However, mention should be made at this point of the restrictive effects of certain governmental practices on company finances. Many of the companies participating in this study had been badly burned by changes in governmental policies, new regulations having been imposed that prevented remittance of funds. Some stated explicitly that, because of such experience, they were not willing to invest in certain countries. Company comments often showed the importance—in the short run even the dominance—of the foreign-exchange situation in investment decisions for certain areas. Clearly, the prospects of remittance of profits and capital, and the hazards of inconvertibility, are major preoccupations of companies planning their foreign investments in countries whose records of currency fluctuations suggest doubts as to exchange stability.

Complementary to the foreign-exchange problem is that of the use of blocked funds. Many companies have used these funds to expand their operations or to go into new enterprises, not wishing to leave funds idle while their value deteriorated through inflation. In some countries, notably in Brazil, investment in fixed assets has become the usual response to U.S. companies to the formidable problems of transfer restrictions and inflation. On the other hand, since companies frequently reported reliance on profits generated in one country to finance new investments in others, as will be noted below, the typing up of money in some countries has sometimes limited new ventures elsewhere, and the blocking of funds in some countries has forced some U.S. companies to rely more heavily on capital from the United States for expansion elsewhere.

(4) Investment Incentives. The use of an assortment of devices to encourage companies to set up new factories is now widespread among the developing countries. Such investment incentives are less important in the developed countries, though even there they are fairly common, especially in countries making deliberate efforts to help depressed areas, e.g., Northern Ireland and Southern Italy. Among the incentives commonly offered are tax reductions (e.g., exemptions from income taxes, for a given period), financial support in the form of loans at low interest rates, plant facilities built to order in preconstructed industrial parks, and help in recruiting and training labor.

(5) Fiscal Policies and Inflation. Most companies have found that they can operate profitably under inflationary conditions, even when they are as extreme as those experienced in Brazil in recent years. But the problems of keeping prices in line with costs, of managing assets and liabilities, and of avoiding losses when currencies are depreciated are so troublesome that a history of inflation in a country deters many investors.

(6) Government Interference and Political Conditions. Expropriation was the most important reported risk of this type. However, this risk was not considered great in most companies for most countries. More common is the risk of excessive government in management, often closely related to political conditions. Government interference is encountered in all functions of management, including labor relations, pricing, and financing. Some countries have become known for subjecting management to constant harassment while others have reputations for leaving business relatively free from interference. These images figure significantly in investment decisions.

(7) Legal Considerations. Laws regulating the registration of companies, right of establishment, and privilege of doing business vary considerably among countries. The benefits realized by U.S. shipping companies operating under foreign flags provide a clear-cut example of the type of tax and other advantages that may be gained by operating through a foreign affiliate. Another group of laws, concerning product specifications, and even origin of goods sold, also favors production in the country where the final sale will be made.

Foreign Economic Factors

The interplay of various economic factors—costs, market prospects, state of competition—that are related to each other, and that can be compared to similar factors in different countries, bears on investment decisions because it affects both the competitive urgency and the commercial feasibility or attractivenss of production abroad.

(1) Costs. The combined effects of the costs of labor, materials, machinery, power, and of "overhead" on costs of manufacturing vary tremendously around the world. As the NICB's earlier study, *Costs and Competition*, has shown, unit production costs are generally higher abroad than they are in the United States, but the cost pattern varies greatly according to industry, geographic region, and type of cost. In this study, the basic costs of production alone were rarely mentioned, in questionnaire responses or in interviews, as the determining consideration in investment decisions. . . . A number of companies reported that in many of the less-developed countries factories have been set up despite much higher production costs, and are making good profits behind protective barriers of prohibitive tariffs or of import restrictions. In other cases, chiefly in Europe, lower costs fostered profitable investments in countries where exports from the United States were not competitive with locally made goods.

In Latin America, for example, local production costs were more often than not reported to be unfavorable to local production, in contrast to Europe where local costs, as affected by local policy, often favor local production. But a high level of restrictions frequently offsets cost disadvantage, making local production necessary where costs are unfavorable. In Latin America restrictions have typically been a major consideration in the decisions to manufacture there despite higher costs, while in Europe the level of restrictions—an important investment-forcing factor in the first decade after World War II—has in recent years become relatively less important than the other considerations.

Some of this intricacy is in the interplay of cost considerations with other local conditions, for example, in the case of one company that had a strong and relatively unchallenged position in the U.S. market until the early 1950s when European producers of its machinery specialty began to enter the market. This company felt the need for expanded production that would reduce the fixed-cost burden (for research and development, administration and so forth) on units produced in order to survive in the United States and, to achieve this, it initiated an export expansion program. At the same time it found that the Europeans had a price advantage based on lower costs abroad. Thus it was forced to establish production abroad so as to be able to serve some foreign markets.

(2) Taxes. Corporate taxes as a cost element affect the profitability of investments, and most companies indicate that they are taken into consideration when there is a choice between two or more alternative foreign sites. Given fiscal efforts to stimulate investment in particular regions within a country, tax considerations may be even more important in determining the location of facilities within a country. In this study, the evidence surprisingly indicated that tax differentials between the United States and foreign countries actually have little to do with U.S. company decisions to produce in foreign rather than in U.S. facilities. These decisions are made primarily on the basis of factors other than cost, and even among cost factors, taxes are usually not the controlling ones.

Parenthetically it should be noted, however, that although tax differentials do not currently appear to be important in company decisions to produce abroad, these differences are potentially important influences in the international movement of factors of production and appear likely to become more so as the continuing movement of factors increases the relative importance of foreign production compared with exports. Discriminatory tax policy can already be observed as the means chosen with increasing frequency to achieve what a given government considers to be an effective balance between resident and nonresident control of production, and between local and foreign employment of locally available capital. Hence the negotiation of adequate reciprocal tax agreements covering foreign production is an important and growing problem of diplomacy. Given the rapid growth of international production, such agreements are conceivably destined to become (perhaps soon) more far-reaching than tariff arrangements.

(3) Market Conditions. The familiar condition required for investment, foreign or domestic, in given production facilities is the expansion of product demand to a level where, in the context of cost considerations as conditioned by local government policies, economic production becomes feasible. The *prospective* level of demand and its rate of *growth* then ordinarily become the key factors in a company's decisions to invest abroad. The level and growth of demand depend on a country's economic development; investment depends on the investor's judgment of the demand (present and potential) and the success of investment depends on the correctness of this judgment. The investor, however intricate his supporting calculations . . . acts basically on his estimate of favorable market potential.

In some cases a secondary but related factor appears: demand in a foreign market may call for a somewhat modified version of a U.S. product adapted to local needs. This circumstance provides a further incentive to set up local production. For example, experience of a company that makes "sophisticated" machinery appropriate for U.S. production fits in this category. This company found that similar but simpler equipment would be more suitable in certain less-developed markets, and cost studies indicated that tooling up for the manufacture of this simpler equipment in the company's U.S. facilities would be unprofitable. But because over-all costs of this production are lower abroad, the company has found it feasible to set up new foreign units to manufacture the product for export to the less-developed areas.

There is no simple formula for determining at what point demand reaches a level that justifies local production. However, when the processes of company investment decisions are studied the familiar historic pattern emerges—a fairly steady progression corresponding to a country's economic growth, during which one product after another moves into the range of reasonably economic local production. At an early stage simple consumer items like textiles can be profitably produced locally, while complex, limited demand items like automatic control machinery come into range toward the end of the industrialization process.

(4) Competition. Competition from local or other foreign producers is often the decisive factor in investment decisions. The competitive threat becomes particularly acute when, in a developing country, it is coupled with the threat of

selective government action to support a limited amount of local production. Left to itself, a firm might defer plans to set up a factory, but when faced with the prospect that a competitor may obtain a favored, or even an exclusive status as a local producer, many firms have felt impelled to hasten their own investments to protect their market positions. For example, a company that makes a variety of industrial products had a good export business after World War II. However, in the late 1940s, the company began to realize that its customers were looking for local sources of supply, particularly its Latin American customers who were prompted by chronic shortages of foreign exchange and their governments' resultant policies of minimizing imports. It was obvious that the company would either have to start local production or to abandon the market. The company responded initially with a licensing operation in Brazil, and has progressively intensified local operations, ultimately establishing a controlling position there and in other countries.

Commonly the companies mentioned—often emphasized—that they expect to obtain important but hard-to-quantify advantages in their competitive position by producing locally in a foreign market—a broader basis for research and development, a close-by observation point for changes in demand and other developments.

Company Factors

A company's examination of investment questions is normally occasioned by basic developments—environmental factors within the foreign markets of the sort described above—but the nature of the company's response is determined by a variety of factors within the firm. Companies differ not only in economic characteristics—their size, stage of growth, pattern of organization, technology—but also in their personalities, their management objectives, their modes of operation. When similar problems are discussed with a number of companies, the individuality of responses is impressive. Investment decisions are affected by the nature of the company's industry and its products, its status and capabilities, its reactions to international conditions, and by its state of mind at the given moment, in short, by an intricate combination of economic and human motives.

The nature of a company's product affects the extent of its international interests. Most manufacturers start to produce abroad only after they have established a market position through exports. Others make products that are less suitable for export trade due to their various bulk-weight-value-perishability-complexity characteristics.

For example, while steel products and textiles have in the past had at least a modest export volume, their production abroad has typically been dominated by local private or government capital. In certain other fields like chemicals and electronics, production abroad has been dominated by U.S. companies along with a few European firms. No clear-cut pattern is demonstrable here, but in general it appears that, other things being equal, the more advanced the technological developments in a line of production, the greater the probability that a firm will undertake overseas production. This bears out the logical conclusion that American competence will be accepted and will succeed in competition with local industry where it can call upon technical developments or skills not available locally. Superior organizational ability arising from greater experience with diversified and coordinated operations in large markets is in itself a significant example of such skills.

Industry characteristics also affect the type of operations, and thus the extent of investments, and the choice that companies make between wholly owned subsidiaries, joint ventures, and licensing agreements. The complexity of the technology involved, questions of pricing of the U.S. and the foreign operations, and the necessity of tightly coordinated marketing management are typically important considerations in determining what type of operation is effective for a particular industry.

Resources Available for International Operations

Beyond industry or product characteristics, what a company does in the international area depends largely on the *state of its development* and on its own *resources*. The decisions of a company are inevitably dominated by consideration of its activities in its main areas of operation. Thus the great majority of U.S. companies are only potentially global enterprises because full international operations are not yet essential to their activities. Most are still essentially U.S. businesses, their international investments being adjuncts of varying degrees of importance. A company's position in the U.S. market has therefore much to do with the extent of the company's interest in foreign markets, and with the resources it employs in serving them. For example, a U.S. company has recently been giving priority to its international operations because, in its opinion, U.S. opportunities are relatively limited after several decades of intensive development, and overseas markets are now more promising. On the other hand, a quite new company that has had spectacular growth in the United States in a new industry is anxious to develop its foreign sales, but has to throw so much of its resources into the domestic market that it has turned its foreign business over to another company, making only limited overseas investments itself. Another company exemplifies the growing intra-corporate rivalry between foreign and domestic divisions observed when companies find that their foreign operations account for a rising share of their market and therefore of their total revenues and profits. A growing number of companies have approached or passed this point in recent years.

The financial resources at the command of a company influence its decisions on foreign activity. Most executives interviewed thought that they would not encounter any difficulty in raising the capital needed for a foreign investment which they considered worthwhile. A few, however, indicated that their capital requirements at home definitely limited their activities abroad. It should be emphasized here that this study covered primarily large, well-financed companies. Among smaller firms, financial limitations are a greater constraint on the extent of foreign investment, and are one of the major reasons why many of these firms rely on licensing. Another form of financial constraint is the practice of some companies to start their foreign operations off with a modest "seed" investment and then to expand them, mostly with profits made overseas. There was only occasional evidence of this practice being followed by the firms in our survey, since most of them were heavily committed to international operations. It is reported that experimental investment-seeding is the usual practice of companies less deeply committed to international business.

The availability of people who have the skills needed to run an international business, both in the home office and abroad, is generally considered an essential requirement for expansion of international investments. A few firms are known to have expanded very rapidly abroad, relying on men recruited quickly in the U.S. job market or hired at the foreign location. Their experiences have shown that this is not a particularly successful method, and most companies think it wise to expand at a pace consistent with orderly recruiting and training of management personnel, and with evolution of international managerial skills. Thus new investments are only undertaken as the management organization is prepared to handle them. This frequently expressed point was emphasized by an executive who observed that the availability of executives with the know-how necessary for newly proposed investment projects was a critical check point in the investment analysis process. In his company, human resources are much more scarce than capital, which can be obtained in a variety of ways. If a newly proposed project is likely to call for the work of a large number of highly specialized people who are already occupied elsewhere, this circumstance might be a major deterrent. As the executive put it, profit is a return on "qualified people."

This observation underscores the important general impression gained in discussing foreign investment activities with businessmen, that "capital export" is in reality a misleading term for the process through which the technique of producing efficiently and responsively for a large, developed, and dynamic market at home is transferred from its original environment in the United States to markets now reaching the level of development to which such experience and skill are fully relevant and perhaps indispensable. The process might well be compared to the domestic expansion of a New York company to a less developed state.

Reactions to International Conditions

One observer summarized the context of investment decisions as follows: "The components of the company system coming from within and the environmental factors coming from outside converge on management in the formulation of international investment decisions. At this convergence the character of the management becomes yet another variable. Executives naturally consider the possibilities through objective analysis, but they inevitably inject subjective opinion and feeling. Some key executives have been aggressively favoring international operations, some have been clearly antagonistic or fearful when confronted by international problems, and most fall somewhere between these extremes."

These attitudes are manifest in a wide range of basic operating policies, governing the extent and form of the international activities of companies. A few firms throw their full energies into developing their international operations, and a steady flow of new investment into overseas plants becomes an established pattern.

In a larger group of companies management, though generally committed to building internationally, has mixed feelings about foreign activities. Some of their executives are anxious to develop activities abroad, some are in principle reluctant to do so, and still others, applying reasonably objective standards, conclude that operations in the United States have greater potential than investments abroad and that therefore foreign investment should get lower priority. In this group of companies each new foreign investment proposal must be argued through a sequence of reviewers offering substantial opposition, and any significant—especially political—change in the environment is likely to prejudice a favorable conclusion.

The policy adopted by a third group of companies is to enter into international operations, but only to a very limited extent. For example, one company reported having made a few small "seed" investments through which it expects to gradually acquire a knowledge of international business that can be used for expanded activities at a later stage. Another firm has been satisfied for some time to earn, with minimum effort, a respectable profit from small minority investments in licensees. As these cases suggest, most companies in this category seem to have restricted their investments according to a well-reasoned plan rather than because they have a negative attitude towards overseas business.

Beyond these general views of international activity, a broad range of reactions to specific environmental situations was found. Within the guidelines set by basic policies, the handling of specific investment opportunities is subject to the reactions of management to the immediate environmental situation. Many types and shadings of attitudes affect decisions at this stage, but the striking feature observed is the contrast between the negative "withdrawal" attitude and the positive "make-the-best-of-it" attitude toward investment in areas that have had troubled conditions in recent years (e.g., Latin America). For example, the financial executive of a company that had had considerable difficulty in Brazil said that had they known in the beginning what they know now, they would not have committed themselves to investment there. Once they had become involved and the money had been invested, they had no choice but to support the Brazilian operations. They still hoped that the situation would stabilize itself. However, the company indicated that it does not, at present, plan to send any additional funds into Latin America, though it is making new investments in other parts of the world; future development of operations in Latin America would depend on earnings generated there.

Those who do not withdraw in this manner are not impervious to adverse developments. They may defer, or decide against, some investments when conditions become too unfavorable, but there is no sweeping adverse reaction. Even in the more troubled Latin American countries, companies have developed practical, and occasionally ingenious, programs to cope with inflation and instability. Many reported continuing profitability, and a few stated that they were willing to invest new dollar funds. Companies typically accept adversities abroad as an inevitable part of the international environment and persist in a long-term program of development, shifting emphasis somewhat from one country to another in response to changing conditions, but in the main going ahead on all fronts, making the best of prevailing conditions.

The attitudes of managements toward international conditions evolve over time so that the response to a given set of investment circumstances is likely to be quite different at different periods. While the course of this evolution varies considerably among companies, one pattern observed with some frequency can be noted.

Executives looking back on early foreign operations recall the air of optimism and enthusiasm surrounding their companies' first producing ventures. The company may have been forced to produce locally by some of the government measures described above, but this may have been mitigated by special investment incentives offered, and by encouragement from various local associates. In the first phase of operations unexpected difficulties were likely to crop up, and would be resolved on an ad hoc basis, but for the moment optimism and assurance prevailed. In this early phase a policy for international business had not yet been formulated, at least not one well thought through. The company had simply been responding to immediate opportunities.

The early period passed quickly, and through a combination of experiences and commitments, management acquired a different view of international business. Numerous problems appeared, some small, some large, but problems were always present. Some of the executives frankly regretted that they had started inter-national operations, and decided not to go any further, at least not in troubled areas like Southeast Asia or Latin America. Others, more convinced of the long-run opportunities, or perhaps by nature more adventurous, kept moving ahead, but with increasing alertness to risks. Some, experiencing even better results than had been anticipated, proceeded at an accelerated pace, having greater confidence in future success because of the experience they had acquired.

At this point the extent of a company's commitment to international investment becomes an important variable affecting new investments. Among the factors favoring new investments are the funds generated by existing investments. Under some circumstances, tax benefits can be obtained by keeping these funds overseas; this provides an incentive to find new ventures abroad in which retained earnings can be invested. If funds are tied up by exchange controls, there is a compelling drive to use them in some new form of local investment. In addition, the protection of the existing commitment may call for further efforts, as was the case of the company cited earlier which, having set up a plant in Brazil, felt impelled to invest in another plant to make raw materials that its original plant needed, but which could not be reliably supplied as imports under the existing foreign exchange regulations. Finally, the creation of some form of international managerial unit within the company almost invariably sets in motion a dynamic force for further expansion. While an international manager may be disillusioned and beset with problems, he usually favors still greater investments.

Thus, as experienced is gained, the international program may be slowed down somewhat by problems and growing disenchantment but its commitments, and the men involved in managing it, generate a momentum which usually carries it forward. This persistence is notably demonstrated by the tenacity with which companies hold on to unduly difficult operations and even to some that are losing money—cases in which a decision to cut one's losses and quit would apparently be well justified.

A late stage of maturity can be distinguished, when the stresses and strains have worked themselves out for the most part and when a fairly stable and sophisticated pattern of policies and management actions has emerged. During the maturing processes, actions may be mainly reactions to current conditions, with gradual disappearance of the early optimism. At the level of full maturity (which only a few U.S. companies have reached), management has become so well conditioned to the problems of foreign production and has evolved such a clear long-range concept of its activities, that individual problems have little impact on its plans. Each difficulty is dealt with as it arises, without altering the main course of a company action. Investment decisions are made within a systematic review pattern, established in a relatively objective manner, and are little influenced by currently acute problems. An example is provided by the attitude of a company that has had international operations for many years and makes a steady stream of new undertakings and expansions part of its general market-penetration program. The only significant area outside the scope of its program is the Far East (though it is active in the Philippines) where it is deterred by cutthroat competition among the foreign companies established there. In keeping with the long view of many experienced companies, and sharply in contrast to the anxious, bearish attitude of newer companies, is this company's generally confident attitude towards Brazil.

The Dominance of Marketing Strategy

There is a striking diversity among the motivations of the investment decisions reviewed. The environmental factors and the company situation introduce so many variables that every decision appears unique, and it is extremely difficult to find a common pattern of investment decision. In a private market economy, the basic and crucial process of allocating resources consists of the varied investment decisions of individual managements, not of estimates of production possibilities made by a central authority trying to attain politico-economic goals.

The various managements are primarily moved, of course, by their responsibility to improve earnings. But their decision must accommodate the various—often conflicting—elements of finance, production, and marketing. This study showed that among these, *marketing strategy* was clearly the dominant element in investment decisions. This fact bears directly on the characteristic view of businessmen that normally investment, even where it appears as new or expansionary, is necessary to maintain competitiveness, and is made to strengthen the continued earning ability of the enterprise as a whole, not just to produce additional profits. Similarly, it accounts for the view that growth is organic, not incremental, and can be arrested only at the cost of viability.

In the great majority of cases, firms that invest abroad view their foreign production facilities as an essential element in maintaining, building, or fortifying the company's position in the foreign market. The situation of one company interviewed, while perhaps representing an extreme, is indicative of the preoccupation of managements with marketing strategy. This company's European operations have, for several years, been operating at losses incurred while trying to introduce new products to some markets and to protect their competitive position in others. Subsidiaries in Brazil and Mexico also encountered financial problems as they attempted to build the company's market position there. While there have been scattered profits, the company's overseas investment can be judged successful only in terms of its contribution to the earning potential of the cumulative investment, not in terms of rates of return on new commitments of funds. On this basis, the company continues investment support of its foreign operations.

A company's marketing position may require investment support for various reasons. Most prominent are instances of foreign governments' blocking further imports. Local production then becomes the only means of remaining in the market. In other cases, local production may be required to meet competitors' prices. Local production of raw materials or components may also be undertaken to assure a reliably regular rate of factory output and better service to the market; or it may facilitate the manufacture of goods adapted to local tastes. Sometimes the establishment of a local plant is helpful or necessary to get import licenses for other company products, or to strengthen the company's general marketing position, so that imports from the United States are increased. One company, whose operations fit a recurrent pattern, became a major exporter of equipment, including an important volume of parts. Under pressures of local tariffs and lower local costs, it moved steadily into foreign production and these operations have been a prerequisite for the admittance of parts from the United States. In this, as in many cases, the expansion of its U.S. exports has been directly contingent upon increases in the company's investment abroad. Typically, companies do not make investment decisions specifically to increase exports, but rather to increase sales. Nonetheless, companies reported with considerable regularity that a growth in exports accompanied investment growth and companies showed a distinct awareness of the fact that new producing ventures abroad are the occasion for extended sales efforts for othe products manufactured in the United States.

Marketing strategy was found to be not only the overriding consideration in company decisions to undertake production abroad, but often was the controlling factor in determining the form of investments. For example, many companies have found that their joint-venture partners or licensees had comparatively ineffective sales organizations; consequently the U.S. companies increased their equity in the foreign enterprises so as to gain control of marketing. An instance of such an experience is the case of a company whose organization is currently in a transitional stage, moving away from its piecemeal licensing operations and toward fully controlled international operations. It recently acquired a major portion of its licensees in the United Kingdom, specifically for the purpose of establishing effective control over the local marketing program. At the same time it shouldered greater responsibility for European sales through a sales subsidiary directly controlled by the U.S. producer. The state of development of the foreign operations is the critical factor in deciding at what point marketing strategy and the company position make investing for control purposes imperative. In some cases a company, recognizing that it lacks the capacity to handle its foreign sales efficiently, turns to a well-established local organization through which greater volume can be achieved than is within the U.S. company's own current capabilities.

All of these considerations influencing investment decisions add up to a common, perhaps universal, approach. A company wants above all to be sure that its products are present in the foreign market and that a competent sales organization promotes them there. It is concerned, not just with the immediate profit from a given product in a given market but, most importantly, with consolidating an effective earning position, in accordance with its evaluation of its capacities. Obviously definite limits must be placed on costs to be carried and risks to be taken as part of this marketing strategy but within these limits marketing considerations govern.

The probing of company motivation produced little to suggest that a differential profit rate is sufficient to induce a company to establish producing facilities abroad, and even less to suggest that a committed company would, because of a decline or the disappearance of this differential, discontinue the investment support required for the maintenance of its market position. Even a continuing decline in total earnings in a market may provoke rather than discourage further investment depending on the company's opinion of what is required to safeguard its longer-range financial intersts.

The Foreign Investment Decision-Making Process

W. Dickerson Hogue

Profit-seeking firms making investments outside their home countries can be broken down by their dominant reasons for going abroad, as is the following chart.

Chart I. Foreign Investors Seeking—

I   *Raw materials*
II   *Production efficiency*
III   *Knowledge*
IV   *Markets*
      a.   *Firms nearing marginal-return points at home*
      b.   *Firms well below marginal-return points at home*

The reason for classifying foreign investors in this way is that these groups use different criteria to judge the attractiveness of foreign investment opportunities. More exactly, the weights put on various criteria change from one group to another. Each of these investors wants the highest obtainable rate of return at the lowest possible risk. However, factors making for high return and low risk vary from one group to another.

Who are these investors?

The raw material seekers include oil producers, miners, lumbermen and the owners of plantations. Until recently, this group accounted for the majority of American investment abroad. Recently, it has taken second place, behind the market seekers.

The production-efficiency seekers look for lower costs of production, frequently through lower labor costs but sometimes through lower costs of power or some other factor. Take, for example, a Philco investment in a Taiwanese plant using low-cost labor to assemble tuners for tv sets; or an aluminum company going to British Columbia to find low-cost power for the refinement of bauxite; or a U.S. jewelry-store chain setting up a diamond-cutting operation in Antwerp.

The small group of knowledge seekers includes such projects as a McGraw-Hill operation in Europe digging out news of European technical developments. Frequently, the search for knowledge is combined with a search for production

---

Reprinted by permission of W. D. Hogue.

411

efficiency, as seems true of the European research laboratories set up by Battelle Institute, Arthur D. Little and others. Or the search for knowledge may combine with a search for markets, as when a British advertising agency sets up shop on Madison Avenue.

The market seekers currently account for most new investment abroad by U.S. companies. Of the two subsets shown in the chart, "a" invests many more dollars than "b" does. "A" includes all the companies which must necessarily look for expansion either to new foreign markets for their present products or to new products in present markets. "B" is made up of companies whose best opportunities for expansion lie in expanding their present products in their home market—but who, for one exceptional reason or another, find it attractive to make one or two special investments abroad.

Because their circumstances differ, these groups differ in the criteria they find particularly important in maximizing their chances of gain or in minimizing their risks of loss.

Let us look at one key difference between them—where their product is sold and, hence, where the profit is being made or is potentially to be made.

Market seekers sell, and make their profits, in the host country. The other groups sell, and make most of their profits, outside of the host country. Because of this difference, the market seeker must be more concerned with the strength of the local economy than other groups need to be. A weak local economy suggests the likelihood of exchange controls and devaluation—both of which affect the market seeker more than other investors. Also, the market seeker needs to estimate carefully the future size and strength of the local market and the likelihood of price control—none of which matters importantly to the other groups.

On the other hand, seekers of raw materials or production efficiency must concern themselves more with factors determining unit cost of production, and transportation cost, than do the market seekers. Products of the first two groups sell on world markets in competition with similar goods from all sources. Market seekers sell inside the host country, which ordinarily protects them with tariffs or quotas.

Another great concern of the first two groups is being shut off from markets by war or political action—which is at most a minor concern of the other groups. When the U.S. imposes quotas on imports of foreign oil, or raises tariffs on watches made in Switzerland by U.S. companies, it is raw material seekers or production efficiency seekers who are hurt.

The raw material seeker is more likely to be subjected to unreasonable labor demands, or to have his investment nationalized, than are the other groups. Raw material seekers produce unbranded commodities for the world market and they are pinned to their physical locations—you can't move a copper mine or oil well or banana plantation. In contrast, the production efficiency investors, for example, tend to supply specific captive markets, and their operations are comparatively portable. The difference makes the raw material operations much more attractive targets for nationalization-minded governments and xenophobic labor leaders. For this reason, a raw-material-seeking investor will be more concerned about future political stability in the host country than will other potential investors.

The knowledge seeker is minor in terms of total dollars invested abroad, but has some interesting special circumstances which influence his choice of where to invest. He is not warmly welcomed by foreign governments, because he imports little foreign exchange, contributes little to the growth of the local economy and employs few low-skilled local voters. At the same time he does employ the scarce high-skilled people the country has spent so much to educate, and he does want to use some of the country's scarce foreign exchange. The knowledge seekers must look for countries with economies strong enough to permit the government to be tolerant. From my observation, it seems that to have sufficient tolerance the government must also be one with a strong cosmopolitan tradition.

I have not attempted to list even the major differences in the circumstances of these groups and the consequent differences in the criteria they weigh heavily in looking at foreign investment possibilities. I have sought merely to show that there *are* important differences in circumstances, with important consequent differences in investment criteria.

Another point I would like to make concerns the group I know best—the market seekers interested in new foreign markets for their present products and, in general, at one point or another on the road to becoming truly global operations. In these companies, foreign investment possibilities are *not* judged in terms of "Is this potential project attractive or not?" The appropriate question is, rather, "Where should this project rank on our priority list of attractive possibilities?"

One of these companies has at any moment hundreds or even thousands of possible projects for expansion at home and abroad. But it has only limited amounts of money and suitable management men (ordinarily, the market seekers run out of men long before they run out of money) available for expansion projects. How should limited resources be used to obtain best results?

Answers start with the particular capabilities a company can devote to expansion. Suppose a company has for years had an enormous U.S. business in canned soups and has recently acquired a small U.S. candy company. In this position, it is reasonable to assume the company would have very adequate capabilities to expand its canned soups abroad. It would have many proven managers with knowledge of how to produce, package and market soups and adjust the formulae, packaging and marketing to suit local tastes. At the same time it might have almost no capability to expand its candy business, either abroad or in the U.S. As a result, projects to expand the candy business abroad would be on the priority list, but would be very far down on the list.

Other basic criteria for "roughing out" a priority list—by "roughing out" I mean putting a small number of projects near the top for more careful examination, and deferring other projects for further consideration later—may be listed as follows:

Chart II. Basic Criteria for Establishing Rough Priority of Expansion Projects

1. Fit available company capability?
2. Size of profits after taxes?
  a. Short-term
  b. Medium-term
  c. Long-term
3. Profit per unit of scarce resource?
4. Future strength of host economy?
5. Future stability of host government?

On the basis of these criteria, projects for present markets compete with projects for new markets as shown in Chart III, and an over-all priority list emerges. As many as practical of the items near the top will be investigated carefully, and implemented if they stand up under careful investigation.

Chart III. Basic Types of Expansion Project

In Present Markets
Increase company capability—increase research, hire personnel, build plant, replace machinery, float bonds, etc.
Market present products more aggressively
Introduce/acquire new products

In New Markets
Market products sold in present markets
Market new products
Manufacture present/new products

Note that two of these basic criteria have broad significance. "Future strength of host economy" indicates likely size of several major risks in the marketing and financial areas—likelihoods of devaluation, rigorous exchange control, rapid inflation, price control and so on. "Future stability of host government" helps determine the size of some additional major risks. Exceptional labor troubles, nationalization, anti-foreign actions of many sorts—these are frequently associated with weak governments seeking to win popular support by belaboring foreign devils. If you can forecast that a certain country will very likely have a strong and growing economy and a reasonably stable government with strong popular support, a potential investor in that country really need not worry about much of anything other than the market for his own products.

In addition to the basic criteria, other criteria may become important during a particular time or in regard to a particular country, as shown in Chart IV.

Chart IV. Examples of Occasional, or Exceptional Major Investment Criteria

Threatened loss of export market
Completion of regional pattern
"Buffering" important markets
Home government pressure
Change in company's long-range strategy

The presence of one of these may promote a previously deferred project to the top of the priority list. Let me clarify the headings with illustrations.

Threatened Loss of Export Market. Here you have a large and profitable export market for your brand of widgets in less-developed Country A. One day it is announced that widgets will be manufactured for the first time in Country A by a competitor of yours. You will lose the market unless you, too, put up a local plant to make widgets.

Completion of Regional Pattern. You have flourishing subsidiaries in Guatemala, Honduras and Costa Rica, but are doing nothing in El Salvador or Nicaragua. Now all five countries are linked in a successful-looking common market. You are likely to raise the priorities, on your list, of projects to establish subsidiaries in El Salvador and Nicaragua.

"Buffering" Important Markets. You have a high and profitable percentage of the market for your type of product throughout the Arab world, except that you do not market in Egypt. A competitor starts to market in Egypt and you feel success there would encourage him to enter other countries in the area. Therefore you raise the priority of entering Egypt with your product.

Home Government Pressure. The U.S. government was concerned in 1949 to see the Japanese economy rebuilt, and asked you to give priority to establishing an operation there. (On the other hand, the U.S. government is currently asking you to reduce sharply the priority ranking for foreign investment projects in most developed countries.)

Change in Company's Long-Range Strategy. You are a large investor in Africa at the time the African nations are becoming independent. It seems to your top management that much too high a percentage of the company's assets is in Africa, and that the company should "shift its weight" to other less-developed countries. Your management has not previously had much interest in South America, but now it begins to give extra priority to South American projects, and to reduce the priorities of African projects.

These are only examples. There may also be patent and trademark considerations, competitive considerations of various sorts and other exceptional circumstances which modify a company's basic calculations of the desirability of a particular project.

In short, what I am saying is that most successful companies approach foreign investments in a rational way. They emphasize those aspects of an investment situation which specially favor or threaten the profits of their particular type of operation. Each foreign investment possibility competes in their eyes with every other investment possibility at home and abroad.

Catalyst for Europe

Christopher Layton

"Rather than be judged a rival, it ought to be considered an auxiliary all the more precious because it alone permits an increased amount of productive labour and useful enterprise to be set to work." Alexander Hamilton's remark on foreign investment in America, made in 1791, might well be quoted by Europeans today. For in a half-century which has seen the near-suicide of Europe, the old world, whose capital assisted the development of the new in the century after Hamilton's death, has been restored and helped towards a new prosperity by a rich return flow, first of American aid, then of American private capital, know-how and technology.

The emergence of America as the world's main supplier of capital has been swift and sudden. In the two postwar decades, American banks have taken over much of the role once played by London in the financing of world development; their lending abroad climbed to a peak of some \$12 billion[1] at the end of 1964. Above all, in the twenty years since 1946, American direct investment[2] abroad has grown sevenfold (to a total of \$44 billion) as American capital has built or brought oil wells, factories, banks and commercial establishments abroad.

A growing share of this American direct investment abroad now takes place in Europe. The process is not new. Even at the turn of the century, while Europeans with their cheap capital and well-developed capital markets were investing in shares and bonds in the United States, Americans, with their new technologies, were investing directly in Europe on a substantial scale. But in the last two decades the move to Europe has gathered speed. In the thirties and forties, Latin America had received the largest share of American direct investment capital. Compared to war-torn Europe, America's back-garden seemed relatively safe. It was both an important source of oil and other raw materials and a favored site for new factories

---

Reprinted from *Trans-Atlantic Investments, The Atlantic Papers,* published by the Atlantic Institute.

[1] Unless otherwise stated, statistics on pages 000–000 are from the U.S. Department of Commerce.

[2] Direct investment as opposed to portfolio investment is usually defined in terms of control. Legally, 51 percent foreign ownership should confer control. In practice, the amount of equity necessary for control depends upon the organization of the enterprise: 99 percent ownership may be too little, and 10 percent may be enough. The various agencies which collect on foreign investment attempt to use the criterion of control in distinguishing between direct and portfolio investment. The data on direct investment which follow should be viewed as approximations because of the obvious difficulties in drawing hard and fast lines between the two.

abroad. But in the fifties the horizon of many industrialists widened as the United States assumed the responsibility of world leadership. A growing number began to appreciate the possibilities of manufacturing abroad. American companies turned increasingly to Canada—near, rich, politically safe; by 1960, Americans owned 43 percent of the capital of Canadian industry and 54 percent of the mining and oil industries. Then, as Europe recovered, the investors began to perceive its potentialities and to realize that, politically, investment might well be less risky there than in Mexico or Argentina. The Marshall Plan Aid which put Europe on its feet was followed by a growing stream of private capital, mainly in the form of factories and plant. Table A shows these developments.

Value of United States Direct Investments Abroad by Main Regions
($ million)

	1950	1957	1962	1963	1964
OVER-ALL	11,788	25,394	37,225	40,645	44,343
Canada	3,579	8,769	12,133	13,016	13,820
Latin America	4,445	7,434	8,424	8,657	8,932
Europe	1,733	4,151	8,930	10,351	12,067
All Other	2,031	5,040	7,738	8,621	9,524

Table A.

It is possible to exaggerate or underestimate the American stake in Europe, depending on the figures used.

Table A gives the Department of Commerce valuation of investment assets abroad, based on figures from the U.S. parent companies of their interest in the "stock," cash surplus, and liabilities of the concern. It underestimates the total, for the figures are only based on companies in which U.S. firms or individuals hold more than a 25 percent interest. Also, valuations on fixed assets are frequently on the low side. But, unlike any other figures, these do have the virtue of comparability. They show us, for instance, that in 1964 U.S. direct investment assets in Western Europe ($12 billion), with its 250 million people, were still smaller than the $13.8 million direct investment assets in Canada, with its population of a mere 19 million.

More accurate assessments of the American stock of direct investment assets abroad have however been made in certain countries. In his useful study of foreign investment in France, Gervais[3] estimated it at some $1,700 million in 1962, (70

---

[3] Jacques Gervais, *La France face aux investissements étrangers,* Editions de l'Entreprise Moderne.

percent over the Department of Commerce figure). He based this figure on stock-exchange valuations. The French Ministry for Industry put total American investment assets in France at $2,500 million in 1965. If the Department of Commerce figures were as much of an underestimate for the rest of Western Europe, American direct investment assets in Western Europe would be nearer $20 billion than $12 billion.

The Bundesbank threw interesting light on the American share in the nominal capital of German public companies in a study published in West Germany in 1965[4]. It concluded that American ownership was about 5 percent though the share is even smaller if the many other enterprises, not quoted publicly, are included in the figures.

How does American direct investment in Europe compare with foreign investment in Europe by other countries? The West German study is a useful reminder of the dangers of identifying "foreign" investment in Eruope with "American" investment.

Two-thirds of the "foreign" investment in Germany is by other, mainly European, countries. When Germans talk of *"Uberfremdung,"* they may in fact be

The American Share in the Stock of Foreign Investment
(Percent)

	France 1962	West Germany 1964	Britain 1962
U.S.A.	45	34	72
Great Britain	12	10	–
Netherlands	11	17	2
Switzerland	5	16	7
Belgium	8	5	1
France	–	7	2
Sweden	1	3	1
Italy	5	included in "others"	1
West Germany	3	–	1
Canada	2	included in "others"	9
Others	8	8	4
Total	$5,000 million (net worth estimate)	$2,780 million (book value only)	$4,200 million (book value without oil and insurance)

Sources: Gervais (*France*), Bundesbank (*West Germany*), Board of Trade (*Britain*).

Table B.

[4] Monthly Bulletin (May 1965).

as much concerned with BP and Unilever as with Dupont and Ford. In France the direct investment assets of other foreign countries are roughly comparable to the American stake. Gervais put them at $2,000 million in 1962 compared to U.S. assets of $1,700 million. Two years later, the French Ministry of Industry put total foreign investment assets in France at $5,000 million, split equally between Americans and others. Only in Britain are American investors responsible for much more than half of foreign direct investment assets.

These figures of accumulated investment assets are interesting. But they are not much help in answering the main question the Europeans ask: Do Americans own a disproportionate share of European industry? After all, if it is hard to put a valuation on the accumulated assets of an American investor, it is even more difficult to guess at the value of total industrial assets in Europe.

But if we look at figures for *new* investment, rather than at the *stock*, we can obtain comparable figures for individual countries which give a meaningful indication of the U.S. share. The best figures to use are those for new investment in plant and equipment, where we can compare annual new investment in individual OECD countries with annual new investment by U.S. direct investors. The results are shown in Table C.

New Investment in Plant and Equipment: Percentage by American Direct Investors

	1963	1966[a]
Canada	36	41
Total Europe	4.9	5.5
Common Market	4.0	5.0
Belgium	3.5	8.0
France	3.2	3.9
West Germany	3.9	4.5
Italy	4.2	3.4
Netherlands	5.0	11.2
United Kingdom	7.1	9.8

[a] Company estimates.
See Appendix Table 3 for further details.
Sources: Department of Commerce, OECD.

Table C.

In fact, even Table C understates the contribution American direct investment makes to fixed capital formation in Europe. In particular, the figures still refer only to companies in which American direct investors have an interest of more than 25 percent. OECD's definition of new investment in plant and equipment includes investment in commercial fixtures. The proportions would look higher if a comparison were made for industry alone. It would not be far off the mark to say that, in 1964, American direct investors were repsonsible for between 5 and 6 percent of fixed capital formation in the industry of Western Europe.

This share is not spectacular, but it is growing fast. In 1950, according to one calculation, U.S. direct investors were responsible for only 2 percent of new investment in plant and equipment in Europe compared with 5.5 percent in 1965. By then, a quarter of total American direct investment assets abroad was in Europe, compared to 10 percent in 1950.

This growth was largely due to the massive increase in U.S. investment in the Common Market. In the first postwar years Britain attracted the lion's share of U.S. direct investment in Europe, thanks to its political stability and traditional ties with the United States. But as the Common Market took shape, a major change became evident. The most rapid growth of new direct investment took place on the continent.

This growth was fed, in particular, by new capital from the United States. American direct investment abroad is of course financed only in part by fresh capital from the United States. In 1957, in the last complete census by the Department of Commerce, 46 percent of the funds available to direct investment enterprises after payment of income to the parent companies consisted of depreciation and ploughed back profits. Funds raised accounted for another 24 percent. New U.S. capital supplied only 30 percent. The broad proportions have not changed greatly since. (See Table D.)

Sources of Finance for U.S. Direct Investments (1957)

	$ Million	Percent
Depreciation	1,616	21
New U.S. Funds	2,023	29
Funds Raised Abroad	1,718	24
Income Retained	1,758	24
Other	167	2
Income Paid Out	1,891	—
Total Available to Enterprises	7,292	100

Table D.

But in the Common Market the proportion of new capital from the United States has been much higher than for the world as a whole in the last five years. While the ploughing back of profits and the raising of local capital have continued to grow steadily in most parts of the world, the flow of new capital from America has switched to continental Europe.

Hence, by 1964, the Common Market was taking far the largest share of the *flow* of United States direct investment capital abroad (excluding ploughing back by subsidiaries)—$787 million compared to $207 million to Britain and $250 million to Canada (see Figure 1). . . .

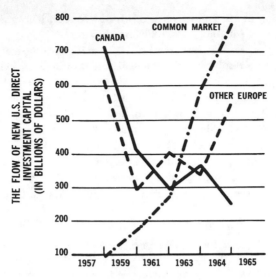

Figure 1

The main weight of this new American direct investment in Europe has been in manufacturing. In the world at large, America's interest in petroleum (32 percent of its direct investment in 1964) is almost as large as in manufacturing (38 percent). In Europe, industry has the main share (55 percent) (see Table E). Investment in manufacturing is also growing faster than that in other fields. In 1965, manufacturing accounted for 65 percent of plant equipment expenditures by direct investments in Europe. Europe will be taking nearly half of United States overseas direct investment in manufacturing plant and equipment (an expected $1.7 billion

U.S. Direct Investment Assets by Main Sectors and Regions (1964)

	Europe		Canada		Latin America		World	
	$ Mil.	Percent	$ Mil.	Percent	$ Mil.	Percent	$ Mil.	Percent
Mining and Smelting	56		1,671	12	1,098	12	3,564	8
Petroleum	3,086	25	3,228	24	3,142	35	14,350	32
Manufacturing	6,547	55	6,191	44	2,340	28	16,861	38
Trade	1,472	12	805	6	951	15	3,736	8
Others	907	8	1,925	14	1,400	11	5,831	14
Total	12,068	100	13,820	100	8,931	100	44,342	100

Table E.

out of $3.8 billion in 1965), or over a tenth of the total investment by American industry in plant and equipment at home and abroad.

It is this major shift in the strategy of American industry toward overseas manufacture which is responsible for the excitement in the last years over American direct investment. American opinion is even more worried than that of the Europeans by the fact that roughly a fifth of United States investment in manufacturing industry goes abroad, with the most advanced industries taking the lead. The American electrical industry spends 21.9 percent of its total investment in plant and equipment overseas, and chemical industry 24.6 percent, rubber 27.4 percent, and the transport equipment industry 29.5 percent; this last is over-whelmingly investment in the European motor industry. . . .

When one looks at particular industries, the United States stake in Europe really appears large. Thus, of the fourteen largest automobile companies in Europe, American companies (General Motors, Ford and Chrysler) are responsible for 30 percent of the turnover. In petroleum, U.S. owned companies had 25–30 percent of the market in Great Britain and in the Six in 1964. Of total expenditures on plant and equipment by American manufacturing firms in Europe in 1964, 74 percent was undertaken in the key growth industries—chemicals, transportation equipment, and electrical and non-electrical machinery. . . .

The commanding position of American firms in many of the newer industries is often due to the simple fact that they introduced them—perhaps as far back as the twenties and thirties. In photographic films, agricultural machinery, office-machinery, oil-refinery equipment, sewing machines, tires and razor-blades, American subsidiaries have led the way, as they have in certain highly specialized branches of chemicals, pharmaceuticals, and in particular antibiotics, oil-refining, toilet preparations and cosmetics. In some of these industries, strong competitive European-owned industries have subsequently grown up. In others, such as computers and carbon-black, they have not, and American firms still have a near-monopoly. In other words, direct American investment in Europe is concentrated in the growth industries where markets are expanding rapidly, profits are large, and American technology has often pioneered the way. The part played by the older industries, such as steel and textiles, is by contrast small. Table F shows the U.S. share in some of the newer industries in France, Britain, and Germany.

A surprisingly large proportion of the American direct investment in Western Europe is undertaken by large firms that have been established there for many years. Forty percent of American direct investment in France, West Germany, and Britain is accounted for by three firms (Esso, General Motors, Ford); and two-thirds of American direct investment in all Western Europe by twenty firms. During the past fifteen years, however, more and more of the other major companies have bought or built their way into Europe. By 1961, 460 of the 1,000 largest U.S. companies had a subsidiary or branch in Europe. By 1965, the figure had risen to 700 out of 1,000.

In the early sixties there were signs of a new trend. A growing number of

Indications of the U.S. Share in Certain Industries

France 1963 (Turnover—Percent)

Industry	Percent
Petroleum Refining	20
Razor Blades & Safety Razors	87
Cars	13
Tires	Over 30
Carbon Black	95
Refrigerators	25
Machine Tools	20
Semi-Conductors	25
Washing-Machines	27
Lifts & Elevators	30
Tractors & Agricultural Machinery	35
Telegraphic & Telephone Equipment	42
Electronic & Statistical Machines	43
(of Which Computers 75 Percent)	
Sewing-Machines	70
Electric Razors	60
Accounting Machines	75

Britain 1964 (Turnover—Percent)

Industry	Percent
Refined Petroleum Products	Over 40
Computers	Over 40
Cars	Over 50
Carbon Black	Over 75
Refrigerators	33-1/3–50
Pharmaceuticals	Over 32
Tractors & Agricultural Machinery	Over 40
Instruments	Over 15
Razor Blades & Safety Razors	Approx. 55

West Germany (Percent of Capital of Public Companies)

Industry	Total U.S.	Total Foreign
Petroleum	38	93
Machinery, Vehicles, Metal Products (of Which Cars† 40 Percent)	15	24
Food Industry	7	41
Chemicals, Rubber, etc.	3	15
Electrical, Optics, Toys, Musical (of Which Computers 84 Percent)	10	23

Sources: Ministry for Industry (*France*), Dunning and Industry Estimates (*Britain*), Bundesbank (*West Germany*)
† Turnover Industry Estimates.

Table F.

medium-sized firms began to catch the fashion for setting up in Europe. Thus, 10 percent of new manufacturing operations abroad by U.S. firms in the years 1961–64 were by firms with a sales volume of under $50 million per year. At the same time, while investment in chemicals and the traditional fields of petroleum, cars and machinery, continued to grow fast in Europe, certain other fields—e.g., the food industry, and such services as hotels and distribution—shared in the expansion.

According to *Libre-Service Actualités* (October 1965), foreign investors "control" almost one-fifth of the French food industry (9 percent of coffee, 11–13 percent of animal foodstuffs, 14 percent of biscuits, 50 percent of non-sweetened milk, and 75 percent of processed milk, soup, instant coffee and margarine). Some of these investments are long-established, and by European firms (Nestlé, Unilever), but a part reflects the new American interest in the last five years.

Direct investment in Europe, in other words, though still based on the great international corporations which have long been established on both sides of the Atlantic, has now become an accepted part of the operations of most large American corporations and many medium-sized companies as well. The number of American corporations with European interests therefore continues to grow.

What proportion of new American direct investment consists of new construction, or the creation of new enterprises, and how much is simply the take-over of existing European firms? Acquisitions certainly rose sharply in Europe between 1960 and 1964. In 1964, they were equivalent to almost a quarter of the total influx of new capital to Western Europe ($1,342 million), or about a seventh as much as was spent by direct investors on new plants and equipment in Western Europe.

Net Acquisitions by American Companies in Foreign Enterprises
($ million)

	1963	1964
Europe	140	318
World	176	263

Table G.

The acquisition of European companies, though significant, is thus seen to be by no means the major part of American direct investment activities.

This picture of the growth of American direct investment in Europe would not be complete without a glance at the reverse-flow European investment in America and elsewhere. Its size comes as something of a shock. American direct investment in Europe is matched by European investments in the United States, and elsewhere, which actually exceed inward investment. In his useful study of foreign investment in France, Gervais put French investments abroad at $8 billion in 1962, compared with $5 billion of foreign investments in France (a figure confirmed by the French Ministry for Industry in 1965). British investments abroad were put at some $10 billion in 1962 by the Board of Trade, compared to inward investment of a mere $6 million. Holland, Belgium, and Switzerland also have a positive balance; only the former defeated countries, Germany and Italy, are in the red.

Even in terms of the bilateral relationship between Europe and America, there is a remarkably even balance. American statistics, given in Table H, put long term European private investments in the United States at $17.7 million at the end of 1964, compared with American assets in Europe of $17.5 million. But, in the composition of the two figures, there is a vital difference that lies at the heart of the European debate. As at the turn of the century, the bulk of the European assets in America take the form of portfolio investments, a notable contrast with the direct American investments that have caused so much stir in Europe. Indeed, European holdings of American securities ($10.8 million at the end of 1964) far exceeded American holdings of European securities and bonds ($3.2 million). European direct investments in the United States, on the other hand, were worth a mere $5.8 million, compared to U.S. direct investments in Europe of $12.1 million. . . . While Europeans continue to salt away capital and savings in American corporations, American management has been bringing its ideas, techniques, and processes to Europe in the form of plant and factories. While European investors in the United States are often sleeping partners, the new American direct investors in Europe plan an active evident part in the industrial life of Europe.

The Investment Balance Between America and Western Europe

($ billion)

	Investments in Europe American		European Investments in the U.S.	
	1963	1964	1963	1964
Long Term	15.3	17.5	16.2	17.7
of Which Direct	10.4	12.1	5.5	5.8
Corporate Stocks	2.3	2.1	9.2	10.2
Bonds	0.8	0.8	0.5	0.6
Banking Claims and Other	1.8	2.5	1.0	1.1
U.S. Government Credits and Claims	7.0	7.4	−	−
Short-Term Assets	2.9	3.0	13.7	15.6
Total	25.2	27.9	29.9	33.3

Source: U.S. Department of Commerce.

Table H.

That part has been growing far more rapidly, too, placing a strain on America's balance of payments and bringing major changes in the structure of European industrial life. Thus, while the over-all figures show a remarkable balance between European and American investment across the Atlantic, the growth of American investment in Europe, its part in key new industries, and the element of control that direct investment brings make it a catalyst of controversy and change.

The Motives

Why has American business been taking this growing interest in Europe? In 1960, the McGraw-Hill Department of Economics asked a sample of American industrialists what was the principal consideration behind their decision to invest abroad. The answers were: opening new markets, 48 percent; profit differences, 20 percent; trade restrictions, 16 percent; acquiring supplies of raw materials, 13 percent; the competition, 10 percent; differences in labor costs, 6 percent; others, 3 percent.

The answers came in the same order when the question was asked again in 1963. And the "opening of new markets" was the overwhelming motive in the industries of principal concern to Europe (electrical and mechanical engineering, chemicals and transport equipment).

These answers provide a useful guide to the motives of the sixties. They are less satisfactory as an explanation of the movement to Europe in the early postwar years. In these years, the years of dollar shortage, the motives of American investors were often protective or defensive—the need to replace exports frustrated by import restrictions, the need to have a production base for certain products in European Governments were to be sympathetic to other exports of the same firm. "Trade restrictions," third on the list today, were of cardinal importance then. But, as the Common Market took shape, other more dynamic motives began to play a larger part. Europe after all was the world's most swiftly growing market, the one market outside America which would soon be sufficiently rich to buy on a large scale the kind of products America produced—high-income products for the consumer, from cars to washing-machines, and sophisticated machinery and plant. In many of these products the American market appeared to be nearing saturation; Europe, by contrast, was on the threshold of the age of affluence.

From 1950 to 1960, the gross national products of the Common Market nations were growing at a rate of about 5 percent per annum. The EFTA nations, with the exception of the United Kingdom, were not far behind. In contrast, the United States was dawdling along at about 3 percent per year. Europe's skilled labor force and management were capable of applying American techniques, yet costs per unit of labor were little more than a third as high. As the Common Market took shape, a new dramatic advantage would be added. For the first time outside America, the large-scale techniques developed in the United States—in marketing as well as in production—could be applied on a comparable continental scale.

During the fifties, high profit margins and interest rates in Europe provided

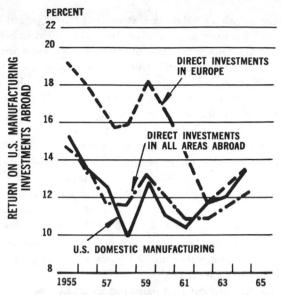

PERCENT

DIRECT INVESTMENTS
IN EUROPE

DIRECT INVESTMENTS
IN ALL AREAS ABROAD

RETURN ON U.S. MANUFACTURING INVESTMENTS ABROAD

U.S. DOMESTIC MANUFACTURING

1955 57 59 61 63 65

Note: Return on domestic manufacturing represents net income applied to net worth at the start of the year (First National City Bank of N. Y.). Return on direct manufacturing investments abroad and in Europe represents the U.S. share of net earnings for the year applied to book value of these investments at the beginning of the year.

Source: Department of Commerce.

Figure 2

classic evidence of these opportunities and of an unsatisfied European demand for capital. As Figure 2 shows, return on capital for American direct investors was substantially higher in Europe than at home. But in the last five years a major change has taken place. The boomtime profits in Europe now seem over, while America's own dramatic boom is producing record profits at home; thus, the gap between profitability in Europe and America has virtually closed. Yet the desire to invest in Europe has not weakened, for now the pull of extraordinary profits has been replaced by the desire simply to find a rewarding outlet for the large cash flow companies have enjoyed during the long American boom. Further, a lower rate of profit today has as much pull as the higher rate of the fifties because of the substantially lower risk element. The fifties were characterized by inconvertibility, discrimination, manifold trade restrictions, exchange controls, and so forth. It takes the promise of large profits to overcome the reluctance of private investors under such conditions. Today, there is convertibility among the major Western currencies, most restrictions and controls have been dismantled, and several European currencies are considered if anything harder than the dollar. So, investment in Europe remains attractive to American direct investors, even if it is no longer markedly more profitable than investment at home.

High profits were possible not only in new industries, where American firms could introduce new techniques to the emerging European market and combine them with lower European labor costs, but also in some of the "older" sectors of the European economy where habits and structures have changed little in recent years, and investment has been negligible. In the French food industry and hotels, for instance, big profits could obviously be made by the enterprising newcomer prepared to invest in new equipment, introduce new management techniques, cut profit margins, and increase his turnover. To take one example, biscuit manufacture does not seem on the surface to bring in a new technology, but sizeable profits are to be made through the application of new techniques in production, management, packaging, and distribution.

Changes in the behavior of American corporations in the past decade have also encouraged the move into Europe. Increasingly swift communications are making international business easier and increasingly normal for large and medium corporations. Slowly, the organization of American corporations is changing to make international operations an integral part of their business instead of a haphazard appendage of the domestic firm. Political divisions and national prejudices have a diminishing importance in management calculations. Increasingly, direct export and local manufacture mix inextricably in the international strategy of the large or medium-size concern.

Large companies have found that manufacture in Europe, designed at first to replace direct exports, has carried an even larger load of new exports on its back. . . . This is particularly true of industries like chemicals, with a wide range of interrelated products. Plants in Europe import American semi-finished products, sophisticate them, and then sell a range which includes both imported and European-manufactured products. In other words, it pays to manufacture in Europe as a bridgehead to penetrate the market.

In the engineering industries, in particular, where a very wide range of medium-sized American producers has filtered into Europe to produce everything from pumps to new types of electronic components, relatively low European labor costs, savings on transport, and the need to provide service near the customer have

U.S. Exports to Subsidiaries in Europe

($ billion)

	1962	1963
Total U.S. Exports to Europe	7,106	7,598
(a) U.S. Exports of Selected[a] Manufactures to Europe	3,680	4,028
(b) Exports to Manufacturing Subsidiaries	681	728
Exports to Distributing Subsidiaries	610	511
(b) as percent of (a)	35%	30%

[a] Comprises those manufactures in which the U.S. subsidiaries abroad are concerned.

Table I.

all combined to encourage production in Europe. In the production of specialist equipment, large scale is often not of decisive importance. For the American manufacturer of a new product not made in Europe, to set up a branch here seems an obvious first step.

Thus, the strategy of a large corporation today cannot be defined merely in the narrow classical terms of comparative return on capital. Where there are a few large competitors, they must think in terms of a worldwide strategy to match their rivals, and in doing so they must take an increasingly long-term view. Maintaining or increasing a share of the market may be a more immediate consideration than short-run return on capital. The practices of "oligopolistic competition," as economists describe it, are not the same as those of a marketplace with a large number of small firms. Thus, a large firm in the United States may invest in Europe to hold down a European rival's profit margins and divert his energies from discomforting competition in the United States. Shell, Unilever, or Olivetti may invest heavily in the United States, despite lower profit margins, in order to maintain a balance with their American rivals. A second-rank American firm (Chrysler in automobiles, General Electric in computers) may invest heavily in Europe in an attempt to prevent a dominant American rival (General Motors, IBM) from achieving a commanding position in the new and potentially rich European market which might one day react on its own competitive position in the United States. The largest American biscuit company went into the Common Market partly because it was afraid that the huge conglomerate corporation, General Foods, would get there first. Defensive as well as offensive motives thus play a part.

Direct investment between developed regions, such as Europe and America, often serves as a means of acquiring or selling know-how and skill. Olivetti believe that their initially unprofitable Underwood investment in America has in the end paid off as a means of acquiring American management techniques. International acquisitions, like domestic ones, can serve the purpose of gaining a new product or process or technique and then exploiting it by the addition of capital and management skill.

The search for diversity is a prevailing motive of American business—to spread risks, gain strength in a market sector less vigorously contested by competitors, and make wider use of know-how developed in a particular field. For an American firm with a substantial cash reserve, a European subsidiary, perhaps in a quite different line of business, can offer an ideal diversification. But if one wishes to isolate a single significant factor in American direct investment in Europe, it is expansion-mindedness. A recent PEP pamphlet divided British managements into two classes—"sleepers" and "thrusters."[5] The American "thrust" into Europe has been driven by men whose basic philosophy is one of expanding and creating new markets, and who see in Europe the great expanding market of today.

---

[5] *Sleepers and Thrusters: Political and Economic Planning* (January 1965).

All this reflects a change of attitude in the American business community, a new awareness by American firms that their market is the world, and a new realization that, to keep pace with rivals, the opportunities outside America must be seized. In the five years between 1960 and 1965, the Chrysler Corporation, for instance, changed its entire strategy and became a worldwide concern. A new, dynamic management took over, made inroads into their rivals' markets in the United States, built up a strong cash position, and, by acquisition and direct investment, established a network of overseas subsidiaries or affiliates from South America to France.

The Benefits

The influx of American capital has brought inportant benefits to Europe. The $10 billion invested by U.S. firms in plant and equipment in the three years 1962–64, for instance, has obviously contributed to economic growth.

The stimulus has been particularly valuable in backward regions, where the effect of the original investment has spread outwards, bringing idle resources into use. American newcomers have also been particularly responsive to European policies of regional development—at least in those areas where financial incentives have been effective and strong. Just over half of the American firms that have come to Britain since 1945 are in Development Districts. A British national computer company, seeking Government orders, may find that an American competitor who has brought a new industry to Scotland has the Secretary of State for Scotland on his side. In Belgium, 30 percent of the 1963 investment, under the 1959 laws for promoting investment, was foreign, most of it American.[6] Holland and Luxembourg have had similar successes. Whatever the view of competitors, the old steel town of Bochum, competing fiercely with other German towns, has been glad to persuade General Motors' Opel subsidiary to set up its new plant there and thus provide badly needed diversity of industrial employment. In France, Firestone at Béthune, Kodak at Chalon-sur-Saône, Esso, with its major oil discovery at Parentis, have significantly improved the economic life of backward regions.

New American firms start with mobile resources, few geographical preconceptions, and no roots in Europe. Far from being unresponsive to regional planning, they are thus more open to planning inducements at the start than established European firms, provided the right kind of instrument is used. Strong tax incentives, for instance, can be very effective in persuading American firms to settle in a particular region. But control of credit is obviously less effective as a means of guiding firms which have ample supplies of capital of their own.

In areas where there already is full employment, the economic value of an American investment can be measured by the extent to which productivity is higher

---

[6] *Investissements Etrangers en Belgique, Rapport 1963,* Ministère des Affaires Economiques.

than it would have been if the resources had been used in other ways. There is abundant evidence of this "productivity differential."

New technology and management methods are perhaps America's biggest contribution to Europe's economy. In his study of American investment in Britain, John Dunning[7] gives a long list of new productive processes and new materials introduced by American firms, from the manufacture of automatic transmissions for cars to pneumatic road-drills.

In old industries, new American methods have introduced striking advances in productivity. The $10 million to be invested by Libby's in canning and food processing in ten years in the Rhône Basin has begun to revolutionize not just food processing, but the marketing and distribution methods of French agriculture as well. The French Government has welcomed this, despite the initial resistance of the French food industry. With equal intelligence, an article in the May 1964 edition of "L'Information Agricole," by Gerard Burgard, argued that American capital might usefully be brought in to help modernize French agriculture itself.

Mr. Dunning's book provides strong evidence that American firms in Britain have made a more than average contribution to higher productivity. Over half the U.S. firms consulted had enlarged their share of the market. Two out of three exported more of their output per head in the relevant sector of industry as a whole; in fact, by 34 percent in Mr. Dunning's sample of firms. However many allowances one makes for size of firm and other special circumstances, it is an impressive figure. On the average, the American subsidiaries invested two and a half times as much per man employed.

High profitability provides further evidence of the comparative efficiency of U.S. firms in Europe. In 1957, U.S. firms accounted for 5 percent of manufacturing sales in Britain, but 10.9 percent of all company taxes,[8] a measure of their higher profits. There are other indications of the high profitability of American firms in Europe. In 1964, return on capital by U.S. firms in Europe was some 14 percent, still a little higher than the return at home, and a good deal higher than the average return from European companies. For instance, in the motor industry the four largest European firms had a return on sales ranging between 2.4 percent and 3.8 percent. The three largest American concerns had a return on their world sales ranging between 4.6 and 9.7 percent. . . .

The potential lead in efficiency of American firms may have been increased by the advent of the Common Market. Large American firms with major subsidiaries in several European countries are more flexible and thus better able to rationalize their production to fit the emerging Common Market than European firms with one fixed home base. Thus, IBM has for many years integrated production of components in its different European plants. Ford is slowly rationalizing its world

---

[7] John Dunning, *American Investment in British Manufacturing Industry.*
[8] Source: *U.S. Business Investment in Foreign Countries.* Department of Commerce.

production and will, for instance, concentrate truck production for the non-American market in its British plant. Concentration between European firms has been slow to develop, and is hampered by many obstacles, while American firms, with subsidiaries in several countries, can at once begin to rationalize output on a continent-wide basis. Many have Europe-wide distribution networks which also help. Already familiar with the large-scale techniques of a continental market, American firms have enabled European consumers to benefit economically from the Common Market more quickly than they could have done on their own. In this sense, they have proved more "European" than the Europeans.

The presence of these vigorous newcomers has undoubtedly increased the pace of competition, and thus helped European productivity as well. In car and tire production, for instance, American manufacturers have in several European countries been the main competitive mitigation to the domination which a single large national producer would otherwise enjoy. The same is true, in Britain at least, of some branches of chemicals. In industries and services where there is already a large number of European firms, American newcomers have often pioneered the introduction of large scale and new methods and thus precipitated, by competition, a major change in the structure of the industry. Woolworth's, early in the century, pioneered high-turnover, low-margin retailing and thus brought mass-produced goods within the range of a new section of British society. North American tractor manufacturers have forced the entire European industry to adopt large-scale methods. American competition in the food industry has at last set moving a concentration of the incredibly divided food industry in France.

All this has had a social as well as an economic impact. Woolworth's, or the new American-owned service industries like launderettes, have brought new industrial services and products within reach of a wider circle of European consumers. IBM pioneered the introduction of "staff" salaries and fringe benefits for all employees in its European firms.

American firms in Britain pay higher wages on the average than their competitors. At Fawley and Coriton refineries in Britain, American managements have pioneered a revolution in productivity and labor relations by bargaining on a plant basis with the unions and persuading them to sweep away a mass of restrictive practices and overtime in return for massive wage increases.

No doubt the down-to-earth American management sometimes prompts superior jokes in the local pub. No doubt there are some nearby employers who grumble at the massive increases in wage levels that the two refineries are introducing. Yet the instinctively democratic attitudes of American management and the bold willingness to grant really massive pay-increases have helped to sweep away wasteful practices that other British industries have been struggling vainly to remove for decades. Bold new trans-Atlantic attitudes, plus a new social technique, have miraculously broken down the inherited fears and class resentments of an old European society.

Finally, the political value to Europeans of American direct investment cannot be ignored. Opponents of foreign direct investment sometimes allege that this makes their country alarmingly dependent on its guests. But the guests are very dependent on them, too. American corporations with interests in different European countries have an immense interest in the stability and strength of Europe, and in good relations between the two continents. If they sometimes lobby European governments in their own interest, they will also be found lobbying the United States government in favor of amicable policies which make for good relations. Direct investment enhances America's interest in the security of Europe, strengthening a commitment which most European governments regard as vital. It is a cement of unity for the Atlantic world.

The European Welcome

Since 1945, most European countries have been well aware of these benefits, and have indeed done all they could to persuade American firms to settle in. In the first postwar years, European policies were not very different from those of underdeveloped countries seeking to build up their infant industries.

Just as Australia and India have imposed import quotas to force General Motors or Daimler-Benz to set up factories, so the dollar-gap made it axiomatic in most countries to force or persuade American firms to produce in Europe instead of exporting directly. Europe's overwhelming need was to save dollar imports, increase investment, spur growth, and introduce new technologies. American direct investment seemed the answer. Britain was for many years the main European host. Its own massive overseas investments (worth $10 billion today, or twice inward investment) and traditions as a capital market encouraged it to welcome capital from abroad. Chronic balance of payments difficulties and a depressingly low rate of investment have all helped to make American capital welcome to whatever government has been in power. Competition from go-ahead American concerns and the new management methods they brought seemed an invaluable medicine for the sluggish British economy. In Britain, where direct investment is subject to authorization by the Treasury and Bank of England, permission has never been refused in the twenty postwar years. Transfer of earnings is automatically permitted.

All this has helped to give Britain easily the largest slice of American direct investment in Europe. It was the one European country in which American industrial assets emerged from the war relatively unscathed, and it seemed the safest base for American investment in Europe in the first postwar years. An investment in Britain provided access to the Commonwealth market. Common language, common units of measurement, and all the intangible qualities of the "special relationship," still at that time significant, helped to make Britain an obvious European site for the large American concern, and sometimes a base for its world operations outside America. In 1950, Britain was host to $847 million or almost half the total American direct investment assets in Europe ($1,733 million). Even today the stake in Britain ($4,550 million) is not a great deal smaller than the American interests in the entire Common Market ($5,398 million).

As Europe recovered, continental countries became more attractive to American investment and most of them went out of their way to get it. In the early fifties, the Dutch pioneered a system of industrial estates and regional tax incentives, offering these to American investors and attracting them with handsome brochures and expert advice. In Belgium, a similar policy was developed later in the fifties. As in Britain, American direct investment seemed an ideal means of modernizing an old nineteenth-century industrial structure. In engineering and pharmaceuticals, in computers, office-machinery and automobiles, American investors brought new products and processes, supplementing Belgium's traditional textiles, steel, and coal. During the fifties American direct investment grew fastest of all in Western Germany, attracted by a dynamic economy and a policy of complete freedom for capital movements without even the exchange control practiced by the Dutch and British. Old established American firms in Germany and newcomers as well sought a share in the German "miracle."

In Italy, inflation and political uncertainties at first discouraged American investment. But two laws were passed (in 1948 and 1956) to guarantee repatriation of capital and dividends. After the passage of the second, American direct investment began to flow in on a larger scale. Today, even under a left-centre government, Italy remains as keen as ever to attract American direct investment, both to spur growth in its undeveloped South and to improve its shaky balance of payments.

Even tiny Luxembourg has made its own special and highly successful attempt to break away from its one-crop (steel) economy, by bringing in American capital. Dupont, Goodyear, and new firms in electronics and engineering have been coaxed in by special tax facilities and by the efforts of the Prince of Luxembourg, working from an office set up in New York.

In the years up to 1958, in short, only one country remained relatively unattractive to American investment. France's tight exchange controls were mainly designed to stop French capital from bolting, but in practice bureaucratic complications and the instability of the franc provided a severe deterrent to foreign direct investors attempting to surmount France's high tariff wall.

The *volte-face* in French policy in 1958–1959, when the opening of the Common Market began to spark off a new wave of American investment on the Continent, was all the more remarkable. The freeing of capital movements seemed a natural part of the liberal bonfire of restrictions as France joined the Common Market. At that time, France's foreign exchange reserves were at a pitifully low ebb. If foreign capital could be attracted by the new stable franc, it could make a notable contribution to the replenishment of French reserves.

The change worked beyond all expectations. In the years from 1958 to 1962, capital movements made a significant contribution to the soaring growth of French reserves from virtually nothing to $3 billion. On January 1, 1959, restrictions on both imports and exports of capital in France were virtually removed. For the next four years, though foreign direct investments were subject to "authorization" by the Bank of France, the French authorities emphasized that this was a pure formality and no application was refused. Foreign residents could also freely buy and sell French securities, subject only to formal declaration for those listed on the Bourse. The proceeds of sales of securities could be freely transferred.

The result has been a steady net influx of foreign capital. Some fifty French securities are listed on foreign stock markets. Part of the capital which Frenchmen had tucked away in Switzerland and elsewhere came home. In 1960, there was a net influx of 227 million francs ($47 million). Ninety percent of this was accounted for by other European countries; but half of the transactions were Swiss, and much of this must have been for American account. Thus at last, albeit modestly, in investment in securities, France began to share more substantially in the flow of American capital to Europe. Between 1958 and the end of 1961 there were 250 new American investments in France, more than in any other European country. The trends of American investment by country are shown in Table J.

The Stock of U.S. Direct Investment in Europe by Country

($ billion)

		1950	1961	1962	1963	1964
Common Market		637	1,680	3,722	4,471	5,398
Belgium-Luxembourg	69	192	286	351	452	
France	217	464	1,030	1,235	1,437	
Germany	204	581	1,476	1,772	2,077	
Italy	63	252	554	668	845	
Netherlands	84	191	376	445	597	
Other Europe		1,096	2,471	5,208	5,880	6,669
of Which						
United Kingdom	847	1,974	3,824	4,216	4,550	
Switzerland	25	69	553	668	944	
Total Europe		1,733	4,151	8,930	10,351	12,067

Source: Department of Commerce.

Table J.

As the Common Market got under way, the propaganda by individual European countries, seeking American capital and skills, began to be replaced by "European" propaganda. In New York, members of the Common Market Commission told American audiences of the potentialities of their vast new market—a market which had been expanding at 5 percent per annum even before the Common Market was formed—and invited American direct investment. The influx of American capital was proclaimed as evidence of the Common Market's strength and welcomed as a contribution to its growth.

Thus, in the postwar years, Europe aided and encouraged the influx of American direct investment. The American interest in sharing in the prosperity and markets generated by the recovery of Europe seemed matched by a deep European interest in acquiring capital, skills, and know-how from the richest industrial economy in the world. How is it then that this mutually beneficial process has led, in more recent years, to recurrent outbursts of European ill-feeling and some persistent underlying doubts? In the last five years, some Europeans have begun to feel like the "sorcerer's apprentice": the American capital they conjured up seemed to be becoming too much of a good thing. Real as well as fanciful problems lay behind this feeling. . . .

Impact of
Foreign Investments:
The Canadian—U.S. Case

Melville H. Watkins

The extent of foreign ownership of Canadian industry is unique among the industrialized nations of the world. At the end of 1964, the last year for which comprehensive statistics are available, long-term foreign investment in Canada stood at $27 billion—a conservative estimate since the figure is based on book values. At least 80 percent of the foreign direct investment represented ownership and control by U.S. companies. Foreigners owned over one-half of Canadian manufacturing; more than two-thirds of mining and smelting, petroleum and natural gas. Foreign ownership approached 100 percent in such major industrial sectors as automobiles and rubber. The only key sectors of the economy largely immune from foreign control are agriculture, banking and the communications media. The last two, banking and media, are specifically protected by public policy.

Direct investment is not a new phenomenon in Canada. At least as early as the 1850s, more than a century ago, U.S. entrepreneurs had penetrated the Canadian lumber industry in eastern Canada. The flow of direct investment picked up with Canada's move to high protective tariffs in 1879. Indeed Canada pioneered, although largely unconsciously, the use of protective tariffs to attract branch plants—notably of U.S. firms. The intent of this policy was to reduce Canadian dependence on foreign trade. It is, of course, riddled with paradox. What it really did, apparently, was increase the extent of foreign, and particularly U.S., ownership and, in what may be a more important dimension, to increase rather than decrease dependence.

The 1920s saw a major spurt in foreign investment in Canada both in primary products, such as newsprint, and in the manufacturing sectors, such as automobiles. It was widely believed in Canada at the end of the 1920s that there would not be such heavy reliance on foreign investment in the future. In fact, there has been another major round of expansion by direct investment firms in the years since World War II, an expansion that still goes on. These successive waves of foreign capital have been associated with rapid growth in the Canadian economy and large-scale immigration.

The extent of U.S. investment that has taken place in Canada can be explained in very broad terms by a number of interrelated factors which comprise the

Reprinted with permission from the March-April 1970 issue of the *Columbia Journal of World Business*. Copyright © 1970 by the Trustees of Columbia University in the City of New York.

so-called Second Industrial Revolution of the late nineteenth century—a revolution in chemicals, electrical goods and a broad range of commodities. There is considerable evidence that at this point Canadian entrepreneurs began to lag seriously behind the advanced countries of the world. The late nineteenth century saw the growth of big business in the United States when U.S. firms based in the eastern United States went national. In the process they tended more or less automatically to go continental, to spill over the border into Canada partly because it is not a very visible border and it was hard to believe that Canada was really a foreign country. The Canadian tariff facilitated the process, which may also be explained by apparent deficiencies within the Canadian business class. Foreign ownership may actually intensify those deficiencies. Entrepreneurship is a kind of learning process for society. When astute foreigners move in and undertake to do the work that nationals are neglecting, the incentive to learn tends to disappear.

In spite of its long history, direct investment has only become politically controversial in Canada in the past fifteen years. It is an interesting example of a thesis that we only begin to perceive issues after it is too late to do anything about them. Marshall McLuhan, who is a Canadian-based multinational guru, argues that our environment is always invisible, and it only becomes visible (certainly to politicians) after it is much too late to do anything. Clearly, fifteen years ago the presence of U.S. ownership in Canada was already established since the ratios were as high on the whole then as they are now.

The publication of official statistics on foreign ownership and control in the mid-1950s triggered a political debate—a circumstance which may indicate that statisticians are not as apolitical as they appear. The debate went through various phases and culminated in a Task Force Report, issued last year. This paper has become known as the Watkins Report.

A Policy Needed

The Report attempts to analyze Canadian experience with foreign ownership and to prescribe policy. It is written around the major theme of the harmonies and tensions between the multinational corporation and the nation-state. Explicitly, the Report insists that Canadians must recognize the existence of the multinational corporation and should discuss foreign ownership less in terms of the importation of capital and more in terms of the operation of large foreign-based corporations. Implicitly, the Report insists that Americans need to admit the reality of nation-states other than their own. It is essentially a report about the need for a national policy by host countries such as Canada. The major problem it has created, as far as can be seen from any coverage it has had in the U.S. press, is a tendency to label it a nationalistic document. This is unrealistic. It implies a failure to recognize that there are legitimate national interests other than the U.S. national interest.

Perhaps the outstanding exponent of the other point of view is George Ball, who creates headlines whenever he comes to Canada and sometimes when he doesn't come. Mr. Ball has said, and in doing so reflects a broadly held position, that the nation-state is old-fashioned and obsolete in contrast with the futuristic multinational corporation. This view needs to be challenged by Americans as well as Canadians. The nation-state has a much longer history than the multinational corporation. People have talked about the obsolescence of the nation-state for a long time, but it lives on in the present and will presumably live on in the future. It will not go away because Mr. Ball labels it old-fashioned. Nation-states exist to pursue various kinds of policies in the economic field: full employment, stability in prices, redistribution of income. None of these are things which multinational corporations are able to do.

The policy framework of the Report is *simpliste* and predictable since the Task Force consisted only of economists. Basically what it said was that Canadian policy should be directed toward increasing the benefits from foreign direct investment and decreasing the costs. It is impossible to measure benefits in a precise way. There is always the problem that benefits are mostly economic while costs are political. How do you compare apples and oranges?

The Right to Know

Among its recommendations, the Report suggests that there should be more disclosure by all firms in Canada, many of which of course are foreign. This is not an attempt to discriminate in any way against foreign firms but simply an effort to get a great deal more disclosure than is possible at present. The point is that Canadian policy has been far less effective in this area than U.S. policy.

Since over half the large firms in Canada are foreign controlled and a large percent of these are wholly owned subsidiaries, they have only one shareholder, their parent company. Under Canadian law they are private companies and do not have to tell anybody what they are doing except the tax authorities who won't tell anybody else. When, for example, the *Financial Post*, a Toronto publication, a few months ago issued a list of the 100 largest Canadian corporations, General Motors of Canada, one of the largest corporations in Canada, wasn't on the list. Under these circumstances it is impossible to compile a list of the largest companies in Canada. Anyone wanting information on a Canadian firm owned or controlled by a U.S. company must get it from official or private sources in the United States. It is not available in Canada.

The Trudeau government has announced that it is going to insist on more disclosure in the future and will perhaps implement recommendations made in this field by the Task Force.

The Report specifically proposes that an agency be set up by the federal government to collect information and coordinate policy with respect to foreign ownership. The logic here is simply that most governments have such agencies. In collecting information, they at least have the possibility of exercising policy. Canada, for example, needs a stronger antitrust or anti-combines policy, but one which will permit large Canadian controlled companies to emerge.

The Task Force also gave consideration to lowering Canadian tariffs. Canada participated in the Kennedy Round, but a recent study indicates that effective rates of protection are today as high or higher than they used to be. This also explains why, although an elaborate procedure for giving adjustment assistance to firms was set up, few firms have applied. Now we know why.

Rationalization Agreements

The Report recommends that Canada should attempt to negotiate specific "rationalization" agreements with the United States to raise Canadian productivity, which is significantly lower than U.S. productivity. The automobile industry case is a good precedent. In the opinion of the Task Force, branch plants of foreign firms are somewhat inefficient. Completely free trade could create serious unemployment problems, but rationalization agreements would permit free trade on a controlled basis with guarantees built in to protect Canadian employment. This is what happened in the automobile industry agreement.

The Task Force took a strong stand on the so-called issue of extraterritoriality—the situation in which the U.S. government, by law and by policy, uses U.S. firms and their subsidiaries as a means of exercising foreign policy under the Trading with the Enemy Act, Foreign Assets Control Regulations, the Clayton and Sherman Acts, all of which reach outside the United States to control firms which, while subsidiaries of U.S. firms, also happen to be incorporated in other countries.

Trade with China

The most controversial proposal concerned exports to communist countries. The Report stated that Canada should insist strongly on its right to trade freely with the communist world, particularly with China. The Task Force worked out a scheme which technically solved the problem. Most likely it is not a politically satisfactory solution, but it received a great deal of publicity which may persuade governments to move toward a solution. The Report said that if a U.S. subsidiary refused an order because of U.S. law, this would not be an acceptable argument in Canada. If the firm continued to decline the order and no Canadian company could fill it, the Canadian government should place the order on behalf of the communist customer. In these circumstances the U.S. firm would find itself in the position of defying the Canadian government. This is called confrontation. The then Prime Minister, Lester Pearson, was most unhappy with the proposal. The present Prime Minister, Pierre Trudeau, ignores it, and the idea is undoubtedly dead.

Another set of proposals sought to secure more benefits for Canadians from foreign ownership. Part of the problem lies in the field of taxation. As in the United States, Canada confers special tax treatment on the oil, natural gas and mining industries, many of which are controlled by U.S. interests. Consequently, it can be argued that the benefits derived from this special tax treatment do not come to Canadians but are passed along to foreign shareholders. Since these industries are characteristically capital intensive, they offer few jobs. A Royal Commission on

Taxation has since recommended on different grounds that all industries and economic activities should be taxed on a uniform basis. The Task Force endorsed this recommendation and insisted that Canada should not be in the position of subsidizing foreign shareholders.

The most contentious issue which the Task Force faced was the question of minority participation in foreign subsidiaries. The Report argued that such participation was not only desirable but that firms should be given incentives to issue shares. The fact is that at present Canada does not have a large equity market. If a Canadian wishes to buy shares in some key sector—business equipment or airlines, for example—he has little choice but to buy stock in a foreign company. Canada would thus seem to be in the curious position of becoming a capital exporter rather than a capital importer. It is a sort of colonial situation in which foreigners control the economy which exports capital to them as it once did raw materials. It would also seem that a balance-of-payments problem will eventually emerge from these circumstances. The Report suggests that the tax system be used to create the necessary incentives for the firms. The present Minister of Finance has been urging mutual and pension funds to buy more Canadian securities. This, of course, may drive up their prices and encourage foreign firms to issue shares.

A Development Corporation

An alternative vehicle for Canadian participation is the Canadian Development Corporation (CDC) a proposal which has had a stormy five-year non-existence in Canada but which the Task Force adopted. It was originally thought of as a means to buy back Canadian enterprises from the foreigners. It is probably too late to do that. The current thinking is more modest. The Corporation is conceived of as an agency which in the future will give Canadians an opportunity to own more Canadian industry.

An example of the role for a CDC occurred in the 1950s. Some Canadian firms were involved in a large iron ore development in Labrador. They could not stay the course, and the ultimate consortium came under U.S. control. A Canadian Development Corporation could have moved in there to preserve a national presence in the project. There is already an embryonic CDC operating in the north. The Prime Minister is interested in it, and the government is taking equity positions with foreign firms in the development of Arctic oil.

As the Task Force worked its way toward a basic strategy of increasing economic benefits to Canadians and decreasing political costs, its thinking was influenced by an earlier study which concluded that the benefits were not as large as might perhaps be imagined. There appear to be few significant differences in the performance of foreign-controlled and Canadian-controlled firms in terms of many criteria of economic behavior. The press and business community interpreted this conclusion as implying that foreign firms perform as well as Canadian. Therefore, Canada could stop worrying about foreign ownership. From another point of view, the findings can be interpreted as saying that foreign firms perform as badly as domestic firms. Many outside the business community are not impressed with the performance of Canadian companies. The question then to be answered is: why should the political costs known to inhere in foreign direct investment be borne when foreign firms create only the same economic benefits as domestic?

What is the relevance of the Canadian experience for other countries? For the United States the lesson would appear to be that Canadian nationalism, although weak, is real. There is reason to expect continuing tension and periodic crises in Canadian-American relations associated with U.S. involvement in Canadian economic activity. Canada will probably take some action, possibly even in the area of extraterritoriality, but it is unlikely that there will be any substantive change in policy. For other host countries the lessons are unclear, primarily because of the special relationship of Canada to the United States growing out of geography and history.

Relevant Policy

However, two points may be suggested that might be applicable to policy in host countries generally. First, host countries need a national economic policy if their citizens are to benefit fully from foreign direct investment. No policy, or the wrong policy, means that they will bear the political costs of foreign direct ownership with no assurance of the economic benefits. Secondly, policies in host countries must be formulated to come to grips with the reality of these political costs. If the issue is extraterritoriality with respect to trading with China, the country must have a definite policy which comes to terms with it. In the long run this may mean an international policy, but in the foreseeable future there is no alternative to positive national policies.

Looking back at the Report and trying to put it in perspective, it seems to be a bland document. In Canada, it has been treated as a radical document, in the United States as an example of nationalism and anti-Americanism. To the Task Force the Report reflects the conventional wisdom of North American economists and is in the best tradition of twentieth century liberalism when it argues that Canada should do something to control big business and create an environment in which the public receives maximum benefits from the operations of big business. The Report then is a bland, liberal document.

It is possible to visualize a more radical document advocating one of two theses. There is the Servan-Schreiber position which admires U.S.-style capitalism and wants to imitate and compete with it. An alternative policy promotes national economic planning, or what might be regarded as socialism. Both are viable options in Canada, and either may be a better solution to the problem than the present one of no policy. But for the immediate future, and perhaps in the long run, Canada will probably continue to follow a middle course between the two.

The Investment in the LDC: Asset with a Fixed Maturity

Peter P. Gabriel

There is widespread agreement today that the economic growth of the less-developed countries depends upon their ability to attract the skills and techniques which support the higher productivity levels of the industrialized nations. While foreign-aid programs can supplement capital formation in developing lands, the efficient utilization of foreign aid requires a technical and administrative infrastructure, and the catalyzing effects of foreign capital inflow presuppose a base of local entrepreneurship, which are absent in many of the recipient countries and severely limited in most.

The traditional carrier of the required industrial know-how has been foreign private direct investment. Therefore, it is not surprising that donor nations never tire of advising the recipients of foreign aid that a climate inhospitable to foreign private investment is apt to be a serious deterrent to economic growth.

The advice has met with a decidedly ambivalent response. Government guarantees to the foreign investor in one industrial sector are made suspect by arbitrary cancellation (or "reinterpretation") of contracts with foreign investors in other industries. Special tax concessions are offset by exchange restrictions. Official welcome to the foreign businessman is marred by toleration of popular outbursts against him.

The foreign investment community can react to this state of affairs in three ways: It can pack up and go home, it can try to change the environment in its favor, or it can try to adapt itself to existing conditions.

The first of these alternatives—withdrawal or retrenchment—has been elected by a substantial number of investigators in recent years. The second embraces a wider range of responses. The more direct approach is to pressure one's home government to make foreign aid contingent on a clearly demonstrated sympathetic attitude toward the foreign investor. More fashionable, sophisticated approaches to foreign investment attempt to influence the local climate indirectly, through policies of "enlightened self-interest" and "good neighborliness" aiming at maximum integration with the local economy. Because these latter approaches involve adaptation to local conditions and sensitivities, they may superficially resemble the third alternative mentioned above. But their basic objective in most cases is more to influence the direction of environmental change than to adapt to it.

Reprinted by permission of the author and publisher from *Columbia Journal of World Business* (Summer 1966).

The distinction has a parallel in the controversy that has swirled around the purposes of foreign aid. As governments have learned that stimulating economic growth in the developing nations does not necessarily promote the development of western-style political and social institutions, private business has experienced a comparable revelation. Foreign investors have learned that, however "progressive" their conduct has become in the developing world, the investment climate has not materially changed in their favor. Inescapably, this realization has led to withdrawal or stagnation of private investment in many areas.

The third alternative outlined above—adaptation of investment planning and execution to prevailing environmental conditions—remains to be considered. What forms might such adaptation take?

Analysis of this question may well begin with a review of some recent changes in the situation of foreign investors in the developing countries. These changes, I believe, have largely destroyed the relevance of conventional approaches to foreign investment—including even the so-called "new departures" in current investment thinking. As a result, fresh analytical approaches to investment planning and risk evaluation are needed.

Why Investors Turn Away

The reasons for the decline in the rate of private foreign investment in the less-developed nations, relative to the remarkable expansion of capital flows within the industrialized world, vary from country to country. Yet most of them can be traced to two historical developments:

(1) The abandonment of the gold standard in the aftermath of the First World War. Under the gold standard, exchange rates remained stable and currency convertibility assured as countries adjusted to balance-of-payments surpluses or deficits by tolerating internal inflation or deflation. Today, in contrast, domestic political pressures for sustained economic expansion have shifted the burden of adjustment to the external position. Particularly in less-developed countries, balance-of-payments deficits are no longer allowed to induce internal economic retrenchment. Instead, they are combated with foreign-exchange restrictions and, ultimately, manipulations of the exchange rate. The effects of such measures on the repatriation of earnings and principal of foreign investments have naturally become of concern to long-term investors abroad.

(2) The change in relative bargaining power between foreign investors and host governments. Vis-à-vis the foreign investor, the less-developed nations now possess bargaining power out of all proportion to their relative economic and military strength.

This remarkable accretion of bargaining power can be traced to three sources. First, the east-west stalemate has imposed on the industrial states a new code of conduct toward the "poor" countries, and has sharply limited the responsiveness of their foreign policy to private business interests. Second, the ubiquity and intensification of international economic competition among the industrial countries often permits a "host" country to play off one potential foreign investor against another to secure the terms most advantageous to itself. Finally, the growth in underdeveloped countries of local entrepreneurship, both public and private, in areas once the domain of foreign capital confronts the foreign investor with this dilemma: his very success in the host country promotes the growth of local capabilities that threaten his continued presence.

The rising bargaining power of the less-developed countries in their relations with foreign investors finds its clearest reflection in their "investment climate"— that complex of environmental factors which characterizes a country's *general attitude* toward the foreign investor.

Much of this attitude is rooted in the culture, social fabric, and historical experience of the country concerned. But to a crucial extent, a nation's attitude toward foreign ownership of domestic business is determined by government policy. Or put differently, since the real or alleged national consensus with respect to the foreign investor is interpreted and implemented by the government, it is governmental action which gives these attitudes expression, which sets the investment climate. Political instabilities may affect the exercise of this power but do not change its ultimate locus.

What Government Can Do

Host governments can influence their investment climate in ways ranging from guarantees against expropriation and discrimination to diverse forms of taxation, foreign-exchange regulations, and labor legislation. These policies need not relate exclusively to foreign investment. The foreign investor usually attributes equal importance to the way local private enterprise is treated in general, and to the contemplated size of the public sector relative to the size of the private sector in particular. By explicit regulation or by default, a host government will manifest *some* policy in all these areas.

If, then, a nation's investment climate is largely manipulable by government fiat—if it were not so, the admonition to governments of less-developed countries to take positive action about their investment climates would not make sense—two conclusions immediately follow. First, any investment climate—favorable or unfavorable—is reversible to the extent that an about-face in government policy can be made credible to the foreign investor community. Second, it is essentially a short-term factor, of no more relevance as a criterion for a long-term investment decision than current market size or current consumer preferences.

Hearty Welcome, Heavy Letdown

The fickleness of host government attitudes has become painfully clear to foreign investors. The underlying reasons, however, are not always so apparent. Sheer political instability or governmental opportunism are often part of the explanation—though not a part the foreign investor can do very much about. The more significant part of the explanation frequently relates to historical forces. For the evidence of Brazil, Mexico, and to some extent even Canada and Europe suggests that *the more unqualified the welcome to foreign business, and the better the "climate" has been in any country over a given period of time, the more likely is a subsequent change for the worse.*

This apparent paradox has two explanations. In the first place, unrestricted admission of direct investment from abroad tends to lead to the establishment of foreign-controlled firms not only in industries for which foreign investment is deemed "essential," in the sense that they are uniquely exploitable by imported corporate know-how and capital, but also in areas in which the foreigner competes with existing or nascent local entrepreneurship. Sooner or later, these local interests will pressure the government to check the expansion of established foreign firms and to keep others out—to the detriment of the investment climate.

In the second place, foreign investment in less-developed economies (indeed in advanced countries as well) shows a bias toward "new" industries having considerably greater growth rates than traditional lines of business. For this reason, the stock of foreign-owned capital tends to increase more rapidly than industrial investment held domestically. Inevitably, this raises the specter of "foreign domination" and generates hostile political pressures[1] and persistent local rhetoric equating the foreigner's presence with imperialism and the conduct of his affairs with exploitation.

Good Neighborliness Won't Do

Foreign businessmen in the underdeveloped countries are frequently perplexed at these charges, which seem totally at odds with current realities—in particular, with the well-documented efforts of foreign investors to identify their economic interests with those of the local community. At one time, corporate policies designed deliberately to contribute to the social and economic welfare of the host country may have been avant-garde curiosities; today, they have matured to established orthodoxy.

Corporate actions consistent with these policies include the training of nationals not only for subordinate but also for managerial positions; promotion of local entrepreneurship through local procurement and technical and financial assistance; the setting of examples in business ethics, product quality, and employee relations; financial and other contributions to local welfare and community activities; respect for local culture and patterns of living. All these actions, of course, are only ancillary to more immediate aspects of the *raison d'être* of the foreign presence: its part in the economic development of the host country and the consequent

---

[1] See E. T. Penrose, "Foreign Investment and the Growth of the Firm," *Economic Journal* (June 1956).

contributions to national income, employment, and foreign trade—multiplier effects and all.

Why is it, then, that the foreign investor's contributions avail him so little? Why do developing countries so often bite the foreign corporate hand that feeds them? Beyond the much-publicized nationalistic sentiments in the emerging countries and their psychological reactions to the overpowering might of the rich nations, three broad reasons may be singled out:

First, "good behavior" on the part of the foreign corporation—in fact, *exceptionally* good behavior—is now being taken for granted. It no longer attracts special recognition, let alone special reward. Anyone who has lived long enough in a less-developed country to become attuned to the local mood will attest to the deep-seated feeling of most nationals—sometimes realistic, sometimes cynical, sometimes neurotic—with respect to the inadequacy of local institutions, and the concomitantly high expectations of the intrinsic quality of anything foreign. The foreign corporation is *expected* to be more punctilious in observing the law, to pay higher wages, to be more responsive to appeals for charity, to share its superior know-how with local competitors, actual or potential. The larger the foreign corporation, the higher the standards popularly applied to the firm's public posture.

And yet, along with these high expectations often goes a suspicion that the foreign company's operations do not, on balance, redound to the maximum benefit of the host economy. However "enlightened" the foreign investor's policies may appear to be, they cannot be divorced—his detractors will claim—from the goals they serve. His other actions in support of these goals, so the argument runs, tend to nullify whatever benefits he brings.

As Benefits Fall, Costs Rise

Second, it is characteristic of direct-investment projects that their first-order benefits are greatest, certainly most spectacular, in the initial stages of the undertaking; capital flows in, plants are built, local workers are hired and trained, local supply contracts are let. Subsequently, the benefits from the investment change in nature and become diffused. The straightforward inflow of capital is followed by export production or domestic production of goods formerly imported (import substitution). Job creation shifts from the foreign enterprise to local contractors and suppliers. The importance of new technology changes from its direct use by the foreign firm to the more subtle demonstration effects on local entrepreneurship. These benefits seldom phase out completely. Yet over time they lose much of the impact associated with the inception and initial operation of the enterprise.

The explicit *costs* of the foreign investment to the host economy generally behave in an exactly opposite fashion. They accrue almost imperceptibly at first, rise with the usual increase in the company's capital stock through plowback of earnings, and finally begin to abrade national sensitivities—in the form of dividend payouts—when the front-page benefits of the foreign investment have already sunk into oblivion, and discussion of second-, third-, and fourth-order benefits continues only in economic journals. True, remissions of earnings—though perhaps huge in comparison with the amount of capital originally brought into the country—are often modest compared with total profits realized or total capital employed. But these distinctions do not usually inform public controversy, acknowledged as they may have become in theoretical analysis.

Why Investment Is "Tolerated"

The third factor to be considered here is more substantive. It relates to local conceptions of the self-interest of the host country with regard to foreign investment in domestic industry. To argue this matter through to generally valid conclusions, if feasible at all, is beyond the intent of this analysis. But some possible ways of thinking about the problem can be suggested. Let's look that this question from the standpoint of the host country.

Why should *any* country play host to a business enterprise owned and controlled by foreign interests? Surely, direct investment from abroad is not *inherently* preferable to domestically owned business. On the contrary, all other things being equal, it has several disadvantages. Foreign ownership, by definition, will cause part of the wealth the firm creates within the country to flow abroad ultimately, and the presumption that corporate policies will be consistent with national economic interests is, *a priori*, less readily sustainable with a foreign-owned enterprise than with its domestic counterpart. Why, then, does a nation tolerate the inflow of private direct capital?

It does so for one or both of two reasons: first, national commitment, rationalized in economic or political terms, to free trade and free international capital flows; second, recognition that "all other things" are *not* equal, that foreign investment helps make up for domestic capital deficiencies, thereby mobilizing resources which would otherwise remain idle, and that it supplies skills and techniques that are unavailable locally.

The first reason, clearly, is not likely to be espoused by the developing countries in the foreseeable future as an argument to permit foreign investment. Few of the developing nations feel that they can yet "afford" a stance of classical liberalism in their international economic relations, or have recently adopted such a stance for any length of time. So far as these countries are concerned, foreign investment has to prove its own case in terms of specific contributions to the host economy.

If so, how is this contribution to be valued in relation to the price it exacts? And is it reasonable, from the host country's standpoint, that the payments to the foreign investor should continue indefinitely, even though his net contributions to the economy may decline or even cease over time? The latter question brings up fundamental issues of property rights—issues which cannot be explored here, although they are obviously central to the ongoing polemic in the developing countries on the subject of private capital inflows. With regard to the first question, however, several points may be made.

Assuming that the total contribution of the foreign direct investor could be defined with sufficient precision, it might be quantified in terms either of "intrinsic" value or of "market" value. One approach to *intrinsic* valuation might be to estimate what it would cost the host country to generate with its own resources the export production or import substitution made possible by the foreign investment, the domestic jobs it creates, the capital formation it promotes, the education and training of management and technical personnel provided by the foreign firm, the duplication of the sum total of research and development represented by the investment, the provision of all the supporting services supplied by the parent concern, and many other things—with due allowance for the assumption of risk. Such a calculation would generally reveal the price paid to the foreign investor, whatever its definition, as a most satisfactory bargain indeed to the receiving nation. It is this sort of calculation which is implicit in much of the conventional argument put forward by the foreign business community to justify the costs to the host country that its investments entail.

Alternatively, the foreign contribution may be viewed as a package of services the value of which is determined in the *marketplace*. In the international investment market, foreign corporations compete for investment opportunities, access to which host governments control. These in turn compete for foreign private investments, i.e., for the benefits that only such investments can supply. In this model, the price which the receiving nation will ultimately pay is a function of (1) the number of foreign firms independently competing for the investment opportunity; (2) the *recognized* measure of uniqueness of the foreign contribution (as against its possible provision by local entrepreneurship, public or private); (3) the *perceived* degree of domestic need for the contribution. The terms the foreign investor will accept, on the other hand, depend on (1) his general need for an investment outlet; (2) the attractiveness of the specific investment opportunity offered by the host country, compared to similar or other opportunities in other countries; (3) the extent of prior commitment to the country concerned (e.g., an established market position[2]).

Like the approach to intrinsic valuation discussed earlier, this market-value concept is presented here not for practical application, in the sense of putting specific currency amounts on each of the multiple elements it includes, but as an

---

[2] The desire to protect established interests in foreign markets is no doubt the most powerful factor inducing many international corporations to continue investing in a country which, from the standpoint of an *initial* commitment, may have become a relatively poor risk. The strategic implications for a host country intent on improving its bargaining position vis-à-vis foreign investors are obvious. (See L. Gordon and E. L. Grommers, *United States Manufacturing Investment in Brazil*, Division of Research, Harvard Business School, Boston, 1962, pp. 147–148).

underlying rationale for analysis of the problem. If the "contribution" of the foreign investor to the host country defies quantification, so surely does it "cost" (or "price"). Just as the former goes beyond the mere financial and physical assets brought into the receiving nation, so—in the host country's view—does the latter transcend the earnings and fees remitted abroad by the foreign investor. One cannot summarily dismiss, for example, the real or alleged preemption by foreign business of local resources (scarce bank credit, scarce skilled manpower, etc.) and of business opportunities to which domestic entrepreneurs may feel they have first title. Nor can the host government safely ignore the possible political hazards of admitting foreign ownership to major, exposed sectors of local industry.

A Question of Framework

Clearly, these two ways of thinking about the value of foreign investment to the recipient economy lead to sharply different conclusions about the "reasonableness" of the price the host country has to pay for the foreign presence. The foreign investor, who tends to think in terms of "intrinsic" value, concludes that his contribution to the host country far outweighs its costs. But the host countries, aware of their new bargaining position, naturally take the "market" value approach. In other words, their notion of a "reasonable" price is defined by the terms they can freely negotiate in a competitive international investment market (where, ideally, competition is restricted to the investor side, while the bargaining country holds some measure of monopoly power) for services that are deemed essential to the local economy and cannot be duplicated by domestic resources.

Now, it is characteristic of a developing country that all these conditions change radically with time. A "fifty-fifty" agreement with a foreign corporation that is seen as highly advantageous today, in comparison with previous arrangements in the same country or concurrent deals in other countries, will look intolerably onerous if other countries successfully bargain for 75 percent tomorrow. Moreover, both the need for and the uniqueness of the contribution made possible by a given foreign investment are bound to be vitiated by the very process of industrial development it was typically called in to assist.

It is not surprising, therefore, that host governments should continually be tempted to try to renegotiate or unilaterally alter existing contracts and long-term arrangements with foreign investors, or to revoke or "reinterpret" laws and regulations affecting them. Governments in the less-developed countries are subject to severe pressures to extract the best possible deal from the foreign businessman, even if it means taking liberties with specific contracts made or general promises given. It may be a matter of sheer economic necessity. In times of desperate foreign-exchange shortages, guarantees of free profit remission are more easily suspended than imports of essential goods. It may be a matter of political survival for incumbent governments, or of redeeming campaign pledges for newly elected governments. It is easier to marshal popular support by squeezing additional levies out of the foreigner on grounds of alleged "exploitation" than by acknowledging responsibility for domestic fiscal problems or failures. And there are the pressures from local business interests for protection from "unfair competition" unleashed by the allegedly more powerful foreign firm, or for license to participate in industries which the foreigner may have pioneered in the economy.

The Proverbial Straw

At what point is a host government likely to succumb to any one or a combination of these pressures? Resistance to pressures from *outside* the government will probably crumble when the latter's own stability is at stake. Second thoughts *within* the government on existing contracts or regulations concerning foreign capital are likely to be translated into administrative action when it can plausibly be argued that national interests demand the abrogation of these commitments, and when it seems that the action can be taken with impunity. The latter condition, in turn, is satisfied when a host government such as Cuba, or Sukarno's Indonesia, decides it can continue without foreign private capital; when the action can be convincingly represented as aiming only at specific sectors of the foreign investor community (e.g., an extractive industry or a public utility); or when, even after deliberate disturbance of the investment climate, remaining opportunities are so attractive, the longer-term future appears so promising, and existing foreign commitments are so large, that an effective boycott by foreign private investors is unlikely.

The complexity of all these questions is apparent. Though the single investor may be intimidated by a host country's power to tax, confiscate, or discriminate at will, the situation is different where the host country confronts a multitude of foreign investors whose solidarity sometimes proves more real than apparent, whose reactions to outside infringement are unpredictable, whose expectations constantly change. For both parties, it is an uncertain world.

The Irrelevance of Ethics

From the standpoint of the less-developed country, exhortations from abroad to establish and maintain "favorable investment climates" are often less than realistic counsels of perfection. Insistence on long-term promises designed to attract a magnitude of foreign capital inflow that inevitably will radically modify the conditions under which the promises are given is bound to be resisted by these countries, or to tax their sincerity. Nor is it helpful, from a practical standpoint, to reflect upon the morality or justice of governmental breaches of contract. As Churchill has written, "The Sermon on the Mount is the last word in Christian ethics. Everyone respects the Quakers. Still, it is not on these terms that Ministers assume their responsibilities of guiding states."

Considering the problem from the foreign investor's side, I suggested, at the beginning of this article, three ways in which the international corporation can react to the current realities in the less-developed countries: (1) it can completely withdraw or slowly retreat; (2) it can attempt to change the environment in desired directions; (3) it can accept environmental factors as given and try to adapt the planning and execution of investment projects to them. The first of these alternatives may undeniably be warranted in situations where the investment in question is concretely and specifically in jeopardy, but it is not appropriately based on general judgments of "investment climates." As for the second, we have seen that the results of past corporate efforts "to win friends and influence people" have not been encouraging.

The third alternative, the adaptation of investment planning and execution to existing environmental factors, suggests a somewhat different way of thinking about investment risks and opportunities in the less-developed countries. In formulating this approach, I shall distinguish between the risks associated with the safety of the investment *principal* and the less formidable risks related chiefly to future proceeds from the foreign investment. I shall then consider how the foreign investor might evaluate and deal with such risks. The major parts of the argument will be presented in the form of summary propositions derived from the points previously raised.

"Solvency" and "Conversion" Risks.[3] In analyzing foreign investment risks, it is useful to distinguish between the *solvency* risk of the commitment and its *conversion* risk. Solvency risk relates to the safety and profitability of the foreign venture per se. This risk is a function of political and economic developments in the host country that specifically affect the investment in question. Conversion risks are usually related to the future of the host country's international payments position and affect the entire business community, though in different ways. Of course, since "economic developments" include the international payments position, solvency and conversion risks are interrelated.

Viewed in terms of outright confiscation or expropriation, severe government discrimination, and even lesser threats to long-term profitability, the solvency risk is *absolute* in character. In contrast, the conversion risk is relative. Currency controls or fluctuations are usually—or are believed to be—more or less temporary. They can be adapted to or "lived with." By definition, the solvency risk, if it materializes, cannot.

Thus, of the two types of risk, the solvency risk is clearly the more forbidding. It is probably the single most important obstacle to international capital flows today, especially in underdeveloped countries. The conversion risk, though certainly present in investors' calculations of risk premiums, apparently does not

----

[3] These terms were suggested by R. E. Caves' paper, "Flexible Exchange Rates," *American Economic Review* (May 1963), 120–129.

detract from foreign direct investment if market prospects are sufficiently bright. Witness the huge number of new commitments undertaken in Brazil in the late 1950s, when the country's international payments position and prospects were steadily deteriorating.

Conversion risks can be explained largely in terms of the theory of international finance. The solvency risk, on the other hand (or those elements of it that are unique to foreign investment), pertains to what might be called a theory of international politico-economic *bargaining power.*

Criteria of Acceptability

Investment Risks and Opportunities and Their Appraisal. The foreign corporation in a less-developed country no longer operates under the protection of its home government but at the sufferance of the host country. Hence, in order to maintain his tenure the foreign investor has to justify, from the host country's standpoint, not only his entry but his continued presence.

The traditional argument that the associated benefits conferred on the host economy directly or indirectly outweigh their costs is rapidly losing its relevance. Net gain to the host economy from the foreign investment is a necessary but no longer sufficient condition of its acceptability. Host governments not only want the foreigner "to earn his keep"; they want to be satisfied that the price paid to him, in whatever form, *is as low as possible.*

In other words, the "solvency" risk (of confiscation, expropriation, or severe discrimination) is inversely proportional to the investor's ability to demonstrate to the host country that the cost-benefit ratios associated with his investment are more attractive than those of any alternative that appears to offer equivalent benefits.

The risks of direct investments in underdeveloped countries are conventionally assessed in terms of (1) near- or longer-term currency stability and (2) the present and prospective "investment climate." The investor's over-all assessment of these risks, which determines the premium on the rate of return he will consider acceptable, is typically colored by the assumption that, in the eyes of the host country, all foreign direct investments—at least within major categories, such as extractive industries versus manufacturing—must be of like virtue (or like anathema). Encroachment by a host government on any one member of the foreign business community is generally viewed as a threat to all.

Such generalizations, as I have argued, are seldom tenable in evaluating the risks of specific investments. Barring the *total* collapse of the legitimacy of private capital (as in Cuba), the status of a foreign direct investment depends ultimately upon the bargaining power of its owner vis-à-vis the host government. This bargaining power, in turn, is contingent on the demonstrable importance and uniqueness of the essential functions it performs.[4]

These arguments suggest certain implications for the businessman seeking to assess the "solvency" risks of a direct investment in a developing nation.

First, it is unrealistic to try to justify foreign direct investment on the basis of a general presumption of economic net advantage to the host economy—let alone to argue its sanctity in terms of an ideology of private enterprise rooted in social and historical patterns that are alien to most underdeveloped countries and utterly irrelevant to their current emergencies. Pragmatic nationalism, not theoretical socialism, is the force with which the foreign investor must reckon.

Always on Trial

Second, the foreign investor should look upon his investment as being continually "on trial" against other alternatives open to the host country, not only at the time the investment is made but even more so after it has matured. This proposition points up the precarious tenure of foreign-owned enterprises in developing countries. In proportion as such an enterprise meets stated demands or more or less vaguely perceived "obligations" to spread its technology and know-how within the country, its indispensability to the economy—from the standpoint of bilateral bargaining with the host government—will appear less plausible. If on the other hand, the foreign firm seeks to *withhold* techniques and general assistance from potential local competitors, it will provoke active hostility, and the host government will sooner or later seek to improve its bargaining position by establishing a competitive enterprise of its own, or by inducing other firms to enter.

"Plan for Impermanence"

The practical significance of this proposition has two aspects. In the first place, the direct investor will generally be well advised to balance the nature and magnitude of his resource commitment against the time span within which returns can "safely" be expected. In this sense, the direct investment, theoretically of

---

[4] Egypt, for example, could "get away with" the nationalization of the Suez Canal because, contrary to predictions, the government proved capable of running the operation efficiently. Iran, on the other hand, failed to make the seizure of foreign petroleum properties stick because she could not duplicate the functions performed by integrated international oil companies. Eventual renegotiation of contracts with the oil industry did, to be sure, result in raising Iran's share in profits from 15 percent to 50 percent and more. But the bargaining power of the companies proved too strong for Iran to compel the companies to grant more than they had already conceded to Venezuela and, subsequently, to Saudi Arabia. Nothing, in fact, more clearly demonstrates the remarkable accretion of bargaining power to the "new" nations over the last fifteen years than the recent history of the oil industry's international operations.

infinite duration, assumes some of the characteristics of a security with fixed maturity. Secondly, this time span should, under certain conditions, be regarded as a variable over which the investor himself has some potential control. The conditions in question are these: (1) if the particular technology, skills, know-how, or processes which the investment introduces into the country are *unique to the firm*, not merely to the industry; (2) if these resources are critical to the efficient operation of the enterprise created in the host country; (3) if through the continous application of intrafirm research and development the "spread effects" mentioned earlier do not materially weaken the initial investor's leadership position. All these conditions might well be met, for example, in electronics and communications industries. They are less likely to be satisfied in food processing, basic chemicals, standard construction materials (cement, paints, glass, etc.).[5]

Analyzed in these terms, the risks of foreign direct investment in developing and "unstable" countries are directly related to the nature of the contribution which the investment makes to the host economy. Conventionally, this contribution is defined in terms of effects on the foreign balance (export creation and import substitution) and/or less readily quantifiable effects on the growth of real national income. Whatever the importance of these contributions, there is no historical or current evidence to suggest that they alone can alleviate the risk of host government infringement.

On the other hand, if the foreign investor's contribution is evident in terms of a continuous stream of valuable innovations, as well as of balance-of-payments and real-income effects, the risks of expropriation or discrimination are correspondingly likely to be held in check. Once that continuous stream subsides and the accumulated store of previously imported techniques has been effectively transferred to the local community, the host government will become more susceptible to the pressure of nationalist charges that the foreign investor has outlived his usefulness.

This approach to the analysis of investment opportunity and risk in the less-developed countries contains many elements that in practical contexts must be judged subjectively, by individual investors as well as by host governments. My purpose is not to add one more checklist for the management of foreign operations, but to propose a way of thinking that may be helpful in weighting the items contained in standard prescriptions on investment planning—revealing the significance of some and exposing the irrelevance of others to specific investment problems or projects.

---

[5] Demonstrable essentiality of a particular foreign direct investment need not be based on technological monopoly through effective process differentiation or patent protection. The logistics of vertical, intercountry integration—if requisite for the operation of the enterprise—will confer as much bargaining power on the foreign investor, as is clearly the case in the petroleum industry.

A Confidence in Rationality

Over the long term, I believe, a basic rationality and consistency can be discerned in the seemingly inconsistent behavior of the nations now struggling for social stability and economic growth. The kind of corporate decision making here suggested is designed to appeal to this long-run rationality and consistency. It cannot protect the individual investor from precipitate government actions impelled by the urge to experiment or the irresistible pressures of circumstance. But however large and unpredictable these environmental risks may be, they do not threaten all investments alike.

That foreign private investment in the less-developed countries will enjoy safety from government infringement and popular hostility in proportion as it identifies itself with the needs of the host economy is almost a tautology. The point is that this identification will actually result in greater investment security only if it relates to corporate *goals*—not merely to the means of achieving them.

Uphill Struggle for World Enterprise

This argues the necessity of reexamining some implications of the concept of the "world enterprise." This concept has done much to illumine the opportunities and *technical* complexities of international operations. But too little has been said about its long-run implications for the countries which world enterprises are urged to consider their domain. If the term "world enterprise" is intended to mean the international movement of investment, manufacturing, sales, and procurement activities according to some centrally perceived dictates of optimum division of corporate labor, the idea of the international firm is not likely to win favor with the developing nations. Almost without exception, these are intent on promoting their industrialization in accordance with their own development plans and priorities, rather than the classical doctrine of comparative advantage.

On the other hand, a private firm will only convict itself of hypocrisy if it denies the primacy of long-run profitability or stresses the "good-neighbor" rationale to the point of suggesting that anything beneficial to the recipient should raise a presumption of philanthropic motives in the giver. A private corporation is not, cannot be represented to be, and certainly is nowhere accepted as a foreign-aid institution.

Why should it be? If the substance of my argument is correct, the foreign private investor has no need to be defensive about the legitimacy of his basic profit motive. If he accepts the fact that the quality and essentiality of his contribution will be continually challenged by the host country, and if he plans the extent, nature, and duration of his resource commitment accordingly, it is likely that his objectives abroad—not only his manner of pursuing them—will coincide with what host countries view to be their best interest. And to the extent that they do, the safety of his investment will be assured.

This "happy ending" is more easily described than consummated. To identify these kinds of opportunities, and to integrate their uncertain or limited time horizons into the long-range, worldwide planning of an international corporation does indeed require business statesmanship. It is a task of awesome complexity. But so is any task of statesmanship in the world of today.

Interdependence on a Small Planet

Emile Benoit

We now live in a world in which all men are so close that only a few minutes' communicating, orbiting, or shooting time separates them—a world which is only a tiny footstool for the beginning of man's exploration of the universe. Yet we are still trying to make do with a system of international relations based on a much earlier order, one that could accommodate scores of "independent" self-centered nation-states, each claiming the absolute rights of a Machiavellian "sovereign" to do what its own interest appeared to dictate, to withdraw from (or ignore) prior agreements when inconvenient, and to be bound solely by its own judgment in international disputes—including disputes about the meaning of its promises and agreements.

The tension between these two worlds—the vast one of petty "independent" quarreling human groups, and the small one inextricably linked for good or for ill by modern technology—is the central drama of our era; it is unimaginable that these two concepts of the world can coexist for long. One or the other—or both—must go. It is the writer's belief that the universe of seemingly sovereign political entities will gradually disappear as mankind grows to understand the basic facts of its interdependence and learns to fashion political tools more consistent with them. This interdependence is both military and nonmilitary. The first variety has been accorded greater publicity, but even in this area the nature and strength of the ties that bind mankind are but imperfectly understood.

Few truly comprehend that we are now in the strange position of being militarily dependent upon our opponents. This paradoxical situation has arisen out of the contemporary revolution in military technologies. Contrary to Alfred Marshall's soothing adage, nature does make jumps; they are rare, but when they occur, a new system emerges and that new system is no longer understandable and predictable by the laws that governed the old one.

Anatomy of a Quantum Jump

The main features of the current military revolution need no detailed exposition here. As every modern schoolboy now unfortunately knows, the

Reprinted from *Columbia Journal of World Business* (Spring 1966), pp. 9–18, and Chapter 1 of *Disarmament and World Economic Interdependence*, edited by Emile Benoit, with the assistance of P. Gleditsch, Columbia University Press, 1967.

Hiroshima bomb was thousands of times more powerful than earlier weapons, and the first hydrogen bomb a thousand times stronger than that. These nuclear explosives, of continuously improving efficiency, were then incorporated into missiles capable of delivering havoc at least forty times more quickly than World War II planes. Their effectiveness was again raised by another large factor with the development of inertial guidance systems that can direct the missiles to their targets with fantastic precision. When the possibility of an active antimissile defense arose, decoys and jamming devices were quickly installed on the incoming missiles to make the chance of intercepting any significant percentage of them exceedingly remote. As a final step, missile launchers have been hardened, dispersed, concealed, or kept in motion beneath the oceans or in the air so that there is little hope of preventing any decisive proportion of them from functioning by means of a preclusive attack.

All this adds up to a true quantum jump of the order of hundreds, or thousands, of millions. Changes of that magnitude are comparatively rare in cosmic experience: they may be likened to the gathering of forces behind the explosion of stars, or the mutation which led to the emergence of the human brain in the evolutionary process. Certainly the magnitude of the present weapons revolution completely dwarfs that of the invention of gunpowder, cannons, and muskets which in its time destroyed the viability of feudalism. It is surprising that, in the light of these developments, so many people can expect a political system based on war as the means of settling major disputes to go on much as before.

In effect, what has occurred is a *mass exchange of hostages*, leaving the population of the world's major cities subject to sudden slaughter by hostile governments. This is interdependence on a new plane of intensity: to an unbelievable and gruesome degree we now depend on each other's leaders to be rational, to be predictable, to be sane. One has only to imagine for a moment what the situation would be like today if Hitler and the Nazi Party were in charge of a military force like that of the U.S. or the USSR to appreciate how desperately we now depend on each other's leaders to be relatively free of paranoia, and endowed with humane qualities.

Breaking the Language Barrier

It would be a mistake, however, to overemphasize military interdependence to the exclusion of other types. Military interdependence is simply one facet of the technological revolution which, by overcoming the obstacles of distance and time, is in an operational sense "shrinking" our planet. Already the jet plane and modern electronics have greatly reduced the girth of our globe: electronic advances can transmit the essential raw material of human intercourse—exchange of thought—as well as the impulses for aiming weapons. The presence of Telstar in the sky is a reassuring omen, preparing us for a day in the near future when international communication, and indeed when television and facsimile pictures—which are so much more readily comprehended across linguistic boundaries than are mere words—will flow easily over national boundaries, enlarging the community of experience out of which the community of feeling and of trust needed for political cooperation must grow. But this will require cooperation; hostile use of such facilities could quickly create chaos in the airwaves.

Geographic and physical aspects of human interdependence will increasingly obtrude on our attention and demand solutions. Recognition has gradually emerged that nuclear fission explosions in the air raise the radioactivity of the atmosphere and can spread malignancy and death far from where they initially were set off. We are now becoming more aware that the atmosphere is also subject to gradual deterioration from the effects of the wastes dumped into it by a rapidly growing industrial civilization. The world's rivers and seas may be similarly affected, especially if better technical solutions are not found for disposal of nuclear wastes before there is large-scale use of nuclear fission for electric power generation. Already the conservation of ocean food resources poses an acute problem for international cooperation.

Dealing with Overpopulation

Another serious danger arises from the unchecked growth of population which not only imperils living standards in the overpopulated countries themselves but raises intractable long-term problems for their neighbors—which as a minimum will have to continue raising larger and larger food surpluses for relief programs, or accept the horror of large-scale famine in the world community. Further, all too soon in the time scale of human history, nations will probably be able to modify their own climate, and—intentionally or unintentionally—the climate of their neighbors. We have already seen how diversion of river water can threaten to become a *casus belli*. Imagine the implications of changing a neighbor's mean temperature by, say, fifteen or twenty degrees, or lowering the average rainfall by several inches! Finally the exploration of space is emotionally felt by most people as a generically human rather than as a merely national enterprise. Increasingly, it will provide a perspective against which national divisions will appear secondary and irrelevant to man's ambitions.

Nor are the triumphs of understanding and invention in the twentieth century by any means confined to the realm of physical realities. Our knowledge of how to create and distribute goods and services has also taken giant steps forward. This includes not only the vast progress in applying physical technology to production, but also—and not less significant for man's welfare, I think—the tremendous progress in economic theory, policy and administration. It is only within my adult lifetime that national accounts and related statistical series have provided the market economies with a reasonably clear picture of what was going on, and that Keynesian insights and neo-Keynesian techniques have enabled us to avoid the depressions that made the *laissez-faire* economy violently and dangerously unstable, unbearably wasteful, and morally unsupportable.

The centrally planned economies also are improving their knowledge of aspects of economic reality and performance (such as standards of quality and the preferences of consumers) hitherto undeservedly ignored. They are reconstructing their planning methods to make better use of such information, and also to liberate the creative power of individual incentive and inventiveness—which can never be entirely preplanned, but which add so much to the quality of a society's output, if only the plans are flexible enough to accommodate them.

At the same time, great improvements in the techniques of managing the individual production unit have been developing both in the market and the centrally planned economies. Examples are the use of computers to solve technically difficult problems of inventory management as well as production layout and sequencing; the precise identification of the skill requirements of different categories of jobs; the effective matching of such requirements with employee capabilities; the use of programmed learning and simulation techniques for industrial training and retraining; the precise measurement and accounting analysis of elements in the cost structure and their variation with scale of production; the influence of worker morale on production, and the factors affecting such morale, etc.

This vast progress in economic understanding and management has greatly enhanced the possibilities of cooperation. In the first place, it has so enormously increased the potential output of goods and services through the normal processes of economic activity that it makes any possible gains from the use of force seem trivial by comparison. Not only wars, but colonialism and other forms of exploitation through political power fade in attractiveness, even to the least humanitarian spirit, as the human contribution to production becomes less and less a matter of simple repetitive physical effort (which can easily be measured and coerced) and more and more a positive, creative expression of skill and imagination, within a complex and subtle team activity in which the individual's contribution is hard to isolate and measure, let alone impose by force.

Moreover, the outpouring of material benefits available in this way is so vast that the struggle over the division of these benefits should subside, with a concomitant softening of class hostility. Even if injustices in distribution are slower to be eliminated than our consciences desire, it is easier to bear them if there is enough so that even the poorest of the world receive what is essential for human dignity and development.

An End to Polarity

Secondly, the improvements being made both in the market economies and in the centrally planned economies are gradually drawing the two systems together. In essence this "depolarization" may be characterized as a movement toward centralization in the west, and away from it in the east. The convergence of the two systems may help to weaken the widespread ideological illusion of total opposition and conflict between the two types of economy, which is so dangerous a feature of contemporary life—distorting and exaggerating as it does the inevitable conflicts of power politics between national states.

With convergence arises a greater possibility of fruitful economic cooperation. So long as the two economic types are viewed as deadly rivals locked in a blind struggle for survival, cooperation is difficult. Even mutually beneficial activities are suspect, since they will almost invariably be (or seem to be) more helpful to one side than to the other, and will therefore be opposed by the other side. Indeed, even a willingness of one side to accept a given agreement is likely to arouse the suspicions of the other that there must be some asymmetry in the benefits—even if it cannot be readily identified.

Investment Displacing Trade

But the process of convergence will not merely enhance the possibility of routine economic cooperation; of perhaps even greater significance, it will open vast geographic areas to a relatively new type of business association—one that is proving increasingly valuable in the west. Hopes of improved economic cooperation among western nations had hitherto centered mainly on the possibility of a balanced expansion of commodity imports and exports. I would like to register my conviction, however, that trade in the conventional sense of a balanced two-way flow of goods is now being displaced in importance by a different, though little noticed, mode of economic cooperation.

Essentially, what seems to be happening is that conventional international trade, involving autonomous "untied" exchange of exports and imports, has been rapidly losing in importance to a type of international economic activity dependent on private or public investment or grants. Thus, of the $21.9 billion of U.S. nonmilitary exports in 1963, a third were either financed by government loans or grants ($2.7 billion) or involved sales to U.S. foreign affiliates (estimated at $5 billion) and were thus to a degree dependent on earlier investment. Only $14.2 billion were balanced exports of the conventional autonomous sort, not the result of prior investment or aid-giving decisions.

Moreover, even the total export figure is completely dwarfed by *production abroad by American-owned enterprises.* U.S.-owned foreign manufacturing enterprises alone showed sales of $31.3 billion for 1963. My own rough estimate (based on the ratio of foreign investment and earnings in manufacturing to total foreign investment and earnings) suggests that total 1963 sales of goods and services produced abroad by American-controlled companies were of the order of $60–$70 billion, which is about the size of the national income of France, the United Kingdom, or Germany. (Value added by these companies would, of course, be less than sales. On the other hand, a substantial additional amount of output was obtained as a result of technical and managerial assistance by U.S. companies under licensing and management contract agreements, and is not reflected in the above foreign investment and earnings estimates.) Incidentally, this foreign production of

American-owned companies is not only much larger than U.S. exports, but seems to be growing twice as fast.

Why is this so? What has happened to give such growing emphasis to producing abroad in place of exporting? I suspect that this trend reflects a fundamental change now occurring in the determinants of comparative advantage and specialization. Conventional economic analysis lays great stress on differences in factor endowments as the source of international division of labor. Particularly emphasized were gross geographic differences of climate, soil and mineral or other natural resources. The tropics would, in this view, export tropical fruits, coffee and tea, petroleum, rubber, silk, tin, etc., because their climate and raw material endowments gave them a unique ability to produce such items at low cost. Similarly, it was thought that the industrial countries had the capacity to produce and export steel because of the availability, in close proximity, of high quality deposits of coal and iron ore.

Manufactures Dominating Commerce

While this concept may have been adequate to explain trade patterns in agriculture or basic metals, it never shed much light on the pattern of trade in manufactures. It could not, for example, explain why the three leading producers and exporters of machinery, the U.S., U.K., and Germany, also bought such a large quantity of machinery *from each other*. It is becoming even less useful as manufactures grow to constitute a far larger share of world trade. This process is the inevitable result of the displacement by synthetics of tree rubber, silk, wood and other natural products, as well as continued technical improvements reducing the amount of raw materials per unit of output and permitting the use of lower-grade material. The industrialized countries have also insisted on developing their own agriculture and reserves of oil, gas and other natural resources, even when adequate imported supplies at low cost were available. Thus, the explanation of trade in terms of gross geographic advantage applies satisfactorily to an ever smaller part of the world's commerce.

Triumph of the Superior Firm

Competitive advantage in manufactures is only indirectly and partially dependent on possession of the required raw materials or other strictly geographic advantage. Rather it is now primarily an attribute of *particular firms, or even particular product lines*. It rests on the capability of a given company, establishment or production unit to produce a superior bundle of goods and services—including such services as speedy delivery, favorable terms of payment, availability of spare parts, technical advice on using the product and technical servicing to keep it operating efficienly during its normal life period. Such advantage is the fruit of superior technical knowledge, new products, and better product specification resulting from past research and development activities, and from greater efficiency in meeting the varied needs of customers. Sometimes, this is accompanied by lower prices, but often it is not, since the buyer may be more concerned with the dependability of the product, or the quality of the services provided, than with marginal savings on the original price.

To provide such services reliably, a company must command resources that will enable it to extend meaningful service guarantees far into the future and a vast organization which can offer a variety of personnel opportunities for a lifetime career. Such enormous, virtually permanent, world-wide organizations as General Motors, Jersey Standard, Unilever, Philips' Gloeilampen, etc., with assets and life expectations paralleling those of nation-states, completely transcend the competitive-market assumptions of classical economics.

As the key competitive advantages become essentially matters of skill, knowledge and organization rather than of climate or natural resource location, the economies of scale are altered. It becomes less advantageous to complete a production operation in one central place and ship bulky goods for long distances to where they will be used. Opportunities will increasingly be found to sell or rent the superior knowledge or skills and ideas that convey the crucial competitive advantages. Alternatively, efforts will be made to establish new production affiliates close to where the goods and services will eventually be utilized and where the particular needs and desires of the user can be given consideration, and the essential servicing provided in a reliable and economical manner. In effect what is now being demonstrated is that the long-run cost of transferring ideas, skills, and organizational patterns from one place to another is far lower than the cost of continuously transporting merchandise.

Cash Is Secondary

People not in international business rarely understand the extent to which international direct investment today involves such a transfer rather than the mere migration of surplus capital. Much of the capital from U.S. direct investment in recent years has come from local and other non-U.S. sources: local investors and suppliers, banks, governments, and international agencies. The American investor's most valuable contribution hasn't been cash but know-how and management skill. Moreover, as restrictions on capital exports diminish, European, Japanese and other non-U.S. investors are beginning to emulate U.S. companies, with parallel benefits to the economies in which their investments are made. The U.S. has, of course, no monopoly on advanced technology and management, and will itself benefit from direct investments made by European and other foreign companies in this country. An interesting example of such reverse flow of technology and management is offered by the acquisition, reorganization and modernization of The Underwood Typewriter Company in the U.S. by the pioneering Italian firm of Olivetti.

Abstract But Compelling

It is thus not amiss to argue that the increasingly abstract character of competitive advantage is the chief reason that international investment tends to displace exports in importance. While such investment also creates further opportunities for the export of components, raw materials, supplementary models, etc., the relative importance of overseas production steadily increases.

What benefits have foreign countries gotten out of the supplementation of management, skill and technology represented by the over $40 billion (by 1963) of U.S. investment in foreign enterprises? First, an enormous increase in production—as indicated, perhaps $60–$70 billion per year, including wages and salaries paid almost entirely to workers and employees of the host countries. Secondly, substantial interest and profit payments to local lenders and equity investors participating in the projects. Third, $1.5 billion of reinvested U.S. profits in 1963, representing new savings and investment. Fourth, a large volume of profits taxes collected, which could easily have totaled around $1.5 billion, or even more, in that year. Fifth, and crucially important, an enormous contribution to foreign exchange earnings: these came to $4.7 billion from exports of manufactures alone generated by these investments. Adding the exports generated by mining and petroleum would easily double this figure. Furthermore, that part of overseas production which was not sent out of the country may be regarded as in some sense a substitute for imports that the host country would otherwise have had to purchase. The cost to the host country for all this was $4.5 billion of U.S. profits, of which, as we have noted, only $3 billion was withdrawn. Moreover, nearly $2 billion of this $3 billion was offset by new U.S. direct investment.

Private Investment in Public Enterprise

Demonstrably, international investment is a fruitful source of cooperation for economic progress among western nations. But of what relevance is this to countries where the means of production are not privately owned? Certainly, communist society would appear to provide little place for foreign private investment. However, if we remember that the essential aspect of such investment may be viewed as a transfer of skills, ideas, and techniques—to be paid for with fees or royalties—rather than primarily as a migration of capital—to be remunerated by a dividend or an interest payment—it is possible to discern a basis for east-west collaboration. Such a basis already underlies many joint-venture situations. Here, the foreign investment process is looked upon as an export of equipment paid for in installments over an extended period, plus royalty payments for the licensing of new technology, know-how or trademarks, and management fees for the costs of advising and administering the new operation, transferring the new technology, etc. Comparable arrangements can also be made between east and west. Alternatively, one can avoid the need for an agreement in financial terms altogether by simply deciding to divide the physical output of the joint venture in agreed proportions, with the private-enterprise partner free to retain the foreign exchange proceeds from the foreign marketing of his share of the output. There are a number of other formulas that will serve equally well.

This mechanism has come to be called "co-production." Such an arrangement usually involves the use of advanced western technology, equipment and management by a productive enterprise in an East European country in a partnership arrangement with a capitalist production unit. The East European partner normally contributes the labor, the raw materials, and the plant—and often some of the components. The western partner supplies advanced equipment and know-how, product design, often at least part of the management, and—what is extremely important—international marketing channels.

This concept is certainly rather a startling one. Not only is it hard to see how a communist society could accept private foreign investment, it is equally difficult to understand how western managers could participate in running a unit of centrally planned economy which would presumably issue directives to the enterprise inconsistent with the profit-maximization objectives of western entrepreneurs. Yet surprising or unbelievable as the idea of co-production may seem, the fact is that such ventures actually exist, that they are increasing in number, and that many more are currently being explored as possibilities, or are in the stage of active negotiation. Let me mention a few examples.

Curious Combinations

The West German firm of Rheinstahl has entered into a joint venture with the Hungarian Ministry of Machine Building for the construction in Hungary of quarrying equipment, machine tools, and other steel products, utilizing Hungarian as well as German semifinished components. The Austrian firm of Simmering-Graz-Pauker has a joint venture with the Hungarian group called Komplex to build power plants in India, financed through Hungarian-Indian bilaterial clearing arrangements. IKEA, a Swedish furniture company, supplies machinery and designs for the semimanufacture of furniture in Poland under its own technical control. The semimanufactures are shipped to Sweden for finishing and marketing. The British firm of Walmsley (Bury) Group Ltd. has agreed with Poland's Metalexport to supply paper-making machinery to Poland (and thereafter to sell it to other Soviet bloc countries) which will after a time contain components made in Poland with Walmsley technical assistance. The British firm of Callaghan & Son, Ltd., and the Czech firm of Kdynske Strojirny have an agreement to manufacture jointly a line of automatic textile machinery, and to market and service the machinery throughout the world on a prearranged basis. A great many other examples could be cited.

It is important to be clear about the economic bases of such ventures. What is in it for each side? For the east the answer is obvious. The eastern partner is enabled to produce the sort of items for which there already exists a large demand in western markets, to reach and maintain the necessary quality standards, and to make and service the goods as they must be manufactured and serviced to win and hold western customers. But what offsetting special advantages can be offered by the eastern countries to the western partners? Why bother to produce in Eastern Europe items to be sold in the west?

Surprisingly, the most important advantage offered is the eastern labor force. Overfull employment in Germany, Switzerland, and other countries of Western Europe has generated severe manpower shortages, relieved only by expensive importation and on-the-job training of foreign workers, with considerable social dislocation and expensive new requirements for housing, schools, etc. The Eastern European countries, on the other hand, still have considerable labor surpluses in agriculture, or even inefficiently employed in industry, owing to the requirement that enterprise directors find employment for a given work force whether they really need them or not. (Of late, the growing freedom granted to managers to disregard such considerations has begun to create overt unemployment, especially in Poland.)

Cheap, Stable and Skilled

What is more, the East European labor force has some especially valuable properties from the point of view of western management. First, it is relatively cheap. Living standards are still considerably lower in Eastern than in Western Europe, and workers in communist countries are not free to have independent unions or strike. Thus the cost of labor is not only low, but is relatively stable over the production planning period. Finally, the East European work force contains a high ratio of relatively skilled people; it is particularly strong in middle-grade technicians, engineers, and scientists, who have been trained in large numbers as part of the communist ideological commitment to education and science.

Boon to Trader

A second advantage that co-production ventures can offer western firms is markets. While the eastern partner will ordinarily reserve for itself the marketing of the joint venture's finished products in the countries of Comecon (Council for Mutual Economic Cooperation), the western firms may gain important eastern outlets for components and materials. Moreover, through its growing familiarity with trade and other officials of the communist country, it may obtain orders (directly or as an intermediary) to supply other finished goods that the communist country needs to import. In the case of the joint venture between Simmons Machine Tools in Albany, N.Y., and the Czech industrial complex, Skoda, Simmons found an advantageous and inexpensive source of supply in Skoda for certain machine tools which Skoda could deliver in three to five weeks (compared to over a year for comparable items from western firms), while Skoda is to provide an East European market for some Simmons tools that are superior to eastern models.

A third, and potentially quite important, benefit to the western partner is specialized technology. In a growing number of cases, the eastern partner has made certain technological improvements from which the western partner could benefit, and this return flow of technology becomes a significant *quid pro quo*.

The partners in these co-production arrangements can increase their returns in the same manner as returns are normally augmented (whether in international or domestic investment)—by raising productivity sufficiently to repay the costs of financing the productivity increase, including the costs of the machinery, inventions, stocks of goods, and other forms of capital invested. The role of profits—both as an indicator of and as a stimulus to success—is equally important whether the process is carried on by private or by public enterprises, or by a partnership arrangement using both types, as suggested above. Nor is there any reason to doubt that the full modernization of the Soviet bloc economies could be a highly profitable operation for all participants. In some respects the Soviet bloc is technologically and economically at about the stage of Western Europe of the early postwar period. Modernization is an enormous, but by no means impossible task, and assistance from the advanced private enterprise economies could greatly shorten the time and sacrifice required to achieve the goal. A very large amount of private business would be involved.

Ideology's Irrelevant

The beauty of these co-production arrangements from the point of view of one who welcomes more interdependence is that they require a great deal of communication and mutual understanding on matters which are taken seriously, because they are of obvious importance to both sides. In such ventures, practical results count, and ideological differences are pushed into the background. According to a former student of mine who has planned and carried out a number of such operations in Yugoslavia, ideological differences have proved remarkably irrelevant and easy to ignore in this context. Thus, such ventures *can* do much to stimulate interdependence and cooperation.

If co-production succeeds in reducing interbloc tensions and increasing the prosperity of the east, then both east and west can settle down to solving what is perhaps a more fundamental problem than their mutual hostility: closing the gap in living standards between north and south (the developed and the less-developed). The poorer countries of Asia, Africa and Latin America have begun to view their historic poverty as by no means inevitable, but subject to improvement by their own efforts, and with the help of the developed countries. The resulting "demand for development" is a relatively new but already vastly powerful political force in the world, one that contributes enormously to the world's progress, but which may also lead to catastrophic conflict if not accommodated.

While the developed countries have inspired, through example and precept, the demand for development, they have unwittingly acted to frustrate that demand by exposing the less-developed countries most intensively to a single extremely potent sector of advanced technology, namely, public health measures to eliminate epidemics and reduce infant mortality. Such measures have been given priority for humanitarian reasons, and also because they are relatively inexpensive. It is these measures, however—and not any rise in the birth rate—that are responsible for the so-called population explosion, which, unless contained, threatens to swamp all constructive efforts to raise living standards and achieve rapid self-sustaining economic growth in the developing countries.

Fortunately, remedies are at hand or visible over the horizon. Essentially, they consist of a more balanced exposure of the less-developed countries to the whole range of medical capabilities of the developed countries in the public health field, including new inexpensive technologies for restraining births—such as the intra-uterine loop—along with new informational and public health clinics for diffusing the new knowledge of fertility control, and dispensing assistance in contexts which inspire confidence and engender willingness to change social attitudes and personal habits. It has been calculated that such aids to population stabilization are a great many times more effective in raising per capita incomes than an equal dollar volume of foreign aid of the conventional variety. Since it was the intervention of the developed countries—no matter how well motivated—that created the problem in the first place, there is clearly a moral obligation on the part of the developed countries to do what they can to right the balance.

As for the traditional economic aid programs, they have been basically undermined by having been so largely planned and administered in the spirit of the cold war. Most of the resources made available for foreign aid have been actually used to obtain or support foreign "client states," ideological converts, military bases, U.N. votes, revolutionary or counterrevolutionary movements, etc. The resulting scandalous confusion of objectives has been extremely prejudicial to a serious attack on the problem of economic development, which is, in any case, a vastly more difficult enterprise than was thought until a few years ago.

The communists can make political gains, no doubt, by cultivating the harvest of hatred arising from past colonialism and neglect. But political gains of this sort are obtainable only at the risk of escalating minor conflicts into major military confrontations; and victories—even if attained—are likely to be evanescent and burdensome. When it comes right down to it, communism has no more of a solution to the demand for a simple and quick route to economic development than capitalism. (Indeed, as even Marx perceived, a rather high degree of economic development is probably a prerequisite for the effective running of a centrally planned economy.) A long-term and responsible view by the Soviet bloc leaders could therefore lead them to pass up such easy but illusory "victories," and to turn, in partnership with the west, if indeed the latter is willing, to coping with the real and vast problems of world economic growth.

If this partnership were to be effected, the problems of world economic development would begin to look manageable. Even if disarmament remained elusive, one could count in such a case on tens of billions of dollars in savings from an arms freeze, and from the phasing out of obsolescent weapon systems. Moreover, much of the released resources in research and development, systems analysis, and large-scale program administration capability could usefully be diverted to the basic analytic, innovational and creative programs required to achieve the needed breakthroughs in the field of economic development. Examples of such potential breakthroughs are the inexpensive desalination of water, the effective tapping of unconventional energy sources, sharply reduced building costs via prefabricated modules, the speedy achievement of universal literacy and advanced skills through the use of teaching machines and satellite-transmitted TV programs, etc. Dramatic progress will probably be required in a number of such fields to enable the tasks of development to be accomplished within a politically tolerable time span.

For many, therefore, everything depends in the end on the capability of both west and east to make the enormous intellectual adjustments to the technological imperatives of the new interdependent world in which we live. Such mental changes, it is clear, are made only with difficulty. The most menacing aspect of the problem is the fantastic speed with which our environment has been changing and the fact that if we fail to meet a single test we may not have a second chance. There is little room for learning by trial and error. Whether the human race possesses the flexibility to adapt to such a rapidly changing environment no one can foretell. Our job is to try.

Special Aspects of International Management

7

The problems of international business are, of course, basically the same as business problems in various other settings. All management people, whether they manage locally or internationally, must be continually on the alert for unexpected problems, and unexpected opportunities, in their markets, in the organizations they manage, in their relations with suppliers, competitors, government officials, and with all those other people with whom business must live. Decision making must go on—continuously, promptly, effectively—in all business organizations, whether they are large or small, bilingual or multilingual, uninational or multinational. Production must be kept up to schedule, the staff must be recruited, trained, and inspired, markets must be found and developed, accurate records must be kept, and taxes must be paid on time.

All of this is common ground to the businessman, wherever he may be. No business can prosper unless these functions are performed smoothly and well. But in international business we have all of this, plus much more. No one can expect to carve out a successful international business career unless he excels in one or more of these traditionally important business skill areas. But internationally, a man must be a superior manager, and, in addition, he must have developed a set of special antennae for sensing those special risks and opportunities that are unique to international business. He should know at least two modern languages—his own and at least one other—but in addition he must have acquired the "special language," or special art, of living with a vast array of environmental differences.

The international businessman must be a man of many interests; he must have, or acquire, a cosmopolitan viewpoint. He will find himself eating "strange" foods, imbibing drinks the local bartender never made, and rubbing shoulders with many different, non-American types of people. Some will be adept at keeping different sets of books, one for themselves and one for the tax collector; some will expect him to cross their palms when he least expects it; some will be avid followers of Karl Marx while others will reminisce about how "orderly" things were under Hitler and Mussolini; some will call themselves socialists; some will live in palaces surrounded by squalor and misery; some will regard him as an ambassador of his native country, whether he wishes them to do so or not, while others will take it for granted that he is a "filthy capitalist imperialist."

Unless a man can keep his cool when caught in these crosscurrents of ambivalences, ambiguities, and misunderstandings, and unless he can function effectively as a business manager in the midst of it all, he may not be the type that will succeed in international business. The international manager must be a man who can see through the different appearances that surround him and grasp the essentials of the business problems that confront him. The fast-growing new world of international business, in short, is bringing along new types of management problems which require, for their solution, new types of management men.

Each of the main areas of management takes on a special, novel character when it is projected onto the international scene—for instance, personnel management. If only unskilled labor is available for production operations in a less-developed country, one can expect that both personnel practices and production management will be different from what is practiced in the United States. The firm may have to develop more elaborate training facilities for its workers, and machines may have to be redesigned so that an unskilled man cannot make errors or hurt himself through lack of operating experience.

If money markets in a given country are inadequate, capital needs must be met in very different manners than in the United States. In this case, the firm might also run into various international constraints dealing with capital flows into or out of various countries.

The various functional managers of multinational firms have to be aware of environmental differences in overseas operations which make such adjustments mandatory. As with other parts of international business, many of these adjustments are fairly obvious, but most are not. It is usually quite clear when high skill manpower, such as engineers and other technicians, is unavailable, and steps are usually taken to assure proper supplies of such manpower, either through intensive training or through foreign recruitment. But it is not so obvious that a truck driver or production line worker in the United States has additional skills and attitudes which his foreign counterpart may lack, or that a widely accepted marketing symbol in the United States might be considered offensive or even illegal in another country.

If a man is a marketer he will need to be alert not only to different customs in different markets, but also the possibility that exchange rate changes may drastically alter the relative attractiveness of different markets, that regional groupings like the European Common Market may enter the picture and upset traditional ways of doing business, and that his own country and other countries may embark upon far-reaching tariff reduction schemes (like the "Kennedy Round") or slap on new import quotas as the U.S. has done for oil and some important nonferrous metals, and as it may do some day for textiles and shoes. Whatever a man's management specialty may be, he will find that it entails new kinds of fun and games when practiced internationally.

In this concluding set of readings we have selected works that, we think, catch the flavor of what it is like to be one of the new international management men, and to live with the problems they live with.

In the first selection, Professors Robock and Simmonds ask "What's New in International Business?" and proceed to identify at least four "new" areas in which unique problems arise when business crosses national boundaries. They point out also that international business is, itself, a major change agent in the environments in which it operates, and they wind up with some words of wisdom for the student seeking to prepare for an international business career.

In the next selection Alan Reid describes "The New Men in Overseas Management" who have come to replace the legendary European expatriates of a bygone colonial era. International firms have been able to ride out political storms in many host countries, he points out, by internationalizing their managements. Future management men of whatever nationality are identified as early as possible and are then systematically cross-posted to different countries at appropriate stages of their careers. In one large multinational company a young man from Japan gets a three-year assignment in Brazil, his job in Japan being filled by a high potential man from Venezuela. In this way cadres of talented men for international management posts are built up.

But, as Professor Simmonds points out in our third reading, in these matters there may be a wide gulf between *middle* management and *top* management. He presents detailed statistics covering almost 4,000 top executives of the 150 largest U.S. companies to show that, in American-based multinational companies at least, the path to the top is more difficult for a foreigner than for an American to tread. Although from one-fifth to one-third of the employees of these companies were foreigners, less than 2 percent of their top managers were non-Americans. Professor Simmonds ventures some tentative explanations for what he found, and even advances some thoughts about how it might be changed.

In studying international management we must investigate the flows of management talent in both directions—from subsidiary companies toward the corporate headquarters and from the central offices to assignments in foreign posts. In our fourth selection Professor Schöllhammer looks into the outward flow in an article dealing with "The Compensation of International Executives." He examines the experience of twelve large international U.S.-based companies in compensating executives working outside their home countries. He finds that such employees— there were some 40,000 Americans holding managerial positions abroad when he wrote—receive recurrent compensation that is about twice as high as they would receive at home, but that the foreign premium is designed to compensate them for the increased costs of living abroad. The broad policy goal of most companies is that, for the executive concerned, a foreign assignment should produce neither an undue financial gain nor a loss compared to similar employment at home.

In a final selection we reprint an article by Professor Farmer, "Nuts, Bolts and Economic Progress," on a previously little-noticed aspect of managing a business operation in a less-developed country. Building on his own experiences when he managed a business in a middle-Eastern country, Professor Farmer describes how the unavailability of needed machinery parts and components can be a serious drag on economic efficiency in the less-developed countries. Inevitably, the use of machinery proliferates with economic progress but because most LDC's do not have large inventories of parts readily available, when expensive machinery breaks down, it may have to be kept out of operation for a considerable time until replacement parts can be secured, often from abroad. Much economic waste occurs in this way because the utilization rate of scarce capital equipment turns out to be much lower than it needs to be. Both international businessmen and economic development economists have taken an active interest in realizing the substantial savings that Professor Farmer shows can be had by attending to this apparently mundane aspect of international business management.

What's New in
International Business?

Stefan H. Robock
Kenneth Simmonds

The tremendous growth in international business represents one of the most dramatic and significant world events of the last decade. International business operations have become massive in scale, are expanding rapidly, and are influencing patterns of political, economic, and social development throughout the world.

At the same time this phenomenon has confronted the business executive with new and unique management problems. He must deal with new elements of risk, of conflict, of environmental adjustments, and of influence over social and economic change—elements he has not been facing in purely domestic operations. And, until recently, the international business executive was not able to look to the academic centers of business research and education for much help.

Although an educational lag still persists, a significant new trend has been gaining momentum in American business education—to give explicit attention to the international dimension of business. The new trend is supported by the view that existing theories, generalizations, principles, methods, and techniques, developed in response to norms in the United States, are neither general nor universal and that the international dimension of business involves unique aspects that need to be explicitly treated in business education.

This new emphasis on international business studies has important implications for the businessman, because he can utilize both the knowledge being developed and the personnel being trained. How the field of international business is being defined, what materials and ideas are being developed, and how the international dimension of business is altering the business school curriculum are issues that should be of interest to the businessman.

The Field of International Business

The label "International Business" covers the evolving multidimensional pattern of international activities by business firms. As a field of study, it supersedes and extends beyond the traditional field called "Foreign Trade." Until recently, because the international dimension of business consisted mostly of importing and exporting, courses in foreign trade were the mainstay of the international dimension in business education. But since the end of World War II, investment has

---

Reprinted by permission of the authors and publisher from *Business Horizons* (Winter 1966), Indiana University.

begun to displace trade.[1] Many firms have established industrial and commercial operations in a number of different countries. These operations involve direct foreign investment and direct managerial responsibility. Furthermore, much of the import and export activity of multinational corporations depends directly upon having business operations in many countries.

Business firms differ significantly in their degree of direct and indirect international involvement. The international dimension for some firms may be limited to importing or exporting; other firms may be purely domestic but subject to considerable foreign competition. At the end of the spectrum is the multinational business firm that has its home in one sovereign national state but operates and lives under the laws and customs of other countries as well.[2] The multinational corporation may operate on a world scale without a dominant commitment to a particular country, but it is more common at present for the international firm to have close ties to its home country. Although few, if any, business firms are isolated from the effects of international business activity, the field of international business gives major, but not exclusive, attention to the role of the multinational corporation.

Business firms operating within only one country, whether it is the United States or a foreign country, are generally covered by the concepts and ideas being taught in the functional fields of marketing, finance, production, and control. And where necessary, the substance of these fields may need to be adapted to the peculiar conditions of different foreign environments. Yet, where the operations of a domestically owned company or a foreign subsidiary influence or are influenced by a relationship with a foreign firm or institution, problems arise that fall within the scope of the international business field.

In a broad sense, then, the field of international business focuses on unique problems that arise when the business firm crosses national boundaries—whether through the movement of goods, services, investment capital, money flows, or personnel. The field also includes problems of decision making by public officials who must understand the effects of government policies and actions on international business activities and take such effects into account in the formulation and implementation of public policies. These problems all require special concepts, theories, ways of thinking, and methods of analysis not developed in existing areas of business concentration.

Separate Identity of International Business

Although unique variables and considerations of business have fostered the development of the field as a separate entity in the business area, not everything

---

[1] For an interesting discussion of why investment is displacing trade see Emile Benoit, "Interdependence on a Small Planet," *Columbia Journal of World Business* (Spring 1966).

[2] David E. Lilienthal, "The Multinational Corporation," in Anshen and Bach, eds., *Management and Corporations 1985* (New York: McGraw-Hill Book Co., Inc., 1960).

concerning international business must be studied separately under that heading. Some aspects of international business may be covered most effectively by extending existing fields; others can be better developed as a unified whole than as segmented appendages to existing fields. For example, an understanding in depth of cultural differences as they affect international business operations is more likely to develop when the subject is treated as a unified whole than if the scholars of finance, marketing, production, and management were each to study separately the adjustment of their function to different cultures.

There are four aspects of international business activity around which new types of thinking are beginning to emerge. These four aspects overlap to some degree and do not exhaust the potential for new approaches that may evolve. But each stems from unique problems that develop when business crosses national boundaries, and each gives rise to a new body of study and concepts.

International Risk Elements

The special risk elements confronted in international business activity include financial, political, regulatory, and tax risks. They arise from causes such as the existence of different currencies, monetary standards, and national goals, but they are all measurable through their effect on profitability or ownership.

The financial risk elements involve balance-of-payments considerations, varying exchange rates, differential inflation trends among countries, and divergent interest rates. In the political area, the risk of expropriation or lesser harassment directed toward the foreign firm must be considered for many years ahead when heavy capital investments are being contemplated. The regulatory risks arise from different legal systems, overlapping jurisdictions, and dissimilar policies that influence such conditions as the regulation of restrictive business practices and the application of antitrust laws. In the tax field, unforeseen changes in fiscal policies can significantly affect the profitability of the multinational corporation. Furthermore, uncertainty as to application of tax laws frequently creates a risk of double taxation.

International economics provides essential tools for understanding the risks arising from balance-of-payments considerations, foreign exchange regulation, problems of international liquidity, tariff policies, and trade restrictions. Political theory is developing new insights into nationalistic tendencies and the preferences of different societies for varying mixes of public and private sector activities. Legal research on international business transactions has been expanding, and a growing amount of international tax research is enlarging the general understanding of different tax systems and practices.

But the coverage in these related fields does not yet meet many of the major needs of international business. For example, the emphasis in international economics is still predominantly on international trade rather than on international investment. Also, the extension and application of the materials and concepts in the related fields to multinational business operations has been slow. Public policy has been even slower to adopt ideas and analyses that recognize the implications to international business activities of international economic and political variables.

The vigorous business and academic criticism of recent U.S. policies to restrict direct foreign private investment in order to improve the balance of payments suggests that the international business effects of such policies must be better identified in the formulation of governmental policies.[3] In the case of foreign investment controls, the recipient countries need to examine more rigorously the effect of such controls on international business and the question of how much and what kind of outside investment benefits the country.

The international risk elements are beginning to be identified and evaluated.[4] Some work is underway on the prediction of these risks. And the need is becoming recognized for a continuing business intelligence activity of considerable complexity to identify and predict international risks. Ideally, international risks should be analyzed for underlying causal forces, and projections into the future should be formulated in terms of probabilities and quantified in terms of potential costs.

Multinational Conflict Elements

Of major concern to international business are the conflicts that arise because of different national identities of owners, employees, customers, and suppliers and because of divergencies between national interests and the business goals of multinational corporations.[5] Some of the conflicts occur within the international firm, and others involve the firm's relationship to the external environment.

An extremely troublesome area of external conflict concerns profit maximization decisions that result in the transfer of funds, types of production, and employment from one country to another. The results of these decisions may at times run contrary to the national economic policies of one or all the countries involved. For example, extension of credit to foreign subsidiaries at times when the foreign nation is attempting to dampen purchasing power through monetary restrictions and exchange controls can undermine national objectives as well as place local firms at a competitive disadvantage.[6] The list of areas in which conflicts occur also includes such matters as contribution to local exports or reduction of imports, national interests in strengthening local research and management, or the country's international competitive position.

---

[3] For example, Judd Polk, Irene W. Meister, and Lawrence A. Veit, *U.S. Production Abroad and the Balance of Payments* (New York: National Industrial Conference Board, 1966).

[4] John G. McDonald, "Minimizing the Risks of Moving Abroad," *Business Horizons*, IV (Spring 1961).

[5] Howe Martyn, "Multinational Corporations in a Nationalistic World," *Challenge Magazine* (November–December 1965).

[6] See, for example, Raymond Vernon, "Saints and Sinners in Foreign Investment," *Harvard Business Review* (May–June 1963): 157.

External conflicts frequently arise in decisions concerning a firm's allegiance to national defense policies. A recent example is the French subsidiary of an American computer manufacturer, which, in deference to American allegiance, did not solicit computer sales from Eastern Europe. Another recent example resulted from the different national security policies followed by the United Kingdom and the United States in dealing with Cuba. As a result of this difference, a British subsidiary of an American firm was persuaded to maintain American allegiance and not sell motors that would be installed in passenger buses going to Cuba. Conflicts on defense matters are likely to increase with the growing numbers of foreign-owned subsidiaries in technically advanced fields.

Within the international corporation the mixture of national allegiances raises further issues. Better preparation of Americans for business posts tends to perpetuate American management abroad, and expansion from a parent organization in a developed country tends to retain research and administration functions in the developed countries. Disparity in wage and salary rates has also led to widely practiced discrimination on the basis of nationality. A number of nations have already placed restrictions on the numbers of foreign expatriates they will allow in local operations.

The conflict aspect of international business requires thinking that will relate a multiplicity of interests, each with different objectives and different criteria for evaluating potential outcomes. Specific attention to the development of this way of thinking can be a valuable contribution of international business study. No other business field covers this very successfully. The international businessman, trained to identify each conflicting interest and to think through the possible actions and reactions from each viewpoint, will be better prepared to plot his own best strategy in a complex situation. One of the functions of international business study should be to erase any tendency to make blindly nationalistic decisions or revert to pure economic arguments. There is currently a gradual emergence of an international framework for establishing legal validity of claims and actions of different parties involved in these conflict situations.[7]

Multiplicity of Environments

The most pervasive distinction between international and domestic business lies in the environmental framework. As business activity transcends a national setting, its environmental framework becomes more complex, more diverse, and more significant in influencing the effectiveness of business operations.[8] Aside from its

---

[7] W. G. Friedmann and R. C. Pugh, eds., *Legal Aspects of Foreign Investment* (Boston: Little, Brown and Co., 1959); A. A. Fatouros, *Government Guarantees to Foreign Investors* (New York: Columbia University Press, 1962).

[8] Roy Blough, *International Business: Environment and Adaptation* (New York: McGraw-Hill Book Company, 1966).

relationship to the elements of risk and conflict discussed above, the multiplicity of environments in international business creates a wide range of operational problems that require new tools, concepts, analytical methods and types of information. The wider the scope of the firm's international activities, the greater become the environmental diversities and the more crucial becomes the task of identifying, evaluating, and predicting environmental variables.

The environmental framework must be enlarged to include forces operating at a supranational level—such as the European Common Market—and forces involving relations between pairs of countries. Variables associated with different national settings must also be included. The need to understand the effect of environment on international business activity in both business decision making and public policy formulation has begun to produce analytical approaches peculiar to international business.[9]

One important category of environmental variables relates to business activity open to the international business firm and the form of business organization that must be used. The field of public utilities, including electric power, communications, and transportation, is not open to private enterprise in many countries. Business activity in the natural resource field, such as petroleum and mining, is restricted by many nations to domestic private enterprise or public enterprises. In some situations, the options open to international business firms require joint ventures with majority local ownership or joint ventures with government.

A second major category of environmental variables involves the diversity of the institutional settings. Labor unions, for example, are organized on different philosophical foundations and play different roles from country to country.[10] Patterns of national, regional, and local economic planning vary greatly in scope and in their influence over business activity. Capital markets and financial institutions are in different stages of development and, in some cases, are evolving along different paths.

Another broad environmental variable involves cultural differences that affect business management. International business needs to know how cultural differences influence the behavior of customers, suppliers, and employees, and how these influences on behavior will change. This aspect of international business involves the full range of communication problems arising out of different languages, different customs, and different values.[11]

International business has begun to develop its own body of cultural analysis following the functional division of business, with marketing questions receiving

---

[9] Richard N. Farmer and Barry M. Richman, *Comparative Management and Economic Progress* (Homewood, Ill.: Richard D. Irwin, Inc., 1965).

[10] Arthur M. Ross and Paul T. Hartman, *Changing Patterns of Industrial Conflict* (New York: John Wiley & Sons, Inc., 1960).

[11] Edward T. Hall, "The Silent Language in Overseas Business," *Harvard Business Review* (May–June 1960).

most attention. Considerable management literature has focused on the cultural adjustment of expatriate management and on the differences in foreign management and work force that might require adjustment of organization or procedures.[12] While concern for specific problems initially channeled cultural analysis along these functional lines, the common need throughout many business functions to understand cultural factors is leading toward a more unified approach, which might be titled "Cultural Analysis for Business Decisions." In the same way, other customary segments of environmental study such as educational, political, economic, and legal aspects can be explored in a unified manner.

International Business and Development

International business is frequently a major change agent and a key force in the economic and social development of a nation. This can be true for developed countries, such as those of Western Europe, as well as for underdeveloped countries. Thus, international business needs new concepts that provide an understanding of what can and cannot be achieved by the change agent and what are the potential contributions that international business can make to development.

In the case of the underdeveloped countries, the need to identify and justify the contribution that a proposed international business activity will make to the country has been forcefully stated by Richard Robinson as follows:

> The reason for attempting at least a semi-rigorous analysis of what a firm proposes to do in an underdeveloped country within the context of the national interest of that country lies in the near certainty that the host government will analyze the project in similar terms—if not at first, then later. The Western businessman must be prepared to defend the utility of his local enterprise in terms of sustained economic growth and political modernization.[13]

The large diversified international corporation that has flexibility in its selection of countries and products to offer within those countries is much in need of a body of expertise to guide its global operations. Although economists have given some attention to the divergence between social benefit and the firm's profit maximizing alternative, they have stopped far short of the specific calculations needed by the international business decision maker. Although economists have also given some attention to the costs and benefits to a country from foreign private investment, they have not yet developed an adequate and objective framework for decision making on such questions by the host countries.

---

[12] John Fayerweather, *The Executive Overseas* (Syracuse: Syracuse University Press, 1959).

[13] Richard D. Robinson, *International Business Policy* (New York: Holt, Rinehart and Winston, 1964), p. 100.

One facet of the contribution of international business to development that requires more attention is its role in encouraging indigenous entrepreneurial opportunities external to the firm for local suppliers and merchants. On the other hand, it may attract much of the entrepreneurial potential in a country and thereby inhibit the possibilities for development of other national enterprises.

The role of international business in development also raises moral and ideological issues. It is frequently true that profit maximization will keep the firm away from the less developed markets. Yet the opportunity for the greatest long-term good from the viewpoint of both the corporation's home country and the developing nations may well be to enter the developing countries.

Once a corporation has entered a developing market, a whole new range of considerations arise that are beginning to draw attention in international business studies. One such issue is the degree to which the firm should become involved in the community and undertake expenditures normally the function of the public sector.[14] As a number of studies have demonstrated, the paternalistic firm, which provides much of the normal functions of the public sector, can foster animosity among the local population.[15]

International Business Training

The Student

International business training has advanced most in the United States at the postgraduate level and in programs leading to the master of business administration degree. Some steps have been taken in undergraduate business programs and in executive development programs to include the international dimension of business. In addition, some business schools have programs at either the undergraduate or the graduate level for the student to complete part of his course work in a foreign university. The approach may internationalize the student by exposing him to a different foreign environment, yet foreign study per se does not necessarily include specific consideration of the substantive aspects of international business.

At the M.B.A. level, the kinds of students and their training needs will vary greatly. Most business schools structure their programs on the assumption that they are training future top business executives. In reality, however, many, if not most, of the M.B.A. students will make their careers as specialists in particular functional activities of business or as second-level managers.

Some students will want to study international business as a field of

---

[14] Clifton R. Wharton, "Aiding the Community: A New Philosophy for Foreign Operations," *Harvard Business Review* (March–April 1954): 64–72.

[15] Stacy May and Galo Plaza, *The United Fruit Company in Latin America* (Washington, D. C.: National Planning Association, 1958), pp. 240–43.

concentration; others will want international business courses as a supplement to their concentration in the traditional fields of accounting, marketing, finance, and so on. Some students specializing in international business hope to follow a career working in foreign countries. Others will take positions in the headquarters operations of a multinational firm that uses nationals for operating foreign subsidiaries. In schools with a sizable graduate program, courses and study programs can be designed to satisfy the international business training needs of the varied student body.

Having identified the kinds of concepts and materials required for international business as well as the different training needs of the students, a business school must develop an appropriate strategy for preparing these students to deal effectively with the international dimension of business. Ideally, the approach adopted should endeavor to achieve two goals: to internationalize the student as an individual so that he develops special sensitivities, attitudes, flexibility, and tolerance, and to make available the body of knowledge on international business.

Ethnocentrism and personal parochialism can be attacked in several ways. Living and working experience in a foreign environment through student exchange programs such as that of AIESEC (Association Internationale des Étudiants en Sciences Économiques et Commerciales), which arranges summer internships in foreign countries for students in commerce and business, can provide some of the necessary personal reconditioning. Recruiting a good mix of students from various countries will expose the international business student to other cultures and values through class discussion and through team projects, where the teams are composed of different nationalities.

In a personal and emotional sense, the international businessman must have a special kind of radar that alerts him to situations where specific values and ways of action that he takes for granted in his own environment are different in other cultures and nations. The businessman must develop enough flexibility to understand what underlies these differences, and he must have enough tolerance to recognize that types of behavior and sets of values different from his may be valid for other people.

The Curriculum

To inject the substantial materials of international business into a curriculum, one line of attack is to enlarge the international experience of members of the business school faculty, in the hope that increased international content of existing courses will result.[16] Attempts simply to tack international content onto existing courses are doomed to failure if the faculty is not convinced of its merit and if this addendum fails to mesh with the real purpose of the course.

---

[16] Borje O. Saxberg, "International Business and Economics Faculty Internship Exchange Programme," *The Quarterly Journal of AIESEC International, II* (February 1966).

Addition of specialist courses in international aspects of existing fields, such as international finance and international marketing, is another alternative. However, these courses usually require a number of prerequisite courses in the same field. Without this requirement a course in international marketing, for example, can degenerate into a course in marketing taught with international examples. Prerequisite requirements naturally limit the number of international courses a candidate without prior business training could take in a two-year master's program.

The more direct approach is to introduce courses, not necessarily tied to existing fields, that are aimed specifically at emerging concepts in international business. Such an approach offers more opportunity to those students with special international interests, and enables the faculty to concentrate both their teaching and research directly on international problems.

All of these approaches for internationalizing the business school can be complemented by making greater use of international study resources in other parts of the university. Languages, social sciences, history, law, and area studies all can be used fruitfully in building specific dimensions for the individual business school student. Specialist business graduates will be increasingly needed in work such as prediction of social unrest and resulting risk to international business or changing cultural attitudes and their long-run effect on demand.

Only a few years ago, American business schools did not recognize the international dimension of business except through traditional courses on foreign trade. Now the teaching of international business is growing rapidly, and considerable discussion is underway as to what the field should embrace, how international business can be developed as an academic discipline, and how the subject matter should be included in the business school curriculum.[17]

New concepts, theories, ways of thinking, and methods of analysis needed in multinational business operations and public policy formulation are becoming identified. A small but growing amount of research is underway. The results are finding their way into the curriculum of American business schools and executive development programs through a variety of patterns. The field is in an early stage of development and the opportunities for contributions by business educators are immense. Hopefully, we will be able to meet the challenge.

---

[17] Stefan H. Robock and Lee C. Nehrt, eds., *Education in International Business* (Bloomington, Ind.: Bureau of Business Research, Indiana University, 1964).

The New Men in Overseas Management

Alan Reid

"Sales down half stop send two more cricket blues" reads the legendary pre-war cable from Singapore to the London head office. There is a strong element of probability in this tale, calling up Imperial visions of gins downed in the infernal heat as immunity against the flies and the blundering natives. But overseas branches and subsidiaries have progressed as the countries themselves have progressed, and though there have been political storms, industry has largely kept out of trouble by riding before the wave.

Industry's ability to advance more rapidly than politics is based partly on common business sense, and partly on genuine philanthropy; but it is only achieved through skillful management. Branches and subsidiaries in the developing countries are prone to numerous special and extremely frustrating problems calling for talents and attitudes rarely required at home. Frequently these problems are of a purely geographical and physical nature; transport, spares, communications and technical assistance are seldom as easily available as at the parent plant, and these problems are only solved by initiative or, frequently, time and patience.

But there are also politically and socially oriented problems, and much of Africa is representative of all developing countries. Nigeria is a typical example. It has all the foundations for a vigorous industry and a thriving economy—a large population, rich natural resources, ports, rivers, power, and it is comparatively accessible to the industrialized world. It also has all it needs to hold it back—unstable government, tribal strife, large scale illiteracy and poor education, and inferior communication systems.

For many, these problems seem great enough to scare them away altogether. Since 1958 British private investment abroad has averaged about £300 million per year, but although at that time almost half was for developing countries, in 1963–1964 only about £90 million was thus accounted for, and the figure is still falling.

But although the advanced economies are usually considered to be more promising for quick returns on investment, there are numerous incentives such as tax holidays, low rent periods, protection from competition, tariff privileges and many others. Companies are further attracted by the lower degree of saturation or by completely untapped markets, and by new sources of good raw materials. These

Reprinted from *Business, The Management Journal* (recently changed to *Business Management*) (January 1967): 50–55.

pros and cons to industrial development exist in varying degrees in all the developing countries, and determine not only their desirability as investment areas, but also the ease of management of subsidiaries in them.

How to Prepare for Nationalization of Personnel

The career British expatriate is almost an extinct figure. Gone is the man with a permanent post in some far colonial corner. "Before the war, we used to recruit separately and especially for overseas service," says Shell International Petroleum Company's Mr. J. M. B. Corfe, head of personnel planning. "This 'international' staff, mainly British and Dutch, spent their whole Shell career abroad filling technical and management jobs in countries where suitable nationals were not available. But those days are past."

Increasingly, it is locals that are in managerial positions and it is the declared policy of every newly independent government to nationalize jobs as soon as possible. But industry itself has long striven for this. There are obvious economic reasons for employing nationals as extensively as possible, and these reasons are reinforced by the easier conditions and negotiations that result from like dealing with like, as nationalization progresses. And very often there is a strong desire to improve the lot of the native countrymen. What causes the problems is not pressure to employ nationals but the lack of a trained or educated work force.

The national governments are generally realistic about these problems, though determined to achieve their own ends. Representative of most attitudes is the statement by the government of the United Republic of Tanzania in March 1965: "There can be no compromise on our national aim to get real control of the Tanzanian economy by the people of this country." But it adds the qualification "this does not imply any opposition to private enterprise, whether local or foreign. . . . What our nation must quite deliberately avoid is the attempt to Africanize management with untrained people. This would be as disastrous to the economy of the country as the Africanization of hospitals with witch doctors would be to the health of the nation."

The pace at which job nationalization can take place varies from country to country. India and Malaysia, for example, both pressing for job nationalization, have long histories of trade, commerce, and advanced cultural development, which aid faster changeovers.

The Dunlop Company's policy is to fill managerial positions from local talent where the experience and skills are available, and to train for that purpose. "In India, nationals have steadily filled high administrative and managerial positions," says Mr. F. G. W. Jackson, overseas works director, "and the number of senior expatriates has considerably decreased. Many of the younger men are working under senior nationals, and others go out on a short-term basis to implement technological advances or introduce new products."

In many truly international firms, like the oil companies, the top management positions are becoming internationalized, and to a considerable degree this takes the pressure off nationalization. Shell International now finds that as more and more of the nationals in the countries in which it operates are gaining the necessary training to take over higher positions, the need for the old type of "career expatriate" is rapidly disappearing. But it is not just a matter of finding the suitable nationals for reasons of economy or broader local knowledge, for in an international business like the oil industry, it is important that its managers should also be internationally minded. "For the new-type potential 'national' manager to gain international experience," says Corfe, "opportunities have to be created to give him assignments outside his own country as part of his career development plan."

This is achieved by early identification of future managers of all nationalities and then arranging cross postings at appropriate stages in their careers. "Thus we might have a high potential Japanese serving a three-year assignment in Brazil, and replaced in the Japanese company by a promising Venezuelan, and so on." This interchange benefits not only Shell and the people concerned, but also the countries themselves. For although many governments resent too many foreigners, such a mutual exchange system broadens the experience of the nationals of these countries, and does not do any nationals out of a job.

The Problem of Technical and Clerical Staff

But while international movement takes care of the high potential personnel, it still leaves a vast body of junior technicians, clerks, typists and other posts that have to be filled locally. There are two ways to deal with this.

One is to accept lower standards, and adjust estimates and budgets accordingly. The other is to insist on worldwide equivalent standards and go all out to achieve them as fast as possible, as Dunlop does. A specially established overseas centre in the UK correlates all the experience and special techniques learned in Dunlop's various companies abroad, and this central source is invaluable in assisting each self-contained overseas company to take the necessary steps to ensure the rapid development of its staff to the required standards.

The first managerial positions Dunlop strives to nationalize as soon as possible are those on the shop floor; apart from the economic advantages of such a step, the abolition of any traces of "white overseer" impressions greatly help worker attitudes. Some positions, however, such as in personnel selection take longer due to adverse tribal conditions, for example, where the need for complete impartiality supersedes the desire to nationalize.

Biggest Stumbling Block: Absence of Industrial Education

"At the moment it is easier to get a foreigner a permit to work in northern Nigeria than it is to employ eastern region Ibos or southerners," says EMI Ltd.'s Mr. W. J. Richmond, supervisor for Africa, India and Pakistan, at a time when tribal strife adds to communication and transport problems at the remote Jos plant, EMI and other concerns are now in considerable difficulties owing to the absence of Ibos, who made up a very high percentage of technical and office workers, northerners being largely untrained in this type of work. Northerners coming out of school with even rudimentary knowledge are therefore generally snapped up by the Northern Government, and those with technical or accounting qualifications can demand very high salaries which could not be met by small manufacturing units.

Low education standards are usually a bigger brake on industrial development than political problems. Even in potentially wealthy Swaziland, where an elected and inherited leader, Paramount Chief Sobhuza II, rules over a multiracial country where the large majority is a single tribe, and where there is a close proximity to South Africa's industrial resources, a frustrating problem is the poor education of the Swazis. Obviously, more could be spent on education, but it is unrealistic and unreasonable to expect private enterprise to continue to take on much of the task of even basic teaching. As it is they spend enormous sums on the sort of training that in industrialized countries would normally be available in technical colleges.

Moreover, the natives of many developing countries lack the motivation towards technological education. The average African's aspirations are essentially white collar, that is towards those activities previously associated with top people, whether tribal chiefs or colonial administrators. Few want to be engineers or factory workers—the popular posts are lawyers or doctors, or at least clerks. When a lowly paid clerk has a far higher social standing than a highly paid plant supervisor, it is difficult to industrialize at the true potential rate. Even loading the wage structure abnormally in favor of engineering jobs does not help where social levels are based mainly on title, and it may take many years of industrial growth before there are significant changes.

The Industrial Missionaries

The degree of assistance in industrial education given by local governments can depend very largely on the evidence a firm can show of its desire and intent to benefit the country. "If you are going flat out on training, and really trying to get nationals into positions of responsibility and authority, then there is a good chance that the government may be sympathetic to your needs," says Mr. D. L. Roberts of Arthur Guinness Ltd., which started its brewing operations in Nigeria in 1962. And all firms echo the conviction that you only get out of a country, in goodwill, what you put into it.

However, the ever present threat of drastic political changes, and for some the possibility of nationalization, does mean that companies investing in developing countries must plan, as far as possible, to recover their investment in the shortest possible time. As areas for long-range, safe investments, the developing countries do not draw many supporters. Many firms would not be there at all were it not for the fear of losing what will doubtless one day be a good market, and international companies cannot afford to neglect the developing countries, even though the risks might seem great.

Sometimes the incentives offered brighten up the gloomy prospects, but as Mr. J. E. Hornsby, principal of Barclays Bank DCO economics department says, "There are some countries that dangle too many carrots in front of overseas investment—it arouses suspicion. Incentives are the trimmings. What companies base their decisions on is the way in which foreign investment has previously been treated in that country." These incentives can also be offered too optimistically in the enthusiasm of the moment. The setting up of a factory might appear to have immediate advantages in the form of new jobs and the rippling effect of large construction work; but the long-term results are what will determine whether the country will be able to continue to offer investment incentives.

Companies already in these countries are doing much of the spade work for those that will follow. Firms like The Metal Box Co. act as catalysts for industry—many companies can start up on even the smallest scale once a packaging service is provided. But it is not only by its products that Metal Box lays the foundations for other industry. It spends a great deal on training, though a pioneering industry cannot hope to keep everyone it trains for itself. Other, smaller firms arrive, or are set up by locals, that cannot afford the same training facilities; but they can afford to pay just a little more in wages, and so attract workers from the larger companies. Metal Box would not enter into a wage war with new industries, for this would just push up the cost of living, to the detriment of the whole country.

This employee loss is not regarded as a bad thing by firms like Metal Box, even though some experience a loss as high as 70 percent over five years, for it at least means that the pool of skills available in an economy is improved particularly if several firms operating training schemes find themselves in the same position.

Mr. D. R. B. Mynors, Coutaulds' overseas director, emphasizes that foreign industry cannot wait for local governments in undeveloped countries to educate at a sufficient pace. "You've got to be prepared to spend a great deal on training. It's in your own interests directly, but indirectly it shows your determination to make your investment a long-term one, not a get-rich-quick-and-then-pull-out exploitation. It also gets you more support from local business as well as the government, as well as the knowledge, always satisfying, that you are really doing something for the country."

While in many instances overseas branches and subsidiaries are risky investments, often making little or no profit and causing much frustration, they can be financially rewarding. The developing countries can become vast, untapped markets, and offer potentially enormous fields of development. And if nothing else, they are excellent proving grounds to test the mettle of aspiring managers. As one executive said, with a gleam in his eye like a researcher confronted with a new source of data, "They can be enormously interesting—there's a different thing every day. And sometimes there are enjoyable challenges solving really unforeseen problems—like Rhodesia, for instance."

Multinational?
Well, Not Quite

Kenneth Simmonds

The multinational corporation is widely described as an entity capable of transcending national interests to operate for the benefit of a worldwide group of investors, employees and customers. Its internationalistic character is reinforced by a top management team composed of unusually adaptable and peripatetic executives who are chosen with a praiseworthy indifference to national origins. These managers, it is even suggested, will eventually decide all conflicts of allegiance between corporation and country of origin in favor of the former.

Such is the idyll. The reality is something else. There are a number of reasons to suspect that, particularly in large U.S. corporations with extensive international operations, internationalization of top managements is not expanding in step with worldwide employment, but follows only gradually as individual foreign subsidiaries and affiliates approach the size of their U.S. parents.

A tendency for a self-perpetuating management to fill vacancies with men of a similar cultural background would be one reason to expect a lag in movement of foreigners into top management. Altogether apart from any prejudice, such a tendency may be a simple necessity if management does not feel capable of evaluating the potential of someone from a different background. When selecting a top replacement in a billion dollar corporation, it's no time to gamble.

Another advantage of the domestic national is that he has been closer to the head office for a longer time than his foreign counterpart. Unless it seeks replacements among men in their forties or fifties, top management would change so frequently that there would be little opportunity to observe, design, implement, and adjust the corporate course. A foreign national in his mid-forties, regardless of his outstanding record in subsidiary management, is unlikely to have had much exposure to the operation of top corporate management. This lack of exposure is compounded in those worldwide corporations that follow the suggestions of the "how-to-do-it" school of international business and centralize strategic planning and decision making. International Telephone & Telegraph is an example of such a company. As reported recently:

> Geneen eliminated much of the autonomy of ITT's operating managers, and replaced it with a control system tautly run from New York headquarters. From what was once described as a kind of

---

Reprinted from the *Columbia Journal of World Business*, Vol. 1, No. 4 (Fall 1966), pp. 115–122, by permission of the author and publisher.

The domestic national, on the other hand, is more likely to have been recruited as a management trainee directly from a business school, and to have spent time in corporate headquarters. He will probably have been involved in the details of strategic planning at the corporate level, perhaps helping to establish new plants, integrate new acquisitions and the like. In short he will have a better opportunity to prepare for top management posts than the foreigner.

The more rigid management structure that seems endemic to some foreign countries also makes it difficult for the young foreign executive to climb as rapidly as his American colleague. While he may come into a firm from an educated elite marked for top posts, much as the American comes in as a management trainee from a graduate business school, he is likely to be regarded as young and inexperienced for ten years longer than the American, and he is more accustomed to wait his turn for promotion rather than grab it as and where he can, or sidestep rungs in the ladder by transferring to other firms.

Furthermore, although he generally has a quality university education, the lack of a business education hampers the foreigner in competing with an American for the same top post. The foreigner is not made as vividly aware as are the 7,000 U.S. M.B.A. students graduating each year that it doesn't take forty years of apprenticeship at lower levels of the hierarchy to handle a top-level decision in a competent fashion.

U.S. Policies Hurt

The policies of many American corporations toward their foreign subsidiaries tend to reinforce the relative disadvantage of the foreign executive in several ways. True, the American firm makes a determined effort to get the brightest and best foreign management material, if anything because the cost of keeping U.S. nationals overseas is extremely high. ("Hardship" benefits may bring their salaries in uncomfortable cities such as London and Paris up to the level of the top 1 percent of local executives.) Moreover, the firm needs someone who knows how the foreign culture operates and can find his way around the centers of power and influence. And once it gets this talent the American firm spares no effort in grooming it. But adequate grooming for management of a subsidiary is a different thing from preparation for headquarters management. Subsidiary top management is normally a castrated top management with the truly entrepreneurial function removed. [2] It is

---

[1] Stanley H. Brown, "How One Man Can Move A Corporate Mountain," *Fortune* (July 1, 1966): 82.

[2] Allen W. Johnstone presents carefully collected evidence of this in *United States Direct Investment in France: An Investigation of the French Charges* (Cambridge, Mass.: The MIT Press, 1965).

usually too costly to create a second or third research establishment at the subsidiary level and more profitable to copy the success of the parent than to mold the subsidiary into a completely different shape. Elementary economic reasoning points to international expansion of activities for which the domestic corporation is well along on the learning curve and has a lead on the competition. Backed by the experience of the parent, the subsidiary stands to do better if it remains in these fields than if it pursues untrodden ways. This is reinforced by the overbearing size and purchasing power of the U.S. market and the keen competition for it, which usually means that new ideas are exploited there first.[3]

In many cases internationalization of top management may be hindered by the reluctance of the foreign manager himself to move from his subsidiary status. Why leave the top position in a large subsidiary in one's own cultural environment where the headaches of operating at the top are lessened by the load assumed by parent leadership? Furthermore, in seeking educated men, the American firm will in many countries have obtained men from the social and cultural elites for its subsidiary managers. While these men may feel some underlying rancor at continual subjugation to an absent corporate deity, they may find it equally unpalatable to seek a "place in the sun" that involves relocation to what seems to them a cultural vacuum—say, the American Midwest.

Finally, the foreigner who has not spent a considerable time in the United States may be at a considerable disadvantage in a top management post in a company that is responsible to American shareholders, still has a large percentage of its sales in the United States, and therefore requires that the incumbent possess an intimate knowledge of American institutions. This would be particularly true on the government relations side. What foreigner would feel at home with the pantomine performance required at congressional investigating committees before banks of television cameras? Less than a polished grasp of English would also hinder many of the executives who have spent their working life using principally other languages.

The Matter of Proof

Proof that these difficulties currently face foreign executives in moving to the top of the U.S. international corporation would require a careful study of statistics of employment and promotions for different executive levels. As a first step, a study was made of the national origins of the top management of the 150 largest U.S. industrial corporations in terms of sales. These were taken from the 1965 Fortune Directory.[4] All top *corporate* officers and directors listed for these firms in

---

[3] See Raymond Vernon, "International Investment and International Trade in the Product Cycle," *The Quarterly Journal of Economics* (May 1966): 190–207.
[4] *Fortune* (July 1965): 149–168.

Moody's under the management heading were included in the survey.[5] With double-counting eliminated, this covered 3,847 executives, an average of twenty-five per corporation. Table 1 summarizes these results.

Foreign Participation in Top Corporate Management
(150 largest U.S. industrial corporations)

Classification	Number of Managers
U.S. Citizens by Birth	3,593
Born Outside U.S., not Identified as U.S. by Birth:	
Entered U.S. Permanently Before Age 26[a]	81
Entered U.S. Permanently at Age 26 or Above	34
Resident Outside U.S.[b]	25
Insufficient Data for Classification	114
Total	3,847

[a] Includes roughly 50 percent identified as non-U.S. citizens at birth.

[b] Excludes corporate officers of Shell and Unilever; also board members of their U.S. subsidiaries.

Table 1.

Biographical particulars were taken from a range of standard references and for the large number of executives for whom insufficient data were available from these sources (over 20 percent), particulars were requested directly. Sufficient information was collected to classify all but 3 percent of the total. In this manner most of the foreign participation in top corporate management in the sample corporations has been traced. Any allowance for errors in published biographies or for executives with "shrinking violet" tendencies should thus not affect the conclusions materially.

Executives who transferred to the U.S. up to age twenty-five have been shown separately. Many of these came to this country in their early years, perhaps born of American parents outside the U.S. Only a minority had any business experience outside the U.S. before they arrived. Every future top executive who was in the United States permanently by age twenty-six climbed the ladder essentially on the basis of American performance. Only those who came here after twenty-five can be classified as representative of a corporation's foreign employment. Subsequent reference in this article to "foreign participation" will exclude those who emigrated to the United States before age twenty-six.

---

[5] *Moody's Industrial Manual* (New York: Moody's Investors Service Inc., 1965). Group and divisional managers not also holding corporate posts, and some lesser corporate offices such as assistant treasurers and assistant secretaries were not classed as top corporate management and hence omitted from the study.

Before examining the results in detail, a few comments are needed in defense of the most common objections to any conclusions from these figures. First, it is true that top corporate posts in firms of this size both omit many important executive positions and include some relatively unimportant posts in terms of day-to-day operation. But they do take in the presidents, chairmen, vice presidents and internal directors who make up the top echelon. Second, it may be argued that the top-management picture in 1965 does not take into account that many non-U.S. employees are now rapidly climbing the ladder, that most of these large firms had little international activity at the time the foundations for promotion of current top management were being laid, or that, even in those that had, internationalization was impeded by the war. These points may be valid and suggest that the findings of this survey should not be projected into the future without more testing. Even so, many of those in the survey reached top corporate management in the 1960s, and foreign activity of a number of these corporations has for many years been quite substantial.

About one-fifth of the total employment in these firms is foreign; yet only 1.6 percent of their top corporate management entered as foreigners after age twenty-five or remain outside the United States (see Table 2). If we had data on companies that do not disclose their foreign employment, those that do not include subsidiary employment in their employment figures, and those that do not classify Canadian employment as foreign, the comparison would become even more dramatic. For seventy-one corporations with heavy foreign activity, foreign employment jumps to 33 percent while foreign participation in top management remains at 1.6 percent. The fairly even dispersion of foreign executives among the three groups of corporations listed suggests that promotion of foreigners to top posts is less dependent on the size of the company's foreign employment than it is on the availability of foreigners in the general pool of competent executives.

No attempt was made to collect figures for foreign sales or sales of foreign production. A *Business International* study of 117 U.S. corporations operating abroad, however, recorded foreign earnings of these firms for 1964 as 26 percent of total earnings and foreign net assets as 25 percent of total net assets.[6] This selection of firms included many of those in the top 150, so the foreign employment figure of 20 percent shown in the table seems a reasonably representative indicator of "foreign activity," however measured.

The major discrepancy between the percentage of total employment which is foreign and the percentage of foreign participation in top corporate management lends strong support to the contention that the path to the top is more difficult for the foreigner. Even if we allow that many of these firms have penetrated overseas markets only recently, this conclusion still appears valid.

Table 3 contains a further breakdown of the figure of thirty-four foreigners in top management who transferred to the United States after age twenty-five. Of

---

[6] *Business International* (June 11, 1965): 186.

Comparison of Foreign Participation in Employment and Corporate Management

(150 largest U.S. industrial corporations)

	Significant Foreign Employment	Little or No Foreign Employment[a]	Data Not Obtained	Total
Number of Corporations	71	55	24	150
All Employees (millions)[b]:				
Total	4.66	1.79	1.10	7.54
Foreign	1.54	.03	—	1.56
Percent Foreign	33.0	1.7	—	20.7
Top Corporate Management:				
Total Classified[c]	1,815	1,263	655	3,733
Foreign				
Employees	21	10	8	39
Outside Directors	9	7	4	20
Total Foreign	30	17	12	59
Percent Foreign	1.6	1.3	1.8	1.6

[a] These include firms in steel, airframe, petroleum, tobacco, packaging, and food industries.
[b] Subject to differences in treatment of employees of subsidiaries and probably undercounting.
[c] Foreign is defined as non-U.S. at birth and not entering U.S. permanently before age 26.

Table 2.

Management Who Transferred to U.S. after Age 25— Type of Transfer and Country of Origin

Country of Origin	Changed Employment at Time of Transfer	Transferred While with U.S. Corporation	Transferred While with Foreign Corporation	Transferred When Foreign Corporation Merged into U.S. Corporation	Total
Canada	2	5	—	4	11
U. K.	4	5	2	—	11
Germany	5	—	—	—	5
France	—	1	1	—	2
Holland	1	—	1	—	2
Austria	1	—	—	—	1
Mexico	—	1	—	—	1
Australia	—	1	—	—	1
Total	13	13	4	4	34

Table 3.

these only thirteen were shifted from a foreign subsidiary activity by American firms with whom they were then employed—not a very large number out of 3,847 executives surveyed. Five of these were transferred in the crucial age period 36–45, three at a younger age, and five later in their career. Of those who were not transferred from a foreign subsidiary, thirteen seem to have transferred at their own volition, four were initially moved to United States subsidiaries of foreign firms, and four became directors when Canadian firms merged with U.S. corporations. It is noteworthy that of the thirteen transferring of their own accord none came after age forty-one, suggesting a nontransferability of top foreign management skills and experience.

The nationality distribution is far from a representative collection of American subsidiary activity even as it existed fifteen years ago. The only South American had an MIT degree, and the Europeans came mainly on their own. As might be expected, Canadians and Englishmen make up a large proportion of the total, and if these were excluded there would be only three executives promoted from overseas. While promotion from subsidiary to top management is more common for Canadians than others, few Canadians have come to the United States on their own later in their careers and made it to the top of the corporations included in the survey. Both Canadians shown in this category were under age thirty at the time they transferred.

A further twenty-five members of top corporate management who have not transferred to the United States were shown in Table 1. These are analyzed more fully in Table 4. Here again Canadians predominate and there is a surprising lack of any attempt to add nationals of other countries to the top corporate group even where they hold top posts in subsidiaries or affiliates.

It might be thought that some firms would have quite advanced foreign representation in top corporate management, even though the top 150 corporations

Foreign Management Who Have Not Transferred to USA

Country of Origin	Officers of Subsidiaries on Parent Board	Foreign Outside Directors	Total
Canada	5	14	19
U. K.	1	2	3
France	1	—	1
Switzerland	1	—	1
Argentina	1	—	1
Total	9	16	25

Table 4.

as a group show such small participation. But there are no outstanding exceptions. Only one or two corporations had more than three members of their top team who were either nonresident foreigners or had transferred after age 25.[7] Moreover, a study of the biographies of the foreign executives concerned ruled out any possibility that these firms were beginning a concerted effort to internationalize at the top. Of the thirteen foreigners actually transferred from a subsidiary or an affiliate of a U.S. corporation, no firm had more than two. These are surprising results from a group of companies that contains ITT, which has a foreign employment of around 165,000 out of 200,000; Ford, with 160,000 foreign employees; and Singer, with 63,000 to mention but three examples. Of none of these three corporations could it be argued that their international activities have just taken root. Each has had significant foreign employment for thirty years.

This picture suggests that a determined effort will have to be made to promote foreign personnel into top management ranks if, within the near future, there is anything approaching an international team in the 150 top corporations investigated. Even if all foreseeable vacancies were to be filled with foreigners, the snowballing of American foreign investment, coupled with existing managerial turnover patterns, may mean that the proportion of overseas employment for some firms will continue to increase faster than their foreign participation in top management.

But it is unlikely that many firms will switch rapidly to favor foreigners in promotions to top management. Besides those arguments mentioned earlier, two further reasons may be advanced. A number of executives interviewed in the course of this study expressed a firm conviction that it was right and necessary to retain what is American for Americans. Another group pointed out that American business is not run for charity, and that the firm should always look for the "best" man regardless of nationality, but be quite contented if this usually means an American.[8] The argument that an international top management should be internationally planned seems to carry little weight with these respondents.

Also emerging from discussions with executives of international corporations was a feeling that there were few, if any, ways in which subsidiary management could bring pressure to bear on corporate management without taking actions that were not in the best interests of the firm as a whole. And to take such actions invites dismissal, not promotion. As long as corporate management retains a firm grip on strategic planning and decision making, the power seems to lie all on its side.

---

[7] Excluding Shell and Unilever for which foreign corporate officers sit on the boards of the U.S. subsidiaries.

[8] These men were quick to claim that foreign international firms were even more parochial, although the example of Royal Dutch Shell, which recently appointed an American to join a Dutchman and an Englishman as managing directors, would seem to belie this.

Solution: Get Big Quick

Pulling these ideas together, sketchy though the evidence may be, leads to the conclusion that only as individual subsidiaries become large and complex, generating new products and large income, will the subsidiary executive gain the status and experience that will lead to promotion into top corporate management. As decentralization of top decisions grows, internationalization of top management will follow. With the business literature pointing toward centralized strategy formulation, however, this seems likely to come about more as a result of very gradual evolution than as a consequence of planned internationalization.

The alternative to internationalization is an American "master race" of top executives ultimately controlling a large segment of business activity outside the United States. Any reasonable projection of foreign direct investments of U.S. corporations shows astronomical figures even ten years hence. With this the case, candid advice to the bright young foreigner starting his career may increasingly take the following lines: "If you are thinking of working up the ladder in an American-owned subsidiary, don't. Buy a one-way ticket to New York and get on the right escalator."

It's Just Bad Business

Another consequence of the noninternational top corporate team is that it is likely to be less effective than if it were to be internationalized. Whatever the top American manager may wish to believe, he is a creature of his American culture and no amount of overseas experience can stimulate the depth of understanding of the foreign environment that the foreign national himself possesses.

But the major problem will be an increasing strain between corporate and subsidiary management that affects corporate performance. Even though the subsidiary executive may not have the power to engineer his promotion, he may adopt a more nationalistic stance than would otherwise be necessary, fail to tell corporate headquarters the full story, or vent his dissatisfaction with permanent subsidiary status in many other ways. An example of the sort of problems that can arise is illustrated in a *Sunday Times'* article on Ford's operations in Britain. Whether these claims are just or not, the significant point is that they were made, and have reflected on the firm's reputation and performance:

> Four directors have quit Ford U.K. in a year: those of finance, sales, industrial relations and the head of the Basildon tractor operations. All but the last resigned largely because of the tightening American control.
>
> In two years, more than twenty key men in Ford U.K.'s finance department have left. They include the investment analysis manager, the purchase analysis manager and within a few months, three successive administrative managers under the American director of engineering.
>
> From Ford U.K.'s product-planning section, the manager has

left. So have the market research chief and the product-planner of the Cortina. With the labor relations director went one of his top executives. Ford U.K.'s controller of metal stamping has left, so has his right-hand man. So has the manager of operations in Ford U.K.'s new foundry, technically ahead of any other in Europe.

"This is not wastage; this is a haemorrhage," said one of the most senior men who have left. All these, with other less significant executives who have also left, have gone to excellent, even superlative jobs—Ford executives have a usually justified and always expensive mystique. But virtually all had one motive in common. One ex-manager said: "I know of no British senior Ford executive who any longer believes that there is a real future for a Briton in Ford."

To all this, Ford has an adamant answer: "We have been since 1960 wholly an American company," said one director, "but we are run in Britain by Britons. We are world-wide; our attitudes and needs are not therefore those of Little Englanders. There is not dictation from Detroit."

But the total American domination of Dagenham—and the evidence of former executives is too strong to deny—is not a Detroit conspiracy; it is the logical result of Ford U.K.'s own history, Ford Detroit's world plans, the American lead in techniques of management and mass production, and a certain British bloody mindedness. Detroit's 1960 guarantee to the British Government when it sought 100 percent of Ford U.K.—the promise that "the majority" of Ford U.K.'s management would remain British—has not been broken. It was irrelevant.

Ford U.K. now has Americans as managing director, financial director, engineering director, and production planning and styling director. Only four Americans are on the ruling Policy Board of fifteen, but they are the men with power.

"You control a company if you control its capital expenditures, its products, and in great detail its operating budgets," said one senior ex-finance man. "All these are controlled by Americans over here, and ultimately in Detroit. The amount of paper flowing to Detroit and back is unbelievable."

The other Americans at Dagenham control strategic functions— chief stylist, body construction, paint, data processing, the foundry, a welding and manufacturing engineer, three plant layout men, and a bevy in the truck group. "The technical men are mostly first-class," said one departed. "Ford management is correct when it says Detroit has much technically to teach us. What causes the friction is that the Britons the Americans work with know that it is the American who has the ear of Detroit."[9]

Ensuring that top corporate management in the international corporation does become truly international requires planned action. There are many ways to start.

---

[9] Extracted from John Barry, "Ford's Top Britons Quit as U.S. Grip Tightens," *The Sunday Times* (November 21, 1965).

Noteworthy steps include: international executive development programs that concentrate on top management problems, rotation of younger foreign executives through corporate headquarters, decentralization of staff functions to foreign sites, or adoption of policies that treat all executives as internationalists regardless of origin.

The first physical transfer to a foreign site of the corporate head office of any major U.S. international corporation is still a thing of the future. There are plenty of regional offices but these are not the same. Although the foreign executives in regional offices will be better prepared to step into corporate management for having had more experience in policy formulation, the imposition of another executive layer can compound the inaccessibility of the American "gods" at corporate headquarters.

Of course, there are costs attached to passing over more advanced U.S. nationals in order to train foreigners for entry into top posts. But in the longer run there may be greater costs from failure to ensure not only equality of opportunity, but equality of preparation. The far-sighted worldwide firm will be the one that makes sure that its top management is both the best *and* the most international it can get.

The Compensation of International Executives

Hans Schöllhammer

It is generally recognized that the single, most important determinant of a firm's success is the quality of its executives. While this holds true for all business ventures, it is most clearly demonstrable in a firm's international operations. These operations are subject to a variety of social, economic, and political-environmental conditions and restrictions considerably different from those that affect purely domestic business activities. Inevitably, the staffing of a firm's foreign subsidiaries and affiliates with competent and creative executives is of extreme importance. Practically all international firms follow a staffing policy which commits them to use local personnel to the maximum extent. The rationale of this policy is obvious, and most companies are successful in implementing it. A number of studies have shown, however, that most international firms staff a rather large portion of the higher and decisive management positions with nationals of the company's home base who are familiar with the parent company's policies and operating procedures, and who are the agents for the transfer of the firm's managerial and technical skills to the foreign operation.[1]

As an international firm's operations expand, it acquires in its reservoir of managerial talent *foreign* executives who again can be employed in countries other than their own. An international executive is by definition a member of one or the other group. For the purpose of this study, an executive who is a citizen of the home base of the company and who is working in one of the company's foreign subsidiaries or affiliates is referred to as a foreign service employee. An executive who is a citizen of a country other than the home base of the company and who is working in a country other than his home country (for instance, a British citizen

Hans Schöllhammer, "The Compensation of International Executives," *MSU Business Topics* (Winter 1969), pp. 19–31. Reprinted by permission of the publisher, the Bureau of Business and Economic Research, Division of Research, Graduate School of Business Administration, Michigan State University.

[1] See e.g., E. R. Barlow, *Management of Foreign Manufacturing Subsidiaries* (Boston: Division of Research, Graduate School of Business Administration, Harvard University, 1953), p. 174 ff; Thomas D. Cabot, *et al.*, *Cooperation for Progress in Latin America* (New York: Committee for Economic Development, 1961), p. 43; Theodore Geiger, *The General Electric Company in Brazil* (New York: National Planning Association, 1961), p. 58; R. F. Gonzalez and A. R. Negandhi, *The United States Overseas Executive: His Orientations and Career Patterns* (East Lansing: Bureau of Business and Economic Research, Graduate School of Business Administration, Michigan State University, 1967).

working for an American company in India) is referred to as a third country national.

It is a common notion, supported by empirical evidence,[2] that international executives receive compensation higher than that of domestic executives having similar functional responsibilities. There are a number of reasons for this situation. Primarily, it is the relative scarcity of qualified managers who can cope effectively with the increased demands which overseas positions pose, such as knowledge of the local language, familiarity with local business practices, the ability to get along with people of different backgrounds, initiative, and willingness to assume greater responsibility.

Other Factors

There are other factors as well which account for the higher remuneration of international executives. One, which U.S. international firms frequently emphasize, is the reluctance with which many qualified U.S. executives accept an assignment abroad because of the inconveniences of the transfer, the frequently lower standards of living overseas, a perceived inferiority of the educational system in many foreign countries, and inadequate health services. In addition, many executives feel that being absent will not enable them to compete for a rise in the organization as effectively as if they are working in the firm's headquarters. For all these reasons, multinational firms may find it necessary to make overseas assignments attractive by offering a favorable compensation. In this connection, a number of interesting questions can be raised. What are international company policies as to the determination of the base salary for their foreign service employees and third country nationals? Are these groups treated equal? If not, what are the differentials and what determines them? What specific premiums and allowances of a recurrent as well as non-recurrent nature are paid to international executives? What factors determine these allowances or premiums? What non-financial *privileges* are granted to them?

In order to find answers to these questions, fifty large international U.S. based firms were asked to provide relevant information. Twelve of these manufacturing firms participated in the survey. All these firms have more than two foreign subsidiaries and each of the firms has at least 100 of its American employees in management positions abroad. Together, the twelve firms have 3,207 foreign service employees, not including their American employees in Canada, and 670 third

---

[2] See, e.g., E. R. Barlow, *op. cit.*, p. 163; E. R. Floyd, *Compensating American Managers Abroad* (New York: American Management Association, Inc., Research Study No. 31, 1958); A. Patton, "Executive Compensation Here and Abroad," *Harvard Business Review*, XL (September–October, 1962), 144 ff; G. F. Dickover, "Compensating the American Employee Abroad," *Financial Executive* (April 1966), 40–49; A. Patton and J. Lock, "Executive Compensation: Trends Here and Abroad," *The McKinsey Quarterly*, IV, 2 (1967), 22 ff.

country nationals.[3] The following report on the policies and practices of compensating international executives is based on information these firms provided.

Determination of Base Salary

For the purpose of a uniform administration of compensation matters applicable to their international executives, all of the firms in the sample declared that they follow a set of explicitly stated policies and regulations. The main policy in this respect is that executives who accept foreign assignments should not substantially gain or lose money or property because of a transfer to an overseas operation, while at the same time minimizing related company costs. Apart from various allowances, all companies stated that they attempt to maintain the same base salary for comparable positions at home and overseas which are staffed with foreign service employees. For the determination of the base salary, which largely depends on the scope of responsibility and job content plus required background and experience, the firms use the same job evaluation plans on the foreign management positions as on the jobs at home. The base salary of third country nationals, however, is generally different from the salaries paid to foreign service employees because in their case, the going rate for comparable positions in their home country is used as a determinant of the base salary.

The companies pointed out that in general they do not transfer an executive from a higher paid position at home to a position with a lower base pay abroad, and if he is reassigned to the parent company, every effort is made to assign him to a position with responsibility and base salary at least equal to the one in his previous position and contingent on his past performance. However, the majority of the firms state that as a matter of policy, foreign assignment does not, by itself, obligate the parent company to give any individual special consideration, nor does it guarantee the reassigned executive any predetermined status in the parent organization.

Considering the various premiums and allowances which companies usually pay to their international executives while on assignment abroad, it becomes obvious that the firms' strong emphasis on the maintenance of a base pay has mainly two reasons. First, it serves as a basis for the determination and allocation of the various allowances and premiums. Second, it should eliminate salary problems at some future date when the executive is again transferred to his home base. The companies' policy of equal compensation for equal positions at home or abroad refers only to the base salary.

In addition to the base salary, international executives are generally granted a variety of allowances either for specific reasons such as the frequently higher costs of living abroad, or for more intangible ones such as severance of an established way

---

[3] The firms participating in this survey noted that they generally compensate their expatriates in Canada in the same way as they compensate domestic employees.

of life, or simply as a financial inducement for qualified executives to accept an overseas assignment. The purpose of the following paragraphs is to analyze that portion of an international executive's compensation which he receives above and beyond the base pay as well as to describe and evaluate the methods which are used for determining it.

Allowances and Bonuses

A study published in 1958, based on information by sixty-seven companies, has revealed that almost 80 percent of U.S. executives assigned to foreign subsidiaries or affiliates receive in addition to their base salary two or more separately calculated premiums or allowances. Only 3 percent of the foreign service employees (mainly employees of firms that had no more than ten executives abroad) received a single adjusted salary but no extra allowances.[4] The twelve large firms on which this study is based confirmed that the same situation still prevails. Although no two companies have exactly the same compensation system, they show considerable similarities as to four major recurrent allowances: foreign assignment allowance, cost of living allowance, housing allowance, and educational allowance.

Foreign Assignment Allowance

Companies generally pay their international executives a foreign assignment allowance (sometimes referred to as an overseas premium) which is intended to be a foreign service incentive and a compensation for the inconveniences of having to live in a foreign environment, separated from an accustomed way of life, the family, friends and associates, and of having to work under more difficult conditions such as a language handicap, having greater responsibilities, and frequently less assistance. The firms determine this allowance as a percentage of the base salary, generally between 10 and 30 percent. Two-thirds of the firms pay the same percentage (in almost all cases either 15 or 20 percent of the base salary) regardless of the location. One-third of the firms vary the foreign assignment allowance either by taking into account the particular attractiveness of a certain location, and consequently allowing only 10 to 15 percent of the base salary as foreign assignment allowance, or by increasing the allowance to 25 to 30 percent in cases where the international executive has to work under unaccustomed climatic conditions, inadequate health services, lack of sanitation, and geographical isolation. Companies which set different rates pay the highest foreign assignment allowances plus hardship allowances to their employees in India and in African countries. Half of the firms grant the same foreign assignment allowance (in terms

---

[4] See Floyd, *op. cit.*, p. 18.

of percentage of the employee's base salary) to foreign service employees as well as third country nationals. The rest of the firms differentiate between the two groups of international executives. In the majority of cases, third country nationals are granted a somewhat lower percentage than that accorded foreign service employees.

Cost of Living Allowance

Since cost of living can vary greatly from one country to another (and even within a country) and since all of the international firms have a policy that the employees should neither lose nor unduly gain from an overseas assignment, it follows that they take into account the differences in the cost of living abroad in the form of a cost of living allowance. The purpose of this allowance is to enable the international executive to maintain, as nearly as possible, the same standard of living which he would have in his home country. For the individual firm it would be difficult, expensive, and time consuming to investigate the comparative cost of living level for every one of its foreign operations to which it assigns international executives. The large majority of U.S. based multinational firms use, therefore, for the determination of the cost of living allowance, the so-called local (cost of living) index, which is periodically computed by the U.S. Department of State for the many foreign cities where the U.S. government has a diplomatic or consular staff. The local index compares the cost for required goods and services as purchased locally with the cost of the same items in Washington, D. C. Firms using this index may find it appropriate to allow for differences between their foreign location and Washington, D. C. In foreign locations for which no local index has been computed by the U.S. Department, firms may use their own formula and calculate an index, for instance, on the basis of a sample of goods and services for which the overseas employees themselves periodically report the local prices.

Salary Spent Abroad

In order to come up with an equitable cost of living allowance, the companies must not only find out the foreign cost of living level as compared with the home country, but they must also determine what percentage of the base salary the employees spend for goods and services abroad. This percentage depends, of course, largely on family size and the actual pay the employee receives. According to budget studies in several foreign areas made by the Industrial Relations Counselor Service, Inc., U.S. executives abroad tend to spend only between 45 and 55 percent of their base salary in the foreign area.[5] If it is established that the cost of living in a particular foreign location is 5 percent higher than at home, an equitable cost of living allowance would amount to 5 percent of about one-half of the base salary.

---

[5] See Dickover, *op. cit.*, p. 46.

Flexible Allowances

The firms which provided information for this survey determine the cost of living allowances in the manner shown in Tables 1 and 2.

Table 1 indicates that the majority of the firms keep the determination of the cost of living allowance rather flexible due to their definitions of foreign spending. All firms (with the exception of the three using the IRCS rates) declared that they do not pay a cost of living allowance where the local cost of living index is lower than in the United States, but neither do they deduct the saving from the monthly remuneration; it is simply considered as an additional incentive to work abroad. When determining the cost of living allowance, all firms take into account the number of dependents of the foreign service employees simply by using different percentages of the spendable income as a basis for the allowance.

Cost of Living Allowance To Foreign Service Employees

Number of Firms	Basis of Allowance
3	Local index as computed by the U.S. State Department applied to base salary
6	Local index as computed by the U.S. State Department applied to company-determined foreign spending level (which varies from 30 percent to 85 percent of the base pay)
3	According to scale computed by Industrial Relations Counselors Service, Inc., N.Y.[a]

[a] In general, U.S. Department of State local index applied to 30–60 percent of the monthly base pay plus an adjustment, depending on how difficult it is to get the required goods and services locally.

Table 1.

Policies Employed

Table 2 shows that half of the firms treat third country nationals the same as foreign service employees. They provide them with a cost of living allowance as if their home country were the United States. On the basis of a policy which emphasizes neither gain nor loss because of a foreign assignment, the approach which the group of four firms uses is certainly more complicated, but it is the correct one. It is noteworthy that the incidence of a cost of living allowance to third country nationals is higher than a foreign service allowance paid to this group of international executives.

Cost of Living Allowance to Third Country Nationals	
Number of Firms	**Basis of Allowance**
6	Cost of living allowance to third country nationals computed in the same way as for foreign service employees. Same percentages of spendable income are used.
4	Cost of living allowance depends on the cost of living index of the employee's home country. For this purpose the U.S. State Department's index of the employee's home city is divided into the local index of his present employment to obtain the relative index. Percentage of spendable income, to which the cost of living allowance is related, is the same as for foreign service employees.
2	No general rule; cost of living allowance handled on an individual basis.

Table 2.

Housing Allowance

The purpose of a housing allowance is to compensate international executives for comparatively higher housing costs abroad. As with the determination of any other allowance, the basic problem is to find reasonably accurate data as to the cost of housing in foreign locations. In addition, it must be determined how much of his income the employee spends for housing in his home country. One possibility for the determination of shelter costs at a particular foreign location is to use again the information on housing allowances which U.S. government personnel abroad receive. They are compensated for about 90 percent of their actual housing expenditures.

A U.S. based multinational firm may use again the information on housing allowances as published by the Department of State, add 10 percent to this figure, and arrive at reasonably reliable housing expenditures at particular foreign locations. In order to determine whether a housing allowance is justified it is necessary to compare this figure with the actual expenditures of the employee at home. In the United States housing expenditures amount in general to 10–15 percent of a family's income. Therefore, under a policy of neither gain nor loss a company could expect that its foreign service employees contribute about 15 percent of the base salary as their share to the actual shelter costs. The positive difference is then the required housing allowance. In case of a negative difference (lower housing expenditures for a comparable standard of housing abroad, for example) the savings could be deducted from the foreign service allowance. Three-fourths of the firms stated that they reimburse their foreign service employees for all housing costs which are in excess of a certain percentage of the base salary (varying between 8 and 20 percent, usually 15 percent). The rest of the firms pay a general housing allowance regardless of location or actual housing costs amounting to 10 percent of the base salary of the foreign service employee. None of the companies indicated any provision for deducting a negative difference in the case where the employee's standard of housing could be maintained at lower cost than in his home country. The savings are simply considered as an additional compensation for the other hardships of a foreign assignment. The majority of the firms do not, at least not explicitly, fix an upper limit for their housing allowance. It must be recognized that under these circumstances the companies do not provide any incentive to their foreign service employees to find lower cost housing; on the contrary, it is an inducement to look for high cost housing accommodations and the status which goes with it. A few companies even encourage this by pointing out that their employees abroad are representatives of the company whose public relations may be enhanced by the status of their representatives in the community, which is in part due to their living standards.

The investigation of the companies' policies on housing allowances paid to third country nationals revealed that 40 percent of the firms use the same formula as for foreign service employees. One-fourth of the firms use a similar formula but make adjustments on an individual basis; the rest of the firms determine the housing allowance for their third country nationals by estimating the housing cost difference between the employee's home country and the new location.

Even though all companies provide their third country nationals with a housing allowance in cases of a positive difference between a predetermined amount of housing expenditures and actual costs, these practices reflect again a less fixed and much more flexible compensation policy with regard to international executives. By inquiring about the individual adjustments, two companies indicated that the percentages used for determining the housing allowances were not as favorable as the ones used for determining the housing allowance for foreign service employees— the reason being lower housing expenditure in the third country nationals' home countries.

Educational Allowances

Most companies are aware that one major factor affecting a manager's decision on whether he willingly accepts an overseas assignment is related to the educational possibilities for his children. To provide schooling that is comparable or better to that in the home country frequently necessitates added expenses, which the executive's firm may be willing to share in some form of educational assistance or allowance. The firms contributing to this survey reported the following practices:

All companies provide some form of assistance toward the cost of elementary and high school education of the children of their foreign service employees at the location of assignment. All twelve firms contribute in varying degrees to the educational fees which foreign service employees have to pay for such education. Nine firms pay a flat amount—on the average, $300 per year for each child attending elementary or high school. One firm reimburses 75 percent of the education costs up to $800 per year per child, and another company reimburses all educational expenditures except $300, which is considered the proper contribution of the parents. Four firms declared that they do not automatically reimburse educational fees if the parents choose to send their children to an English-speaking private boarding school when adequate public schools are available locally. On the other hand, eight companies recommend that foreign service employees send their children, wherever possible, to an English-speaking school. The companies also reimburse, if applicable, additional educational expenditures such as school uniforms, textbooks, examination fees, and transportation costs to and from school.

Educational allowances in cases where children of foreign service employees go to colleges or universities are much more restricted. Only five out of twelve companies offer some form of assistance toward college costs, mainly in the form of an annual round trip from the U.S. college which the child attends to the foreign location of its parents.

Concerning an education allowance to third country nationals, seven out of the twelve firms stated that they reimburse elementary and high school costs which exceed those normally incurred in the home country for comparable education. Three companies pay 100 percent of the educational costs in case the schools which the children attend have been authorized by the company. Two of the twelve firms provide no educational allowance to their third country nationals.

Other Allowances

Foreign assignment, cost of living, housing, and educational allowances are the major and most common payments granted to international executives in addition to their base salary. Some companies grant additional recurrent allowances such as an automobile allowance, an allowance for social or professional club memberships, an entertainment allowance, a separation allowance in case the family of the international executive does not move abroad, or special hardship allowances for particular conditions. The international executives of the twelve firms which supplied information receive between four and seven different recurrent allowances. It is thus no surprise that most personnel people find that determining the compensation of international executives is a complex, time consuming cumbersome task.

Bonuses

Ten out of twelve companies in this survey had bonus plans. Their foreign service employees receive a bonus according to the same formula as the employees of the parent organization. The bonuses vary between 10 and 35 percent of the base salary. Third country nationals receive bonus payments in two-thirds of the cases, according to the formula used for determining the bonus of foreign service employees. One-third of the firms pay bonuses to third country nationals in accordance with the bonus scheme of the firm's subsidiary in the third country national's home country.

While an international executive's compensation is determined by his base salary and his recurrent allowances and bonuses, his actual take home pay can be influenced considerably by paying attention to tax and currency matters, which all multinational firms take into account, but in different degrees.

Currency Considerations

All companies providing information declared that they calculate and state their foreign service employees' base salary as well as allowances in U.S. dollars. With regard to third country nationals, practices are more diversified. All three possible methods are used: stating base salary and allowances in the currency of the country of assignment, in the currency of their home country, or in U.S. dollars. Stating the international executive's compensation in dollars is obviously the advisable practice for U.S. based multinational firms for the sake of simplicity, uniformity, and comparability. A decision must be made whether the remuneration should actually be paid in U.S. dollars, in the currency of assignment, or a mixture of both. The following practices have been reported:

Five of the twelve firms pay their foreign service employees in U.S. dollars only, and the rest of the firms pay part (generally between 30 and 40 percent) in U.S. dollars and part in local currency. None of the foreign service employees are paid only in local currency. On the other hand, third country nationals receive their compensation predominantly in local currency; only two firms pay in U.S. dollars, and two firms pay part in local currency and part in the currency of the third country nationals' home country. The difference in payment procedure with regard to foreign service employees and third country nationals does not necessarily indicate any discrimination to the disadvantage of the latter; this could, however, be the case with regard to those currencies which are not fully convertible and whose purchasing power depreciates rapidly, such as the currencies of some Latin American countries. Two of the companies which pay their foreign service employees only in U.S. currency said they would prefer to compensate them in part in local currency, but that the employees would resist this change. Obviously, for international executives working in a country where the currency is not freely convertible or whose exchange rate is under pressure, it is advantageous to get as much of their salary and allowances in dollars as possible; in this way they protect the value of their income and, in addition, in certain countries they may be able to exchange dollars at a premium for those expenditures for which local currency is needed. Many international companies operating in countries with currency restrictions are faced with a paradoxical situation. On the one hand, the foreign subsidiaries are generating a cash surplus but cannot exchange it into dollars and transfer it to the parent company. On the other hand, their overseas executives frequently insist on being paid in dollars instead of in local currency by the foreign subsidiary where they are working. In general, it would seem to be a defensible policy for every U.S. based multinational firm to pay a maximum of 20 percent of an international executive's base salary in dollars, and the remainder and all allowances in local currency through the organization to which he is assigned.

Tax Considerations

Tax considerations are of eminent importance to an international executive's compensation since in quite a number of countries the rates of personal taxation are so high that it would be unreasonable to expect an employee to serve there unless the company takes these differences into account. A policy that an executive should neither gain nor lose because of a foreign assignment leads necessarily to a solution of the personal tax question in such a way that the company deducts from the taxable salary of the employee an amount equivalent to what he would have to pay in his home country and, in turn, assumes full liability of whatever taxes he has to pay locally. This approach seems to be simple, but it is not. For instance, a U.S. based company will have to decide what it considers as taxable income or what kind of deductions it is willing to recognize. Standard deductions, for example, may do injustice to an executive who usually can claim more than merely the standard deduction. The question then is, should the company also recognize them? The investigation as to the relevant practices among twelve U.S. based international firms showed that five companies reimburse their foreign service employees for income taxes exceeding those which would have to be paid in the United States. Relevant decisions are taken on an individual basis. The rest of the firms principally deduct estimated U.S. taxes and assume full liability for any income taxes levied on foreign service employees.

This indicates that all companies shelter their foreign service employees from higher tax liabilities abroad as compared with U.S. taxes. Half of the firms let advantages derived from lower income taxes abroad accrue to their foreign service employees as an additional financial payoff of a foreign assignment. With regard to third country nationals, the seven companies which principally assume the tax liabilities for their foreign service employees and which deduct an amount closer to or equivalent to U.S. taxes, apply the same method to the compensation of the third country nationals. The rest of the companies do not follow a general rule, which again suggests a somewhat unequal treatment between the two groups of international executives.

Relocation Expenditures

The transfer of an executive to a foreign position necessitates a variety of costs which can be classified as relocation expenditures. These expenditures are not a part of an international executive's compensation and thus seem to be of no direct concern within the framework of this study. Nevertheless, it seems justifiable to consider these expenditures, particularly since these data contribute to obtaining a complete picture as to the total cost burden caused by giving executives foreign assignments.

The main relocation expenditures for which the employee generally expects reimbursement are connected with (1) possible sale of the home and the monetary losses which it may entail, (2) the sale and storage or shipment of household effects or other items such as automobiles, (3) transportation costs to the foreign location for the executive and his family, and (4) the expenditures encountered in finding suitable housing abroad and related incidental expenses.

All firms declared that they assist their foreign service employees with the sale of their homes if they so desire. For instance, all twelve firms reimburse their employees for the necessary and unavoidable expenditures incurred by selling a home, such as commissions charged by real estate agencies, legal fees, and federal, state, or local taxes. In addition, eight out of twelve firms reimburse their foreign service employees to some extent for a financial loss incurred on the sale of their homes.

With respect to third country nationals, the firms pointed out that it happens rather infrequently that someone who owns a house is transferred and therefore arrangement for the reimbursement of related losses are made on an individual rather than on a general basis. However, the firms provide third country nationals in this respect with the same type of assistance as foreign service employees.

Shipment Costs

An employee being transferred to a foreign position expects to be reimbursed for the shipment costs of household goods and personal effects. Two-thirds of the firms pay practically 100 percent of the shipment costs for household goods and personal effects, whereas the rest of the firms stipulate a maximum (averaging about $10,000), which is so high that an employee will seldom have to pay a substantial part of the shipment expenditures out of his own pocket.

All companies also contribute to the cost of storing household goods. Nine firms stipulate no limitations in this respect, three firms pay storage costs only up to eighteen months. In addition, seven of the twelve firms also pay all expenses for shipment, insurance, import duties, and clearance charges to ship one automobile to the employee's new location. The other five firms follow a policy not to compensate for these expenditures, but to provide financial assistance in case an employee transferred to a position abroad sells his car at a loss. Most companies either supply high ranking international executives with an automobile or assist them in purchasing one.

Travel costs for the international executive and his family are also part of the relocation expenditures. Half of the firms compensate only air travel, economy or tourist class; one-fourth of the firms pay first class fares in the case of a flight of more than eight hours; one-fourth of the firms allow principally first class travel.

The various relocation expenditures alone can easily amount to more than the *annual* salary of the employee who is assigned to an overseas position, and it thus shows very clearly how important it is to investigate carefully whether it is necessary to assign a foreign manager instead of a locally available executive to a particular overseas position.

Fringe Benefits

Most large companies provide their executives with various benefits such as pensions, contributions to life insurance, and compensation of medical expenses. Obviously, a policy of neither gain nor loss because of a foreign assignment means that a company must grant international executives benefits comparable to those received by the parent company personnel. All firms provide their foreign service employees with life insurance covering generally two times the annual base salary. The companies pay either all or two-thirds of the insurance costs. The same benefits are also granted to third country nationals in seven out of twelve companies. Eleven of these firms reported having the same type of pension plan for their foreign service employees as for their domestic personnel. Only four companies also provide third country nationals with pension plans, which in three cases are related to the U.S. company's plan, and in one case related to a pension plan as established by the company's subsidiary in the third country national's home country.

Besides the fringe benefits which international executives generally receive in the same way as the company's domestic personnel, they frequently are granted supplementary fringe items, which can make an overseas assignment more attractive. Longer vacations, as well as periodic home leaves, are the most common in conjunction with certain financial benefits. Six out of twelve firms have special vacation schedules for their foreign service employees. For them the paid vacations are generally one week longer than if they were not working abroad. One of these six firms does not grant this same privilege to its third country nationals who get vacations according to local practice. Four firms follow the parent company's vacation schedule; for two firms the vacation period for foreign service employees is determined by local practice.

All of the U.S. based multinational firms included in this survey also grant their foreign service employees paid home leave. Only six of these firms also grant this privilege to their third country nationals; three other companies only under certain conditions (for example, the third country national's home country must be on a continent other than where he works), and three firms so far have no provision for home leave for third country nationals.

The average annual home leave period is about three weeks. In addition to the home leave, seven of twelve companies allow an additional two days for traveling. The majority of the companies require that home leave be actually spent in the employee's home country. Only three firms do not stipulate such a condition. Most of the firms also allow the regular vacation period and home leave to be taken consecutively, although two firms require that both be taken separately. Two firms do not grant the regular vacation period in the year of home leave.

Conclusions

An attempt has been made in this survey to investigate and analyze the policies of a representative sample of large U.S. based multinational firms concerning the compensation of their international executives and those major cost items which are the result of an employee's foreign assignment and which the firms are willing to absorb.

These general conclusions can be drawn:

By all counts, international business activities have been expanding rapidly in recent years. This expansion has brought about a remarkable increase in the number of business executives given foreign assignments. The chief reason for this is that the transfer of an organization's technological knowledge and managerial skills to a new foreign venture depends largely on the executives who have already worked for the parent company for some time and have acquired the necessary company related know-how. At present, U.S. based multinational firms have about 40,000 Americans in managerial positions abroad. Only ten years ago this group was estimated to number 25,000.[6] In fact, the evolution of a managerial class of international executives symbolizes most drastically the revolution which is taking place: A large segment of the business community in all developed countries is becoming more and more outward looking and is pursuing business opportunities on a global rather than a national scale. One consequence of this development is that the compensation of international executives becomes a major policy issue in a growing number of firms. Until recently even the very large multinational firms were deciding compensation questions concerning employees who were given foreign assignments on an individual basis. Today, many of these firms have manuals covering the most pertinent situations which may be encountered when assigning employees to foreign operations.

Equitable Remuneration

Their main purpose, however, is to provide a basis for consistent and equitable remuneration. This means that the individual-centered approach to determining the compensation of an international executive is giving way to a more general, organization-centered approach, although most companies are quite prepared to grant their international executives special allowances in response to particular needs.

From the data and information presented in this survey, it becomes clear that because of a variety of necessary allowances and transfer costs, international executives are considerably more expensive than local management personnel. Of course, the individual firm establishing new operations abroad frequently has no

---

[6] See H. and M. Krosney, *Careers and Opportunities in International Service* (New York: E. P. Dutton, Inc., 1965), p. 62.

alternative; qualified personnel are not available locally and the firm must rely on the personnel of the parent company or on personnel of well-established subsidiaries. The relative scarcity of qualified management personnel for foreign operations is certainly a sufficient reason for the higher remuneration which international executives generally receive—quite apart from the special adaptive abilities which are expected of them and other hardships of foreign assignments. As a result, all firms offer international executives a premium of about 15 percent to 25 percent of their base salary (generally the amount which they would receive for a comparable position in their home country) as a compensation for an array of elusive factors involved in an overseas position but not found in a similar position at home. In addition, it has been shown that all the firms contributing to this survey had developed rather elaborate schemes for calculating a variety of allowances, which generally are designed to compensate the international executive for higher expenditures abroad or for cost items which he would not encounter at home. Compensatory items of this nature (such as cost of living allowances, housing allowances, educational allowances, and in some cases special hardship allowances) amount in most cases to another 45–70 percent of an international executive's base salary. On the average, the recurrent compensation of a U.S. executive working abroad is roughly twice as high as the remuneration he would receive in a comparable position at home, and in certain cases this amount is three times as high.

Cost Absorption

In addition, the transfer of executives to a foreign operation causes a variety of relocation costs which are absorbed by the company and which, particularly in cases of a transfer to another continent, come close to, or are even in excess of, one year's salary of the employee concerned.

All top managers of multinational firms with whom this subject has been discussed agree that international executives are generally considerably more expensive than locals. They are quick to point out that, nevertheless, multinational firms have to absorb these higher costs not only because they have in many cases no other alternative, but also because they expect that work abroad will provide these executives with experiences that may later be valuable to the parent company and the organization as a whole. Despite this, all companies emphasize their determination to rely to the maximum extent possible on local personnel. This leads most multinational firms to undertake a considerable training effort which ultimately allows a reduction in the number of international executives. In this respect, however, it should be kept in mind that a firm's commitment to pull out the international executives as soon as sufficiently qualified local managers are available may have positive as well as negative effects. For instance, this policy may lead, on the one hand, to salary savings and may reduce a company's vulnerability against charges of remote control where nationalist sentiments are high. On the other hand, international executives may be able to show (in the interest of the company) greater resistance against certain governmental pressure than local managers who may not want to be suspected of lack of patriotism.

High Salaries

During the course of collecting empirical data on this project, a number of personnel directors of multinational firms expressed concern about the high salaries and allowances paid to employees assigned to a foreign operation. Generally they expressed regret that they were unable to do very much about it except to reaffirm their company's policy that an overseas assignment should neither lead to an undue financial gain nor a loss for persons concerned, and that local personnel should replace international personnel as soon as possible. However, in some cases, a company's high salaries and allowances to international executives are simply a remnant from a time when the international operations were limited, and thus the generous compensation to the few international executives was of little significance. As the international activities of a firm expanded and the number of foreign assignments increased, these companies neglected or found it difficult to reduce the allowances to a more reasonable level. The only solution in these cases is to use an objective approach to the calculation of cost differentials and then to reduce overseas allowances to these new justifiable levels. These difficulties also show how important it is that a company uses a rational approach to the determination of international executives' salaries and allowances even if for the time being it has only a few executives abroad.

Financial Inducements

Some companies found that they have formidable difficulties in persuading good managers to accept foreign assignments, and thus they offer generous financial inducements. In many of these cases the high compensation to a firm's overseas personnel appears to be mainly a necessary consequence of the failure to eradicate among the firm's potential international executives the notion that they will miss opportunities for advancement at home, or that when their foreign assignment is over they may find themselves at loose ends. In these cases, a reduction of what seems to be an unduly high compensation can be accomplished by proper career planning and careful attention to the reabsorption of international executives into the domestic organization. The better a company succeeds in keeping open the channels of advancement within the domestic firm for the international executive, the easier it will be to attract the organization's best men to overseas assignments at a lower cost burden than would otherwise be necessary.

Two Distinct Groups

The increasing multinationality of many firms and their policies of selecting their international executives company-wide rather than only from the parent company's pool of managerial talent has led to two distinct groups of international executives—foreign service employees and third country nationals. Only fifteen years ago the latter group was numerically rather insignificant. In the meantime, as more and more companies became truly international in scope and philosophy, the proportion of third country nationals increased rapidly. Among the large multinational firms, about one-fourth to one-third of their international executives are third country nationals. The distinction between the two groups of international executives is of no relevance from the point of view of their required activities. However, with respect to their compensation, this survey provides evidence that although in the majority of cases these executives are remunerated according to the same formula or methods, there is a certain degree of discrimination against the third country national as compared to the foreign service employee. For instance, it has been shown that some companies do not provide third country nationals with the allowances they grant to foreign service employees; in other cases, the formers' allowances are lower. Even in the cases where the two groups of executives seemingly receive the same treatment, the third country nationals actually get a lower allowance in cases where it is calculated as a percentage of the base salary which, for comparable positions, is generally lower than the base salary of foreign service employees. The discrimination is particularly noticeable among firms with a low share of third country nationals among their international executives. The higher the percentage of third country nationals in a firm's pool of international executives, the lower is the intergroup discrimination with respect to their compensation.

This survey also provides evidence of a clear trend among the multinational firms to internationalize the upper management ranks by making an overseas assignment part of the executive career development plan. Increasingly, firms attempt to identify managerial talent of all nationalities where they are operating and then arrange cross postings at appropriate stages in their careers—an interchange which benefits the individuals concerned as well as the organization. Multinational firms which follow this route are faced with the necessity to develop centrally administered, systematic, and equitable compensation schemes which should have two main characteristics: (1) they should be based on the principle that an executive should neither gain nor lose because of a foreign assignment, and (2) they should facilitate the executive's reintegration into the parent organization or any other part of the total organization to which he may be assigned. It is hoped the information in this survey can be of use in developing a rational and equitable system for a firm's international executives.

Nuts, Bolts, and Economic Progress

Richard N. Farmer

For want of a nail the horse was lost . . . goes the old saying. The modern version of this phrase might be, "For want of part number 32-57896-B-12 (Kingpin, Dodge-Fargo Models D-200-300, 1959–64) the truck was lost . . ."

Most of us who have worked in less developed areas are keenly aware of the very high cost of maintenance, often directly connected with the unavailability of parts in remote areas. As countries attempt to modernize their societies, an inevitable mark of progress is the proliferation of every type of modern industrial equipment, often obtained from numerous sources in the Western and Eastern industrialized countries. Whatever the pattern or orientation of development may be, trucks, pumps, machines, electronics gear, and endless other complex items begin to be utilized for productive purposes. Almost equally inevitably, the problems of maintenance grow geometrically as the new materials are put to use.

One typically finds that down time is high on such equipment, resulting in low utilization rates. Maintenance tends to be expensive, since parts often are not available and must be flown in at high cost, and workers must constantly acquire new skills to handle the rapidly improving machinery which steadily becomes more numerous and important. One cannot normally pick up the phone and call a distributor for advice, assistance, or that key bolt which prevents the machine from operating. The small number of any given piece of equipment in many smaller countries prevents the accumulation of large stockpiles of parts which could prevent downtime. And one also detects a general lack of interest in such mundane problems as this. To obtain new capital equipment is exciting, relevant, really the essence of development. But to struggle to maintain a rusty, banged up 1957 Lorraine Crane, which also is doing its part in the development process, is something which can safely be left to lower level technicians as a problem of small consequence.

This might well be true except that the result of inept maintenance leads to overinvestment, often on a major scale, in countries which can ill afford it. If half a fleet of fifty $30,000 trucks is idle on the average for lack of parts, defective maintenance practices, and poor planning, when the expected portion of the fleet down for maintenance should be ten percent, then an additional half million dollars must be invested to get the same output. One of the major (and generally

Reprinted from *International Development Digest*, Vol. III, No. 1 (March 1966): 17–18.

unreported) reasons for high capital-output ratios is that firms must overinvest in equipment because so much of it will be down for repairs at any given time.

This apparently minor point tends to become a major one in many less developed countries, in large part because the problem appears so simple on the surface. When a part is needed, you get it and put it in place—what could be easier? This tendency to overlook the problem may also be related to the fact that relatively few development strategists are trained in engineering or mechanics, and what appears on the surface to the layman to be a simple problem often turns out to be a question whose subtlety and complexity defies the most advanced mathematical analysis.

The Problem

Consider a relatively simple piece of equipment, such as a diesel engine. Such items are used all over the world, although production tends to be concentrated in a few developed countries. A diesel engine will have from 600 to 1,000 individual parts, ranging from such big items as cylinder blocks to minute pieces such as small special fasteners. The majority of items will be special, in that they will not fit any other engine (except perhaps a few related models of the same manufacturer). Perhaps half the parts will be critical, in that if they are not in place in good condition, the engine will not run. Many parts are also special in that they are prepared to very close tolerances out of closely controlled materials. A bearing cap bolt is not just any bolt of a given size—it is made of special steel, heat treated in a very special manner.

Even smaller manufacturing firms may have five or six different models or engines on hand, each requiring its own block of spares. Often, in part reflecting the lack of interest in this sort of problem, each type of engine will be from a different manufacturer, frequently from countries using different measurement standards (metric or English). To complicate the problem still further, firms may be relatively short of working capital, forcing them to economize on inventories on hand, and operators of equipment may also be relatively unskilled in operations and unfamiliar with routine preventive maintenance procedures.

Multiply this single item by hundreds, and one has a picture of a moderate sized enterprise attempting to maintain its equipment. A familiar and depressing pattern emerges: A worker, not realizing the importance of the step, neglects checking the oil filter. Shortly, the main bearings are scored, and the engine is down for maintenance. What is needed for this rather routine repair are several dozen of the 800 parts in the engine. Main bearings in general will not do—what is needed is a set of .010" oversize bearings for the specific engine. Unfortunately, these are not on hand, any place in the country. The engine (and its allied equipment) sits idle while frantic air freight orders are rushed to the site. Perhaps thirty or forty days later, the parts arrive (often the wrong ones—developed nation firms have a lot to learn on this point as well!), and finally the equipment is placed back in operation. The result? In effect, lost income for the firm, lost growth for the country, and excess capital investment needed to accomplish needed tasks. Trivial? Perhaps, except that the author has seen routinely large contractors in the Middle East who normally have half to two-thirds of their total capital equipment down for repairs. The capital costs must be paid, whether the firm is public or private, and the resulting higher operating costs become a burden on the entire economy.

The difficulty is compounded when it is realized that if fifty-six out of the fifty-seven needed parts are on hand, the engine still won't go. The issue gets worse when one considers the fairly rapid changes in models and designs. Dead inventory, representing parts not used for now worn out equipment, tends to be large. I would estimate that about half of all parts ordered for industrial equipment in the Middle East (including those ordered by firms based in developed countries) never get used. When one considers that a set of injectors for a diesel may cost $400, or a crankshaft may be $1,000, this also is not a trivial item.

The Technical Librarians

All of these points noted above are understood, if not resolved, by men working in this area. A vast body of production literature exists to give the techniques and tools necessary to work creatively on the problem. Inventory models, statistical analysis of parts use, and similar concepts are available for the direct analogy between librarianship and parts warehousemen. Both types of people tend to file, catalog, order, and store items in a systematic way. Both groups are swamped with new items, previously uncataloged species, irate customers, and items which are around someplace, only no one knows where (a striking, and totally frustrating phenomenon in this business is to try to find a misfiled part, particularly when it is critical to the operation of some essential item of equipment. Scholars searching for misfiled books are not the only ones frustrated in this sense!). But perhaps reflecting our values on this issue, a librarian or archivist is a respected, university trained specialist, while the warehouseman will be a young man with (hopefully) a secondary school education, who is frantically trying to learn his demanding trade.

A relatively small parts warehouse in any country will contain as many separate items as a good sized library. Our operation in Saudi Arabia carried about 150,000 separate listed and filed items, valued at over $500,000, and the firm was relatively small by any standard. Oil companies in the region have had inventories of over $30 millions at times. With capital values at even 6 percent, it is easy to see what improvements here could do to the investment potential of the country. Physical distribution specialists estimate that it costs about 25 percent of investment per year to maintain inventory.

With due respect to librarians, it could be argued that the harrassed parts men have a much harder, and certainly less appreciated job in developing economies. Perhaps, heretically, it might even be argued that the job is more important. Failure here directly results in cost increases, and frequently strikes directly at the heart of the development process. One might also comment on the tragedy of a country in deep foreign exchange difficulty who spends millions of dollars of precious foreign currency for parts which never will get used. An unread (to date) book is always potentially useful, but what does one do with the new set of pistons for a 1948 Chevrolet truck which has long since been scrapped?

Examination of tables of organization of many kinds of public and private firms in developing countries also often indicates the low status and implied unimportance of this parts problem. Warehousemen are rarely considered managers, except perhaps on the lowest levels. When financial allocations are made, spare parts inventories often get much less than other, relatively less important functions. I have seen firms order new equipment almost without discussion in the Middle East, often for millions of dollars, when half of what they already had was deadlined for repairs, and when much smaller sums spent on maintenance would accomplish the same result. We are all fascinated with what is new and dramatic, but to lavish attention on (apparently) decaying and obsolescent equipment appears rather silly.

Some Modest Proposals

What is involved here is more a state of mind and a reflection of values in development economics than any tangible issue. Perhaps it is relevent that no one bothers to keep adequate statistics on the national level on the amount of capital equipment which is currently not operating for maintenance reasons. One suspects that such data, if collected, would stagger planners everywhere.

Any firm which is willing to spend some time and energy on maintenance problems can usually show striking improvements in a very short time. Indeed, this may be one of the easiest development programs which can be instigated. The number of highly skilled, trained men required is relatively small, and the techniques and tools needed for improvements are readily available from a variety of sources.

Equipment manufacturers in most developed countries, anxious to improve the image of their products abroad, are usually willing and eager to proffer relevant advice and assistance. Another group which could help a great deal is the librarians and archivists. This professionally trained group could advise and assist warehousemen in many phases of their activities, given the close relationship of the two fields. Economists, familiar with recent operations research techniques and inventory models, also could make major practical contributions if they became actively interested.

What is needed is the recognition of the problem. One hopes that this note may lead to more creative thinking about a situation normally left to the lower levels of persons engaged in economic development.

47154